THE
boat
galley
COOKBOOK

800 Everyday Recipes and
Essential Tips for Cooking Aboard

THE
boat
galley
COOKBOOK

Carolyn Shearlock

Jan Irons

INTERNATIONAL MARINE/McGRAW-HILL
Camden, Maine • New York • Chicago • San Francisco • Lisbon •
London • Madrid • Mexico City • Milan • New Delhi •
San Juan • Seoul • Singapore • Sydney • Toronto

The McGraw·Hill Companies

7 8 9 10 11 12 13 14 15   QTN/QTN   1 9 8 7

ISBN   978-0-07-178236-4
MHID   0-07-178236-2

e-ISBN   978-0-07-178235-7
e-MHID   0-07-178235-4

Library of Congress Cataloging-in-Publication Data

Shearlock, Carolyn.
        The boat galley cookbook : 800 everyday recipes and essential tips for cooking aboard / Carolyn Shearlock, Jan Irons.
            p.   cm.
        Includes indexes.
        ISBN 978-0-07-178236-4 (pbk.)—ISBN 0-07-178236-2 (pbk.) —
        ISBN 978-0-07-178235-7 (eISBN)—ISBN 0-07-178235-4 (eISBN)
        1. Cooking on ships.   2. Quick and easy cooking.   I. Irons, Jan.   II. Title.

    TX840.M7S54 2012
    641.5'55—dc23   2012008420

Beef Made Easy and Spanish English Beef Cuts charts on pages 30–31 from the Beef Checkoff. Used with permission.

Pork Basics and El cerdo es bueno charts on pages 32–33 from the National Pork Board. Used with permission.

Omnia stove-top oven image on page 75 courtesy of Anna N Kjellgren/www.annafolio .com. Used with permission.

Cooking guidelines chart on page 258 courtesy of The Beef Checkoff. Used with permission.

Portions of the section on canned meat and seafood was written for the "Galley Gourmet" section of *Latitudes & Attitudes*. Part of it was published in September 2004 (Issue 52, page 176) and more in April 2005 (Issue 59, page 163) as "Un-Canny Meals."

McGraw-Hill products are available at special quantity discounts to use as premiums and sales promotions or for use in corporate training programs. To contact a representative, please e-mail us at bulksales@mcgraw-hill.com.

This book is printed on acid-free paper.

contents

preface

No matter what anyone tells you, boat cooking *is* different from cooking ashore. The space is smaller, there's no grocery store five minutes away, you have fewer prepared foods, and electric appliances and food storage are much different.

Over the years we've learned this the hard way. Decades ago, we were two couples living in different states, spending summers racing small one design sailboats against each other. Then we decided to take a wild jaunt to Strictly Sail Chicago. When the weekend was over, we'd signed up for a "big boat" charter together in the British Virgin Islands.

Stepping aboard the charter sailboat, we wondered what we'd gotten ourselves into. Were we nuts? As the wind filled the sails, the rumbling diesel was silenced and we were left with the mesmerizing sounds of crystal blue water sluicing past the hull. All four of us were grinning from ear to ear.

At anchor that night, we got our first lesson in galley management. It is *not* a good idea to dump all the food into the refrigerator, pour 20 pounds of ice over it, and then run the engine-driven refrigeration for an hour. Everything froze into a solid block of ice and we spent an hour chopping our "first night celebration steaks" out of the mess.

The rest of the week was magical—sailing, snorkeling, hiking, and even making some pretty good meals. All of us knew that someday we'd go cruising again. And we did, first chartering and then each buying our own boat a few years later.

Fast forward to now, with 20,000+ miles of cruising between us. Jan and her husband, David, were aboard *Winterlude* in the western Caribbean to Cartagena and the San Blas islands, and Carolyn and her husband, Dave, were aboard *Que Tal* in the Sea of Cortez and south to El Salvador. Despite cruising different oceans, we had both faced the same challenge: eating well while having time to enjoy all the other great aspects of cruising—snorkeling, swimming, kayaking, exploring—or just sitting and admiring the view.

We learned with the cookbooks we both had aboard and wished for information we didn't have—such as the time when Jan ended up with a frozen chicken complete with head and feet and no instructions on how to cut it up. Bit by bit, we filled in the gaps.

When we couldn't get foods such as sour cream, English muffins, spaghetti sauce, or yogurt, we adapted recipes to make our own. We experimented with substituting ingredients. Maybe the result wasn't identical, but it was still tasty. We learned easier ways to make things by hand, without electrical appliances. We tried various methods for storing foods and learned from our failures. When the tropical heat got to us, we developed strategies that not only reduced the heat in the boat but also conserved propane. We asked the local fishermen how to prepare the seafood. Most of all, we had fun!

As we traded recipes and knowledge with each other and cruisers, we realized that the information we were compiling would be useful to others. *The Boat Galley Cookbook* is designed to help you every step of the way. We hope it becomes a trusted reference on your boat and a source of many enjoyable meals.

Fair winds and following seas!

Carolyn   Jan

how to use this book

The *Boat Galley Cookbook* is a comprehensive guide to cooking in a small boat, with tons of features to make cooking aboard easy and enjoyable. We've divided the book into two parts, as follows:

A Galley Frame of Mind includes helpful galley information—tips, tricks, and cooking techniques—that we learned through experience. We hope you will read through all the chapters in this section to familiarize yourself with our approach.

Recipes provides recipes organized by type of food, but with a few non-traditional groupings, like our "Holiday Cheer" chapter in which we provide recipes for that special occasion or holiday. If a recipe includes unusual cooking techniques, we provide step-by-step instructions.

A Galley Frame of Mind

- "Boat Cooking *Is* Different" highlights some of the important differences in cooking aboard your boat—and provides tested tips to make the transition easier.
- "Equipping a Galley" shares insights on what to look for when buying various pieces of gear, how to make do if you don't have a particular item (we're big on using what you have), and troubleshooting common galley problems.
- "Provisioning" includes A Stroll through a Central American *Supermercado*—if you're cruising outside the United States or Canada, it can be intimidating to head into a store in a foreign country. Even if you're not in Central America, we hope that our pointers will make foreign stores a little less confusing.

- "Food Storage" provides detailed, tested information on how to stow your provisions so they'll still be good a day or a month from when you brought them aboard.
- When you're missing an ingredient, check out the "Food Substitutions" chapter, where we list more than 150 tested possibilities.
- The "Measurements and Conversions" chapter can help whether you need to convert ounces to cups, tablespoons to teaspoons, quarts to liters, or anything else. We also include eyeball estimates in case you're missing a measure.
- Want to know how to bake without an oven, cook in a thermos, or use a pressure cooker? "Special Galley Cooking Techniques" provides step-by-step directions for methods rarely used ashore.

The Recipes and Their Features

- The **Recipes** section begins with "Meal Ideas for the Boating Life," where we provide ideas for those times when you just don't know what to make. These quick reference lists provide recipe ideas (and page links) for such categories as Five-Minute Appetizers, Mexican Quick Ideas, and Asian Quick Ideas. There is also a "Potluck" chapter with tips, ideas, and cross-references for recipes.
- Recipes are organized by food type and into logical groupings within each chapter. Where a particular preparation or cooking method may be unfamiliar to many, we've begun the chapter or section with detailed how-to information.

- Recipes show alternative ingredients with an uppercase OR when the amounts of the alternative ingredients are different: for example, ½ teaspoon ground chilies OR ¼ teaspoon chile pepper flakes. When the amounts are the same but the ingredients vary, lowercase "or" is used: for example, ½ teaspoon ground chilies or chile pepper flakes. We've learned that availability varies widely in remote cruising locations with small stores, and we want recipes to be as flexible as possible. Alternate ingredients are listed in order of preference.
- Page numbers in parentheses following an item indicate where to find a substitution (typically used for hard-to-find ingredients), a recipe to make it from scratch, or detailed information on a cooking technique.

- Cross-reference lists at the end of each recipe chapter provide links to recipes in other locations that could have been included in the chapter. For example, Red Beans and Rice is in the "Beans, Rice, and Pasta" chapter, but since it's a main dish, we also cross-referenced it in the list at the end of the "Meat Main Dishes" chapter.

NAVIGATING THIS BOOK

- Tabs keyed to each chapter make browsing easy; see the tabs key at the end of the book to easily locate the different chapters.
- Two detailed indexes (one for recipes and ingredients and the other for topics) make finding a specific recipe or technique a snap.

A GALLEY FRAME OF MIND

*We each faced a huge learning curve
when we first began cruising—everything
from what gear we needed to how
to provision and even how to
cook in a limited space. In these
chapters, we've tried to pass on
all the things we wish we'd known!*

BOAT COOKING
IS DIFFERENT

No matter what anyone tells you, cooking on a boat is different from cooking ashore. That doesn't mean it has to be difficult, though. We want to give you the information you need for success—information we both wish we'd had when we began cruising.

In this chapter we explore the following challenges in cooking aboard:

- What's On Board Is What You Have
- Limited Space
- Cooking from Scratch
- Few or No Electrical Appliances
- Small or No Refrigerator/Freezer
- The Motion of the Boat
- Limited Water
- Heat in the Boat

Also be sure to read our chapter "Special Galley Cooking Techniques."

WHAT'S ON BOARD IS WHAT YOU HAVE

Once you leave the dock, you're generally not able to run to the store if you suddenly realize you're missing something—or to the Internet if you need to find out something. Whether it's provisions, pans, tools, or recipes, you have to make do with what you have until the next time you are at a store.

To some, this is scary: what if I forgot something? I (Carolyn) prefer to see it as a chance for innovation: what can I do with what I have? I've developed some

of my best "recipes" simply because I was making do. Now they've become family favorites!

I have three basic coping strategies for dealing with the challenge of being away from stores:

- **Planning and list-making**—these make it less likely that I'll forget something I really need. You can download my free Inventory and Provisioning Spreadsheet from TheBoatGalley.com. Some cruisers constantly update their inventory so they know exactly what's available; we both prefer to just do an inventory before a big provisioning run.
- **Innovation and creativity**—substitutions don't have to perfectly re-create the original recipe; they just have to produce a good meal. Our Food Substitutions chapter can give you lots of ideas for alternatives. And most of our recipes list alternative ingredients. Where you see "(page XX)," the reference is either to a substitution or a recipe to make the ingredient yourself.
- **Prioritizing**—would we rather spend more time in a great anchorage, or reprovision? Usually we opt for more time in the anchorage, but at some point the balance tips in favor of reprovisioning.

LIMITED SPACE

Limited space refers not just to stowing provisions but also to limited space for food prep and for pans and utensils, fewer burners on the stove, less space in the oven (if you have one), and a smaller sink.

You're likely to have less equipment than when you're ashore.

Our ways to cope:

- Buy versatile items. This is obvious with things like a can opener that also has a bottle opener on it, but how about using a wine bottle as a rolling pin? And buying basic ingredients that can be used in lots of different recipes, instead of single-purpose prepared foods?
- Many kitchen gadgets aren't really necessary. You can do the same thing with more basic, all-purpose tools. See our gear substitutions in the section Equipment Substitution: Making Do (page 7).
- Think about stowing equipment when you buy it. Read more about this in the section Buying Galley Equipment (page 6). Nesting pans and bowls will help; there are also collapsible bowls, colanders, and measuring cups that take up less space than their traditional counterparts.
- Don't give space to things you don't need. For example, throw away the cereal box on the dock—it takes up more space than the bag inside. Buy boneless meat, or bone it before freezing it (see page 256 for details on boning meat). One caveat, though: sometimes things that seem to be just "taking up space" are actually protecting something from breakage, so don't discard things without thinking about their purpose.
- Check out our tips for storing provisions in the limited space available in our "Food Storage" chapter.
- Think beyond the galley when you're looking for space to prepare food. I used the engine cover as an extra counter, and sometimes the nav table, too. Many galleys have covers that can be put over the stove or sink to make additional counter space when needed.
- Plan ahead for space limitations. If you have only two burners on the stove, don't plan a menu that requires three. Don't buy a turkey that's bigger than your oven, or if you do, plan to cut the turkey into pieces so it will fit.
- If one of your "space limitations" is no oven, learn to bake on the stove top (pages 74–79) or on the grill (page 78).

COOKING FROM SCRATCH

If you usually use prepared food and package mixes, the idea of cooking from scratch can be intimidating. Few of us cook from scratch on a daily basis anymore; cooking from scratch is seen as something that "foodies" and gourmets do. But it doesn't have to be that way: you can cook simple meals from scratch every day, without spending forever in the galley.

As we wrote this book, we tried to keep in mind the cruiser who, like Jan, tended to just heat up prepared food when living ashore. We've worked to provide detailed directions for making everyday dishes to give you the confidence that you, too, can create good meals without a lot of fuss. Start with simple things like chili and spaghetti sauce. With some basic ingredients aboard—and this book—you can make anything you want.

FEW OR NO ELECTRICAL APPLIANCES

Many cruisers find the idea of no (or few) electrical appliances to be even more intimidating than the idea of cooking from scratch (and many find the combination overwhelming). But virtually anything that you can do with an electrical appliance, you can do by hand.

There are two critical keys to success:

- Good tools. Sharp knives and a grater can replace a food processor, and a good mixing spoon and a potato masher can do the work of an electric mixer. You don't need a lot of tools, but don't skimp on quality. See the section Buying Galley Equipment (page 6).
- Recipes designed to be made without electricity. That's where this book comes in. We don't assume that you have a microwave, blender, food processor, or electric mixer, although you certainly can use them if you have them. We give you the step-by-step directions you need to prepare food by hand, even if you've never done it before. And our recipes are designed to be made with hand utensils so you won't be exhausted by the process.

SMALL OR NO REFRIGERATOR/FREEZER

Your boat may not have a refrigerator and/or a freezer. If it does, it's likely to be much smaller than what you're used to ashore, yet you're likely to go longer between trips to the grocery store than when you're ashore.

The obvious way that cruisers cope with this is to use less prepared frozen food and cook far more from scratch. But there are many other ways to meet the challenge, and we've included a lot of information to help you in other chapters of this book:

- Tips on using a boat refrigerator and freezer in the section Coolers/Refrigerators/Freezers: Using and Troubleshooting (page 20).
- How to use a cooler for food storage (page 22).
- Storing produce without refrigeration (page 41).
- Making tasty meals from canned meat, which doesn't need refrigeration (page 303).
- Lots of recipes for canned goods and foods that don't require refrigeration.

THE MOTION OF THE BOAT

Everything you do is affected by the motion of the boat—some days more than others!

Things like standing (or needing a hand to hold on with), pots sliding on the stove, bowls and cutting boards sliding on the counter, bottles tipping over, and holding a knife are all affected by the motion of the boat. Then there are the stowage issues: produce bruising, pans and plates clanking in lockers, items breaking or becoming missiles. It's all a challenge!

The first week is a huge learning curve, as is the first bit of rough weather. But it's not that bad once you get the hang of a few coping techniques. With time, these come naturally.

- Always assume that the boat is going to move erratically, so use stove gimbals and pot restraints (see page 14) no matter what the conditions are. Even in a calm anchorage, a fishing boat can come flying by and put up a big wake.
- Never set anything down where it's not restrained, particularly items that could cause injury if they fell (knives, boiling water) or could break (anything in glass).
- Use non-slip materials liberally—cutting boards with non-slip edges, knives with non-slip handles, dishes with non-slip materials on the bottom, and so on.
- Sit down to work when you can. And when you can't, find ways to brace yourself so that if the boat rolls, you won't lose your footing. This is particularly important when you're doing something that could result in an injury, such as using a knife or pouring boiling water.
- When pouring boiling water or other hot liquids, put the container that you are pouring into in the sink and wedge it in, rather than hold it in your hand. Make sure the stream of liquid is going fore and aft, not athwart-ships. This way, spills and splashes won't burn you.
- For tips on stowing provisions so they won't be harmed by the motion of the boat, see the chapter "Food Storage."
- Keep pots, pans, dishes, silverware, cans, and all noisy gadgets quiet with lots of padding. See the chapter "Equipping a Galley" for tips on stowing particular items.

LIMITED WATER

Even if you have a watermaker, chances are that you don't have as much water as you'd really like due to the power it requires. And without a watermaker, you're limited to what your tanks will hold.

The two biggest things that you can do to reduce your water consumption:

- Don't waste water. Don't run the faucet longer than it needs to, don't cook food in more water than it needs, and don't make more coffee or other drinks than people will drink. When washing dishes, make a small bowl of soapy water (in one of your dirty dishes) rather than a sink full. Use a small houseplant watering can to rinse dishes.
- Re-use water when you can. For example, use the pasta water to rinse dishes or make bread, use leftover coffee to rinse dishes or soak a pan. When

you drain liquid from canned food, save it to use in other dishes (it will add flavor, too).

The topic of conserving water always turns to whether or not you should use seawater in cooking and washing. Neither of us does. The question is whether it is sufficiently pure that it won't make you ill. I would never use seawater while coastal cruising; it's my understanding that there are pollutants that are not totally removed by boiling or treating with bleach. Having said that, veteran circumnavigators Lin and Larry Pardey use seawater for cooking regularly without boiling and with no ill effects.

If you do decide to use seawater in cooking, it should be boiled and used in a 1:2 ratio with fresh water, even for foods that you would otherwise add salt to, such as when cooking pasta or vegetables. To use seawater to wash dishes, either boil it or add bleach (eight drops per gallon of clean-looking water; double the bleach for "dirty" water). Again, we don't recommend using seawater. You do so at your own risk.

HEAT IN THE BOAT

The biggest source of heat in the boat is the galley. On a hot day, you're trying to keep as much of that heat out of the boat, and on a chilly day, you're trying to keep it in. Without air-conditioning or an auxiliary heater, managing the heat from cooking plays a big role in staying comfortable.

On hot days, use the stove or oven as little as possible. Eat cold foods, cook on the grill, and, if you do use the stove, choose foods that cook fast or can have a large part of their "cooking" done in a thermos. A couple of good 12-volt fans and a wind scoop will help, too.

Cold days are the time to indulge your cooking desires: make soups and stews that need to cook for a long time, and bake bread and cookies. You can eat well and stay warm!

EQUIPPING A GALLEY

Equipping a galley is different from setting up a home kitchen. There's a lot less space. You won't have as much—if any—electricity. You'll have to conserve water. It's a moving platform. You may be doing a lot more cooking from scratch, and there may be fewer options for buying new gear.

We'll assume you're not designing your boat from the keel up or doing a major refit. As we both did, you're probably going to use your galley with the fixed items—the overall layout, the stove/oven, and the cooler/refrigerator/freezer—more or less unchanged. Instead, we'll focus on choosing other galley gear and in using the stove/oven and the cooler/refrigerator/freezer. Specifically, this chapter covers:

- General things to think about when buying galley equipment
- Safety considerations
- Ways to get by with less gear
- Tips on specific items, based on our experience and preferences
- Ways to get the most out of your stove/oven and cooler/refrigerator/freezer and solving common problems with each

BUYING GALLEY EQUIPMENT

What gear should you have in your galley? There's no one-size-fits-all list. Every boat and every person is different. What works on a 60-footer with a family of five heading out for three years wouldn't be appropri-ate for a singlehander on a 25-foot boat who spends occasional nights on board.

Your style of cooking, and what you like and dislike, won't change just because you're on a boat. If there is something you really feel you can't live without, you'll find a way to take it. Conversely, if you didn't use it on land, you're not likely to use it on a boat.

That said, you need less than you think. Great meals don't depend on lots of fancy equipment. If you're starting from scratch, don't buy everything at once. Buy the true essentials first, then add items as you're frustrated by not having them.

Before buying anything for the galley, and in determining whether a particular item will work well aboard, ask yourself these questions:

- **Do I really need it, or can I use something already on board?** Think about how often you'll actually use a piece of gear and see the section Equipment Substitution: Making Do (page 7). At the same time, trust your judgment. You know what you consider critical gear, so don't worry about what some "expert" (yes, even us) says you do or don't need.
- **Can I stow it in the space available?** Carefully measure your stowage areas and potential purchases. Many times, product specs don't include handles, so measure items yourself.
- **Can I use it in the space available?** Most galley counters, sinks, and ovens are smaller than their "house" counterparts. For example, a standard-size cookie sheet won't fit in many boat ovens. Measure carefully!

- **Will it work when I need it to?** Items that break are a pain anytime, but they're even worse when you won't find a store for a month or more.
- **Is it likely to break or rust?** Boat life is hard on standard kitchen gear. High-quality items are often cheaper in the long run. Stainless steel and soft plastic are least likely to have problems, but we both have some carefully considered breakable items in our galley—just not critical items.
- **Is it non-slip?** Will I be able to hold on to it? With the motion of the boat, it's important that things stay where you put them on counters and won't slip out of your hand. See the following section, Galley Safety, for ways to make items non-slip.
- **How hard will it be to clean?** Everything has to be washed by hand on most boats, and lots of little nooks and crannies take time and water to clean. Opt for things that can be completely disassembled. Nonstick pans take much less water to clean.
- **Does it take power? How much?** It's fine to have some electrical appliances aboard if your setup can handle it, but realize they are luxuries and have manual backups.

GALLEY SAFETY

The galley has the potential for accidents, but many of these can be avoided with some thinking as you're outfitting your galley and deciding where things will go.

- Have a working fire extinguisher and a fire blanket; arrange your galley so both are located where you could quickly and safely grab them if there was a stove fire.
- The stove and its fuel are potentially the most hazardous items on the boat—not just for burning the cook, but the risk of explosion and/or a fire. Read the owner's manual, follow all safety precautions, make sure the stove is installed correctly, and perform any necessary maintenance and fuel leak testing at the recommended intervals.
- When planning where you'll stow items, never place things behind the stove that you'll need when the stove is on. Reaching over a lit burner is asking for a disaster if the boat moves just a bit.

- Another important consideration is planning where you'll stow things when under way so they don't become missiles. Anything that would injure someone if it fell on his or her foot or was flung through the air (heavy pots, cans, and knives, to name a few) must be 100 percent secure when under way.
- Make sure you have pot restraints (page 14).
- Buy non-slip items and use non-slip mats. You can make your own non-skid items (for example, the bottom of dishes, or even throw rugs) by brushing contact cement on the surface where you want the non-skid, then letting it dry without letting anything else touch it.

EQUIPMENT SUBSTITUTION: MAKING DO

One of the challenges of cooking aboard a boat is that you generally have less gear than in a "shore" kitchen. Before buying more equipment than you have room or power for, look at these gear substitutions—particularly for items you don't use often. Save the precious space you have for things you'll use every day.

Pots and Pans

We were both amazed at how few pans we really needed. For the first several years aboard *Que Tal*, I (Carolyn) only had three nesting pans/bowls that came in a Magma set. I found I could cook anything in them. A few of my tricks:

- **Bread pan.** Bake bread in anything that can go in the oven—a casserole, a Pyrex bowl, a cake pan, a cookie sheet, or even on aluminum foil.
- **Cookie sheet or pizza pan.** Turn a cake pan upside down, or use a piece of aluminum foil.
- **Dutch oven.** An ovenproof skillet or saucepan with a lid works well. You may have to cut a large piece of meat in two or three to fit.
- **Pan lids.** Unless the recipe requires a tight-fitting lid (such as for rice), you can use a piece of aluminum foil. For a tighter-fitting lid, try a plate—just

be careful if it's rolly that the plate doesn't slide off and break.

- **Wok.** Anything you'd cook in a wok, you can cook in a skillet.

Substituting a Different Baking Pan

With only three pans, I almost never had the baking pan called for in a recipe. I learned how to alter the time and temperature so I could use what I had.

Most casseroles, meat dishes, and vegetables don't care what size pan they are baked in. As long as it's reasonably close, the final product will be fine.

With baked goods, however, changing the size of a baking pan can greatly alter the finished product. In general, the best pan substitutions are those that end up with the batter being the same depth as originally called for. You shouldn't have to change the temperature or time. But if that's not possible, you can compensate for the difference:

- If the batter is shallower, the center will dry out faster. Decrease the baking time and raise the temperature so the outside will brown in the shorter time.
- If the batter will be deeper, it will take longer for the center to bake. Lower the temperature and increase the baking time.

The key is the area of the bottom of the pan. The larger the area, the shallower the batter. The smaller the area, the deeper the batter. Anything within 10 percent of the pan size that's called for doesn't need compensation.

For example, if a recipe calls for baking in an 8-inch-square pan (64-square-inch bottom) but you have a 9"×5" loaf pan (45 square inches), the batter is going to be almost 1½ times as deep. (Divide the square inches of the original pan by the square inches of the new pan (64/45 = 1.4). Since the batter will be deeper, lower the temperature 25°F and begin testing for doneness at the original baking time plus 10 percent (it probably will take about 25 percent more time, but start checking sooner).

The important thing is how deep the *batter* will be in the new pan compared to in the original pan, not how deep the actual pans are in comparison to

each other or what the total pan volume is. Many online pan size conversion charts talk about using a pan with the same total volume (perhaps they copied one another; every word is identical), but the reality is that what's important is the batter depth, not the total volume of the pan.

This also applies if you halve a recipe or double it. For example, if you make half a recipe, you want a pan that has about half the area of the original pan, or you'll have to compensate for the difference.

SQUARE INCH EQUIVALENTS OF COMMON PAN SIZES

PAN SIZE	SQUARE INCHES
6" round	28
4"×8" loaf	32
5"×9" loaf	45
8" round	50
9" round	64
8" square	64
7"×11"	77
9" square	81
9"×13"	117

To calculate the area of a pan with sloping or curved sides—such as a pie pan—measure the length, width, or diameter halfway down.

Formulas for calculating your own:

- Square or rectangular pan: area = length × width
- Round pan: area = $(\frac{1}{2} \times \text{diameter})^2 \times 3.14$

Glass pans bake hotter than metal pans. If you are using the same size glass pan instead of metal, decrease the temperature 25°F but don't change the time.

Other Gear Substitutions

Innovation is important here. Look around and see what you have available. Our recipes that call for uncommon equipment usually give an alternate method to make the dish.

- **Beach BBQ grate.** Use a rack from your oven (usually the grate from a boat grill is too small).
- **Blender.** You can usually chop ingredients finely,

then mix with a whisk or a fork. Some things won't be quite as smooth without a blender, but most are perfectly acceptable (and some we prefer "chunkier"). A hand potato masher works with most fruits and steamed veggies. An immersion blender will also do many "blender" tasks, if you have the power for it.

- **Bread machine.** It's not hard to make bread by hand. There are detailed directions and lots of recipes in the "Yeast Breads" chapter.
- **Cooling rack.** If the stove is not on, set things on a burner so air will flow underneath. Otherwise, place a couple of table knives on hot pads on the counter and set the hot pan on top. If you have a fan in the galley, move it so it blows on the food.
- **Corkscrew.** Screw a large screw into the cork, then use a pair of Vise-Grip pliers and pull the screw straight out. If the cork crumbles into the wine bottle, put a clean cloth or a coffee filter over the mouth of the bottle and hold it firmly around the neck as you pour the wine. It will act as a strainer. Pour slowly!
- **Electric mixer.** A good mixing spoon will mix anything, although it may take a bit more time and effort.
- **Garlic press.** Use a knife and finely mince the garlic, or use the side of the knife and crush it.
- **Grater.** Many times, you can use a vegetable (potato) peeler to make long strips, then chop the strips into shorter lengths.
- **Insulated bag.** To take a hot or cold dish to a pot-luck, wrap several towels around the pan or bowl and use duct tape to secure the towels in place.
- **Meat grinder.** For most recipes, you can chop items very finely instead of putting them through a grinder.
- **Potato masher.** You can use a fork (best) or spoon to mash and whip things up, particularly if you let the items cook longer or, in the case of butter or cream cheese, let them warm up and soften.
- **Rolling pin.** Use a wine bottle or a clean piece of PVC.
- **Toaster.** See the section Toast Without a Toaster (page 117).

TIPS ON CHOOSING SPECIFIC GEAR

Here are our thoughts on what has—and hasn't—worked well for us and others we know. For more details on many of these as well as others, see "Outfitting" on TheBoatGalley.com.

Dishware and Glasses

Do you want plastic or breakable? If you really want "good" dishes and real glasses, you'll figure out a way to stow them so they don't break. The trade-offs are basically these: plastic won't break as easily (nothing is immune), it's lighter, and it's less likely to cut you if it does break, but it's also more likely to scratch and "look worn" after a while. Breakable dishes and glassware are more prone to shattering, need more protection when they are stored, and are heavier, but they feel less like camping and don't show as many scratches from wear. If you opt for breakable, you should also have a few non-breakable (paper or plastic) items in case of rough weather.

Corelle is an option chosen by many cruisers. It feels like real dishware but is much harder to break (though not impossible). If you choose white, you don't have to worry about the pattern being discontinued if you want more pieces in the future. And a solid color is good if you pick up some interesting placemats or tablecloths along the way—the designs won't clash.

Include a couple of flat-bottom serving bowls to use as your primary "plates" when under way. It is easier to eat out of a bowl if the boat is rolling, and bowls are easy to hold when the conditions are such that nothing will stay on the table. They'll also do double duty as serving bowls when you're anchored in calm waters.

Watch out for "super-size" plates that won't fit in the built-in cubbies on many boats. If you are buying pieces separately, consider buying "lunch" plates instead of dinner plates. It's easier to control portion sizes with smaller plates, and they take up less room.

Although ceramic mugs are nice in a calm anchorage and warm weather, an insulated mug with a narrow base (designed for car cup holders) will fit in standard cockpit drink holders and is better for use under way or in rough anchorages.

Pots and Pans

Pots and pans are the heart of the galley. Don't skimp here—it will just cost you more in the long run when you decide you can't stand the first ones you bought, pitch them out, and buy new ones. You need pans that won't rust, with thick bottoms that won't develop hot spots. For stowing, nesting pans with detachable handles can't be beat—and Magma makes them with an excellent nonstick coating that will cut down on the water (and time) for cleanup.

There are two primary considerations in buying pans for a boat galley. First, make sure the pans won't rust. High-quality stainless steel is your best bet. Second, if you are going to get nonstick, get good nonstick. Cheap nonstick will just chip, wear away, and peel off. Even if you don't buy online, read online reviews of any cookware and baking pans you're thinking of buying.

To eliminate clanking with pans, and to prevent scratches to nonstick, buy some fleece fabric (you can find inexpensive remnants if you don't care about the color) and cut it into pieces about 18 inches square (or another size as needed). Place a piece between stacked pans—no noise and no scratches. You can also use paper towels or placemats for the same purpose.

When buying oven pans, remember that boat ovens are generally smaller than home ovens. A 9"×13" pan is realistically the largest you're going to get inside most boat ovens (pan measurements generally don't include lips or handles). A standard cookie sheet won't fit; neither will a full-size roasting pan. Measure your boat oven before buying anything!

If you don't have an oven on board, consider an Omnia stove-top oven. We normally don't recommend specific brands, but there isn't anything else on the market remotely similar. It weighs about a pound, can be used on any type of stove or on the grill, and will bake almost anything you would bake in an oven (see page 75 for a picture and more details).

A teakettle is best for boiling water (even if you don't drink tea). Yes, it's more heat efficient than a saucepan, but the bigger benefit is a greatly decreased risk of spilling boiling water. Whistling teakettles conserve propane by letting you know when the water is boiling.

Pressure Cooker

A pressure cooker is a large pot with a locking lid and a seal, and a steam vent with weights on it to increase the pressure within, leading to higher cooking temperatures and shorter cooking times. You put the pressure cooker on a stove like any other pan. It is typically used for soups, stews, and other things that like long, slow cooking.

Cruisers, it seems, either love pressure cookers or never use them. If you like meals that simmer for a long time, a pressure cooker typically cooks dishes in one-third the time of a conventional pot. That translates to less propane (or other stove fuel) used and less heat in the galley. If you decide to get a pressure cooker, buy one that fits inside your pot restraints, and is small enough to store conveniently. Most pressure cooker recipes are designed for a 6-quart pan.

Neither one of us used our pressure cooker much to speed cooking, but we did like it as a pot that food wouldn't slosh out of in rough weather, due to the locking lid.

Thermos

I (Carolyn) consider a thermos essential. I own three of them—one to make yogurt (see page 101), one for coffee, and one for thermos cooking (see the sidebar "What's Thermos Cooking?" on page 11). We all call these bottles "a thermos," but Thermos is actually one brand of vacuum-seal bottle. There are many brands, qualities, and sizes available. A few things to consider:

Material. Thermos bottles come in stainless steel, glass lined, and all plastic.

- **Stainless.** The stainless bottles are unbreakable but also the most expensive. In kitchen-counter tests we did, all stainless bottles are not created equal. Thermos Nissan—the top-end line made by Thermos—is absolutely wonderful at retaining heat, with boiling water cooling just 26°F in five hours; the popular green Stanley bottles are much worse for heat retention, dropping 118°F in the same time. (Source: http://theboatgalley.com thermos-testing.) Further, if the stainless itself is not top grade, the inside of the bottle can rust in salty air.

- **Glass lined.** The glass-lined bottles also do a good job of retaining heat and cost less than most stainless, but they are more prone to breakage. In our test, the glass-lined bottle made by Thermos dropped 37°F.
- **All plastic.** The all-plastic bottles, with a plastic liner, are the worst at retaining heat. Some have no insulation between the inner and outer shell; others have various insulating materials. The advantage is that they are cheap. In many cruising locales outside the Unites States, these are all you find.

What grade you need depends a lot on where you are and how you plan to use the bottle. In the tropics, you can probably get by with one of the plastic ones, although a better one will be much more satisfactory. If you're cruising Alaska or the Chilean fjords, you're really going to need at least a glass-lined bottle, and a top-notch stainless one will perform just that much better.

Mouth Size. The best bottles have a wide mouth the same size as the rest of the interior. To use the bottle for anything other than liquids, you need a wide mouth. Narrow-mouth containers are hard to get food in and out of, and they're harder to clean if something sticks inside the bottle. A denture tablet and boiling water can do wonders to clean otherwise impossible messes out of bottles.

Bottle Size. A vacuum bottle retains heat best when it is full. Remember Goldilocks? You want one that's "just right" for what you're cooking. A three- to four-cup (quart or liter) size is good for most thermos cooking for two people and is also a good size for coffee. A two-cup (pint) size is perfect for yogurt.

Bottle Brush. Be sure to get a bottle brush (sold in the baby department, not housewares) to scrub the inside of the bottle. The longer the handle, the better.

What's Thermos Cooking?

A thermos is the cruiser's Crock-Pot, good for foods that require long simmering. It saves propane, keeps heat out of the boat, and frees you to do something else while the food cooks.

Thermos cooking makes using foods that save space and weight aboard—such as dried beans—a reasonable alternative to canned foods. We also love it for cooking brown rice, which is nutritionally superior to instant white rice but takes far longer to cook. Learn more in the chapter "Special Galley Cooking Techniques."

Coffeemaker

There are lots of ways to make good coffee on a boat. The only one we don't recommend is trying to use a 12-volt coffeemaker. They simply take way too long to brew a pot of coffee. One friend said that when she switched from a 12-volt to a 110-volt coffeemaker with an inverter, she actually used less power.

When choosing your coffeemaker, an important consideration may be the amount of coffee each type makes. Remember that a mug is equal to two "cups" of coffee, so if there are two of you, and you each like two mugs of coffee, that's not four "cups"—it's eight cups. The options include:

- A 110-volt coffeemaker and an inverter. The benefit is that it's the same coffeemaker you are used to. The downsides are the power usage, the glass pot that can break (unless you opt for the Thermos type of pot), and stowage space. Jan's choice is a new single-cup coffeemaker that takes less space and uses 2 amp-hours per cup with a refillable K-cup, eliminating the need for expensive—and impossible to find outside the United States—K-cups.
- The Coleman Camping Coffeemaker is fairly new on the market but getting rave reviews. It is a drip coffeemaker that sits on a gas stove (or camping stove). The downsides are the glass pot, stowage space, and the fact that it's tippy.
- Stove-top percolator. You can make good coffee with a stove-top percolator, but you have to watch

it and turn the heat down before the grounds escape the basket. The benefits are energy efficiency, no breakable parts (with a metal pot), and smaller stowage space.

- Pour-through cone and pot/thermos. You put a filter in a plastic or metal cone, add ground coffee, and pour boiling water through into a pot, thermos, or even straight into your mug. We found the filters everywhere we cruised (you can also use a paper towel or a piece of cotton fabric). The benefits are no breakable parts, easy stowage, and energy efficiency. The downsides are that it takes time and attention, it's possible to spill boiling water, and it can be hard to manage in a rolly anchorage.
- French press. Some people swear by them; others swear at them. I've never had good luck with one, but you may have a better experience.
- Instant coffee. The benefits are that it's cheap, quick, and energy efficient, and there's nothing extra to stow. The downside is the flavor.

Grater

If you're in foreign countries, you'll use a grater far more than you do in the United States, as you generally can't buy things already shredded or grated. Look for one made of stainless steel, with sharp cutting surfaces. Flat ones or A-frame ones stow best. Just make sure it has a comfortable handle.

Knives

You don't need a lot of knives, but you do need good ones. You're likely to chop and dice a lot more food by hand aboard a boat. I found that I needed just four knives: a serrated knife for bread and tomatoes, a chef's knife for chopping and slicing, a fillet knife, and a paring knife. Don't forget a sharpening stone or steel, as well as a sheath for each knife to protect the blade and to protect your hand when reaching into the drawer where the knives are stored.

Meat Thermometer

A meat thermometer is useful for making yogurt and baking bread in addition to checking when meat is done, but not everyone makes these things. The

digital instant-read ones are nice, and you can generally get batteries for them, but the analog (dial) ones work just as well.

Silicone Versus Nylon Cooking Utensils for Nonstick Pans

If you have nonstick pans, you need compatible utensils. The question comes down to silicone or nylon. For anything that you might use in a pan on the stove top, silicone has greater heat resistance. Nylon can melt and bubble. The one exception is pancake turners, where nylon is best. Manufacturers simply coat a piece of metal with the silicone, and in time (sometimes a surprisingly short time), the metal will wear through and scratch your pans. Nylon is stiff enough that it does not need a metal core.

Mixing Spoon

You need a good mixing spoon that's comfortable in your hand and sturdy enough to mix heavy batters. It's hard to find a good hand-mixing spoon, but they are out there. If you are using nesting pans as mixing bowls (I did for several years), make sure that your mixing spoon won't scratch them if the pans are nonstick.

Bowls

Many nesting pots with removable handles work well as bowls—for mixing and serving—with the extra benefit of adding nothing more to stow. You can also use some of your plastic storage containers.

However, since you do a lot of hand mixing on a boat, it's nice to have a bowl designed for that. Several styles incorporate some type of a handle (usually called a batter bowl or a mixing bowl). I prefer plastic since it's unbreakable, easy to keep clean, and quiet when stowed. There are also collapsible bowls (and colanders), which are great for saving stowage space. Jan has some she loves.

Measuring Cups and Spoons

There are lots of nesting sets of measuring cups and spoons, which save space. Plastic ones are usually inexpensive and quiet in the cupboard, but the markings will quickly wear off if they are not raised or indented. Stainless sets generally have less of a problem with markings wearing off, but they can clank in a drawer. Stuffing a towel in the drawer can help. Collapsing measuring cups are available, but they have the same problem as other plastic cups with markings wearing off.

Pepper Mill

Inexpensive pepper mills with metal grinders will quickly rust in salt air, making them unusable. Try to find ones made of plastic, or buy more expensive ones with stainless blades. If you opt for a pepper mill, keep some ground pepper on hand in case the mill stops working.

Plastic Storage Containers

Plastic food storage containers are another area where you don't want to skimp on quality. Lids simply have to stay on securely and containers not crack. The movement of the boat makes it much tougher for lids to stay on, so you need to really look at lids before you buy the containers. Ask yourself, "Would I be willing to fill this with oil, then carry it all day in a backpack with a bunch of other stuff?" If the answer is yes, it will probably work on the boat.

Soft Cooler

You need a cooler aboard for lots of things: carrying meat and other refrigerated items back from the grocery store, carrying cold food to a potluck (it can also be used to keep hot foods hot), going on hikes and other side trips, maybe even holding a stash of drinks in the cockpit.

A soft-sided cooler can be stowed much more easily than a hard one, and it's easier to carry any distance resting on your hip with the strap across your chest. Get one with the best insulation possible if you are going to be in a hot climate. A cooler in the 18- to 24-can size was good for times when I had to carry it a mile or more. It was large enough to hold the meat, cheese, and butter (along with some ice), but it was still a size I could manage. A shoulder strap that's long enough to go across your chest instead of just over your shoulder will help on those long treks, too.

Expect one of these coolers to last two to three years before developing leaks.

Vacuum Sealer

A vacuum sealer is wonderful to have aboard if you're going to remote locations for any length of time. It removes the air from the bag, leading to less spoilage, and makes a seal that won't pop open accidentally.

Before deciding to buy a vacuum sealer, consider three issues. First is whether you have enough power to use one—or will you always be at a marina with shore power when you'd be sealing things? Second is getting the bags. I never saw any outside the United States, and I brought extras back to the boat from every trip back to the United States. Third is the style and price of the bags. There are several types and they are not interchangeable; some styles are much more expensive than others. Often you can get large quantities of bags cheaper online, particularly if you buy "generics."

If you decide to get a vacuum sealer, read reviews. Some make it hard to get a good seal. Pay particular attention to how large various models are if storage space is an issue. This is not something to buy based just on price, and often the less expensive brands of vacuum sealer use the most expensive bags, which can make them extremely expensive in the long run. I loved the luxury of having one, but that's just what it is—a luxury.

Shopping Bags

You'll need a variety of bags. In addition to making it easier to carry your purchases, having reusable bags cuts down on trash. Three types work well, and I use all three:

- **Standard reusable shopping bags**. Some are fabric, some are mesh.
- **Backpacks**. These are great for heavy stuff, like cans of pop or beer, if taxis aren't available.
- **Dry bags**. These are perfect for transporting anything that shouldn't get wet in the dinghy—flour, sugar, toilet paper. You get the idea. They're also very good for clean laundry! Within reason, the larger, the better—just put the heavy stuff on the bottom.

Serving Items

Many food storage items or pans can be used for serving. For example, a mixing bowl lined with a pretty piece of fabric does well as a cracker bowl. Since you already have the bowl, the only "extra" item is the fabric or napkin. Much easier to stow than a separate basket!

For potlucks, you want serving dishes with secure lids for transporting dishes in the dinghy or even just down the dock. Most often, you'll use good food storage containers, not fancy serving bowls.

STOVES AND OVENS: USING AND TROUBLESHOOTING

Most of our tips in this section are equally applicable no matter what type of fuel you're using. Whatever type of stove you have, read the owner's manual carefully and pay special attention to the safety precautions.

Using Galley Stoves and Ovens

Galley stoves and ovens (particularly propane ones) are quite similar to home stoves and ovens, but with a few added features.

Pot Restraints. Virtually any stove designed for use in a boat comes (originally) with pot restraints, also known as pot holders, pan holders, or pot/pan clamps. These are the first half of the equation for keeping your cooking on the stove and not on the galley sole or, worse, spilling hot food on the cook.

Pot restraints are generally metal bars that screw into each side of the stove and "hug" a pan on a burner. You loosen the knob a little to swing the bars into the correct position, then tighten the knob so the pot doesn't slide with the motion of the boat. Various brands have different mechanisms, but these are the most common. Pot restraints aren't just for use under way. They're also great in rolly anchorages or those with lots of boat traffic.

Unless you spend almost all your time at a very sheltered marina, leave your pot restraints in place and use them all the time—if you always use them,

you won't forget when conditions are marginal. You never know when a fishing boat is going to roar past you, even in a glassy calm anchorage.

We generally refrain from saying you "need" a particular item, but these are an exception. They are truly a safety item. (Note: my experience is based on sailing a monohull, which has a very different galley motion than a multihull.) Without them, every pan on the stove is a potential major burn on the cook if it slides while hot.

The restraints that came with my stove were always fine for the coastal cruising we did. However, I've heard reports of pans flying out of the typical types of restraints when a boat hard on the wind "fell off a wave"—not so much a rolling action but a sudden drop and stop—or when the back of the stove, swinging on its gimbals, hit the side of the boat hard. If you expect to encounter such conditions (and think you'd be trying to cook in them), you may want to engineer more sturdy pot restraints specific to your boat. That's beyond the scope of this book, but I've seen some good discussions and designs on the sailnet.com and Seven Seas Cruising Association (SSCA) bulletin boards.

If you are trying to bake while under way or in a rolly anchorage, you'll need to wedge the pan in place so it won't slide as the boat moves, as well as using the gimbal to keep things level. Many cruisers take up the extra space in the oven with additional pans or crumpled aluminum foil, but these interfere with the heat and airflow in the oven and can lead to hot spots. Instead, I used small binder clips (yes, the ones for holding a bunch of papers together; make sure they're 100 percent metal with no plastic!) on the oven rack to hold the pan in place. (If the wires in your rack are too small for the clip to hold, wrap the wire with a few layers of aluminum foil.)

Stove Gimbal. The stove gimbal is the second half of keeping your pans on the stove or level in the oven. Basically, it's an attachment system to the boat (often a pivot point running fore and aft) that lets your stove/oven stay level, even when the boat is heeled or rolling.

Generally, gimbaled stoves have a latch that keeps the stove from swinging when it's not in use or not needed. These are usually some form of barrel latch that you slide to release. Once released, the stove will swing with the motion of the boat.

In using a gimbaled stove, keep in mind:

- Most gimbal systems will let the stove swing 20 to 30 degrees, at which point it will crash against a bulkhead or the side of the boat. If it hits with any force, pans can fly off the stove onto the galley sole or onto the cook—even with pot restraints—because the sudden jolt may bounce the pot right out of the restraint. It's also not good for the stove to crash into the hull.
- If you are using the gimbal on the stove and have just one pot on the stove top, the stove isn't going to stay level. It's going to tilt in the direction of the pan.

Thus, if conditions are rough, you need to check the swing of the stove before actually putting a pan on it and lighting the burner. Begin by releasing the stove and watching it for several minutes. If the stove crashes into the bulkhead or hull, forget about cooking and find something cold to eat.

If you decide that it's safe to use the stove, you'll have to equalize the weight on both sides of the gimbal system's pivot point. If you want to cook something on a front burner, fill the teakettle or a saucepan with water and set it on an unlit back burner (using its pot restraints). Adjust the amount of water until the stove is approximately level.

Once you are finished cooking, latch the stove again so that if conditions worsen, the stove won't hit the hull.

Oven Door Latch. Most, but not all, oven doors on marine stoves have some sort of latching mechanism. If not, tie the handle so the door won't swing open with the motion of the boat (or install some sort of a latch). Even if you're not using the oven, you don't want the door to open unexpectedly and hit you; it's even worse if you're using the oven and a hot pan comes flying out.

Troubleshooting

There are dozens, if not hundreds, of models of boat stoves, and we can't begin to cover all the problems

that can arise. We do have a few tips for the three most common problems, though.

Can't Turn Down a Burner Low Enough. If your stove burner goes out before the flame is as low as you'd like, your best bet is to use a heat diffuser (also called a flame tamer or a simmer ring).

Other options include using a double boiler, getting a piece of aluminum from a machine shop (about the thickness of a cookie sheet and the diameter of your pan), or folding several layers of aluminum foil into your own heat diffuser (this is better than nothing, but the other options work much better).

The least expensive style of flame tamer works just as well as the more expensive ones, plus you can cut off the wooden handle to make it easier to stow and so it won't catch fire if it slides over a lit burner.

Oven Won't Heat Hot Enough. Newer (say, since 2000) ovens built for marine use seem to be much better than older ones. If your oven just doesn't get hot enough:

- Read the troubleshooting section in the owner's manual and follow its advice.
- Check out the FAQs or knowledge base on the manufacturer's website and see if it provides any clues. If possible, contact the manufacturer and describe your problem.

- Go over the installation instructions and make sure the oven is installed properly and the gas connections to it are all proper.
- Clean the gas jet(s) for the oven.

If all that doesn't get the oven working properly:

- Use the broiler (if you have one) to get the heat up to what it should be. The difficulty is that when you open the door to put in the food, some of the heat will escape. If you leave the broiler on for a few seconds after you put in the food, you can bring it back up to temperature, then turn off the broiler. But for anything that has to be baked more than 10 to 15 minutes, it's likely to cool down below the desired temperature again.
- Bake the item at the highest temperature you can achieve, for a longer time. In general, the result will be drier and won't have as crunchy an exterior.
- Some claim that using a baking stone (see below) and preheating it for 30 minutes will have the effect of baking as though the oven were 25° F hotter.

Uneven Oven Heat. The other common complaint about boat ovens (typically older ones) is that they have uneven heat, or hot spots that cause some areas to burn while other areas are undercooked. Generally, this is due to one (or both) of two reasons: a small heat shield over the flame in the bottom of the oven and/or the short distance from the flame to the rack where the pan is, both of which cause the heat to be concentrated in the center of the oven.

There are three "nothing-to-buy" solutions to try, but they generally provide only a partial solution:

- Move the rack your pan will sit on as high as possible in the oven.
- Turn the pan 180 degrees halfway through the baking process. If it's a small pan, put it first on the left side of the oven, then on the right.
- If you have a cookie sheet, put it under the pan or on the lower rack. This will help to diffuse the heat, but it does not do as good a job as a baking stone.

The best solution is to use a baking stone, also known as a pizza stone. These will also retain heat in the oven when you open the door, which can also be a problem with the small size of most boat ovens.

Baking stones are available at most kitchen stores and online through Amazon and other places. (If you can't find a stone where you are, see below for using unglazed tile.) Despite being called a "stone," they are actually a ceramic. The best ones for boats are rectangular and about 1" smaller all around than your oven, so air can move in the oven. If you can't find a stone that's the perfect size, buy one slightly too large and take it to any ceramic tile store or installer and have it cut to size. (Unless you have a tile saw, it's hard to do it yourself.) Otherwise, get the largest stone that will fit in your oven.

The stones come in various thicknesses, from about $1/4$ inch to almost 2 inches. The thinner ones have more of a problem with breaking but are faster to heat. In general, one at least $1/2$ inch thick seems to be the best for boat use, but they can be hard to find; most are thinner.

To stow the stone, just leave it in the oven! If it is slightly smaller than the oven and slides with the movement in the boat, use binder clips as discussed in the section on pot restraints, above, to keep it in place.

Put the stone in the oven before you light it (or immediately after if you have to light it manually and can't get to the burner with the stone in the oven). If you have two racks, put the stone on the lower one. Otherwise, put the rack low enough that your pan will fit in the oven on top of the stone, with at least 1 inch (preferably 2 inches) of airspace on top. Bake when the oven comes up to temperature.

Just place your pan directly on the stone. *Never* place a cold item (from the refrigerator or freezer) onto the hot stone; it will crack. Equally, never let liquids drip on a hot stone.

Cleaning the stone: The stone needs little care. Unless you spill something on it, you don't need to clean the stone. It will turn a little darker over time, but that's no reason to clean it. If you do spill something on it, wait until the stone is cold, then scrape off what you can with a plastic scraper (don't use metal).

Without a baking stone, the cookies in the center would have been burnt and the ones on the ends still raw.

Small binder clips will keep the baking stone from sliding—wrap a little aluminum foil around the wire if needed to keep the clip on.

A spatula for nonstick pans or a plastic putty knife works well. Then soak the stone in water if what's left won't just bake off. Don't use soap! Soap will permeate the stone and be impossible to rinse out. The stone must be totally dry before using again or it's likely to crack.

If you can't get a baking stone, you can create the same effect by using unglazed ceramic tiles (the key being *un*glazed). They can be cheaper but also thinner and easier to break or crack and don't hold heat as well. Unless they are quite large, they can also shift with the movement of the boat. However, they are definitely better than nothing. Sometimes you can get a large, heavy sheet of aluminum or stainless that you can use. Metal can still have some hot spots, but it will help.

Conserving Propane or Other Fuel

If you're cruising in hot climates, the following tips will not only help you conserve fuel, but you'll put less heat into the boat. Of course, if you're cruising where it's cool or downright cold, you may want your cooking to help keep the boat warm.

- **Measure water.** Measure it into the pan or teakettle so you're not heating more than you need.

- **Use less water.** If you're boiling something, you can usually use less water than you may be used to. Generally, barely covering a food with water cooks it just as well as covering the food by several inches. And every extra ounce of water takes just that much more propane to make boil.

- **Boil water for several dishes at once.** If you need hot water for several things about the same time (for example, in the morning I might make oatmeal and coffee, start yogurt, and brew concentrated tea for iced tea later in the day), plan ahead and heat the water all at once.

- **Keep hot water in a thermos.** Related to the above tip, if you know you're going to need more hot water in an hour or two, keep it in a thermos. Even if it needs to be freshly boiling when you use it, it will boil much faster if it starts out hot.

- **Thermos cooking.** Many foods requiring long cooking can be fully or partially cooked in a thermos. Although they have to be initially heated on the stove, it's a far shorter time than completely cooking the dish on the stove top. Check out "Special Galley Cooking Techniques."

- **Making iced tea tip #1.** Make Sun Tea (page 91).

- **Making iced tea tip #2.** If the weather doesn't allow you to make Sun Tea, make a concentrated brew with just 1 to 2 cups boiling water, and then add cool water to make the full amount desired.

- **Cover pots.** Water will boil faster in a covered pot, and you can generally cook at a lower heat.
- **Cooking pasta.** "Perfect" pasta requires lots of water and cooking without a lid. I honestly don't notice a difference in using about half the recommended water (and I have some friends who use even less) and covering the pan—this uses less water, less propane, and puts a LOT less steam in the boat (a real plus on hot days).
- **Rice, pasta, and couscous.** If you're looking for a starch to serve something else over, be aware of the relative cooking times of rice, pasta, and couscous:
  - Traditional brown rice simmers for about 45 minutes.
  - Traditional white rice simmers for about 20 minutes.
  - Instant brown rice simmers about 10 minutes.
  - Instant white rice simmers about 3 minutes.
  - Most dried pasta cooks in 8 to 10 minutes.
  - Couscous just has to be brought to a boil, then the fire is turned off.
- **Turn off the stove early.** Your pans and their contents retain a lot of heat and will continue to cook after the heat is turned off. You can often shut off the heat 5 to 10 minutes before the end of the cooking time (particularly if you have a lid on the pan) and let the pan sit on the stove, where it will finish cooking.
- **Cut foods in smaller pieces.** Smaller pieces cook faster than large ones, no matter what the cooking method—baking, boiling, sautéing, steaming, whatever. But if you make the pieces too small, everything turns to mush.
- **Pressure cooker.** Anything that needs to simmer for a long time, such as stews and soups, will cook in about one-third the time in a pressure cooker.
- **Use cold water for dishes.** Yes, the dishes *do* get clean!
- **Heat dishwater on the stove.** If you really prefer hot water for dishes, put about an inch of water in a dirty pan, add a squirt of dish soap, and heat it on the stove until it's warm. You can clean all the other dishes by dunking the sponge in the warm water, washing them, and rinsing with cold water. By the time the rest of the dishes are washed, the dirty pan has nicely soaked and is easy to clean.
- **Use a solar shower to heat dishwater.** If you're in a sunny locale, get an extra solar shower and use it to heat water for dishes. Leave it on deck and run the hose down through a porthole to the galley sink.
- **Baking.** First, don't preheat the oven longer than you have to. Time the preheating so the oven is just coming to the right temperature as you're ready to put in the food. Second, don't preheat for things that don't need it, such as most casseroles. Baked goods always need a preheated oven (unless the recipe states otherwise). Third, if you're baking a small dish for a meal, think about whether you can bake something else in the oven at the same time.

How to Gravity-Fill Propane

In most cruising locales, refilling your propane tank means sending it out to be refilled. Most cruisers will never need the information in this section. However . . .

Some otherwise wonderful cruising locales simply have no "normal" way to refill a propane tank. The problem is not a lack of propane, but that the local propane distributor can't refill your bottle. He only exchanges or rents full bottles that he gets from somewhere else.

Innovative cruisers have figured out how to gravity-drain propane from a full foreign propane tank (which usually has different fittings from the US tank) into an empty US/cruiser tank by utilizing a hose with special connections.

Get the supplies before you head into an area without propane refills. It's a good idea to assemble the transfer hose while you're still where you can get parts in case something doesn't quite fit (items 1 through 4 make up the transfer hose). You'll need:

1. The foreign-country propane adapter to fit on one end of the flexible hose, so you can connect the hose to the foreign tank.
2. Clean, clear PVC flexible hose tubing—so you can see the propane flowing—sized so the adapters fit

Safety Considerations

You are dealing with raw propane during this process, usually in or near your cockpit. Ideally, it's better to get it away from your boat, but if that's not possible, guard against propane leaking into the boat. Propane is heavier than air, so it sinks. It is also *extremely flammable* and probably one of the biggest causes of boat explosions and fires.

Attempt this at your own risk (we will not be liable for any damage or injuries), and *please, please* be careful! It's best to do it the first time with someone who has done it before. Ask on the radio. Someone is usually willing to help a first-timer.

If you smoke, do not smoke anywhere near this set-up, and be very careful in the area where the tank overflows once full. Make sure the propane is completely gone before lighting up!

and are long enough to reach between the tanks when arranged as described in the directions below.

3. Two stainless steel hose clamps (sized to attach the fittings on each end of the hose).
4. A brass pipe-to-hose fitting to go on the other end of the hose and connect the transfer hose to the hose on your tank (either male or female depending on the fitting on your existing hose to your tank).
5. Your hose to your propane tank.
6. A full local propane tank.
7. Your empty propane tank.

The transfer usually takes between one and three hours but depends greatly on how much of a temperature differential you can achieve. It's not unheard of to take overnight.

Step 1: Get a full propane tank and choose a location for the transfer. Just as in the Unites States, you can "rent" a tank, use it, and bring it back empty. You may be charged a refundable deposit for the tank.

Some propane providers insist you do the gravity drain on their premises, which isn't all bad because it keeps the dangerous fumes away from your boat. In this situation, you will need to bring with you your empty tank and all the apparatus to hang the full tank

and connect the tanks. If you transfer the propane ashore, be sure not to get sand in the fittings!

Step 2: The full bottle needs to be higher than the empty bottle and at a higher temperature. The temperature differential will determine how quickly the transfer will occur. The best transfer is where the full bottle is in full sun on a warm day and the empty bottle is in a very cool location, such as having the bottom of it in the water. But beware of potential corrosion problems with salt water and the metal of the tank.

Hang the full propane bottle upside down. Don't put it so high that you can't connect the hose or open the tank valve. If you use a halyard to hoist the full bottle, figure out some way to keep the bottle from swinging.

Put your empty tank below the full tank in as cool a location as possible and where any propane overflow will not go into your boat (propane is heavier than air and will cause explosions). Some cruisers leave the empty tank in the propane locker while others hang the empty bottle over the side of the boat in the water. Take care not to get water in the fittings.

Step 3: Attach your tank hose to the transfer hose and the transfer hose to the foreign tank. Propane is liquid. A key is to keep the clear flexible PVC hose hanging *down* with no kinks or curves to inhibit the gravity flow of the liquid.

Step 4: Open the valve on the empty tank and then open the valve on the full tank.

Step 5: The propane will begin flowing from the foreign tank into your tank. You will be able to see the propane flowing since it is a liquid moving through a clear hose. At a certain point the pressure in the two tanks will equalize and the propane will stop flowing. Release the pressure from your tank via the pressure relief valve until the propane flows again. Close the pressure relief valve.

Step 6: Continue the pressure relief step as often as needed until propane begins to flow out of your tank. At that point you have a "full" tank. It won't be as full as a pressurized refill, but you have propane again!

Step 7: Shut off the valve on your tank and then shut off the valve on the foreign tank. Disconnect the transfer hose from the foreign tank and then from your tank. Return the foreign tank to the distributor.

COOLERS/REFRIGERATORS/FREEZERS: USING AND TROUBLESHOOTING

The majority of long-term cruisers have refrigerators, and many have a freezer as well. Some have only an icebox or a cooler, although these tend to be those who cruise for shorter periods at a time (say a weekend to a week). Although I (Carolyn) had a refrigerator and a freezer on board, I've done several two- to three-month camping trips with only a cooler and will offer some tips on iceboxes and coolers as well.

Since most cruising boats have refrigeration, I'll start there. Most boat refrigerators are top loading, the theory being that (1) stuff won't fall out when the door is open and the boat moves a bit, and (2) since cold air sinks, you won't lose as much each time you open the refrigerator.

Reduce Energy Used by Refrigerators and Reduce Ice Needed in Iceboxes and Coolers

Refrigeration is generally the biggest energy drain on a cruising boat and can easily use 100 amp-hours a day or more in tropical climates. A few simple things can reduce the energy usage considerably. Many of these ideas apply to iceboxes as well as coolers.

Add Insulation. For some reason, boat designers like to put refrigerators next to the companionway, where the hot noon sun beats down on them. If this is the case with your boat, put some type of insulation— even a blanket or a towel will help—over the top. If your refrigerator is surrounded by teak, as mine is, which heats up and retains heat when the sun shines on it, you can drape it with a car windshield reflector or even more towels. You'll be surprised at how these lessen the energy consumption, particularly if your refrigerator was not well insulated to begin with.

Buy a sheet of rigid foam insulation, cut it to fit the inside of your refrigerator, and use a bit of silicone caulk or tape to hold it in place. Even if you don't have room to completely line the refrigerator, putting foam under the top and on the inside of the lid and on any common walls with the engine compartment will really help.

In tropical areas, it can also be helpful to hang a piece of white canvas or auto windshield reflector over the hull where the refrigerator is.

Drain. Does your refrigerator have a drain in the bottom? If so, close it or put a cork in it. Cold air falls, and if the drain isn't sealed off, you're just dumping cold air into the bilge or wherever your drain line leads. Just this one simple item cut more than 10 amp-hours a day from our energy needed.

Organize. Rummaging around in the refrigerator wastes a lot of energy. Figure out an organization plan that works for you so that you always know where things are. See the chapter "Food Storage" for more tips on organizing the refrigerator.

Fan. Adding a small fan (such as a 4-inch 12-volt computer fan) inside your refrigerator can help to circulate the cold air.

Keep It Full. Although it takes energy to chill foods down when they are first put into the refrigerator, once they are cold they help keep the area cold. If you have extra space in your refrigerator, add water bottles or soda cans to keep the refrigerator full and operating efficiently. In a hot climate, fill the refrigerator with warm drinks in the evening, when the cooler ambient temperatures make it easier for the refrigerator compressor to work.

Front-Loading Refrigerators

You can avoid much of the problem with food falling out if the refrigerator is installed so that the door opens forward or aft instead of toward the center of the boat. It's a good idea to use bins to put like foods together so that small jars won't slide around with the movement of the boat.

To avoid cold loss, you can use a plastic strip curtain (those clear plastic hanging strips used inside commercial refrigerators). Buy a few of the "replacement strips" (generally 8 inches wide and 8 feet long or more). Cut each into strips 3 to 4 inches wide and as long as the opening, then hang them from the top of the opening (exactly how depends on the refrigerator). The strips should overlap one another by at least one-quarter of a strip (half a strip is better)—in other words, two layers offset from each other. Since the strips are clear, you can see through them to locate what you want, then slide your hand in and grab it.

Top-Loading Refrigerators

Usually, a top-loading refrigerator is just one large space with a chill plate or a small freezer compartment in it, although some have a separate freezer. In general, it's coldest nearest the chill plate and colder at the bottom of the space than the top. If your refrigerator is one big box and you want more freezer (or almost-freezer) space, you can put a vertical divider in the refrigerator compartment, using insulating foam board (use duct tape to hold it in position so it's easy to remove when you defrost). The side that has the chill plate is an almost-freezer good for meats and other things that need to be kept very cold, and the other side is cool storage for produce. Adjust the relative temperatures by making holes in the divider so that the cold air circulates to some extent. After making one hole, wait a few days to see if it has the desired result or if you need to make another one. Continue until you're happy with the temperature in each section.

Making the Most of the Space

Due to the energy requirements, most boat refrigerators aren't large. There are several keys to making the best use of the space you do have:

- **Prioritize.** Think about what's most important to you to have cold: drinks, fresh veggies, cheese, meat, ice, or something else? How much of it has to be in the refrigerator? For example, you may decide to have only four cans of soda in the refrigerator, and then replace one each time you take one out. Or you may want a dozen cans of beer, so you're always ready to offer a cold one to guests.

- **What doesn't have to be refrigerated?** See the chapter "Food Storage" for more information on what does and does not need to be refrigerated.
- **What can go in a smaller container?** Many times, leftovers and things that you are chilling before serving can go in a plastic freezer bag, which takes up a lot less space than a whole bowl. Put the plastic bag into one of your storage bins, so that if a bag should leak, the mess is easy to clean up.

See the chapter "Food Storage" for tips on organizing the refrigerator.

Defrosting

Your refrigerator will run much more efficiently if you defrost whenever there is $1/4$ inch of frost built up. In the tropics, I had to defrost about once a month to keep the refrigerator operating efficiently. This doesn't have to be a huge chore. With a hair dryer and an inverter, I could defrost ours in about 35 minutes. It helps if all your food is already in bins.

Here are my tips on defrosting:

1. If you're in a hot climate, work fast so that food won't spoil.
2. Put your most perishable foods in the best coolers you have. Take the other bins out of the refrigerator and cover them with quilts, towels, pillows—whatever you have to insulate the contents.
3. Turn off the refrigerator and remove all dividers. If there is a drain in the bottom, open it.
4. Use a hair dryer to melt the ice buildup. Be careful not to actually get the hair dryer in any water, due to the electrocution risk. Many times, the hair dryer will cut off before all the ice is melted. This is a safety feature to keep it from getting too hot. Turn it off for a few minutes and let it cool off, then use it again.
5. Break off as many chunks of ice from the chill plate as possible and dump them in the sink. It is much easier to dry out the refrigerator if you don't let the ice melt in the bottom of the box.
6. Be very careful around the chill plate or freezer compartment not to puncture a tube. Use a dull knife to gently poke ice out of hard-to-reach places. Use the hair dryer to loosen it up

if necessary. Never use force, as you're likely to break something and then you'll be without a refrigerator.

7. When all else fails, you can pour hot water over a stubborn bit of ice. But this will create a lot more work to mop it all out of the bottom of the refrigerator if you don't have a drain.

8. Totally dry out the refrigerator, close the drain, and replace any dividers. Any moisture left in the refrigerator will quickly turn to frost and ice, necessitating another defrosting job.

9. Spray the evaporator or chill plate and all the nooks and crannies around it with nonstick cooking spray so that the next time the ice can be broken off much more easily.

10. Put the food back in.

11. Don't forget to turn the refrigerator back on!

Iceboxes and Coolers

How you use your icebox/cooler depends a lot on how readily you can get more ice. If you're just going out for an overnight, planning the cooler setup is a lot less complicated than if it's going to be a week before you can get more ice. Assuming that it will be at least five days before you get more ice, here are some tips:

- Keep drinks in a separate cooler. You'll get drinks out far more often than food, and keeping them separate means that the ice in the food cooler will last a lot longer.

- Get the best cooler you can. If you have an older cooler, it can pay to buy a new one. Coleman makes a line of Xtreme and Ultimate coolers that really work well. I used one on a car camping trip in 100-degree heat and could go five days or more before needing to buy more ice (this was using block ice and using the cooler for food, not drinks). There are other brands that also make superinsulated coolers that are tougher for long-term use.

- If you are buying a cooler, get the lightest color one you can. You don't need the cooler absorbing heat!

- When you pick out a cooler, remember that about half the space inside will be taken up by ice if it's going to have to last five days. Get a cooler that's large enough.

Using racks and ventilated bins in an icebox or a cooler will keep your food out of the meltwater and organized so you can quickly find what you need.

- Whether you're using an icebox or a cooler, put as much insulating material around it as you can, and try to keep it out of the sun.

- If you can, pre-chill as much of the food as possible in a regular refrigerator. Putting room-temperature items into the cooler will use up a lot of the ice's cooling power.

- Block ice lasts much longer than cubes, although cubes will chill things faster.

- Find racks to fit inside the cooler. Put ice under the racks, and then put your food in bins on the racks. This will keep your food out of the meltwater and organized so that you can find things quickly.

MISCELLANEOUS GALLEY SETUP TIPS

Over our years of cruising, we have learned a number of "tricks" that make galley life a little easier but which don't fall into any major category. Rather than leave them out, we grouped them together here.

Ventilation

In the galley, ventilation is necessary to get rid of cooking odors and to keep the cook (not to mention the rest of the boat) cool.

- If it's not buggy out, leave the screens off the portholes and hatches. Screens cut down on airflow.

- A venting exhaust fan over the stove can move a lot of hot air and food odors out of the boat.

A passive system, such as a dorade vent, won't do as much but is better than nothing.

- A wind scoop in a hatch can put a lot of air through the boat. Both of us use an omnidirectional scoop (also known as a 3-way or 4-way wind scoop) and think they are excellent, particularly in areas where currents hold you at an angle to the wind, where the wind frequently changes direction, and at docks.
- Fans go a long way, too. Put one in the galley where you can point it directly at yourself when cooking. I really like the 12-volt Caframo fans; they move a lot of air and use little power.

Water

Whether or not you want a watermaker depends a lot on where you cruise and for how long. In remote areas, particularly hot areas, or if you're living aboard away from the dock full time, a watermaker makes life much nicer. There are lots of pros and cons to having one, and it's way beyond the scope of this book to go into a detailed discussion of the merits.

A second issue is a water filter. Regardless of whether you have a watermaker, you probably put something (chlorine or another chemical) into your water tanks to keep "crud" from growing. It doesn't taste too good to drink, however. We both have Sea Gull water filter systems, which provide a dedicated tap of drinking and cooking water that is filtered to remove chorine, bacteria, and a host of other things. The water tastes great and is safe. However, the Sea Gull is fairly expensive initially, and replacement filters are also expensive—and almost impossible to find outside the United States.

A good alternative is to put a 10-inch water filter housing on the supply line to the galley. If you just want to reduce the chlorine taste in the water, any type of charcoal filter will do. If you want to remove almost as much bacteria and other things as the Sea Gull, use a 0.5 micron carbon block filter. The 10-inch filters can be found in most major cruising ports, although you may have a hard time finding the higher-quality ones.

Reduce Your Paper Towel Usage

Paper towels can be hard to find and/or expensive in many places. Get a 12-pack of "bar towels" or cheap terrycloth washcloths instead. They're easy to wash and work just as well for most things. There's also the environmental aspect to using fewer throwaway items, as well as less onboard trash.

The half-sheet size of paper towels can be hard to find outside the United States, but they're good for lots of things and will also conserve your supply. Although it's hard to tear a paper towel in half crosswise as it's coming off the roll, it's easy to tear them lengthwise!

Extra Counter Space

Think outside the box, or in this case outside the galley, for extra counter and food prep space. For example, on *Que Tal* I often use the middle companionway step (which is actually the top of the engine box) as an extra counter if we're in a calm anchorage. Aboard *Winterlude*, Jan has a cutting board that fits over the galley sink, increasing counter space by 25 percent.

Microwave

If you have a microwave on board and sometimes use it running off an inverter while you're away from the dock and sometimes on offshore power at a marina (or directly from a generator), be aware that it will have less power when running off an inverter.

Snack Bin

Keep a snack bin of stuff that's okay for anyone to eat without asking. This will lessen the chances of planning cashew chicken for dinner and discovering that someone ate the cashews as a snack, and your boat mates won't feel like they're three years old and having to ask for a snack.

Change What You Hate

If something in the galley just doesn't work for you, no matter how many other people say it's "right," change it.

Before we bought *Que Tal*, I read about galleys. Double sinks were considered essential, although I'm not quite sure why. So when the boat we liked for lots of other reasons also had a double sink, I thought it was perfect. After moving aboard *Que Tal*, I came to hate that double sink: the two halves were each so small that I couldn't put a dinner plate in the sink— even on edge, diagonally—let alone a pan. Our first boat improvement project was to install a single-bowl sink (custom made at a local machine shop). Suddenly, I could dump dirty dishes and hot pans in the sink. I loved it, even though the "experts" said it was wrong!

PROVISIONING

Discovering the differences of provisioning between various cultures can be one of the most fun adventures in cruising. Before we left the United States to go cruising, I (Jan) was convinced I had to bring vast quantities of certain provisions. But, believe it or not, people eat in all parts of the world; they also use toilet paper, paper towels, and other supplies. So while you may choose to stock up from home with special treats, be sure to be open-minded as you travel and provision. Trying new things and leaving some things to chance is a wonderful part of the cruising adventure.

To help you organize your purchasing needs, The Boat Galley website has a Downloadable Provisioning Spreadsheet at http://theboatgalley.com/downloadable-provisioning-spreadsheet/. You may prefer another setup, but this format has worked for *Que Tal* and *Winterlude*.

A STROLL THROUGH A CENTRAL AMERICAN *SUPERMERCADO*

One quick note: this chapter is based on my (Jan's) experiences. Some items that I could find easily, Carolyn almost never found, and vice versa. And availability of various items—and where you might find them—literally changes from week to week. So take this stroll as an example and learn from our experiences, but don't expect things to be the same where you are.

Before going to a supermarket in a country where you don't speak the language, take a pocket dictionary or a calculator-size translator. Standing in the baking section, searching for yeast, I discovered the importance of my forgotten translator when I accidentally purchased baking powder, not yeast.

General Provisioning Tips

- Take shopping bags with you. Some of the newer *supermercados* provide plastic bags; some of them charge extra. Besides, it's green to bring your own.
- Bring a thermal cold bag. You will probably need to bring these from the United States. You can keep meat, cheese, and yogurt chilled as you make your way back to the boat.
- Beer and pop don't always come in easy-to-carry cases; they are often sold by the individual can or bottle. We stuff them into a backpack. Just remember, you have to be able to carry the pack once you load it—particularly important in areas with no taxi service.
- Don't forget your own egg cartons in all the local markets or when buying from the veggie boats. If you buy unrefrigerated eggs, use the plastic camping egg containers with holes punched in the top and bottom to retard mold. Large modern supermarkets will have eggs in cartons, but they are often refrigerated. Once they've been refrigerated, you must continue to refrigerate them or they will go bad.
- If there's no taxi service, plan your shopping by how much you can carry. Often the bag boys are willing to help carry stuff to the boat—for an extra tip, of course.

- If you have a potentially wet dinghy ride back to the boat, take dry bags or oversize garbage bags to keep the salt spray off the food. The same oversize dry bags can be very helpful in getting clean, dry laundry back to the boat without salt spray.
- Try the local brands. You may like them better than US brands and they are almost always less expensive. But be careful if you are buying in bulk. Buy one of something first and try it before you have two dozen cans of edible but awful tuna taking up valuable space.
- If something is not in the location where you would generally find it, that doesn't mean the store doesn't have it. Always ask for something you need. Other countries put foods in the strangest places based on what you may be used to in the United States. For example, chocolate chips may be in the candy aisle instead of with baking supplies.
- Keep a stash of foods that you can eat if you become sick, since you may not be anchored in a place that's convenient to a supermarket or a *farmacia* (pharmacy) when you catch a cold or the flu. We always keep a few cans of chicken noodle soup, six cans of 7 Up or ginger ale, and regular saltines on hand just in case.
- You may need to go to several stores to find everything on your list. I am rarely successful in finding everything on my list, so be flexible and plan accordingly. Some items may be in grocery stores, but also look in *farmacias, carnicerias* (butcher shops), dollar stores, hardware stores, candy stores, *panaderias* (bakeries), and restaurant supply houses. Restaurant supply houses are often a source of otherwise hard-to-find items if they cater to resort hotels and restaurants in the area. Separate dairy and produce stands/stores may have surprisingly large selections of not just their specialty items but other things as well.

Ready to go through the doors of the *supermercado* with your translator or dictionary? Wait! Two more things . . .

First, where are the shopping carts? Look around. If they're available, they're often in very odd locations, frequently outside.

Second, immediately upon entering most stores in Latin American countries, you must surrender all packages and bags. Often there's a sign reading *Paqueteria* over a window. You leave the packages and bags and get a number—usually a plastic tag. The employee puts your packages in a bin labeled with the same number. You retrieve them on your way out of the store. Most stores strictly prohibit tipping. We have never had a problem with anything missing from our belongings. Note that if you carry a backpack as a purse, you may be asked to surrender it. Make sure your money and any personal identification are on your person.

Health and Beauty

Often the first section encountered is Health and Beauty, which includes such essentials as shampoo, soap, deodorant, lotions, and maybe items forgotten in your medical kit. If you take any vitamin supplements, bring them from the United States as they are often impossible to find in Latin American countries. Be sure to bring enough for the extent of your cruise.

Sunscreen is generally available but very expensive. Same goes for bug spray and lotions. If you have a preferred brand, bring it from home.

Bakery

The wafting aromas of freshly baked bread will draw you to the next area, the bakery. The goodies will not last (mold will set in shortly), so buy only enough to enjoy in the next day or so.

Household Goods

The household goods sections are often next, and we stock up on paper towels such as Scott Duramax (which I have yet to find in the United States, but they're wonderful), toilet paper, and plastic bags. (If you want to buy the local brand of plastic bags, be sure to buy one box and try them first. Some brands can be superior to US brand names, but others literally would not hold anything without splitting.) The try-one-first rule goes for all paper products, including toilet paper, paper towels, and tissues. For cleaning supplies, we usually buy white vinegar, bleach, ammonia, Joy dish soap (it lathers in salt water), and a gallon or more of vegetable oil for the head. White vinegar cleans lots of stuff and helps you avoid buying expensive US-brand task-specific cleaning items. Be careful, though, because vinegar can ruin the coating on some sunglasses. We know from experience.

Breads and Crackers

The breads and crackers section is often hidden in the recesses of the *supermercado* and is generally much smaller than similar-size supermarkets in the United States. Be aware that store-bought bread molds in a couple of days in the tropics. The exception to this rule is Bimbo brand bread. It must be chock-full of all kinds of preservatives, but it tastes good. In the last few years, Bimbo has come out with *integral* (wheat) and whole-grain breads. We have had Bimbo bread keep up to three months aboard in the tropics of Panama—unopened. Once you open a loaf, it lasts two to three days, a week at the most, before mold sets in.

Also in the breads section are things like bread crumbs and special mixes used to coat fish for frying.

Crackers are usually in this section as well, although not always. We stock up on any whole-grain crackers we can find; they are becoming more common. *Integral* (wheat) crackers, usually Nabisco Club Social *Integral* (similar to Club crackers in the United States) are tasty.

Also note that in Spanish the word *galletas* can mean sweet cookies or regular crackers, so make sure you know what you're buying. Crackers (and cookies) in Central America are often individually packaged. This type of packaging works well in the humidity of the tropics.

Spices

Spices add flavor and store easily, allowing us to add a wide variety of flavors to canned as well as fresh food.

One thing to keep in mind: spices do not last forever, and in the heat and humidity found in tropical cruising grounds, they may congeal or lose flavor faster than normal.

Nothing tops fresh spices, such as cilantro, ginger, garlic, and basil, but they are generally fragile, do not store well (with the exception of garlic and ginger),

and are unavailable in remote parts of the world. For this reason, some cruisers grow their own herbs, although neither of us has. Don't forget to buy extra bay leaves to slip into flour, pasta, rice, and any other dry foods to help keep out weevils (see more about this in the chapter "Food Storage").

In many smaller markets, salt is available only in plastic bags, and it does not have the fine-grained consistency of iodized salt. Sea salt, which has larger crystals, is becoming more common. See the chapter "Food Storage" for tips on storing it.

Available spices vary widely from country to country, but readily available ones usually include garlic powder, garlic salt, salt, and ground pepper. Luckily, your other favorites are easily packed and take little space to bring from home. In some places, spices and herbs are sold in bulk, and you'll be given a little bag of your chosen spice.

Condiments

The condiment aisle is another place where the selection will vary widely by where you happen to be. For the most part, you can always get ketchup. Some local brands are good, but others leave you wishing you'd sprung for the extra money to buy Heinz, so try one bottle of the local brand before you buy more. In general, local brands will have a lot more sugar and taste sweeter.

Also readily available in many areas are mustard (sometimes Dijon or horseradish mustard), sweet pickle relish, mayonnaise, barbecue sauce, honey, and jelly. Hellman's makes a handy disposable plastic squeeze pack of mayonnaise that fits easily in the fridge. Jelly can be readily available—again try local brands. We like some better than US brands, but some are horrid. It's best to stick with US brands for peanut butter; the local brands are often very sweet, or are dry, tasteless paste.

The two things that we regularly could not get were dill pickle relish and real horseradish (not horseradish sauce). If you want to make tuna salad with dill relish or mix real horseradish with ketchup for your shrimp cocktail sauce, bring these items from home.

Be careful of buying seasoning packets such as taco seasoning. Due to the humidity on the boat, these packets turn into a sticky mess, often before you can eat them. We limit the quantity of packets (we don't buy a six-month supply) and put them in a plastic freezer bag to reduce the humidity infiltration. See the chapter "Food Substitutions" for ways to make your own seasonings.

Juice/Drinks/Beer/Wine/Spirits

Soda pop, juice, and other drinks are all widely available. If you want a certain brand, buy it when you see it. The next stop may have only the "other" brand. Beer and wine are usually available in the larger *supermercados*, and, just as in the United States, the prices may be slightly higher than at the distributor. But the convenience may be worth the extra expense.

V-8 or other vegetable juice will provide two servings of vegetables—a consideration if you're out of fresh produce. The recipes in this book can use V-8 as a substitute for tomato sauce; just be sure to compensate for the extra liquid.

Local brands of coffee can be very good, or very bad. In Central America, most of the grade A coffee is exported to Europe or the United States, so buyer beware. If you're in Panama, try the yellow-packaged Duran coffee.

Drinks are usually available in plastic containers and, even better, Tetra Paks—foil-lined cardboard containers perfect for storage aboard a boat.

We stock only enough water bottles to keep four in the fridge because they're smaller and more space flexible than a larger container of water. With the watermaker, we simply refill the bottles. Same with Gatorade—we buy a few bottles ready-made and then refill them with powdered Gatorade and water. Powdered Gatorade can be found in most (but not all) larger provisioning areas. We bring our own just in case.

If you are cruising Belize, be sure to try Squash, a liquid drink concentrate available in a variety of flavors. Lime Squash is particularly prized amongst cruisers who enjoy an occasional margarita. Margarita mix is very expensive and difficult to find, but Lime Squash fills in nicely.

Keep in mind your cruising area when buying all drinks; for example, in Panama you can find most items in Panama City or Colon, but provisioning in the San Blas islands is quite a challenge. Cruisers bring a six-month supply of Coke or especially Diet Coke—diet, or diet without caffeine, is rarely seen outside major markets.

Don't forget to stock up on wine plus any special spirits that you enjoy. As an example, gin is not available anywhere in the western Caribbean except the Rio Dulce or Panama City. Likewise, tonic water is difficult to find outside the larger cities, so if you enjoy gin and tonics, bring your supply. (Note from the editor: the small, individual cans of tonic, so readily available in New England, are great to stock up on since they prevent the flat-tonic syndrome.) Beware that drink cans outside the United States are generally *very* thin—so thin that holes can be worn in the aluminum cans if they are stored where they can rub together, creating a sticky mess!

Wine is available in most places, but if you're a real connoisseur, better stock the boat with your favorite vintages when you're in a big city. We buy several cases of Clos, wine that comes in one-liter Tetra Pak type of boxes: no bladder, just foil-lined cardboard. It stows easier than bottled wines. Keep in mind that heat and motion seem to prematurely age wine, so, often younger wines taste much better after being aboard and aged wines can go to vinegar much more quickly.

Canned Vegetables, Fruits, and Soups

Supplement fresh provisions with canned goods. Be sure to take more than you anticipate needing. Canned goods don't go bad and are very useful when unanticipated circumstances arise, such as getting trapped by weather in a remote anchorage.

Many canned goods that are easily available "everywhere" are simply not available in some cruising areas. Canned green beans are virtually non-existent in Belize, Guatemala, and Honduras. Condensed cream soups and canned tomatoes can be difficult to find on the Pacific side of Mexico, including La Paz and the Sea of Cortez. (Note that availability can change rapidly—for the better or the worse!)

One of my favorite discoveries is pre-seasoned tomato sauce, which has a big burst of flavor. Tomato *criolla* is in a foil packet, which stores very easily. It has the consistency of a thick tomato sauce, but it has peppers, onions, and spices already mixed in for a nice base flavor.

Rice, Beans, and Spaghetti

This aisle will provide the staples of your provisioning.

We like beans, and with so many variations including a variety of lentils, we'll eat them twice a week for the six-month duration of our cruise. Rice and Beans (see page 185) is a favorite because there are always leftovers—which means just a bit of reheating for overnight passages or for those days when maintenance projects turn out to be never-ending. Luckily, rice, dried beans, and pasta are generally available in most smaller *tiendas* (stores).

Couscous, orzo (rice-size pasta), and specialty pastas are very difficult to find. Whole-grain pasta is becoming increasingly available. Not surprisingly, quinoa is found everywhere in South America since it originated as a South American staple, but it is not found in other parts of the Caribbean.

Baking Supplies

In large *supermercados* you will find prepackaged goods; in smaller markets, you may find only white flour and sugar in barrels. We make sure to stock up on the other items such as cocoa, brown sugar, baking powder, and baking soda while we're doing major reprovisioning. Also, keep in mind that the humidity will affect baking essentials more than other provisioning items. Store your baking soda in its paper box in a plastic freezer bag to help keep out humidity.

Be careful when buying baking supplies from tiny *tiendas*. Whether buying in bulk from open barrels or items in plastic bags with twist ties, there is an increased likelihood of getting more than you paid for in the way of bugs or critter eggs.

Cereals

In the past, the only cereals available were sickeningly sweet or local stale corn flakes. More recently, I found Total Raisin Bran and had many other choices.

Snacks, Chips, Cookies, and Candy

Sometimes you just have to have a Tostito or an Oreo. Our favorite snack is Snyder's Pretzel Pieces, readily available in larger provisioning markets. The package size is about right for happy hour for four. Plus they come in yummy flavors such as Hot Buffalo Wing, Garlic, Honey Mustard, Jalapeño, Cheddar Cheese, and others.

Depending on where you are, you may find chips only in single-serving packages, even in large stores. We guess that the intent is to keep them fresh from the humidity, but it's annoying to find an entire aisle stocked with nothing but individual packages. The Honduran Bay Islands are a prime example of this practice.

Be sure to try local brands; they will often be as good, if not better than, US brands at a fraction of the price. But try one before you get a six-month supply. One of our favorites is Zambos Chili Cheese Plantain Chips, available only in Honduras (at least that's the only place we found them, and we were on the lookout).

We always keep a supply of trail mix on hand. Mixing salted peanuts, raisins, and M&M's together satisfies a sweet and salty snack craving all at one time.

Frozen Foods

Since our freezer aboard will freeze meat and ice cubes with no room for anything else, the frozen foods aisle offers nothing of interest, unless you count a small container of ice cream eaten on the way back to the boat.

Meat Counter

The meat counter often feels like an alien adventure. Virtually nothing looks familiar, and the smell can be overwhelming even in a refrigerated case. Some meats are prepackaged and available to pick up, but for most meats you will have to take a number and speak in a foreign language to someone who doesn't speak English. Fear not—it's not as overwhelming as it seems.

The first thing to realize is that in most countries meats do not come in pounds; they come in kilos. The basic conversion is 1 kilogram = 2.2 US pounds. Ask for a half or media-kilo and you'll get a bit over a pound US.

Chicken is available everywhere. Unfortunately it's usually a whole chicken, sometimes with the head and feet intact. To learn what to do with such a monstrosity, see the chapter "Meat Main Dishes." You'll not only learn how to get rid of the head and feet,

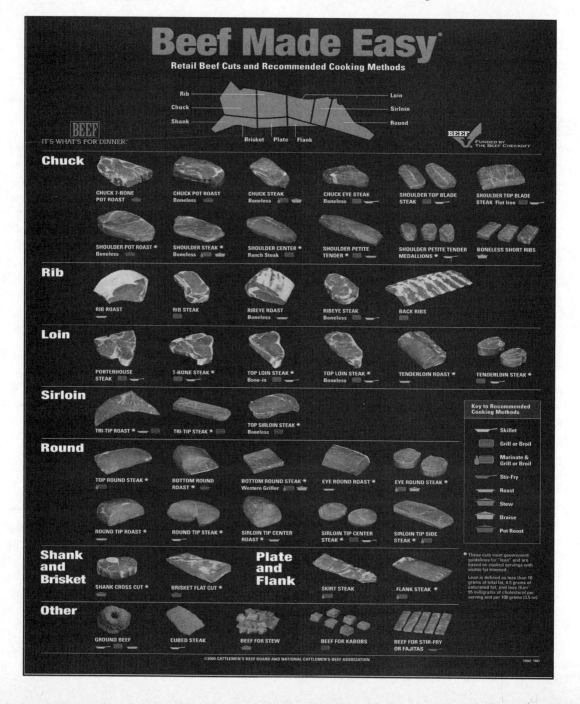

Provisioning

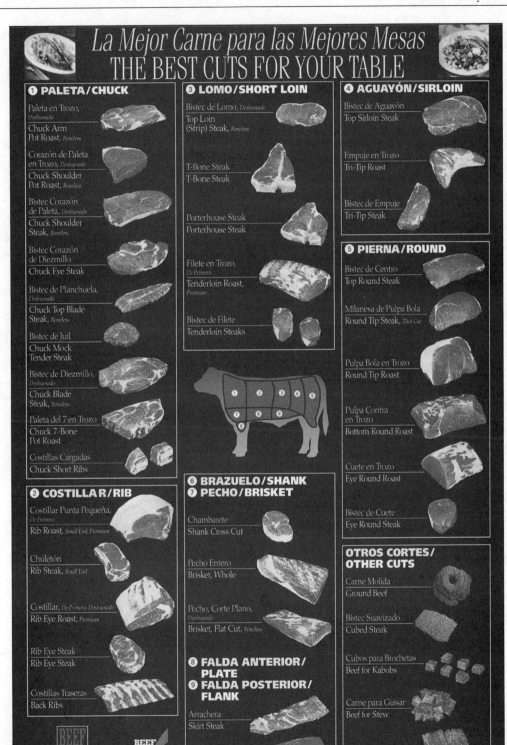

La Mejor Carne para las Mejores Mesas
THE BEST CUTS FOR YOUR TABLE

❶ PALETA/CHUCK

Paleta en Trozo, *Deshuesada*
Chuck Arm Pot Roast, *Boneless*

Corazón de Paleta en Trozo, *Deshuesado*
Chuck Shoulder Pot Roast, *Boneless*

Bistec Corazón de Paleta, *Deshuesado*
Chuck Shoulder Steak, *Boneless*

Bistec Corazón de Diezmillo
Chuck Eye Steak

Bistec de Planchuela, *Deshuesado*
Chuck Top Blade Steak, *Boneless*

Bistec de Juil
Chuck Mock Tender Steak

Bistec de Diezmillo, *Deshuesado*
Chuck Blade Steak, *Boneless*

Paleta del 7 en Trozo
Chuck 7-Bone Pot Roast

Costillas Cargadas
Chuck Short Ribs

❷ COSTILLAR/RIB

Costillar Punta Pequeña, *De Primera*
Rib Roast, *Small End, Premium*

Chuletón
Rib Steak, *Small End*

Costillar, *De Primera, Deshuesado*
Rib Eye Roast, *Premium*

Rib Eye Steak
Rib Eye Steak

Costillas Traseras
Back Ribs

❸ LOMO/SHORT LOIN

Bistec de Lomo, *Deshuesado*
Top Loin (Strip) Steak, *Boneless*

T-Bone Steak
T-Bone Steak

Porterhouse Steak
Porterhouse Steak

Filete en Trozo, *De Primera*
Tenderloin Roast, *Premium*

Bistec de Filete
Tenderloin Steaks

❻ BRAZUELO/SHANK
❼ PECHO/BRISKET

Chambarete
Shank Cross Cut

Pecho Entero
Brisket, Whole

Pecho, Corte Plano, *Deshuesado*
Brisket, Flat Cut, *Boneless*

❽ FALDA ANTERIOR/PLATE
❾ FALDA POSTERIOR/FLANK

Arrachera
Skirt Steak

Falda
Flank Steak

❹ AGUAYÓN/SIRLOIN

Bistec de Aguayón
Top Sirloin Steak

Empuje en Trozo
Tri-Tip Roast

Bistec de Empuje
Tri-Tip Steak

❺ PIERNA/ROUND

Bistec de Centro
Top Round Steak

Milanesa de Pulpa Bola
Round Tip Steak, *Thin Cut*

Pulpa Bola en Trozo
Round Tip Roast

Pulpa Contra en Trozo
Bottom Round Roast

Cuete en Trozo
Eye Round Roast

Bistec de Cuete
Eye Round Steak

OTROS CORTES/OTHER CUTS

Carne Molida
Ground Beef

Bistec Suavizado
Cubed Steak

Cubos para Brochetas
Beef for Kabobs

Carne para Guisar
Beef for Stew

Tiritas de Carne
Beef for Stir-Fry

BEEF
IT'S WHAT'S FOR DINNER:
Funded by America's Beef Producers.

BEEF

Pork Basics

The Other White Meat
Don't be blah.

Upper row (l-r):
Bone-in Blade Roast,
Boneless Blade Roast
Lower row (l-r):
Ground Pork (The Other Burger®),
Sausage, Blade Steak

Cooking Methods
*Blade Roast/Boston butt –
  roast, indirect heat on grill,
  braise, slow cooker
Blade Steak –
  braise, broil, grill
Ground Pork –
  broil, grill, roast (bake)*

Shoulder Butt

Upper row (l-r):
Smoked Picnic,
Arm Picnic Roast
Lower row:
Smoked Hocks

Cooking Methods
*Smoked Picnic Roast –
  roast, braise
Arm Picnic Roast –
  roast, braise, slow cooker
Smoked Hocks –
  braise, stew*

Picnic Shoulder

Top:
Spareribs
Bottom:
Slab Bacon, Sliced Bacon

Cooking Methods
*Spareribs –
  roast, indirect heat on
  grill, braise, slow cooker
Bacon –
  broil, roast (bake),
  microwave*

Side

Upper row (l-r):
Bone-in Fresh Ham,
Smoked Ham
Lower row (l-r):
Leg Cutlets,
Fresh Boneless Ham Roast

Cooking Methods
*Fresh Leg of Pork –
  roast, indirect heat on grill,
  slow cooker
Smoked Ham –
  roast, indirect heat on grill
Ham Steak –
  broil, roast*

Leg

Loin

Chops

Roasts

Upper row (l-r):
Sirloin Chop, Rib Chop, Loin Chop
Lower row (l-r):
Boneless Rib End Chop, Chef's Prime Filet™ –
Boneless Center Loin Chop, America's Cut™ –
Butterfly Chop

Cooking Methods
*Cutlets (⅛ to ¼ inch) – sauté
Thin (½ to ¾ inch thick) – grill, broil,
Thick (1¼ to 1½ inch thick) – grill, broil, roast*

Upper row (l-r):
Center Rib Roast (Rack of Pork),
Bone-in Sirloin Roast
Middle:
Boneless Center Loin Roast
Lower row (l-r):
Boneless Rib End Roast,
Chef's Prime™ – Boneless Sirloin Roast

Cooking Methods
roast, indirect heat on grill, slow cooker

Tenderloin & Canadian-Style Bacon

Left: Tenderloin **Right:** Canadian-Style Bacon

Cooking Methods
*Tenderloin – roast, grill, pan broil
Canadian-Style bacon – roast, broil, sauté*

Ribs

Left: Country-Style Ribs **Right:** Back Ribs

Cooking Methods
roast, indirect heat on grill, braise, slow cooker

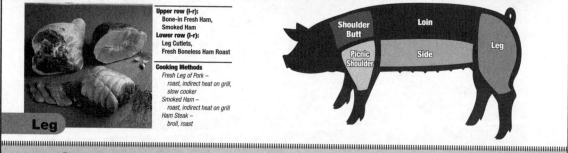

Shoulder Butt   Loin
Picnic Shoulder   Side   Leg

Roasts
No-fuss family dinner or holiday favorite

THE MANY SHAPES OF PORK
Cut Loose!

When shopping for pork,
consider cutting traditional
roasts into a variety of
different shapes

Chops
Dinner, backyard
barbecue or
gourmet entree

Cubes
Great for kabobs,
stew and chili
grill, stew, braise, broil

Strips
Super stir fry,
fajitas and salads
grill, sauté, stir fry

Cutlets
Delicious breakfast
chops and
quick sandwiches
1/8 to 3/8 inch thick –
sauté, grill

El cerdo es bueno™

U.S. Pork - Datos de Nutrición

U.S. Pork es sano

- Los productores de U.S. pork usan mejoradas técnicas de genética y producción para producir carne de cerdo que es 31% más magro que el cerdo de hace 20 años atrás*.
- El filete de lomo de cerdo tiene sólo 1 gramo de grasa más que la pechuga de pollo sin piel.
- El cerdo también es una gran fuente de proteínas, aminoácidos esenciales, hierro, zinc y vitaminas B.
- Usted no tiene que memorizar los nombres de los cortes más magros del cerdo. Sólo busque "loin" en el nombre (en inglés), tal como "pork loin" o "pork sirloin roast."

*Fuente de información de nutrición: USDA Handbook 8 Series.

U.S. Pork - Facts on Nutrition

U.S. Pork is Healthy

- U.S. pork producers utilize improved genetics and production techniques to produce pork that is 31% leaner than 20 years ago*.
- Pork tenderloin has only one more gram of fat than a skinless chicken breast.
- Pork is a great source of high-quality protein, essential amino acids, iron, zinc, and B vitamins.
- You don't have to memorize the names of the leanest pork cuts. Just look for "loin" in the name (in English), such as pork loin chop or pork sirloin roast.

*Source for Nutrition Information: USDA Handbook 8 Series.

Pig diagram labels:
- Cabeza de Lomo (Shoulder - Butt)
- Lomo (Loin)
- Filete (Tenderloin)
- Pierna (Leg)
- Espaldilla (Shoulder - Picnic)
- Costillar (Side)

LOMO (LOIN)

- Caña Regia — Boneless Center Loin
- Chuleta Prime — Chef's Prime
- Chuleta Sirloin — Boneless Sirloin Chop
- Chuletón — Bone-in Center Cut Loin Chop
- Chuleta Núñe — Thin Cut Boneless Loin Chop
- Chuleta Emperador — Stuffed Chop
- Chuleta Michigan — Butterfly Chop
- Sirloin — Top Sirloin
- Costilla de Lomo — Rack of Pork
- Chuleta de Costilla — Bone-in Rib Chop
- Chuleta de Centro sin Hueso — Center Cut Boneless Chop
- Rib Eye — Rib Eye
- Sirloin Roast — Sirloin Roast
- Costilla Barbecoa — Barbecue Ribs
- Punta de Costilla — Back Ribs

FILETE (TENDERLOIN)

- Filete de Cerdo — Tenderloin
- Filete Francia — Thin Cut Tenderloin
- Medallón Monarca — Tenderloin Medallions
- Mignon — Filet Wrapped
- Trocito de Filete — Tenderloin Tips

CABEZA de LOMO (SHOULDER - BUTT)

- Roast — Bone-in Blade Roast
- Chuleta Arriera — Blade Steak
- Trocito — Stew Meat
- Entera — Boneless Blade Roast
- Costilla Asadera — Butt Steak
- Costilla Ranchera — Country Style Ribs
- Deshebrada — Strips
- Medallón del Rey — Boneless Pork Butt Steak w/Bacon

PIERNA (LEG)

- Entera — Bone-in Whole Ham
- Pierna Ahumada — Smoked Ham
- Pierna Regia — Ham Roast
- Chamorro — Ham Hock
- Molida — Ground Pork
- Milanesa — Thin Cut Ham Steak
- Cubito — Cubes
- Tampiqueña — Thin Cut Ham Strips
- Fajitas — Fajita Strips
- Tablilla con Hueso — Bone-in Ham Steak
- Chuleta de Contra — Butterfly Ham Steak
- Chuleta de Bola — Boneless Ham Steak
- Alambre — Kabobs
- Bisteck Suave — Tenderized Steak / Cutlet

COSTILLAR (SIDE)

- Entera — Spare Ribs

pork
Calidad U.S. Pork.™

but you'll also learn the essentials in cutting up your chicken.

Always remember that in smaller *tiendas*/stores, meat may have been frozen and refrozen several times due to electrical outages, making it less safe than in the United States. Keep an eye out for freezer burn and ice crystals, which indicate that maybe the meat hasn't always been in a frozen state.

To facilitate beef and pork choices, we have included selection charts from the National Cattlemen's Beef Association (see pages 30–31) and the National Pork Board Des Moines Iowa (see pages 32–33). While the cuts you see at the meat counter may not be exactly as illustrated, hopefully this will give you an idea of what cut you have purchased and how best to cook it.

Although canned meats are not found at the meat counter, don't forget to stock up on them. Tuna, salmon, chicken, corned beef, and turkey are all generally available and will go a long way toward making delicious meals if fresh meat is not available. See chapter "Canned Meats and Seafood" for dozens of tasty recipes.

Dairy

Milk in other countries is not always kept in the refrigerated section. Without reliable refrigeration, "fresh milk" as Americans think of it may be virtually impossible to find. But there are acceptable alternatives, including boxed milk or powdered milk. For more details, see chapter "Dairy."

Eggs. Eggs are rarely refrigerated. These eggs may be the freshest and best you've ever eaten. Unrefrigerated eggs don't need refrigeration once you get back to the boat. See the chapter "Food Storage" for more specifics.

Butter. If you're cruising in most places except Mexico (which has only US and local brands), butter is a huge treat. For whatever reason, many foreign brands of butter are better than US brands. They will normally be in the refrigerated section, although you can get blue tins of New Zealand butter that do not have to be refrigerated. New Zealand Anchor butter is among the best. Danish butter also ranks among the

top brands. Sometimes, the local butter (i.e., butter made in the country you are cruising) can be flavorless, so buyer beware! Buy just one of a brand until you know you like it.

Also, with butter you'll find "*con sal*" and "*sin sal.*" This is another time when it's imperative to know the language or get out the translator. *Con sal* translates to "with salt" and *sin sal* is "without salt." Butter packages look more like a typical Philadelphia cream cheese package than a stick of butter. And a "stick" of butter is not the same size as in the United States— see the chapter "Measurements and Conversions." Recently, we've found some brands of butter that are mixed with canola oil to make a "spreadable" butter in tubs similar to US brands.

Produce

Fresh produce doesn't keep well and requires cool storage, a real challenge from many cruisers' perspective. Take advantage of every possible opportunity to get fresh produce.

Before shopping for fresh produce, talk to cruisers already in the area for any local knowledge. For example, after not having lettuce for months, we anchored in West End, Roatan. Other cruisers were raving about the hydroponic lettuce mix bags that were available only on certain days in certain *tiendas*. Not just iceberg lettuce, but radicchio, romaine, shredded carrots, and spinach. This mix was better than anything found in the United States.

Tomatoes are readily available from veggie boats as well as stocked in the smallest village shops.

Bananas are mostly available everywhere (not always in Mexico), a lot of times by the stalk in the bottom of a wood *cayuco* (canoe) in outlying islands. Be careful when buying bananas. Locals will tell you that what you're looking at is a banana when actually it is a plantain. We usually asked for "bananas dulce" (sweet bananas). If you're buying a stalk of bananas, beware—once they start to ripen, the entire stalk often lasts only a day or two before turning black.

Plantains, the food that masquerades as a banana, can be a valuable addition to your larder. There are a variety of ways to fix plantains, not all of which are fried. Try steaming them for ten minutes, then throw on some spices and drizzle with olive oil as a replacement for potatoes/starch.

Other readily available vegetables are cabbage, potatoes, onions, and carrots (sometimes the biggest I've ever seen, and bigger does not mean bad; the carrots were sweet, juicy, and delicious!). Also cucumbers, a variety of peppers, *christophene* (also called *chayote*, a squash), and garlic. Occasionally you'll find broccoli, cauliflower, or zucchini, but not regularly. I found asparagus once.

Other readily available fruits include apples (except in Mexico). We like Gala because they stay crunchy and juicy longer than Red Delicious, which are the most readily available but can be mushy. Oranges and limes (or *limónes*—the smaller ones we call "Key limes") are also readily available.

Checking Out

When you check out, a bag boy or girl will bag your goods. They may offer to take everything out of your cart and put it on the conveyor before you go through the checkout process. They may also take the cart outside and help you load groceries into a taxi or a bus. Be sure to give them a tip. Carolyn bases a tip on the price of a Coke locally—a tip equal to the price of one Coke for a normal amount of groceries, two Cokes for a big load or extraordinary service, and three Cokes if it's a big load and exceptional service, such as calling a taxi, helping load the taxi, etc.

Don't forget to pick up any packages or bags you left at the *paqueteria* on the way out!

This concludes our trip to the *supermercado*, but this is not the most fun place to buy provisions. Be sure to explore the local markets, the tortilla *tienda*, and the local *carniceria* (butcher) and *panaderia* (bakery). While you're at it, don't forget to enjoy some street food.

Travel advice is often to avoid local foods because of the possibility of Montezuma's revenge. But we have enjoyed street food for years without any trouble, and we have gotten food poisoning at swanky restaurants. Choose street vendors who seem to have lots of customers (always a good sign at restaurants, too). High turnover means that the food won't sit and develop bacteria, and that's the key to successful local food fun.

TIPS FOR BUYING IN AN OUTDOOR OR FARMER'S MARKET

We've both bought from outdoor markets, farmer's markets, veggie boats, and local fishermen.

- Have fun! This is where you get to join in the culture and have a good time. Do not be afraid to ask the woman behind the stall what something is if you don't recognize it. And don't stop there; ask how to cook it. Even if your language skills are marginal, most times with pantomime and broken language, you'll get the essence. Do not miss this part of the cruising experience.
- The advice that markets are "dangerous" can be misleading. Take normal precautions and you'll have a great experience. Do not wear jewelry or carry a purse or anything that screams "grab me."
- Sometimes locals will be offering samples of fruits or vegetables and you have no idea what they are. Be adventurous and try them. You may find a new favorite.
- Bring your own bags; vendors rarely have them.
- Carry small change; the volume of business they do rarely allows them to have change for $5 or $1, let alone $20.
- Buying in bulk increases the risk of encountering critters. Be sure to store flour and other bulk purchases separately, and put bay leaves in the container to control any "extras."

OTHER SHOPS FOR PROVISIONING

Outside of very major cities, you probably will need to make some other stops to find everything you need.

Local *Tortillaria*

The *tortillaria* is wonderful for tortillas that you'll use in the next couple of days; they go bad quickly. You can buy flour tortillas or corn tortillas, usually in a couple of different sizes. They're hot right off the grill, and we eat a couple as we walk down the street.

Local *Carniceria*

This is the butcher shop. The "meat counter" may not have anything displayed since local *carnicerias* usually do not have "excess" refrigeration. Usually there are oversize chest freezers lining a wall or two. Open them and look to get an idea of what is available. Ask for what you want; meat is generally cut to order. Use the Spanish/English cuts of beef chart earlier in this chapter for reference. If your language skills aren't top-notch, bring this book; pointing to a photo often yields results.

Local *Panaderia*

You'll recognize the local *panaderia* (bakery) by the fabulous tempting aromas drifting for blocks around. Often they're in someone's back room or just in the house. Our experience in Central America is that while the aroma is amazing, the baked goods often lack the melt-in-your-mouth flavor, and no preservatives means you probably can't buy more than a day or two days' worth of baked goods. That's fine—usually warm out of the oven is best anyway. Just come back tomorrow.

Some great baked goods can be found in the strangest places. In Placencia, Belize, a local entrepreneur baked the most amazing coconut bread and cinnamon buns. She packed them all up in a battered black wheelbarrow, and at 4 P.M. her son pushed it down the main street singsonging, "Anybody can buy, anybody can buy, don't miss the treats." Of course tempting aromas wafted down the street as he passed! Needless to say, the load of baked goods disappeared quickly.

FOOD STORAGE

Storing food on a boat is different than in a house. For one thing, the storage areas are different. There is no large pantry, and a lot of your food will be stored outside the galley—under settees, in lockers, or even in the bilge. Most likely, your refrigerator opens from the top, so organizing it is different. And there's more that you have to protect your food from.

There are five goals in food storage aboard a boat:

1. Protect food from the motion of the boat—crushing, chafing, breakage.
2. Protect food from heat and humidity.
3. Store foods so they don't harbor or attract bugs.
4. Make foods and ingredients as easy to access as possible.
5. Make efficient use of space to have sufficient food for the trip.

Every boat is different, and there's no one perfect layout. In this chapter, we give you some tips and insights that we've learned. Still, expect to rearrange things a few times before you get it right for you. Both of us have made several changes as we discovered what did and didn't work and as we traveled from one country to another and found that food availability and packaging changed.

In this chapter, we'll look at the supplies for effective food storage on a boat, developing a food storage plan, the specifics of storing different types of food, and finally some special precautions to take in bringing food aboard and accessing it to avoid pests.

STORAGE CONTAINERS AND SUPPLIES

To effectively store food on your boat, you're going to need some supplies:

- Food storage containers
- Bins and possibly gear hammocks
- Plastic bags and, if desired, a vacuum sealer (see page 13)
- Permanent markers
- Non-skid shelf paper
- Tube socks or other padding material
- Bug deterrents

Food Storage Containers

Initially, you will need a LOT of storage containers as you plan and organize your food storage. They'll serve as your canisters for everything—not just flour and sugar as when you're ashore, but also for things like pasta, baking mixes, and all your extra stocks of food. Getting good storage containers can be a significant expense in outfitting your galley.

Containers with square corners and straight sides make the most efficient use of space, but the primary concerns have to be that they are heavy enough not to crack and lids will stay sealed. See the section Plastic Storage Containers (page 13) for tips on selecting containers.

Bins and Gear Hammocks

You'll use plastic bins to organize lockers and the refrigerator. Solid ones are good to contain things that would be messy if they broke, such as oils and honey (and on a boat, any container can break). Use ventilated bins for things that need airflow. In addition to things marketed as storage bins, I (Carolyn) used milk crates, small wastebaskets with air holes drilled in them, and plastic juice and water containers with the tops cut off.

Gear hammocks are wonderful for stowing all sorts of lightweight and breakable items, such as bread, eggs, produce, chips, and so on. I hung four gear hammocks from the overhead handholds in *Que Tal*'s saloon. Best of all, they're cheap!

Plastic Bags and Possibly a Vacuum Sealer

Good plastic bags are essential; a vacuum sealer is not. Vacuum sealers are better than zippered plastic bags when it comes to getting the air out of bags and making sure that they don't pop open, but you can get close to the same results with plastic bags. If you are interested in getting a vacuum sealer, see the section Vacuum Sealer (page 13).

You'll need high-quality plastic zipper bags in one-quart and one-gallon sizes. Bags labeled as "freezer" bags are heavier and less likely to tear. Good bags can be expensive and/or hard to find, so reuse as many as possible. Bags holding meat shouldn't be reused; there is too much chance for food poisoning.

Permanent Markers

I label bags where the contents look confusingly like something else (flour and baking mix, for example) and also the tops of cans that I will be storing upright in top-loading lockers so it's easy to find what I want without removing every can. Be sure to use a *permanent* marker; water-based ones will run from any dampness on your hands, resulting in no labels and, literally, a mess on your hands.

Non-Skid Shelf Paper

Non-skid shelf paper is the first line of defense against cans and other items making noise as the boat moves. You can get rubbery, waffle weave shelf "paper" in every housewares department and in many grocery stores. Use it to line not just your shelves, but also your drawers and the bottom of every locker.

Tube Socks

Old tube socks make wonderful padding for any breakable jars and bottles. The socks can be slipped right over the item and won't slide off.

Pest Control

I don't want to use toxic sprays where I'm going to store food. See below for more detailed information on controlling bugs, but you'll need the following supplies:

- Bay leaves (to put in with all dry goods to keep weevils out)
- Whole cloves, clove oil, or ground cloves (in every locker to prevent ants)
- A paste-type ant and roach killer containing borax (very mildly toxic to humans and pets, but deadly to pests). You can make your own from powdered nondairy coffee creamer or powdered milk and borax. Use a tongue depressor to smear a bit in the crevices of lockers where food is stored, and also put a bit into empty beer or pop bottle caps and set these on the bottom of lockers.

YOUR FOOD STORAGE PLAN

Exactly what you store where is a highly personal decision, based on what foods you like, your style of cooking, the size of your boat, and the boat layout. But the chances are good that some of your storage areas just aren't that convenient, and there isn't as much space as you'd like.

Spend a little time looking at the various storage spaces and think about what could go where. Planning food storage has to happen in parallel with buying your bins and storage containers, so that you've got the ability to put things where you want to. A few other things to keep in mind:

- **Access.** Keep things you use frequently in the most accessible places. Many times, you can't keep your entire stock of something in an accessible place, but you can store enough for a few days or a week. I kept canisters of pasta and rice right in the galley, but extra stores were in big plastic tubs under the floorboards. Once a week, I'd get in that locker and replenish stocks of everything stored there.

- **Protection.** Consider what type of "protection" various foods need. For example, flour and sugar need to stay totally dry while bread and chips need to be protected against crushing. The following section deals with the specifics of storing many foods and should be considered when creating your plan.
- **Weight.** Heavy items, such as canned food and drinks, need to be kept low and toward the center of the boat, as well as evenly distributed from port to starboard. Poor placement of heavy items will affect the boat's performance.
- **Areas that have to stay clear.** Sometimes, part of a compartment simply has to stay "unused" so that cans don't bump into equipment, block air-flow, or get in the way of something else. For these, you can make upright dividers to section off shelf or locker areas. Planning for this gives you a better idea of the usable space in various lockers.
- **Think outside the box.** Or, in this case, the locker. Can you "create" other storage areas? For example, I put a lidded storage bin under the nav station and just put my feet up on it when using the computer.
- **Cooking equipment.** As you're planning where you'll put various foods, don't forget to leave space for your pots, pans, plates, and other galley equipment!
- **Nothing is set in stone.** It's hard to get all your stowage right the first time, and your preferences may change over time. It takes a bit of work to move stuff if you don't like the organization, but it's a good opportunity to clean out lockers.

STORING YOUR FOOD

The actual process of storing food begins as you bring it aboard. The basic procedure is a little more involved than just carrying it aboard and finding places to stow it:

- Discard cardboard and excess packaging ashore if possible. It's less trash aboard your boat and you'll get rid of any bugs that may be lurking in the packaging.
- Repackage food into smaller containers where possible. Meats are a good example of this; get rid of the trays and put the meat into bags.
- Wash cans, if necessary. In many places, cans will be dirty and will attract bugs. Further, if it's a drink can, you don't really want to drink from a dirty can. A dilute bleach solution of one capful of bleach in one to two gallons of water works well as a disinfectant. Make sure to dry the cans thoroughly or they can develop pinholes.
- Wash produce (see page 42).
- Put anything that needs it into a plastic bag and seal it. This will protect the items against moisture and also contain any spills if a top loosens or a container cracks.
- Label! And if you keep an inventory or map of locations, update it.
- Finally, put the food where it goes. Be sure to do the cold foods first!

Food in the Refrigerator and Freezer or the Cooler

On some boats, the refrigerator and freezer are all one box, with the freezer being a small compartment in it. On others, they are totally separate. And on some—generally those with engine-driven refrigeration—there is only a refrigerator (that is, no area where food will reliably stay frozen). Other boats only have a cooler or an icebox. Consequently, there are no universal rules about storing "cold food" on a boat, but I'll offer some tips that can be modified to fit your situation.

Few boat refrigerators are as good as "shore" refrigerators at holding a steady temperature. For most foods, this isn't a problem. But for meats and seafood, it means that anything that won't be used within two days (or less, depending on how good your refrigerator is) needs to go in the freezer. If you don't have a freezer, though, don't despair:

- Meats that are commercially vacuum sealed (such as bacon or hot dogs) will still be safe (unopened) for two weeks in the refrigerator, according to the FDA (http://www.fda.gov/downloads/Food/ResourcesForYou/HealthEducators/ucm109315.pdf). This assumes that the refrigerator is at 40°F.

- Canned meats don't require any refrigeration and stay good for years. They are perfect for boats without refrigeration as well as boats with only a tiny freezer. We have an entire chapter on making delicious meals from canned meats. See the chapter "Canned Meats and Seafood."

I'll first provide tips for foods in the freezer, then go on to the rest of the refrigerator or cooler.

Meat in the Freezer. If your boat doesn't have much freezer space, buy boneless meat or bone it yourself before putting it in the freezer (page 256). To save freezer space, repackage any meat that wasn't vacuum sealed when you bought it, getting rid of any plastic trays. Label the packages. I try to mix things up as I put food in the freezer so that all the packages of one thing (such as ground beef) aren't on the bottom, requiring me to take everything else out when I want one of those packages.

Seafood. Seafood must be cleaned before going into the refrigerator or freezer. If you won't eat it that day, it's best to freeze it unless your refrigerator is capable of holding a temperature under 40°F. When freezing seafood, use towels or paper towels and pat it dry as much as possible; the more water you remove, the less ice there will be and the better the texture will stay. Vacuum seal the seafood or use heavy-duty plastic bags—and use a double layer with either one for things with sharp spikes (like lobster shells) that could poke a hole in the plastic, leading to freezer burn.

Other Food in the Freezer. If space is limited, putting food into bags instead of hard containers will result in less wasted space.

Organizing the Refrigerator in General. The first time that Jan and I—and our husbands—chartered a boat for a week, we just piled all the cold stuff in the refrigerator with a couple of bags of ice to "help out the chill plate." What a mistake! Everything froze together in a big glob and we spent hours breaking it apart and then trying to figure out what was what ("Is this a chicken breast?"). Labeling food and using bins to organize it avoids this problem.

It's important to note that the coldest areas of the refrigerator are lowest and nearest the chill plate. Cold air falls, and thus the higher areas will be warmer.

Drinks. If you're in a hot climate, probably half your refrigerator will be devoted to cold drinks. Opening the refrigerator to get them out and put new ones in can be a significant source of cold loss. If you like canned drinks (soda, juice, beer), develop a system of loading the cans so that you can quickly get the right can and don't have to fumble around forever. We used two large plastic bins and used one for beer and one for pop.

If you like cold water or drinks made from cold water, have multiple bottles in the refrigerator (space permitting). For each drink, we like one that's "in use" and one that's in a less accessible place, chilling down. We kept the "in use" bottles of water, Gatorade, and iced tea right under the locker lid and always kept them in the same order, left to right, so that we could quickly grab the one we wanted. Labeling the bottle tops helps, too, if you have guests or a crew member who just never remembers.

Be sure to stock up the refrigerator before going to bed so that the new stock will have all night to chill down. This also puts less strain on the refrigerator compressor as it's the coolest time of day. Keep drinks at the bottom of the refrigerator. It's coolest there and the weight is best there.

Yeast and Eggs. Yeast has a much longer life if stored in the refrigerator. You have to do everything you can to protect it from moisture and condensation as well, as dampness will cause yeast to deactivate.

Eggs need to be stored in the refrigerator only if they've already been refrigerated; in other words, if you can get eggs that haven't been refrigerated, you can leave them at room temperature. Many people turn the eggs (or just the carton) anywhere from every other day to once a week, but I usually forgot and they were still fine for several weeks. I always break eggs first into a small bowl. Your nose will let you know if the egg is bad—there's no question.

If your eggs were refrigerated when you bought them, you'll need to store them in the refrigerator. Regular egg cartons provide some protection against breakage, but plastic camping egg carriers are better, and the ones with true locking latches are the best (they also tend to be the heaviest plastic and offer the most impact resistance). Don't put eggs where they might freeze.

Butter and Cheese. Any portions that won't be eaten in the next few days should be vacuum sealed or put in plastic bags with as much air removed as possible. I like to put all the butter and cheese together in a plastic bin just so it's easier to find. It can be kept in almost any area of the refrigerator from the coldest to the warmest, although cheese will be "crumbly" if allowed to freeze (but it will taste just fine).

Cream cheese will keep for four to six weeks if you put the foil pouch in a vacuum-sealed bag; other cheeses can last even longer. Any cut cheese surfaces should be wiped down with vinegar (any type will work, but white vinegar doesn't leave a taste) to prevent mold. If cheese does develop mold, just cut it off and wipe the remaining part with vinegar.

Fruits and Vegetables. Put produce in its own plastic bin(s). Don't use metal containers as they will get too cold and damage the food. I prefer plastic tubs with solid sides and bottoms, as they tend to bruise items less than ones with ridges. I pad the bin with rags and/or bubble wrap to also protect against bruising. A great deal of produce that has never been refrigerated—at any time, from farmer to you—will last a surprisingly long time without being refrigerated. See our tips on storing fruit and vegetables outside the refrigerator (or cooler) in the next section.

In a hot climate, you'll find that produce in plastic bags rots quickly as condensate forms inside the bag when it goes from hot tropical air to the cold refrigerator. If you open the bag and wrap a paper towel or a rag around the produce, it will absorb the water; replace it in a day to keep the food dry. Hang the paper towels to dry, then reuse them on the following day. Note that produce should go in the warmest area of your refrigerator—high and away from the chill plate.

Condiments. Most condiments don't actually need to be refrigerated, although you can if you have sufficient room. The two that really need refrigeration to keep more than a couple weeks are wasabi and horseradish; both lose their bite in tropical heat. And yes, they need to be refrigerated even before they're opened. However, they don't pose a food safety threat if they are not refrigerated.

I never refrigerated open containers of jams, jellies, syrup, soy sauce, Worcestershire, ketchup, and mustard. They lasted for six months or more, even in tropical heat. I always had enough room in the refrigerator to keep mayonnaise there; cruisers with more limited space usually buy small containers and use the "clean spoon" rule. (Do this at your own risk; the FDA of course says "never" use mayonnaise that's not refrigerated.) The clean spoon rule means never putting a utensil in the jar if the utensil isn't perfectly clean. No spreading some mayo with a knife and then getting more out of the jar with that knife. Others use squeeze bottles to avoid contamination.

Storing Produce Outside the Refrigerator or Cooler

Even if your boat has refrigeration, storing some of your vegetables outside the refrigerator helps considerably with the problem of "my refrigerator's not large enough!" And if you don't have a refrigerator or cooler, well, you have to store them otherwise.

The good news is that with a bit of care, many vegetables can be stored anywhere from a week to a month or sometimes even more. No, not everything will last that long— but enough will that you can still have some fresh veggies to mix with the canned!

Buying Produce. Having fruits and veggies last a reasonable amount of time without refrigeration actually begins with how you choose them in the first place. This is probably the most important part of the process and the one usually overlooked.

- **Buy never-refrigerated produce.** This is most often available at farmer's markets or on veggie trucks. Once something has been refrigerated, it needs to stay refrigerated, or it will quickly go bad. In general, produce that's been refrigerated has less than half the life outside the refrigerator of something that has never been refrigerated. Below, when I talk of how long something will last, I'm talking about items that have never seen the inside of a refrigerator.
- **Be very picky.** Don't accept any that are bruised, rotten, overripe, have insect holes, or look "old."
- **Don't buy too much.** If you buy more than can comfortably fit in your storage areas, your produce will get bruised as you try to fit the extra in. Be realistic about how much room you have.
- **Transport the produce gently.** If you're carrying them in a backpack, bring along some towels to pad the veggies and don't cram them in. If you're going by cab, make sure nothing will fall on them and they won't roll around. You don't want to bruise them before they even get to the boat.

Bringing Produce Aboard. To wash, or not to wash? The argument for washing is to get any critters off before they cause damage or infest other food, and also to have food ready to use when you want it. The argument against it is that produce lasts longest with the least handling and left in the dirt it was pulled from. Both sides have merit.

I wash my veggies regardless of where I'll store it. Even at farmer's markets, I've rarely found produce that hasn't been washed at least once, so it's not in its own dirt. BUT if you wash it, you have to get it totally dry before storing it. Even in ventilated bins, it won't totally dry if put in damp—it will just start to rot.

As you stow the produce, double-check each item to make sure it's still in good condition. I usually find an item or two that need to be eaten right away, which can be worked into the dinner menu.

Storage Basics. Storage areas need to be well ventilated, dry, and as dark as possible. Bins need to be something that can be easily washed—plastic works the best as you can use bleach on it and it dries quickly. Wire baskets and gear hammocks cause

"pressure points" that will bruise, so these need to be well padded. Gear hammocks should be hung in locations where they won't bump into anything in rough seas but will just swing unencumbered. Don't store non-refrigerated produce in plastic bags; they simply trap any moisture and the food rots.

Bins and other storage containers need to be located where you can see into them to check on the produce daily. If you see something that's bruised, put it on the dinner menu. Anything that you missed and is now rotting or molding needs to be thrown out immediately—and the container wiped out with bleach.

Storage Specifics for Various Vegetables

- **Onions.** Store in a dark, dry area to keep from sprouting. Do not store onions and potatoes together as the potatoes will sprout.
- **Potatoes.** Store in a dark, dry area with good ventilation. Light will make them go green, and any green parts should be cut off along with any eyes and not eaten.
- **Cabbage.** Keep cool. Cabbage will last several weeks as long as you protect it from too much bruising.
- **Tomatoes.** Store them in a dark place or wrap with paper towels or newspaper or put them in tube socks. They need darkness to ripen. Unwrap when ripe and use within two days. (Buying in various stages of ripeness provides you with a supply for two weeks or more.)
- **Carrots and celery.** Wrap in aluminum foil, but don't totally seal the packet; leave little openings at the end for moisture to escape (otherwise, they'll rot). If they dry out some, rejuvenate in water. They'll easily last one week, often two weeks or more.
- **Cucumbers and bell peppers.** Pad these well so they don't bruise and they will last at least a week, often two weeks.
- **Summer squash and zucchini.** Small ones last much longer (10 days or more) than larger ones. If they start to wilt a bit, use them in a cooked dish instead of eating them raw; you won't notice that they're not crisp.

- **Broccoli and cauliflower.** Both can last a week. Broccoli may get a little yellow and cauliflower may get some black spots, but just cut both out. If either starts to wilt, use it in a cooked dish and it won't be noticeable.
- **Lettuce.** Lettuce is so susceptible to bruising and rot that it's best to eat it within a day or two of buying it.

Storage Specifics for Various Fruits

- **Citrus fruits.** Wrap individually in aluminum foil and do not store near apples (which will cause the apples to overripen or rot). Make sure that any fruit is 100 percent dry before wrapping it in foil. It will last several weeks to a month. If left unwrapped, it will last a week to 10 days. Minor mold on the skin can be wiped off with a mild bleach solution.
- **Bananas.** We were never able to keep bananas longer than two days. Buying a stalk of a hundred or so green bananas and tying a bag around it to allow just one round to be exposed—and ripen— at a time sounds like a wonderful idea for a Pacific passage. However, the cruisers that I've known to try this have ended up with them all ripening at once—not to mention the bugs that came out of the stalk. I don't recommend trying this.
- **Avocados.** These are hard to keep from bruising. Put them in a sock, then in a gear hammock; otherwise, the strings on the gear hammock will bruise them. Even if they're purchased rock hard, avocados won't last much longer than a week to ten days in tropical heat; if you buy them ripe, they'll last only a couple of days.
- **Mangoes.** Buy in varying stages of ripeness from ripe (to eat right now) to rock hard (to eat in 10 days to two weeks). As the rock-hard ones ripen, they'll ooze a bit of sugary juice, so store them in their own bin with towels that can be easily washed.
- **Apples.** Apples will last up to a month if you can protect them from bruising. Don't store them with citrus (which will cause the apples to overripen or rot) or bananas (which will cause the bananas to overripen). If apples are not chilled, they won't have as much crunch.

- **Pineapple.** Will last up to two weeks if purchased green. Pad well against bruising and keep upright.
- **Strawberries.** Will last only two days at most— only one day if fully ripe when purchased. My suggestion: buy and eat the same day.
- **Grapes.** Will usually last at least two days, often as many as four days or sometimes more. After that, they may start to dry out (on their way to becoming raisins), but they still won't mold for several more days—sometimes never. The older, drier ones are good in coleslaw or tuna salad.

Other Food Not in the Refrigerator

The bulk of your provisions don't need to be in the refrigerator, freezer, or cooler. But we still have a few tips on the best way to store them—or at least a few things to think about.

Canned Goods. Most cruising boats carry a significant stock of canned goods: vegetables, fruits, meats, soups, evaporated milk, and more.

- Cans are heavy and should be stored low and in the center of the boat.
- Be careful of corrosion from saltwater spray or drips (lockers under deck fittings, etc.). If there is any chance of salt water getting into a locker, use a lidded plastic bin to protect the cans.
- Use bins to divide up large lockers so cans don't move too much with the motion of the boat. Movement will result in dented cans, possibly broken cans, pinholes, and noise.
- In smaller lockers, it helps to put something nonskid under cans so they don't move around.
- Store cans upright so they don't roll; the sound of cans rolling is really annoying.
- If you store cans upright in a top-opening locker, label the tops of cans with a permanent marker so you don't have to pull out every can to see what it is.

Pop and Beer. Pop and beer cans are generally very thin outside the United States (and sometimes in the United States). Watch out for chafe and salt water making tiny pinholes in the cans, leading to nasty messes to clean up and bug infestations as well. We both store cans in solid plastic bins (even if they are in a locker) so that if one can does develop a hole, the mess is contained.

Drink Powders. If the humidity is high where you are, put containers of powdered mixes (whether packets or larger containers) in sealed plastic bags or airtight plastic boxes. The powder may get clumpy from humidity in the air, but it's safe to use unless it smells moldy.

Wine (and Other Liquids) in Glass Bottles. We took a length of 4-inch PVC and cut it into 8-inch sections. These we glued together standing upright in a locker in sort of a honeycomb pattern. We slipped the wine bottles into tube socks and stuck one in each PVC tube. We never had one break, and they're quiet, too!

Boxed Drinks. Boxed drinks such as milk, juice, and wine in boxes, last about six months in tropical heat and can be tucked in anywhere. The two keys are to remember where you put all the boxes and to always use the oldest ones first, not just those that are most handy.

Cereal, Crackers, and Chips. These should be kept in the original packaging and then put in vacuum-sealed bags or airtight plastic bags so they don't pick up moisture and taste stale. If they do pick up some moisture, rejuvenate them by putting them in the oven on low for five to ten minutes. Put them in plastic immediately when you take them out of the oven, or they'll pick up moisture again. Store in gear hammocks or lidded bins to prevent crushing.

Baking Supplies. The two big issues with baking supplies are keeping out moisture and bugs. A few recommendations:

- **Flour**—use bay leaves to keep out weevils; use double plastic bags to keep out moisture.
- **Sugar**—if you get ants, put whole cloves in sugar; use double plastic bags to keep out moisture.
- **Box mixes**—take the mixes out of the cardboard packaging if possible, cut the directions from the box and put it with the contents, and put the bag of mix inside a plastic bag or a lidded storage container. Use bay leaves to keep out weevils.

- **Baking soda and baking powder**—both react with moisture; if humidity gets to either one, it won't work in baking. Put them in double plastic bags and remove from the bags just long enough to use. Screw-top jars are not sufficiently moisture proof.
- **Yeast**—store in the refrigerator or cooler if you have one (page 40). Otherwise, store in the coolest and driest location you have, such as for spices.

Spices, Herbs, and Mix Packets. These need to be kept cool and dry. They lose their flavor quickly when kept in warm places. Lots of boats have spice racks over or very near the stove, but that's just too hot to be good for spices. Mix packets (taco seasoning, gravy mixes, etc.) should be kept in sealed plastic containers or bags so they don't absorb moisture and turn to hard lumps (that often can't be reconstituted) and then to moldy messes. Salt needs to be kept in an airtight container or it will turn into a hard lump. I put the large container in a sealed plastic bag and decant it as needed into a shaker with a tight lid over the holes (look for these shakers made for camping, picnics, or travel, and read reviews to determine how tightly they seal in actual use). I keep a few grains of rice in with the salt to absorb any moisture.

Dried Beans, Pasta, Rice, Couscous, and Ramen Noodles. These need to be overwrapped with a sealed plastic bag but can pretty much be stored anywhere.

Dry Dog and Cat Food. Pet food should be stored like flour, with a few bay leaves to prevent weevils and put in airtight containers to keep from getting stale.

Paper Goods. Paper goods such as paper towels, napkins, and toilet paper shouldn't all be stored in one locker in case of a leak. It's never fun to discover you have a leak, but it's that much worse when you discover that your entire stock of toilet paper or feminine hygiene supplies has been ruined.

Olive Packets, Dried Fruit, and Nuts. These are some of the easiest items to store, as they aren't easily crushable and aren't overly sensitive to heat. If they don't come in tough vacuum-sealed bags, put them in sealed plastic bags. I put them in an open-topped bin (actually an old gallon water bottle with the top cut off) just to keep all like items together in the locker.

Bread and Tortillas. Bread products get moldy fast in hot climates unless you buy brands with lots of preservatives. Read more about bread and tortillas in the chapter "Provisioning." The best places to store bread are in the microwave, oven, plastic bread box, or gear hammock so it doesn't get crushed.

AND ONE FINAL TIP . . .

Whatever you do, don't ignore problems in your food storage. Any sort of problem that you discover needs to be addressed immediately. Whether it's finding "just a couple" of ants, a cockroach, a rotten potato, or a couple of drops of syrup that leaked out of the bottle—not to mention anything more serious—it *will not* get better on its own. It *will* get worse. And "worse," in the context of food, usually involves a bug infestation.

Clean things up immediately, no matter how inconvenient. Use a bleach solution to disinfect. Check everything nearby to see if the problem is larger than first suspected. And then double up on all your usual pest control measures.

Food Storage

FOOD SUBSTITUTIONS

Although some substitutions almost duplicate the original (margarine and butter, for example), most simply make an agreeable alternative to the original. If you don't expect the finished dish to taste exactly the same as the original, you're less likely to be disappointed. When looking at the possible substitutions listed in this chapter, think about the role of the ingredient in the dish and what the substitution will do to the flavor, texture, color, cooking time, and other variables. Some recommendations may work well in a particular recipe while others won't.

Since substitutions are a way of life on a boat, where you usually can't just run to the store for a missing ingredient, we've compiled an extensive list. We've divided this monster list into sections:

- Spices, Herbs, Flavorings, and Packet Mixes
- Fruits, Vegetables, and Juices
- Dry Foods (baking supplies, crackers, and the like)
- Soups, Broth, and Bouillon
- Liquids
- Syrups, Honey, and Molasses
- Condiments
- Dairy (milk products, eggs)
- Other Foods

SPICES, HERBS, FLAVORINGS, AND PACKET MIXES

Allspice, 1 teaspoon
- ¹/₂ teaspoon ground cinnamon and ¹/₂ teaspoon ground cloves

Apple pie spice, 1 teaspoon
- ¹/₂ teaspoon ground cinnamon, ¹/₄ teaspoon ground nutmeg, and ¹/₈ teaspoon ground cardamom or extra nutmeg *or*
- 1 teaspoon ground allspice

Bay leaf, 1 whole
- ¹/₄ teaspoon crushed bay leaf

Beau Monde seasoning, 1 teaspoon
- 1 teaspoon seasoned salt *or*
- 1 teaspoon Mrs. Dash *or*
- ¹/₂ teaspoon salt plus dash of garlic powder, onion powder, and celery powder

Cajun spice mix, slightly more than ¹/₂ cup
Mix together:

- 2 tablespoons cayenne pepper
- 2 tablespoons paprika
- 1¹/₂ tablespoons onion powder
- 2 tablespoons ground pepper
- 1 tablespoon garlic powder
- 2 teaspoons dried basil
- 1 teaspoon chili powder
- ¹/₄ teaspoon dried thyme
- ¹/₄ teaspoon dry mustard
- ¹/₈ teaspoon ground cloves

Cardamom, 1 teaspoon
- ¹/₂ teaspoon ground cinnamon plus ¹/₂ teaspoon ground ginger (the flavor is not identical, but the substitute works well in most recipes)

Chili powder, 3 tablespoons
Mix together:

- 3 teaspoons ground chilies (what chilies you use will determine the spiciness)
- 2 teaspoons ground coriander
- 1 teaspoon ground cumin
- ¾ teaspoon garlic powder
- 2 teaspoons dried oregano (crushed or ground)
- ¾ teaspoon ground cloves

Chinese 5-spice powder, 4 teaspoons
Mix together:

- 1 teaspoon ground Szechuan pepper or ground black pepper
- ½ teaspoon ground cinnamon
- ½ teaspoon ground cloves
- 1¼ teaspoons ground fennel
- 1 teaspoon ground star anise or ground anise

Chives, chopped
- Use an equal amount of chopped green onion tops, scallions, or leeks.

Cilantro, fresh, 1 cup
- ½ cup dried cilantro

Cinnamon, ground, 1 teaspoon
- ½ teaspoon ground allspice *or*
- 1 teaspoon ground cardamom

Cream of tartar, ½ teaspoon
- 1½ teaspoons lemon juice or lime juice *or*
- 1½ teaspoons white vinegar or cider vinegar

Curry powder, 1 tablespoon
Mix together:

- ¼ teaspoon ground cinnamon
- ¼ teaspoon ground cardamom
- ¼ teaspoon ground cloves
- ¼ teaspoon ground coriander
- ¼ teaspoon ground cumin
- ¼ teaspoon ground ginger
- ½ teaspoon ground chilies
- ½ teaspoon garlic powder
- ½ teaspoon ground black pepper

Extracts (almond, orange, lemon, etc.), 1 teaspoon
- Almost all extracts can be substituted one for another, although the flavor will be different.
- 1 or 2 drops of the same oil *or*
- For citrus fruits, 1 teaspoon grated rind (zest) from the same or other fruit *or*
- Up to 1 tablespoon juice from the same fruit (but be careful about the added liquid in some recipes) *or*
- 1 teaspoon rum or other liquor with complementary flavor *or*
- Orange extract: 1 teaspoon Cointreau or Triple Sec

Garlic, 1 clove (1 teaspoon), minced or pressed
- ⅛ teaspoon garlic powder *or*
- ¼ teaspoon dried (dehydrated) minced garlic *or*
- ¼ teaspoon garlic salt, and reduce salt in recipe by ⅛ teaspoon

Garlic powder, ½ teaspoon
- 4 cloves garlic, minced or pressed *or*
- 4 teaspoons minced or pressed garlic *or*
- 1 teaspoon dried (dehydrated) minced garlic *or*
- 1 teaspoon garlic salt, and reduce salt in recipe by ½ teaspoon

Garlic salt, 1 teaspoon
- ½ teaspoon garlic powder plus ½ teaspoon salt *or*
- 4 cloves minced or pressed garlic plus ½ teaspoon salt *or*
- 4 teaspoons minced or pressed garlic plus ½ teaspoon salt *or*
- 1 teaspoon dried (dehydrated) minced garlic plus ½ teaspoon salt

Ginger, ⅛ teaspoon ground
- 1 tablespoon fresh (raw) grated or minced ginger *or*
- ⅛ teaspoon ground allspice plus dash of ground cloves (flavor will be different) *or*
- 1 tablespoon minced candied ginger (rinse in water first to remove as much sugar as possible, then pat dry)

Ginger, 1 tablespoon fresh grated or minced
- ⅛ teaspoon ground ginger *or*
- ⅛ teaspoon ground allspice plus dash of ground cloves (flavor will be different) *or*
- 1 tablespoon minced candied ginger (rinse in water first to remove as much sugar as possible, then pat dry)

Herbs, dried, not ground (oregano, basil, dill, cilantro, chives, etc.), 1 teaspoon

- 1 tablespoon of the same fresh herb, finely chopped *or*
- ½ teaspoon of the same dried ground herb

Herbs, fresh, 1 tablespoon

- 1 teaspoon dried, not ground *or*
- ½ teaspoon dried ground

Horseradish, 1 tablespoon fresh grated

- 1½ to 2 tablespoons prepared horseradish (white or red) *or*
- 2 to 3 tablespoons horseradish "sauce" in a bottle *or*
- 1 teaspoon wasabi paste (or enough powder to make 1 teaspoon). Watch out, strength varies! *or*
- In many recipes, you can substitute 1 tablespoon spicy prepared mustard or 1 teaspoon dry mustard, although the taste will be different.

Italian seasoning, 1 teaspoon

- ¼ teaspoon *each* dried oregano, dried marjoram, and dried basil plus ⅛ teaspoon ground sage *or*
- ½ teaspoon dried oregano, ¼ teaspoon dried basil, and ¼ teaspoon ground thyme

Mint, ¼ cup fresh chopped

- 1 tablespoon peppermint or spearmint extract

Mrs. Dash salt substitute/seasoning, ¼ cup

Mix together the following and keep in an airtight container or shaker:

- 1 tablespoon garlic powder
- 1 teaspoon dried parsley flakes
- 1 teaspoon dried basil
- 1 teaspoon dried marjoram
- 1 teaspoon dried thyme
- 1 teaspoon ground sage
- 1 teaspoon ground pepper
- 1 teaspoon onion powder
- ½ teaspoon ground mace
- ½ teaspoon cayenne pepper

NOTE: If you are missing one or two of the spices, just use the others. It will still be a good mix, just not quite the same.

Mustard, dry, 1 teaspoon

- 1 tablespoon prepared mustard *or*
- ½ teaspoon mustard seeds

Nutmeg, ground, 1 teaspoon

- ½ teaspoon ground allspice *or*
- ¼ teaspoon ground cloves plus ½ teaspoon ground cinnamon *or*
- ½ teaspoon ground mace
- All the above substitutions will change the flavor.

Old Bay Seasoning

The following will make about 1 cup:

- ¼ cup pickling spice
- ¼ cup salt
- 2 tablespoons dry mustard
- 2 tablespoons ground pepper
- 2 tablespoons hot red pepper flakes
- 1 tablespoon celery powder
- 1 tablespoon minced dried chives or dried onion flakes
- 2 teaspoons ground ginger
- 2 teaspoons dried oregano
- 5 bay leaves, broken into small bits

Also see the "Seafood" chapter for other crab and shrimp boil recipes (page 235).

Onion powder, 1 tablespoon

- 1 medium onion, chopped
- 1½ tablespoons onion salt, and omit 1½ tablespoons salt from the recipe

Orange zest, dried, 1 tablespoon (zest is the colored part of the rind, grated)

- 2 to 3 tablespoons fresh orange zest *or*
- 1½ teaspoons orange extract *or*
- Zest of 1 medium orange *or*
- 1 tablespoon lemon or lime zest *or*
- 1 teaspoon chopped candied orange peel, and decrease sugar in recipe by 1 teaspoon

Orange zest, fresh grated from 1 medium orange (zest is the colored part of the rind, grated)

- 1 tablespoon dried grated orange peel *or*
- 2 to 3 tablespoons fresh orange zest *or*
- 1½ teaspoons orange extract *or*
- 1 tablespoon lemon or lime zest *or*
- 1 teaspoon chopped candied orange peel, and decrease sugar in recipe by 1 teaspoon

Parsley, dried, 1 teaspoon

- 1 tablespoon fresh chopped parsley

Peppermint, extract, 1 teaspoon

- 4 teaspoons fresh chopped mint

Poultry seasoning, 1 teaspoon

- ¼ teaspoon dried ground thyme (or 1 teaspoon fresh) and ¾ teaspoon dried ground sage (or 3 teaspoons fresh chopped sage)

Pumpkin pie spice, 1 teaspoon

- ½ teaspoon ground cinnamon, ¼ teaspoon ground ginger, ⅛ teaspoon ground allspice, and ⅛ teaspoon ground nutmeg *or*
- ½ teaspoon ground cinnamon, ¼ teaspoon ground ginger, ¼ teaspoon ground nutmeg, and ⅛ teaspoon ground cloves *or*
- 1 teaspoon ground allspice

Ranch Dip Mix, 1 packet

See Ranch Dressing in the "Salads" chapter (page 161).

Rum, as flavor in cooking, 1 tablespoon

- 1 teaspoon rum extract and 2 teaspoons water

Salt, 1 teaspoon

- Table salt, kosher salt, sea salt, and coarse grained salt can be substituted equally one for another.
- 1 bouillon cube OR 1 teaspoon bouillon powder (tastes less salty than straight salt; bouillon flavor is great in meat dishes)

Sherry, for cooking, 2 tablespoons

- 1 to 2 teaspoons vanilla extract *or*
- 2 tablespoons orange or pineapple juice

Soy sauce, ½ cup (called *salsa chino* in Latin America)

Mix together in a saucepan and boil down to ½ cup:

- 2 cups beef broth (can be made from bouillon cubes)
- 2 teaspoons cider vinegar (in a pinch use white or wine vinegar, but it's not as good)
- 1 teaspoon molasses
- ⅛ teaspoon ground ginger
- Dash ground pepper
- Dash garlic powder or garlic salt
- Dash onion powder or onion salt

Spearmint, extract, 1 teaspoon

- 4 teaspoons fresh chopped mint

Taco Seasoning, 1 packet

Mix together the following:

- 1 tablespoon chili powder*
- 2 teaspoons onion powder OR 2 tablespoons dried onion flakes
- 1 teaspoon ground cumin
- 1 teaspoon garlic powder
- 1 teaspoon dried oregano
- 1 teaspoon sugar
- ½ teaspoon cornstarch
- ½ teaspoon salt

Chili powders vary considerably in their heat. If yours is particularly spicy, use less to start and add more to taste if desired.

To use for tacos, brown 1 pound ground beef and drain fat. Add ½ cup water and mix into the above mixture. Simmer for 10 minutes or until thick.

Vanilla bean, whole bean

- 2 teaspoons vanilla extract

Food Substitutions

Vanilla extract, 1 teaspoon

- $1/2$ vanilla bean, split and simmered in liquid used in recipe *or*
- 1 teaspoon imitation vanilla flavoring *or*
- $1/2$ teaspoon powdered vanilla extract plus 1 teaspoon additional liquid *or*
- 1 teaspoon rum, Triple Sec, Cointreau, or other liquor (consider flavor in substitution) *or*
- 1 teaspoon fruit juice or fruit juice concentrate (consider flavor) *or*
- 1 teaspoon wine (consider flavor) *or*
- 1 teaspoon strong coffee (consider flavor)

Wasabi, 1 teaspoon paste

- 1 teaspoon fresh grated horseradish *or*
- $1^{1}/_2$ teaspoons prepared horseradish *or*
- 2 to 3 teaspoons horseradish "sauce"

Worcestershire sauce, 1 teaspoon (called *salsa inglesa* in Latin America)

- 1 teaspoon bottled steak sauce

FRUITS, VEGETABLES, AND JUICES

Bell pepper, 1 tablespoon dried

- 3 tablespoons fresh chopped bell pepper

Coconut, dry grated

- Use $1^{1}/_2$ times as much fresh grated coconut

Corn on the cob, 1 ear

- Approximately $1/4$ cup cooked corn, sliced off the cob or canned

Currants, 1 cup

- 1 cup chopped raisins, dates, or other moist dried fruit

Lemon juice, 1 teaspoon

- $1/2$ teaspoon white vinegar. Don't use for flavoring. *or*
- 1 teaspoon lime juice or *limón* (Key lime) juice

Lemon, juice from 1 lemon

- 2 to 3 tablespoons lemon juice, lime juice, or *limón* (Key lime) juice (bottled or fresh) *or*
- $1^{1}/_2$ tablespoons white vinegar (plus $1/2$ to 1 tablespoon water if liquid volume is crucial). Don't use for flavoring.

Lemon or lime zest, fresh grated, 1 teaspoon (zest is the colored part of the rind, grated)

- $1/2$ teaspoon dried lemon or lime zest *or*
- $1/4$ teaspoon lemon or lime extract *or*
- 1 teaspoon lemon or lime juice

Mushrooms, 1 pound (16 ounces) fresh

- 3 ounces dried mushrooms *or*
- 1 can (6 or 8 ounces) mushrooms, drained

Mushrooms, powdered, 1 tablespoon

- 3 tablespoons dried mushrooms *or*
- 4 ounces fresh mushrooms *or*
- 2 ounces canned mushrooms, drained

Onion, 1 small

- 1 tablespoon instant minced onion *or*
- $1/4$ cup fresh chopped onion *or*
- $1^{1}/_3$ teaspoons onion salt, and omit $1/2$ teaspoon salt from the recipe *or*
- 1 teaspoon onion powder *or*
- $1/2$ medium onion *or*
- $1/4$ large onion

Orange, 1 medium

- 6 to 8 tablespoons orange juice (will change texture) *or*
- $3/4$ cup canned oranges or mandarin oranges, drained

Orange juice concentrate, $1/4$ cup

- 1 cup orange juice, and omit $3/4$ cup other liquid from recipe

Peppers, bell (sweet: green, red, yellow, or orange), 3 tablespoons fresh chopped

- 1 tablespoon dried green, red, yellow, or orange bell pepper *or*
- 2 to 3 tablespoons other mild peppers (will be slightly spicier) *or*
- $1/2$ can chopped green chilies, drained (will be a little spicier) *or*
- 2 tablespoons chopped pimiento

Pumpkin, canned, 1 cup

- 1 cup cooked, mashed sweet potato (peeled), carrots, squash (peeled and seeded), or turnip

Raisins, 1 cup

- 1 cup chopped moist dried fruit, such as dates, currants, cranberries, cherries, blueberries *or*
- 1½ cups diced fresh fruit, and reduce liquid in recipe by ¼ cup or more as appropriate for the moisture in the fruit

Tomato juice, 1 cup

- 1 cup V-8 or Clamato juice *or*
- ½ cup tomato sauce plus ½ cup water *or*
- 3 tablespoons tomato paste plus enough water to make 1 cup

Tomatoes, canned, 16-ounce can (typical US can)

- 2 cups chopped fresh tomatoes *or*
- About 3 medium tomatoes, chopped
- Diced and stewed tomatoes can be substituted for each other. Whole canned tomatoes can be used— just chop them up.

Tomatoes, fresh, 2 cups, chopped

- About 3 medium tomatoes, chopped *or*
- 1 can (16 ounces) tomatoes, drained

Tomato paste, ¼ cup

- ½ cup tomato sauce (cook down to ¼ cup) *or*
- ½ cup tomato sauce, and reduce water in recipe by ¼ cup

Tomato puree, 1 cup

- ⅓ cup tomato paste plus ⅔ cup water

Tomato sauce, 1 cup

- ½ cup tomato paste plus ½ cup water

Tomato sauce, 15-ounce can

- 6-ounce can tomato paste plus 1 cup water

DRY FOODS

Arrowroot, 1 tablespoon

- 1½ tablespoons cornstarch *or*
- 3 tablespoons flour

Baking mix (like Bisquick or Jiffy)

See Baking Mix in the chapter "Quick Breads, Muffins, and Biscuits" (page 376).

Baking powder, 1 teaspoon

- ¼ teaspoon baking soda plus ½ teaspoon cream of tartar *or*
- ¼ teaspoon baking soda plus ½ cup buttermilk, sour milk, or yogurt, and decrease liquid by ½ cup *or*
- ¼ teaspoon baking soda plus 1½ teaspoons white vinegar or lemon juice *or*
- ¼ teaspoon baking soda if recipe already calls for an acidic liquid such as lemon juice, buttermilk, vinegar, yogurt, or citrus juice

NOTE: Basic rule of thumb is that you need 1 teaspoon baking powder (or its substitute) for every 1 cup of flour.

Baking soda

- Use three times as much baking powder (for example, a recipe calling for 1 *tea*spoon baking soda will require 1 *table*spoon baking powder).
- If you use baking powder instead of baking soda, you can substitute milk or water for any acidic liquid in the recipe, such as vinegar or lemon juice. You can also eliminate any cream of tartar.

NOTE: Basic rule of thumb is that you need ⅓ teaspoon baking soda (or its substitute) for every 1 cup flour.

Bisquick

See Baking Mix in the chapter "Quick Breads, Muffins, and Biscuits" (page 376).

Bread crumbs, ⅓ cup dry

- 1 slice bread, crumbled *or*
- ¾ cup soft bread crumbs *or*
- ¼ cup cracker crumbs *or*
- ¼ cup cornmeal *or*
- ⅓ cup matzo meal *or*
- ⅓ cup crushed cornflakes *or*
- ⅓ cup crushed potato chips (decrease salt in recipe)

Make your own dry bread crumbs by leaving bread out to dry and turning slices over every 6 hours until totally dry. Grate into a bowl. Store tightly covered or in a plastic bag.

Bread crumbs, ³/₄ cup soft
- 1 slice bread, crumbled

Brown sugar, low calorie, 1 cup
- 1 cup sugar substitute (such as Splenda) that substitutes one-for-one for sugar plus 1 teaspoon to 1 tablespoon molasses or honey

Brown sugar, 1 cup
- 1 cup white sugar and 1 teaspoon to 1 tablespoon molasses (depending on how dark you want it) *or*
- 1 cup white sugar and 1 teaspoon honey (more like light brown sugar) *or*
- 1 cup raw sugar

Carob powder, 3 tablespoons
- 1 ounce (1 square) unsweetened baking chocolate and decrease liquid by 2 tablespoons *or*
- 3 tablespoons cocoa (regular or Dutch processed)

Chocolate, unsweetened (baking), 1 ounce (1 square)
- 3 tablespoons cocoa plus 1 tablespoon shortening, margarine, or butter *or*
- 3 tablespoons carob powder plus 2 tablespoons water *or*
- Can use an equal amount of semi-sweet chocolate but the taste will be different

Chocolate, semi-sweet (baking), 1 ounce (1 square)
- 3 tablespoons semi-sweet chocolate chips *or*
- 1 ounce (1 square) unsweetened baking chocolate plus 1 tablespoon sugar *or*
- 1 tablespoon cocoa powder, 3½ teaspoons sugar, and 2 teaspoons butter, margarine, or shortening

Chocolate, German sweet baking, 1 ounce
- 3 tablespoons cocoa powder, 4 teaspoons sugar, and 1 tablespoon butter, margarine, or shortening

Chocolate chips, semi-sweet, 1 ounce
- 1 ounce semi-sweet baking chocolate, chopped or broken into chunks *or*
- 1 ounce sweet baking chocolate, chopped into chunks *or*
- 1 ounce milk chocolate, broken into pieces *or*
- For baking and garnishing, use an equal amount of M&M's or Reese's Pieces

NOTE: 6 ounces chocolate chips equals 1 cup; 3 tablespoons chocolate chips equals 1 ounce (1 square)

Chocolate chips, 6-ounce package, melted
- 2 ounces (2 squares) unsweetened baking chocolate, ½ cup sugar, and 2 tablespoons butter, margarine, or shortening *or*
- ½ cup plus 1 tablespoon cocoa powder, ¼ cup plus 3 tablespoons sugar, and 3 tablespoons butter or margarine, melted

Chocolate, white
- Use an equal amount of milk chocolate or semi-sweet chocolate. Color and flavor will be different from the original.

Chocolate, in general
- 12 ounces chocolate or chocolate chips will make 1 cup melted chocolate

Cocoa, ¼ cup (4 tablespoons)
- 1 ounce (1 square) unsweetened baking chocolate, and omit ½ tablespoon butter, margarine, shortening, or oil in the recipe *or*
- ¼ cup Dutch-processed cocoa *or*
- ¼ cup carob powder

Cooking spray, nonstick
- Evenly spread a little oil, butter, margarine, or shortening on the pan.

Cornmeal, 1 cup
- ½ to ¾ cup corn flour (known as masa harina or *harina de masa* in Latin countries, where it is used to make corn tortillas; don't confuse it with corn tortilla mixes that contain other ingredients). **NOTE:** The exact amount for replacement depends on how finely the corn flour is ground. The finer it is, the less it will take. *or*
- 1 cup polenta *or*
- 1 cup corn grits *or*
- 1 cup maize meal *or*
- If using cornmeal to "flour" a baking pan, you can substitute finely crushed cornflakes or oats. This won't work for recipes where the cornmeal is incorporated into a batter.

Cornstarch, 1 tablespoon

- 2 tablespoons flour *or*
- 2 teaspoons arrowroot *or*
- 2 tablespoons tapioca (texture will be different) *or*
- 1 tablespoon corn flour (known as masa harina or *harina de masa* in Latin countries; don't confuse it with corn tortilla mixes that contain other ingredients) *or*
- 1 tablespoon rice flour *or*
- 1 tablespoon potato flour

Cracker crumbs, ¾ cup

- 1 cup dry bread crumbs

Croutons

- Substitute coarsely crushed dry ramen noodles (the type with a separate seasoning packet; don't use the seasoning). This works well in many salads. To make your own croutons, see Croutons in the chapter "Salads" (page 162).

Espresso Instant Powder (for recipes, not for a drink), 1 tablespoon

- 1 tablespoon instant coffee granules or powder *or*
- 2½ tablespoons instant cappuccino mix

Flour, for thickening, 1 tablespoon

- 1½ teaspoons cornstarch, potato starch, or rice starch *or*
- 2 teaspoons arrowroot *or*
- 1 tablespoon tapioca (texture will be different) *or*
- 1 tablespoon rice flour *or*
- 1½ teaspoons corn flour (known as masa harina or *harina de masa* in Latin countries; don't confuse it with corn tortilla mixes that contain other ingredients) *or*
- 1½ tablespoons whole wheat flour

Flour, for cooking or baking, 1 cup sifted

- 1 cup minus 2 tablespoons unsifted flour

Flour, for baking (yeast breads, quick breads, muffins, etc.), 1 cup

NOTES: The following substitutions make interesting variations, but the finished product is usually smaller and heavier. Counter this by adding an extra ½ teaspoon yeast per cup of substituted flour (for yeast breads) or an extra 1 teaspoon baking powder per cup of substituted flour (for baking powder products).

Do not substitute more than half the total volume of wheat flour (white or whole wheat) with a non-wheat flour, particularly in yeast breads. Other flours have virtually no gluten and won't rise properly. Instead, use a recipe designed for the type of flour you have.

The following are approximations. Due to differences in milling and storage conditions, you may need more or less. It helps if you've made the recipe before without the substitution, as you then know the proper texture of the dough.

- 1 cup whole wheat flour (best to use half white and half whole wheat) *or*
- 1¼ cups rye flour (rye flour should be no more than a quarter of the total amount of flour in a recipe) *or*
- 1½ cups oat flour *or*
- ½ cup corn flour *or*
- ¾ cup cornmeal *or*
- ⅝ cup potato flour *or*
- 1 cup plus 2 tablespoons (1⅛ cups) cake flour *or*
- 1½ cups dry bread crumbs *or*
- 1 cup oats (no more than half the total amount of flour in a recipe) *or*
- 1½ cups barley flour *or*
- 1 cup wheat germ (substitute no more than a third of the total amount of flour in a recipe) *or*
- 1 cup self-rising flour (eliminate the salt and any baking powder from the recipe)

Flour, cake or pastry, sifted, 1 cup

- 1 cup less 2 tablespoons (⅞ cup) unsifted cake flour *or*
- 1 cup less 2 tablespoons (⅞ cup) sifted white flour *or*
- ¾ cup unsifted white flour

Flour, self-rising, 1 cup

- 1 cup minus 2 teaspoons flour plus 1½ teaspoons baking powder and ½ teaspoon salt

Flour, whole wheat, 1 cup

- 1 cup white flour *or*
- 1 cup graham flour *or*
- ½ cup rye flour plus ½ cup white flour *or*
- ¾ cup white flour plus ¼ cup wheat germ

Gelatin, 1 envelope unflavored (1 tablespoon)
- 4 leaves of leaf gelatin (gelatin is sold in "leaves"—about 3" × 8" and as thick as paper—in some countries, particularly in Europe) *or*
- 2 teaspoons agar

Gelatin, flavored, 3-ounce package
- 1 tablespoon (1 envelope) unflavored gelatin plus 2 cups fruit juice, and omit 2 cups of other liquid in recipe

Maple sugar, 1 cup
- 1½ cups white or brown sugar (taste will be different) *or*
- 2 cups maple syrup, and decrease liquid in recipe by ½ cup *or*
- 1½ cups white or brown sugar plus 2 teaspoons maple extract

Oats
Stone-cut, old-fashioned, quick-cooking, and instant oats can be used interchangeably in recipes, although the cooking time may vary. If the oats are flavored (such as instant apple and cinnamon packets), be sure to adjust the amount of sugar and spices.

Polenta, 1 cup dry
- 1 cup cornmeal *or*
- 1 cup maize meal *or*
- 1 cup corn grits

Sugar, brown—see Brown sugar

Sugar, confectioner's (powdered), 1 cup
- ¾ cup white or brown sugar. This will not work in frostings and will change the texture of many dishes.

Sugar, white, 1 teaspoon
- ¾ teaspoon honey or molasses *or*
- 1 teaspoon brown sugar

Sugar, white, 1 cup
- 1 cup packed brown sugar or raw sugar *or*
- 1¼ cups corn syrup, and decrease liquid in recipe by ½ cup. For cookie recipes that have no other liquid to reduce, increase the flour by 3 tablespoons per cup of syrup used. *or*
- 1 cup honey, and decrease liquid in recipe by ¼ cup. In baked goods, add ½ teaspoon baking soda for each cup of honey substituted, and lower the baking temperature by 25°F. For cookie recipes that have no other liquid to reduce, increase the flour by 2 tablespoons per cup of honey used. In cakes, no more than half the sugar can be replaced with honey. *or*
- 1 cup molasses, and decrease liquid in recipe by ¼ cup. Do not replace more than half the sugar in a recipe with molasses. For cookie recipes that have no other liquid to reduce, increase the flour by 2 tablespoons per cup of molasses used. *or*
- ¾ cup maple syrup, and decrease liquid in recipe by ⅛ cup

NOTES:
- Molasses and maple syrup will change the flavor of the dish considerably; honey and brown sugar will change the flavor somewhat.
- In many recipes, sugar does not just sweeten, it also works to add volume when beaten with a liquid and also aids browning. Substitutions can thus affect the texture and appearance of the finished dish.

Tapioca, granular, 1 tablespoon
- 2 tablespoons pearl tapioca *or*
- 1 tablespoon instant or quick-cooking tapioca *or*
- 1½ tablespoons flour (for thickening) *or*
- ¾ tablespoon cornstarch (for thickening) *or*
- 1½ teaspoons arrowroot (for thickening)

Yeast, 1 package
- 1 cake yeast *or*
- 2¼ teaspoons bulk or bread-machine yeast

Do not try to substitute baking powder or baking soda for yeast. Instead, find a recipe formulated for what you have.

SOUPS, BROTH, AND BOUILLON

Bouillon, 1 cube
- 1 teaspoon powdered bouillon

Broth, 1 cup
- 1 bouillon cube OR 1 teaspoon powdered bouillon dissolved in 1 cup boiling water

Broth, 1 can (10$\frac{1}{2}$ ounces), undiluted
- 4 teaspoons powdered bouillon (or 4 cubes), dissolved in 1$\frac{1}{4}$ cups water

Condensed cream soup (such as Campbell's), undiluted

Mix together:

- $\frac{1}{4}$ cup powdered milk
- 1$\frac{1}{2}$ tablespoons cornstarch
- 2 teaspoons dried onion OR 1$\frac{1}{2}$ teaspoons onion powder
- Dash black pepper
- 1$\frac{1}{2}$ teaspoons chicken bouillon powder OR 1$\frac{1}{2}$ chicken bouillon cubes
- 1$\frac{1}{4}$ cups water

Mix all the dry ingredients in a small pan. Add the water and stir to combine. Cook over medium heat, stirring frequently, until thickened. To substitute for cream of mushroom soup, add a 6-ounce can of mushrooms, drained, and use the liquid from the canned mushrooms as part of the water.

Onion soup mix, 1 packet

Mix together:

- 8 teaspoons dried onion flakes
- 1$\frac{1}{2}$ teaspoons dried parsley flakes
- 1 teaspoon onion powder
- 1 teaspoon ground turmeric
- $\frac{1}{2}$ teaspoon celery powder or celery salt
- $\frac{1}{2}$ teaspoon salt
- $\frac{1}{2}$ teaspoon sugar
- $\frac{1}{4}$ teaspoon ground pepper

OR mix together:

- 4 teaspoons beef bouillon granules OR 4 beef bouillon cubes mashed to a powder
- 8 teaspoons dried onion flakes
- 1 teaspoon onion powder
- $\frac{1}{4}$ teaspoon seasoned pepper

Tomato soup, condensed, 1 can (10$\frac{3}{4}$ ounce)
- 1 cup tomato sauce plus $\frac{1}{4}$ cup water

LIQUIDS

Balsamic vinegar
- For 1 tablespoon balsamic vinegar, use 1 tablespoon red wine vinegar plus $\frac{1}{2}$ teaspoon sugar *or*
- For $\frac{1}{4}$ cup balsamic vinegar, use 3$\frac{1}{2}$ tablespoons red wine vinegar plus 2 teaspoons sugar *or*
- For 1 cup balsamic vinegar, use $\frac{7}{8}$ cup red wine vinegar plus 2 tablespoons sugar *or*

Coconut milk, $\frac{1}{4}$ cup
- $\frac{1}{3}$ cup milk plus 1 teaspoon cornstarch (mix well and boil until thick) plus $\frac{1}{2}$ teaspoon coconut extract *or*
- 1 tablespoon canned cream of coconut plus 3 tablespoons water or milk *or*
- $\frac{1}{4}$ cup coconut juice (sometimes called coconut water) drained from the center of a fresh coconut *or*
- $\frac{1}{4}$ cup milk (you'll lose the coconut flavor) *or*
- 3 tablespoons milk plus 1 tablespoon fresh or dried coconut *or*
- Line a cup with a clean cloth and place 2 to 4 tablespoons grated coconut (fresh or dried) in it. Pour $\frac{1}{4}$ cup hot milk (or water) over the top and let stand 30 minutes. Gather up the cloth and squeeze out all the liquid; use the liquid as coconut milk.

NOTE: These substitutions do not work for the "cream of coconut" used in piña coladas and other drinks. Cream of coconut is a commercially prepared product, and substitutes just don't match up. The substitutions listed above work well in cooking and baking.

Oil (vegetable, canola, or olive), 1 cup
- 1 cup other type of oil (olive oil has a distinctive flavor that may not work in all dishes) *or*
- 1 cup butter or margarine *or*
- In baking, you can usually replace up to half the total amount of oil with an equal amount of unsweetened applesauce.

Vinegar, 1 teaspoon
- 1$\frac{1}{2}$ teaspoons lemon juice *or*
- 1 to 2 teaspoons wine (not sweet) *or*
- Most vinegars (white, cider, wine, balsamic) can be substituted for one another one for one, but the flavor of the dish will change slightly.

Wine, in cooking, 1 cup

- 3 tablespoons lemon or lime juice plus 1 tablespoon sugar and enough water to make 1 cup *or*
- 1 cup grape or cranberry juice is a good substitute for red wine. *or*
- 1 cup white grape or apple juice is a good substitute for white wine. *or*
- In some recipes, 1 cup wine vinegar or white vinegar works well. *or*
- In some recipes, 1 cup chicken broth works well. *or*
- 1 cup water or other liquid used in the recipe

SYRUPS, HONEY, AND MOLASSES

Corn syrup, 1 cup

- 1 1/4 cups white sugar or packed brown sugar plus 1/4 cup liquid *or*
- 1 cup golden syrup *or*
- 1 cup treacle *or*
- 1 cup honey (flavor will be affected) *or*
- For dark corn syrup, substitute 3/4 cup light corn syrup and 1/4 cup molasses *or*
- You can substitute 1 cup light corn syrup for 1 cup dark corn syrup and vice versa. The color and flavor will be slightly different.

Golden syrup, 1 cup

- 1 cup corn syrup (light or dark) *or*
- 1 cup light molasses *or*
- 1 cup treacle *or*
- 1 cup honey

Honey, 1 cup

- 3/4 cup maple syrup plus 1/2 cup sugar *or*
- 3/4 cup light or dark corn syrup plus 1/2 cup sugar *or*
- 3/4 cup light molasses plus 1/2 cup sugar *or*
- 1 1/4 cups white or brown sugar plus 1/4 cup additional liquid in recipe

Maple syrup, 1 cup

- 1/2 cup maple sugar (increase liquid in recipe by 1/4 cup) *or*
- 1 cup honey *or*
- 3/4 cup plus 1 tablespoon light molasses or corn syrup plus enough water to make 1 cup (plus 1 teaspoon maple extract if desired) *or*

- Boil 1/2 cup water and 1 cup sugar. Add 1/4 teaspoon maple extract and boil 3 minutes more. Let cool.

Molasses, 1 cup

- 3/4 cup sugar plus 2 teaspoons baking powder, and increase liquid in recipe by 5 tablespoons *or*
- 3/4 cup sugar plus 1 1/4 teaspoons cream of tartar, and increase liquid in recipe by 5 tablespoons *or*
- 1 cup honey *or*
- 1 cup dark or light corn syrup *or*
- Light and dark molasses can be substituted for each other. *or*
- 3/4 cup brown sugar (light or dark) plus 1/4 cup water *or*
- 1 cup maple syrup

NOTE: None of the substitutions has the same flavor as molasses. Don't substitute where the flavor is important (such as in molasses cookies).

Treacle (golden syrup), 1 cup

- 1 cup dark or light molasses *or*
- 1 cup light or dark corn syrup

CONDIMENTS

Chili sauce, 1 cup

- Mix 1 cup tomato sauce with 1/4 cup brown sugar, 2 tablespoons vinegar, 1/4 teaspoon ground cinnamon, dash of ground cloves, and dash of ground allspice *or*
- 1 cup ketchup, 1/4 teaspoon ground cinnamon, dash of ground cloves, and dash of ground allspice

Ketchup, 1 cup (for cooking, not as a condiment)

- 1 cup tomato sauce plus 1/2 cup sugar and 2 tablespoons vinegar

Mayonnaise, 1 cup, for salads, salad dressings, and dips

- 1 cup sour cream (page 99) *or*
- 1 cup Miracle Whip salad dressing *or*
- 1 cup plain, unsweetened yogurt (page 101) *or*
- 1 cup cottage cheese, blended until smooth

Mustard, prepared, 1 teaspoon
- ⅓ teaspoon dry mustard plus 1 teaspoon white vinegar *or*
- Make your own prepared mustard (about 1 cup):
  - ½ cup finely ground mustard seed (brown or Oriental are hotter)
  - ¼ cup cold water
  - ¼ cup vinegar (white, cider, or wine)
  - ½ teaspoon sugar
  - ¼ teaspoon salt

Pickle relish
- Finely chop a bread-and-butter or sweet pickle to equal the amount needed (for dill relish, use a dill pickle)

Pimiento, chopped, 2 tablespoons
- 3 tablespoons chopped fresh red bell (sweet) pepper *or*
- 1 tablespoon chopped dried red bell pepper *or*
- If the color is not critical, use 3 tablespoons any color chopped bell (sweet) pepper. *or*
- 2 tablespoons canned green chilies (will be spicier and texture will be different)

DAIRY

Butter, 1 cup
- ⅞ cup shortening plus ½ teaspoon salt *or*
- 1 cup margarine *or*
- ⅞ cup lard plus ½ teaspoon salt *or*
- ⅞ cup oil plus ½ teaspoon salt (Oil is not a direct substitute for solid fats in baked products. The texture of the item will be odd. Instead, use recipes formulated for oil.) *or*
- In baked goods, you can generally substitute a third to half the total amount of butter, margarine, or shortening with an equal amount of unsweetened applesauce, and use butter, margarine, or shortening for the remainder.

Measurements: See the section Butter/Margarine Sticks in the chapter "Measurements and Conversions" (page 62).

Butter, salted, 1 cup
- 1 cup unsalted butter plus ½ teaspoon salt

Butter, unsalted, 1 cup
- 1 cup salted butter, and omit ½ teaspoon salt from the recipe

Butter, melted
- An equal amount of melted shortening or lard *or*
- An equal amount of canola or vegetable oil *or*
- An equal amount of olive oil, but be careful of the stronger flavor of olive oil

Buttermilk
- Use the same amount of unsweetened plain yogurt. *or*
- Use half unsweetened plain yogurt plus half milk. *or*
- Use the same amount of sour milk. *or*
- Mix ½ teaspoon cream of tartar per ¼ cup milk. Let stand for 5 minutes. Use the same amount as the amount of buttermilk called for. *or*
- Mix 1 teaspoon white vinegar or lemon or lime juice per ¼ cup milk. Let stand for 5 minutes. Use the same amount as the amount of buttermilk called for.

Cream, 1 cup
- ⅓ cup melted butter or margarine and ⅔ cup whole milk *or*
- 1 cup *media crema* (a canned half-and-half sold in Latin American countries and in the Mexican aisle of most US supermarkets) *or*
- 1 cup evaporated milk (undiluted) *or*
- 1 cup powdered milk (not nonfat or low fat), mixed with enough water to make 1 cup

NOTE: None of the above will whip like whipping cream, but you can use them in cooking and some baking.

Cream, sour—see Sour cream

Food Substitutions

Cream, whipping, 1 cup

- Chill 1 cup evaporated milk for at least 12 hours. Add 1 teaspoon lemon or lime juice and beat until stiff using an electric mixer or hand beater (a whisk won't work). *or*
- Mix ½ cup ice-cold water (it has to be cold, not room temperature) and ½ cup powdered milk and beat until stiff using an electric mixer or hand beater (a whisk won't work). Continue to beat while slowly adding ½ cup sugar, then 2 tablespoons lemon or lime juice.

Cream cheese

- Equal amount of ricotta cheese *or*
- Often, you can find a local cheese that is similar in taste and texture. *or*
- Many times, an equal amount of sour cream or unsweetened plain yogurt can be substituted.

Egg, 1 whole

- 3 tablespoons beaten egg *or*
- 2 egg whites OR 2 egg yolks *or*
- ¼ cup egg substitute *or*
- 1 egg white plus 2 teaspoons oil, butter, or margarine *or*
- 2½ tablespoons powdered egg plus 2½ tablespoons water *or*
- In cake batter, 2 tablespoons mayonnaise (not Miracle Whip) *or*
- In baking, ½ teaspoon baking powder plus 1 tablespoon white vinegar and 1 tablespoon water or other liquid *or*
- In baking, ¼ teaspoon baking soda plus 1 tablespoon white vinegar and 1 tablespoon water or other liquid

Measurements:

- 1 large egg = approximately ¼ cup
- 8 to 10 egg whites = 1 cup
- 12 to 14 egg yolks = 1 cup

Egg substitute (Egg Beaters type), 1 egg

- 2 egg whites plus 1 to 3 teaspoons canola or olive oil (optional) *or*
- 1 egg white, 2¼ teaspoons powdered milk, plus 2 teaspoons canola or vegetable oil *or*

- For items already calling for baking powder (such as cookies, cakes, and muffins), use 2 tablespoons water plus an extra ½ teaspoon baking powder

Ghee, 1 tablespoon

- 1 tablespoon clarified butter *or*
- 1 tablespoon canola or vegetable oil (or olive oil if the flavor is acceptable)

Half-and-half, 1 cup

- ½ cup whole milk plus ½ cup cream *or*
- ¼ cup skim milk plus ¾ cup cream *or*
- 1 cup undiluted evaporated milk *or*
- ¾ cup powdered milk (whole milk type, not low fat or nonfat) and enough water to make 1 cup *or*
- 1 tablespoon canola oil, vegetable oil, melted butter, or margarine plus enough whole milk (fresh, boxed, or from powdered milk) to make 1 cup

Margarine—see substitutes for Butter (page 57)

Milk, evaporated, 1 can (about 12 ounces: 1½ cups)

- 1 cup powdered milk plus 1⅓ cups water *or*
- 1½ cups half-and-half *or*
- 1⅓ cups whole milk plus ¼ cup powdered milk

Milk, for cooking and baking, 1 cup

- 1 cup fruit juice (obviously, the taste will be different) *or*
- 1 cup vegetable juice (taste will be different) *or*
- 1 cup water (the finished product won't be as creamy. Often, you can improve it by adding up to 2 tablespoons oil, butter, or margarine) *or*
- 1 cup potato water or other water from cooking vegetables *or*
- ½ cup evaporated milk plus ½ cup water *or*
- 1 cup pureed zucchini (about ¾ pound zucchini, peeled)

Milk, sweetened condensed, 1 can (about 14 ounces: 1¼ cups)

See Sweetened Condensed Milk in the "Dairy" chapter (page 99).

Parmesan cheese, as topping

The following is good as a topping for pasta, but it won't work in recipes where the Parmesan is mixed in:

- 2 tablespoons olive oil, canola oil, or vegetable oil
- 1/2 cup bread crumbs (the drier the better)
- 1 teaspoon garlic powder or garlic salt OR 1 to 2 cloves garlic, minced
- 1 teaspoon salt (or to taste; use less if you use garlic salt)

Heat the oil in a pan over medium-high heat. Add the bread crumbs and toast until they just start to turn golden. Add the garlic and salt. Toast until medium brown, then turn onto a paper towel to cool.

Ricotta cheese, 1 cup

- Make your own or see recipe for Yogurt Ricotta in the "Dairy" chapter (page 102) *or*
- 1 cup dry cottage cheese (place in strainer and let drain for 30 minutes or more)

Sour cream, 1 cup

- See the sour cream recipes in the "Dairy" chapter (page 99) *or*
- 3/4 cup sour milk or buttermilk plus 1/3 cup butter *or*
- 1 cup unsweetened plain yogurt (don't use if the dish will be heated; it will curdle) *or*
- 1 tablespoon lemon or lime juice or white vinegar plus enough whole milk or evaporated milk to make 1 cup; let stand for 5 minutes (this is thinner than sour cream) *or*
- In dips, 1 cup mayonnaise or Miracle Whip often works well.

Yogurt, in cooking, 1 cup plain unsweetened

- 1 cup buttermilk *or*
- 1 cup sour cream *or*
- 1 cup milk plus 2 teaspoons lemon juice or white vinegar; let stand until thick *or*
- 1 cup mayonnaise or Miracle Whip *or*
- 3/4 cup ricotta cheese plus 1/4 cup milk, mixed until creamy *or*
- 1 cup cottage cheese, stirred until creamy

Also see how to make your own (page 101).

OTHER FOODS

Lard, 1 cup

- 1 cup shortening *or*
- For frying, use the same amount of cooking oil. *or*
- For baking, use the same amount of butter or margarine. The texture and flavor will be different.

Macaroni

- 1 cup uncooked equals 2 cups cooked.
- Substitute the same amount of any medium-size pasta (rotini, penne, etc.).
- In some recipes, you can substitute half the amount of small pasta (it will change the texture of the finished dish).
- Break spaghetti, linguine, or fettuccine into 2-inch pieces and substitute an equal amount.
- Cooked spaghetti squash can be equally substituted for cooked macaroni.
- Use 1 1/2 times the quantity of uncooked noodles; the same quantity of cooked noodles.

Marshmallows

- Substitute 10 miniature marshmallows for 1 large.
- Substitute 10 large marshmallows for 1 cup miniature marshmallows.

Marshmallow cream (or Fluff), 1 cup

See Marshmallow Fluff in the chapter "Sweet Tooth" (page 432).

Preserves, 1 cup

- 1 cup jam or jelly (The consistency will be thinner; you may need to reduce other liquid in the recipe.)
- Depending on the recipe, you can often substitute fresh fruit (for example, as a dessert topping).

Rennet, 1 tablet

- 1 tablespoon liquid rennet

Pasta, cooked, semolina, 4 cups

Semolina pasta is the "typical" pasta. This conversion works for medium-size pasta such as spaghetti, angel hair, linguine, fettuccine, bow ties, rotini, penne, mostaccioli, macaroni, shells, twists, and similar types.

- 8 ounces uncooked pasta of any type listed above

Food Substitutions

Rice—see the "Beans, Rice, and Pasta" chapter (page 175) for detailed information on substituting brown and white rice, cooked for uncooked, and water ratios
- Substitute equal amount of cooked barley, bulgur wheat, couscous, or pasta, depending on the dish.

Salsa, 1 jar (American type)
Mix together 1 (16-ounce) can diced tomatoes or 2 cups fresh diced tomatoes, 1 teaspoon to 1 tablespoon finely diced chile peppers (to taste, depending on how hot the peppers are) OR 1 (4-ounce) can chopped green chilies, $1/4$ cup finely diced onion or green onion, 2 tablespoons cooked corn kernels (optional), $1/4$ cup Recipe-Ready Beans (page 176) or canned black or kidney beans. Add salt to taste; can also add ground cumin, chili powder, or red pepper flakes to taste.

Sausage, breakfast or Italian
Make your own Fish Sausage (page 233)—it tastes virtually identical!

Shortening, for baking, 1 cup
- $1\frac{1}{8}$ cups butter or margarine, and decrease salt in recipe by $1/2$ teaspoon *or*
- 1 cup minus 2 tablespoons lard

NOTE: Do *not* use oil unless the recipe calls for melted shortening; find a recipe designed for oil.

Shortening, melted, 1 tablespoon
- 1 tablespoon canola or vegetable oil (olive oil can also be substituted if taste is acceptable) *or*
- 1 tablespoon butter or margarine, melted

MEASUREMENTS AND CONVERSIONS

We've tried to provide all the equivalents and metric conversions you'll ever need, as well as "eyeball estimates."

We'll also give you ideas for makeshift measuring cups, some frequently used rules of thumb, tips for measuring butter and margarine, and oven temperature metric conversions and makeshift "thermometers."

BASIC KITCHEN MEASURES

TEASPOONS	TABLESPOONS	CUPS	PINTS	QUARTS	GALLONS	FLUID OUNCES	METRIC
⅛	—	—	—	—	—	—	½ ml
¼	—	—	—	—	—	—	1 ml
½	⅙	—	—	—	—	—	2 ml
1	⅓	—	—	—	—	—	5 ml
3	1	1/16	—	—	—	½	15 ml
6	2	⅛	—	—	—	1	30 ml
12	4	¼	—	—	—	2	60 ml
16	5⅓	⅓	—	—	—	2⅔	80 ml
—	8	½	¼	—	—	4	125 ml
—	16	1	½	¼	—	8	250 ml
—	—	2	1	½	—	16	500 ml OR ½ liter
—	—	3	1½	¾	—	24	750 ml (std. wine bottle)
—	—	4	2	1	¼	32	1 liter
—	—	8	4	2	½	64	2 liters
—	—	16	8	4	1	128	4 liters

NOTE: The metric conversions are "everyday" conversions—in other words, they are not exact but work well in most situations. For example, a gallon is actually 3.8 liters, but most people use 4 liters in everyday galley situations.

ESTIMATES

Good to know in a pinch (or when you just don't feel like digging out the measuring spoons):

1/8 teaspoon	1 pinch using your thumb, index, and middle finger
1/4 teaspoon	2 of the above pinches OR nickel-size mound poured into the center of your cupped hand (cupped as though you were holding water in it)
1/2 teaspoon	quarter-size mound poured into your cupped hand
1 teaspoon	a mound 1/4 inch larger than a quarter poured into your cupped hand OR an "eating" teaspoon about half full
1 tablespoon	slightly rounded soup spoon OR turn a 12-ounce pop or beer can upside down; the depression in the bottom holds exactly 1 tablespoon

MAKESHIFT MEASURING CUPS

Just in case you've lost your measuring cup, or someone decided that it was the perfect thing in which to mix epoxy:

- **Coffee mug.** A typical coffee mug holds 12 ounces—1 1/2 cups—totally full. Filling it 2/3 full is about 1 cup.
- **Gatorade scoop.** The scoop that makes 1 quart (or 1 liter) of Gatorade is 4 1/2 tablespoons, or just a little more than 1/4 cup.
- **Yogurt container.** A single-serving yogurt container usually holds 1 cup, measured to about 1/4 inch below the rim.
- **Water bottle.** Many reusable water bottles have measuring marks on the side.

RULES OF THUMB

There are lots of helpful rules of thumb in the "Food Substitutions" chapter (about how many asparagus spears in a pound? how much coleslaw will a head of cabbage make?), but we've repeated a few of the most often asked about here:

- **Garlic.** 1 clove yields about 1 teaspoon minced.
- **Ginger.** A 1-inch piece, when peeled and grated or minced, yields about 1 tablespoon.
- **Herbs.** You need about three times as much fresh as dried and *un*ground, or six times as much fresh as dried and ground. See also specific herbs in the "Food Substitutions" chapter.
- **Cheese.** 1 pound yields 4 to 5 cups grated or shredded.
- **Egg.** 1 egg is about 1/4 cup. If you're halving a recipe that calls for one egg, you can usually use a whole egg and use 1/8 cup less of any other liquid in the recipe.
- **Lemons and limes.** 1 lemon or lime yields 2 to 3 tablespoons juice. A Key lime (also called a *limón*) yields a little less than 1 tablespoon juice.
- **Pasta.** Will approximately double in volume when cooked.
- **Rice.** Instant rice will approximately double in volume when cooked; standard rice will approximately triple in volume when cooked.

BUTTER/MARGARINE STICKS

Butter and margarine sticks outside the US are often not the same size as in the US; be on the lookout for differences. When they're not the same, any recipe you may have that calls for something like "1 stick of butter" has to be translated into a definite measurement, and then you have to measure the butter or margarine.

US STICKS	TABLESPOONS	CUPS	OUNCES (WEIGHT)
1/8	1	—	1/2
1/4	2	1/8	1
1/2	4	1/4	2
2/3	5 1/3	1/3	2 2/3
3/4	6	3/8	3
1	8	1/2	4
2	16	1	8 (1/2 pound)
4	32	2	16 (1 pound)

DRINK MEASUREMENTS

NOTE: A jigger is 1½ ounces or 3 tablespoons.

FLUID OUNCES	TABLESPOONS	CUPS	METRIC
½ ounce	1 tablespoon	—	15 ml
¾ ounce	1½ tablespoons	—	22½ ml
1 ounce	2 tablespoons	⅛ cup	30 ml
1½ ounces	3 tablespoons	³⁄₁₆ cup	45 ml
2 ounces	4 tablespoons	¼ cup	60 ml
3 ounces	6 tablespoons	⅜ cup	90 ml
4 ounces	8 tablespoons	½ cup	120 ml
5 ounces	10 tablespoons	⅝ cup	150 m
6 ounces	12 tablespoons	¾ cup	180 ml
8 ounces	16 tablespoons	1 cup	240 ml (often rounded to 250 ml)
10 ounces	—	1¼ cups	300 ml
12 ounces	—	1½ cups	360 ml (often rounded to 375 ml)
16 ounces	—	2 cups (1 pint)	480 ml (often rounded to 500 ml OR ½ liter)
32 ounces	—	4 cups (1 quart)	1,000 ml OR 1 liter
64 ounces	—	8 cups (2 quarts OR ½ gallon)	2 liters

WEIGHT

American		Metric	
Ounces	Pounds	Grams	Kilograms
½	—	15	—
1	—	30	—
4	¼	115	just under ⅛
8	½	225	just under ¼
12	¾	340	just over ⅓
16	1	450	a little under ½
17.6	1.1	500	½
35.2	2.2	1,000	1
—	11	—	5
—	22	—	10
—	55	—	25

Measurements and Conversions

OVEN TEMPERATURES

AMERICAN	METRIC	DESCRIPTION
250°F	130°C	Very low oven
300°F	150°C	Low oven
350°F	180°C	Moderate oven
400°F	200°C	Hot oven
450°F	230°C	Very hot oven
500°F	250°C	Extremely hot oven

Practical Tests for Oven Temperature

Here are a couple of tests used for woodstoves back in pioneer days. They work just as well for boat ovens:

- If you can hold your bare hand in the middle of the oven for a count of 20, it's about 350°F.
- If you can hold your hand in the oven only for a count of 5, it's about 450°F.
- Place a small piece of white paper in the oven for 5 minutes. If it turns golden brown, the oven is about 350°F. If it turns dark brown, the oven is over 400°F.

MEALS ON PASSAGE

Regardless of whether you love or hate passage-making, you still need to eat. It is appalling to hear stories of multi-day passages where the menu is nothing but junk food and/or sandwiches. A hot meal raises morale aboard, especially during a difficult passage. Impossible, you say? Not at all. By pre-planning and pre-preparing your underway cuisine, you can actually look forward to tasty meals.

This chapter is written for the multitudes of primarily coastal cruisers who occasionally have an overnight passage or even a weeklong passage. Clearly it is not written for serious passagemakers who are crossing oceans for weeks or months at a time.

Advance planning and preparation are the keys to eating well while under way. Here are some tips followed by a cross-reference list of recipes that we have found work well for passagemaking.

WHAT MEALS, WHEN?

Determine how many of each meal will be needed. We always plan for at least one extra of each meal, and usually much more, on board. Depending on our destination, we may not be able to leave the boat for a day if we're checking in to a new country, or we may be arriving at a destination where we don't know what provisions are available.

Many cruisers, such as Carolyn, prefer less structured meals and eat small meals throughout the day. They still emphasize at least one meal per day together—usually a hot meal during a watch change.

CREATE SPECIFIC MEAL PLANS

Although we never eat elaborate meals, I (Jan) at least try to make sure we get a balanced nutritional meal since diet plays such a big part in morale.

Sample meal plans might include:

- **Breakfast:** Oatmeal with fruit. Regular cereal with milk can be difficult to keep from sloshing out of a bowl. It's easy to boil water for oatmeal in the stove-top teakettle. Add the water to the oatmeal and let it stand for 5 minutes in a bowl; wedge it in the sink so it doesn't spill. Add raisins, cinnamon, and even a dash of brown sugar for flavor.

   An alternative is bran/fruit muffins or a yogurt and fruit mixture.

- **Lunch:** Try a salad such as a Black Bean, Corn, and Tomato Salad (page 156). Choose a salad that "sticks" to the spoon as opposed to salads that are loose and difficult to spear. Another alternative is a sandwich, but sandwiches are surprisingly difficult to make or eat in some seas.

- **Dinner:** Dinner is usually a hot, one-pot meal. We plan watches so we can sit in the cockpit together for dinner. One of our favorites is Rice and Beans (page 185), a delicious combination incorporating meat (usually chicken or spicy sausage), onions, peppers, garlic, kidney beans, and brown rice. Another favorite is a pasta and shredded chicken one-pot meal. Aboard *Que Tal*, Carolyn and Dave's favorites are chili, jambalaya, Spanish rice, and goulash. We try to add a salad of some sort to the meal, although it becomes optional depending on conditions. Applesauce or fresh fruit, if available, is good.

Aboard *Que Tal*, Carolyn would prepare in advance a huge bowl of rice or pasta salad as well as a big bowl of cabbage salad with ramen noodles. Both keep for several days and are easy to dish out whenever you get hungry.

PRE-PASSAGE FOOD PREPARATION

Once you have identified your menu, you can begin pre-preparing everything. Think in terms of making everything easy to eat. That may entail cleaning and chopping vegetables so they're ready to munch as a snack. It definitely includes pre-cooking all the hot meals (except for morning oatmeal). When you pre-cook, plan to put exact portions needed in a pan to reheat; it takes longer to reheat a lot of food.

Pre-prepare hard-boiled eggs; carrot and celery sticks; GORP; Black Bean, Corn, and Tomato Salad; any pasta salad; Spanish rice; and Rice and Beans. You can even pre-wash any fruit; apples are easy and nutritious. In short, anything that will need any type of preparation before you eat it should be done before you pull up the anchor.

Pre-preparation also includes thinking through all the details. The seasick meds don't do you much good if they're hidden in a locker all the way forward. If you're prone to motion sickness, be sure to take any advance measures necessary.

And don't forget advance preparation for the ditch bag. We assemble an oversize waterproof bag at the base of the companionway. Inside are all the ditch bag items that can be pre-assembled. This includes water and extra food. Even if you have a life raft, don't count on the food inside. Pack extra. We usually pack hardy items such as apples and nutrition bars.

DECIDE WHO COOKS

Aboard *Winterlude* and *Que Tal*, cooking responsibilities do not change from normal life. We deliberately plan our watches with a half-hour "slack" period so we can eat together. So, for example, 12N–3P, 3P–6P—with a half hour for dinner, 6:30P–9:30P, 9:30P–12:30A, and so on. Except for longer passages, both of us are usually up during the day with maybe a nap in the afternoon, so we eat breakfast and lunch together.

PLAN TO STAY HYDRATED

Don't forget drinks, especially if the passage will be hot. It's important to stay hydrated, as dehydration contributes to motion sickness. We fill our refrigerator with more drinks than normal and make sure to refill them daily so there are always cold drinks in the refrigerator. Powdered Gatorade in a water bottle is a great change from plain water. Other alternatives may be Kool-Aid, Crystal Light, powdered lemonade, or iced tea.

Both *Que Tal* and *Winterlude* have a rule against any alcohol consumption on passage. We break out a celebratory beverage as soon as the anchor is firmly set, but not before.

The few times we had a chilly passage, hot chocolate was great in the middle of the night; those little packets were perfect. Spiced cider packets are also good middle-of-the-night treats.

COOKING AND GALLEY SAFETY TIPS WHILE UNDER WAY

- **Cooking on an angle or in rolly/pitching seas.** Remember that it takes only 5 minutes or less to heat up an already prepared one-dish meal. So in rolly or pitching seas, make sure your pot restraints are in place on each side of the burner that you intend to use, then light the burner. After lighting the burner, unhook the gimbal restraints and let the stove swing.

- **Think safety!** Sloshing food can splash out and cause third-degree burns, so you may want to wear long sleeves or long pants or at least stand away while the pot is clipped securely to the swinging stove. Or use your pressure cooker to warm up dinner, not for the pressure but for the locking lid if the pot accidentally departs the burner in an ill-timed pitch or roll.
- **Use your sink.** The galley sink is the perfect place to wedge most anything when you're preparing a meal. In calmer seas, a non-skid pad or even a damp chamois cloth will usually stop pots and dishes from sliding on your counters, assuming that the counters have borders.
- **Morning coffee.** There's no reason not to enjoy hot coffee if you normally have coffee in the morning. We prefer our Mr. Coffee with a stainless pot, which fits perfectly in the deep one-section sink, and we brew coffee in all but the nastiest of conditions. Other cruisers prefer to make the coffee and put it in a thermos for hot coffee all day long. Carolyn always keeps a small jar of good instant coffee on hand in case it's too rough to use her Melitta cone. Instant coffee is better than nothing.
- **Teakettle.** For other hot beverages, use your teakettle (instead of a saucepan) to heat the water. It fits securely inside the pot restraints on the burner, and you can fill the thermos with the boiling water, keeping it hot all day or all night long.
- **Pre-prepared snacks.** Think finger foods, and make a variety available 24/7 from the cockpit so you don't have to leave to go below (and wake the off-watch crew) when you get a snack. Have veggies and fruits cut up and ready. It's easy to munch a carrot stick. Carolyn always keeps a big Tupperware bowl full of snack stuff near the companionway—almonds, individual packages of olives, crackers, M&M's, cookies, GORP, and whatever can be grabbed and munched easily. (Her Dave is a real snack-o-holic!) Make sure your snack selection contains some healthy choices as well as your favorite snack foods!
- **Dark chocolate.** Dark chocolate is a natural mood enhancer, which is useful during a difficult night watch, and a great excuse to justify more chocolate!
- **Flat-bottom serving bowls.** Prepare nothing that you can't eat from a flat-bottom serving bowl. And choose foods that stick together, are easy to scoop on a spoon, and will·stay there on the trip to your mouth.
- **Use your thermos.** You can use the thermos to keep boiling water hot enough to make hot chocolate or cider anytime you want a treat (or to warm up in a cold night passage). Or you can make rice or pasta ahead of time in the thermos—see Thermos Cooking (page 70).

IDEAS FOR MEALS ON PASSAGE

Here are some of our favorites for passages.

Breakfast and Brunch
Boatmeal, *page 104*
Boiled Eggs, *page 108*

Appetizers and Snacks
GORP, *page 144*
Various energy bars, *pages 144–146*
Protein Balls, *page 145*

Salads
Black Bean, Corn, and Tomato Salad, *page 156*
Picnic Pasta Salad, *page 159*

Soups and Stews
Chili, *page 169*

Rice, Beans, and Pasta
White Chicken Chili, *page 180*
Lentil Chili, *page 181*
Rice and Beans, *page 185*

Canned Meats and Seafood
Classic Tuna Salad, *page 304*
Cold Macaroni Tuna Salad, *page 306*
Black Bean Tuna Salad, *page 307*

Sweet Tooth
Ginger Snaps, *page 416*

Meals on Passage

STORM PREPARATION
IN THE GALLEY

Whether you're at sea or at anchor, a storm or heavy weather takes a bit of galley preparation. While a few of the following tips will apply even in a brief squall (such as securing anything that would become a missile if the boat rolls gunwale to gunwale), most won't. Here, I'm thinking more of a weather system such as a tropical storm, a hurricane, or a norther that blows for days, any of which can keep you aboard (hopefully in a safe anchorage) while the boat is bounced around by the waves.

PREPARE THE DECK FIRST, AND THEN THE GALLEY

Taking care of the boat itself is always the first priority if a storm is coming. While there are a few things that you need to do almost simultaneously (such as getting food out of lockers before you pile sails on top of them), most of the galley work can happen after the deck work is done. *Getting food is no excuse for failing to prepare the boat.* I've seen this happen twice as hurricanes hit where we were cruising. People were running to town to buy fresh veggies instead of prepping their boats. The consequences of not prepping the boat are much more severe than anything that can happen in the galley!

- **Get food out of lockers that will be inaccessible.** Some lockers will become inaccessible when stuff gets piled on top of them; others because they're hard to get to in a rolling boat (such as one where you have to lift the bed mattress while you dive in

headfirst). If you're going to need anything out of these lockers, get it out now and put it in a safe but accessible location.
- **Make sure seasickness medications and the first-aid kit are accessible.** If you need either of these, you want them right at hand. If you take any daily medications, keep them available, too.
- **Secure potential missiles.** Make sure that knives can't go flying and cans are really secure. Both can cause serious—even life-threatening—injuries if they are hurled across the boat at you. Use duct tape over the latches. If you pile sails on a settee, tie them down so that they won't slide off when the boat rolls. Stuff rags in everywhere you can to keep locker contents quiet.
- **Secure the TP.** A bad day is just that much worse if you suddenly discover that your entire stock of toilet paper is soggy (ditto for feminine hygiene products). Split it up between a couple of different lockers in case one develops a leak. And put some, a roll or two, in a Ziploc bag or dry bag.
- **Top up water tanks if possible.** If you have a watermaker, top up your tanks before the storm so you won't have to run the watermaker for several days after the storm passes. If you're at anchor, the water is likely to be very disturbed after a storm, possibly with a lot of dirt or other debris having been blown in. This will quickly plug your watermaker's prefilters.
- **Keep a stock of "storm food."** If you're gunkholing in an area where storms are a distinct possibility, you need to have enough reserve food aboard

so you can wait an extra week—or, better, two—to get to your next reprovisioning. You also need some food that needs no cooking, doesn't have to be refrigerated, and can be eaten without utensils. If the boat is really rolling, you don't want to have to try to get into the refrigerator. You're sure not going to cook, and utensils will be too hard to use. We found that peanut butter and crackers could be eaten even in the roughest weather, as could energy bars, nuts, olives, M&Ms, and GORP.

- **Make snacks and drinks accessible.** Before the storm hits, make sure that you have a stash of easy-to-eat snacks and drinks in a place that is easily accessible but safe (you don't want drink bottles becoming missiles).

- **Pre-prepare food.** If you have time (and you may not after preparing the boat, which is the biggest priority), you can pre-prepare several meals just as you would for a passage (see the chapter "Meals on Passage"). The same types of easy-to-heat, easy-to-eat meals work well when the weather isn't at its absolute worst.

- **No alcohol.** Both *Que Tal* and *Winterlude* have a rule that if we're preparing for or in bad weather, no one aboard consumes alcohol. You just don't need even slightly impaired reactions if a problem develops.

- **Pot restraints and stove gimbals.** If you do decide to cook in rough weather, be prepared. See our notes on pot restraints and stove gimbals in the section Stoves and Ovens: Using and Trouble-shooting in the chapter "Equipping a Galley" (page 14). The bottom line is that there is no totally guaranteed method to secure pots on the stove (or in the oven) that will avoid the danger of them flying, spilling, or causing burns in rough conditions.

- **Ditch bag.** While none of us wants to think about the possibility of being evacuated off the boat, or leaving the boat voluntarily into either the dinghy or life raft, if it's a severe storm forecast, you may want to think about preparing a food/water ditch bag to supplement your normal ditch bag. The food/water ditch bag should be waterproof and contain daily medicines you'd need plus food and drink items that don't require cooking or refrigeration. Make sure the bag can be easily grabbed from the cockpit.

Storm Preparation in the Galley

SPECIAL GALLEY COOKING TECHNIQUES

While many cooking techniques used ashore are also used on a boat, there are several techniques we learned that we'd never heard much about in a "house" kitchen.

- Thermos Cooking—the cruiser's Crock-Pot
- Pressure Cookers—dramatically cut the cooking time of many foods
- Omnia Stove-Top Oven—the best way to bake on the stove—or grill
- Dutch Oven Stove -Top Baking—probably the best-known way to "bake" on the stove
- Pizza in a Skillet—make a great pizza without an oven
- Baking on the Grill—a great way to keep heat out of the boat in hot climates

THERMOS COOKING

Thermos cooking saves propane, keeps heat out of the boat, and you get to do something else while the food cooks. Thermos cooking makes using dried beans—which take up a lot less space and weight than canned—and brown rice—nutritionally far superior to white—a snap. While there are many other things you can cook in a thermos, these are the two standout uses—along with making your own yogurt (page 101).

Keys to Success

The basic technique is simple: heat the ingredients, put them in a thermos, let it sit, then eat. As with everything, the devil is in the details. We've learned five key points for successful thermos cooking.

1. **Plan ahead.** Thermos cooking takes time, so you can't decide to cook dinner in a thermos an hour before you want to eat.
2. **Select the right thermos.** You need one that is well insulated, sized right for what you want to cook, and preferably widemouthed. See the section Tips on Choosing Specific Gear in the chapter "Equipping a Galley" (page 10) for tips on choosing a Thermos bottle.
3. **Cook appropriate foods.** It must be something that is cooked in liquid. Thermos cooking is best for single foods or dishes where everything needs to cook the same length of time, or to pre-cook part of a dish, such as:
   - Soaking and cooking dried beans for use in a recipe
   - Rice
   - Soups, stews, and chili
   - Spaghetti sauce
   - Reconstituting dried and freeze-dried foods

Don't even try to cook foods that are easily over-cooked; dishes that require many additions of extra ingredients, which causes heat to escape each time; dishes with cheese in them (unless you can add it after removing the food from the thermos) because it sticks to the inside of the thermos and is hard to get out; or food that cannot be brought to a full boil before putting it into the bottle (yogurt, page 101, is one exception to this).

4. **Don't skip parts of the method** (below). Preheating the thermos and pre-cooking the food are necessary.

5. **Cleaning the thermos.** A bottle brush and soapy water will generally keep the bottle clean. If you need a little more muscle, use a denture tablet in water; leave the cap off and let the contents sit several hours or overnight.

The Method

This is the general method for cooking in a thermos. In the following section, there are three recipes that detail the steps for particular foods. This will get you started. But don't limit yourself to just those recipes. Most soups can be cooked in a thermos, as can chili, spaghetti sauce, and similar dishes.

Preheat the Bottle. Before preparing the food to be cooked, boil water, fill the thermos, and stopper it. Let it sit at least 5 minutes to thoroughly heat the inside of the bottle; otherwise, a lot of the heat in the food will be used up to heat the bottle rather than in further cooking the food. Don't empty the water until you're ready to fill the thermos with food (save the water to use in something else).

SAFETY TIP: Fill the thermos in the sink. Whenever you're pouring hot water or a hot mixture into the thermos, put the thermos in the sink first. This way, anything that spills or splashes will be contained in the sink. It also helps to use a canning funnel when pouring hot food.

Brown the Meat, Onions, and Other Ingredients (if needed). Anything that must be browned—such as meat and onions for chili—should be browned before being mixed with the other ingredients. Meat and other ingredients will cook in the thermos, but they won't brown.

Pre-Cook the Food. Pre-cooking doesn't just mean putting things into a pan and heating them to boiling, then pouring them into the thermos. The cooking has to actually begin before you put the food into the bottle. Cook things right up to where you'd turn the heat down and let them simmer. Then put the food in the Thermos, stopper it, and put it in a secure location.

Cooking Times. Cooking times will vary, depending on how well the thermos retains heat, the temperature where the thermos sits, and how large the food pieces are in the thermos (smaller pieces cook faster).

THERMOS COOKING TIMES FOR BASIC INGREDIENTS

ITEM	STOVE TIME (AT A BOIL)	THERMOS TIME
White rice (not instant)	5 minutes	1½ hours
NOTE: Because rice expands beyond the volume of water it soaks up, leave an extra inch of room at the top		
Brown rice (not instant) (see note above)	5 minutes	4 to 5 hours
Beef stew meat, 1-inch cubes	15 minutes	4 hours
Chicken, 1-inch pieces	8 minutes	3 hours
Beans, dried— to soak	5 minutes	2 hours
Beans, dried— after soaking (change water)	10 minutes	3 hours
Potato, 1-inch cubes	5 minutes	2 hours

For soups, stews, chili, spaghetti sauce, and other things like that, cook them as usual on the stove up to the point where the recipe says to "simmer for *x* hours." Instead, bring the food to a full boil for at least 5 minutes, then put it in the thermos for two to three times the originally specified cooking time.

Reheat if Necessary. Depending on the temperature around the bottle (40°F in the boat versus 100°F in the boat), the quality of the bottle, and the total time needed to cook the food in the bottle, you may need to reheat the contents so that they will continue cooking. Check the contents halfway through the allotted time if the total thermos time is over 3 hours. If steam does not rise up when you open the bottle, you need to reheat the contents.

To reheat, pour the thermos contents into a pan and re-stopper the bottle to keep the heat in. Unless you're in a very cold climate, you don't need to re-preheat the bottle. Bring the food to a full rolling boil, then put it back in the thermos and re-stopper it.

Finishing on the Stove. If you desire, you can cook the dish traditionally for 5 to 10 minutes after taking it from the thermos. Add more water or boil some away if needed and add any extra spices that a taste reveals are needed. But if you're trying to conserve propane or want something to take along on a hike, it certainly isn't necessary!

Recipe-Ready Beans in a Thermos
Makes 1³/₄ cups

Recipe-Ready Beans replace a can of beans, to be used in another recipe such as Chili or Three-Bean Salad. Throughout this book, you'll see references to "Recipe-Ready Beans," and you can use either these or the stove-top version (page 176).

Total Time: approximately 6 hours, including about 5¹/₂ hours "sitting"
Prep Time: 30 minutes (15 minutes each at two different times)

³/₄ **cup dried beans such as black, pinto, kidney, red, lima, butter, Great Northern, etc.***
water

*Do not use this recipe for lentils; they require much less cooking!

1. You need at least a 2-cup (pint or half liter) vacuum bottle for this recipe. If you have a 4-cup bottle, you can make a double batch and put half in the refrigerator for future use (they will be good for 3 to 5 days or even longer if you can put them right against the cold plate), or you can make just a single batch but use enough water to fill the bottle.
2. Boil enough water to fill your thermos. Put the thermos into the sink and fill it with the boiling water. Stopper the bottle and let it sit, preheating, while you ready the beans.
3. Measure out the beans and pick out any stones and debris. Put the beans in a pan and just cover them with water. Swish the pan around a little to rinse off the beans, then discard the water.

4. Cover the beans again with water and bring to a boil. Boil for 5 minutes. *Do not add salt or any other ingredients that may contain salt;* it will toughen the beans and they'll take much longer to cook.
5. Pour the hot water out of the thermos into a pan or other suitable container so that you can re-use it. Again set the thermos into the sink, then pour the hot beans and water into the thermos. If the thermos is not full, add some of the saved hot water up to the fill line (if there is no fill line, the contents should come about ¹/₂ inch below the stopper).
6. Let sit for at least 2 hours (4 hours or more won't hurt). This is the "soak" stage.
7. Drain the beans and discard the water. **NOTE:** If you have a shortage of water and re-use this water to cook the beans instead of discarding it, your beans will be gassy!
8. Put the beans back in the pan, cover with new water, and bring to a boil. Again, don't add any salt. Boil for 10 minutes. While the beans are cooking, be sure to keep the stopper in the thermos to keep it warm so you don't have to preheat it again.
9. Put the beans back into the bottle, again adding hot water to the fill line if needed. Stopper and let sit for at least 3 hours (again, extra time won't hurt). This is the "cook" stage.
10. Unstopper the bottle and look at the beans. At least some of them should have split their skins. Try a bean. It should not be hard, although it will be firmer than canned beans. If you are used to canned beans, you'll also think that it tastes flat, as no salt has been added yet (most canned beans are loaded with salt). If the beans are still hard, recap them and let them sit an hour longer. If the beans weren't steaming when you unstoppered the bottle, reheat them in a pot on the stove before letting them sit longer.
11. Drain the beans and discard the water. Use the beans in place of 1 can of beans in any recipe. Add salt as needed.

12. If you are not using the beans in the next few hours, keep them in the refrigerator or cooler, or leave them "cooking" in the thermos.

Brown Rice in a Thermos
Makes about 1½ cups

Total Time: 5½ hours, including about 5 hours "sitting"

¾ cup brown rice (not instant or quick cooking)
1 teaspoon bouillon powder OR 1 bouillon cube, crumbled, OR 1 teaspoon salt
water

1. Put water on the stove to boil; you'll need enough to fill the thermos. This will be the water used to preheat the thermos.
2. While the water is coming to a boil, put the rice in the thermos and fill with more water to about 1 inch below the stopper (this gives more clearance than usual because of the rice's tendency to swell). This step is just to "measure" the water needed to cook the rice. Pour the rice and water from the thermos into a pan and add the bouillon powder. Bring the rice and water to a boil and let boil for 5 minutes while you are preheating the thermos.
3. To preheat the thermos, put it in the sink (to contain any spills) and fill with the plain boiling water. Cap and let it sit while the rice mixture is coming to a boil and starting to cook.
4. When the rice has boiled for 5 minutes, empty the hot water from the thermos, retaining it for other uses. Fill the thermos with the hot rice mixture. Cap and let it sit for about 3 hours. Reheat the contents and replace them in the thermos for another 2 hours.
5. The rice should be done, but check it before serving. Depending on the size of your thermos, the rice will probably not have absorbed all the water, so do not use the amount of water left as a guide to "doneness." Taste the rice. If it is not quite done, you can either recap it and let it sit awhile longer, or cook it for a few minutes on the stove. Drain the excess water. Serve the rice or use it in any recipe calling for cooked rice.

Split Pea Soup in a Thermos
Serves 2

This recipe is designed for a thermos that holds approximately 4 cups/1 quart/32 ounces. You can use the same ingredients and make it on the stove, simmering for 1 hour.

Total time: 4½ hours, including 4 hours "sitting"

¾ cup dried split peas
1 teaspoon chicken bouillon powder OR salt
4 to 6 ounces ham or smoked sausage OR 1 chicken breast OR 1 6-ounce can ham or chicken
½ cup diced onion OR 1 teaspoon onion powder OR 1 tablespoon minced dried onion
1 carrot, diced
2 or 3 bay leaves
ground pepper, to taste
water

1. Boil enough water to fill your thermos. Put the thermos into the sink and fill it with the boiling water. Stopper the bottle and let it sit, preheating, while you get out the other ingredients and otherwise ready them.
2. When all the ingredients are measured and diced as needed, pour out the water from the thermos and save it. Put all the ingredients except the water into the thermos. Add the saved water until the thermos is full (this will not be the full amount of water that you used for preheating).
3. Pour all the ingredients into a pan and then recap the thermos to keep in the heat. Warm the split pea mixture on the stove until it is boiling. Boil for 3 minutes, then pour the mixture back into the thermos. Cap and let it sit for about 4 hours (it can sit up to 12 hours).
4. Check after 2 to 3 hours to make sure that the mixture is still hot. If it's not steaming, reheat the mixture on the stove and then put it back into the thermos for the remaining time.
5. If desired, simmer the soup on the stove for the last 10 minutes, adding a little water if it seems too thick. When the peas and carrots can

be easily mashed with a spoon, the soup is done. Remove the bay leaves and serve the soup.

NOTE: This is a great soup to take along on a cool-weather hike. It does not have to be cooked on the stove for the last 10 minutes. However, try making this the first time where a stove is available as all thermos bottles are different as to how fast the soup will cook in them. Once you know how long your particular bottle takes, you can time it correctly for a hike.

PRESSURE COOKERS

Pressure cookers appeal to cruisers for their ability to save time and save fuel, which translates into less heat in the boat. As a general rule (*very* general), food cooks in a pressure cooker in about one-third the time it would take conventionally.

Converting Recipes to Use a Pressure Cooker

This section is not intended to be a substitute for the owner's manual that came with your pressure cooker, or for a dedicated pressure cooker cookbook. Both will provide far more detailed information, and you'll note that we do not include any recipes that require a pressure cooker. If you would like to make one of the recipes in this book in a pressure cooker, your owner's manual is the best place to look for information on converting the cooking times and methods. The second-best place is to find a similar type of recipe in a pressure cooker cookbook and adapt it to use the ingredients here.

A few notes in general on converting recipes:

- Don't use canned meats in a pressure cooker. They will turn to mush by the time it's up to pressure. Canned vegetables will also usually get mushy.
- Very little liquid will evaporate in a pressure cooker, so you usually have to reduce the amount used.
- Any milk or cream in the recipe should be added after the pressure is released, as it is likely to scorch otherwise.

- Before trying to convert a recipe for use in a pressure cooker, make some recipes designed for a pressure cooker. You'll gain invaluable experience.
- Soups and stews are the easiest to convert, along with other dishes that require long, slow simmering without needing to be stirred or having other ingredients added frequently.
- Foods that can easily be overcooked are not suitable for pressure cookers.
- Many pressure cooker recipes call for quickly cooling the pan with cool water. If you're short on water, seawater works well as it won't touch the food inside the pan.

Baking in a Pressure Cooker

It seems that a staple of cruiser lore is the concept of baking in a pressure cooker if the boat does not have an oven. Frankly, we think the results are much better using an Omnia stove-top oven or Dutch oven, or baking on the grill, all of which are explained below. If you want to bake in your pressure cooker, there are three ways to do it. (Note that none of them involves pressurizing the pot.)

1. Use the pressure cooker in the same fashion as a Dutch oven, below. This is likely to warp your pressure cooker, however, and we strongly discourage it.
2. Steam breads. Remove the gasket from the pressure cooker and the weights if possible. Put 1 inch of water in the bottom of the pressure cooker and put the trivet (usually used with the steaming basket) in the bottom. Put the bread dough in a smaller pan that will fit inside the pressure cooker and set it on the trivet. Put the lid on the pressure cooker and bring the water to a boil. Cook for approximately the same length of time that you would in the oven. If you notice that the pot is not steaming, open it and carefully add more water. Since the bread is steaming, it won't develop a crunchy crust. This method works best with quick breads (made with baking powder) rather than yeast breads.
3. "Bake" yeast bread in the pressure cooker. Prepare dough for yeast bread as normal. When it comes time to put it in the pot, coat the inside of the pressure cooker with oil and then oats or cornmeal,

then put the dough in the pot for the final rising. When it has risen, remove the gasket and weights from the lid of the pressure cooker, then put the lid on. Place the pressure cooker on the stove over medium heat for 5 minutes, then turn the heat down to the lowest setting for another 40 minutes. If you want the top of the loaf brown, very carefully slide the loaf out of the pot, turn it upside down, replace it in the pot, and cook for 10 minutes more.

NOTE: It's very easy to blacken the bottom of the bread before the top is done. A thick coating of oats on the pot helps avoid this.

OMNIA STOVE-TOP OVEN

The Omnia stove-top oven makes it easy to bake without a regular oven. While baking in a pressure cooker or a Dutch oven is fairly commonly discussed amongst cruisers, few have heard of the Omnia, although that is beginning to change. And while we normally don't specifically endorse a particular brand of gear, there just isn't anything else similar. If your boat doesn't have an oven, we think this is a far better solution than "baking" in a pressure cooker (discussed above) or a Dutch oven (see page 76).

- The whole thing is smaller and much lighter than a good cast iron Dutch oven (it's about 10 inches in diameter, 5 inches high, weighs about a pound, and comes with a little storage bag).
- You can bake about twice as much in the Omnia as in a Dutch oven (about what would fit in an 8-inch square pan or a 9"×5" loaf pan versus about a 6-inch round pan).
- The results are better and easier to achieve.

There are three pieces to the Omnia oven: a steel base, an aluminum ring-shaped baking pan, and the lid. The picture at right shows how it works. The burner directly heats the steel base, which in turn heats the air trapped between the base and the baking pan. The burner also heats air that goes up the center of the baking pan, and the lid serves to distribute that hot air over the top of the food. Thus, there's hot air under and above the baking pan and in the center.

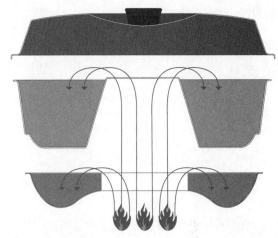

The Omnia puts hot air under, over, and on the inside of the special tube pan. (Courtesy Omnia/Anna N Kjellgren/ www.annafolio.com).

A few air holes in the lid allow steam to escape. The Omnia can be used with virtually any type of stove burner—gas, electric, or even various other fuels used with camping and backpacking stoves. And it can be used on a grill, which makes it easier to keep the cooking heat out of the boat.

With a Dutch oven or a pressure cooker, it is difficult to keep the top of the baked food from being steamed by the moisture being driven out of the food. The Omnia takes care of that, with the lid being high enough over the food to have quite a bit of hot air there, as well as having holes to let the steam escape. My bread and baked goods were very similar in texture to what they were in a conventional oven.

Even better, the system isn't limited to just breads and cakes. I've baked chicken, beans, appetizers, and pretty much everything I would bake in a regular oven. Pizza has a hole in the center, and you can bake only a few cookies at a time (or make them as bar cookies), but the quality is excellent.

The system is simple: you place the steel base on the burner and let it heat for about 3 minutes on high. Put your food into the baking pan and put the lid on it, then set it onto the base. The instructions say to then turn the burner down to medium or lower. I found that I had better results if I left it on high for about a minute (to heat the air on top of the food) and then turned it down to slightly higher than medium. The cooking time is then about the same as with a conventional oven. Don't take the lid off too often to check, as you let out the hot air from the top each time.

The most important thing is not to overfill the baking pan when making cakes and breads. Even after the item rises, there needs to be air space between it and the lid. With cakes and breads, making a batch sized for an 8-inch square pan or a 9"×5" loaf pan works perfectly.

DUTCH OVEN STOVE-TOP BAKING

For years, cruisers without an oven have "baked" in a Dutch oven—more bread than anything else. The technique is more complicated than with the Omnia, but it does work. Quick breads (batter breads made with baking powder) turn out just as well on the stove top as in the oven. Yeast breads can also be baked this way, but I recommend baking quick breads a few times first to get the general method down before trying yeast breads.

Equipment

- **Dutch oven.** Heavier is better, with a cast iron one being the best. If yours isn't particularly heavy, put a flame tamer (see the section Stoves and Ovens: Using and Troubleshooting in the chapter "Equipping a Galley"—page 15) under it.
- **Tuna can or metal trivet.** Place an empty tuna can or a trivet in the Dutch oven to support the bread pan. This will raise the bread pan off the bottom of the Dutch oven so that the bottom of the bread won't burn.
- **Pan for the bread.** You need a pan for the bread that will fit inside the Dutch oven with an inch or more of air space around it. I used a backpacking pan with the handle removed. You can also use a "personal" size loaf pan; it's okay if the corners of the pan come close to the Dutch oven, as long as there is plenty of air space around it otherwise. The heavier the bread pan, the better.

  Make sure that the bread pan (sitting on the tuna can) isn't too tall to put the lid on the Dutch

oven. There needs to be some air space between the bread pan and the lid. Make sure that there is nothing on the bread pan (such as a handle) that is not heat resistant.

The Bread

- Unless you have a very large Dutch oven, you'll probably need only a half batch of the bread recipe for the smaller pan.
- Prepare the bread pan by greasing or oiling the bottom and sides (nonstick spray isn't enough). Use this method for nonstick pans as well. Then sprinkle cornmeal or oats in the bottom of the pan (you can put it on the sides as well). This will help "insulate" the bottom of the bread from the heat of the flame. My experience is that oats work better, and are easier to find than cornmeal in many places.
- Don't overfill the pan. If there is only a small amount of air space between the bread pan and the lid, you have to make sure that the bread won't rise above the sides of the pan as there has to be some air space over the top of the bread.

The Method

This method uses the Dutch oven dry. Over time, the bottom of the pan will discolor from the heat and possibly warp as well. Flame tamers (page 15) are inexpensive; I recommend one to save your pan.

Preheat the Dutch oven. Put it on your largest burner, with the flame tamer underneath it. Put the tuna can in the Dutch oven and put the cover on. Heat the pan over high heat (the highest setting on your stove) for 5 minutes. Use your pot restraints and stove gimbal to make sure that the whole thing doesn't slide around.

As the Dutch oven is preheating, put the bread batter in the bread pan. When the Dutch oven is preheated, quickly lift the lid and set the bread pan on the tuna can, then replace the cover.

Turn the heat down just a little bit. My stove has seven numbers on the burners—1 being the lowest, 7 the highest. I turn it to 6. "Bake" the bread for 5 minutes at this setting.

After 5 minutes, take the lid off for just a second to let out built-up steam, then replace the lid. Turn down the heat to a little higher than medium (on my stove, 4) and continue baking. You'll have to experiment; it depends on how hot an oven the recipe calls for.

My experience is that the total baking time (including the first 5 minutes at the higher temperature) is about the same as with a conventional oven. But until you know how it works with your pans and stove, I'd check the bread about 10 minutes before you expect it to be done.

Partway through the remaining baking time, again remove the lid to let out steam. This is also a good time to check how it's baking and adjust the burner setting if necessary.

Test the bread for doneness with a toothpick, or use an instant-read thermometer (it will read between 190° and 200°F when the bread is done). The top of the bread won't brown, although it shouldn't look raw either.

Turn off the stove and remove the bread pan. Cool and serve. Don't touch the Dutch oven until it's cooled off!

It may take making a couple of batches of bread before you get the technique down pat. I can only give a general methodology, as every set of pans and stove is a little different.

Changes Needed to Bake Yeast Breads

Yeast breads are a little trickier to bake on the stove top than breads made with baking powder. With yeast breads, we expect a dry, crunchy crust. But when I "baked" bread in the Dutch oven using the same method as for quick breads, I got a crust that was more like that of a bagel—in other words, a chewy crust. The bread was good, but it wasn't quite the same as when I had baked it in a conventional oven—and that's what I wanted. After a lot of experimentation, I've been able to consistently obtain a drier crust.

The basic problem is that in a Dutch oven, bread tends to "steam" rather than "bake." The moisture comes from the dough itself, but my question was why this was a bigger problem in a Dutch oven than in a conventional oven. I've come to the conclusion that "steaming" resulted from three differences between conventional baking and Dutch oven baking:

- A Dutch oven is smaller.
- Conventional ovens have a vent, which allows the steam to escape.
- A typical pan sitting on a tuna can in the Dutch oven has little space between the sides of the pan and the lid, which traps the moisture right over the baking loaf.

Another problem is that the top crust does not really brown, as it does in a conventional oven. The solution was fourfold:

- Bake the bread on a flat sheet instead of a pan with high sides. This allows the humidity to dissipate through the entire volume of the Dutch oven.
- Bake denser bread (less yeast, more flour) so the loaf won't overflow the flat sheet.
- Bake darker breads (whole wheat and rye) that have color of their own.
- Periodically lift the lid to let accumulated steam escape.

The result is still not quite a French baguette-style super-crunchy crust, but it's very comparable to a typical loaf of homemade bread.

All that said, there is nothing wrong with baking yeast bread using the same technique as for baking quick breads on the stove top as long as you don't mind a chewier crust. Since that technique uses a pan with sides, it's much easier to get the bread in and out of the Dutch oven without burning your hand. And since it doesn't use as high a heat, you do less damage to your Dutch oven.

So now on to step-by-step directions for baking yeast breads in a Dutch oven so they have a more traditional yeast-bread crust.

The equipment is basically the same, except that as a "pan," you'll need a metal disk or a flat pan that's at least 3 inches less in diameter than the Dutch oven. Four inches smaller is even better. The heavier the metal, the better. I used the bottoms from two metal coffee cans, one on top of the other. A small pizza pan would be perfect.

Special Galley Cooking Techniques

A dark, heavy bread dough is best. Unless you have a very large Dutch oven, a loaf made from $1/2$ cup water is about the right size (it will make a "personal" loaf just right for two people). While I normally caution against adding too much flour to bread dough, my caution here is against too wet a dough. If it doesn't hold its own shape to some extent, it will overrun the edges of your "pan" and cause a big mess. No-knead breads are too wet and cannot be baked this way; you'll have a huge mess if you try it.

Make your bread dough as usual, being sure to size the batch to your pan. When it comes time to put it in the pan, prepare the pan with a coating of oil and a thick layer of dry oatmeal.

Shape the dough into a round ball and put it in the center of the disk. Let the dough rise slightly. Remember that it will still get larger when you put it in the Dutch oven, and you don't want it to overflow the disk.

Place the Dutch oven on the flame tamer and put the tuna can in it, then place the cover on the pot. Preheat over the highest possible heat for 5 minutes (time it). Place the bread on top of the tuna can, being very careful not to burn your hand on the hot sides of the Dutch oven. Replace the lid. Leave the burner at its hottest setting for 5 minutes (again, time it).

Without removing the lid, turn the heat down to just slightly over medium (on my stove, $4^1/2$, where 7 is hottest). Let it bake another 5 minutes, then briefly remove the lid to release the accumulated steam.

Replace the lid and let the bread bake for the remainder of the allotted time (with my equipment, a loaf takes almost exactly the same time in total that it would have for a full-size loaf in a conventional oven).

It's hard to test the loaf for doneness by tapping on it as you would do in a conventional oven. If you have an instant-read meat thermometer, you can poke it into the center of the loaf. For a heavy bread, a temperature of 190° to 200°F means that it is done.

When the bread is done, very carefully remove it from the Dutch oven (again, watch your hands on those hot sides) and place it on a cooling rack, cutting board, or plate.

PIZZA IN A SKILLET

Pizza cooks amazingly well in a skillet. It's fairly easy to get to good, crispy crust, but almost impossible to really get the cheese golden, although it will melt. And it will taste great!

Again, a heavy pan works much better than a thin one. Have the dough, sauce, and all toppings ready before starting the "baking." Press the pizza dough (no sauce or toppings yet) into the bottom of the skillet, then carefully remove the dough, keeping its circular shape. Set the dough aside while you preheat the pan in the next step. Have everything ready to go before starting.

Oil the pan or spray it with nonstick spray. Heat it over high heat for 3 to 5 minutes or until hot. Turn the heat to medium-high and carefully put the pizza dough back into the hot pan. Let it cook, uncovered, for 4 to 5 minutes. The top should not be done, but the bottom should be a little golden.

Carefully flip the crust over and quickly spread the sauce, toppings, and cheese on it. Cover and turn down the heat to medium-low. Cook for about 8 minutes or until the cheese melts (it won't brown).

All stoves and pans are different, so you may have to experiment a bit to get the heat level and times correct for your equipment.

BAKING ON THE GRILL

Jan and her husband, David, are grilling experts. When Jan wanted to make homemade bread but didn't want to heat up the boat, they figured out how to "bake" bread on the grill.

Since every grill is different, you'll need to get to know your grill before you have that perfect loaf of bread. But after a couple of trial runs, everyone will be asking how you did that! Use any of the recipes in Yeast Breads (page 385) or Quick Breads (page 375). Rolls and buns will probably bake in 15 to 20 minutes; loaves will take 20 to 30 minutes depending on their size and the baking temperature. Be sure to check periodically to monitor progress.

A few tips:

- Smaller loaves or rolls are better because they bake all the way through before burning on the bottom. Try using a half recipe of the Whole Wheat Bread (page 392). It will make a nice "personal" loaf, perfect for two for dinner.
- Slash the top two or three times to release the steam while the bread is baking. If you forget, the bread will be good but a bit soggy inside.
- Grills don't circulate hot air as well as your oven. You may need to move the pan around the grill during the baking process for the bread to bake evenly. Be sure to put the lid on to keep the hot air in!
- Burning the bottom is the most common mistake in grilling bread—as I discovered on my first

attempt. Do *not* set the bread in the middle of the grill unless you have a grill that has better temperature control than most. I turned a metal loaf pan upside down, placed a piece of foil on top for insulation, and set the loaf directly on that. You can try putting two metal pans together to get the bread farther away from the heat. Or put it on an elevated rack if you have one. If not, just experiment. If the bottom of the bread is burning, move it away from the hottest point of heat and elevate it more.

Be sure to check out Jan's recipe for Pizza on the Grill (page 343).

Special Galley Cooking Techniques

RECIPES

From Everyday to Special Occasions

And now, 800 boat-friendly recipes with ingredients that are easy to find and stow. We're not gourmet chefs, but we like good food that can be made aboard the typical boat without electrical appliances or other special gear. We've included everything from meals that can be made in five minutes to special holiday treats!

MEAL IDEAS FOR THE BOATING LIFE

Lunch is by far our most boring meal only because I (Jan) can never think of something quick, easy, and not the same as yesterday. We developed the quick reference lists that follow to provide ideas for a variety of situations where you just can't think of what to make.

If your taste buds are calling for Mexican but you don't have a specific dish in mind, there's a list for all the south-of-the-border recipes. If you drop anchor and the boat next to you calls on the VHF inviting you to sunsetters in five minutes, there's a Five-Minute Appetizers list. If it's so hot you can't bear the thought of eating, let alone fixing, anything for dinner, there's a Hot-Weather Meals list.

Whenever you're just looking for inspiration, scan our nine idea lists—and add your own inside the front and back covers!

LUNCH IDEAS

You don't have to limit yourself to sandwiches or leftovers for lunch!

Salads

Asian Cabbage Salad, *page 147*
Mixed Cabbage Chicken Salad, *page 150*
Black Bean, Corn, and Tomato Salad, *page 156*
Vegetable Salad à la *Que Tal*, *page 157*
Mediterranean Pasta Salad, *page 158*
Picnic Pasta Salad, *page 159*
Hawaiian Ham Salad, *page 160*
Apple Chicken Salad, *page 160*

Soups and Stews

Chicken Tortilla Soup, *page 166*
Hearty Chicken Vegetable Soup, *page 166*
Quick Southwestern Chicken Soup, *page 167*
Vegetarian Black Bean Taco Soup, *page 168*
Tuxedo Soup, *page 168*
Too Many Veggies Soup, *page 169*
Main Dish Minestrone, *page 172*
Carolyn's Gazpacho, *page 173*
Jan's Gazpacho, *page 173*

Beans, Rice, and Pasta

Black Bean and Avocado Quesadilla, *page 178*
White Chicken Chili, *page 180*
Lentil Chili, *page 181*
Veggie Jambalaya, *page 183*
Fried Rice, *page 185*

Meat Main Dishes

Sloppy Joes, *page 262*

Canned Meats and Seafood

Middle Eastern Tuna Salad Pitas, *page 304*
Grilled Tuna and Cheese Sandwich, *page 306*
Tuna Pasta Salad Without Mayonnaise, *page 306*
Apple Tuna Salad, *page 307*
Mediterranean Tuna Stuffed Tomato, *page 307*
Chicken Salad Sandwiches, *page 312*
BBQ Chicken or Beef Sandwiches, *page 314*
Vegetable Beef Soup, *page 315*
Reuben Sandwich, *page 317*

ONE-POT MEALS

One-pot meals are great for busy days or on passage.

Breakfast and Brunch

Although these are listed as breakfast or brunch, they also work well as a light dinner.

Breakfast Casserole, *page 115*
Spinach Breakfast Pie, *page 115*
Quiche, *page 115*

Soups and Stews

Chicken Tortilla Soup, *page 166*
Spicy Chicken Corn Chowder, *page 167*
Quick Southwestern Chicken Soup, *page 167*
Tuxedo Soup, *page 168*
Chili, *page 169*
Campfire Stew Casserole, *page 170*
Michele Carruthers' Famous Potato Soup, *page 171*
Main Dish Minestrone, *page 172*
Taco Soup, *page 172*

Beans, Rice, and Pasta

Ham and Beans, *page 179*
Red Beans and Rice, *page 180*
White Chicken Chili, *page 180*
Jambalaya, *page 184*
Fried Rice, *page 185*

Meat Main Dishes

Pot Roast, *page 266*
Ground Beef, Potatoes, and Carrots in a Skillet, *page 269*
Potluck Burger 'n' Rice, *page 271*
Zesty Chicken Stir-Fry, *page 278*
Chicken Pot Pie, *page 282*
Chicken and Rice Casserole, *page 285*
Spicy Corn and Sausage Skillet, *page 290*
Sesame Pork Stir-Fry, *page 291*
Southwestern Frittata, *page 297*

Canned Meats and Seafood

Hobo Dinner, *page 320*
Chicken, Rice, and Beans Hash, *page 313*
Corned Beef Veggie *Criolla*, *page 316*
Crustless Hash Quiche, *page 319*
Jambalaya, *page 320*

Meatless Main Dishes

Ratatouille (French Veggie Stew), *page 350*
Lentil Chili, *page 354*

HOT-WEATHER MEALS

After strolling the beach or snorkeling the crystal-clear waters and you're too hot to cook, here are some ideas for refreshing drinks and easy meals.

Beverages

Iced Coffee, *page 89*
Sun Tea, *page 91*
Tang-o-rade, *page 92*
Rehydration Drink, *page 92*
Lemonade from Scratch, *page 92*
Tropical Painkiller, *page 93*
Mojito, *page 93*
Gin and Tonic, *page 95*
Long Island Iced Tea, *page 95*

Dairy

Yogurt, *page 100*
Frozen Yogurt, *page 103*

Appetizers and Snacks

Traditional Hummus, *page 131*
Bacon and Cheddar Ranch Dip, *page 134*
Sour Cream Dip for Fruit, *page 137*
Green Olive Anchovy Dip, *page 136*
No-Bake, No-Refrigerate Granola Bars, *page 145*

Breakfast and Brunch

Yogurt Granola Parfait, *page 106*

Salads

Asian Cabbage Salad, *page 147*
Basic Vinegar and Oil Coleslaw, *page 149*
Company Coleslaw, *page 149*
Broccoli Cauliflower Salad, *page 152*
Marinated Zucchini Salad, *page 153*
Pita Pockets with Chick-Pea Salad, *page 158*
Fruit Pasta Salad (if the pasta is made ahead of time), *page 159*

Meal Ideas for the Boating Life

Soups and Stews

Summer Shrimp Soup, *page 173*
Carolyn's Gazpacho, *page 173*
Jan's Gazpacho, *page 173*

Seafood

Most seafood and fish take a very short time to cook or grill, making it perfect for hot weather! Try scallops for the shortest cooking time.

Basic Ceviche (Jan's favorite hot-weather meal), *page 228*
Chilled Shrimp (Plan ahead and boil the shrimp so they're waiting in the fridge), *page 233*
The Cat's Meow Scallops, *page 247*
Conch Salad, *page 254*

Meat Main Dishes

Although no meat main dish may sound appetizing when the heat index hits 110°F, some dishes, especially stir-fry, are quick and easy.

Mexican-Style Tacos, *page 267*
Asian Skillet, *page 273*
Sesame Chicken, *page 278*
Zesty Chicken Stir-Fry, *page 278*

Canned Meats and Seafood

Classic Tuna Salad, *page 304*
Middle Eastern Tuna Salad Pitas, *page 304*
Cold Macaroni Tuna Salad, *page 306*
Apple Tuna Salad, *page 307*
Mediterranean Tuna Stuffed Tomato, *page 307*
Nicoise Salad, *page 308*
Chicken Salad Sandwiches, *page 312*
Couscous Chicken, *page 312*
Mexican Crab Salad, *page 323*

Grilling

Grilling keeps the heat out of the boat and often is a great solution to a "too hot to cook day." Make an entire meal on the grill by grilling a meat or seafood and a veggie packet!

Grilled Margarita Grouper, *page 338*
Basic Grilled Fish, *page 339*
Sesame-Crusted Tuna, Salmon, or Mahi Mahi, *page 339*

Grilled Lobster Tails, *page 339*
Grilled Shrimp Wrapped in Bacon, *page 340*
Grilled Herbed Vegetables, *page 341*
Grilled Sweet Potato Slices, *page 341*

Sweet Tooth

Chocolate-Oatmeal No-Bake Cookies, *page 421*
No-Bake Booze Balls, *page 423*

FIVE-MINUTE APPETIZERS

Getting together with another boat is often a spur-of-the-moment decision, but you don't want to go empty-handed. Or friends may have just stopped by to return a book they borrowed, and you invite them aboard. For whatever reason, you need something to serve—now!

- Sliced pieces of fruit (fresh or canned) and a dish of yogurt (slightly sweetened) to dip them in. Cut fruit into bite-size bits and use toothpicks as skewers.
- Plate with cheese, crackers, dried apricots, and almonds (or whatever you have that's similar)
- Olives—stock black olives in cans and green olives in little vacuum-sealed pouches. They will last almost indefinitely.
- Crab Dip (page 135) and crackers. Also good made with ham, tuna, or clams.
- Any sort of nuts. I've found that small packages keep best in general.
- A block of cream cheese covered with jam (peach, apricot, or jalapeño are best). Serve with crackers. *NOTE:* Cream cheese lasts almost indefinitely if you vacuum seal it before you put it in the refrigerator. Leave the original foil packaging on and wrap it in plastic.
- Chex Mix (made ahead—see page 143).
- Almost any of the sour cream dips (page 133) can be made quickly. If you don't have sour cream on hand, you can substitute mayonnaise or yogurt in most of the recipes. Serve with veggies or crackers.

The following appetizers take five minutes or less to prepare:

Black Bean and Corn Salsa, *page 127*
Red Kidney Bean Dip, *page 130*
Spicy Tuna Dip, *page 133*
Chipotle Cream Cheese, *page 133*
Quick Veggie Dip, *page 133*
Clam Dip, *page 136*
Green Olive Anchovy Dip, *page 136*
Creamy Corned Beef Dip, *page 137*

QUICKIE MEALS

When cruising, it's rare that you can call out for a pizza after a long day. It's late, you're hungry, and you don't want to spend time cooking. These dishes aren't going to be confused with fine dining, but they *are* filling and fast. And these types of evenings are the best reason for leftovers!

Breakfast and Brunch
Breakfast for dinner is often a meal aboard *Winterlude* after a long day—easy and quick.

Scrambled Eggs with Stuff, *page 109*
Breakfast Burrito, *page 109*

Salads
Even without a recipe, we often throw together a "chef's salad" as a quick meal—lettuce, chopped whatever meat we happen to have left over, tomatoes, mushrooms, carrots, sliced almonds or grated cheese, and voila—dinner! Here are some other ideas:

Black Bean, Corn, and Tomato Salad, *page 156*
Ham Salad, *page 159*

Soups and Stews
These can be made quickly and easily.

Quick Southwestern Chicken Soup, *page 167*
Vegetarian Black Bean Taco Soup, *page 168*
Tuxedo Soup, *page 168*

Meat Main Dishes
Southwestern Frittata, *page 297*

Canned Meats and Seafood
Tuna Melt, *page 305*
Grilled Tuna and Cheese Sandwiches, *page 306*
Black Bean Tuna Salad, *page 307*
Couscous Chicken, *page 312*
Corned Beef Omelet, *page 316*
Reuben Sandwich, *page 317*
Mexican Crab Salad, *page 323*

Grilling
Aboard *Winterlude*, grilling is one of our favorite ways to have a quick dinner. Throw a piece of meat on the grill with slices of potato, wait ten minutes, and dinner is ready! Easy, quick, and no big cleanup.

MEXICAN QUICK IDEAS

Sooner or later everyone has a taste for south of the border. Try these ideas!

Beverages
Margarita, *page 96*

Breakfast and Brunch
Breakfast Burrito, *page 109*
Huevos Mexicana, *page 110*

Appetizers and Snacks
Tortilla Chips, *page 124*
Mexican Casserole Dip, *page 125*
Quesadillas, *page 125*
Chorizo and Manchego Quesadillas, *page 126*
Refried Bean Dip 1, *page 126*
Salsa, *page 127*
Black Bean and Corn Salsa, *page 127*
Pico de Gallo, page 128
Guacamole, *page 129*

Salads
Black Bean, Corn, and Tomato Salad, *page 156*
Lime Lettuce Salad Dressing, *page 160*

Soups and Stews
Chicken Tortilla Soup, *page 166*
Quick Southwestern Chicken Soup, *page 167*
Vegetarian Black Bean Taco Soup, *page 168*

Meal Ideas for the Boating Life

ASIAN QUICK IDEAS

Taste buds calling for Asian flair with no takeout in sight?

PASTA IDEAS

Feel like pasta?

Meal Ideas for the Boating Life

Beans, Rice, and Pasta
Chinese Noodles, *page 189*

Seafood
David's Cioppino, *page 229*
Shrimp and Pasta, *page 237*
Linguine with Red Clam Sauce, *page 242*
Greek Seafood Pasta, *page 243*
Scallops Carbonara, *page 247*

Meat Main Dishes
Spaghetti Sauce, *page 261*
Cruiser's Lasagna, *page 261*
Baked Ziti, *page 263*
Beef Stroganoff, *page 265*
Goulash, *page 265*
Chicken and Sesame Noodles, *page 274*
Cajun Chicken Pasta, *page 280*
Bacon and Tomato Pasta Florentine, *page 295*
Chorizo Pasta, *page 296*

Canned Meats and Seafood
Classic Tuna-Noodle Casserole, *page 308*
Stove-Top Tuna Penne, *page 310*
Italian Chicken Pasta, *page 314*
Rice or Pasta Salad with Ham, *page 321*
Seafood Lasagna, *page 325*
Linguine and Clam Sauce, *page 327*

Meatless Main Dishes
Bahamian Mac and Cheese, *page 346*
Spaghetti Pie, *page 347*
Minestrone Pasta Salad, *page 348*
Italian Pasta Skillet, *page 349*

CABBAGE IDEAS

Cabbage lasts forever and is a staple on many cruising boats. How many times have you thought "what am I going to do with cabbage *today*"?

Salads
Asian Cabbage Salad, *page 147*
Abidjan Cabbage Salad, *page 148*
Cabbage Bacon Salad, *page 148*
Ham-Coleslaw Salad, *page 148*
Company Coleslaw, *page 149*
Thanksgiving Cabbage Salad, *page 150*
Mixed Cabbage Chicken Salad, *page 150*

Soup and Stews
Too Many Veggies Soup, *page 169*
Cabbage Soup, *page 171*
Main Dish Minestrone, *page 172*

Vegetables
Garlic Smushed Potatoes and Veggies, *page 194*

Seafood
Grilled Fish Tacos, *page 229*

Meat Main Dishes
Cabbage Lasagna, *page 262*
Zesty Chicken Stir-Fry, *page 278*

Canned Meats and Seafood
Cabbage and Corned Beef Soup, *page 318*

Grilling
Grilled Pork Tenderloin "Roast," *page 333*

Meal Ideas for the Boating Life

BEVERAGES

Whenever sailors gather, it seems that some type of beverage is involved, be it sipping coffee or latte in the morning, hiking with a sports drink, or enjoying cocktails at sunset. Typically, we know the recipe by heart—or we just open an ice-cold bottle—but when you want to change it up a bit, here are some suggestions.

A GOOD-MORNING COFFEE

For many of us, a good morning includes a good cup of coffee. Regardless of how you make it, there's just nothing better than the aroma of a freshly brewed cup wafting up through the companionway to signal the start of a new day.

Since fresh coffee beans are essential to the perfect cup of coffee, not every cup aboard *Winterlude* can be classified as perfect. If you're a true aficionado and want to grind your own beans, go ahead and bring a coffee grinder. Storing the beans below the waterline will keep them cooler, hence fresher longer.

One of the big dilemmas for cruisers is how to dispose of coffee grounds and paper filters. Many cruisers simply dump them overboard. However, if you'd prefer to be more green, coffee grounds make good fertilizer.

Basic Drip Coffee

Here are directions in case you pick up a "new" coffeemaker at a swap meet and it doesn't have instructions.

1 heaping tablespoon ground coffee per 8 ounces water (1 cup)

1. Place a filter or paper towel in the grounds basket, then put the appropriate amount of coffee in the filter.
2. Fill the coffeemaker with water, plug it in, turn it on, and let it drip.

Old-Fashioned Percolator Coffee

When you bought your boat, if you (like me) found a metal coffee percolator that looks like a leftover from some cowboy's campfire, here's what to do with it.

1 tablespoon ground coffee for each cup (a cup of coffee is typically 6 ounces; a mug is usually double that, or 12 ounces)

1. Place the ground coffee in the top metal casing. Slide the casing over the metal waterspout. Fill the percolator with water and slide the coffee casing and the metal "pipe" into the water. The water should be at least an inch below the coffee casing (otherwise, the boiling water will cause the coffee grounds to come out the top of the casing). Secure the lid and place the percolator on the stove burner.
2. Turn the burner on high until the percolator begins to perk. Reduce the heat so that the water just gently perks, and perk for 4 minutes or until the color in the perk bubble is the strength you prefer.

Melitta-Type Coffee

A Melitta cone is a manual drip cone. You may have had one in college or seen one in camping stores. It uses a cone filter and makes great coffee, just like an electric drip coffeemaker except that you boil the water separately and pour it through the cone bit by bit—by hand.

**1 to 2 tablespoons medium-grind coffee per
  6-ounce cup**

1. Place a paper filter in the cone; in a pinch you can use a paper towel. Add the ground coffee. Place the cone over a thermos, mug, or other container.
2. Bring water to a boil in a teakettle. The best temperature for brewing coffee is between 195° and 205°F. If using a manual drip coffeemaker, this can be achieved by letting your kettle rest for 30 seconds after the water comes to a boil before pouring the water through the cone.
3. Pour the water into the cone—slowly to allow it to drip into the thermos or other container.

French Press Style Coffee

**2 level tablespoons ground coffee for every
  6 ounces water**

1. Bring water to a boil in a teakettle. When you pull the kettle off the flame, let the water cool slightly, maybe 30 seconds, so it reaches the optimum temperature.
2. Meanwhile, place the appropriate amount of coffee in the press container. Pour the water directly over the ground coffee.
3. Put the French press lid on the pot, but do not depress the plunger. Putting the lid on the French press will retain heat and let the coffee "steep" for 3 to 5 minutes.
4. Gently press the plunger to separate the grounds from your coffee. Pour the coffee into a mug and enjoy!

Iced Coffee

1 tablespoon sugar
4 ice cubes
²⁄₃ cup warm or cool brewed coffee
²⁄₃ cup milk

1. Put the sugar in a large glass and drop in the ice cubes.
2. Pour the coffee over the ice and add the milk. Stir until the sugar dissolves.

Specialty Coffee Mixes

You can make your own specialty instant coffee mixes. It's easiest with a blender, but you can do it with any container that's large enough to vigorously shake the ingredients.

1. To make any of the following mixes, place the ingredients in a plastic container with a leakproof lid and shake until the ingredients are well blended.
2. Each recipe makes about 2 cups of mix. To use, place 1 tablespoon of the mix in a 6-ounce cup, or 2 tablespoons in a 12-ounce mug, and fill with boiling water. Stir and enjoy! Store the mix in a cool, dry place.

Café Latte Mix

¹⁄₂ cup instant coffee
¹⁄₃ cup sugar
1 cup powdered milk
¹⁄₂ cup powdered coffee creamer
2 teaspoons vanilla extract

Variation: For a toffee-coffee mix, use brown sugar and skip the vanilla.

Café Vienna Mix

¹⁄₂ cup instant coffee
²⁄₃ cup sugar
¹⁄₂ cup powdered milk
¹⁄₄ cup powdered coffee creamer
1 teaspoon ground cinnamon
**¹⁄₄ cup instant butterscotch- or vanilla-flavored
  pudding mix (optional)**

Beverages

Mocha Espresso Mix

$\frac{1}{2}$ cup instant coffee
$\frac{1}{2}$ cup sugar
2 cups powdered milk
$\frac{1}{2}$ cup powdered coffee creamer
$\frac{1}{4}$ cup unsweetened baking cocoa
$\frac{1}{4}$ teaspoon ground cinnamon (optional)
$\frac{1}{4}$ cup instant vanilla- or chocolate-flavored pudding mix (optional)

Unlike the previous mixes, use $1\frac{1}{2}$ tablespoons for a 6-ounce cup or 3 tablespoons for a 12-ounce mug.

PREFER TEA, HOT CHOCOLATE, OR HOT CIDER?

Tea is growing in popularity and has less caffeine than coffee. Iced tea is a refreshing change from soda pop and much easier to store on a boat, so stock up on tea bags even if you don't drink hot tea.

Sipping a mug of hot chocolate after hours of snorkeling can warm you right up. And on a chilly morning, hugging a mug of hot tea, hot chocolate, or hot cider can be a nice change.

Donna Wagner's Russian Hot Tea
Makes 4 cups mix

Donna was a Y-Flyer sailing friend of ours, known for her sense of humor and go-get-'em attitude. Sadly, Donna lost her fight against cancer in December 2011. We will miss her.

Yield: 96 cups or 48 mugs of tea

2 cups powdered Tang
1 cup powdered instant tea (plain)
1 to 2 cups sugar, to taste
$\frac{1}{2}$ teaspoon ground cloves
1 teaspoon ground cinnamon
dash of ground mace, ground allspice, and ground nutmeg

1. Combine all the ingredients and store in a sealed container.
2. Use 2 teaspoons per 8 ounces boiling water to make hot tea.

Ice Aboard: The Never-Ending Debate

Ice or no ice, cold drinks are still an important part of many cruisers' lifestyles. In our Adler Barber Cold Machine jerry-rigged freezer, we have space for two vertical ice cube trays that prop against the cold plate and freeze easily. These old-fashioned ice cube trays make giant ice cubes that don't easily melt, so they don't water down our drinks while they're keeping them cold.

Friends on larger boats with generators sometimes have a separate ice machine capable of making enough ice cubes for the entire anchorage. When you meet boats like these, be sure to make friends so as to be invited over for cocktails. We happily bring our own ingredients, but our vertical ice cube trays make only enough ice for eight drinks total.

A lot of boats have minimal or no freezer space and can't spare room to make nonessentials like ice cubes. But you can still make up a batch of your favorite cold drink ahead of time, place it next to your refrigerator cold plate for an hour or two, and voila—cold drinks without ice cubes!

Whichever way you do it, remember that the view from your cockpit at sunset is better than that of most five-star hotels costing far more than onboard drinks!

Ginger Tea
Makes 1 cup

Great for mild seasickness!

$1\frac{1}{2}$ cups water
$\frac{1}{2}$ teaspoon fresh ginger, crushed with the back of a spoon
1 tea bag
$\frac{1}{2}$ teaspoon honey
dash of milk (optional)

1. Combine the water and the ginger and bring to a boil. Then reduce the heat to medium and simmer for 5 minutes.
2. Place the tea bag in a cup and pour the mixture into it through a strainer. Discard the ginger. Stir in the honey and the milk if desired.

Southern Sweet Tea   Makes 1 gallon

Total Time: 15 to 35 minutes, including steeping for
10 to 30 minutes

1 cup sugar
1 gallon water
10 tea bags OR 3 or 4 "family-size" tea bags
ice cubes
mint leaves (optional)

1. Heat the sugar in a bit of water in a saucepan over
low heat until the sugar dissolves.
2. Fill the saucepan ⅔ full of water and bring it to a
boil. Turn off the heat and add the tea bags to the
water. Let the tea steep until it is the strength you
prefer.
3. Pour the tea into a large pitcher. Add the rest of the
water to make 1 gallon. Add the ice cubes, or chill
the tea and enjoy. For a different flavor, add some
mint leaves if desired.

Sun Tea   Makes 2 quarts

*Sun tea doesn't use any propane or heat up the boat. Try
different types of tea for differing results. Because the
water isn't boiled, the tea will not last as long as regular
tea. Refrigerate for the longest life.*

Total Time: 4 to 6 hours
Prep Time: 3 minutes

water
4 to 6 tea bags
sugar (optional)

1. Fill a 2-quart container with cool water. Put in the
teabags with the tags hanging over the neck and
put the cap on tightly. Set outside in full sun for
4 to 6 hours.
2. When the tea is the strength you like, bring it
inside and remove the bags. Add sugar if you prefer
sweet tea.

Stove-Top Iced Tea   Makes 2 quarts

*Rather than boiling all the water, this method makes a
tea concentrate that is then diluted. It uses far less propane and puts a lighter load on the refrigerator.*

Total Time: 35 to 65 minutes, including steeping
30 to 60 minutes

2 cups water
6 to 8 tea bags
¾ cup sugar (optional)
½ cup lemon juice (optional)

1. Heat the water to a boil in a large saucepan.
2. Remove from the heat and add the tea bags. Cover
and steep from 30 to 60 minutes, depending on
the strength you prefer. (Remember, this is concentrated, so decide accordingly. The tea should look
quite dark.)
3. Combine the steeped tea, sugar, and lemon juice in
a 2-quart juice bottle or pitcher. Add enough water
to top off the container.
4. Refrigerate, or serve over ice cubes for chilled tea.

Hot Chocolate Mix   Makes 3 cups mix

Yield: 12 mugs hot chocolate

2 cups powdered milk
⅓ cup unsweetened baking cocoa
⅔ cup sugar
dash of salt

1. Combine the powdered milk, cocoa, sugar, and
salt; mix well. Store in a tightly sealed container.
2. To serve, put ¼ cup mix in a coffee mug and fill
with hot but not boiling water.

"Almost" Hot Apple Cider   Serves 1

8 to 12 ounces apple juice
cinnamon stick, grated nutmeg, or ground pumpkin pie spice

Heat the apple juice with the spices until the juice is
almost hot. This is especially good if you've become
chilled after snorkeling too long.

Beverages

SPORTS AND REHYDRATION DRINKS

One of the challenges facing many cruisers is hydration, especially when cruising in far tropical latitudes.

Tang-o-rade
Makes ½ gallon

In many places, Gatorade is hard to find. In these same places, it's often easy to find packets of powdered rehydration mix (usually flavored for kids) in the pharmacy. You can mix these with powdered Tang. One of our favorite combinations is pineapple rehydration mix and orange Tang. This drink will help replace electrolytes, just as Gatorade does.

1 packet powdered Tang (the size that makes
    1 quart)
1-quart or 1-liter packet rehydration mix
½ gallon water

Combine Tang, rehydration mix, and the water and mix well. Store in the refrigerator if you'll be keeping it longer than a few hours.

Homemade Sports Drinks
Makes 2 quarts

½ cup orange juice
9 tablespoons sugar (½ cup plus 1 tablespoon)
½ teaspoon salt
2 quarts water

Combine the juice, sugar, salt, and water. Stir until the salt and sugar are dissolved. Chill for the best flavor.

Variations

• Honey Lemon Sports Drink. Substitute ¼ cup lemon juice for the orange juice and use ½ cup honey instead of the sugar.
• Citrus Delight Sports Drink. Mix 12 ounces orange juice, 1 tablespoon lemon juice, 1 tablespoon lime juice, and ¾ teaspoon salt. Stir until the salt dissolves. Add enough water to make 2 quarts.

Rehydration Drink
Makes 1 quart

Gatorade it isn't, but when you need a rehydration drink, this one will work. You must plan ahead by having the "lite" salt (which contains potassium) aboard.

4 cups water
½ teaspoon salt
3 tablespoons sugar
¼ teaspoon "lite" salt or salt substitute (bring it
    from the United States if necessary. Regular salt
    does not contain the potassium that this does)

Combine the water, regular salt, sugar, and lite salt until the salt and sugar dissolve. Take small sips rather than large gulps to help get it down. The funny thing is that if you're really dehydrated, this tastes quite good!

Lemonade from Scratch
Makes six 8-ounce servings

Total Time: 1 hour, 20 minutes (if you're squeezing
    your own lemons—the best kind!)

1 cup sugar
water
1 cup lemon juice (fresh squeezed is best!)*

1. Add the sugar to 1 cup water and heat until the mixture boils and the sugar dissolves.
2. Combine the lemon juice and the sugar water in a large pitcher. Add 4 cups water and stir well.

*The juice from 5 to 8 lemons, depending on size and
    juiciness.*

HAPPY-HOUR DRINKS

Watching the sunset and enjoying a "sunsetter" drink while lounging in the cockpit with or without friends is a tradition aboard *Winterlude*.

Be sure to store the ingredients for drinks in a cool place. Aboard *Winterlude* we keep a "liquor locker," a locker behind the settee slightly below the waterline. Since liquor often comes in glass bottles, we store each one in a heavy knee-high athletic sock, which so far has kept the bottles safe, even in heavy seas.

All drinks in these recipes serve one unless otherwise noted.

Drink Measurements

Many of the drink measurements are given in ounces—particularly for alcoholic drinks—but not everyone has ounce measures. Use the chart below to convert to whatever you have:

FLUID OUNCES	TABLESPOONS	CUPS	METRIC
½ ounce	1 tablespoon	—	15 ml
¾ ounce	1½ tablespoons	—	22½ ml
1 ounce	2 tablespoons	⅛ cup	30 ml
1½ ounces	3 tablespoons	3/16 cup	45 ml
2 ounces	4 tablespoons	¼ cup	60 ml
3 ounces	6 tablespoons	⅜ cup	90 ml
4 ounces	8 tablespoons	½ cup	120 ml
5 ounces	10 tablespoons	⅝ cup	150 m
6 ounces	12 tablespoons	¾ cup	180 ml
8 ounces	16 tablespoons	1 cup	240 ml (often rounded to 250 ml)
10 ounces	—	1¼ cups	300 ml
12 ounces	—	1½ cups	360 ml (often rounded to 375 ml)
16 ounces	—	2 cups (1 pint)	480 ml (often rounded to 500 ml OR ½ liter)
32 ounces	—	4 cups (1 quart)	1,000 ml OR 1 liter
64 ounces	—	8 cups (2 quarts OR ½ gallon)	2 liters

Cuba Libre

¾ ounce lime juice
twist of lime
2 ounces rum
ice
5 ounces Coke or cola

Put lime juice and a twist of lime in a glass. Add rum, then ice, and fill with Coke.

Tropical Painkiller

Painkillers are designated by numbers: #2 indicates 2 parts rum; #3 stands for 3 parts rum; and #4 is reputed to contain 4 parts rum. Cheers!

2 parts any good rum you have aboard
ice
4 parts pineapple juice
1 part coconut cream (found in 16-ounce cans as CocoCasa or Coco Loco or other brands; not coconut milk)
1 part orange juice
ground nutmeg

Pour the rum into a glass. Fill the glass with ice and add the pineapple juice, coconut cream, and orange juice. Stir gently. Sprinkle with nutmeg.

Mojito

Fresh mint may be difficult to come by aboard, but in the off chance you find it, as we did one day at a street veggie stand in Placencia, Belize, here's a great mojito recipe that doesn't require simple syrup.

fresh mint (optional, but without the mint you don't get the mint versus lime flavor)
2 tablespoons superfine sugar or regular sugar
3 ounces light rum or gold rum
1 lime OR 3 to 4 tablespoons lime juice
3 ounces club soda
ice cubes

1. Put 2 or 3 sprigs of mint and the sugar in a glass and crush the mint with a spoon.
2. Stir in the rum. Squeeze the lime into the glass. Add the club soda and stir gently. Add the ice and serve.

Beverages

Piña Colada

4 ounces fresh or canned pineapple juice *or* canned pineapple

3 ounces rum (light, dark, or a mix)

2 ounces coconut cream (not coconut milk; it's not thick enough)

2 cups ice (crushed ice is good if you have the extravagance of an icemaker and a blender to crush it)

fresh pineapple, for garnish

Maraschino cherry, for garnish

1. In a blender, add the juice, rum, coconut cream, and ice and whirl for a few seconds on high speed.
2. If you don't have a blender, stir together the juice, rum, and coconut cream or put them all into a plastic bottle, cap it, and shake. Pour over ice.
3. Garnish with fresh pineapple and a cherry, and serve.

Bahama Mama

½ ounce light rum

½ ounce gold rum

½ ounce dark rum

½ ounce coconut rum or liqueur

ice

orange juice

pineapple juice

grenadine (optional)

Maraschino cherry, for garnish

fresh pineapple, for garnish

1. Combine the rums and mix well. Pour into a tall glass filled with ice.
2. Fill the glass with half orange juice and half pineapple juice. Add a splash of grenadine if desired. Garnish with a cherry and pineapple, and a paper umbrella if you have one aboard!

Sex on the Beach

ice cubes

1 ounce vodka

½ ounce peach schnapps

cranberry juice

pineapple juice

Partly fill a tall glass with ice and add the vodka and peach schnapps. Fill the glass with half cranberry juice and half pineapple juice. Stir and serve.

Orange Cranberry Vodka

ice cubes

2 ounces vodka

cranberry juice

orange juice

Fill a tall glass with ice and add the vodka. Fill the glass halfway with the cranberry juice and top with the orange juice. Mix well and serve.

Salty Dog

5 ounces grapefruit juice

1½ ounces gin or vodka

¼ teaspoon salt

ice cubes

Combine the juice, gin, and salt, and mix well. Add the ice cubes and serve.

Cosmopolitan

1½ ounces vodka

1 ounce Cointreau

½ ounce lime juice

¼ ounce cranberry juice

ice cubes

orange zest, for garnish

1. Combine the vodka, Cointreau, lime juice, and cranberry juice in a cocktail shaker. Add ice cubes and shake well.
2. Pour into a chilled glass, garnish with the orange zest, and serve.

Classic Martini

If you don't have a cocktail shaker, you can still have a martini, but it will be stirred, not shaken.

ice cubes

2½ ounces gin

¼ ounce dry vermouth

twist of lemon

1. Put some ice cubes and a little water in a cocktail shaker and shake to chill it.
2. Empty the shaker. Add the gin and vermouth and shake. Pour the mixture into a chilled martini glass and garnish with the twist of lemon.

Dirty Martini

ice cubes
2 ounces gin
1 tablespoon dry vermouth
2 tablespoons olive juice
2 olives

1. Put the ice cubes and a bit of water in a cocktail shaker and shake to chill it. Then pour out the water and ice cubes.
2. If you don't have a cocktail shaker, add the ice, gin, vermouth, and olive juice to a glass jar. Shake hard.
3. Ideally, you'll have a martini glass chilling in the freezer and can fill it with the "dirty martini." If not, just pour it into whatever glass you prefer. Garnish with the olives and serve.

If, like me, you like a lot of olive juice in your dirty martini and end up with a jar of olives and only a third of the juice remaining, dissolve 1 teaspoon salt in a cup of water and add it to the jar. Wait a couple of days for the olives to flavor the added liquid.

Gin and Tonic

Tonic water, agua tonica, can be difficult to find in some parts of the Caribbean. If you do find it, be careful. It comes in cans made of very thin aluminum, which can easily get pinholes when stored anywhere they can rub against one another or anything else, including the bottom of the lazarette where you stored them. If you're cruising in Belize, tonic water is found only in bottles from Fanta, and it's pink! But it tastes the same and is just as refreshing at the end of a hot day.

ice cubes
2 ounces gin
4 ounces tonic water
slice of fresh lime

Fill a glass with ice cubes and add the gin, then the tonic water. Squeeze a slice of fresh lime over it all, and stir gently so you don't lose those refreshing bubbles!

Variation: Use vodka instead of gin to make a Vodka Tonic.

Long Island Iced Tea

ice cubes
1 ounce vodka
1 ounce tequila
1 ounce rum
1 ounce gin
1 ounce Triple Sec
1 1/2 ounces premixed sweet and sour mix*
splash Coca-Cola
lemon wedge, for garnish

*Sold wherever you'd buy margarita mix, or see below to make your own.

1. Fill a tall glass with ice and set aside. Combine the vodka, tequila, rum, gin, Triple Sec, sweet and sour mix, and Coca-Cola. Pour the mixture into a large shaker and give it one good shake. Then pour the mixture back into the glass; make sure there's a bit of fizz at the top.
2. Garnish with a lemon wedge and serve.

Sweet and Sour Mix   Makes 3 ounces mix

3 tablespoons sugar
2 tablespoons water
1 tablespoon lemon, lime, or *límón* (Key lime) juice

Combine the sugar, water, and lemon juice. Mix well until the sugar is completely dissolved.

Margarita

lime wedge
coarse salt
ice cubes
1 ounce lime juice or sweetened lime juice
1 ounce tequila
1 ounce Triple Sec, Cointreau, or Grand Marnier

1. Moisten the rim of a glass with the lime wedge. Put some coarse salt in a small plate, invert the glass, and dip the top into the salt to create a salt rim on the glass.
2. Fill the glass with ice cubes and add the lime juice. Add the tequila and Triple Sec and stir gently.
3. Let the mixture sit for a minute for the ice to chill the ingredients. Enjoy!

Mimosa

chilled champagne
orange juice

Pour the champagne and orange juice into a chilled glass in any proportion you prefer. I like one-third champagne to two-thirds orange juice.

NOTE: As a good alternative, substitute cranberry juice for the orange juice, or combine some of each. Very refreshing!

Irish Cream   Serves 4

This drink is similar to Bailey's Irish Cream.

Total time: 5 minutes (better if it can be refrigerated for a few hours)

1 can (14 ounces) sweetened condensed milk (page 99)
1 cup whipping cream or half-and-half (*media crema*)
1¼ cups whiskey
3 teaspoons unsweetened baking cocoa
1½ teaspoons instant coffee
2 eggs

1. Combine the condensed milk, cream, whiskey, cocoa, coffee, and eggs. Mix well using a blender, an electric or hand mixer, or a whisk. Or put all the ingredients into a container with a tight lid and shake well.
2. For the best flavor, refrigerate the mixture for a few hours to let the flavors combine. Be sure to mix it again just before pouring.

CAUTION: There is a slight risk of a food-borne illness such as salmonella from consuming uncooked eggs.

Homemade Kahlua   Makes about a fifth of Kahlua

Total Time: 30 minutes, plus 3 weeks to age

2 cups water
1½ cups packed brown sugar
1 cup white sugar
½ cup instant coffee (the better the quality, the better the Kahlua)
2 tablespoons vanilla extract
3 cups vodka (inexpensive vodka will make Kahlua with an edge)

1. Combine the water and both sugars in a medium saucepan. Bring to a boil and cook for 5 minutes. (The syrup will try to boil over, so make sure that your pan is big enough.) Remove from the heat.
2. Add the coffee gradually. Let cool.
3. Add the vanilla and vodka. Stir well to combine.
4. Transfer the mixture to an airtight container and let stand for 3 weeks to age before using (insufficient aging may produce "rot gut" Kahlua!).

Homemade Amaretto   Makes approximately 6 cups

Total Time: 5 minutes, plus 1 month to age

2 cups white sugar
1 cup packed brown sugar
2 cups water
2 cups vodka
2 cups brandy
4 teaspoons almond extract (not flavoring)
4 teaspoons vanilla extract

1. Combine both sugars and the water in a medium saucepan and bring to a boil. Reduce the heat and simmer until the sugar is dissolved. Let cool.
2. Add the vodka, brandy, almond extract, and vanilla to the syrup. Stir well. Pour the mixture into a bottle, seal it, and let it age at least 1 month before serving.

Easy Eggnog   Serves 8

Total Time: $3^{1}/_{4}$ hours

6 eggs
3 cups milk
8 tablespoons sugar
3 teaspoons vanilla extract
$^{1}/_{2}$ teaspoon ground nutmeg

1. Beat the eggs in a large bowl. An electric mixer or at least a hand-operated eggbeater will have somewhat better results than a fork or a whisk.
2. Add the milk and sugar. Continue beating until the mixture thickens slightly. Add the vanilla and nutmeg and stir to combine. Cover the bowl and refrigerate for 3 to 5 hours or until the mixture is chilled. Pour into glasses and serve.

Variation: For holiday cheer, add a shot of brandy.

CAUTION: Be aware that there is a slight risk of food-borne illness such as salmonella when consuming uncooked eggs.

HOLIDAY BEVERAGES

The only other beverage recipes in this book are for holidays:

Holiday Cheer
St. Patrick's Day Green Beer, *page 371*
Mint Julep, *page 373*

Beverages

DAIRY

Fresh milk is hard to keep aboard a boat for any length of time. But there are plenty of good alternatives to fresh milk that are readily available in most cruising grounds.

- **Boxed milk.** Outside the US, boxed milk is available almost everywhere. Recently I've found it in the US (in Walmart Supercenters, it's in the baking aisle). The boxes are the same Tetra Paks that we're used to seeing for kids' juice cartons, except they're usually one quart or one liter in size. Boxed milk is ultrapasteurized. It doesn't have to be refrigerated until it is opened, and it lasts up to a year unopened. I don't notice a difference in taste between boxed and fresh. Most cruisers use boxed milk for their primary milk supply.

  Depending on your store, you can get Tetra Paks of whole, 2 percent, and skim milk. Many places also carry boxed cream, light cream (half-and-half, called *media crema* in Latin America), evaporated milk, and even sour cream. In this chapter, we've included an easy way to make your own sour cream or buttermilk from boxed products.

- **Canned milk products.** Just as in the US, evaporated milk and sweetened condensed milk are often sold in cans, which work well for keeping on a boat. *Media crema* (half-and-half) is often available in cans in the Latin foods aisle in US supermarkets.

- **Powdered milk.** Most of us have horrid memories of powdered milk we've had as a kid or on a camping trip. Surprise! Other countries have developed really good powdered milk. Although we used boxed milk for most of our drinking milk, we used powdered milk in many recipes as it takes less room to stow.

In Latin countries, you can almost always find Nido powdered milk, made by Nestlé. There are other good brands, too. In the US, you can buy it in many supermarkets in the Latin food aisle. There is Nido Classic, which is whole milk. There are also several specialty products, such as Nido for Kids (Nido Kinder). Many times, the specialty products have added fat (to raise the caloric intake) and/or vitamins and/or flavorings. The varieties with added fat don't work well for many of the recipes in this chapter (yogurt and cheese won't set up properly).

With good powdered milk, you can easily make substitutes for evaporated milk and sweetened condensed milk, and make your own cheese. Another good use for powdered milk is to make a substitute for condensed cream soups (page 54). But the best thing to make is yogurt (page 101). It's delicious and is great for breakfast, lunch, snacks, or dessert. And we've included an easy way to make frozen yogurt—one of the best treats you can have aboard on a hot day!

All the recipes in this chapter are easy to do aboard a family-size cruising boat without unusual ingredients or hard-to-carry equipment.

BUTTERMILK, SWEETENED CONDENSED MILK, EVAPORATED MILK

With a few basic ingredients on board, you can make your own buttermilk, evaporated milk, and even sweetened condensed milk for use in other recipes.

Buttermilk Substitute
Makes ¼ cup

This is actually just soured milk. It does not taste like buttermilk when you drink it, but it's a very good substitute in recipes.

Total Time: 7 minutes

1 teaspoon white vinegar, lemon juice, lime juice, or Key lime (*limón*) juice
¼ cup milk* less 1 teaspoon

*The milk can be fresh, boxed, or made from powdered.

Put the vinegar in a measuring cup, then fill with the milk to the ¼-cup mark. Mix and let stand 5 minutes. This can be made in any multiple needed for a recipe:

TO MAKE . . .	VINEGAR	PLUS ENOUGH MILK TO TOTAL
⅓ cup	1½ teaspoons	⅓ cup
½ cup	2 teaspoons	½ cup
⅔ cup	2½ teaspoons	⅔ cup
1 cup	4 teaspoons	1 cup

Sweetened Condensed Milk
Makes 1⅓ cups

Special Equipment: Blender or immersion blender (a hand mixer or beating with a spoon will not produce as good results)
Total Time: 1 hour, including 55 minutes to chill
Prep Time: 5 minutes

½ cup hot water
1 cup sugar
1 cup powdered milk
3 tablespoons butter or margarine, melted (do not substitute oil; it won't thicken properly)

1. Combine the hot water, sugar, powdered milk, and melted butter. If using a blender, whirl for 1 minute. If using a hand mixer, mix 3 to 5 minutes. With a spoon, beat as long as your arm holds out.

2. The mixture will seem thin. For the best results, refrigerate for an hour to allow it to thicken. It will also thicken somewhat even if not refrigerated. If thickness is not important, you can use it immediately. It can be stored in the refrigerator for up to 4 days.

Evaporated Milk
Makes 1½ cups

If you use low-fat or nonfat milk, you'll get a low-fat or nonfat evaporated milk substitute. Using regular powdered milk will make a creamier finished product, although it will raise the calorie count.

Total Time: 5 minutes

1⅓ cups water
1 cup powdered milk

Combine the water and milk. Keep stirring until all the lumps are gone.

SOUR CREAM FROM SCRATCH

With a few non-refrigerated ingredients, you can have sour cream whenever you want it.

Sour Cream 1
Makes 1 cup

This is a classic cruiser "recipe!" You can use the sour cream immediately, but it's even better (and will thicken some more) if you refrigerate it for 15 minutes or more.

Total Time: 5 minutes (tastes much better if refrigerated for 15 minutes or more)

1 box or can (8 ounces/250 ml) cream or half-and-half (*media crema*)
1 to 2 teaspoons white vinegar, lemon juice, lime juice, or *limón* juice

Put the cream in a small bowl and mix in the vinegar 1 teaspoon at a time. As you add the vinegar, the cream will thicken and become sour. Different brands of cream will require different amounts of the acidic ingredient. Stop adding the vinegar before it starts to thin the cream.

Sour Cream 2

I've had good results with this when using very high quality powdered milk such as Nido or some of the New Zealand products. These dissolve quickly in water. Any brand that says to "refrigerate overnight before serving" requires extra time to totally dissolve the milk powder and isn't suitable for this recipe.

Total Time: 35 minutes, including 30 minutes chill time
Prep Time: 5 minutes

²/₃ **cup powdered whole milk (low-fat milk won't work)**
³/₄ **cup water**
2 teaspoons white vinegar, lemon juice, lime juice, or Key lime (*limón*) juice

1. Combine the powdered milk and water and mix until there are *no* lumps. Add the vinegar 1 teaspoon at a time and mix well.
2. Refrigerate at least 30 minutes to let the mixture thicken. Stir again just before serving.

HOMEMADE RICOTTA CHEESE

Ricotta is a simple cheese to make from scratch, as it doesn't require rennet or long curing. Be sure to check out the recipe for Yogurt Ricotta (page 102), too.

Ricotta Cheese   Makes about ¹/₂ pound or 1¹/₂ to 2 cups

This can be used in place of store-bought ricotta in any recipe and can also substitute for cream cheese in many dishes. Avoid making this cheese if your boat is rolling a lot. The mixture needs to sit relatively motionless to curdle.

Special Equipment: Cooking thermometer for liquids; cheesecloth
Total Time: 1 hour (probably longer the first time you do it)

6 cups water (1¹/₂ quarts)
3 cups powdered milk*
1 to 1¹/₂ cups white vinegar
¹/₂ teaspoon salt

*This can also be made with fresh milk instead of powdered. However, it won't work with boxed milk, which is ultrapasteurized and won't curdle.

1. Warm the water and powdered milk in a large saucepan over low heat until the mixture reaches 120°F. Stir often so that the milk does not scorch.
2. When the milk reaches 120°F, add 1 cup of the vinegar and turn off the heat. Allow the mixture to sit undisturbed for 10 minutes. Avoid stirring it because the cheese will be developing curds.
3. After 10 minutes, you should see a lump of cheese in the center of a pool of liquid. If the liquid is clear, proceed to the next step. If the liquid is still cloudy, add a couple more tablespoons of vinegar and stir; you'll see more curds form. Continue doing this until the liquid is clear and no additional curds form.
4. Line a colander or strainer with cheesecloth or other clean cloth. Pour the curds and their liquid (it's the whey) into the colander. Pour a little additional water over the curds to rinse them, then gather up the cheesecloth and squeeze to get rid of as much moisture as possible. Continue to squeeze for 2 to 3 minutes to thoroughly dry the curds.
5. When the curds are dry, transfer them to a bowl or plastic storage container. Add the salt and mix well.

Variations

- You can make a good approximation of cottage cheese by mixing a little evaporated milk or plain yogurt with the curds.
- You can also add various "flavorings," but be careful not to add too much, as the flavor will intensify as the cheese sits. Some good additions to try include Italian herbs, chile peppers, green onions, or garlic.

YOGURT FROM SCRATCH

Store-bought yogurt is hard to carry on a cruising boat. It has to be refrigerated to store it more than a day, and that takes up valuable refrigerator space. Luckily, it's easy to make your own, and the results are even better than store-bought.

Dairy

Yogurt

The basic recipe for yogurt is very easy. All it takes is warm milk and a little yogurt from the last batch, kept in a warm place while the culture grows. As with many things, the devil is in the details, and attention to detail is crucial to successful yogurt-making. A good thermos and a thermometer are essential, as are the right ingredients.

Thermos

You don't have to have a fancy yogurt maker, but you do need a thermos to keep the mixture warm while the culture grows. And since a thermos works best when it's full, you want one big enough to make a reasonable-size batch for your needs. Most cruisers find that a pint (2 cups/16 ounces/500 ml) to a quart (4 cups/32 ounces/1 liter) size works well. It's easier to make the yogurt with a wide-mouthed thermos, but you can use a narrow-mouthed one with good results. Read about buying a thermos in the chapter "Equipping a Galley."

Thermometer

An instant-read or candy-type thermometer is essential. Guessing at the right temperature of the milk just doesn't work. A few degrees too hot and the culture will be killed; too cool and it won't grow. You need a thermometer that can read between 110° and 120°F.

Powdered Milk

Using powdered milk produces excellent results, but not all powdered milk will work.

- For your initial efforts, avoid using low-fat or nonfat milk. It is much harder to obtain satisfactory results. Once you have the technique down, you can gradually transition from full-fat milk to nonfat.
- Avoid brands with "added vegetable fat." These are widely available in Latin American countries, but the culture will not grow.
- The higher the fat content in the milk, the creamier the end result—and the more calorie laden.
- Nido Classic milk is widely available in Latin American countries (and in the Latin food aisle in many US supermarkets) and works quite well.

Yogurt Starter

You need yogurt with a live culture as a starter. Your best bet is to get some from a cruiser who makes his or her own. In some places, you may be able to buy "homemade" yogurt. Here are a few tips if you have to buy commercial yogurt:

- It must contain a *live* culture.
- It *must not* contain gelatin.
- The fewer the additives, such as flavors, the better.

Often, I've found that yogurt drinks work best as a starter, especially ones promoted as digestion aids. Because they have a thinner consistency, use at least twice as much of a drink for starter as you would a thick yogurt.

In the US, you can buy special "yogurt starter cultures" in health food stores and online. Although these get great reviews (I've never used one), they are much more expensive and are not needed.

Water

The issue with water is that the stuff we put in the water tanks to kill bacteria (bleach, for example) will also kill the yogurt culture. If your water has a chlorine smell or taste to it, the best thing to do is to heat it close to a boil to quickly dissipate the chlorine before using it in yogurt. If you use carbon-filtered or bottled water for drinking, it is usually fine.

Basic Yogurt Recipe

The following recipe is for a 3-cup thermos. If yours is larger or smaller, you will have to adjust the amounts accordingly, as the thermos must be full to within 1 inch of the stopper for the contents to stay at an even temperature and the yogurt to culture well.

water
1¼ cups powdered milk
1 to 2 tablespoons yogurt starter OR 2 to
   4 tablespoons yogurt drink

1. Heat 3 cups water to almost boiling (it's okay if it does boil). Pour the water into the thermos and put on the stopper. Let the thermos sit to preheat while you're doing the next step.
2. In a small bowl combine the powdered milk and ½ cup water. Stir until the mixture is smooth.

Dairy

3. Pour the hot water out of the thermos and reserve it in a container. Return about ½ cup of the hot water to the thermos.

4. Add the milk mixture to the thermos and gently shake to combine. Put a candy thermometer into the thermos. Alternately add hot water and regular-temperature water, mixing after each addition, so that the thermos is almost full (about an inch below where the stopper will come) and the temperature is between 110° and 120°F. If the temperature is higher, let the mixture sit until the temperature has dropped into the correct range. If temperature is lower, remove some of the mixture and heat it, then return it to the thermos and check the temperature again. If the temperature is too low or too high, the yogurt will not culture.

5. Once the temperature is correct, add the yogurt starter and stir it in. Be sure to read the notes above about yogurt starter. Put the stopper back on the thermos and put the thermos in a place where it can sit undisturbed for 4 to 5 hours.

6. After about 4 hours, remove the stopper and look inside. If the yogurt does not appear thick, replace the stopper quickly so as not to lose the heat and check it again in 1 to 2 hours.

NOTE: I usually find that when I start a new batch of yogurt from commercial yogurt or yogurt drink, it takes longer to culture the first few batches. In fact, the last batch I started from a yogurt drink took 11 hours! I think it's because many commercial products have a relatively low concentration of live yogurt cultures—even those that prominently advertise their health benefits.

7. When the yogurt is thick, pour it into a storage container and keep it in the refrigerator. If you leave it in the thermos, it will continue to ferment, resulting in a very tart yogurt.

8. You will notice a watery liquid on top of the yogurt. That is the whey. You can stir it into the yogurt or pour it off. If you intend to make frozen yogurt or yogurt ricotta (below), you should pour it off.

NOTES

- When eating the yogurt, be sure to reserve at least a tablespoon for use as a starter in your next batch.

If the yogurt took longer than 6 hours to culture, use 2 to 3 tablespoons as a starter for your next batch. I have found that the flavor and consistency of the first several batches get better and better, and the yogurt will culture more and more quickly until it takes only 4 to 5 hours.

- This recipe makes a very thick yogurt, which is what we like. If you prefer a thinner yogurt, decrease the amount of powdered milk by 2 tablespoons at a time until it reaches the consistency you prefer.

- To make low-fat yogurt, very gradually substitute low-fat powdered milk for an equal amount of regular milk, and make it two or three times at each new level before increasing the amount of low-fat milk powder. I have never been able to just switch to low fat all at once and have found that making a slow transition produces the best results. I have also never been able to make a totally nonfat yogurt; it has simply not cultured for me. I'm guessing that it has to do with the particular strain of yogurt culture and the conditions in which it will reproduce.

Here are some ways to serve yogurt:

- With honey drizzled over the top
- With fresh or dried fruit mixed in (you can add a little sugar to the yogurt)
- Mix with fruit juice as a drink
- Serve over cereal instead of milk (try ⅓ fruit, ⅓ bran cereal, and ⅓ yogurt)
- In place of sour cream in dip recipes
- Over a baked potato instead of sour cream
- Mix in 1 teaspoon vanilla extract and a little sugar and use as a dessert topping in place of whipped cream
- Also see the list of add-ins for frozen yogurt; all are equally good not frozen

Yogurt Ricotta or Cream Cheese

Place yogurt in a colander or a strainer lined with a clean cotton rag (such as from an old sheet or T-shirt) or a paper towel. Put the colander in the sink or over a bowl for 6 to 8 hours to drain all the excess liquid. Use in any recipe that calls for ricotta or cream cheese.

Frozen Yogurt

If you are in a hot climate and have even a small amount of space in your freezer, this is one of the best treats you can make! Yogurt will freeze rock solid if sugar isn't added. Use 2 to 3 tablespoons sugar per cup of finished frozen yogurt. My experience has been that Splenda works just as well; I have not tried other no-calorie sugar substitutes.

2 to 3 tablespoons sugar per cup of yogurt

Combine the yogurt, sugar, and any add-ins (see following for ideas) in a small container,* cover it, and place it in the freezer for about 6 hours or until it is frozen to about the consistency of ice cream. The exact time will vary depending on the temperature of your freezer, how full it is, the container you're using (for example, a metal container will chill its contents much faster than a thick plastic container), and how large a batch you're making. On a hot day, it doesn't matter whether it's "perfect" or not!

*A small margarine tub (1 cup or less) with a lid works best as the freezing container. A thick plastic bag can also work, if you are very careful to check for holes.

Add-Ins

Here are some of our favorite add-ins:

- Fresh or canned fruit, cut into cubes no larger than 1/2 inch
- Soft dried fruits like raisins, dates, apricots, prunes, figs, or cranberries. If necessary, cut into bite-size pieces
- Nuts
- A swirl of honey, peanut butter, or Nutella
- Almost any chocolate candy, cut into bite-size bits
- M&M's or Reese's Pieces
- Oreos or other cookies, broken into bits
- Granola or bran cereal (good with honey instead of sugar)
- Vanilla, rum, Homemade Kahlua (page 96), Homemade Amaretto (page 96), or orange liqueur
- Nestle's Quick or other flavorings for milk (if they contain a lot of sugar, decrease or eliminate the sugar)
- A swirl of Hershey's syrup (wonderful with a few peanuts thrown in). See our recipe for Chocolate Syrup (page 410) for an easy way to make your own from powdered milk and unsweetened baking cocoa.

Dairy

BREAKFAST AND BRUNCH

Think of breakfast and most Americans think of boxed cereal, eggs and bacon, bagels or English muffins, and maybe yogurt. In this chapter, we've included a number of ways to make your own breakfast dishes as well as alternatives.

Brunch is often a fun time for entertaining, so we've included many recipes that are boat-friendly. Most don't require things like refrigerated rolls or overnight refrigeration of a big pan. Instead, they can be made quickly and easily from ingredients that you can find almost anywhere.

CEREALS AND ALTERNATIVES

Here's an easy way to prepare non-instant oatmeal and some alternatives to boxed cereal.

Boatmeal—
Oatmeal on a Boat   Serves 1

When I told a friend this way to make oatmeal, she immediately dubbed it "boatmeal."

Total Time: 7 minutes

¹⁄₃ cup old-fashioned oats or quick-cooking oats
1 cup water
salt

Combine the oats, water, and salt in a saucepan. Cover and bring to a boil over high heat. When it boils, turn off the heat and let sit for 5 minutes (3 minutes for quick-cooking oats). The longer the oatmeal sits, the thicker it will get. Serve it plain or

with milk or cream. A little brown sugar over the top is good.

Alternate Method: Place the quick-cooking oats in a large mug and sprinkle with any desired additions. Pour boiling water over it and stir once. Let sit for 5 minutes.

Variations:

- Add ¹⁄₄ cup dried fruit before cooking. Almost everyone likes raisins, dates, and apricots, but dried apples, bananas, cranberries, blueberries, mango, papaya, and even prunes are good, too.
- Add a few chopped nuts such as almonds, walnuts, or pecans after cooking.
- Add ¹⁄₄ teaspoon ground cinnamon and/or ¹⁄₈ teaspoon ground nutmeg after cooking.
- Add 1 tablespoon maple syrup after cooking.
- Add ¹⁄₄ cup fresh fruit over the top after cooking.
- Add 2 tablespoons applesauce after cooking.

Rice and Raisins   Serves 1

Total Time: 7 minutes

³⁄₄ to 1 cup cooked rice (leftovers are perfect)
¹⁄₄ cup milk, soy milk, or water
¹⁄₄ cup raisins
1 tablespoon brown sugar, white sugar, or honey

In a small saucepan combine the rice, milk, and raisins. Heat almost to boiling. Serve in a bowl and sprinkle the brown sugar over the top.

Variations: Add dried fruit, fresh fruit, a few tablespoons of applesauce, and/or a few nuts. A dash of ground cinnamon is good, also.

Rice and Yogurt   Serves 2

Total Time: 10 minutes

1 cup cooked rice (leftovers are great)
1 cup plain yogurt (page 101), or use flavored yogurt and adjust other add-ins to suit
1 teaspoon honey or brown sugar
1 apple, cored and chopped, or other fruit prepared in bite-size bits
1 teaspoon ground cinnamon
2 tablespoons raisins or other dried fruit

Combine all the ingredients in a medium bowl; mix well. Serve in bowls or mugs.

Rice and Eggs   Serves 2

Total Time: 10 minutes

1 teaspoon butter, margarine, or canola oil
1 cup cooked rice (leftovers are good)
4 eggs
salt and ground pepper

1. Melt the butter in a skillet over medium-high heat. Add the rice and sauté just until it starts turning golden brown on the bottom.
2. With a spoon, make four wells in the cooked rice. Break an egg into each well. Sprinkle with salt and pepper. Cover, turn down the heat to low, and let cook 2 to 4 minutes, depending on how done you like your eggs.
3. Use a spatula to transfer the eggs to plates, trying not to break the yolks.

Alternate Method: Instead of making wells in the rice and cooking the eggs whole, beat all the eggs lightly in a small bowl with the salt and pepper. Pour the egg mixture over the rice in the skillet and sauté, turning occasionally, until the eggs are cooked to your preferred degree of doneness.

Variations:
- Add chopped bits of almost any vegetable (cooked or raw) to the rice. Onion, tomato, bell pepper, corn, broccoli, and many others are good.
- Add ¼ cup chopped cooked meat (ham, fish bits, or sausage) to the rice.
- Almost any leftovers can be added to the rice.
- Spoon some salsa (page 127), tomato sauce, or leftover spaghetti sauce (page 261) over the eggs just before serving.
- Add a little curry powder (page 47), hot sauce, or soy sauce to the eggs.
- Toss a few ¼-inch to ½-inch pieces of cheese in with the beaten eggs before adding them to the pan.
- Use leftover pasta instead of rice.

Breakfast Granola   Serves 6
(approximately ½-cup servings)

Great over yogurt or as a cereal with milk.

Total Time: 90 minutes

1½ cups oats (old-fashioned, quick cooking, or instant)
½ cup chopped or sliced almonds
½ cup cashews, walnuts, or pecans, whole or broken
⅜ cup shredded coconut
3 tablespoons brown sugar
½ teaspoon salt
3 tablespoons maple syrup
2 tablespoons canola oil or vegetable oil
cooking spray
½ cup raisins or other moist dried fruit

1. Preheat oven to 250°F.
2. In a large bowl combine the oats, nuts, coconut, brown sugar, and salt. Pour the maple syrup and oil over the dry ingredients and mix well.
3. Coat a 9"×13" pan or a baking sheet with cooking spray. Spread the mix in the pan.
4. Bake for 1¼ hours, stirring every 15 minutes. Remove from the oven and let cool. Place in an airtight container or a plastic bag, add the raisins, and close the container. Shake well to mix.

Yogurt Granola Parfait   Serves 1

Total Time: 5 minutes

$\frac{1}{2}$ **cup yogurt (plain, vanilla, or flavor of your choice; page 101)**
$\frac{1}{4}$ **cup granola (page 105)**
$\frac{1}{2}$ **cup fresh fruit chunks, such as banana, strawberries, mango, pineapple**
$\frac{1}{2}$ **tablespoon honey**

Use a wine glass or a juice glass. Layer half the yogurt, half the granola, and half the fruit into the glass; repeat with the remainder of each. Drizzle the honey over the top.

Variation: To make a frozen parfait, use a small plastic container with a lid (a small butter tub works well). Increase the honey to 2 tablespoons and mix it into the yogurt if the yogurt is not already sweetened. (The yogurt will freeze rock hard if it does not contain sugar.) Layer as above, then freeze for 4 to 6 hours. This is fantastic on a hot day!

EGGS

Eggs also work well for a quick and easy dinner after a long day!

Eggs Sunny-Side Up   Serves 1

Total Time: 5 minutes

2 tablespoons canola oil, vegetable oil, butter, or margarine
2 eggs

1. Heat the oil in a pan over medium-high heat until a drop of water sizzles. Gently break the eggs into the pan from just above the pan. If you drop them from any distance, you're likely to break the yolks. Turn the heat down to medium.
2. As the whites start to turn white, tilt the pan to one side so that the oil makes a little puddle. Use a spoon to scoop up some of the oil, then position the pan back flat on the burner and gently pour the oil over the yolks and whites. Do this several times as the eggs cook, until the white is fairly firm but the yolk is still runny.

3. Gently slide the eggs out of the pan onto a plate. Serve hot.

Fried Eggs   Serves 1

Total Time: 5 minutes

1 tablespoon canola oil, vegetable oil, butter, margarine, or bacon grease
2 eggs

Decide if you like your eggs:

- Over Easy—White a little runny, yolk runny
- Over Medium—White solid, yolk soft
- Over Hard—White and yolk solid (some cooks deliberately break the yolk, too)

1. Heat the oil in the pan over medium-high heat until a drop of water sizzles. Tilt the pan so that the oil covers every bit of the pan.
2. Gently break the eggs into the pan from just above the pan. Reduce the heat to medium. (The egg white should not turn totally white within seconds of going into the pan. If that is the case, turn the heat down and know for the next time to use a lower heat. Every stove is different.)
3. Cook the eggs for 1 to 2 minutes, or until the egg white is white on the bottom but still clear over the yolk. The more well done you like the eggs, the more of the white should be cooked.
4. Just before you are ready to flip the eggs, cut them apart with the edge of the spatula and jiggle the pan a bit to see if the eggs are free or sticking. If you like your yolks broken, break them before flipping.
5. Hold the pan handle in one hand and use the other hand to slide the spatula under one of the eggs. To reduce the chance of breaking a yolk, use the thinnest spatula you have, and keep the entire leading edge in contact with the pan. Try to center the yolk over the spatula. Don't try to do this super slow and carefully. Believe it or not, a quick move is less likely to break the yolk. Carefully roll the egg over, keeping one edge of the spatula very near the pan. Dropping the egg from any distance is more likely to break the yolk. Forget any of those wild "flip in the air" moves! After flipping, jiggle the pan just a bit to make sure the eggs are not sticking.

6. Here's where it will take some experience to get your eggs just perfect. It's hard to say exactly how long to let them cook on the second side because of differences in eggs, pans, and stoves. In general, it will take about 30 seconds more for Over Easy, 1 minute more for Over Medium, and 2 minutes or more for Over Hard.

7. Gently slide the eggs out of the pan and onto a plate. Serve hot.

Easy Fried Eggs

Have a "fried egg" without worrying about flipping it!

Special Equipment: For this technique, your pan *must* have a tight-fitting lid.

Cook as above for Fried Eggs, but at the point where you would flip the eggs, add 1 tablespoon water and put the cover on the pan for the remaining time.

Poached Eggs   Makes 3 eggs

Some recipes use a little vinegar in the poaching water. We've learned that using milk seems to work more reliably to "keep the whites together."

Total Time: 7 minutes

½ teaspoon butter or margarine
1 tablespoon milk
salt
3 eggs

1. Grease a saucepan with the butter. Add cold water to a depth of 2 inches. Add the milk and a pinch of salt to the water; bring to a boil, then reduce to a light simmer.

2. Holding the egg as close as possible to the simmering water, break the eggs one at a time into the water. Some find it easier to break the egg into a small cup or saucer, then slide the egg into the boiling water.

3. Simmer over very low heat for 5 minutes, or until the egg reaches the desired doneness. Carefully remove the egg with a slotted spoon. Repeat for the other eggs.

French Toast   Serves 2

Total Time: 10 minutes

4 slices bread (any type)
2 eggs
1 tablespoon milk or water
salt
1 teaspoon ground cinnamon (optional)
dash of ground nutmeg (optional)
cooking spray OR 1 tablespoon butter, margarine, canola oil, or vegetable oil
butter and maple syrup, for serving

TIP: Lay out the bread slices while preparing the eggs so that the bread dries out just a bit and will absorb more of the egg mixture. Also check to see if your skillet will hold two slices of bread at once. If not, you can cut the slices in half, or cook one slice at a time.

1. Mix the eggs, milk, salt, cinnamon, and nutmeg in a pie pan or a bowl just large enough for one slice of bread.

2. Coat a skillet with cooking spray and place it over medium-high heat until a drop of water sizzles.

3. Dip one slice of bread into the egg mixture and then flip it over so both sides are fully coated with egg. I find that using my fingers works best for this, but if you prefer to use a fork, you'll have better luck with the bread not tearing if you insert the fork into one of the bottom corners of the slice. Place the bread in the skillet. Repeat with a second slice.

4. Let each slice cook until it's golden brown on the bottom. Depending on your pan and stove, this will take about 1 minute. Flip the slice and cook until the second side is golden.

5. Remove the slice and place it on a serving plate. Repeat with the remaining slices. Depending on the size of your eggs and bread, you may be able to make five slices.

6. Serve hot with butter or margarine and maple syrup.

Variations:

• Replace the maple syrup with confectioners' sugar.
• Add 1 tablespoon vanilla, Homemade Kahlua (page 96), or Homemade Amaretto (page 96) to

Breakfast and Brunch

the egg mixture. (This is particularly good if you don't have maple syrup.)
- Top the slices with Maple Spread (page 121) or Cinnamon Butter (page 121).

Boiled Eggs

Let's begin with descriptions of the three types of "boiled" (or, more correctly, "cooked") eggs:

- A soft-cooked egg has a firm white and a runny yolk.
- A medium-cooked egg has a firm white and a slightly firm yolk.
- A hard-cooked egg has a firm white and a firm yolk.

The basic cooking technique is the same for all three types of "boiled" eggs. The technique described below will avoid that nasty green layer of yolk we've probably all experienced in hard-boiled eggs, which is a result of cooking at too high a temperature for too long.

1. Place the eggs in a single layer in a pan (having more than one layer will cause the eggs to cook unevenly). Add enough water to just cover the eggs completely (using deeper water will throw the timing off). Add a splash of white vinegar to the water (this makes the eggs easier to peel).
2. Cover the pan and put it on the stove over high heat. Watch for the water to come to a full rolling boil.
3. To avoid the dreaded green line, as soon as the water comes to a full boil, turn off the stove (on an electric stove, remove the pan from the burner) and begin timing according to the chart below for the size of the eggs and the desired doneness. Leave the cover on the pan until the time is up.
4. At the end of the time, transfer the eggs from the hot water to a bowl of cool water (cold or ice water is even better).
5. Tap an egg against the side of the sink or on the counter, then peel it, being sure to remove all the membrane as well as the shell. As you peel, periodically dunk the egg back into the water to rinse off tiny shell fragments—and to cool it down a bit if it gets too hot for your hands.

6. If you get an egg that just won't peel, use a spoon to scoop the egg out of the shell.

TIMING CHART FOR BOILED EGGS

Begin timing when you turn off the gas or remove the pan from the heat. Subtract 30 to 60 seconds from the time below if your eggs were not refrigerated.

EGG SIZE	DONENESS	TIME
Medium	Soft	3 minutes
	Medium	5 minutes
	Hard	12 minutes
Large	Soft	4½ minutes
	Medium	6 minutes
	Hard	17 minutes
Jumbo	Soft	5 minutes
	Medium	7½ minutes
	Hard	19 minutes

Egg Boiling Tips

- Fresh eggs are much harder to peel. Eggs that are at least one week old, preferably two, peel more easily.
- Eggs will rarely crack if you put them into cool water, then heat the water. Eggs will almost always crack if you place them in boiling water.
- That green ring around the yolk of a hard-boiled egg is caused by overcooking—specifically, when the yolk reaches a temperature above 158°F. It won't hurt you to eat the green part, but hard-boiled eggs look better without it. To avoid the green, remove the eggs from the hot water according to the above table and put them into cool water to stop the cooking process.

Scrambled Eggs   Serves 2

Total Time: 10 minutes

4 eggs
2 tablespoons milk or water
⅛ teaspoon baking powder (optional, but it makes the eggs much fluffier; page 376)
salt and ground pepper
cooking spray OR 1 tablespoon butter, margarine, canola oil, or vegetable oil

1. Whisk the eggs, milk, baking powder, salt, and pepper in a small bowl.
2. Coat a skillet with cooking spray and warm it over medium-high heat until a drop of water sizzles. Pour the egg mixture into the pan and let cook, scraping and flipping over with a spatula every 30 seconds, or until the eggs reach your desired doneness.

Serve at once.

Scrambled Eggs "with Stuff"

Whether you're trying to stretch the eggs you have, want to increase your daily veggie intake, or just have a more substantial meal, there are all sorts of things that you can add to the Scrambled Eggs in the above recipe. Rather than give specific recipes, I've listed below some of our favorite combinations. If you choose to add sauce and it has been refrigerated, warm it to at least room temperature ahead of time.

1. In a small bowl combine the eggs, milk, baking powder, salt, and pepper as for regular Scrambled Eggs, above.
2. Heat the skillet and sauté any meat, vegetables, rice, or pasta until done.
3. Add the egg mixture and any cheese (either grated or in $\frac{1}{2}$-inch chunks) to the skillet. Let cook about a minute, then use a spatula to turn the eggs over (sort of stirring them). Cook to your desired degree of doneness, turning the eggs every 30 seconds or so.
4. Remove the eggs to serving plates and top with any warmed sauce.

Add-Ins: Here are some of our favorite additions to scrambled eggs. Almost any leftovers work well. Create your own combinations!

- Ham and mushrooms
- Ham, spinach, and cheese
- Feta, black olives, tomatoes, basil, and oregano
- Pasta and spaghetti sauce (great for using up leftovers)
- Spaghetti sauce and ricotta
- Leftover chili

- Sausage crumbles (small pieces of bulk sausage OR $\frac{1}{4}$-inch-thick slice of sausage cut into quarters), tomato, and onion
- Sausage crumbles, diced potato, and onion
- Diced potato, diced green bell pepper or chile pepper, and diced tomato
- Artichoke hearts and cheese

Breakfast Burrito   Serves 2

Except for the eggs and tortillas, all the ingredients are optional. You can even add other items you might have on hand. Look at Scrambled Eggs with Stuff (previous recipe) for good combinations!

Total Time: 15 minutes

cooking spray
4 ounces sausage, ham, or bacon, cut into small pieces
$\frac{1}{4}$ onion, diced
$\frac{1}{4}$ green bell pepper, diced, OR a little bit of minced chile pepper OR 2 tablespoons canned green chilies
1 tomato, diced
2 eggs, lightly beaten
2 tortillas (any type)
$\frac{1}{4}$ cup shredded cheese, any type
salsa (optional; page 127)

1. Coat a skillet with cooking spray. Warm it over medium heat and add the meat, onion, bell pepper, and tomato. Sauté a couple of minutes, or until the meat is done. (If you're using bacon, cook it to about 75 percent of doneness, then add the other items and finish cooking.)
2. Add the eggs and scramble them to your preferred doneness. At the same time, heat another dry skillet over high heat. When it is hot, heat the tortillas one at a time by placing them in the skillet for about 15 seconds per side (they will get a few light brown spots on them; if they have any black spots, cook the rest a few seconds less).
3. Place a hot tortilla on a plate and add half the egg mixture, half the cheese, and a bit of salsa. Roll up the tortilla. If you use a large tortilla, you can first fold the bottom up about one-quarter of the way, then roll it the rest of the way. If you use a small

Breakfast and Brunch

tortilla, you may have leftover egg and can either serve it on the side or heat an extra tortilla to hold it.

4. If you need to keep the burritos warm (and tidy) for someone on deck, wrap each one in aluminum foil.

Huevos Mexicana   Serves 2

Total Time: 15 minutes

2 tablespoons olive oil, canola oil, vegetable oil, butter, or margarine

2 green onions, sliced, including tops, OR ¼ cup diced onion

1 tomato, chopped, OR 8 ounces canned diced tomatoes, drained (half a 16-ounce can)

1 jalapeño pepper, seeded and finely diced, or to taste, OR 2 tablespoons finely diced spicy chile pepper or milder pepper

½ teaspoon dried oregano

salt and ground pepper to taste

4 eggs

1. Heat the oil in a skillet over medium-high heat. Add the onion and brown it for a minute or two. Add the chopped tomato and jalapeño and cook for a few minutes more. Add the oregano, salt, and pepper.

2. Break the eggs into a small bowl and beat slightly. Add them to the tomato mixture in the pan. Use a spatula to turn the eggs periodically until they're cooked to the desired doneness. Remove them from the heat and serve.

Breakfast Sandwiches

A breakfast sandwich is basically bread, egg, and meat all in one. There are lots of ways to make these, depending on what you have on hand. Here are some ideas:

Bread: Use a bagel, an English muffin (page 120), two slices of English muffin bread (page 121), or a biscuit (page 376). Toast and butter it, if desired.

Meat: A slice of ham or bacon or a sausage patty is typical. However, you can use a slice of lunch meat, bacon crumbles, or even leftovers. If you don't have a "slice" of meat, it's often easier to cook smaller pieces of meat with the eggs so that the meat won't fall out of the sandwich.

Eggs: Either scrambled or fried. If you scramble the eggs, you can add meat or vegetables to the mix as well as spices. If you fry the eggs, it's easiest to eat if they are done Over Medium or Over Hard.

If you want your eggs to be perfect rounds (whether scrambled or fried), you can do this in one of two ways:

- Cut the top and bottom off a tuna (or similar) can and place the can in the hot skillet. Pour the eggs inside the can until they firm up enough to hold the shape.
- Put the eggs (whole or scrambled) in greased muffin tins and bake at 350°F for about 5 minutes (depending on how done you want them).

Another good way to prepare the eggs is to make the Baked Denver "Omelet" (page 111). Add anything you like, such as:

- A slice of cheese (or mix shredded cheese with scrambled eggs)
- A spoonful of salsa (page 127) or spaghetti sauce (page 261)
- A few drops of hot sauce
- A slice of tomato

To assemble, start with half a bagel or other bread. Place any meat on it, then the egg, then any extras. Put the remaining bread on top. If you're making these to eat later (such as a mid-watch or mid-hike snack), wrap each sandwich tightly in foil.

Fluffy Cheese Omelet   Serves 2

There are two tricks to success with omelets: an exceedingly clean and well-seasoned pan (there should be no "sticking spots") and the willpower to let the egg mixture cook without too much stirring. If you stir too often, it will end up more like scrambled eggs; the finished product will taste good, but it won't look like an omelet.

Adding just a touch of baking powder will cause your omelet to rise up beautifully. You can make one large omelet, or divide the egg mixture in two and make two small omelets.

Total Time: 10 minutes

4 eggs

$1/8$ teaspoon baking powder (page 376)

2 tablespoons milk or water

1 green onion, including top, finely chopped, OR
   1 slice onion, finely chopped (optional)

salt and pepper

2 tablespoons butter or margarine

$1/4$ cup shredded cheese (any type that will melt)

1. In a small bowl combine the eggs, baking powder, milk, green onion, salt, and pepper.
2. Heat an 8-inch skillet over medium heat. Add the butter and tilt the pan so the melted butter covers the bottom completely. When the butter begins to bubble, pour in half the egg mixture and again tilt the pan so the mixture covers the bottom.
3. When the eggs have begun to set up, use a spatula to pull the egg mixture from the edge of the pan into the center, then tilt the pan to cover the exposed pan bottom with uncooked egg. Repeat two or three times until all the egg mixture is set (don't overcook).
4. Sprinkle half the cheese down the center of the omelet, then use a spatula to fold the left and right sides of the omelet over the cheese.
5. Gently slide the omelet out of the pan and onto a serving plate. (You may have to use the spatula if any places stick.) Repeat for the second omelet.

Variations:

- Add cooked bacon, ham, or sausage
- Add diced tomato and bell pepper
- Add tomato sauce, salsa (page 127), or spaghetti sauce (page 261)
- Add mushrooms (best if sautéed first)
- Add spinach (if using canned, squeeze out as much water as possible)
- Add cooked diced potato
- Top with hollandaise (page 207) or enchilada sauce (page 213)

Baked Denver "Omelet"

Serves 2 to 4, depending on appetites

To make a "true" Denver omelet, add ham and green bell pepper to the Fluffy Omelet, above. You can use the baking technique below with an infinite variety of add-ins to make all sorts of "omelets."

Total Time: 25 minutes
Prep Time: 5 minutes   **Bake Time:** 15 to 20 minutes

4 eggs

$1/4$ cup water or milk

$1/2$ teaspoon salt

$1/2$ teaspoon ground pepper

cooking spray OR 1 tablespoon butter or
   margarine

4 green onions, sliced (including tops), OR
   $1/2$ medium onion, diced

1 cup diced cooked ham OR 1 can (6 ounces) ham, crumbled

1 green bell pepper or chile pepper, seeded and diced

12 ounces any meltable cheese, cut into $1/2$-inch cubes or shredded (cheddar, Monterey Jack, Colby, and mozzarella are all good, or you can use slices of American cheese or Velveeta)

1. Preheat oven to 400°F.
2. Beat the eggs, water, salt, and ground pepper. Set aside.
3. Coat an ovenproof sauté pan with the cooking spray and sauté the onions, ham, and pepper over medium-high heat for 3 minutes; the onions and pepper should still be a little crisp. (**TIP:** If you don't have a pan that can go from stovetop to oven, sauté the onions, ham, and pepper in a skillet, then transfer them to a prepared baking pan.)
4. Pour the egg mixture over the ham mixture and then sprinkle with the cheese.
5. Bake for 15 to 20 minutes, or until the eggs are cooked through and the cheese is melted and golden. Cut into quarters to serve.

Breakfast and Brunch

Omelet in a Bag

This is a great way to make breakfast for lots of people, such as a beach festival or a large brunch. Ziploc's official position is that its bags are not intended for cooking in this way, but several cruiser get-togethers that I've been with have done this with no ill effects. Kids love it!

Required per person:
- 1 quart-size freezer Ziploc-type bag
- 2 eggs

Required for a group:
- Permanent marker to write names on plastic bags
- Large pot of boiling water (for more than about 10 people, you may want two pots of water)
- Tongs

Add-Ins: amounts will vary depending on the number of people, their preferences, and the size of their appetites. Set out whatever is available. Some ideas:

- One or more types of grated cheese
- Ham
- Bacon crumbles (precooked)
- Sausage crumbles (precooked)
- Diced onion
- Sliced green onion
- Diced green bell pepper
- Minced hot chile peppers (be sure to label that they are hot)
- Sliced mushrooms (best if sautéed, but not required)
- Diced tomato
- Diced cooked potato (not raw). Sweet potato is good, too!
- Salt and pepper
- Hot sauce

1. Have everyone write his or her name on a Ziploc bag. Have each person break 2 eggs into the bag, then squish the egg around to break up the yolk. Don't use more than 2 eggs per bag.
2. Have everyone choose whatever add-ins he or she wants, then close the bag and get out as much air as possible. Shake the bag to mix the ingredients.
3. Immerse the bags in boiling water in batches of four to eight, depending on the size of the pot. Add the bags to the water one at a time so the water

stays at a boil. The bags should not be crowded. Let each batch boil for exactly 13 minutes. Use tongs to retrieve the bags from the boiling water.

4. Remove the bags from the pot. Everyone can open his or her bag and roll out the omelet onto a plate. Be sure to help kids with the hot bags, as the bags will still have some drops of very hot water on them.

Ham and Cheese Breakfast Casserole   Serves 8

Total Time: 1 hour, 30 minutes
Prep Time: 30 minutes   **Bake Time:** 50 minutes

1 pound sausage OR 2 cups cubed ham
cooking spray
6 cups cubed bread (French bread is best, but any type will work)
¼ pound cheddar cheese, shredded or cubed*
¼ pound Swiss cheese, shredded or cubed*
8 eggs
2 cups milk
1 teaspoon salt
⅛ teaspoon ground pepper
¾ teaspoon dry mustard OR 1 tablespoon prepared mustard
¼ teaspoon Worcestershire sauce

You can substitute ½ pound of almost any cheese for both of these.

1. Remove the sausage from its casings. Sauté in a skillet over medium-high heat, breaking it up with the side of a spoon as it cooks. When it is no longer pink, remove the pan from the heat and drain off the fat.
2. Coat a 9"×13" baking pan with cooking spray and arrange the bread cubes in the pan. Scatter the cubed cheese and cooked sausage evenly over the bread.
3. In a large bowl slightly beat the eggs with the milk, spices, and Worcestershire. Transfer the egg mixture to the pan, pouring slowly so as not to make "holes" in the layers of bread, cheese, and sausage.
4. Let the casserole sit while the oven preheats to 350°F. This lets the egg mixture soak into the

bread. If desired, the casserole may be refrigerated overnight at this point.

5. Bake the casserole for 45 to 50 minutes, or until completely set. The best way to test for doneness is to cut into the center to see if the eggs are cooked as desired.

6. Remove the casserole from the oven and let sit for 5 minutes before cutting. Serve hot.

Egg Casserole for Two   Serves 2

Total Time: 25 minutes
Prep Time: 5 minutes   **Bake Time:** 20 minutes

cooking spray
3 eggs
3 tablespoons milk or water
2 slices bread, cut into 1-inch cubes
1 green onion, with top, thinly sliced, OR 1 slice onion, diced
$\frac{1}{3}$ cup shredded cheddar cheese or other cheese that melts
$\frac{1}{3}$ cup chopped ham OR 2 slices cooked bacon, crumbled

1. Preheat oven to 350°F.
2. Coat a small baking dish (a small loaf pan also works well) with cooking spray.
3. Beat the eggs in a large bowl. Add all the other ingredients and mix well. Pour the egg mixture into the prepared baking dish. Bake for 20 to 25 minutes, or until the egg mixture is cooked through.

Variation: Use any combination of the add-ins listed for Scrambled Eggs "with Stuff" (page 109).

Eggs Benedict from Scratch   Serves 4

This recipe is for real, true Eggs Benedict. I haven't listed substitutions for the key ingredients, but you can certainly substitute a packet of hollandaise sauce mix instead of making it from scratch, or use soft-boiled eggs instead of the poached eggs, or use bagels or toast instead of the English muffins. You'll have a special treat, just not "true" Eggs Benedict.

Total Time: 45 minutes to 1 hour

hollandaise sauce (page 207)
8 poached eggs (page 107, but alter the recipe to make 8)
4 English muffins, split (page 120)
soft butter
4 slices fully cooked ham

1. Prepare the hollandaise sauce and the poached eggs according to the recipes.
2. To assemble, spread the English muffins with butter, and wrap the ham in aluminum foil.
3. Arrange the muffins and ham on a broiler pan and broil until the muffins are browned and the ham is hot. If you don't have a broiler, toast the English muffins, and heat the ham in the oven or in a skillet.
4. Place two muffin halves on each plate, buttered side up. Top each half with a half slice of ham and one well-drained poached egg. Spoon 2 tablespoons hollandaise sauce over each egg. Serve hot.

Healthier Eggs Benedict   Serves 2

Although still not a "health food," this version has leaner meat, a far lower calorie substitute for hollandaise sauce, no butter on the English muffins, and a smaller serving size. An added bonus is that it's far faster to prepare.

Total Time: 15 minutes

2 slices Canadian bacon or lean ham*
$\frac{1}{4}$ cup lemon yogurt or plain low-fat yogurt (page 101)
$\frac{1}{2}$ teaspoon lemon or lime juice
$\frac{1}{2}$ teaspoon dry mustard
salt
cayenne pepper
1 tablespoon milk
2 eggs
1 English muffin (page 120)

*If you're being really healthy, you can substitute $\frac{1}{2}$ cup fresh spinach leaves or asparagus pieces for the Canadian bacon

1. In a skillet over medium heat, lightly brown the Canadian bacon. Remove from the pan and keep warm.
2. Meanwhile, in a small saucepan over low heat, combine the yogurt, lemon juice, dry mustard, salt,

and cayenne, and cook until heated through and smooth. Set aside and keep warm. Don't let it get too hot or the yogurt will curdle.

3. Poach the eggs, using the milk (page 107).
4. Meanwhile, toast the English muffin. Place half on each plate, and top with the reserved Canadian bacon.
5. When the eggs are ready, place an egg on top of the Canadian bacon, then spoon the sauce over the top. Serve immediately.

Eggs Benedict Cups   Serves 4

Not true Eggs Benedict, but tasty and much easier!

Total Time: 20 minutes
Prep Time: 7 minutes   **Bake Time:** 13 minutes

cooking spray
4 thin slices ham (lunch meat also works well)
3 slices Swiss cheese or other meltable cheese, cut in half
4 eggs
4 tablespoons cream, half-and-half, evaporated milk, or milk
2 English muffins (page 120)

1. Preheat oven to 400°F.
2. Coat four muffin tins with cooking spray. Place a ham slice in each depression like a nest. Place a half slice of cheese on each ham slice.
3. Break an egg over each of the cheese slices in the muffin cups, then spoon 1 tablespoon cream over each.
4. Slice the remaining cheese into strips ¼ inch wide or less. Sprinkle evenly over the eggs.
5. Bake for 10 to 13 minutes, depending on the degree of doneness preferred for the eggs. Remove from the oven and let sit for 5 minutes to firm up.
6. Meanwhile, toast the English muffins and arrange on the plates.
7. Remove the egg cups from the muffin pan and place each on a toasted English muffin. Serve hot.

BREAKFAST CASSEROLES, QUICHE, AND PANCAKES

All of these recipes are good for guests or just for a special breakfast or brunch.

Baked French Toast with Praline Topping   Serves 8

Total Time: 55 minutes
Prep Time: 15 minutes   **Bake Time:** 40 minutes

1 loaf unsliced white bread (French or Italian bread works best, but almost anything will do)
cooking spray
8 eggs
2 cups half-and-half (*media crema*), evaporated milk, or cream
1 cup milk
2 tablespoons sugar
1 teaspoon vanilla extract
¼ teaspoon ground cinnamon
¼ teaspoon ground nutmeg
dash of salt
maple syrup (optional), for serving

Praline Topping
1 cup butter or margarine, softened
1 cup packed brown sugar OR white sugar with 1 tablespoon honey
1 cup chopped pecans or walnuts
½ teaspoon ground cinnamon
½ teaspoon ground nutmeg

1. Cut the loaf of bread into 1-inch slices.
2. Coat a 9"×13" baking dish with cooking spray. Arrange the bread slices in the pan. You will probably have two or three layers, depending on how thick your slices are. Set aside.
3. In a large bowl beat the eggs, half-and-half, milk, sugar, vanilla, cinnamon, nutmeg, and salt until well blended but not frothy. Pour the mixture over the bread slices in the pan. If desired, refrigerate the pan overnight, but it is not necessary.
4. Preheat oven to 350°F. Let the egg mixture soak into the bread as the oven preheats. Also while the oven is preheating, in a small bowl mix the ingredients for the Praline Topping.

5. Sprinkle the topping over the bread mixture and immediately bake the French toast uncovered for about 40 minutes, or until the bread is golden on top.
6. Cut into squares. Serve warm with maple syrup or plain.

Breakfast Casserole   Serves 6

Although this recipe uses a package of crescent rolls, which can be hard to find in some cruising locales, we included this recipe for those who can get the rolls easily. (If you can't get crescent rolls, try making the Ham and Cheese Breakfast Casserole, page 112.)

Total Time: 35 minutes
Prep Time: 15 minutes   **Bake Time:** 20 minutes

½ pound sausage, fish sausage (page 233), or ground beef
cooking spray
1 package refrigerated crescent rolls
1 cup shredded mozzarella cheese or other meltable cheese
3 eggs
⅓ cup milk
salt and ground pepper

1. Preheat oven to 350°F.
2. Cook the sausage (if it's in casings, remove the sausage and crumble it). Drain and set aside.
3. Coat an 8-inch square baking dish with cooking spray. Unroll the crescent rolls in the bottom of the dish, pressing the edges together. Sprinkle the sausage and cheese over the rolls.
4. In a medium bowl combine the eggs, milk, salt, and pepper. Pour the egg mixture over the sausage and cheese.
5. Bake for 15 to 20 minutes. Test for doneness by cutting into the center of the casserole and making sure that the eggs are cooked as desired. Let cool for 5 minutes before cutting and serving.

Spinach Breakfast Pie   Serves 4 to 6

Total Time: 45 minutes
Prep Time: 10 minutes   **Bake Time:** 35 to 40 minutes

cooking spray
1 large flour tortilla or corn tortilla
1½ cups shredded cheese
3 cups fresh (raw) spinach OR 1 cup frozen spinach, pressed and drained
5 eggs
3 slices cooked bacon, crumbled, OR ¼ cup diced ham (optional)
2 tablespoons milk or water
3 garlic cloves, crushed, OR ¼ teaspoon garlic powder
¼ teaspoon ground pepper
dash of salt

1. Preheat oven to 375°F.
2. Coat a pie pan with cooking spray. Lay a tortilla in the pan as a crust. Sprinkle alternating layers of the cheese and spinach over the tortilla, ending with spinach.
3. In a large bowl combine the eggs, bacon, milk, garlic, pepper, and salt; mix well.
4. Gently pour the egg mixture over the spinach, keeping all the mixture inside the tortilla shell.
5. Bake for 30 to 40 minutes. Test for doneness by inserting a knife into the center. When the pie is done, the knife will come out clean. Cut into wedges and serve hot.

NOTE: I've tried making this with canned spinach (1 can). It's okay but not nearly as good as when made with fresh or frozen spinach.

Quiche   Serves 6 (using a 9-inch pan)

Rather than giving recipes for a number of different quiches, this is a general "recipe" so that you can put one together based on what you have available. A recipe for Quiche Lorraine follows as well.

Total Time: approximately 1 hour, 40 minutes, including 10 minutes "stand" time
Prep Time: 45 minutes (depends on ingredients and whether you make a piecrust)
Bake Time: 45 minutes

A quiche is an egg pie without a top crust. A quiche made in a 9-inch pie pan will serve about 6 people, depending on their appetites. For smaller or larger pans, adjust the

Breakfast and Brunch

amounts of ingredients accordingly. You can also make a quiche in a square pan, a loaf pan, or even an ovenproof bowl. You'll just have to roll the piecrust into a suitable shape. Or you can make an "almost quiche" without a crust if you prefer; just bake the egg mixture in a greased pan. This approach cuts the time involved and the calories.

unbaked piecrust (see page 425)

4 eggs

2 cups cream, half-and-half, evaporated milk (page 99), milk, or soy milk

spices such as salt, ground pepper, cayenne pepper, garlic, onion powder, oregano, basil, and ground nutmeg

dash or two of hot sauce (optional)

Add-Ins

- Cooked ham, bacon, Canadian bacon, sausage, ground beef, or chicken
- Cooked fish, shrimp, or clams
- Spam or canned hash
- Diced onion, or sliced green onion, including tops
- Spinach (if using frozen, defrost and squeeze out as much water as possible)
- Cooked broccoli and/or asparagus
- Mushrooms (sautéing them first is best)
- Diced tomato, tomato sauce, spaghetti sauce, or salsa
- Peppers—bell or chile
- Black olives
- Leftovers
- Pasta (cooked) or potato (diced and cooked)
- Cheese—grated, shredded, or in ½-inch chunks

1. To make a quiche, place an unbaked piecrust (page 425) in your pan. Let the oven preheat to 450°F as you prepare the other ingredients. If your oven won't get this hot, get it as hot as you can and pre-bake the piecrust for about 3 minutes, then let the crust cool before adding the other ingredients. If your oven will get to 425°F or 450°F, you do not need to pre-bake the crust.
2. Place the add-ins in the crust. They should fill it halfway. Any meat should be pre-cooked. All items should be cut into pieces no larger than ½ inch or

be grated or shredded. If not using a crust, grease the pan before putting the add-ins into it.
3. In a medium bowl combine the eggs and cream. Add the spices of your choice and a dash or two of hot sauce, if desired.
4. Pour the egg mixture over the add-ins in the pan. Don't overfill the pan or the mixture will spill as you place it in the oven—and as the boat moves while baking the quiche.
5. Bake for 15 minutes, then reduce the temperature to 300°F and bake an additional 30 minutes, or until a knife inserted in the center comes out clean.
6. Remove from the oven and let sit for 10 minutes before cutting into wedges. Quiche should be served warm, not hot.

Quiche Lorraine   Serves 6

This makes an elegant brunch with a tossed salad, a slice of homemade bread, and a glass of white wine. It helps to serve it in a beautiful anchorage!

Total Time: 1 hour, 25 minutes (includes 10 minutes "stand" time; add time to make piecrust if needed)

Prep Time: 30 minutes   **Bake Time:** 45 minutes

The first listed ingredient is traditional; the substitutes listed still make a great quiche, but it won't be a true "Quiche Lorraine."

12 slices bacon (about ½ pound) OR ¼ pound ham or sausage

1 unbaked piecrust (page 425); frozen or refrigerated is fine

1 cup shredded Swiss cheese or other meltable cheese

⅓ cup minced onion or sliced green onion with or without tops

4 eggs

2 cups cream, half-and-half, evaporated milk (page 99), milk, or soy milk

¾ teaspoon salt

¼ teaspoon ground nutmeg

⅛ teaspoon cayenne pepper or ground black pepper

1. In a skillet or microwave, cook the bacon until crisp. Let drain on paper towels, then crumble.
2. Follow the general quiche instructions above for the remainder of the preparation.

Pancakes   2 to 3 servings

Total Time: 15 minutes (depending on pan size)

1 cup flour
2½ teaspoons baking powder (page 376)
¾ teaspoon salt
2 teaspoons sugar
1 egg plus enough milk to total 1 cup (this will be about ¾ cup milk)
2 tablespoons canola oil or vegetable oil, or butter or margarine, melted

For 4 or 5 servings:
1½ cups flour
3½ teaspoons baking powder (page 376)
1 teaspoon salt
1 tablespoon sugar
1 egg
1¼ cups milk
3 tablespoons canola oil or vegetable oil, or butter or margarine, melted

1. In a medium bowl combine the flour, baking powder, salt, and sugar; mix well. Add the egg, milk, and oil; quickly mix until smooth.
2. Heat a lightly oiled skillet or griddle over medium-high heat until a drop of water sizzles. Pour the batter into the pan: ¼ cup batter makes a typical 4-inch pancake; a little over 1 tablespoon batter makes a "silver dollar pancake." The number of pancakes you can cook at once will depend on the size of the pan. Don't press down on the pancake as it cooks!
3. The first side is done when bubbles on the top are just starting to break. Gently turn over each pancake with a spatula (forget those wild flips in the air) and cook about 30 seconds more on the second side. Both sides should be golden, with no raw dough in the center. Serve hot.

If you don't have syrup available, try:
- Honey
- Jam or jelly warmed until just pourable
- Butter and cinnamon sugar
- Fresh fruit topping (with a dollop of yogurt if desired)
- Chopped nuts, butter, and sugar
- Applesauce
- Peanut butter or Nutella
- Cream cheese
- Any spread at the end of this chapter (see page 121)

TOAST WITHOUT A TOASTER

All these methods produce good results if you pay constant attention to the toast. Unlike using a toaster, you just can't pop the bread in and leave it. The key to good toast (golden and crunchy on the outside and soft and moist on the inside) is high heat, and that means the bread can go from white to burnt in just seconds.

Method 1: Broiler

1. Move the oven rack to the top position. Preheat the broiler until it is red hot.
2. Slide out the rack, place the bread slices on it (no pan), then slide it back in.
3. Keep the oven door cracked, and watch for the bread to become golden. The exact time will depend on the heat of your broiler, the distance between the broiling unit and the rack, and the moisture in the bread. It generally takes somewhere between 30 and 60 seconds.
4. Slide out the rack, quickly flip the bread, and slide the rack back in. (Don't try to reach into the oven to flip the bread; it's too easy to burn yourself!) Watch for the second side to turn golden. It will take less time than the first side. Remove the toast and serve hot.

Method 2: Skillet 1

Warm a dry skillet over high heat. Place the bread in the skillet (no oil). Turn the bread over when the first side is golden. When the second side is golden, remove the toast and serve hot.

Method 3: Skillet 2

Warm a dry skillet over medium-high heat. Lightly butter one side of a slice of bread, as you would for a grilled cheese sandwich. Place the bread in the skillet, buttered side down. While the first side is cooking, lightly butter the second side. When the first side is golden, flip the bread with a spatula. When the second side is golden, remove the toast from the pan and serve hot.

Variation: You can make garlic toast by sprinkling the butter with a little garlic powder, or mixing finely minced garlic or garlic paste into the butter.

Other good flavorings are ground cinnamon, minced onion, or dried or fresh dill.

Method 4: Camping Toaster

Coleman and other companies make camping toasters that can be used over a gas stove. You can find them cheaply at Walmart and camping stores. Get one that folds flat for efficient storage.

Set the "toaster" over medium-high heat and prop the bread on it. Watch carefully: when the "inside face" of each slice is golden, flip it around to toast the second side. The time will vary by the type of bread and how hot your burner gets, but expect it to take 30 to 60 seconds for the first side, and the second side taking about half the time of the first side.

BREAKFAST BREADS, MUFFINS, AND COFFEE CAKES

When the delicious aroma of fresh baking breakfast bread, muffins, or coffee cake drifts over the anchorage, every boat will wish they'd thought of baking in the morning!

Apple Breakfast Bread   Serves 6

Total Time: 45 minutes
Prep Time: 15 minutes   **Bake Time:** 30 minutes

2 cups flour
4 teaspoons baking powder (page 376)
1 teaspoon salt
4 tablespoons brown sugar or white sugar
4 tablespoons shortening
2 cups chopped raisins or dates
1 egg, beaten
$3/4$ cup milk or water
cooking spray
2 tablespoons butter or margarine, melted
3 apples, peeled and thinly sliced
1 tablespoon ground cinnamon

1. Preheat oven to 350°F.
2. In a large bowl combine the flour, baking powder, salt, and 2 tablespoons of the sugar. Cut in the shortening. Add the raisins and stir to combine.
3. Combine the egg and milk and add to the dry ingredients to make a stiff batter.
4. Coat a shallow pan (a 9-inch pie tin is perfect) with the cooking spray. Spread the batter in the pan.
5. Brush the batter with half the melted butter. Arrange the apple slices in rows, allowing their edges to overlap; there may be several layers. Brush the slices with more melted butter. Combine the cinnamon and the remaining 2 tablespoons brown sugar and sprinkle over the top.
6. Bake for 30 minutes, or until the apples are tender. This is best served warm, but it's not bad cold, either.

Gingerbread Muffins   Makes 12 muffins

Delicious anytime, these are great to make ahead for a middle-of-the-night snack on a passage. Ginger is a natural remedy for queasy tummies!

Total Time: 30 minutes
Prep Time: 10 minutes   **Bake Time:** 20 minutes

cooking spray or paper muffin cup liners
$1/4$ cup packed brown sugar or white sugar
$1/2$ cup molasses or honey
$1/3$ cup canola oil or vegetable oil
1 egg
$1/2$ cup milk or water
2 cups flour
1 teaspoon baking powder (page 376)
$1/2$ teaspoon salt
$1/2$ teaspoon baking soda
2 teaspoons ground ginger
1 teaspoon ground cinnamon
$1/2$ teaspoon ground allspice

Add-Ins (optional)

- ½ cup broken walnuts or pecans
- ½ to 1 cup raisins or chopped dates
- 1 apple, peeled and diced

1. Preheat oven to 400°F. Coat the muffin tins with cooking spray.
2. In a medium bowl combine the brown sugar, molasses, and oil. Add the egg and milk and beat until well mixed and light.
3. In a small bowl or measuring cup, combine the flour, baking powder, salt, baking soda, ginger, cinnamon, and allspice. Mix well to ensure that the spices are evenly distributed.
4. Add the flour mixture to the sugar mixture along with any optional add-ins. Mix just until everything is well combined.
5. Fill the muffin cups evenly to about two-thirds full. Bake for 15 to 20 minutes, or until a toothpick inserted in the center of one of the muffins comes out clean.
6. Remove the pan from the oven and immediately turn the muffins out of the pan. Cool a bit on a wire rack or a plate. Serve warm.

Streusel Coffee Cake
Makes 8 to 10 slices

Total Time: 60 minutes, including 10 minutes cooling time
Prep Time: 15 minutes   **Bake Time:** 30 to 35 minutes

Batter
cooking spray
1½ cups flour
¾ cup sugar
1 teaspoon salt
2½ teaspoons baking powder (page 376)
½ cup raisins, chopped dates, or other chopped dried fruit or fresh or frozen fruit
1 egg
½ cup milk or water
¼ cup canola oil or vegetable oil, or butter or margarine, melted

Topping
½ cup chopped walnuts or pecans or chopped dried, fresh, or frozen fruit
2 tablespoons brown sugar or white sugar
1½ teaspoons flour
1½ teaspoons butter or margarine, softened
1 teaspoon ground cinnamon

1. Preheat oven to 375°F. Coat a pan with cooking spray; use a loaf pan (best), pie pan, or other baking pan up to 8 inches square.*
2. To make the batter, in a medium bowl combine the flour, sugar, salt, baking powder, and fruit. Add the egg, milk, and oil; stir until well mixed. The batter will be thick.
3. To make the topping, in a small bowl combine the nuts, sugar, flour, butter, and cinnamon to form a crumbly mixture (it will not all clump together). Set aside.
4. Pour the batter into the prepared pan. Sprinkle the topping over the batter. Bake for 30 to 35 minutes, or until a toothpick inserted in the center comes out clean. Cool at least slightly before cutting.

If you're using a 9-inch square pan, make a double batch; otherwise, the coffee cake will be too thin. A 9"×13" pan needs a triple batch.

BAGELS AND ENGLISH MUFFINS

These are my favorite breakfast treats!

Homemade Bagels
Makes 12 bagels

These taste wonderful, but they take a lot of work! With the boiling water and baking, it's a good way to warm up a boat on a cold day. In the tropics, though, it's a hot and humid chore.

Total Time: 2½ hours

IMPORTANT: Because the bagels are partially cooked in an open pot of boiling water, these should not be made while you're under way or in a rolly anchorage.

Breakfast and Brunch

1½ cups warm water
4½ teaspoons yeast (2 packages, page 387)
3 tablespoons sugar
1 tablespoon salt
3½ cups flour (white or up to half whole wheat)
2 quarts water, to boil
cooking spray
1 egg white, beaten (optional)
sesame seeds, poppy seeds, coarse salt, or any
    other desired toppings

1. In a medium bowl combine the warm water, yeast, sugar, and salt. Let the mixture proof for 5 minutes (page 388). Add the flour little by little and stir in.
2. Knead the dough in the bowl for about 5 minutes, adding more flour if needed. The dough should be fairly stiff but not dry. See page 390 to learn more about kneading dough.
3. Remove the dough from the bowl. Rinse the bowl, dry it, and coat it with a little oil. Replace the dough in the bowl and turn the dough to completely coat it with oil. Cover the bowl and let the dough rise until doubled. The time will vary considerably depending on the ambient temperature.
4. Divide the dough into 12 roughly equal balls (the dough will deflate as you handle it; that's okay). Let the dough balls rest for 5 minutes.
5. Use your finger to make a hole in the center of each piece of dough, then pull the hole open 1 to 2 inches to make a bagel shape. Place the shaped bagels on plates, baking sheets, or the countertop and let rise for 10 minutes.
6. Meanwhile, pour 2 quarts of water into a large pot and bring to a boil. The water should not fill more than half the pot. If necessary, use less water (but it has to be at least 1½ inches deep) and cook fewer bagels at a time.
7. Meanwhile, preheat oven to 350°F. Coat two baking sheets with cooking spray.
8. Reduce the heat to medium under the pot of water. Place the bagels, two or three at a time (or fewer if your pot is smaller), into the boiling water. Cook for 30 seconds, turn them over with a spatula, and cook for another 30 seconds.

Remove with a spatula, and let excess water drain back into the pot for a few seconds.

9. Place the bagels on the baking sheets. Brush the tops of the bagels with the beaten egg white and sprinkle with the sesame seeds.
10. Bake for 30 to 35 minutes, or until golden. Serve warm or cool. Store in an airtight container.

Variations:

- For cinnamon raisin bagels, add 1 teaspoon ground cinnamon and ½ cup raisins to the mix (or more to taste).
- For onion bagels, add 1 tablespoon dried onion.

English Muffins   Makes 8 muffins

These taste wonderful, but it can take a few tries to get the texture right. Be sure that your yeast proofs really well (page 388); otherwise, the desired holes will not form in the dough. Before making these muffins, collect some empty tuna cans (or a similar size) and cut out the bottoms to use the cans as cooking rings. Plan on baking these muffins in a couple of batches.

Total Time: 1½ hours (depends on temperature and rising time, estimated at 30 minutes)
Prep Time: 15 minutes   **Cook Time:** 36 minutes

1⅓ cups warm water*
½ cup powdered milk*
1 tablespoon sugar
½ teaspoon salt
1 tablespoon canola oil, vegetable oil, shortening, butter, or margarine
2¼ teaspoons yeast (1 packet, page 387)
2 cups flour
cooking spray
approximately ¼ cup cornmeal (optional)

1½ cups milk can be substituted for the powdered milk and water.

1. In a large bowl combine the water, powdered milk, sugar, salt, oil, and yeast. Let proof for 10 minutes (page 388). Add the flour and beat thoroughly with a spoon. **NOTE:** This dough will be much "wetter" than typical bread dough.

2. Cover the bowl and let the dough rest in a warm spot for 30 minutes. The dough should at least double in size, but if the temperature is less than 70°F, it's likely to take longer than 30 minutes.

3. Coat a skillet with cooking spray and warm over medium-high heat. Coat the tuna can rings with cooking spray and place them on the skillet. Sprinkle about ½ teaspoon cornmeal on the skillet inside each tuna can ring if desired.

4. Place a scant ¼ cup dough into each ring. Quickly sprinkle ½ teaspoon cornmeal over each. Cover with the pan lid (or another pan, such as a baking sheet or cake pan). Cook for 6 minutes, or until the bottom side is golden. Flip, using a spatula or tongs. Cook another 6 minutes on the second side.

5. Remove the filled rings and place them on a cooling rack (or put them in a cold oven). When the cans are cool enough to handle, remove the rings. Repeat for the remaining dough.

6. To serve, split the muffins and toast each half.

English Muffin Bread   Makes 1 loaf

This bread is much easier to make than true English muffins and tastes every bit as good.

Total Time: 1½ hours (depends on temperature and rising time, estimated at 45 minutes)
Prep Time: 10 minutes   **Bake Time:** 35 minutes

1 cup milk or water
½ cup water
2½ teaspoons yeast* (1 packet, page 387)
1½ teaspoons sugar
1 teaspoon salt
1 teaspoon baking powder (page 376)
2½ cups white flour (or up to half whole wheat flour)
cooking spray
cornmeal

The yeast must be fresh to achieve the big holes typical of English muffins.

1. If the temperature in the boat is cool, warm the milk and water to 110°F.

2. In a large bowl combine the yeast, sugar, salt, baking powder, and about half the flour. Add the warmed milk and water and stir until thoroughly mixed. Add the remaining flour and stir it in. *Do not knead the dough.*

3. Coat a loaf pan with cooking spray. Sprinkle a little cornmeal in the bottom of the pan.

4. Transfer the dough to the pan. Cover and place in a warm spot to rise until doubled. Time will vary considerably, but will take about 45 minutes if the temperature is around 70°F.

5. When the dough is almost fully risen, preheat oven to 375°F.

6. When the dough is fully risen, bake the loaf for 35 minutes, or until golden.

7. Let cool for at least a few minutes before cutting. Serve warm or toasted.

JAMS AND SPREADS

Top off your fresh baked breakfast breads with tasty jams or spreads.

Cinnamon Butter   Makes about ½ cup

Great on toast, bagels, English muffins, and zucchini or pumpkin bread. The list is endless!

¼ cup butter or margarine, softened
¼ cup brown sugar or white sugar
1 teaspoon ground cinnamon
¼ teaspoon ground nutmeg

Thoroughly combine all the ingredients. Store any extra in the refrigerator.

Maple Spread   Makes about 2 cups

Maple syrup can be hard to find in some places, but a bottle of maple extract is easy to tuck in your luggage on a trip to the US or Canada. It makes a spread that's great on pancakes, muffins, toast, English muffins, and bagels.

Total Time: 10 minutes

2 cups packed brown sugar
½ cup flour
1 cup milk
2 tablespoons butter or margarine
1 teaspoon maple extract

Breakfast and Brunch

In a medium saucepan over low heat, combine the brown sugar, flour, milk, and butter. Cook, stirring constantly, until the butter is totally melted and the mixture is smooth and thick. Remove from the heat and stir in the maple extract. Use at once or store in the refrigerator.

Cream Cheese and Jam Breakfast Spread   Makes about 2¼ cups

8 ounces cream cheese, softened (regular or light)
1 cup butter or margarine, softened
4 to 6 tablespoons jam (any kind), or to taste

In a small bowl cream together the cream cheese and butter using the back of a spoon until it is well mixed. (The softer the cream cheese and butter, the easier it will be to mix them.) Add the jam to your taste. Use at once or store in the refrigerator.

Banana-Peanut Spread   Makes about 1¼ cups

A good way to use over-ripe bananas! Use on toast, bagels, English muffins—whatever.

2 large bananas
⅛ cup peanut butter
1 teaspoon honey
⅛ cup raisins

Mash the bananas in a medium bowl. Add the peanut butter, honey, and raisins and mix well. Use at once. Although this can be stored in the refrigerator for a short time, the mashed bananas quickly lose their texture.

Cranberry-Orange Spread   Makes a little over 2 cups

8 ounces cream cheese, softened
½ cup dried cranberries
¼ cup orange marmalade OR ¼ orange, peeled, seeded, and diced
½ cup chopped pecans or walnuts

In a medium bowl, thoroughly mix all the ingredients. Store in the refrigerator, but let it come to room temperature before spreading.

Date-Orange Spread   Makes about 1½ cups

1 cup chopped dates or raisins
2 tablespoons orange juice
½ teaspoon ground cinnamon
dash of salt
4 ounces cream cheese, softened

In a medium bowl combine all the ingredients until well blended. Refrigerate any unused portion.

Fruit and Cheese Spread   Makes about 1 cup

3 dried figs or other dried fruit, such as raisins or chopped dates or apricots
2 tablespoons shelled sunflower seeds or other nuts
4 ounces cream cheese, softened
1 teaspoon honey

1. Chop the figs and sunflower seeds into small pieces.
2. Mix together the cream cheese and honey until smooth. Stir in the figs and seeds.

Store in the refrigerator, but bring to room temperature before spreading.

Honey Walnut Cream Cheese Spread   Makes about 1½ cups

Total Time: 5 minutes

8 ounces cream cheese, softened
2 tablespoons honey
2 tablespoons brown sugar or white sugar
1 teaspoon vanilla extract
dash of ground cinnamon
2 tablespoons finely chopped walnuts or pecans

In a small bowl combine the cream cheese and honey until completely mixed. Add the sugar, vanilla, cinnamon, and nuts and mix well. Store in the refrigerator, but bring to room temperature before spreading.

Pineapple Spread

Makes a little less than 3 cups

Wonderful on bran bread and raisin toast.

Total Time: 5 minutes

8 ounces cream cheese, softened
1 can (8 ounces) crushed pineapple, drained,
 OR 1 cup diced fresh pineapple
½ cup chopped pecans or walnuts
⅓ cup packed brown sugar or white sugar

Combine all the ingredients and mix well. Store in the refrigerator.

BREAKFAST AND BRUNCH RECIPES IN OTHER CHAPTERS

Here are additional breakfast and brunch recipes in other chapters.

Beverages
Several ways to make coffee, *pages 88–89*
Specialty Coffee Mixes, *page 89*

Appetizers and Snacks
Chewy Granola Bars, *page 144*
Fruity Energy Bars, *page 144*
Vanilla Granola, *page 145*
No-Bake, No-Refrigerator Granola Bars, *page 145*
Choco-Peanut Butter-Oatmeal Energy Bars, *page 146*

Sauces, Gravies, Marinades, and Rubs
Sausage Gravy, *page 222*

Canned Meats and Seafood
Corned Beef Omelet, *page 316*
Corned Beef Scramble, *page 317*
Corned Beef Hash with Eggs, *page 318*
Crustless Hash Quiche, *page 319*
Crab and Mushroom Quiche, *page 324*

Holiday Cheer
Hot Cross Buns, *page 368*

Quick Breads
Various Biscuits, *page 376*
Any of the muffins, *page 378*
Healthier Banana Bread, *page 382*
Banana Bread, *page 383*
Pumpkin Bread, *page 383*
Zucchini and/or Carrot Bread, *page 383*
Healthier Zucchini and/or Carrot Bread, *page 384*

Yeast Breads
Almost all the breads are great sliced or for toast,
 pages 392–395
Cinnamon-Raisin Coffee Cake, *page 401*
Totally Decadent Cinnamon Rolls, *page 402*

Breakfast and Brunch

APPETIZERS AND SNACKS

Appetizers are an essential part of cruising, whether you're socializing or relaxing. We're active enough that we want a snack in the late afternoon. It's a chance to relax, sit in the cockpit, and enjoy the beauty of an anchorage. Here, we've put together more than 75 appetizer and snack recipes, from very simple appetizers to those suitable for major celebrations, and several bar-type snacks that you can take on hikes.

Although we've included approximate servings on each recipe, the actual number of servings will vary, depending on what else is served, how active the group has been, whether they had a big lunch, whether this is their favorite snack, etc. For dips, we've simply listed how many cups the recipe will make.

If you need a quick appetizer, look at the Five-Minute Appetizers list on page 84.

WHAT TO DIP?

Many appetizers are dips or spreads. In addition to the traditional chips and crackers, there are lots of things that can be served with a dip or spread—and most are easier to store than a bag of potato chips!

- Vegetables, cut into bite-size pieces
- Corn chips, which are sometimes sold as 6-inch rounds that you break into chip-size pieces
- Bread or pita bread, torn or cut into bite-size pieces

Tortilla Chips   Makes any number

Total Time: 15 minutes

flour or corn tortillas (each medium tortilla will make 8 chips)
cooking spray
salt (coarse salt like margarita salt works well, but you can use any kind)

1. Preheat oven to 350°F.
2. Cut each tortilla into quarters and then each quarter in half again. Place in a single layer on a baking sheet or a piece of aluminum foil. Spray with cooking spray and sprinkle liberally with salt.
3. Bake for about 10 minutes, or until golden brown and crunchy. The exact time will vary with how moist the tortillas are. Watch carefully so they don't burn!

MEXICAN DIPS, SALSAS, AND GUACAMOLE

Make these as spicy (or not) as you wish!

5-Layer Dip   Serves 8 to 10

You can omit almost anything except the refried bean layer and still have a good dip.

Total Time: 10 minutes

1 can (16 ounces) refried beans
1 tablespoon chili powder
1/2 teaspoon ground cumin
1 cup sour cream (page 99), plain yogurt (page 101), or mayonnaise
1 cup shredded cheddar, Monterey Jack, or similar cheese
1 tomato, chopped
3 green onions, including tops, sliced
black olives, sliced or whole (optional)

Combine the refried beans, chili powder, and cumin; mix well. Spread the mixture on a serving plate (a dinner plate or a pie plate works well). Top with layers in this order: sour cream, cheese, tomato, and green onion. Garnish with the olives, if desired. Serve with tortilla chips or crackers.

Mexican Casserole Dip   Serves 10

This also works well without baking and takes only 15 to 20 minutes to put together!

Total Time: 1 hour, 15 minutes
Prep Time: 20 minutes   **Bake Time:** 50 minutes

1 can (16 ounces) corn, drained
1 can (16 ounces) black beans, rinsed and drained, OR Recipe-Ready Beans (page 176)
1 cup sour cream (page 99)*
1 jar (8 ounces) picante sauce OR 1 cup salsa (page 127) OR 1 can (4 ounces) green chilies
2 cups shredded Monterey Jack or other cheese that will melt
1 can (16 ounces) diced tomatoes and green chiles, not drained, OR 1 can (16 ounces) diced tomatoes OR 2 to 3 fresh tomatoes, diced, and 1/4 chile pepper, diced, or to taste
1/4 teaspoon ground pepper
1 or 2 green onions, sliced thinly
sliced black olives, for topping (optional)
1/2 cup shredded cheese, for topping (optional)

You can substitute plain yogurt (page 101) if you're not baking this dip. (The yogurt will curdle if it's baked.)

1. Preheat oven to 350°F.
2. In a large bowl combine the corn, black beans, sour cream, picante sauce, cheese, tomato, ground

pepper, and green onion. Transfer to a baking dish. A 10-inch or 12-inch circular cake pan works well, but you can use anything that the mixture will fit in, from an 8-inch square pan to a 9"×13" pan. With a smaller pan, increase the baking time; with a larger one, decrease the time.
3. Cover the dip with any toppings. Bake for about 50 minutes. Serve warm.

Southwestern Corn and Cheese Dip   Serves 12

This dip may be made up to a day ahead and refrigerated.

Total Time: 5 minutes

3 cans (16 ounces each) whole kernel corn, drained well
2 cups shredded cheddar or other cheese
1 can (4 ounces) diced green chilies, drained, OR chile peppers, to taste
3 green onions, including tops, sliced, OR 1/2 cup minced onion
3/4 teaspoon ground cumin
1/2 teaspoon ground pepper
3/4 cup mayonnaise*
1 cup sour cream* (page 99)

Use any combination of mayonnaise, Miracle Whip, sour cream, and/or yogurt (page 101) to make a total of 1 3/4 cups.

Combine all the ingredients; mix well. Serve with corn chips, tortilla chips, crackers, or veggie sticks.

Quesadillas   Serves 1

A Mexican grilled cheese sandwich!

Total Time: 5 minutes per quesadilla

1 flour tortilla
meltable cheese, sliced 1/8 inch thick (mild white cheese is traditional, but any type that melts will work)

1. Warm a dry skillet over medium-high heat. Place the tortilla in the pan and place the cheese on half the tortilla. Flip the other half of the tortilla over the cheese.

Appetizers and Snacks

2. Cook until golden brown, then use a spatula to flip the quesadilla and cook the other side until golden.

3. Serve warm. As an appetizer, it is often cut into 4 or 6 wedges and served with *Pico de Gallo* (page 128).

Variations: Add cooked meat such as chicken, ham, shrimp, taco meat, and/or salsa (page 127). To make with corn tortillas, use two tortillas per quesadilla—one on top and one on the bottom—because corn tortillas break when folded.

Chorizo with Dates   Serves 4

Total Time: 30 minutes

$^{1}/_{2}$ **pound chorizo or other sausage**
2 tablespoons olive oil, canola oil, or vegetable oil
1 small onion, chopped
$^{1}/_{4}$ **pound dates, diced**
$^{3}/_{4}$ **cup red wine**

1. If the sausage is in casings, remove the meat and crumble it.

2. Warm the oil over medium heat. Add the onion and cook about 5 minutes, or until translucent but not brown. Add the chorizo and cook 5 minutes more. Add the dates and wine and continue cooking until the sausage is cooked through and the wine is reduced by half.

3. Serve by placing small spoonfuls of the mixture on quarter slices of bread, tortillas, or crackers.

Chorizo and Manchego Quesadillas   Serves 10

Total Time: 40 minutes

1 teaspoon olive oil, canola oil, or vegetable oil
1 red onion, sliced $^{1}/_{8}$ inch thick
$^{1}/_{2}$ **pound chorizo sausage, cut into $^{1}/_{8}$-inch-thick slices**
10 large flour tortillas OR 20 small flour tortillas (corn tortillas can be substituted)
$^{3}/_{4}$ **pound Manchego cheese, thinly sliced or shredded, or any cheese that melts easily**

1. Warm the oil in a pan over medium-high heat. Add the onion slice and cook until lightly browned. Remove the onion from the pan, separate it into rings, and place them on paper towels to drain.

2. Without washing the pan, place it back over medium-high heat and add the chorizo slices. If the chorizo was precooked, you'll need to cook it only about 1 minute per side. If it is fresh, cook about 3 minutes per side, or until cooked through. Then place it on a paper towel to drain.

3. Lay out one tortilla on a plate or cutting board (I've found it's easiest to make one at a time and slide them into the pan). Cover with thin slices of cheese, then top with one-fifth (or one-tenth if using small tortillas) of the cooked onion and chorizo. Add a little more cheese, and finish by placing one of the remaining tortillas on top. It's important not to overstuff the quesadillas, as the ingredients may fall out during flipping.

4. Wipe out the skillet and then reheat it over medium-high heat. Carefully slide the quesadilla into the skillet. Cook about 2 minutes on the first side—or until it is golden—then flip and cook for about 2 minutes on the second side. (You'll notice that once the cheese starts to melt, it's easier to flip the quesadilla without the meat and onions falling out.) Remove from the pan and cut into 8 wedges (for large tortillas) or 4 wedges (for smaller tortillas). Repeat with the remaining tortillas. Serve warm.

Refried Bean Dip 1   Makes about 3 cups

Total Time: 10 minutes

1 can (16 ounces) refried beans
2 ounces cream cheese
$^{1}/_{4}$ **cup sour cream (page 99)**
$^{1}/_{2}$ **cup shredded cheddar or other cheese that will melt**
5 green onions, including tops, chopped
1 tablespoon minced onion OR 1 teaspoon onion powder
1 small tomato, seeded and chopped
few drops hot sauce (optional), to taste

Mix all the ingredients together in a saucepan and warm over low heat until the cheese is melted and everything is well combined. Serve warm.

Refried Bean Dip 2 — Serves 6

Total Time: 10 minutes

1 can (16 ounces) refried beans
½ cup shredded Monterey Jack or other meltable cheese
⅓ cup beer, chicken broth (may be made from bouillon), or chicken stock (page 164)
1 tablespoon minced onion
1 clove garlic, minced, OR ½ teaspoon garlic powder
2 teaspoons chili powder, or to taste

Combine all the ingredients in a saucepan and warm over low heat until heated through and the cheese is melted. Serve warm.

Refried Bean Dip 3 — Serves 15

Total Time: 10 minutes

2 cups shredded cheddar cheese*
2 cups shredded mozzarella cheese*
2 cans (16 ounces each) refried beans
1 can (4 ounces) chopped green chilies

You can substitute any cheese that will melt.

1. Reserve ¼ cup of each shredded cheese for garnish.
2. Mix the rest of the cheese, the refried beans, and the chilies in a saucepan and warm over low heat until the cheese is melted. Transfer the dip to a serving dish and garnish with the reserved cheese. Serve warm.

Salsa — Serves 4 (Makes 2+ cups)

Total Time: 30 minutes, plus 1 hour to chill (optional)
Prep Time: 30 minutes

2 large tomatoes OR 4 Roma tomatoes, diced, OR 1 can (16 ounces) diced tomatoes, not drained
½ onion, finely chopped
1 to 3 jalapeños or other chile pepper, seeded and minced, or to taste
2 tablespoons chopped fresh cilantro
1 clove garlic, minced, OR 1 teaspoon minced garlic OR ¼ teaspoon garlic powder

2 tablespoons lime juice, lemon juice, or *limón* juice
1 teaspoon olive oil, canola oil, or vegetable oil
¾ teaspoon salt
½ to 1 teaspoon ground cumin, or to taste
¼ teaspoon ground white pepper or black pepper

You can also add in any of the following:
- Finely chopped green bell pepper
- Sliced or chopped black olives
- Small can of corn (drained)
- Chopped avocado
- Sliced green onion

Combine all the ingredients and serve with chips, crackers, or vegetable dippers. The flavor is even better if you mix the salsa ahead of time and refrigerate it for an hour or more.

Black Bean and Corn Salsa — Serves 8 to 10

Total Time: 5 minutes

2 cans (16 ounces each) black beans, drained and rinsed, OR Recipe-Ready Beans (page 176)
2 cans (16 ounces each) corn, drained
2 cups salsa* (page 127)
¼ teaspoon ground cumin
1 tablespoon lime juice, lemon juice, or *limón* juice
4 tablespoons chopped cilantro, or to taste (optional)

You can substitute 2 tomatoes, ¼ green bell pepper, and 1 chile pepper (to taste), all finely chopped, and ¼ cup finely chopped onion.

Mix all the ingredients together. If a spicier dip is desired, add more cumin and some cayenne pepper or chili powder. Or finely chop part of a chile pepper and add it. Serve the salsa with tortilla chips or crackers.

Pico de Gallo
Serves 4

Translated from Spanish, pico de gallo means "rooster's beak." The origin of the name is unclear, but this is a very old and very common salsa in Mexico with many slight regional variations. In restaurants, it's as common as ketchup is in the US, both as an appetizer with tortilla chips and as a condiment for tacos and other dishes.

Total Time: 10 minutes, plus 20 minutes chill time (optional)
Prep Time: 10 minutes

3 medium tomatoes, seeded and diced
2 cloves garlic, minced, OR ½ teaspoon garlic powder
¼ medium onion, chopped fairly finely
1 jalapeño, seeded and diced, or to taste
juice from 2 *limónes* (Key limes) OR half a lime or lemon (about 2 tablespoons juice)
½ teaspoon salt
2 to 3 tablespoons chopped fresh cilantro OR 1½ teaspoons dried cilantro

Mix all the ingredients in a small bowl. Refrigerate for 20 minutes to let the flavors blend. Serve with tortilla chips as an appetizer, or as a garnish for tacos or other Mexican dishes.

Mango Salsa
Serves 6 to 8

Total Time: 15 minutes

2 mangoes, peeled and diced
¼ cup pineapple chunks (fresh or canned)
¼ red bell pepper, finely diced*
¼ green bell pepper, finely diced*
1 jalapeño or other chile pepper, seeded and finely chopped (optional)
2 tablespoons canola oil or olive oil
1 clove garlic, finely minced, OR ¼ teaspoon garlic powder
1 green onion, including the green top, thinly sliced
2 tablespoons chopped fresh cilantro
2 teaspoons *limón* juice, lime juice, lemon juice, or orange juice
½ teaspoon red pepper flakes OR dash cayenne pepper, to taste (optional)
½ teaspoon salt

*You may use all red or all green bell pepper or another mild pepper.

Mix all the ingredients in a small bowl.
Serving Ideas:
• With tortilla chips or crackers
• With Baked Cinnamon Chips (see below)
• Spread over a block of cream cheese and served with crackers
• As an accompaniment to pork or chicken

Fruit Salsa
Serves 6 to 8

Total Time: 15 minutes (plus 15 minutes to make optional cinnamon chips)

juice of 1 orange OR ¼ cup orange juice
2 tablespoons brown sugar or white sugar
2 tablespoons apricot jam, peach jam, or apple jelly
2 apples, peeled and diced*
1 pint strawberries, finely diced*
2 or 3 kiwifruit, peeled and finely diced*

*You can substitute any mix of fresh fruits.

In a small bowl combine the orange juice, sugar, and jam; mix thoroughly. Add the apples, strawberries, and kiwi and stir to mix. Make sure that the apples are well coated or they will turn brown. Serve the salsa with sweet chips or crackers, or cinnamon chips (below).

Baked Cinnamon Chips
Makes 32 wedges

Total Time: 15 minutes

cooking spray
4 flour tortillas
1 tablespoon ground cinnamon
¼ cup sugar

1. Preheat oven to 400°F. Coat a cookie sheet or other baking pan with cooking spray.
2. Cut each tortilla into 8 wedges and spray with water. Arrange the wedges in the baking pan, overlapping them as little as possible. Mix the cinnamon and sugar together and sprinkle over the tortillas.

3. Bake the tortillas for about 10 minutes, or until the edges are brown and the wedges crisp. Remove from the oven and allow to cool before serving.

NOTE: These do not store well, even in a plastic bag. Make them just before serving.

Guacamole Serves 8

Total Time: 15 minutes

2 avocados
juice of 1 lime, 3 *limónes* (Key limes), or 1 lemon
2 medium tomatoes, chopped (discard some of the seeds)
1 medium onion, chopped fine
1 teaspoon salt
2 cloves garlic, minced, OR $\frac{1}{2}$ teaspoon garlic powder
$\frac{1}{4}$ teaspoon ground cumin
$\frac{1}{8}$ teaspoon cayenne pepper, or to taste, OR very finely minced chile pepper OR a few drops of hot sauce

1. Peel and seed the avocados. Place in a bowl and pour lime juice over them. If they're soft enough, mash with a fork; otherwise, finely chop right in the bowl to keep the avocados covered in juice (otherwise, they'll turn brown quickly). Mix in the remaining ingredients.
2. Serve immediately, or cover tightly and refrigerate up to 6 hours. If you need to store longer than that, add more lime juice to ensure that the guacamole won't turn brown.

Guacamole Without Tomatoes Serves 4

Total Time: 10 minutes

1 avocado
2 teaspoons lime juice, *limón* (Key lime) juice, or lemon juice
$\frac{1}{4}$ cup chopped cilantro OR 4 teaspoons dried cilantro (optional)
$\frac{1}{4}$ cup finely chopped onion
2 cloves garlic, minced, OR $\frac{1}{4}$ teaspoon garlic powder

2 serrano chilies or other chile, seeded and very finely chopped, or to taste
$\frac{1}{4}$ teaspoon salt

Prepare as for Guacamole, above.

Creamy Guacamole Serves 6 to 8

Total Time: 10 minutes

1 avocado
1 to 2 cups sour cream (page 99) or mayonnaise
1 teaspoon garlic salt OR salt and garlic powder, to taste

1. Peel and seed the avocado. Place in a bowl. If it's soft enough, mash with a fork; otherwise, finely chop. Quickly cover with the sour cream so the avocado does not turn brown. Mix in the remaining ingredients.
2. Serve immediately, or cover tightly and refrigerate up to one day.

BEAN DIPS

Beans can be found virtually everywhere there are cruisers, and they form an excellent "base" for a variety of tasty dips.

Black Bean and Mango Dip Serves 10 + (Makes 5 to 6 cups)

Total Time: 10 minutes, plus 1 hour to chill (optional)

1 red onion or any other onion, chopped
1 red bell pepper or any other colorful sweet bell pepper, chopped
1 jalapeño pepper or any other chile pepper, minced, or to taste
2 cans (16 ounces each) black beans, drained and rinsed, OR Recipe-Ready Beans (page 176)
1 mango, peeled and chopped
$\frac{1}{2}$ can (8 ounces total) corn, drained (optional)
4 cloves garlic, crushed, OR $\frac{1}{2}$ teaspoon garlic powder OR 4 teaspoons minced garlic
juice of 2 limes OR 6 tablespoons lime juice, lemon juice, or *limón* (Key lime) juice
1 bunch fresh cilantro, chopped, OR 1 tablespoon dried cilantro

Combine all the ingredients. If you have time to refrigerate the dip for an hour before serving, the flavors will be even better. But it's still good if you serve it immediately. Serve with corn or tortilla chips, or crackers. Also good with chicken or pork.

Baked Bean Dip   Serves 10 to 12

With its ground beef and cheese, this is a hearty dip. It's great for occasions where dinner is billed as "heavy hors d'oeuvres."

Total Time: 1½ hours (plus time to make Recipe-Ready Beans if needed)

Prep Time: 30 minutes   **Bake Time:** 1 hour

1 tablespoon olive oil, canola oil, or vegetable oil
½ pound ground beef or ground turkey (may be omitted for a vegetarian version)
1 small onion, finely diced
1 can (28 ounces) pork and beans, not drained, OR 1 can (16 ounces) kidney beans, drained and rinsed, OR Recipe-Ready Beans (page 176)
1 can (16 ounces) butter beans, lima beans, Great Northern beans, or pinto beans, drained and rinsed, OR Recipe-Ready Beans (page 176)
2 tablespoons molasses
¼ cup packed brown sugar
½ cup ketchup
2 teaspoons prepared mustard
1 to 2 tablespoons chili powder
1 cup shredded cheese (cheddar is ideal, but anything that will melt works; otherwise, omit the cheese)

1. Preheat oven to 350°F.
2. Warm the oil in a skillet over medium heat. Add the meat and onion and cook until browned. Add all the other ingredients; mix well.
3. Transfer the mixture to a casserole dish or baking pan, and bake, uncovered, for about an hour. Serve warm with tortilla chips or crackers.

White Bean Dip   Serves 4 to 6

Total Time: 15 minutes

1 clove garlic, minced, OR 1 teaspoon garlic powder, or to taste
½ teaspoon salt

1 can (16 ounces) cannelloni beans, navy beans, or pinto beans, drained and rinsed, OR Recipe-Ready Beans (page 176)
2 tablespoons olive oil, canola oil, or vegetable oil
1 tablespoon lemon juice
dash of cayenne pepper, to taste
ground pepper, to taste
1 tablespoon chopped fresh sage OR 1 teaspoon dried sage or poultry seasoning

In a large bowl combine all the ingredients. Mash them together with a potato masher, or use a food processor, mixer, or blender. Serve with crackers, or veggies such as carrots, celery, and bell pepper strips.

Variations:
- Use rosemary or tarragon instead of sage.
- Add 2 or 3 sun-dried tomatoes packed in oil, chopped.
- Add ⅛ to ¼ cup black or green olives, sliced.
- Add ¼ cup chopped and toasted walnuts or pine nuts.

Red Kidney Bean Dip   Serves 10 to 12

Delicious served with veggies such as carrots and celery sticks, with olives on the side.

Total Time: 5 minutes, plus 1 hour to chill (optional)

1 cup low-fat mayonnaise
¼ cup olive oil, canola oil, or vegetable oil
1 tablespoon red wine vinegar
¼ teaspoon sugar
salt and pepper
1 cup chopped onion
1 cup chopped celery
3 cans (16 ounces each) red kidney beans, drained and rinsed, OR Recipe-Ready Beans (page 176)
¼ cup sweet pickle relish, drained

1. In a small bowl combine the mayonnaise, oil, vinegar, sugar, salt, and pepper.
2. Add the onion and mix well. Add the celery, beans, and relish and stir to combine.
3. The dip may be served immediately, but it's even better if refrigerated anywhere from 1 hour to overnight.

Red Kidney Bean Sour Cream Dip
Serves 4 to 6

Total Time: 5 minutes

2 teaspoons minced garlic
¾ cup finely chopped onion
1 tablespoon horseradish, or to taste (start with half this amount and taste)
1 teaspoon prepared mustard
¾ cup sour cream (page 99) or mayonnaise
⅓ cup sweet relish, not drained
1 can (16 ounces) red kidney beans, rinsed and drained, OR Recipe-Ready Beans (page 176)

Combine all the ingredients and mix well. Cover and refrigerate if not serving immediately. Serve with crackers.

HUMMUS

Traditionally a Middle Eastern dip, hummus is growing in popularity as a healthy dip for everything from veggies to crackers. Be careful, though, tahini in hummus actually adds more fat than most people realize! Because tahini can be difficult or impossible to find in many places, we've included several hummus recipes that do not use it.

Traditional Hummus with Tahini
Serves 12

Although a blender or a food processor will produce the smoothest hummus, you can mash the beans by hand for a perfectly acceptable dip with a chunkier texture.

Total Time: 15 minutes

2 cans (16 ounces each) garbanzo beans (chick-peas), drained (reserve the liquid)
½ cup tahini (sesame seed paste)
6 tablespoons lemon juice, lime juice, or *limón* juice
3 cloves garlic, minced as finely as possible
1 teaspoon ground cumin
salt and pepper

1. Combine all the ingredients and process in a blender or food processor until smooth. You can also use a hand mixer or simply mash the beans by hand (although the mix won't be as smooth as a commercially prepared hummus).
2. Add the reserved chick-pea liquid as needed for the desired dipping consistency, and adjust the spices to taste.
3. Great served with tortilla chips, veggies, pita wedges, or crackers.

Hummus Without Tahini
Serves 6

Total Time: 10 minutes

1 can (16 ounces) garbanzo beans (chick-peas), drained (reserve the liquid)
3 tablespoons lemon juice, lime juice, or *limón* juice
2 tablespoons reserved chick-pea liquid or water
1 tablespoon sesame oil, olive oil, canola oil, or vegetable oil
2 cloves garlic, crushed or minced very finely, OR 1 teaspoon garlic powder, or to taste
½ teaspoon ground cumin, or to taste
1 dash of hot pepper sauce (optional), to taste
salt and pepper

Mix all the ingredients and serve as above for Traditional Hummus with Tahini.

Creamy Hummus Without Tahini
Serves 6

Total Time: 10 minutes

3 cloves garlic, minced
¼ cup plain yogurt (page 101), sour cream (page 99), or mayonnaise
1 tablespoon lemon juice, lime juice, or *limón* juice
1 teaspoon sesame oil, olive oil, canola oil, or vegetable oil
¼ teaspoon salt
⅛ teaspoon ground pepper
1 can (16 ounces) garbanzo beans (chick-peas), drained

Combine all the ingredients and serve as above for Traditional Hummus with Tahini, adding extra yogurt as needed to achieve the desired consistency.

Appetizers and Snacks

Hummus with Peanut Butter   Serves 6

Total Time: 10 minutes

1 can (16 ounces) garbanzo beans (chick-peas), drained

$\frac{1}{3}$ cup peanut butter (creamy is best, but crunchy will do)

$\frac{1}{4}$ cup lemon juice, lime juice, or *limón* juice

1 teaspoon salt

2 cloves garlic, minced, OR 1 teaspoon garlic powder, or to taste

1 tablespoon olive oil, canola oil, or vegetable oil

Combine all the ingredients and serve as above for Traditional Hummus with Tahini, adding extra lemon juice or olive oil as needed to achieve the desired consistency.

Black Bean Hummus   Serves 6

Total Time: 15 minutes

1 clove garlic, finely minced

1 can (16 ounces) black beans, drained (reserve the liquid), OR Recipe-Ready Beans (page 176)

2 tablespoons lemon juice

$1\frac{1}{2}$ tablespoons tahini (sesame seed paste)*

$\frac{3}{4}$ teaspoon ground cumin

$\frac{1}{2}$ teaspoon salt

$\frac{1}{4}$ teaspoon cayenne pepper

$\frac{1}{4}$ teaspoon paprika, for garnish (optional)

10 black olives, diced, for garnish (optional)

If you don't have tahini, see the recipes above for hummus without tahini, and simply substitute black beans for the garbanzo beans.

Combine the garlic, black beans, lemon juice, tahini, cumin, salt, and cayenne. Serve as above for Traditional Hummus with Tahini. Garnish with paprika and diced black olives, if desired.

TUNA DIPS

Like chick-peas/garbanzo beans, tuna is easy to store and readily available (except in the San Blas Islands!). In any of these recipes, you can substitute canned smoked tuna, other canned fish, or even leftover fish.

Tuna and Bean Dip   Serves 6 to 8

Total Time: 5 minutes

1 can (16 ounces) white beans or other beans, drained and rinsed, OR Recipe-Ready Beans (page 176)

4 cloves garlic, minced, OR 1 teaspoon garlic powder

6 ounces tuna, drained (if you use oil-packed tuna or any other fish packed in oil, omit the olive oil below)

1 tablespoon lemon juice, lime juice, or *limón* (Key lime) juice

$\frac{1}{4}$ teaspoon ground thyme or oregano*

$\frac{1}{8}$ teaspoon dried rosemary or basil*

$\frac{1}{2}$ teaspoon salt

$\frac{1}{4}$ teaspoon ground pepper

1 tablespoon olive oil, canola oil, or vegetable oil

Or use 1 teaspoon total of poultry seasoning.

1. If you're making this dip by hand, place the beans in a bowl and mash somewhat with a spoon or potato masher. Add all the other ingredients and mix well.

2. If you're using a blender or a food processor, put all the ingredients in the container and process until smooth, or as smooth as you prefer.

3. Serve with crackers or veggie dippers.

Easy Smoked Tuna Dip   Serves 6

You can find "liquid smoke" (sometimes called "hickory flavoring") in the spice aisle or sometimes with barbecue sauces in most US grocery stores. It adds a nice smoked flavor to fish and barbecue sauces. There really isn't a substitute for it if it's not available where you are.

Total Time: 5 minutes, plus 1 hour to chill (optional)

2 cans (6 ounces each) tuna (in water or oil), drained

5 tablespoons liquid smoke

3 teaspoons Mrs. Dash or seasoned salt

1/4 cup mayonnaise, Miracle Whip, sour cream (page 99), or yogurt (page 101), or more as needed

Combine all the ingredients. Add a little more mayonnaise if needed to make a thick but spreadable consistency. Serve with tortilla chips, pita wedges, or crackers.

Cream Cheese and Tuna Dip
Serves 4 to 6

Total Time: 15 minutes, plus 1 hour to chill (optional)

1/4 cup milk, soy milk, or water

8 ounces cream cheese, softened

1/2 cup mayonnaise or Miracle Whip

1/4 cup green onion, including tops, thinly sliced, or finely chopped onion

1/2 to 1 teaspoon wasabi paste OR 1 to 2 teaspoons horseradish

dash of Worcestershire sauce

1 can (6 ounces) tuna, drained

1. Combine the milk, cream cheese, and mayonnaise until well mixed. A fork works well. Add the other ingredients and stir to combine.
2. If possible, refrigerate for an hour or more, but it still tastes good if it's served immediately.

Spicy Tuna Dip
Serves 2 to 4

Total Time: 5 minutes

1 can (6 ounces) tuna, drained

1/4 cup mayonnaise or Miracle Whip

2 tablespoons sour cream (page 99), additional mayonnaise, or Miracle Whip

1/2 jalapeño pepper or other chile pepper, seeded and finely chopped, OR hot sauce, to taste

2 tablespoons chopped fresh cilantro (optional)

Combine all the ingredients. Serve at once, or cover and refrigerate.

SOUR CREAM, CREAM CHEESE, OR RANCH DIPS

Some of the quickest and easiest appetizers often involve making a dip and serving it with crackers, chips, or bite-size veggies. Most of our dips can be made with ingredients easy to stock on board just in case you (or your spouse) invite someone to stop by at the last minute and want to serve something to munch. We've kept four or five cream cheese bricks in our refrigerator—usually lining the bottom—for weeks. Also, don't miss how to make your own sour cream, page 99.

Chipotle Cream Cheese Dip
Serves 4

Great with pretzels, crackers, or carrot strips!

Total Time: 5 minutes

8 ounces cream cheese, softened

3 chipotle chilies, seeded and finely minced (we use the canned variety in adobo sauce)

Combine the cream cheese and chilies until thoroughly mixed. Be careful to taste-test as you go. Depending on the brand of chipotle chilies, it's possible to get this dip too hot to enjoy!

Quick Veggie Dip
Serves 4 to 6

Total Time: 5 minutes, plus 15 minutes or more to chill (optional)

1 tablespoon dried parsley flakes

1 cup mayonnaise (Miracle Whip can be substituted, but the flavor is not as good)

1 cup sour cream (page 99) or plain yogurt (page 101)

1 tablespoon dried onion flakes

1 tablespoon prepared mustard

1/2 teaspoon garlic powder

1 teaspoon salt

1/2 teaspoon ground pepper

Combine all the ingredients and mix well. If you have time to let this sit in the refrigerator for even 15 minutes, the consistency will improve as the dried flakes will reconstitute themselves. Refrigerating longer is even better. Serve with any veggies, crackers, or chips.

Appetizers and Snacks

Dill Dip
Serves 6 to 8 (Makes 1½ cups)

This dip is traditionally served in a "bowl" made from a round loaf of rye bread, with chunks of bread removed from the center and used for dipping. However, you can serve the dip with vegetables, crackers, chips, or pieces of other bread for dipping.

Total Time: 10 minutes

1½ cups sour cream (page 99) and/or mayonnaise*
1½ teaspoons dried dill weed OR 1½ tablespoons chopped fresh dill (do not use dill seed)
1 tablespoon dried parsley flakes
½ teaspoon garlic powder OR 1½ teaspoons minced garlic
1 tablespoon dried onion flakes OR 2 tablespoons finely minced onion

Traditionally, this dip is made with 1 cup sour cream and ½ cup mayonnaise. However, you can make it with any combination or all of one and it still tastes great.

Combine all the ingredients. If there is time, chill to let the flavors blend.

Mustard Dip or Spread

Good as a dip or garnish for mini crab cakes, clams, or veggies, or as a sandwich spread.

Total Time: 5 minutes

⅔ cup mayonnaise*
¼ cup Dijon or other mustard (if it's particularly spicy, use less)
1 cup sour cream (page 99)*
¼ teaspoon cayenne pepper OR a few drops of hot sauce, to taste
¼ teaspoon garlic powder

You can use any combination of mayonnaise and sour cream to total 1⅔ cups. You can use low-fat versions of either, or even just one or the other.

Mix all the ingredients and serve. The dip will last 2 weeks or more tightly covered in the refrigerator.

Onion Dip from Scratch
Makes about 2¾ cups

Total Time: 45 minutes, plus 1 hour to overnight to chill (optional)

2 tablespoons canola oil or vegetable oil (olive oil can be used, but it will taste different)
1½ cups finely diced onion
¼ teaspoon salt
1½ cups sour cream (page 99)
¾ cup mayonnaise or Miracle Whip, or additional sour cream
¼ teaspoon garlic powder
¼ teaspoon ground pepper
½ teaspoon salt
dash of Worcestershire sauce

1. Heat the oil in a skillet over medium heat. Add the onion and salt. Cook, stirring frequently, until the onion is caramelized. This will take 20 minutes or longer; don't try to speed it up by increasing the heat, as you don't want the onion to become crispy.
2. Remove the onion from the heat and place in a small bowl. When it is cool, add the other ingredients and mix well.
3. If you have time, cover the bowl and refrigerate. Serve the dip with potato chips, veggies, crackers, tortilla chips, or corn chips.

Bacon and Cheddar Ranch Dip
Serves 6

Total Time: 20 minutes

1 packet ranch dip mix (page 161)
2 cups sour cream (page 99)
2 or 3 slices bacon, cooked and crumbled
1 cup shredded cheddar or other cheese

Combine all the ingredients. Serve the dip with chips, crackers, or veggies. May be made up to a day ahead and refrigerated.

Garlic Dip or Spread   Serves 2 or 4

Also good thinly spread on bread and broiled just until golden. Great with pasta!

Total Time: 5 minutes
Serves 2 (as a dip) or 4 (spread on bread)

3 cloves garlic, minced, OR 3 teaspoons minced garlic OR ¼ teaspoon garlic powder
½ cup shredded cheese (almost any type will work as long as it's firm enough to shred)
¼ cup sour cream (page 99) or yogurt (page 101)*
2 tablespoons mayonnaise

*Don't use yogurt if you'll be broiling the dip; it will either separate or curdle. If needed, you can use all mayonnaise.

Combine all the ingredients and mix thoroughly. Serve with veggies, chunks of bread, or crackers.

Tangy Dipping Sauce   Makes about 1 cup

This is also good as a garnish with almost any kind of fish. Sesame Tuna (page 339) is wonderful with this sauce!

Total Time: 5 minutes

⅔ cup mayonnaise, sour cream (page 99), or plain yogurt (page 101)
2 tablespoons brown sugar or white sugar
2 tablespoons honey
2 tablespoons lime juice, lemon juice, or *limón* juice
1 teaspoon horseradish OR ½ teaspoon wasabi paste, or to taste
dash of hot sauce or cayenne pepper, to taste (optional)

Combine all the ingredients. Serve with veggies.

Broccoli Dip   Serves 8

This is most often served heated, but on a hot day, it's great cold!

Total Time for Hot: 35 minutes (10 minutes prep, 25 minutes baking)
Total Time for Cold: 10 minutes (10 minutes prep)

1 cup chopped broccoli (raw, frozen and thawed, or leftover cooked broccoli)

¼ cup grated or shredded Parmesan cheese
2 tablespoons chopped red or green bell pepper
2 tablespoons chopped onion or green onion
1 cup total mayonnaise and/or sour cream (page 99)
1 cup shredded cheddar or similar cheese
1 clove garlic, minced

Combine all the ingredients in a small bowl. To serve hot, bake in a small pan (a pie plate works well) at 325°F for 25 minutes (no need to preheat oven). It's also good just as is. Serve with tortilla chips, corn chips, or crackers.

Beer Cheese Dip   Serves 6 to 8

Total Time: 10 minutes, plus 1 hour to overnight to chill (optional)

8 ounces cream cheese, softened
1½ tablespoons ranch dressing mix (page 161)
1 cup shredded cheddar or other cheese
1 green onion top, chopped
¼ cup beer (dark, light, or even non-alcoholic)

In a bowl combine the cream cheese and ranch dressing mix. Stir in the cheddar cheese, green onion, and beer. Serve at once, or cover the bowl and refrigerate overnight. The dip is good with crackers, pita wedges, chunks of rye bread, or veggies such as carrots, celery, or green bell pepper strips.

Crab Dip   Serves 6 to 8

Total Time: 5 minutes

8 ounces cream cheese, softened
¼ cup butter, softened (optional)
6 ounces crabmeat (fresh—cook first, frozen—thaw first, or canned—drain first)
Jan's seasonings: garlic powder, salt, pepper, hot sauce
Carolyn's seasonings: Old Bay Seasoning (page 48), dash of Worcestershire sauce, onion powder

Combine the cream cheese, butter, and crab. Season to taste. (We each use different combinations, and your tastes may vary from either of ours.) Serve with crackers, or breadsticks sliced lengthwise and toasted.

Clam Dip
Serves 6

Total Time: 5 minutes

8 ounces cream cheese, softened
1 can (10 to 15 ounces) clams, drained and
    chopped (reserve 1/4 cup juice) OR 12 clams,
    steamed (reserve 1/4 cup of the water they were
    steamed in), shucked, and chopped (page 239)
1 clove garlic, minced, OR 1/4 teaspoon garlic
    powder
2 teaspoons lemon juice, lime juice, or *limón* juice
1 1/2 teaspoons Worcestershire sauce
1/2 teaspoon salt
ground pepper

Mash the cream cheese in a bowl so that it can be
worked. Add the reserved clam juice, garlic, lemon
juice, Worcestershire, salt, and pepper; mix well. Add
the clams, and mix just enough to incorporate. Serve
with tortilla chips or crackers.

Tzatziki
Makes about 2 cups

A Greek cucumber and yogurt dip, tzatziki *works well
both as a dip for veggies such as carrots and celery or flavorful whole-grain crackers, and as a sauce for gyros and
other Greek dishes—or even burgers.*

Total Time: 10 minutes, plus 1 hour to chill
    (optional)

1 cucumber
1 cup plain yogurt (traditional) (page 101), sour
    cream (page 99), or mayonnaise
1 clove garlic, crushed, OR 1/4 teaspoon garlic
    powder
1 tablespoon chopped fresh mint (you can substi-
    tute dill, parsley, or cilantro, or even omit the
    herbs)*
1/2 teaspoon lemon juice, lime juice, or *limón* juice
1/4 teaspoon ground white pepper or black pepper

*Mint is the traditional flavoring, but it can be difficult
    to find in some places. The other herbs will give the
    tzatziki a slightly different flavor.*

1. Wash, peel, seed, and grate the cucumber. Place it
    in a sieve or several layers of towel, squeeze gently,
    and remove as much moisture as possible.

2. Place the cucumber in a bowl with all the other
    ingredients and mix well. If possible, refrigerate for
    an hour before serving to let the flavors blend.

Sweet and Spicy Spread
Serves 8

Total Time: 5 minutes

8 ounces cream cheese
3/4 cup apricot preserves or jam
3/4 cup peach preserves or jam
1/4 cup horseradish OR 1 tablespoon prepared
    wasabi, or to taste
1 teaspoon ground pepper
1/2 teaspoon prepared mustard

1. Place the cream cheese on a serving plate. I usually
    just lay down the block, but you can also spread it
    over the plate.
2. Combine the remaining ingredients in a small bowl
    and spread the mixture over the cream cheese.
    Serve with crackers.

Green Olive Anchovy Dip
Serves 4

*This recipe came about when a cruising friend sent her
husband to the store for olives. He returned with 20 cans
of green olives stuffed with anchovies!*

Total Time: 5 minutes, plus 1 hour or more to chill
    (optional)

1 can (10 ounces) green olives stuffed with ancho-
    vies, drained (reserve the liquid) and chopped
8 ounces cream cheese, softened
1/2 cup sour cream (page 99) or yogurt (page 101)
hot sauce, to taste
ground pepper, to taste

Combine all the ingredients. Add a few drops of the
reserved olive juice to make the desired dipping consistency. If possible, chill a few hours to let the flavors
blend. Serve with crackers, warm bread, or carrot/
cucumber sticks.

Appetizers and Snacks

Sour Cream Dip for Fruit   Serves 4

This makes a great dessert as well as a good appetizer.

Total Time: 5 minutes

1 cup sour cream (page 99) or yogurt (page 101)
2 tablespoons brown sugar, white sugar, or honey
½ teaspoon vanilla extract, rum, Homemade
    Kahlua (page 96), or Homemade Amaretto
    (page 96)

Combine all the ingredients in a small bowl. Serve
with bite-size chunks of fruit and toothpicks for
skewering. The dip can be made up to a day ahead
and refrigerated.

Reuben Dip   Serves 6 to 8

*Great with green beer (page 371) for a St. Patrick's Day
party! But you don't have to save it for just once a year. If
you like Reuben sandwiches (one of my favorites), you'll
love this dip!*

Total Time: 20 minutes
Prep Time: 10 minutes   **Bake Time:** 10 minutes

⅔ cup shredded Swiss cheese or other meltable
    cheese
1 can (12 ounces) corned beef
¾ cup sauerkraut, well drained
¾ cup mayonnaise or Miracle Whip
⅓ cup Thousand Island dressing (page 162)
2 tablespoons horseradish or prepared wasabi, or
    to taste
⅛ teaspoon ground pepper

1. Preheat oven to 400°F.
2. Reserve a little of the cheese for topping. Mash
   the corned beef in a bowl, then add all the other
   ingredients and mix well. Spread the mixture in a
   pie pan or similar-size baking dish. Top with the
   reserved cheese.
3. Bake for 10 minutes, or until the cheese is melted
   and the mixture is bubbling. Serve as a dip with
   crackers, tortilla chips, or pita bits. Or spread it
   on bread or toast that has been cut into bite-size
   pieces. Or serve it in a rye bowl (page 393 and see
   variation for next recipe).

Creamy Corned Beef Dip   Makes 3 to 5 cups

Total Time: 5 minutes

1 can (12 ounces) corned beef
2 to 4 cups total of mayonnaise and/or sour cream
    (page 99) (Miracle Whip is not as satisfactory
    but can be used)
1 to 2 tablespoons finely minced onion OR
    1 teaspoon onion powder
½ teaspoon Worcestershire sauce
½ teaspoon garlic powder

Mash the corned beef in a bowl. Add all the other
ingredients and mix well. If desired, you may refrigerate this dip for up to two days. Serve with crackers,
tortilla chips, or chunks of bread.

Variation: Serve in a bread bowl (rye is really good). To
make a bread bowl, start with an unsliced loaf and tear
bite-size pieces out of the top so that what's left can
serve as a bowl. Arrange the torn-out pieces around
the bowl to use as dippers. When all the torn-out
pieces are gone, start tearing pieces from the "bowl."

Chili Dip   Serves 6 to 8

Total Time: 20 minutes

2 cups leftover chili (page 169) OR 1 can
    (16 ounces) chili
1 cup sour cream (page 99)
1½ cups shredded cheddar or other cheese that
    will melt
1 tomato, chopped, OR ½ cup salsa OR ½ cup
    canned diced tomatoes
¼ cup finely chopped onion or green onion
sliced black olives, for garnish (optional)

1. Warm the chili in a saucepan over medium-high
   heat until it is warm but not boiling. Reduce the
   heat to low and add the sour cream and cheese; stir
   constantly until the cheese is melted. Remove from
   the heat.
2. Add the tomato and onion; mix well.
3. Place the dip in a serving bowl and garnish with
   olives, if desired. Serve with corn chips, tortilla
   chips, crackers, or veggies.

Buffalo Chicken Dip   Serves 8

Total Time: 40 minutes (plus time to cook chicken breasts if necessary—about 10 minutes)

2 cans (6 ounces each) chunked chicken, drained, OR 2 chicken breasts, cooked and shredded
¼ cup hot sauce (or to taste, depending on brand of sauce and personal preference)
8 ounces cream cheese (light is fine; avoid fat free)
6 ounces blue cheese dressing or ranch dressing (page 161)
4 ounces cheddar or other cheese that will melt, grated

1. Place the chicken in a baking dish approximately 8 inches square. (A loaf pan will also work, but bake the dip an extra 5 minutes to compensate for the pan being thicker.)
2. Pour the hot sauce over the chicken and mix well to coat the chicken evenly. Set aside.
3. Preheat oven to 350°F.
4. Melt the cream cheese in a saucepan over low heat. Add the salad dressing and mix well. Remove from the heat and pour the mixture over the chicken. Mix well so that all the chicken is coated.
5. Bake for 10 minutes. Remove the dip from the oven, sprinkle the grated cheese over the top, and return the dip to the oven for another 10 to 15 minutes, or until the cheese is melted and golden.
6. The dip is best served hot, but it's also good cold. Serve with tortilla chips, crackers, pita wedges, or veggies such as carrot or celery sticks.

Variation: If you can get wonton wrappers (in the US, they're usually found in the produce section; outside the US, they can be anywhere that's refrigerated), another good serving option is to mix the cheddar cheese into the assembled dip, then put a spoonful of the mixture into a wonton wrapper. Pinch the corners together over the top (use a drop of water if needed to make the corners stick together). Place on a baking sheet and bake at 350°F for about 15 minutes, or until golden brown. Serve hot.

Hot Pepper Jelly and Cream Cheese Dip   Serves 6 to 8

This is ridiculously easy and always well received.

Total Time: 5 minutes

8 ounces cream cheese, softened
1 jar (4 ounces) hot pepper jelly (red or green)

Combine the cream cheese and hot pepper jelly in a bowl. Serve with crackers, tortilla chips, or pita wedges. Also good with veggie dippers!

Variation: Use ½ cup peach or apricot jam instead of the hot pepper jelly.

Curry Dip   Serves 2 to 4

Total Time: 10 minutes, plus 1 to 3 hours to chill (optional)

½ cup sour cream (page 99) or plain yogurt* (page 101)
¼ cup mayonnaise or Miracle Whip*
1 tablespoon ketchup
½ teaspoon Worcestershire sauce
salt
1 teaspoon minced garlic OR 1 clove garlic, minced, OR ⅛ teaspoon garlic powder
¼ teaspoon curry powder (page 47), or to taste
⅛ teaspoon cayenne pepper OR a few drops of hot sauce

You can substitute any combination of sour cream, yogurt, mayonnaise, and/or Miracle Whip for a total of ¾ cup. It's fine to use just one of the four, too.

In a small bowl combine the sour cream, mayonnaise, ketchup, Worcestershire, salt, and garlic. Add the curry powder and cayenne powder cautiously as their strength varies considerably. It's also possible that you'll want it spicier. Best served with veggies or chunks of fruit.

SPECIAL APPETIZERS

These appetizers require ingredients that may be hard to find and/or take longer to prepare. Perfect for a special occasion!

Bruschetta   Serves 4

Traditionally, bruschetta is small slices of toasted bread topped with chopped tomato, olive oil, and spices, although there are many regional variations. In the past 10 years or so, the usage has changed so that "bruschetta" now often refers just to the topping mixture—probably as more grocery deli counters sell containers labeled "bruschetta," which contains just the topping and which people have come to enjoy not only on toasted bread but on crackers, tortilla chips, and anything else that's handy!

Total Time: 10 minutes

4 medium tomatoes, chopped
½ medium onion, finely chopped
1 clove garlic, minced
2 tablespoons balsamic vinegar OR 2 tablespoons red wine vinegar plus 1 teaspoon sugar
¼ cup olive oil, canola oil, or vegetable oil (olive oil is preferred)
1 tablespoon Italian seasoning (page 48)

Combine all the ingredients. If you've got time to refrigerate the mixture a bit before serving, it will improve the flavor, but you can also serve it right away. Serve with squares of toasted bread, crackers, or any other "dippers." For a special occasion, place thin slices of cheese on crackers and top with a teaspoon of bruschetta.

Deviled Eggs   Makes 1 dozen

Total Time: 40 minutes

6 eggs
3 tablespoons mayonnaise
1 tablespoon prepared mustard
½ teaspoon salt
¼ teaspoon ground pepper
Paprika, for garnish (optional)

1. Hard-boil the eggs (see page 108 for how to cook eggs without getting a green line). Peel the eggs and cut in half. Remove the yolks and place them in a bowl. Let the yolks cool.
2. Mash the yolks with a fork. Add the mayonnaise and mustard a little at a time until the consistency you prefer is reached. Add the salt and pepper.
3. Using a small spoon or spatula, replace the yolk in each egg half with the deviled egg mixture. Sprinkle with the paprika. Chill and serve.

IMPORTANT: The combination of mayonnaise and eggs makes deviled eggs an easy source of food poisoning. Before cutting the eggs, it's a good idea to wipe your cutting board and knife with a bleach solution, particularly if you use the same board for cutting meat. Once the eggs are prepared, keep them well chilled until you're ready to serve them, and don't leave them out longer than an hour (30 minutes if the temperature is over 80°F, and 15 minutes if it's over 90°F).

Killer Bread   Serves 12

This always gets raves!

Total Time: 25 minutes

1 cup mayonnaise (low fat is fine; Miracle Whip does not work well)
1 cup grated or shredded Parmesan or any cheese that will melt
1½ teaspoons minced garlic OR ½ teaspoon garlic powder
1 loaf French or Italian bread, not sliced
½ cup butter or margarine, softened or melted
2 tablespoons finely chopped fresh basil OR 2 teaspoons dried basil OR 2 teaspoons Italian seasoning (page 48)

1. Preheat the broiler.
2. In a large bowl, combine the mayonnaise, Parmesan, and garlic; blend well and set aside.
3. Cut the loaf of bread horizontally in two. Arrange the halves, cut side up, on a large baking sheet. Butter the bread and broil it until it is crisp and brown. Remove from the oven, but leave the broiler on.
4. Spread the reserved Parmesan mixture over the cut sides of the bread. Broil until the top is puffed and golden brown. Sprinkle with the chopped basil. Cut the bread into wedges and serve hot.

Appetizers and Snacks

Seafood "Pizza"   Serves 8

Total Time: 5 minutes

8 ounces cream cheese, softened
½ cup cocktail sauce (page 211)
1 can (6 ounces) shrimp, drained, OR 6 ounces
    fresh shrimp, boiled
1 can (6 ounces) crabmeat, drained
sturdy crackers

1. Spread the cream cheese on a dinner plate or in
   another serving container. (If you have to take this
   in a dinghy, it works well to make in a plastic container with a tight-fitting lid.)
2. Spread the cocktail sauce over the cream cheese,
   not quite extending it to the edge (so it looks like
   the crust of a pizza). Top with the shrimp and crab.
3. Serve with sturdy crackers that can scoop up the
   "pizza."

Baby Pizza Appetizers   Serves 15

Total Time: 45 minutes
Prep Time: 20 minutes
Cook Time: 10 minutes sauté time, 15 minutes bake
    time

1 pound ground beef
1 pound spicy sausage
1 tablespoon garlic salt
1½ teaspoons Worcestershire sauce
1 tablespoon dried oregano or Italian seasoning
    (page 48)
1 pound Velveeta cheese or shredded cheddar OR
    16 ounces Cheez Whiz
1 loaf party rye bread or sandwich bread, each
    slice cut into quarters

1. Preheat the broiler, or preheat the oven to 375°F.
2. Sauté the ground beef and spicy sausage over
   medium heat; drain. Add the salt, Worcestershire,
   oregano, and cheese. Reduce the heat to low and
   cook until the cheese melts and the mixture is a
   spreadable consistency.
3. Spread the mixture on bread and place under the
   broiler or in the oven to brown. Serve hot.

Curried Chicken Tidbits   Serves 6 to 8

Total Time: 20 minutes

2 cans (6 ounces each) chicken, drained, OR 1 or
    2 chicken breasts, cooked and cubed
1 red apple, unpeeled and diced, OR 1 cup diced
    peeled jicama
¾ cup dried cranberries (craisins) or other sweet
    dried fruit such as chopped dates or raisins
½ cup chopped celery (optional)
¼ cup chopped pecans, walnuts, or cashews
1 green onion, including top, thinly sliced
¾ cup mayonnaise or Miracle Whip
2 teaspoons lime juice, *limón* (Key lime) juice,
    lemon juice, or white vinegar
½ to ¾ teaspoon curry powder (start with
    ¼ teaspoon and add more to taste; page 47)
Party rye slices, quarter slices of bread, water
    crackers, toasted tortilla quarters, Ritz-type
    crackers, or Triscuit-type crackers

1. Combine the chicken, apple, cranberries, celery,
   nuts, green onion, mayonnaise, lime juice, and
   curry powder. The mixture may be refrigerated up
   to one day, if desired.
2. When you're ready to serve, place a spoonful of the
   chicken mixture on each rye slice and spread it to
   cover.

Bacon-Wrapped Jalapeños   Serves 12

*The spiciness of the jalapeños is tempered by the cream
cheese and cheddar, with the bacon adding a bit of crunch
as well as flavor. Even people who say they don't like spicy
food like these!*

Total Time: 40 minutes

2 pounds bacon (25 slices needed)
25 fresh jalapeño peppers
16 ounces cream cheese, softened
2 cups shredded cheddar or other meltable cheese
½ teaspoon Worcestershire sauce (optional)

NOTE: It's a good idea to wear gloves while cutting
and seeding the jalapeños.

1. Preheat oven to 450°F. If your oven won't get this hot, pre-cook the bacon in a skillet until it's about half done, and then drain.
2. Remove the stems from the peppers and cut the peppers in half lengthwise. Remove the seeds.
3. Cut the bacon slices in half. In a small bowl combine the cream cheese, cheddar cheese, and Worcestershire sauce.
4. Fill each pepper half with the cream cheese mixture. Wrap ½ slice of bacon around each pepper half.
5. Place the filled pepper halves on baking sheets, cut side up. Depending on the size of the baking sheets, you'll probably have to bake them in at least two batches. You can bake the first batch as you're stuffing the second batch. Bake each batch for about 10 minutes, or until the bacon is fully cooked.
6. Remove the peppers from the oven and place briefly on paper towels to drain any excess bacon grease. Then transfer to a serving plate. Serve warm or cool.

Artichoke Bruschetta   Serves 8

You can substitute almost any bread for the baguette. Pita or tortilla wedges and Triscuit-type crackers also work well. Or serve the artichoke mixture as a dip.

Total Time: 20 minutes
Prep Time: 18 minutes   **Cook Time:** 2 minutes

1 French baguette, cut into ¾-inch-thick slices
1 jar (6 ounces) marinated artichoke hearts, drained and chopped, OR 1 can (16 ounces) artichoke hearts in brine, drained and chopped
1 tablespoon olive oil, canola oil, or vegetable oil
1 tomato (seeds removed), diced
½ cup grated Romano, Parmesan, or other mild cheese that melts
¼ cup finely chopped red onion
2 cloves garlic, minced
5 tablespoons mayonnaise (low fat is fine, but nonfat and Miracle Whip do not work well)

1. Preheat the broiler. Place the bread slices on a baking sheet and toast lightly under the broiler. Remove from the broiler and set aside to cool. Leave the broiler on.

2. Combine all the other ingredients in a bowl. Spoon equal amounts of the artichoke mixture on each slice of cooled bread (still on the baking sheet), and spread the mixture to cover the bread completely. (If the edges aren't covered, they'll burn.)
3. Broil the slices on the baking sheet for about 2 minutes, or just until the cheese is melted and golden. Bruschetta is best when served warm.

NOTE: If you don't have a broiler, you can make this in an oven. It won't be as crunchy, but the cheese will melt and the flavor is delicious!

Artichoke Dip   Serves 8

Total Time: 40 minutes
Prep Time: 10 minutes   **Bake Time:** 30 minutes

2 cans (16 ounces each) artichoke hearts, drained and chopped (not marinated work best, but marinated can be used if you drain them well)
1 cup mayonnaise or light mayonnaise (fat-free mayonnaise or any type of Miracle Whip does not work well)
1 cup shredded Parmesan or other cheese that will melt (shredded Parmesan is better than the grated version in the green can, but the grated will still be good)

Combine all the ingredients, and place the mixture in a greased baking dish. Bake for 30 minutes at 350°F. (The oven does not need to be preheated, but it's okay if it's hot from other baking.) Bake the dip until it is lightly browned and bubbly on top. Serve with your favorite crackers.

Variations:
- Add some hot chilies.
- Substitute canned mushrooms for all or part of the artichokes.
- Add crumbled cooked bacon or diced ham.
- Add up to 2 cups chopped fresh spinach or ½ cup frozen spinach (well pressed to eliminate much of the moisture); canned spinach does not work well.
- Add some minced garlic or garlic powder.
- If you're cooking for someone who can't eat milk products at all, remove a portion of the dip before adding the cheese and bake it separately. It's not quite the same, but it's still tasty!

Appetizers and Snacks

Appetizers and Snacks

Crazy Crust Pizza

Serves 8

Faster and easier than a "true" pizza, and great for a get-together!

Total Time: 35 minutes
Prep Time: 10 minutes   **Bake Time:** 25 minutes

1 cup flour
1 teaspoon salt
1 teaspoon dried oregano
$1/8$ teaspoon ground pepper
2 eggs
$2/3$ cup milk or water
$1/2$ pound ground beef or Italian sausage, cooked and drained*
1 small onion, chopped fine*
$1/2$ cup sliced mushrooms*
$1^{1}/_{2}$ cups pizza sauce or spaghetti sauce (see Pizza in Yeast Breads, page 400, to make your own)
2 cups shredded mozzarella, pizza cheese, or similar cheese

Or substitute your favorite pizza toppings. Except for raw meats, I don't pre-cook any of the toppings, but you can if you like.

1. Preheat oven to 400°F.
2. Grease and flour a pizza pan or 10"×15" baking sheet (with sides). If your pans are smaller, use two pans.
3. Combine the flour, salt, oregano, pepper, eggs, and milk in a bowl and mix well.
4. Pour the batter into a pan and tilt the pan until the bottom of the pan is evenly coated.
5. Sprinkle the cooked meat, onion, and mushrooms (or other pizza toppings), but *not* the sauce or cheese, over the batter. Bake for 20 minutes.
6. Remove from the oven and drizzle on the pizza sauce. Sprinkle evenly with the cheese. Bake for about 5 more minutes, or until the cheese is bubbling.
7. Slice in bite-size pieces (about $1^{1}/_{2}$ inches square works well as finger food) and serve.

Sweet and Sour Meatballs

Serves 8 to 10

Total Time: $2^{1}/_{2}$ hours
Prep Time: 1 hour, 20 minutes
Cook Time: 1 hour, 10 minutes

Meatballs
1 pound ground beef
Worcestershire sauce, to taste
3 tablespoons bread crumbs or shredded bread
$1/4$ teaspoon dried oregano
1 egg
salt and pepper
1 teaspoon minced garlic OR $1/8$ teaspoon garlic powder

Sauce
1 tablespoon canola oil or vegetable oil
$1/2$ cup diced onion
$3/4$ cup packed brown sugar or white sugar
2 tablespoons vinegar (cider vinegar or red wine vinegar work best) or red wine
1 teaspoon lemon juice, *limón* (Key lime) juice, lime juice, or additional vinegar
1 cup ketchup
2 tablespoons soy sauce

1. Mix all the meatball ingredients together. Form into 1-inch balls.
2. Warm a dry skillet over medium-high heat and sprinkle a little salt in the pan. Add the meatballs; gently turn them occasionally so that all sides cook evenly. Cook until lightly browned, then remove the meatballs from the pan and set aside.
3. For the sauce, reduce the heat to medium-low and warm the oil in the skillet. Add the onion and sauté until golden brown and caramelized. Add the sugar, vinegar, lemon juice, ketchup, and soy sauce and stir to combine. Cover, reduce the heat to low, and continue to cook for 20 minutes.
4. Add the reserved meatballs, cover, and cook for 1 hour, stirring occasionally. Serve hot with toothpicks for skewering.

Southwestern Toasties
Serves 10

Total Time: 35 minutes

8 tablespoons butter, softened
1/4 cup finely chopped green onion
1 can (4 ounces) diced green chilies or jalapeños OR 1/4 cup finely chopped mild to spicy chile peppers
1 cup shredded Monterey Jack or other meltable cheese
1/4 cup mayonnaise
1/2 teaspoon garlic powder
1 loaf French bread (baguette) or other loaf of bread OR 5 flour tortillas

1. Preheat the broiler.
2. Combine the butter, green onion, chile peppers, cheese, mayonnaise, and garlic powder.
3. Slice the bread 1/4 inch thick. Spread the slices with the butter mixture. Place the slices on an ungreased baking sheet.
4. Broil about 7 minutes, or until the cheese bubbles. If tortillas were used, cut into quarters. Serve warm.

GRANOLA AND CHEX MIXES

Granola and Chex mixes are great to take along on hikes or any shore excursion. And they're always well received at potlucks or happy hour aboard a friend's boat.

Chex Mix— aka "Nuts and Bolts"
Serves 12 to 15

Way back when I was a child, you couldn't buy Chex Mix; you had to make your own. We called it "Nuts and Bolts" because the stick pretzels and Cheerios looked like, well, nuts and bolts. The first time I had it, I was about eight years old and my next-door neighbor served it instead of the usual popcorn when we came back from waterskiing. Talk about an instant hit!

Total Time: 1 hour, 10 minutes
Prep Time: 10 minutes   **Bake Time:** 1 hour

6 cups total mixture of any variety Chex, Cheerios, pretzels, bagel chips, etc.
1 cup Spanish peanuts or other roasted nuts (you can use dry-roasted peanuts, but they're not as satisfactory)
1/4 cup butter or margarine, melted
1 tablespoon Worcestershire sauce
1 teaspoon salt (more if using unsalted butter)
1 teaspoon onion powder
1 teaspoon garlic powder

1. Place the cereals and nuts in a baking pan. Combine the butter and seasonings and drizzle over the cereals, mixing well.
2. Bake about 1 hour at 300°F (the oven does not need to be preheated), stirring every 10 to 15 minutes. The mix is done when all the cereal is crisp but not browned.
3. Allow to cool completely before storing in an airtight container. If storing in plastic bags, double-bagging is strongly recommended. If the mix loses its crunch, bake at 225°F for about 15 minutes.

Variations:

- Cajun (also called Buffalo): Add 1/2 teaspoon hot sauce and 1/2 teaspoon cayenne pepper, or more to taste.
- Cheesy: Use bite-size cheese crackers or goldfish as part of the dry mix, or add 1/4 cup grated Parmesan.
- Taco: Omit the Worcestershire and garlic. Add 1 package taco seasoning.
- Asian: Omit the Worcestershire and garlic. Add 2 tablespoons soy sauce, 1 teaspoon grated ginger, and 1/4 teaspoon cayenne pepper. Add wasabi to taste (start with 1/4 teaspoon and add more if desired), or use wasabi peas or crackers. Sesame sticks or crackers are good, too.

Appetizers and Snacks

GORP

GORP stands for good ol' raisins and peanuts, and it's great on hikes and overnight passages. And it's always quickly eaten at any get-together!

Total Time: 2 minutes

raisins
peanuts (dry roasted or salted)
M&M's

Mix together roughly equal portions of the raisins, peanuts, and M&M's. Store in a sealed plastic bag or an airtight plastic container.

Chewy Granola Bars   Makes 16 bars

Feel free to vary the ingredients or their amounts. There are all sorts of great combinations.

Total Time: 40 minutes
Prep Time: 15 minutes   **Bake Time:** 25 minutes

cooking spray
1 cup packed brown sugar
1/2 cup butter or margarine, softened, or canola oil
   or vegetable oil
1/4 cup white sugar
2 tablespoons honey
1 teaspoon vanilla extract
1 egg
1 cup whole wheat flour or white flour
1 teaspoon ground cinnamon
1/2 teaspoon baking soda
1/4 teaspoon salt
1 1/4 cups Rice Krispies, cornflakes, or similar
   cereal
1 cup chopped or sliced almonds or other nuts
1 cup chocolate chips or M&M's
1 1/2 cups oats (old-fashioned or instant)
1 cup raisins or other moist dried fruit

1. Preheat oven to 350°F. Spray a 9"×13" pan with cooking spray.
2. In a large bowl mix the brown sugar, butter, and white sugar and beat to combine. Add the honey, vanilla, and egg and beat again.

3. Add the flour, cinnamon, baking soda, and salt and mix well. Stir in the Rice Krispies, almonds, chocolate chips, oats, and raisins; stir until well mixed.
4. Press the mixture into the pan. Bake for 20 to 25 minutes, or until the mixture is light golden brown. Remove from the oven and let cool.
5. Cut into bars. Store in an airtight container or a sealed plastic bag.

Fruity Energy Bars
(No-Bake, No-Cook)   Makes 16 bars

Vary the ingredients to suit what you have available. Chocolate chips or M&M's are also good additions.

Total Time: 2 hours, including 1 1/2 hours to chill
Prep Time: 30 minutes

cooking spray
1 cup peanut butter (creamy or crunchy)
1/2 cup honey
1/4 teaspoon vanilla extract
1/3 cup sunflower seeds or any type of nuts
2/3 cup dried fruit—cherries, cranberries, raisins,
   dates, apricots, or others (chop if larger than
   raisins)
3 tablespoons sesame seeds
1/3 cup shredded coconut
3 cups rice cereal (similar to Puffed Rice or Rice
   Krispies) or cornflakes

1. Spray an 8-inch square pan with cooking spray.
2. In a large bowl mix together the peanut butter, honey, and vanilla. Add the sunflower seeds, dried fruit, sesame seeds, and coconut; mix well.
3. Gradually add the cereal and mix it in. You may have to use your hands.
4. Press the mix into the pan; it helps if you spray your hands with the cooking spray first so that the mix doesn't stick to them.
5. Refrigerate until the mix is solid enough to cut into bars (about 1 1/2 hours).

Protein Balls   Makes about 30

These small bits of energy are delicious, addicting, and good for you!

Total Time: 1 hour, 15 minutes, including 1 hour to chill
Prep Time: 15 minutes

½ cup peanut butter
¾ cup powdered milk
½ cup ground flaxseed, chopped nuts, sesame seeds, or other seeds
½ cup honey
½ cup crushed cereal, such as Honey Bunches of Oats, Rice Krispies, or cornflakes

Add-Ins: Use one or more of the following:
⅓ cup chopped dried fruit
⅓ cup sunflower seeds
⅓ cup chocolate chips or M&M's

1. Combine the peanut butter, powdered milk, flaxseed, and honey in a bowl and mix well. Stir in the add-ins.
2. Roll the mixture into small balls and then roll the balls in the crushed cereal.
3. Place the balls on waxed paper. Chill in the refrigerator for at least 1 hour.

Vanilla Granola   Makes 6 cups

Total Time: 45 minutes
Prep Time: 15 minutes   **Bake Time:** 30 minutes

4 cups oats (any type)
1 cup almonds or other nuts, sliced or chopped
1 cup dried fruit, such as raisins, cranberries, or chopped dates or apricots
½ cup packed brown sugar
1 teaspoon salt
1 teaspoon ground cinnamon
⅓ cup canola oil or vegetable oil
¼ cup honey
2 tablespoons white sugar
4 teaspoons vanilla extract
cooking spray

1. Preheat oven to 300°F.
2. In a large bowl combine the oats, almonds, and dried fruit.
3. In a small saucepan combine the brown sugar, salt, cinnamon, oil, honey, white sugar, and vanilla. Warm over medium heat until the sugars are liquefied and the mixture is pourable. Pour the oat mixture over the sugar mixture and combine well; it may be easiest to mix with your hands.
4. Coat a baking sheet or a large pan with cooking spray. Transfer the mixture to the pan and spread it out. Bake about 30 minutes, or until golden. Stir every 10 minutes, breaking up the clumps as much as you prefer.
5. Let the granola cool in the pan. Store in a sealed plastic bag or a container with a tight lid. It will keep well for up to 2 weeks in a cool spot.

Variation: For crunchier granola, replace the oil with water or apple juice and bake to the desired crunchiness.

No-Bake No-Refrigerator Granola Bars   Makes 24 bars

Total Time: 40 minutes, including 30 minutes to cool
Prep Time: 10 minutes

2½ cups crispy rice cereal (Rice Krispies or similar)
2 cups oats (old-fashioned or instant)
½ cup raisins or other chopped moist dried fruit
½ cup packed brown sugar or white sugar
½ cup corn syrup
½ cup peanut butter
1 teaspoon vanilla extract

1. Combine the rice cereal, oats, and raisins in a large bowl and set aside.
2. In a small saucepan combine the brown sugar and corn syrup. Bring to a boil over high heat, stirring constantly. Remove from the heat and stir in the peanut butter and vanilla. Pour over the cereal mixture and combine well.
3. Press the granola into an ungreased 9"×13" pan. Allow to cool to room temperature (about 30 minutes), then cut into 24 bars. Store in an airtight container or seal in a plastic bag.

Choco-Peanut Butter-Oat Energy Bars
Makes 12 bars

Total Time: 1 hour, 40 minutes, including 1½ hours to chill
Prep Time: 10 minutes

1 cup peanut butter
1 cup honey
3 cups oats (old-fashioned is best, but any type will work)
1 chocolate bar (similar to a Hershey's bar, with or without nuts) OR handful of chocolate chips OR single-serving package of M&M's

1. Put the peanut butter and honey in a medium saucepan. Warm over low heat, stirring constantly until completely mixed. Add the oats and stir to combine; the mixture will be stiff.
2. Take the pan off the stove and let cool 2 minutes. Add the chocolate, breaking the bar as you add it, and stir just until combined.
3. Pat the mixture into about a 9-inch square pan, or you can put it into a sealed plastic bag and then flatten it out. Refrigerate at least 1½ hours, or until the mixture can be cut into bars.

MORE APPETIZERS AND SNACKS

Here are additional Appetizer and Snack recipes that are found in other chapters.

Canned Meats and Seafood
Tuna Bruschetta, *page 310*
Crab Dip or Crab Rangoon, *page 322*
Hot Crab Dip, *page 322*

Holiday Cheer
Coconut Shrimp Appetizers, *page 365*
Pineapple Cheese Ball, *page 366*
Holiday Cheese Ball, *page 366*

SALADS

If there's one food that really complements the essence of cruising, it's salad. It's fresh, natural, crunchy, and perfect for hot tropical days. Cut up a variety of fresh vegetables or fruits, toss them all together, add a zingy splash of flavor for dressing, and voila, salad.

Enjoy a salad as a side dish, or add some protein to it and have a full meal. Nuts add a tasty crunch, and cheese provides extra calcium. Think about using up leftovers; leftover chicken is great shredded on your lunch salad the next day. And don't forget grain, pasta, or bean salads. Use your imagination. The possibilities are endless.

At the end of the chapter, there are recipes for salad dressings made with common ingredients found aboard, such as mayonnaise, olive oil, vinegar, spices, and the juice of *limónes* (Key limes), lemons, or limes. Yogurt qualifies for this list of common ingredients, too, if you make your own! (See page 101.)

CABBAGE SALADS

Available everywhere, cabbage is common while cruising. Unfortunately, many cruisers (like me—Jan—when we began cruising) know only a few ways to prepare cabbage. I've discovered there are many ways to enjoy it!

Asian Cabbage Salad　　Serves 6 to 8

Total Time: 20 minutes, plus 6 hours to marinate (optional)
Prep Time: 20 minutes

1 medium head cabbage OR half head regular and half head red cabbage, all finely chopped
1 carrot, shredded
1 onion, finely chopped, OR 3 green onions, chopped
chopped green bell pepper, chopped celery, or whatever else you have on hand
1 package beef, chicken, or oriental ramen noodles, crumbled
3 tablespoons sesame seeds or slivered almonds, toasted

Dressing
$^{1}/_{2}$ cup olive oil, canola oil, or vegetable oil
$^{1}/_{4}$ cup rice wine vinegar or other vinegar, although the rice wine vinegar makes a difference in the flavor of this salad
$^{1}/_{4}$ cup sugar
$1^{1}/_{2}$ tablespoons sesame oil
ramen noodle seasoning packet
$^{1}/_{4}$ teaspoon salt and $^{1}/_{4}$ teaspoon pepper, to taste

1. Combine the chopped and shredded vegetables in a large bowl. Crumble the ramen noodles into small pieces and add them to the vegetable mixture.

2. Combine all the dressing ingredients. Pour the dressing onto the salad. Add the sesame seeds and toss well. Refrigerate for 6 hours if possible. You can serve the salad immediately, but it is much better after sitting.

Abidjan Cabbage Salad   Serves 6

Total Time: 15 minutes

4 cups thinly sliced cabbage
1 cup shredded carrots
1 cup pineapple chunks
juice of 1 lemon
juice of 1 orange
1/4 teaspoon salt
1/3 cup canola oil, olive oil, or vegetable oil

1. In a large bowl combine the cabbage, carrots, and pineapple.
2. Combine the lemon juice, orange juice, salt, and oil. Pour over the vegetables and toss together. Serve immediately, or refrigerate up to 6 hours.

Grape and Cabbage Salad   Serves 4

Total Time: 10 minutes

2 cups seedless grapes, or seeded grapes cut in half and seeds removed
3 cups shredded cabbage
1 1/2 teaspoons salt
1/8 teaspoon ground pepper
1 tablespoon lemon juice
1/4 cup mayonnaise

Combine all the ingredients and toss gently.

Cabbage Bacon Salad   Serves 4 to 6

Total Time: 35 minutes
Prep Time: 15 minutes   Cook Time: 20 minutes

1/2 pound bacon
1 onion, diced
1 clove garlic, minced
1/2 cup tarragon vinegar or other vinegar
1 medium head cabbage, shredded

1. Fry the bacon in a skillet over medium heat. Remove from the pan, crumble, and set aside.
2. Add the chopped onion and garlic to the bacon fat in the pan and cook until browned. Add the vinegar and bring to a simmer.
3. Add the cabbage and reserved bacon; stir to combine. Sauté briefly and serve warm.

Ham-Coleslaw Salad   Serves 4 to 6

Total Time: 10 minutes

1/2 cup sour cream (page 99) or yogurt (page 101)
2 teaspoons honey
1 teaspoon Dijon or other prepared mustard
1 cup diced cooked ham (optional)
2 cups shredded cabbage
1 carrot, shredded
1/4 cup sliced green onion or any finely diced onion
1/4 cup golden raisins or regular raisins (optional)
1 cup pecan pieces or chopped walnuts

1. In a small bowl combine the sour cream, honey, and mustard to make a dressing.
2. In a large bowl combine the ham, cabbage, carrot, green onion, raisins (if desired), and pecans. Pour the dressing over the ham mixture and toss well.

Basic Creamy Coleslaw   Serves 6 to 8

Total Time: 10 minutes

1 cup mayonnaise
3 tablespoons lemon juice
2 tablespoons sugar
1 teaspoon salt
1 teaspoon ground pepper
6 cups shredded cabbage
1 cup shredded carrot
1/2 cup chopped green bell pepper

In a large bowl combine the mayonnaise, lemon juice, sugar, salt, and pepper. Add the cabbage, carrot, and bell pepper and toss well. Serve immediately, or cover and chill up to one day.

Salads

Basic Vinegar and Oil Coleslaw   Serves 6 to 8

Total Time: 15 minutes

1/2 cup canola oil, vegetable oil, olive oil
1/4 cup vinegar (any type)
1/2 cup sugar
1/2 teaspoon salt
1/2 teaspoon dry mustard (optional)
1/2 teaspoon celery seeds (optional)
1 head green cabbage OR half heads of green and purple cabbage, all shredded
1 small onion, minced (optional)

1. Combine the oil, vinegar, sugar, salt, dry mustard, and celery seeds to make the dressing. Stir until the sugar is dissolved.
2. In a large bowl combine the cabbage and onion.
3. Pour the dressing over the cabbage mixture and toss well.

Company Coleslaw   Serves 4

A little bit nicer than everyday coleslaw.

Total Time: 15 minutes, plus 1 hour to chill (optional)

1/2 cup mayonnaise
1 can (6 ounces) pineapple chunks, drained, juice reserved
3 to 4 cups shredded cabbage
1/4 cup roasted salted peanuts or dry-roasted peanuts

1. Place the mayonnaise in a medium bowl. Add the drained pineapple and mix well. Add just enough of the reserved juice so that the mayonnaise has the consistency of ketchup.
2. Add the cabbage and toss well. Chill before serving if possible. Immediately before serving, add the peanuts and toss to combine.

Substitutions
- Use fresh instead of canned pineapple. Or, instead of the pineapple, use mandarin oranges, sliced mango, seedless grapes, sliced apple, or cooked or canned sliced beets.
- If there isn't enough fruit juice to thin the mayonnaise, use milk.
- Use pecans, slivered almonds, or raisins for peanuts.

Apple Cabbage Salad   Serves 4

Total Time: 3 1/2 hours, including 3 hours to chill dressing
Prep Time: 20 minutes   Cook Time: 5 minutes

1/4 cup sugar
1 teaspoon cornstarch
1/2 teaspoon celery seeds
1/4 teaspoon salt
1/8 teaspoon dry mustard
3/4 cup water
3 teaspoons vinegar (any variety, but different types will produce a different flavor)
2 tablespoons mayonnaise or Miracle Whip
2 tablespoons plain yogurt (page 101)
3 cups shredded cabbage
2 apples, cored and chopped

1. In a small saucepan combine the sugar, cornstarch, celery seeds, salt, and dry mustard. Stir in the water and vinegar to make a smooth dressing. Warm the dressing over medium heat until the mixture boils and thickens slightly. Refrigerate until chilled, or about 3 hours.
2. Stir the mayonnaise and yogurt into the dressing.
3. Combine the cabbage and apple in a serving bowl and add the dressing. Toss lightly to coat. Serve immediately, or refrigerate up to 30 minutes.

Cabbage Salad with Sweet Onion and Peppers   Serves 6

Total Time: 20 minutes, plus overnight to chill (optional)
Prep Time: 20 minutes

1 small cabbage, shredded
3 bell peppers, red, yellow, or green or a combination, julienned
1 onion, quartered and sliced thinly (Vidalia or another sweet variety is best, but whatever you have will do)
1 teaspoon lemon zest*
1/2 cup fresh lemon juice or lime juice
1 teaspoon salt
1/2 teaspoon ground pepper
2/3 cup olive oil, canola oil, or vegetable oil

Salads

1. In a large bowl combine the cabbage, bell pepper, and onion.
2. In a small bowl combine the lemon zest, lemon juice, salt, and ground pepper. Whisk in the oil to make a dressing. Stir the dressing into the vegetable mixture. You can serve it immediately or store it up to 12 hours in the refrigerator to let the flavors meld.

Use a grater to grate tiny "zests" off the colored part of the peel of a lemon.

Thanksgiving Cabbage Salad
Serves 10 or more

This makes plenty for a large crowd and is great for a holiday gathering or a potluck.

Total Time: 1½ hours, including a minimum of 1 hour to chill
Prep Time: 25 minutes

2 apples, cored and chopped
1 tablespoon lemon juice
1 cup cream, half-and-half (*media crema*), or plain yogurt (page 101)
1 tablespoon red wine vinegar
2 tablespoons sugar
2 tablespoons cumin seeds
pinch of salt
dash of pepper
⅓ cup dried cranberries (craisins) or raisins
1 head green cabbage, shredded
1 head red cabbage, shredded

1. In a small bowl toss the apples and lemon juice together (the lemon juice prevents the apple from turning brown).
2. In a large bowl combine the cream, vinegar, sugar, cumin seeds, salt, and pepper.
3. Add the prepared apples and the dried cranberries. Add the cabbage, and gently mix to coat. Chill for 1 to 4 hours before serving.

Mixed Cabbage Chicken Salad
Serves 4 as a main dish or 6 as a side dish

Total Time: 2 hours, 20 minutes, including 2 hours to chill
Prep Time: 20 minutes

3 tablespoons balsamic vinegar or other vinegar
1½ teaspoons olive oil, canola oil, or vegetable oil
salt and pepper, to taste
½ head green cabbage, sliced paper thin
½ head purple cabbage, sliced paper thin
4 or 5 radishes, thinly sliced
1 cucumber, peeled, seeded, and thinly sliced
1 sweet onion, thinly sliced and slices quartered
4 ounces cooked boneless, skinless chicken breast, diced, OR 1 can (6 ounces) chicken, drained

1. In a small bowl make the dressing by combining the vinegar, oil, salt, and pepper; stir well.
2. In a large bowl combine the cabbage, radishes, cucumber, and onion. Add the dressing and toss well. Cover the bowl (or put the contents into a large freezer bag) and refrigerate for 2 hours.
3. Remove from the refrigerator, toss again, and top with the cooked chicken. Serve chilled.

LETTUCE SALADS

While lettuce is not as readily available as cabbage or other produce and is difficult to store, it's nice to have a few recipes just in case you're lucky enough to have it!

8-Hour Salad
Serves 8 to 10

Although this salad requires a tight-fitting lid and a flat spot in the refrigerator to store overnight, it is a treat!

Total Time: Overnight, including overnight chill time
Prep Time: 20 minutes
Cook Time: 10 minutes

1 head lettuce, torn into bite-size pieces
1 head cauliflower, cut into small pieces
1 medium onion, diced
2 cups mayonnaise
⅔ cup grated or shredded Parmesan cheese
¼ cup sugar
12 ounces bacon

1. In a large bowl, place a layer of lettuce on the bottom, then the cauliflower, then the onion.

Salads

2. In a small bowl combine the mayonnaise, Parmesan, and sugar to make a dressing. Spread the mixture over the onion layer in the bowl to seal the edges of the salad.
3. Fry the bacon until crisp, then drain on a paper towel. Crumble it on top of the dressing.
4. Refrigerate for 8 hours or overnight. Mix well just before serving.

Wilted Lettuce Salad with Bacon
Serves 8

This is my favorite salad from childhood. Substitute cabbage or spinach if you can't find leaf lettuce. Variations include one with no garlic. Substituting cider vinegar makes it German cabbage salad. Adding sour cream (page 99) to that makes Danish cabbage salad.

Total Time: 15 minutes

4 to 6 ounces bacon
1 or 2 onions, chopped
1 clove garlic, chopped
$\frac{1}{2}$ cup white wine vinegar, tarragon vinegar, balsamic vinegar, or other vinegar (cut the vinegar with a little water if it's too sour for your taste)
6 cups shredded leaf lettuce OR 1 head cabbage, shredded, OR 6 cups fresh spinach

1. In a skillet over medium heat, fry the bacon until crisp. Remove, drain on a paper towel, and crumble into tiny pieces. Set aside.
2. Add the onion and garlic to the pan and sauté in the bacon grease. Add the vinegar and heat until warm to make a hot dressing.
3. Place the lettuce and reserved bacon in a large serving bowl, pour in the hot dressing, and toss well. If you're using cabbage instead of lettuce, after bringing the vinegar mixture to a simmer, add all the cabbage and the bacon, toss it as you would a salad, and serve. The cabbage won't cook, but it will wilt a little.

Greek Salad
Serves 6 to 8

Even if you don't have all the ingredients to make a true Greek salad, use what you've got with this dressing. It will taste great!

Total Time: 20 minutes, plus 2 hours to chill dressing (optional)
Prep Time: 20 minutes

Dressing
1 cup olive oil, canola oil, or vegetable oil
3 tablespoons lemon juice or lime juice
3 tablespoons dried oregano
3 teaspoons minced garlic
1 teaspoon dried basil
2 tablespoons red wine vinegar
$\frac{1}{2}$ teaspoon salt
1 teaspoon sugar
$\frac{1}{2}$ teaspoon ground pepper

Salad
1 large head romaine lettuce, torn into bite-size pieces
3 Roma tomatoes, cut into wedges
1 cucumber, peeled, seeded, and diced
1 red onion, cut into slivers
1 green bell pepper, seeded and slivered
$\frac{1}{2}$ pound feta cheese, crumbled
1 cup black olives (kalamata are great, but any type work)

1. Make the dressing by combining all the dressing ingredients and whisking until smooth. Chill for 2 hours if possible.
2. Combine the salad ingredients in a large bowl. Add the dressing and toss well.

NOTE: Carolyn prefers a less oily dressing and uses $\frac{1}{2}$ cup olive oil, $\frac{1}{4}$ cup red wine vinegar, and $\frac{1}{2}$ cup balsamic vinegar. The other dressing ingredients are the same.

Salads

Diane Bakelaar's Lettuce Salad   Serves 6

This salad is named for the friend who first served it to us.

Total Time: 15 minutes

1 head romaine lettuce
1/4 head iceberg lettuce
2 green onions, chopped
1 cup chopped celery
1 can mandarin orange slices, drained
toasted almonds

Dressing
1/4 cup vegetable oil, canola oil, or olive oil
2 tablespoons sugar
2 tablespoons cider vinegar or other vinegar
1 tablespoon minced fresh parsley
1/2 teaspoon salt
1/4 teaspoon ground pepper

1. Tear the greens into bite-size pieces. Place them in a serving bowl and add the green onion and celery. Toss to combine.
2. Combine the dressing ingredients in a small bowl; stir well.
3. Just before serving, add the mandarin oranges, toasted almonds, and dressing to the greens. Toss to combine.

VEGETABLE SALADS

Because you never know what vegetables you'll find on the local farmer's truck or in the market, we have provided a variety of salads for veggies.

Japanese Cucumber Salad à la *Bruadair*   Serves 4

Total Time: 2 1/4 hours, including a minimum of 2 hours to marinate
Prep Time: 15 minutes

2 cucumbers, peeled, seeded, and diced
finely slivered onion, to taste (optional)
1 tablespoon sesame seeds, toasted

Dressing
2 tablespoons white vinegar
2 tablespoons sesame oil
1/8 teaspoon dry mustard
1/4 cup soy sauce
1/4 teaspoon Tabasco sauce

1. Combine the cucumber and onion in a large bowl. Add the sesame seeds.
2. Combine the dressing ingredients. Add to the cucumber mixture. Chill in the refrigerator for at least 2 hours (overnight is better) before serving.

Broccoli Cauliflower Salad   Serves 8

Total Time: 50 minutes

6 slices bacon
2 eggs
1 head broccoli
1 head cauliflower
1 cup chopped tomato
1 cup mayonnaise
1/3 cup sugar
2 tablespoons wine vinegar or other vinegar

1. Fry the bacon until crisp. Drain and crumble.
2. Hard-boil the eggs. (See boiled eggs, page 108, to avoid the green line around the yolk.) Peel and chop the eggs, then let them cool while you're chopping the vegetables.
3. Chop the broccoli and cauliflower and place in a large salad bowl. Stir in the chopped tomato and crumbled bacon.
4. Add the eggs to the bowl; mix well.
5. Just before serving, combine the mayonnaise, sugar, and vinegar. Stir until the sugar is dissolved. Pour over the salad and toss well.

Salads

Cucumber Onion Salad   Serves 2

Total Time: 1 hour, 20 minutes, including minimum 1 hour to marinate
Prep Time: 20 minutes

1 cucumber, peeled, quartered lengthwise, seeded, and very thinly sliced
1 stalk celery, diced
$\frac{1}{2}$ onion, very thinly sliced
4 tablespoons lemon juice
4 tablespoons olive oil
4 tablespoons cider vinegar
1 teaspoon dried oregano
$\frac{1}{2}$ teaspoon minced garlic, or to taste
1 to 2 teaspoons sugar, or to taste
feta cheese or any grated cheese (optional)

1. Combine the cucumber, celery, onion, lemon juice, oil, vinegar, oregano, garlic, and sugar. Let marinate in the refrigerator for at least 1 hour; overnight is better.
2. Sprinkle the salad with the cheese just before serving.

Marinated Zucchini Salad   Serves 4

Total Time: 4 hours, 20 minutes, including minimum 4 hours to chill
Prep Time: 20 minutes

1 pound zucchini or similar squash, washed, peeled, and sliced paper thin
1 large lemon, juiced, OR 3 tablespoons lemon juice
2 cloves garlic, minced
1 to 2 tablespoons olive oil, canola oil, or vegetable oil
salt and pepper
2 tablespoons chopped fresh basil or parsley OR 1 tablespoon dried basil

1. Toss the zucchini with the lemon juice, garlic, olive oil, salt, and pepper. Transfer to a zippered plastic bag and seal well. Refrigerate 4 to 8 hours, turning every half hour.
2. Just before serving, transfer to a bowl and toss with the basil.

Firecracker Salad   Serves 6 to 8

Total Time: 1 hour, including time for dressing to cool
Prep Time: 20 minutes   **Cook Time:** 5 minutes

Dressing
$\frac{3}{4}$ cup white vinegar or other vinegar
$\frac{1}{2}$ teaspoon celery salt
$1\frac{1}{2}$ teaspoons mustard seed OR 2 teaspoons prepared mustard
$\frac{1}{2}$ teaspoon salt
$1\frac{1}{2}$ tablespoons sugar
$\frac{1}{8}$ teaspoon cayenne pepper, or to taste (optional)
$\frac{1}{8}$ teaspoon ground pepper
$\frac{1}{4}$ cup water

Salad
6 large tomatoes, cut into chunks
1 green bell pepper, seeded and diced
1 medium onion, diced
1 cucumber, peeled and sliced, each slice cut into quarters

1. Combine all the dressing ingredients in a small pan. Warm over medium heat, stirring often, until the sugar dissolves. Allow to cool to room temperature (or refrigerate to hasten the process).
2. Combine the salad ingredients in a large bowl. Add the dressing and toss well.

If you wish to make the salad for a smaller number of people, the extra dressing will last several days in the refrigerator. It's also good on cabbage, pasta, or rice salads.

Pea and Peanut Salad   Serves 4

Total Time: 10 minutes

$\frac{3}{4}$ cup mayonnaise or Miracle Whip
2 tablespoons minced onion OR 1 green onion, thinly sliced
1 tablespoon lemon juice, lime juice, or *limón* (Key lime) juice
10 ounces frozen peas, defrosted, OR 1 can (10 ounces) peas OR $1\frac{1}{4}$ cups cooked fresh peas*
$1\frac{1}{4}$ cups Spanish peanuts or dry-roasted peanuts

If using fresh peas, bring water to a boil, add the shelled peas, and cook for about 2 minutes, or until just tender. Drain.

Salads

In a large bowl combine the mayonnaise, onion, and lemon juice. Add the peas and peanuts (ideally, about an equal volume of each) and mix well. Serve immediately.

NOTE: If you make this ahead of time, add the peanuts just before serving. They'll get soft if they're covered with the mayonnaise for any length of time.

Variation: Garnish with shredded cheese.

Carrot Raisin Salad

Serves 4

Total Time: 15 minutes, plus 1 hour to chill (optional)
Prep Time: 15 minutes

¾ cup raisins
2 cups shredded carrot
¼ cup mayonnaise
1 tablespoon sugar
3 tablespoons milk

1. Pour boiling water over the raisins to plump them. Let stand for 5 minutes, then drain. (If water is short, this step can be omitted.) Combine the raisins and shredded carrot.
2. In a small bowl combine the mayonnaise, sugar, and milk; stir until smooth. Toss over the raisin mixture and refrigerate until chilled.

Two delicious variations:

- Add ½ cup pineapple tidbits and ½ cup shredded coconut to the carrot/raisin mixture. Increase the mayonnaise mixture a bit and add a spoonful or two of the pineapple juice to add a twist to the flavor.
- Substitute craisins (dried cranberries) for raisins.

POTATO SALADS

Potatoes store easily and are readily available, making them an ideal ingredient aboard a cruising boat.

All-American Potato Salad

Serves 8 to 10

This potato salad may be made up to a day ahead; leftovers will last 3 to 4 days in the refrigerator.

Total Time: 1 hour
Prep Time: 40 minutes   **Cook Time:** 20 minutes

6 to 8 medium to large red potatoes or regular potatoes, with or without skins
6 eggs
1 large onion, chopped
3 stalks celery, chopped
2 cups mayonnaise or Miracle Whip
¼ cup lemon juice
salt and pepper, to taste
garlic powder, to taste
⅓ cup sugar
paprika (optional)

1. Boil the potatoes. Drain and let cool. Chop into ½-inch cubes.
2. Hard-boil the eggs. Let cool and then peel and dice. See boiled eggs (page 108) to ensure you don't get the green line around the yolks.
3. In a large bowl combine the potato, egg, chopped onion, and celery.
4. In a small bowl combine the mayonnaise and lemon juice. Stir in the salt, pepper, garlic powder, and sugar until the salt and sugar are dissolved.
5. Add the mayonnaise mixture to the potato mixture; toss well. Sprinkle with paprika, if desired, before serving.

Salads

Mustard Potato Salad   Serves 8 to 10

Total Time: 5 hours, including minimum 4 hours to chill
Prep Time: 40 minutes   **Cook Time:** 20 minutes

6 medium to large potatoes, boiled, cooled, then diced
3 eggs, hard-boiled and finely diced (page 108)
1 cup chopped celery
1 large Vidalia or other sweet onion, finely diced
3/4 cup finely diced dill pickle
1 1/2 cups mayonnaise
1/2 cup yellow mustard
2 tablespoons dill pickle juice
1/4 cup half-and-half (*media crema*), evaporated milk, or cream
1 1/2 teaspoons salt
1/2 teaspoon ground pepper
2 tablespoons sugar

1. In a large bowl combine the potato and hard-boiled eggs. Mix in the celery, onion, and pickle.
2. Combine the mayonnaise, mustard, pickle juice, half-and-half, salt, pepper, and sugar. Stir until the sugar and salt dissolve.
3. Gently stir the mayonnaise mixture into the potato mixture until everything is coated. Refrigerate for 4 hours minimum; overnight is better.

Variation: Use bread-and-butter pickles (and their juice) instead of dill pickles.

German Potato Salad   Serves 4 to 6

Total Time: 40 minutes
Prep Time: 20 minutes   **Cook Time:** 20 minutes

6 to 8 medium potatoes, with skin on
1/2 pound bacon
1 onion, chopped
1/4 cup cider vinegar or other vinegar (cider vinegar is best)
1/4 cup sugar
1 tablespoon brown spicy mustard or other mustard
1 tablespoon mustard seeds
1/2 cup chicken broth (may be made from bouillon) or stock (page 164)
2 tablespoons flour

1. Cube the potatoes and boil for 10 minutes, or until tender. Let cool, then transfer to a large bowl.
2. In a skillet over medium heat, fry the bacon. Drain and then crumble.
3. Add the onion to the skillet and sauté in the bacon grease.
4. To make the dressing, add the vinegar, sugar, mustard, mustard seed, and chicken broth to the pan. Briskly stir in the flour; increase the heat and bring to a boil.
5. Taste the dressing. If it is too vinegary, add a bit more sugar and stir well.
6. Add the dressing to the potatoes and toss well. Serve immediately, or let the salad chill awhile.

Oil and Vinegar Potato Salad   Serves 4

This potato salad is suitable for hot climates as there is no mayonnaise to spoil.

Total Time: 30 minutes
Prep Time: 10 minutes   **Cook Time:** 15 to 20 minutes

3 large potatoes, peeled and diced small
1 tablespoon minced garlic OR 1 teaspoon garlic powder
1/2 teaspoon salt
3 tablespoons balsamic vinegar or wine vinegar
1/4 cup olive oil (you may need a little more), canola oil, or vegetable oil
1/2 cup chopped fresh parsley or cilantro
Optional add-ins: sliced olives, diced or grated cheese, fresh mushrooms, sliced green onion tops, diced hard-boiled egg

1. Put the diced potatoes in a pan and cover with salted water. Bring to a boil and cook until a fork just pierces the potatoes (do not overcook). Drain and place in a large bowl.
2. In a small bowl make the dressing by combining the garlic, salt, vinegar, oil, and parsley.
3. Include any add-ins to the cooked potatoes, then add the dressing and toss gently. Serve warm, cool, or cold.

Salads

BEAN SALADS

Bean salads are a favorite aboard both *Winterlude* and *Que Tal* as a lunch or even a complete dinner with or without meat.

5-Bean Salad   Serves 12

Total Time: 30 minutes, plus overnight to marinate (optional)
Prep Time: 20 minutes   **Cook Time:** 10 minutes

1 can (15 ounces) green beans
1 can (15 ounces) wax beans
1 can (15 ounces) lima beans
1 can (15 ounces) kidney beans OR Recipe-Ready Beans (page 176)
1 can (15 ounces) garbanzo beans (chick-peas)
$1/2$ cup canola oil or vegetable oil
$1/2$ cup vinegar
$3/4$ cup sugar
1 teaspoon salt
1 teaspoon ground pepper
1 teaspoon dry mustard
1 to 2 teaspoons celery seeds
1 onion, chopped
1 green bell pepper, chopped

1. Drain all the beans and combine in a large bowl.
2. In a small saucepan, prepare the dressing by heating (but not boiling) the canola oil, vinegar, sugar, salt, pepper, dry mustard, and celery seeds.
3. Add the dressing to the bean mixture and let stand overnight in the refrigerator.
4. About an hour before serving, add the onion and bell pepper.

Variation: 3-Bean Salad. Omit the lima beans and garbanzo beans. Use only half an onion and half a green bell pepper. Serves 6 to 8.

Black Bean, Corn, and Tomato Salad   Serves 2

Total Time: 15 minutes, plus 1 hour to marinate (optional)

3 tablespoons lemon juice, lime juice, or *limón* (Key lime) juice
2 tablespoons olive oil, canola oil, or vegetable oil
salt, to taste
1 can (16 ounces) black beans, rinsed and drained, OR Recipe-Ready Beans (page 176)
1 cup corn kernels, cooked, OR 1 can (8 ounces) corn
1 tomato, chopped
1 small onion, chopped
2 tablespoons minced fresh cilantro
dash of cayenne

1. In a large bowl combine the lemon juice, oil, and salt. Stir in the remaining ingredients.
2. Let the salad marinate in the refrigerator for 1 hour to overnight, stirring once or twice, to develop the best flavor. Or enjoy it immediately! If you need a quick meal, add a can of chicken.

Kidney Bean and Corn Salad   Serves 4

Total Time: 15 minutes, plus 1 hour to overnight to chill (optional)

1 can (16 ounces) red kidney beans, drained and rinsed, OR Recipe-Ready Beans (page 176)
1 can (8 ounces) corn, drained
1 can (8 ounces) green beans, drained
2 tablespoons minced green bell pepper
2 tablespoons thinly sliced green onion

Dressing
$1/3$ cup canola oil, vegetable oil, or olive oil
1 tablespoon Worcestershire sauce
2 tablespoons vinegar (any type)
1 tablespoon Dijon or other prepared mustard
$1/2$ teaspoon salt
$1/2$ teaspoon curry powder (page 47)

1. In a large bowl combine the canned vegetables, bell pepper, and onion. Set aside.
2. In a small bowl prepare the dressing by combining the oil, Worcestershire, vinegar, mustard, salt, and curry powder. Blend well.
3. Pour the dressing over the bean mixture, and toss to coat. Cover. If possible, refrigerate for 1 hour to overnight.

Salads

Vegetable Salad à la *Que Tal* Serves 4

In the summer heat, Dave and I enjoy chilled salads, for lunch or with (or even for) dinner. By using some canned and dried vegetables and fruits, I can stretch my stock of fresh items considerably. To make this into a chilled one-dish meal on a hot day, add a 6-ounce can (the size of a tuna can) of ham or chicken. Drain the meat, and break it into bite-size pieces. Mix gently and briefly to avoid turning the meat into mush. Serves two as a main dish for dinner.

Total Time: 20 minutes
Prep Time: 20 minutes

1 cup cooked brown rice
1 can (16 ounces) green beans, drained
8 ounces (half a 16-ounce can) corn, drained
8 ounces (half a 16-ounce can) kidney beans,
    drained, OR Recipe-Ready Beans (page 176)
2 tablespoons chopped onion
1 medium tomato, diced
10 grapes, halved and seeded
2 tablespoons sliced almonds
2 tablespoons quartered dried apricots
½ teaspoon Mrs. Dash (page 48)
1 teaspoon sugar
1 tablespoon olive oil, canola oil, or vegetable oil
2 tablespoons balsamic vinegar

1. In a large bowl combine the rice, green beans, kidney beans, onion, tomato, grapes, almonds, and apricots. Sprinkle with Mrs. Dash and sugar, then drizzle with the oil; mix gently.
2. Add the vinegar and mix gently again. Serve immediately, or place in the refrigerator or other cool place until ready to serve. The salad will last 2 to 3 days in the refrigerator, so it's a good dish to make ahead.

Variations

- Add some diced tofu if you're trying to get more soy into your diet.
- Shredded cheese can be sprinkled over the top just before serving to increase the calcium content.

INSTEAD OF	USE
Brown rice	Any type of rice, pasta, couscous, diced potato, or barley (cooked), or crumbled ramen noodles (uncooked; don't add the flavor packet)
Green beans or beans	Garbanzos, black beans, lima beans, kidney beans, navy beans, peas, spinach (fresh or frozen), or canned or marinated artichoke hearts (all drained)
Tomato	Mushrooms, black olives, or diced avocado
Grapes	Bite-size pieces of any fresh or canned fruit
Almonds	Cashews, walnuts, pecans, raw chopped carrot, chopped jicama, or chopped broccoli or cauliflower
Dried apricots	Almost any other dried fruit, such as raisins, cranberries, or chopped dates
Mrs. Dash	Curry (page 47), ground cinnamon (use a little more sugar), chili powder/cumin mix, garlic, soy sauce, Italian seasoning, tarragon—all to taste because the strength of spices can vary greatly
Balsamic vinegar	Wine vinegar, cider vinegar, white vinegar, or lemon or lime juice (start with 1 tablespoon and add more to taste)

Salads

MIDDLE EASTERN SALADS

Middle Eastern salad flavors offer a welcome change from everyday cruising fare.

Tabbouleh Salad   Serves 4 to 6

Total Time: 2½ hours, including minimum 1½ hours to chill

Prep Time: 50 minutes   **Cook Time:** 5 minutes

1 cup water
6 ounces dry tabbouleh OR 1 box Near East brand tabbouleh
seasoning packet in Near East tabbouleh OR ⅛ teaspoon each, or to taste, ground cardamom, chili powder, ground cumin, and cilantro
1 tablespoon olive oil
2 tablespoons lemon juice
1 large tomato, diced, OR 4 Roma tomatoes, diced
1 cup peeled, seeded, and diced cucumber
½ red bell pepper, finely diced
1 green onion, finely sliced
2 tablespoons chopped fresh basil
salt and pepper, to taste

1. Boil the water. Add the tabbouleh and the contents of its seasoning packet or your own blend of spices; stir to combine. Cover and refrigerate for 30 minutes.
2. Add the olive oil, lemon juice, tomato, cucumber, bell pepper, green onion, and basil. Fluff with a fork. Add salt and pepper to taste.
3. Refrigerate for 1 hour to overnight. Fluff again with a fork, and serve.

Pita Pockets with Chick-Pea Salad   Serves 6

Total Time: 25 minutes

1 cup chopped fresh parsley OR 4 tablespoons dried parsley
1 can (14 ounces) garbanzo beans (chick-peas), drained
½ cup finely chopped green bell pepper
1 tomato, diced
1 green onion, chopped, OR 2 tablespoons chopped onion
¼ cup lemon juice

2 cloves garlic, minced
salt and pepper, to taste
¼ cup olive oil, canola oil, or vegetable oil
4 pita breads, halved, OR 4 tomatoes, cut into wedges

1. In a large bowl combine the parsley, garbanzo beans, bell pepper, tomato, and onion.
2. In a small bowl combine the lemon juice, garlic, salt, pepper, and olive oil. Toss with the garbanzo bean mixture.
3. To serve, fill the pita breads with the mixture, or serve with tomato wedges.

Mediterranean Pasta Salad   Serves 6

Total Time: 30 minutes

14 ounces penne pasta or other pasta such as macaroni or spirals
1 pound fresh green beans, trimmed, OR 1 can (16 ounces) green beans, drained
5 or 6 medium tomatoes, diced, OR 1 can diced tomato
¼ cup olive oil, canola oil, or vegetable oil
1 tablespoon lemon juice
2 cans (6 ounces each) water-packed tuna, drained and flaked
½ cup fresh basil, cut into thin strips, OR 1 teaspoon dried basil
½ cup grated or shredded Parmesan cheese
½ cup black olives, sliced (optional)
salt and pepper, to taste

1. Cook the pasta according to package instructions. Drain and rinse under cold water and allow to cool.
2. At the same time, cook the fresh green beans until just crisp-tender. Drain and cool quickly by rinsing under cold water.
3. Combine all the ingredients in a large bowl. Refrigerate until ready to serve.

PASTA SALADS

Pasta salads are delicious served hot or chilled and can serve as an alternative for lunch or be a great meal for an overnight.

Salads

Fruit Pasta Salad
Serves 6

Total Time: 1½ hours, including minimum 1 hour to chill

Prep Time: 20 minutes   Cook Time: 10 minutes

8 ounces bow-tie pasta or any other medium-size pasta
½ cup mayonnaise (Miracle Whip is not recommended)
6 ounces strawberry preserves or strawberry jam
½ cup diced red, yellow, or green bell pepper
1 can (20 ounces) pineapple chunks, drained, OR 2 cups fresh pineapple chunks
1 cup sliced fresh strawberries
2 cups fresh raspberries (optional)
½ cup shredded Monterey Jack cheese

1. Cook the pasta according to package directions. Drain and rinse under cold water. Allow to cool to room temperature as you prepare the other items.
2. Blend the mayonnaise and strawberry preserves in a small bowl. Set aside.
3. Combine the bell pepper, pineapple, strawberries, and raspberries (if desired). Add to the pasta and mix well.
4. Add the reserved mayonnaise sauce and gently toss together. Chill for 1 hour to overnight.
5. Before serving, gently mix the salad again and then top with the shredded cheese.

Picnic Pasta Salad
Serves 10 to 12

Total Time: 25 minutes, plus overnight to chill (optional)

Prep Time: 15 minutes   Cook Time: 10 minutes

12 ounces tri-colored spiral pasta, penne pasta, or other medium-size pasta
1 pound ham, salami, and/or turkey lunch meat (deli or canned), cubed or slivered
1 large carrot, chopped
1 large stalk celery, chopped
1 large green bell pepper, chopped
4 green onions, thinly sliced
yellow cheese, shredded or cubed, to taste
white cheese, shredded or cubed, to taste

Italian dressing (1 bottle) OR make your own Italian dressing (page 161), Greek dressing (page 151), or Carolyn's Vinegar and Oil Dressing (page 161)
Mrs. Dash seasoned salt or other seasonings of your choice (page 48)
Parmesan cheese, shredded or grated

1. Cook the pasta according to package directions. Drain and rinse with cold water. Place in a large bowl.
2. Add the ham, carrot, celery, bell pepper, green onion, and yellow and white cheeses. Toss together.
3. Drench with ¾ bottle Italian dressing and sprinkle with Mrs. Dash and Parmesan cheese to taste. Cover with plastic wrap or place in a large freezer bag and chill in the refrigerator, overnight if possible.
4. To serve, toss again and add the remaining Italian dressing. The pasta will have soaked up the previous addition overnight.

Potluck Pasta Salad: Add 6 ounces black olives, sliced, and 1 cup sliced almonds. Omit the meat.

HAM AND CHICKEN SALADS

The following ham or chicken salads feature ingredients that are readily available canned, if all the fresh ingredients are gone, or fresh if you just stopped at the market.

Ham Salad
Makes 6 sandwiches

Serve on bread for sandwiches or rolled up in a tortilla. Also great with tomato wedges and sprinkled with chopped fresh basil.

Total Time: 15 minutes
Prep Time: 15 minutes

1 pound ham, finely chopped
¼ cup chopped sweet pickle or sweet relish
½ cup mayonnaise or Miracle Whip
1 tablespoon chopped pimiento (optional)
1 teaspoon dry mustard
¼ teaspoon ground pepper

Combine all the ingredients and mix well. Chill if desired.

Salads

Hawaiian Ham Salad   Serves 4

Total Time: 30 minutes, plus 1 hour to chill (optional)

2 cups cubed smoked ham OR 2 cans (6 ounces each) ham, broken into chunks
1 can (8 ounces) pineapple chunks, drained, OR 1 cup fresh pineapple chunks
2 stalks celery, sliced
1/2 cup black olives, halved
1/4 cup mayonnaise or Miracle Whip
1 tablespoon lemon juice, lime juice, or *limón* (Key lime) juice
1/4 cup peanuts (any kind; we like salted to contrast with the sweet pineapple)

1. In a large bowl combine the ham, pineapple, celery, and olives.
2. Combine the mayonnaise and lemon juice; stir into the ham mixture. Chill for at least an hour if possible.
3. Just before serving, stir in the peanuts. (If you add them before chilling, they'll get mushy.)

Apple Chicken Salad   Serves 2

Total Time: 15 minutes

8 ounces cooked or canned chicken, cubed (drain if using canned)
1/2 cup peeled and chopped apple
1/2 cup thinly sliced celery
2 teaspoons raisins
1/3 cup Italian dressing (page 161)
2 teaspoons brown sugar
almond slivers, walnut pieces, or sesame seeds

1. In a large bowl combine the chicken, apple, celery, and raisins.
2. In a separate bowl, whisk together the dressing and brown sugar. Pour over the chicken mixture and toss gently to coat. Serve sprinkled with slivered nuts of your choice.

FRUIT SALADS

Fruit salad is great for a potluck or makes a delicious dessert aboard.

5-Cup Salad   Makes 6 servings

For a potluck, I usually add one can of each item specified in the recipe rather than the one cup that is suggested. The important thing to remember is equal quantities, except for coconut. Add it according to taste; we don't like a full cup, so we reduced it accordingly.

Total Time: 15 minutes plus at least 1 hour chill time
Prep Time: 15 minutes

1 cup drained fruit cocktail
1 cup drained mandarin orange segments OR 1 orange, peeled, seeded, and chopped
1 cup drained pineapple chunks
1 cup sour cream (page 99) or yogurt (page 101)
1/2 cup shredded or grated coconut
1 cup miniature marshmallows or large marshmallows cut into quarters or eighths

1. Combine the fruit cocktail, mandarin oranges, and pineapple chunks in a large bowl. Fold in the sour cream and coconut. Chill.
2. Just before serving, stir in the marshmallows.

SALAD DRESSINGS

Salad dressings can be difficult to find in certain cruising locales. Even where you can find them, bottled ones usually need to be refrigerated after opening. The good news is that it's easy to make your own from ingredients that you're likely to already have on board and don't require refrigeration. Great taste and more space in the refrigerator—a double win!

Lime Lettuce Salad Dressing   Serves 1

Make your green salad with whatever greens are available, plus any additions you have aboard, such as tomatoes, green onions, shredded carrot, chopped celery, croutons—whatever. Then dress it with this.

1 lime
dash of salt

Cut the lime into quarters. Squeeze two quarters over your salad and toss. Then add salt to taste. The salt and the lime combine to make the easiest and, at least for my palate, tastiest salad dressing available.

Almost Good Seasons Italian Dressing Mix

Makes 1 cup dry mix

Try this when you can't find the real packets.

Total Time: 10 minutes

1 tablespoon garlic salt or garlic powder
1 tablespoon onion powder
1 tablespoon sugar
2 tablespoons dried oregano
1 teaspoon ground pepper
1/4 teaspoon dried basil
1 tablespoon chopped fresh parsley
1/4 teaspoon celery salt
2 tablespoons salt

To make the mix, combine all the ingredients and store in an airtight container.

Almost Good Seasons Italian Dressing
1/4 cup cider vinegar or other vinegar
2/3 cup canola or vegetable oil
2 tablespoons water
2 tablespoons Almost Good Seasons Italian Dressing Mix (above)

Combine the vinegar, oil, water, and dry mix. Blend well.

Carolyn's Vinegar and Oil Dressing

This is a very basic vinegar and oil dressing that can be used for all sorts of things—a tossed salad, rice salad, coleslaw, pasta salad, mixed with tuna instead of mayonnaise, over almost any type of cooked veggies, and so on. Varying the types of oil and vinegar changes the flavor considerably.

olive oil, canola oil, or vegetable oil
salt
sugar or low-calorie sweetener
vinegar (balsamic, wine, rice, cider, white, flavored, etc.)

1. Combine all the salad ingredients in a bowl. Pour 1½ teaspoons oil per serving over the salad. Quickly toss the salad to partially coat everything with oil.
2. Sprinkle the salt and ½ teaspoon sugar per serving over the salad. Then drizzle 1 to 2 tablespoons vinegar (any type) per serving over the top and toss again. Serve immediately.

NOTES
- This is far less "oily" than a true French vinaigrette—and lower in calories. I prefer the taste.
- The amount of vinegar varies by whether the salad will "soak up" the dressing. Pasta and rice will, but lettuce and tuna won't. You can also vary the proportions based on your own preferences.
- You can add cheese or fresh herbs (basil, oregano, and thyme are all good) for even more variations.
- Cider vinegar will give the sharpest taste, while the other vinegars are more mellow.

Ranch Dressing

Makes 2 cups

If you need a packet of dry ranch dressing mix for another recipe, use just the spices and omit the mayonnaise and buttermilk.

Total Time: 1 hour, 10 minutes, including 1 hour to chill

1 cup mayonnaise (Miracle Whip can be used, but the taste will be different)
1 cup buttermilk OR 1 cup milk plus 1 teaspoon white vinegar or lemon juice
1½ teaspoons dried onion flakes
½ teaspoon paprika
½ teaspoon dried parsley flakes
1/4 teaspoon salt
1/4 teaspoon ground pepper
1/4 teaspoon garlic powder

Mix the mayonnaise and buttermilk until creamy. Add the onion flakes, paprika, parsley flakes, salt, pepper, and garlic; mix well. Cover and refrigerate for 1 hour or longer. Refrigerate any unused portion.

Salads

Thousand Island Dressing
Makes ¾ cup

Total Time: 10 minutes, plus 2 hours or more to chill (optional)

½ cup mayonnaise (you can use Miracle Whip, but it will taste different)
2 tablespoons ketchup
1 tablespoon white vinegar, cider vinegar, or wine vinegar
2 teaspoons sugar
2 teaspoons sweet pickle relish, chopped bread-and-butter pickles, or chopped sweet pickles
1 teaspoon minced onion
⅛ teaspoon salt

Combine all the ingredients in a small bowl, and mix well. It will taste better if it's refrigerated for a couple of hours.

French Salad Dressing
Makes 4 cups

Total Time: 10 minutes

2 cups ketchup
2 tablespoons red wine vinegar, balsamic vinegar, or other vinegar
1½ cups canola oil, vegetable oil, or olive oil (the taste will be different with olive oil)
2 teaspoons salt
1 cup sugar
1¼ teaspoons garlic powder
1½ teaspoons ground pepper
1½ teaspoons onion powder OR 1 tablespoon dried onion flakes

Combine all the ingredients in a medium bowl and mix until well blended. Or combine everything in a container with a tight lid, and shake vigorously to blend. Store in a tightly sealed container in the refrigerator.

Parmesan Peppercorn Dressing
Makes 1 cup

Total Time: 5 minutes

1 cup mayonnaise
¼ cup shredded or grated Parmesan or other cheese
2 tablespoons milk
1 tablespoon white wine vinegar or distilled white vinegar
1½ teaspoons minced garlic OR ¼ teaspoon garlic powder
½ teaspoon coarsely ground black pepper (coarsely ground pepper is much better than regular, but in a pinch you can use regular)

Combine all the ingredients, stirring with a fork until thoroughly mixed. Keep refrigerated.

CROUTONS

Croutons may not be readily available in most cruising locales, but they are so easy to make, you can enjoy them anywhere you can find or make bread.

Savory Croutons
Serves 4

Total Time: 35 minutes
Prep Time: 20 minutes   Cook Time: 15 minutes

3 hamburger buns OR 4 slices of any bread—day old is better
6 tablespoons olive oil, canola oil, or vegetable oil
1½ teaspoons seasoned salt, garlic powder, dried oregano, Italian seasoning (page 48), or any other seasoning you prefer

1. Cut the buns into ½-inch cubes. We like to cut off the crust if we're using bread, but it's your choice.
2. Preheat oven to 350°F.
3. Place the bread cubes in a bowl and slowly drizzle them with the oil. Stir to coat uniformly. Use just enough oil to coat lightly and evenly. It may take more or less than the 6 tablespoons listed.
4. Sprinkle with the salt or any other seasonings you prefer.

Salads

5. Spread the bread cubes in a single layer on a cookie sheet. Bake for about 15 minutes, stirring once. Check to make sure they're crisp and crunchy before removing, but don't bake too long or they'll be too brown.

MORE SALADS

Here are salad recipes that appear in other chapters.

Salads

SOUPS AND STEWS

On its own, with a loaf of warm crusty bread, or as an appetizer, a good bowl of soup can't be beat, especially when it's a bit cool outside.

We've included recipes for cold soups as well as hot soups so you can enjoy soup whatever the weather. Several of these soups keep especially well—warm in a thermos for that overnight passage or cold in a plastic container stored in the fridge (be sure to get the kind that seals with no leaks!) for a refreshingly cool lunch.

CHICKEN, BEEF, AND VEGETABLE STOCKS FROM SCRATCH

We use a variety of stocks aboard in a number of recipes, not just soups and stews. I even use stock as a substitute for olive oil when "sautéing" to reduce fat but keep flavor.

Basic Chicken Stock from Scratch
Makes 1 quart

Total Time: 1 hour, 10 minutes
Prep Time: 10 minutes   **Cook Time:** 1 to 2 hours

1 whole chicken or chicken pieces (bone in is best)
1 bay leaf
ground pepper
1 onion, cut into eighths

1. Put the chicken, bay leaf, ground pepper, and onion in a large pot. Cover with about 1½ quarts of water (or whatever it takes to cover the chicken). Simmer for 1 to 2 hours. The longer you simmer, the stronger the flavor.
2. Strain the stock. Ideally, line a colander with a piece of cheesecloth and strain the stock into a larger bowl. I often don't have cheesecloth and just use the colander.
3. Pick the chicken meat off the bones and save for other recipes.
4. Chill the stock. When the fat has congealed on the surface, skim it off and discard. If you don't have room in your refrigerator to chill the stock, simply leave it on the counter until the fat rises to the top. Then take a spoon and skim it off, or use a turkey baster to get the stock out from beneath it. You can also wipe a paper towel or a piece of bread across the surface of the stock to mop up any remaining fat.
5. If you have excess stock and some space in your freezer, transfer the stock to quart-size freezer bags (first make sure they don't leak!). Stock freezes well.

Variations: Consider adding dried thyme (fresh is even better), minced garlic, or chopped celery or carrot as additional flavorings.

Beef Stock from Scratch Makes 1 quart

Total Time: 1 hour, 15 minutes
Prep Time: 15 minutes   Cook Time: 1 to 2 hours

1 tablespoon olive oil, canola oil, or vegetable oil
1 pound beef bones
2 onions, cut into approximately eighths
2 cloves garlic, minced
2 carrots, chopped
2 stalks celery, cut into pieces that are not too big for the pot
2 cups drinkable white wine
ground pepper
2 bay leaves
1/2 teaspoon ground thyme

1. Warm the oil in a large pot over medium heat. Add the beef bones and cook until browned, turning occasionally. Add all the veggies, wine, and spices and cook for 5 minutes. Cover with water and bring to a boil. Turn down the heat and simmer for 1 to 2 hours. The longer you simmer, the stronger the flavor.
2. Strain the stock and skim off the fat. For specific instructions, see Chicken Stock from Scratch (page 164).

Basic Vegetable Stock Makes 1 quart

Total Time: 1 hour, 10 minutes
Prep Time: 10 minutes   Cook Time: 1 to 2 hours

1 carrot, chopped into 2-inch chunks
1 stalk celery, chopped into 4-inch chunks
1 onion, cut into large chunks
1 bay leaf
1/2 teaspoon dried parsley flakes
1/2 teaspoon dried thyme

1. Put all the ingredients in a large pot and cover with water. Bring to a boil, then reduce the heat and simmer, covered, for 1 to 2 hours.
2. Strain the stock through a colander to remove the veggie pieces. For specific instructions, see Chicken Stock from Scratch (page 164).

CHICKEN SOUPS

Chicken soup makes a great lunch or dinner choice.

Chicken Noodle Soup Serves 6

In case of sickness, it's imperative to have these ingredients aboard, or add a couple of cans of chicken noodle soup to your provisioning list.

Total Time: 1 hour, plus time to make your own noodles if needed (page 188)
Prep Time: 20 minutes   Cook Time: 40 minutes

4 chicken breasts
2 cups chicken broth (may be made from bouillon) or stock (page 164)
1 onion, chopped
2 carrots, diced
2 stalks celery, diced
2 cloves garlic, minced
2 to 3 cups dry noodles OR Grandma's Homemade Noodles (page 188)
salt and pepper, to taste

1. Cover the chicken breasts with water in a pot large enough to hold all the ingredients. Add the broth, onion, carrots, celery, and garlic. Cover and bring to a boil over medium heat. Reduce the heat and simmer until the chicken is done and the veggies are tender.
2. Remove the chicken from the pot. Remove any skin or bones. Shred the meat and return it to the pot.
3. Add 2 cups water if needed to cook the noodles. Add the noodles (2 eggs' worth in Grandma's Homemade Noodles) or 2 to 3 cups dry noodles; use more or less to your preference. Increase the heat and bring the water to a boil, then immediately reduce the heat to low to let the noodles swell. Add more water if necessary after the noodles have swelled. Then bring the water back to a boil and boil until the noodles are done, generally 10 to 15 minutes. Add salt and pepper to taste.

Soups and Stews

Chicken Tortilla Soup   Serves 8

Total Time: 1 hour
Prep Time: 15 minutes   Cook Time: 45 minutes

1 cup diced carrot
1 cup diced green bell pepper
1 cup diced celery
1 cup diced onion
2 tablespoons canola oil, olive oil, vegetable oil,
    butter, or margarine
½ teaspoon garlic powder OR 1 clove garlic, diced
⅛ teaspoon salt
¼ teaspoon ground pepper
7 cups chicken broth (may be made from bouillon)
    or stock (page 164)
1 can (15 ounces) diced tomatoes
1 can (10 ounces) diced tomatoes and chilies OR
    1 can diced tomatoes and 1 jalapeño, seeded
    and finely diced, OR 1 can diced tomatoes and
    1 small can diced green chilies
1 packet taco seasoning (page 49)
12 ounces chicken meat, cooked and diced, or
    canned chicken
10 corn tortillas, broken or cut into small pieces
12 ounces Monterey Jack, Mexican blend cheese,
    cheddar, or any similar cheese, shredded
1 cup milk
corn tortilla chips, broken into small pieces

1. Sauté the carrot, bell pepper, celery, and onion in
   the oil in a large pot. Season with the garlic, salt,
   and pepper. Add the chicken broth and bring to a
   boil. Add the tomatoes, tomatoes with chilies, taco
   seasoning, and chicken (if using canned chicken,
   add it with the milk instead of now). Add the tortilla pieces to the broth mixture. Let it boil for
   20 minutes, or until the tortillas are thoroughly dis-
   integrated into the soup. Stir the soup occasionally.
2. Reduce the heat and add most of the cheese;
   reserve enough to sprinkle on top of the soup as
   a garnish. Simmer until the cheese melts. Add the
   milk (and the canned chicken, if used) and simmer
   for an additional 10 minutes.

3. Garnish with the reserved shredded cheese and the
   broken tortilla chips.

Substitution: 1 cup masa harina (masa flour or corn
flour) for one 10-count package of corn tortillas.
Gradually add the masa flour and mix it in to the
broth. If thicker soup is desired, add more masa flour.

Hearty Chicken Vegetable Soup   Serves 8 to 10

Total Time: 1 hour, 25 minutes, including minimum
    1 hour to simmer
Prep Time: 25 minutes   Cook Time: 1 to 2 hours

1 zucchini, yellow squash, or christophene*
    (page 200), thinly sliced
1 large white onion, diced
¼ pound fresh green beans, trimmed and
    snapped, OR 1 can (16 ounces) green beans,*
    drained
1 can (15 ounces) corn,* drained
1 can (15 ounces) white hominy, drained
1 can (15 ounces) garbanzo beans (chick-peas),*
    drained and rinsed
8 whole chicken wings, split, or any other chicken
    you have (include the bones)
3 cups chicken broth (may be made from bouillon)
    or stock (page 164)
5 tablespoons tomato sauce
1 tablespoon garlic powder
2 potatoes, cubed (peeled if desired)
2 jalapeño peppers, seeded and julienned
3½ cups water
½ cup white wine

Substitute whatever veggies are available.

1. In a large pot combine all the ingredients except
   the wine. Bring to a boil, then reduce the heat and
   simmer for 1 hour.
2. Add the wine and simmer until the chicken comes
   off the bones—usually just over an hour. Remove
   the chicken bones and return the meat to the pot.
   Serve hot.

Spicy Chicken Corn Chowder

Serves 4 to 6

Total Time: 55 minutes
Prep Time: 15 minutes   **Cook Time:** 40 minutes

3 tablespoons butter, margarine, canola oil, olive oil, or vegetable oil
3 boneless, skinless chicken breasts, cubed (can use more or less)
1 small onion, chopped
1 jalapeño pepper, seeded and finely chopped
5 cloves garlic, chopped
1½ teaspoons ground cumin
1 cup chicken broth (may be made from bouillon) or stock (page 164)
2 cups half-and-half (*media crema*), evaporated milk, or cream OR 1 cup milk
2 cups shredded Mexican blend cheese or cheddar cheese
1 can (16 ounces) cream-style corn
1 can (4 ounces) diced green chilies
1 can (16 ounces) diced tomatoes, drained, OR 1 large tomato, chopped
seasoned salt or regular salt
ground pepper
hot sauce, to taste

1. Heat the butter in a large pot over medium heat. Add the chicken, onion, and pepper. Cook until the chicken is no longer pink. Add the garlic, cumin, and broth; bring to a boil over medium-high heat.
2. Reduce the heat to low, then stir in the cream, cheese (reserve some for garnish), corn, green chilies, and tomato. Stir until the cheese has melted, then heat for an additional 5 minutes.
3. Add the salt, pepper, and hot sauce to taste. Garnish with the reserved shredded cheese and serve hot.

Quick Southwestern Chicken Soup

Makes 4 servings

Total Time: 35 minutes
Prep Time: 10 minutes   **Cook Time:** 25 minutes

1 jar (12 ounces) salsa verde (green salsa) or red salsa (page 127)
3 cups chicken broth (may be made from bouillon) or stock (page 164)
3 cups shredded cooked chicken
1 can (16 ounces) cannellini beans or other beans, rinsed and drained, OR Recipe-Ready Beans (page 176)
1 onion, diced
2 cloves garlic, minced
1 teaspoon ground cumin
2 green onions, chopped, OR 1 small onion, chopped
½ cup sour cream (page 99)
tortilla chips (optional)

Heat the salsa and broth in a large saucepan over medium heat. Add the chicken, beans, onion, garlic, and cumin. Bring to a boil, then lower the heat and simmer for 20 minutes, stirring occasionally. Serve topped with chopped green onion, a spoonful of sour cream, and tortilla chips around the edges.

Soups and Stews

BEAN SOUPS

Bean soups are filling and can be used to extend your meal plan if you're short on meat.

Vegetarian Black Bean Taco Soup

Serves 4 to 6

Serve with crusty bread and a salad for an easy, filling meal.

Total Time: 45 minutes
Prep Time: 15 minutes   **Cook Time:** 30 minutes

1 medium onion, finely chopped
1 teaspoon minced garlic
1 teaspoon canola oil, olive oil, or vegetable oil
2 cans (16 ounces each) black beans, rinsed and drained, OR Recipe-Ready Beans (page 176)
2 cans (16 ounces each) diced tomatoes and green chilies OR 2 cans (16 ounces *each*) diced tomatoes plus 2 cans (4 ounces each) chopped green chilies
1 packet taco seasoning (page 49)
1 packet ranch dressing mix (page 161)
1 bottle (12 ounces) beer
hot sauce, to taste (I use medium hot)
shredded cheese, sour cream (page 99), and diced onion (optional toppings)

1. Sauté the onion and garlic in the oil in a large pot over medium heat. Add the beans, tomatoes, taco seasoning, dressing mix, and beer; stir to combine. Add the hot sauce, tasting as you add until you get the spiciness you prefer. Then reduce the heat and simmer for 30 minutes.
2. Pour the soup into bowls and top with the shredded cheese, sour cream, and diced onion, if desired. Serve hot.

Spicy Black Bean Soup

Serves 4

Total Time: 60 minutes
Prep Time: 30 minutes   **Cook Time:** 30 minutes

1 onion, diced
1 or 2 stalks celery, chopped
1 or 2 cloves garlic, minced
1 tablespoon olive oil, canola oil, or vegetable oil

1 can (16 ounces) black beans, drained and rinsed, OR Recipe-Ready Beans (page 176)
1 teaspoon dried chipotle powder or chili powder
1 teaspoon ground cumin
1/2 teaspoon salt
1 to 2 teaspoons finely diced seeded jalapeño pepper OR dash of crushed red pepper (optional)
ground pepper, to taste
3 cups chicken broth (may be made from bouillon) or stock (page 164)
2 cups water
1/2 cup shredded cheddar or similar cheese
2 teaspoons dried cilantro

1. Sauté the onion, celery, and garlic in the olive oil in a large pot over medium-high heat. Add the black beans, chipotle powder, cumin, salt, jalapeño, and ground pepper; stir to combine. Add the broth and water; bring to a boil, then reduce the heat and simmer for 30 minutes to thicken.
2. To serve, top with the shredded cheese and a sprinkling of cilantro.

Tuxedo Soup

Serves 4

We both love this soup, and it's very pretty in a bowl. Serve with breadsticks or warm fresh bread. Yum!

Total Time: 1 hour, 15 minutes
Prep Time: 15 minutes   **Cook Time:** 1 hour

1 can (16 ounces) white beans, not drained,* OR Recipe-Ready Beans (page 176)
1 can (16 ounces) black beans, not drained,* OR Recipe-Ready Beans (page 176)
1 can (6 ounces) chunk chicken or turkey, not drained, OR diced leftover chicken
1 large or 2 small green bell peppers, diced
1 onion, diced
1 tablespoon hot sauce, or to taste
2 teaspoons salt
1 tablespoon sugar
2 tablespoons minced garlic OR 1/2 teaspoon garlic powder
3 tablespoons butter or margarine (optional)

*If you drain and rinse the canned white beans and/or canned black beans, add a half cup of water to the soup for each can of drained beans.

Mix all the ingredients except the butter in a large pot over medium-high heat and bring to a boil. Cook for 15 minutes, then turn down the heat and simmer for 30 minutes. Add the butter just before serving.

Chili
Serves 2

Total Time: 45 minutes
Prep Time: 15 minutes
Cook Time: 30 minutes or longer, as desired

salt
$\frac{1}{4}$ to $\frac{1}{2}$ pound ground beef OR 1 chicken breast, shredded
$\frac{1}{2}$ medium onion, diced
$\frac{1}{2}$ to 1 cup beef or chicken broth (may be made from bouillon) or stock (page 164) or V-8 juice
1 tablespoon chili powder, or to taste depending on the "heat" of the chili powder
1 teaspoon ground cumin
$\frac{1}{4}$ teaspoon ground cinnamon (optional)
$\frac{1}{4}$ chile pepper or green bell pepper, seeded and diced, or to taste
1 can (16 ounces) diced tomatoes, not drained, OR 2 or 3 fresh tomatoes, diced
1 can (16 ounces) kidney beans, red beans, or black beans, drained and rinsed, OR Recipe-Ready Beans (page 176)
grated cheese and chopped green onion (optional garnish)

1. Sprinkle salt over the bottom of a large pot and sauté the ground beef (the salt draws the fat out of the meat, so you don't have to add oil unless the meat is very lean). If you use chicken, you will have to use a little oil or cooking spray. When the meat is almost browned, add the onion and continue to brown the meat.
2. Add the broth, chili powder, cumin, and cinnamon (if desired). Add the chile pepper, diced tomato, and kidney beans. Mix well. The amount of broth needed will depend on the amount of liquid in the tomatoes and your preference. Simmer for at least 30 minutes to allow the flavors to blend. To serve, top with the grated cheese and chopped green onion, if desired.

VEGETABLE SOUPS, STEWS, AND CHOWDERS

If you think it'll never be chilly enough to enjoy soups, stews, or chowders, you might be surprised.

Too Many Veggies Soup
Serves 8

Total Time: 2 hours
Prep Time: 20 minutes
Cook Time: 1 hour, 30 minutes

1 tablespoon olive oil, canola oil, or vegetable oil
2 stalks celery, diced
2 large carrots, diced
1 large onion, diced
1 green bell pepper, diced
1 clove garlic, minced
6 cups beef broth (may be made from bouillon), beef stock (page 165), or vegetable stock (page 165)
2 cans (16 ounces each) diced tomatoes, not drained, OR 4 large tomatoes, diced
2 medium potatoes, peeled and diced
$\frac{1}{2}$ small head of cabbage, shredded
1 can (16 ounces) green beans, drained
2 medium zucchini, diced
1 can (16 ounces) red kidney or white cannelloni beans, rinsed and drained, OR Recipe-Ready Beans (page 176)
$1\frac{1}{2}$ cups medium uncooked pasta, such as shells, rotini, or elbows
salt and pepper, to taste
Parmesan or Romano cheese, grated (optional garnish)
green onion, chopped (optional garnish)

1. In a large pot, warm the oil over medium-high heat. Add the celery, carrot, onion, bell pepper, and garlic. Cook, stirring frequently, for 7 to 10 minutes, or until the vegetables are tender. Add the broth, tomatoes, potatoes, cabbage, and green beans. Reduce the heat, cover, and simmer for 1 hour, stirring occasionally.
2. Add the zucchini, beans, and pasta and simmer for 15 to 20 minutes longer, or until the pasta is tender. Season with salt and pepper. Place in bowls

and garnish with the grated cheese and chopped green onion, if desired.

Campfire Stew Casserole Serves 4 to 6

Total Time: 1 hour
Prep Time: 15 minutes   Cook Time: 45 minutes

1 pound ground beef
1 onion, diced
2 cans (10 ounces each) condensed vegetable soup, undiluted
cooking spray
1 pound Velveeta cheese, Cheez Whiz, or any kind of cheese you have

1. Preheat oven to 350°F.*
2. Brown the ground beef and onion in a large pot over medium heat. Pour off the fat.
3. Add the undiluted vegetable soup. Stir to combine and heat through.
4. Coat a baking dish with cooking spray. Pour the soup into the dish. Top with slices of Velveeta and bake until the top of the cheese bubbles, or about 45 minutes.

To make this soup on the stove: Just add the Velveeta to the mixture in the pan and heat it until it melts. Stir and serve. It's not quite as good as baking, but it's much quicker, which is helpful if heat or propane are issues.

Potato and Ham Soup   Serves 2

This is Carolyn's version of potato soup, which doesn't require cheese.

Total Time: 30 minutes

2 potatoes, peeled and cut into large chunks
1 teaspoon salt
¼ cup diced onion
1 tablespoon butter, margarine, canola oil, or vegetable oil
1 cup half-and-half (*media crema*), evaporated milk, cream, or milk
1 can (6 ounces) ham, not drained, and broken into bite-size chunks, OR 6 ounces pre-cooked ham, diced
½ teaspoon ground pepper, or to taste

sprinkle of garlic powder OR ½ teaspoon minced garlic
hot sauce (optional), to taste

1. In a large saucepan over medium-low heat, simmer the potatoes in salted water until tender (about 10 minutes, depending on the size of the potato pieces). Don't overcook to the point where the potatoes are mushy. At the same time, in a small skillet, sauté the onion in the butter until tender.
2. Drain the water off the potatoes and use a fork to break up the pieces. You want a chunky consistency. Add the sautéed onion, half-and-half, ham, ground pepper, and garlic. Mix well and heat just until warmed through; don't allow to boil.
3. Pour the soup into bowls. If desired, sprinkle a few drops of hot sauce over each.

Variation:
• Instead of ham, use bacon (4 strips fried until crisp before adding to the potatoes), canned chicken, or almost any leftover cooked meat.

Crab and Corn Chowder Serves 6 to 8

Total Time: 1 hour
Prep Time: 15 minutes   Cook Time: 45 minutes

2 stalks celery, chopped
2 onions, diced
3 tablespoons olive oil, canola oil, vegetable oil, butter, or margarine
2 cups corn, cooked, OR 1 can (16 ounces) corn, drained
12 ounces canned or fresh crabmeat (drain if canned)
2 potatoes, peeled and finely diced
3 tomatoes, diced
1 cup water
2 cups milk
3 tablespoons flour
salt and pepper, to taste

1. Sauté the celery and onions in the olive oil in a large pot over medium-high heat. Add the corn and crabmeat and sauté for 3 minutes. Add the potato, tomato, and water. Reduce the heat to low; cover and cook for 30 minutes.

2. Add the milk. Increase the heat and bring to a boil. Then turn off the heat, sift in the flour, and stir until the chowder thickens. Add salt and pepper and serve hot.

Cabbage Soup   Serves 8

Total Time: 45 minutes
Prep Time: 15 minutes   Cook Time: 30 minutes

1 stalk celery, diced
3 carrots, sliced
2 bell peppers, diced
6 large green onions, sliced, OR 1 small yellow, white, or purple onion, diced
1 tablespoon olive oil, canola oil, or vegetable oil
1/2 head cabbage, diced
10 cups water
1 package dry onion soup mix (page 55)
2 cups beef or chicken broth (may be made from bouillon) or stock (pages 164–165)
salt, pepper, parsley, garlic powder, and/or Worcestershire sauce, to taste (or any other seasonings you like)
2 cans (16 ounces each) diced tomatoes, not drained

1. In a large pot over medium-high heat, sauté the celery, carrot, bell pepper, and green onion in the olive oil until tender. Add the cabbage, water, soup mix, broth, and seasonings. Cook until the cabbage is tender.
2. Add the tomatoes. Simmer until heated through. Serve hot.

Michele Carruthers' Famous Potato Soup   Serves 6

Total Time: 1 hour
Prep Time: 15 minutes   Cook Time: 45 minutes

4 large potatoes, peeled and diced
1 large onion, diced
3 stalks celery, diced
1 teaspoon dried parsley flakes
3 cubes chicken bouillon
4 ounces Velveeta cheese, Cheez Whiz, or other cheese that will melt

1/4 cup butter or margarine
1 pound pre-cooked ham, cubed
splash of milk
ground pepper, to taste

1. Place the potatoes, onion, celery, parsley flakes, and bouillon cubes in a stockpot. Add water about 1 inch higher than the veggies. Bring to a boil over high heat, then turn down the heat and simmer until the potatoes are almost soft enough to mash (begin testing with a fork 10 minutes after boiling starts).
2. Add the Velveeta, butter, and ham. Cook until the cheese is melted.
3. Stir in a splash of milk until the soup is thinned to your desired consistency. Add ground pepper to taste. Salt is usually not necessary due to the bouillon cubes and ham, but taste and add if necessary.

EGGDROP, TACO, AND MINESTRONE SOUPS

Following are some non-traditional soups that would enhance an Italian, Mexican, or Chinese dinner.

Eggdrop Soup   Makes 2 bowls or 4 cups

I like this soup with a dab of hot spicy Chinese mustard or hot sauce.

Total Time: 20 minutes
Prep Time: 5 minutes   Cook Time: 15 minutes

3 cups chicken broth (may be made from bouillon) or stock (page 164)
1 teaspoon salt
1 dash white pepper or black pepper
1 green onion, chopped
2 egg whites, slightly beaten, OR 1 egg

1. Heat the chicken broth, salt, and white pepper to boiling in a large saucepan over medium-high heat.
2. Stir the green onion into the beaten egg whites. Slowly pour the egg mixture in a very thin stream into the broth, stirring constantly with a fork until the egg whites form shreds. Serve hot.

Soups and Stews

Taco Soup

Serves 8

Total Time: 45 minutes, including minimum 30 minutes to simmer
Prep Time: 15 minutes
Cook Time: 30 minutes to 1 hour

1 pound cooked and shredded chicken or cooked and crumbled ground beef
1 can (16 ounces) pinto beans, not drained, OR Recipe-Ready Beans (page 176)
1 can (16 ounces) navy beans or kidney beans, not drained, OR Recipe-Ready Beans (page 176)
1 can (16 ounces) corn, not drained
1 can (16 ounces) tomatoes and chilies, not drained
2 cans (16 ounces each) diced tomatoes, not drained
1 can (4 ounces) diced green chilies
1 envelope taco seasoning mix (page 49)
1 envelope ranch dressing mix (page 161)
sour cream (page 99), shredded cheese, chopped green onion, and/or tortilla chips (optional garnish)

1. In a large pot combine the chicken, the undrained cans of beans, corn, tomatoes and chilies, diced tomatoes, the diced chilies, seasoning mix, and dressing mix. Stir to mix thoroughly.
2. Bring to a boil and cook for 10 minutes, then reduce the heat and simmer for 30 to 60 minutes. (You can eat the soup sooner, but the flavors won't have blended as well.)
3. Serve hot, topped with sour cream, shredded cheese, chopped green onion, and/or tortilla chips if desired.

Main Dish Minestrone

Serves 4

Total Time: 1 hour, 30 minutes
Prep Time: 30 minutes   **Cook Time:** 60 minutes

1 tablespoon olive oil, canola oil, or vegetable oil
½ pound Italian sausage, casing removed and meat crumbled
1 large onion, diced
1 clove garlic, minced, OR ¼ teaspoon garlic powder
½ cup chopped celery
½ cup chopped carrot
½ cup chopped green bell pepper
1 can (16 ounces) diced tomatoes, not drained
4 cups chicken broth (may be made from bouillon) or stock (page 164)
2 cups shredded cabbage
2 tablespoons chopped fresh parsley OR 1 teaspoon dried parsley flakes
½ teaspoon dried basil
1 bay leaf
1 pinch dried thyme
½ cup elbow macaroni, uncooked
1 can (16 ounces) kidney beans, rinsed and drained, OR Recipe-Ready Beans (page 176)
Parmesan cheese, for garnish

1. Warm the oil in a large stockpot. Add the sausage and onion and cook until browned.
2. Drain off all but 1 tablespoon of fat. Add the garlic, celery, carrot, and green pepper and sauté until the vegetables are soft, or about 5 minutes.
3. Add the tomatoes with their liquid, the chicken broth, cabbage, and herbs. Bring to a boil, then reduce the heat, cover, and simmer for 30 minutes.
4. Add the macaroni and beans and cook for another 30 minutes.
5. Remove the bay leaf. Sprinkle with the Parmesan cheese and serve hot.

Soups and Stews

REFRESHINGLY CHILLED SOUPS

Sometimes it's just too hot to even think about food. Those are the times when chilled soups are ideal.

Summer Shrimp Soup   Serves 4

Total Time: 15 minutes plus 24 hours to chill
Prep Time: 15 minutes   **Chill Time:** 24 hours

1½ pounds shrimp, cooked and peeled (page 233)
2 avocados, peeled and cut into small chunks
3 stalks celery, diced
3 green onions, sliced
¼ cup fresh cilantro OR 1 tablespoon dried cilantro
46 ounces V-8 vegetable juice or tomato juice
dash of hot sauce, to taste
½ teaspoon salt
½ teaspoon celery salt
1 teaspoon ground pepper
1 teaspoon garlic powder
½ teaspoon seasoned salt

Combine all the ingredients. Refrigerate for 24 hours and serve chilled.

Carolyn's Gazpacho   Serves 4 as a side dish, 2 as a main dish

Carolyn's favorite hot-weather meal!

Total Time: Depends on time to chill broth; anywhere from 15 minutes (with ice) to 2+ hours
Prep Time: 10 minutes, exclusive of making and chilling broth

4 cups chicken or vegetable broth (may be made from bouillon) or stock (pages 164–165), well chilled*
2 medium tomatoes, diced, and seeds discarded
½ green bell pepper, diced
½ cucumber, sliced and quartered
½ medium onion, diced
1 clove garlic, chopped finely
½ teaspoon dried oregano
½ teaspoon dried basil
2 teaspoons olive oil, canola oil, or vegetable oil
1 tablespoon lemon juice, lime juice, or *limón* (Key lime) juice

To chill the broth: If you have freezer space, put part of the broth in an ice cube tray and freeze it. Or, if you have ice, make 2 cups of broth double-strength and chill it; use ice to make up the other 2 cups.

1. Place the vegetables in a large bowl, add the spices, and toss well. Add the oil and mix to coat. Chill if not serving immediately.
2. To serve, sprinkle the lemon juice over the vegetables and toss. Divide the mixture between the bowls. Evenly pour the cold broth (or broth and ice) into each bowl. Serve chilled.

NOTE: Most bouillon cubes are high in sodium. Although normally a detriment, this is actually good in very hot weather to help replace salt lost though sweat. If you are in the heat all day without air-conditioning, more salt than normal (as well as lots of liquid) is needed to avoid heat exhaustion and heat cramps.

Jan's Gazpacho   Serves 8

Total Time: 1 hour
Prep Time: 15 minutes   **Cook Time:** 45 minutes

1 cucumber, peeled, sliced lengthwise, seeds removed, and finely diced
1 can (16 ounces) diced tomatoes, not drained
1 green bell pepper, diced
1 onion, diced
1 carrot, finely diced
1 can (12 ounces) V-8 juice OR 1 packet *criolla* (page 213) OR 1 can (8 ounces) tomato sauce and Italian spices
3 cloves garlic, minced
chicken broth (may be made from bouillon) or stock (page 164), to cover
dash of Worcestershire sauce, to taste
salt, to taste (be careful with the salt—the broth and Worcestershire sauce have salt already)
Parmesan cheese, for garnish
ground pepper, for sprinkling

1. Place the vegetables, V-8 juice, garlic, broth, Worcestershire, and salt in a stockpot or large pan. Bring to a boil, then reduce the heat and simmer until the vegetables are the desired consistency (for us the consistency is very mushy).

Soups and Stews

2. Turn off the heat and let cool. When the mixture has cooled a bit, use a potato masher to mush the vegetables as desired. Chill. Sprinkle each bowl of soup with Parmesan cheese and ground pepper and enjoy!

SOUPS AND STEWS LISTED ELSEWHERE

Here are Soups and Stews recipes that appear in other chapters.

BEANS, RICE, AND PASTA

If there were just one food in a cruising boat's provisions, it would probably be rice, beans, or maybe pasta. Staples of cruising boats all over the world, all three store easily and keep indefinitely.

In this chapter, you will find cooking tips for beans, rice, and pasta, followed by our best beans and/or rice recipes. Pasta recipes are spread throughout the book, but we included basic pasta cooking instructions and tips just in case your pasta instructions are in a language you don't comprehend and your recipe says "prepare pasta according to instructions on package!"

TIPS FOR COOKING BEANS

Although throwing a handful of beans in a pot and cooking them is something every cruiser can manage, sometimes it's the nuances that make the difference between truly delicious beans and chewy unappetizing beans. Here are our tips:

- *No salt!* Do not add salt when cooking beans, and do not cook them in seawater. Adding salt changes the outer membrane structure of the bean and results in increased cooking time and *tough* beans. If a recipe calls for salt in any form—ham, bacon, salt, or other seasonings that contain salt—let the beans cook until they're soft before adding the salty ingredients.

- Water quality. Hard water inhibits beans from cooking. Watermaker water is completely pure, so it is fine. Rainwater and bottled water are fine. Dock water or otherwise acquired water varies considerably, depending on the mineral content.

- Check out our Thermos Cooking section (page 70) for an easy way to cook dried beans with less time on the stove—and less heat in the boat.

- Soak dried beans before cooking. Start by rinsing the beans, then cover with 2 to 3 inches of water and soak overnight. Or start with 3 cups of water per cup of dried beans. Check the beans periodically because they will absorb the water, and you want to allow the beans to absorb as much water as they can. This is what changes the insoluble carbohydrate structure, reducing gas and cooking time.

- Most pressure cooker manufacturers recommend not cooking dried beans in a pressure cooker, but we have friends who cook beans in their pressure cookers regularly. Soak the beans, then drain and rinse them before putting them in the pressure cooker. Cover with water at least 2 inches above the beans, and do not add other recipe ingredients until after the beans are cooked. ***IMPORTANT:*** Do not fill the cooker more than half full to prevent clogging the vent, which can lead to an explosion! Add 1 tablespoon canola oil, which will remain on the surface and keep any foam from clogging the vent. Follow the pressure cooker manufacturer's instructions for bringing the cooker up to pressure. Bean varieties vary as to pressure cooking times, but a good rule of thumb is to start with 10 to 12 minutes. Let the pressure release naturally. Taste the beans for doneness. If they're not done, return to pressure for another 3 minutes and naturally release again.

- A pound of dried beans is approximately 2 cups. Since dried beans triple in volume when soaked and cooked, 1 cup dried beans is 3 cups cooked beans. A 1-pound can (16 ounces) of cooked beans contains about 2 cups.

TIPS FOR EATING BEANS

Indigestible carbohydrates in beans cause uncomfortable and embarrassing intestinal gas. Fortunately, the problem carbohydrates are water soluble, and there are several recommended "solutions." Test each to see what works best for you.

- **Soak beans in water overnight and discard the soak water.** Simply soaking beans in water overnight (or as recommended in the Thermos Cooking section, page 72) and then discarding the soak water will eliminate most of the gas.
- **Thoroughly cook the beans.** Thoroughly cooking the beans breaks down more of the indigestible carbohydrates.
- **Always drain and rinse canned beans.** Rinsing canned beans in water (and discarding the water) before adding the beans to a recipe reduces gas.
- **Add "gas-deflating" spices.** Try adding a teaspoon of ground ginger. If you're in Mexico, ask for the spice called epazote (although it adds a bitter "tang" that some people like and others don't). If all else fails, try the commercial product Beano.

Baking soda does not eliminate the carbohydrates, as suggested by a popular theory, so adding it to beans won't really help. Baking soda does reduce cooking time by altering the cell wall structure, but the beans may not have the texture you expect.

RECIPE-READY BEANS

Most recipes calling for beans—kidney, black, navy, red, white, or anything else—work equally well with prepared dried beans or canned beans. Dried beans take a lot less room to stow and also weigh less than canned beans. The trade-off is that it takes at least 2 hours to prepare dried beans for use in another recipe.

We call dried beans that are prepared for use in another recipe "Recipe-Ready Beans." You'll see that option in many of the recipes in this chapter. One batch of Recipe-Ready Beans is the equivalent of one 15- or 16-ounce can of beans.

We've included three versions of Recipe-Ready Beans:

- Traditional, which calls for overnight soaking and will get rid of the most gas-causing indigestible carbohydrates
- Rapid, which can be ready in 2 hours (see following recipe)
- In a thermos, which takes about 6 hours but uses a lot less propane and doesn't heat up the boat (page 72)

Rapid Recipe-Ready Beans

Makes $1^3/_4$ cups, the equivalent of one 15- to 16-ounce can of beans

Total Time: 1 hour, 50 minutes, including 30-minute soak

Cook Time: 1 hour, 20 minutes

$^3/_4$ **cup dried beans (any variety)**

1. Rinse and drain the beans. Put in a large pan and cover with water 1 inch above the beans.
2. Cover the pan, bring to a boil, then reduce the heat and simmer for 10 minutes. Turn off the stove and let stand for 30 minutes.
3. Drain the water and cover with fresh water 1 to 2 inches above the beans. Bring to a boil again, then reduce the heat and simmer for 1 hour, or until the beans are tender. Test as above for doneness.

Traditional Recipe-Ready Beans

Makes 1¾ cups, the equivalent of one 15- to 16-ounce can of beans

Total Time: 1 hour, plus overnight soak time
Cook Time: 1 hour

¾ cup dried beans (any variety)

1. Rinse the beans, put them in at least a 2-quart saucepan, and cover with 1 to 2 inches of water. Soak for 8 hours or overnight. Drain and rinse.
2. Add fresh water to the saucepan to come about 1 inch above the beans. Cover and bring to a boil over medium-high heat; cook for 5 minutes. Turn down the heat to medium and simmer for 50 minutes to 1 hour until "recipe-ready."
3. When testing, keep in mind that "recipe-ready" allows for a bit more cooking in a recipe. If you're merely heating the beans in a recipe, you may want to cook Recipe-Ready Beans for a bit longer.
4. Your results may differ, or you may like your beans a bit firmer or mushier, so start taste-testing earlier rather than later.

BEAN-BASED RECIPES

Everything from Basic Beans and Ham and Beans to Black Bean Burgers and Black Bean Pizza Dough, beans are one of the most versatile ingredients for cruisers everywhere.

Basic Beans

Serves 4

Because there have been too many times when I've purchased bulk beans or rice out of a barrel, or my package has instructions in some foreign language that I cannot decipher, we've included basic instructions for cooking beans.

Total Time: 3 hours, 5 minutes, plus overnight soak time if needed
Prep Time: 5 minutes   **Cook Time:** 3 hours

1 cup dried beans OR Recipe-Ready Beans (subtract 2 hours from Total Time)
1 medium onion, chopped
1 teaspoon ground pepper

1 teaspoon garlic powder OR 2 cloves garlic, chopped
1½ quarts water
2 slices bacon, cut into 2-inch pieces (optional)

1. If using dried beans, soak the beans overnight covered with water. Rinse and drain.
2. Place the soaked and drained beans, the onion, ground pepper, garlic, and water in a large saucepan; cover and bring to a boil.
3. Turn down the heat to medium. Cook for 2 hours, checking periodically to see if more water is needed.
4. Add the bacon. Cook for 30 to 60 minutes longer, adding water if necessary. Serve hot.

Beef and Beans

Serves 2

Total Time: 30 minutes (plus time to make Recipe-Ready Beans, if needed)
Prep Time: 5 minutes   **Cook Time:** 25 minutes

salt
¼ to ½ pound ground beef
¼ medium onion, diced
1 can (16 ounces) kidney beans, red beans, or black beans, drained and rinsed, OR Recipe-Ready Beans (page 176)
½ cup water
1 teaspoon chili powder, or to taste
½ teaspoon ground cumin, or to taste
ground pepper, to taste
sour cream (page 99), sliced green onion, salsa (page 127), and grated cheese (optional garnishes)

1. Sprinkle salt over the bottom of a large saucepan and sauté the ground beef in it (the salt draws the fat out of the meat, so you don't have to add oil unless the meat is very lean).
2. When the meat is almost done, add the onion and continue to cook. Add the beans, water, chili powder, cumin, and ground pepper; mix well. If the beans are particularly dry, you may need to add more water. Simmer for at least 15 minutes to allow the flavors to mix.
3. Serve in bowls. Top with all or some of the garnishes if desired.

Black Bean Burgers

Serves 8

Total Time: 30 minutes (plus time to make Recipe-Ready Beans, if needed)
Prep Time: 20 minutes   **Cook Time:** 10 minutes

3 cans (16 ounces each) black beans, drained and rinsed, OR Recipe-Ready Beans (page 176)
1½ cups uncooked oats, instant or regular
1 medium onion, diced
2 jalapeño peppers, seeded and finely chopped (for milder flavor, use green bell pepper or omit)
½ cup chopped fresh cilantro OR 1 teaspoon dried cilantro
2 eggs, beaten
1 teaspoon salt
¼ cup flour
¼ cup cornmeal or corn flour (masa)
1 tablespoon canola oil or vegetable oil

1. Mash the black beans with a potato masher or fork. Combine the mashed beans with the oats, onion, pepper, cilantro, eggs, and salt.
2. Shape the mixture into patties. Combine the flour and cornmeal on a plate and roll each patty in it to coat.
3. Heat the oil in a skillet over medium-high heat and cook the patties for 5 minutes on each side. Remove the burgers from the pan and place them on paper towels for a minute to absorb any excess oil.
4. Serve just as you would a hamburger. Enjoy!

Black Bean and Avocado Quesadilla

Serves 1 as a main dish, or 2 to 3 as an appetizer

Total Time: 10 minutes
Prep Time: 5 minutes   **Cook Time:** 5 minutes

black or white bean dip (page 130; can use black beans instead of white) to cover tortilla, to taste
½ avocado, peeled and cut into chunks
shredded cheddar or other meltable cheese, to taste
2 flour or corn tortillas

1. Warm a dry skillet over medium-high heat while preparing the quesadilla. Don't add any oil—tortillas cook (or "toast") best in a dry pan.
2. Layer the bean dip, avocado, and cheese on a tortilla. Top with the second tortilla.
3. Place in the hot skillet and cook until one side is golden brown, then flip and brown the other side.
4. Cut into pie-shaped wedges and serve hot.

Black Bean Pizza Dough and Sauce

Serves 4

Total Time: 1 hour, 40 minutes, or 2 hours depending on oven temperature
Prep Time: 30 minutes (not including 60 minutes to let dough rise)
Cook Time: 10 minutes at 500°F; or 20 to 25 minutes at 350°F

Dough
1 teaspoon yeast (½ packet, page 387)
2 cups flour
¼ teaspoon salt
½ cup warm water
½ teaspoon cayenne pepper
¼ cup pureed black beans*

* Mush up a 16-ounce can of black beans, drained, with a potato masher. Use ¼ cup; reserve the remainder of the mashed beans for the sauce.

Sauce
remainder of mushed black beans
½ cup V-8 juice, tomato juice, or similar juice
⅛ teaspoon ground cumin
⅛ teaspoon cayenne pepper
salt and pepper
2 teaspoons minced garlic

Toppings
sausage, pepperoni, chopped olives, diced fresh tomato, sun-dried tomato, diced green bell pepper, minced hot chile pepper, diced onion, diced green onion, sliced mushrooms, cheese

1. Preheat oven to 500°F.
2. Combine all the dough ingredients; knead well. Let rise for 60 minutes.
3. Combine all the sauce ingredients and set aside.
4. Roll the dough into pizza pan size. Sprinkle the pan with cornmeal to prevent sticking. Place the dough on the pan and spread the sauce on top.

5. For a thin crust, place the toppings on the dough immediately. For a thicker crust, allow the dough to rise for 30 minutes before adding the toppings.

6. Place the pizza on the bottom rack of the oven. Bake for 5 to 10 minutes. (If your boat oven is like mine and won't heat to 500°F, bake the pizza at 350°F for 20 to 25 minutes.) Check the bottom for doneness; it should be lightly browned and crisp. Depending on your oven, you may have better luck baking the crust alone for the first 10 minutes, then adding the toppings before finishing the baking.

Ham and Beans   Serves 6

This is traditional comfort food—best served with chopped green onion, coleslaw, and piping hot corn bread with real butter. Yum!

Total Time: 2 hours, 15 minutes, plus overnight soak time

Prep Time: 15 minutes   **Cook Time:** 1½ to 2 hours

2 cups dried Great Northern beans or navy beans OR Recipe-Ready Beans (page 176)
2 cloves garlic, minced
1 bay leaf
2 large onions, chopped
1 pound ham, cut into ½-inch cubes
garlic salt, to taste
ground pepper, to taste

1. Cover the beans with water 1 to 2 inches above the beans and let soak overnight. Drain and rinse.

2. Add 6 cups fresh cold water to cover. Add the garlic and bay leaf. Bring to a boil over medium-high heat and cook for 5 minutes, then turn down the heat to medium and simmer for 45 minutes.

3. Add the onion, ham, garlic salt, and ground pepper, making sure that the water still covers the beans. Bring them back to a boil, then turn down the heat and simmer for another hour, tasting every 15 minutes for bean consistency. If the water is low, add more.

4. Take out the bay leaf. Taste, and add more garlic salt or ground pepper if necessary. Serve hot.

Kidney Bean Chowder   Serves 4

Total Time: 1½ hours (plus time to make Recipe-Ready Beans if needed)

Prep Time: 25 minutes   **Cook Time:** 60 minutes

¼ pound bacon, cut into 1-inch pieces
½ cup chopped onion
½ cup chopped green bell pepper
½ cup chopped celery
1 tablespoon flour
1 can (16 ounces) red kidney beans, not drained, OR Recipe-Ready Beans (page 176)
½ cup chopped carrot
1 tablespoon chopped fresh parsley OR ½ teaspoon dried parsley flakes
1 bay leaf
⅛ teaspoon dried thyme
2 cups beef or chicken broth (may be made from bouillon) or stock (page 164)
salt and pepper
1 chicken breast, cooked and shredded (optional)
1 potato, diced (optional)

1. Sauté the bacon over medium heat until crisp; remove and set aside. Drain all but 3 tablespoons bacon fat from the pan.

2. Add the onion, bell pepper, and celery to the pan and sauté for 5 minutes. Remove from the heat and stir in the flour, mixing until it forms a paste with the bacon fat. Add the beans, carrot, parsley, bay leaf, thyme, broth, salt, and pepper and mix well so that the liquid from the beans and the broth form a smooth paste with the flour. Mash any lumps that form. If chicken or potatoes are to be used, include them here, too (smaller pieces will cook quicker).

3. Return the pan to the stove, increase the heat to medium-high, and bring to a boil. Then reduce the heat, cover, and simmer for 45 minutes, or until the carrot is tender.

4. Remove the bay leaf. Garnish the chowder with the reserved bacon, and serve hot.

Beans, Rice, and Pasta

Red Beans and Rice   Serves 4

Total Time: 1 hour, 30 minutes
Prep Time: 15 minutes
Cook Time: 1 hour, 15 minutes

1 pork chop, cut into 1-inch pieces (if it has a bone,
    save it) OR 6 ounces ham, cut into 1-inch pieces,
    OR 6 ounces sausage, cut into $^1/_4$-inch slices, OR
    1 chicken breast, cooked and shredded
$^1/_2$ cup diced onion
$^1/_2$ green bell pepper or mildly spicy pepper, diced
1 tablespoon minced garlic OR 1 teaspoon garlic
    powder
2 cans (16 ounces each) kidney or red beans,
    rinsed and drained, OR Recipe-Ready Beans
    (page 176)
$^1/_2$ to 1 cup water
2 bay leaves
$^1/_2$ teaspoon ground thyme
$^1/_4$ teaspoon celery powder or celery salt
1 cup chicken broth (may be made from bouillon)
    or stock (page 164)
ground pepper, to taste
dash of cayenne powder
hot sauce, to taste
hot cooked rice to serve 4

1. In a large pot combine the pork (and the bone),
   onion, bell pepper, garlic, beans, water, bay leaves,
   thyme, celery powder, broth, ground pepper,
   cayenne, and hot sauce. Cover and simmer for
   $1^1/_4$ hours, or until the meat and beans are tender,
   stirring occasionally. As it cooks, you may need
   to add more water, depending on how dry the
   beans were and how much steam escapes from the
   pot. The consistency should be similar to that of
   spaghetti sauce or chili.
2. Meanwhile, prepare the rice and keep warm.
3. Remove the bone and the bay leaves from the meat
   mixture and serve the meat mixture in bowls over
   the rice.

White Chicken Chili   Serves 2

*This is a mildly spicy chili that can be made spicier or
milder by varying the chile peppers used.*

Total time: 1 hour (plus time to make Recipe-Ready
    Beans if needed)
Prep Time: 15 minutes   Cook Time: 45 minutes

$1^1/_2$ teaspoons minced garlic OR $^1/_2$ teaspoon garlic
    powder
1 medium onion, diced
$1^1/_2$ teaspoons canola oil or olive oil
$^1/_2$ green bell pepper or chile pepper, diced and
    seeded, OR 1 can (6 ounces) mild or medium
    green chilies (depends on degree of spiciness
    desired—all peppers can be omitted for a very
    mild chili)
1 teaspoon ground cumin
$^1/_8$ teaspoon ground cloves
$^1/_8$ teaspoon cayenne pepper (reduce or omit for
    milder chili)
$^1/_2$ teaspoon dried oregano
2 cups chicken broth (may be made from bouillon)
    or stock (page 164)
1 can (16 ounces) Great Northern beans or
    other white beans OR Recipe-Ready Beans
    (page 176)*
1 chicken breast, cooked and shredded, OR 1 can
    (6 ounces) chicken
1 to 2 cups (4 to 8 ounces) grated white cheese that
    will melt*
sour cream (page 99), for garnish

*You can substitute non-white beans and/or non-white
    cheese and the dish will taste great, but it won't be a
    white chili.*

1. In a large pot sauté the garlic and onion in the oil.
   Add the peppers and spices and cook for 2 minutes. Add the broth, beans, chicken, and half the
   cheese. Simmer for 15 minutes.
2. Serve in bowls, garnished with the rest of the
   cheese and the sour cream.

NOTE: The cheese can be omitted for those who can't
eat it or if you can't find any!

Potluck BBQ Baked Beans

Serves 10 to 12

Total Time: 1 hour
Prep Time: 20 minutes Cook Time: 30 to 40 minutes

6 slices bacon (optional, but yummy)
1 large onion, diced
1 cup barbecue sauce (pages 215–18)
1/2 cup packed brown sugar
1/4 cup cider vinegar or other vinegar
3 cans (16 ounces each) baked beans

1. Fry the bacon until crisp in a pan large enough to hold the three cans of beans. Remove the bacon from the pan and crumble it; set aside.
2. Drain most of the fat, then add the onion and sauté until translucent.
3. Combine the barbecue sauce, brown sugar, and vinegar and add to the pan.
4. Preheat oven to 350°F.
5. Add the beans to the pan and heat until simmering. Let simmer until thoroughly heated, then stir in the crumbled bacon. Transfer to an ungreased baking dish. Bake until bubbling, or about 30 to 40 minutes. Serve hot.

Lentil Chili

Serves 6

Total Time: 1 hour, 30 minutes
Prep Time: 30 minutes   Cook Time: 1 hour

1 1/2 teaspoons olive oil, canola oil, or vegetable oil
2 cups chopped onion
4 cloves garlic, minced, OR 1 tablespoon garlic powder
8 ounces dried lentils
1 can (16 ounces) crushed tomatoes or diced tomatoes OR 2 cups fresh chopped tomatoes
1 can (6 ounces) tomato paste OR packet of *criolla* (page 213)
4 cups water
1 tablespoon chili powder
1 tablespoon ground cumin
dash of paprika
salt, to taste
ground pepper, to taste
1 cup diced carrot

1 green bell pepper, chopped
1 can (8 ounces) sliced mushrooms (optional)
1 can (4 ounces) chopped green chilies (optional)
hot sauce, to taste
shredded cheese and chopped green onion, for garnish (optional)

1. Heat the oil in a large pot over low heat. Stir in the onion and garlic, and cook until tender.
2. Mix in the lentils, tomatoes, and tomato paste. Pour in the water. Season with the chili powder, cumin, paprika, salt, and ground pepper. Bring to a boil, then reduce the heat to low, cover, and simmer for 30 minutes, stirring occasionally.
3. Add the carrot and bell pepper. Continue cooking over low heat for 20 minutes, or until the lentils, carrot, and bell pepper are tender. Add the mushrooms and chopped chilies; cook just long enough to heat through. Add hot sauce to taste, or set out a bottle of your favorite hot sauce for varying tastes.
4. Serve in bowls, garnished with the shredded cheese and chopped green onion if desired.

Southwestern Chicken, Beans, and Rice

Serves 2

Total Time: 30 minutes
Prep Time: 10 minutes Cook Time: 20 to 25 minutes

1 boneless, skinless chicken breast, cut into 1-inch pieces, OR 1 can (12 ounces) chicken, drained
1 medium onion, diced
1 tablespoon canola oil or butter OR cooking spray
2 servings cooked rice (any type)
1 can (14 ounces) kidney or black beans, drained and rinsed, OR Recipe-Ready Beans (page 176)
1/2 teaspoon chicken bouillon powder or salt
ground pepper, to taste
1/2 teaspoon ground cumin, or to taste
1/2 teaspoon chili powder, or to taste
sour cream (page 99), avocado slices, salsa (page 127), or lime wedges (optional garnishes)

1. Brown the chicken and onion in oil over medium-high heat (if using canned chicken, add it at the very end).

2. Add the rice and beans and stir to combine. Add the chicken bouillon powder, ground pepper, cumin, and chili powder and stir again. Sauté over medium-high heat for 5 minutes, then stir and sauté for another 5 minutes. Some of the rice should be browned to a golden color. If not, stir and sauté for another 5 minutes. Don't stir constantly or the rice won't brown.

3. If you're using canned chicken, drain and add the chicken chunks now. Heat just until warmed through, gently stirring as little as possible to mix.

4. Serve with any or all of the optional garnishes.

RICE TIPS AND RECIPES

Contrary to most rice advice, we advocate not rinsing rice unless you're concerned about the cleanliness of foreign purchases, such as out of a barrel at the local outdoor market. Rinsing can eliminate essential nutrients, especially for brown rice.

When you have a choice, select brown rice, basmati rice, or brown basmati rice. These rices retain the nutrients and fiber of the natural rice grain. White rice processing strips out most of the nutrients and almost all the fiber. This results in quicker cooking rice but little nutritional value. Brown rice takes longer to cook, but be sure to check out the Thermos Cooking section (page 73) for a method that takes far less fuel, puts less heat into the boat, and doesn't have to be watched.

As with cooking beans, cooking rice seems like such a simple thing to do: put rice and water in a pot, bring it to a boil, and let it cook. Here are a few tips that will turn "OK" rice into great rice:

- Leave it alone. No stirring or peeking while cooking except to check that the water is not all absorbed.
- Adding a teaspoon of olive oil or other cooking oil to the water helps ensure that the pot doesn't boil over.
- A key for successful rice is figuring out the correct amount of water. As a general rule, use 1½ to 1¾ cups of water per cup of white rice. Brown rice needs more water; start with a 2½ to 1 ratio; that is, for every cup of rice, use 2½ cups of water.

More water gives you softer, stickier rice, such as what you'd want for stir-fries. Less water results in firmer rice—a good consistency for rice salads.

- For more flavorful rice, substitute chicken or beef stock or bouillon for water in any rice recipe.
- Let the rice rest. After the liquid is absorbed and the rice is cooked to your satisfaction, remove the pan from the heat and let it sit undisturbed for at least 5 minutes. That's because immediately after cooking, the rice will be drier and fluffier on top and heavier lower in the pot. Letting it rest allows the moisture to redistribute, resulting in a more uniform texture. Fluff the rice with a fork before serving or adding to another recipe.

Basic White Rice   Serves 4

Total Time: 30 minutes
Cook Time: 30 minutes

1 cup white rice (not instant; see the next recipe for instant)
1½ cups water
½ teaspoon salt (optional)
2 teaspoons butter or margarine (optional)

1. Place the rice, water, salt (if used), and butter (if used) in a large saucepan over medium-high heat. Bring to a boil.
2. Reduce the heat to medium or medium-low and simmer, covered, for about 15 to 20 minutes. While it is simmering, check to make sure it's not burning and there's still a bit of water. If not, add some.
3. Remove the pan from the heat and let stand for 5 minutes. Fluff with a fork, and serve hot.

Instant White Rice   Serves 4

Total Time: 10 minutes

2 cups water
2 teaspoons butter or margarine (optional)
½ teaspoon salt
2 cups instant white rice

Bring the water to a boil in a large saucepan. Add the butter (if used) and salt, then stir in the rice. Cover and remove from the heat. Let stand, covered, for 5 minutes, or until the water is absorbed. Serve hot.

Basic or Instant Brown Rice Serves 4

Total Time: 35 to 45 minutes
Cook Time: 30 to 40 minutes

1 cup brown rice
2½ cups water
2 teaspoons butter or margarine (optional)

Combine the rice, water, and butter (if used) in a large saucepan. Bring to a boil, then reduce the heat to medium. Cover and simmer for 30 to 40 minutes, or until the water is absorbed. Check the pan every 15 minutes to make sure that all the water hasn't been absorbed. But just peek, don't stir! Add water only if necessary. Let sit for 5 minutes, then fluff with a fork and serve hot.

Variation for Instant Brown Rice: Reduce the water to 2 cups and add ½ teaspoon salt. Bring to a boil, then reduce the heat and simmer for 10 minutes. Remove from the heat and let sit undisturbed for an additional 5 minutes, or until all the water is absorbed.

NOTE: Instant brown rice takes longer to cook than instant white rice. Also, all brands are different, so you may need to experiment. However, in the absence of instructions (or instructions only in a language you don't know), this basic recipe will get you started.

Ramona's Rice and Veggie Pilaf Serves 4

Another wonderful recipe from a friend who not only raced Y-Flyers with us but was the first "real person" we knew with a 40-foot cruising boat. Ramona and her husband, Vit, gave us both our first taste of what cruising could be like, with cocktails in their cockpit as the sun set over Kentucky Lake.

Total Time: 45 minutes
Prep Time: 15 minutes   **Cook Time:** 30 minutes

1 teaspoon olive oil, canola oil, or vegetable oil
1 cup sliced fresh mushrooms OR 1 can (8 ounces) sliced mushrooms, drained
1 cup shredded carrot (about 2 medium)
1 cup chicken broth (may be made from bouillon) or stock (page 164)
¼ teaspoon ground pepper

½ cup uncooked white rice (you can use brown rice, but it will take about an hour to cook and require more liquid)
½ cup snipped fresh parsley OR 1 tablespoon dried parsley flakes
2 green onions, sliced

1. Heat the oil in a saucepan. Add the mushrooms and carrot and sauté for 2 to 3 minutes, or until the mushrooms are tender, stirring occasionally.
2. Add the broth and ground pepper; bring to a boil over high heat. Add the rice, then reduce the heat and simmer, covered, for 20 minutes.
3. Remove from the heat. Stir in the parsley and green onion. Let stand for 4 minutes, then fluff with a fork and serve hot.

Veggie Jambalaya Serves 4

Total Time: 35 minutes, plus time to cook rice (and Recipe-Ready Beans if needed)
Prep Time: 15 minutes
Cook Time: 20 minutes (not including rice and beans)

1 medium onion, chopped
1 tablespoon chopped garlic
1 green bell pepper, chopped
½ jalapeño pepper, seeded and finely chopped
1 tablespoon butter, margarine, canola oil, or vegetable oil
1 can (16 ounces) diced tomatoes, not drained, OR 2 medium tomatoes, diced
1 can (16 ounces) corn, drained
1 can (16 ounces) kidney beans, rinsed and drained, OR Recipe-Ready Beans (page 176)
hot sauce, to taste
chili powder, garlic powder, salt, and pepper, to taste
1 cup cooked brown rice or other rice

Sauté the onion, garlic, bell pepper, and jalapeño in butter for about 5 minutes. Add the tomatoes, corn, and beans and mix well. Add the hot sauce and spices and simmer about 10 minutes. Add the cooked rice and simmer until heated through, or about 5 minutes. Serve hot.

Jambalaya   Serves 4

Total Time: 1½ to 2 hours (somewhat less if you use instant rice)
Prep Time: 45 minutes to 1 hour
Cook Time: 45 minutes to 1 hour (less with instant rice)

2 tablespoons butter, margarine, or olive oil
4 ounces ham, cut into ½-inch cubes (lunch meat or canned ham works well) OR 1 pork chop, boned and cut into ½-inch chunks
4 ounces smoked sausage or bratwurst, cut into ¼-inch slices, OR 1 chicken breast, cut into 1-inch pieces
1 medium onion, diced
2 tablespoons minced garlic OR 1 teaspoon garlic powder
5 green onions, including tops, cut into ⅛- to ¼-inch slices
1 green bell pepper, diced
¾ to 1 cup brown or white rice OR 1½ to 2 cups instant rice
2 cups beef broth (may be made from bouillon) or stock (page 165)
ground pepper, to taste
¼ teaspoon cayenne pepper OR small amount of very finely chopped fresh chile pepper*
1 teaspoon chili powder*
4 whole bay leaves
½ teaspoon dried thyme, ground or crumbled, OR 1 teaspoon fresh minced thyme*
¼ teaspoon ground cloves*

Spices vary considerably in their intensity, particularly when purchased at farmer's markets and/or stored in hot places. Ditto for chile peppers. The amounts given here are general guidelines, but vary them as necessary to taste. Remember that you can always add more, but they're impossible to remove. Also, if you don't have all these spices, you can either omit some or use a prepackaged cajun spice mix, a blackening spice mix, or Old Bay Seasoning, or spice up the dish with a shot of Tabasco or other hot sauce.

1. Melt the butter in a large pan. Add the ham, sausage, and onion and cook over medium heat, stirring occasionally until the meat is cooked but not browned.
2. Add the garlic, green onion, bell pepper, rice, broth, ground pepper, cayenne, chili powder, bay leaves, thyme, and cloves. Mix well, then bring to a boil over high heat. Reduce the heat and simmer, covered, for approximately 45 minutes, or until the rice is done (the time will be less if you use instant rice). Stir periodically. Jambalaya should be somewhat "wetter" than rice alone, but not soupy. As it cooks, add more water if necessary.
3. Remove the bay leaves. Serve the jambalaya in bowls.

NOTE: Need to stretch the jambalaya for last-minute guests? Here are a few ideas.

- Use more rice, water, and bouillon, or add a can of black, red, kidney, or pinto beans or Recipe-Ready Beans (page 176).
- Add a can of tomatoes, or cut a tomato or two into chunks and add.
- Just before serving, add a can of corn or mushrooms, or a can of chicken, turkey, ham, or roast beef; handle gently to avoid mushing the meat.
- Be sure to increase your spices accordingly.

Spanish Rice   Serves 2

Total Time: 1 hour, 10 minutes (less for instant rice)
Prep Time: 15 to 20 minutes
Cook Time: 45 minutes (less for instant rice)

½ cup brown rice or white rice OR ¾ cup instant brown or white rice
1 cup beef broth (may be made from bouillon) or stock (page 165)
salt
¼ to ½ pound ground beef
⅓ cup diced onion
1 can (8 ounces) mushrooms, liquid reserved (optional)
½ to 1 tablespoon oil (if ground beef is especially lean)
¼ green bell pepper, diced
1 can (16 ounces) diced tomatoes, not drained, OR 2 tomatoes, cut into chunks
ground pepper, to taste

1. Combine the rice and broth in a large saucepan. Cover and bring to a boil, then reduce the heat and simmer. If using instant rice, follow the package instructions. (The rice will finish cooking in step 3.)
2. Sprinkle the salt in a skillet and place over medium-high heat. Crumble the ground beef into the pan and add the onion and mushrooms (reserve the liquid for step 3). As the beef cooks, the salt will draw the fat from the meat, and the meat, onion, and mushrooms will cook in it. If the meat is particularly lean (as was the case in Mexico and Belize), add the oil so that the mixture sautés nicely.
3. When the mixture is browned, add the bell pepper, tomatoes (including all the liquid from the can), reserved mushroom liquid, and ground pepper. The rice will not be done, but add it and its cooking water to the skillet. Increase the heat to high, and stir to mix the ingredients. When the mixture comes to a boil, reduce the heat and simmer, covered, for another 30 to 45 minutes, checking and stirring every 5 to 10 minutes until the rice is done.

IMPORTANT NOTE: Rice varies greatly in how long it takes to cook and how much water it will absorb. If the rice is getting dry as it cooks, add more water about ½ cup at a time. The finished dish should be moist but not soupy.

Rice and Beans   Serves 6

As opposed to Red Beans and Rice (page 180), where the meat/bean combination is served over the rice, Rice and Beans is a Caribbean medley where all the ingredients are cooked in one pot, including the meat if you decide to include it. This is our favorite passage meal—quick to reheat and easy to serve in a flat-bottom bowl. It's never the same anytime I make it depending on what I have on board at the time.

Total Time: 1 hour (plus time to make Recipe-Ready Beans if needed)
Prep Time: 15 minutes   Cook Time: 45 minutes

1 uncooked chicken breast, cut into 1-inch cubes, OR 1 cup ham chunks or any meat you have OR no meat at all. Hint: chorizo or any spicy meat is a flavorful addition, or use a combination of meats. Chorizo and chicken is my favorite combination.

1 onion, diced
1 green bell pepper, diced
1 mildly hot chile pepper, seeded and diced
1 cup uncooked brown rice, white rice, or instant brown or white rice
3 cups chicken broth (may be made from bouillon) or stock (page 164)
ground cumin, cayenne pepper, red pepper flakes, salt, and ground pepper, to taste
hot sauce, to taste
1 can (16 ounces) diced tomatoes, not drained, OR 2 medium tomatoes, diced
2 cans (16 ounces each) black beans or other beans, drained and rinsed, OR Recipe-Ready Beans (page 176)

1. In a large pot combine the chicken, onion, bell pepper, chile pepper, rice, broth, spices, and tomatoes. Cover and bring to a boil, then reduce the heat and simmer until the rice is cooked. It will take about 35 to 40 minutes to cook brown rice slowly, less time for other types of rice.
2. Add the beans and heat thoroughly. Add more water if necessary. Taste, and add more spice if necessary. Remove from the heat and let stand for 5 to 10 minutes. Serve hot.

Fried Rice   Serves 2

Total Time: 30 to 40 minutes, plus time to cook rice
Prep Time: 15 minutes   Cook Time: 15 minutes

2 eggs
1½ teaspoons canola oil, other oil, butter, or margarine OR cooking spray, for cooking the eggs
2 additional tablespoons canola oil, butter, or margarine
4 ounces meat, cut into bite-size bits (ham, shredded chicken, fish, shrimp, etc.; omit for a vegetarian version)
2 green onions, including tops, finely sliced, OR ½ small onion, diced
½ cup mix of chopped fresh vegetables, such as peas, broccoli, carrots, corn, and mushrooms*
2 servings cooked rice
1 tablespoon soy sauce or oyster sauce

Fresh vegetables are best, but canned will work.

Beans, Rice, and Pasta

1. Slightly beat the eggs in a cup or small bowl. Heat the oil for the eggs in a large skillet. Pour in the beaten egg and twirl the skillet so that the egg thinly covers the bottom of the pan. Cook, stirring with a spatula, until done. Remove from the pan and let cool; shred into small pieces and set aside.

2. Heat the additional oil over medium-high heat until a few drops of water sizzle. Add the meat and stir-fry for 2 minutes. Add the green onion, other vegetables, and cooked rice. Stir-fry for 3 to 5 minutes. Add the reserved egg pieces and soy sauce and stir-fry for another 2 to 3 minutes. Serve hot.

Shipwreck Stew   Serves 6

Total Time: 1 hour, 30 minutes
Prep Time: 15 minutes
Cook Time: 1 hour, 15 minutes

cooking spray
2 medium potatoes, peeled and thinly sliced or julienned
1 medium onion, sliced thinly into slivers
1 can (16 ounces) kidney beans, drained and rinsed, OR Recipe-Ready Beans (page 176)
¼ cup white rice
4 medium stalks celery, diced
3 medium carrots, diced
1 pound lean ground beef, broken into chunks
1 tablespoon Worcestershire sauce
1 beef or chicken bouillon cube, or to taste, crumbled and sprinkled through the layers, OR 1 teaspoon beef or chicken bouillon powder plus chili powder, dried basil, dried oregano, salt, and pepper, to taste
1 can (12 ounces) V-8 juice OR 1 can (10 ounces) tomato sauce plus ½ cup water
½ cup water

1. Coat a 2½-quart casserole dish with cooking spray. Heat oven to 350°F.

2. Layer the potato, onion, beans, rice, celery, carrot, and beef, sprinkling the Worcestershire and the crumbled bouillon cube through the layers. Do not mix or stir. Pour the V-8 juice and the ½ cup water over all.

3. Bake for 1¼ hours, or until done. Serve hot. This dish may be prepared ahead.

NOTE: The first time I made this recipe, it was very bland. Even though the recipe doesn't call for them, I use spices such as cumin, garlic powder, and even a few dashes of hot sauce liberally to add flavor.

COUSCOUS TIPS AND RECIPES

Couscous may be hard to find in some cruising locales. But the ease and rapid cooking time make it ideal for adding to the menu without heating up the galley. Like pasta, couscous does not have much flavor of its own, so the recipes call for chicken or beef stock, herbs and spices, meats and vegetables, or other sauces for flavor. Couscous works really well as a "serve-over" base for many dishes that you'd otherwise serve over rice or pasta.

Most packaged couscous is the instant variety and will cook very quickly off the stove by simply absorbing a boiling liquid. However, real couscous (roughly ground hard durum wheat) will require significantly more time.

- Be sure to identify which type of couscous you have (instant or traditional) to plan the correct cooking time.
- The easiest way to prepare instant couscous is to heat a liquid to boiling and remove from the heat. Add the couscous, cover, and wait for 5 minutes for the liquid to be absorbed, then fluff with a fork to serve.
- Traditional couscous may be cooked like rice. Heat the butter, add the couscous and stir to coat, and add the stock. Bring to a boil, reduce the heat to low, cover, and cook until the liquid is absorbed. Fluff to separate the grains, and serve hot.
- 1 cup dry couscous = 2½ cups cooked.
- As a side dish, plan on ½ to ¾ cup cooked couscous per person.

Beans, Rice, and Pasta

Basic Couscous
Serves 2

Our experience is that couscous seems to vary considerably from one brand to another regarding how much liquid it needs, so experiment accordingly until you know what yours needs.

Total Time: 8 to 10 minutes
Cook Time: 5 minutes to boil and 3 minutes to absorb water

¾ **cup water or any flavor broth (may be made from bouillon) or stock (pages 164–65)**
⅓ **cup instant couscous**
1 **teaspoon olive oil**

1. Combine all the ingredients in a saucepan. Cover and bring to a boil, then turn off the heat.
2. Let sit for 3 minutes and taste. If the couscous grains are still hard, add ¼ cup more water and let sit a few more minutes. There is no need to reheat; there's still plenty of heat in the pan. Re-test before serving.

Couscous Vegetable Pilaf
Serves 4

Total Time: 35 minutes
Prep Time: 15 minutes   **Cook Time:** 10 minutes

2 **cups chicken broth (may be made from bouillon) or stock (page 164)**
2 **carrots, sliced**
1 **onion, chopped**
1 **stalk celery, chopped**
1 **clove garlic, minced, OR ¼ teaspoon garlic powder**
ground pepper, to taste
1 **cup instant couscous**
1 **tablespoon butter (optional)**

1. Bring the broth to a boil in a large saucepan. Add the carrot, onion, celery, and garlic. Cover and reduce the heat to low. Simmer for 10 minutes, or until the carrot is crisp-tender.
2. Remove from the heat. Add the ground pepper and couscous. Cover and let sit for 5 minutes, or until the liquid is absorbed. Add the butter if desired. Fluff with a fork and serve hot.

BASIC PASTA TIPS AND RECIPES

Pasta is quite simple to cook, but many recipes call for you to prepare the pasta ahead of time, and the recipe instructions say "prepare pasta according to instructions on package." This is fine as long as you have the package and/or the instructions are in English! If that's not the case, here are basic pasta instructions and tips.

- 4 ounces of dried pasta is the equivalent of one full cup of dry pasta. When cooked, the pasta will become approximately 2½ cups.
- 4 ounces of "straight pasta"—spaghetti, linguine, or angel hair—is the same as a 1-inch bundle of pasta and turns into approximately 2 cups of pasta when cooked.
- Boiling water is the usual method of cooking pasta. To prepare "perfect" pasta, it is critical to use enough water—about a quart of water for every 4 ounces of dry pasta. More water will not harm anything. If you need to conserve water, using less won't be disastrous, just not "perfect." But if you don't use enough water, the pasta may not have enough to absorb, leaving it "tough."
- Add 1 tablespoon of salt to the water when it begins to boil to bring out the most flavor in your pasta.
- When the water begins to boil vigorously, add the pasta and stir immediately to keep the pasta from sticking together.
- We do not recommend adding oil to the water to keep pasta from sticking together, as it will also prevent the sauce from clinging to the pasta.
- Do not let the water cool after the pasta is added. It is important to keep it at a constant boil. If the water is not boiling, the pasta may absorb too much water, making it soggy.
- It is your choice whether or not to cover the pot. If you choose to cover the pot, make sure it doesn't boil over, leading you to turn down the heat too far, which then risks making the pasta soggy. However, using a cover will take far less propane and put less humidity into the boat!
- Be sure to stir the pasta a couple of times during cooking to ensure that it doesn't stick together.

Beans, Rice, and Pasta

- Pasta should be cooked al dente—an Italian term for tender but still slightly firm—not mushy. The amount of time for pasta to boil depends on the size, shape, thickness, and even the ingredients used to make it.
- Fresh pasta will cook much quicker than dried pasta, so check it often.
- Pasta that will be added to a salad or used in another recipe requiring more cooking should be undercooked slightly—maybe 75 percent of the time that you'd normally cook it. Slightly under-cooking salad pasta will help it not absorb as much of the dressing.
- Ravioli and other stuffed pastas should be cooked at a gentle boil rather than a vigorous boil to keep them from falling apart. Cooking times will be longer.
- When the pasta is done, drain it as quickly as possible and rinse with cold water to prevent the pasta from continuing to cook and becoming mushy.

Originally we had planned on including a table showing each type of pasta and its recommended cook time. Unfortunately, it is almost impossible to give correct cooking times in a cookbook due to the variations in thickness and ingredients in pasta. Instead, start timing when the water comes to a boil.

Test dry pasta after boiling only 4 minutes by tasting it. Most pastas cook in 8 to 10 minutes, but small types (such as stars) and thin types (such as angel hair) take far less time.

Watch the pot carefully; it is easy to overcook pasta. Pasta should be tender but firm when you eat it, not mushy or soft. It also should not have a hard center.

Grandma's Homemade Noodles
5 to 10 servings

Each egg makes enough noodles for 1 or 2 servings, depending on what else is being served.

Total Time: 1 hour, plus drying time (typically 4 to 6 hours)

Prep Time: 30 minutes   **Cook Time:** 30 minutes

5 eggs
1 teaspoon salt

3 or 4 drops yellow food coloring (optional)
sifted flour
bouillon cubes (beef or chicken depending on what else you're serving), and as many cubes as you had cups of water)

1. Beat the eggs with a fork. Add the salt and food coloring if desired. Add the sifted flour until you can no longer stir the dough with a fork. Then continue adding the flour, mixing by hand.
2. Separate the dough into 5 sections (1 section per egg) and continue working in the flour by hand until each ball of dough is very stiff.
3. Roll each ball into at least a 12-inch circle (the dough should be very hard to roll). Let sit until the edges of the dough are very dry—4 to 6 hours depending on humidity levels.
4. Roll up each 12-inch circle and cut the roll into strips $1/16$ inch to $1/8$ inch wide. Unroll the strips and let them dry until very stiff. Freeze them in an air-tight bag if not cooking immediately.
5. To cook the noodles, put them in a pan and add water to about an inch over the noodles. Note how much water you added. Add as many bouillon cubes as you had cups of water. Let the noodles swell by letting them simmer over low heat, then add more water so that there is still an inch over the noodles.
6. Cook until the noodles are done, about 15 to 30 minutes depending on their thickness. Grandma's were paper thin.

Grandma's Homemade Beef 'n' Noodles
Serves 4 to 6

Special Equipment: Pressure cooker, although you can make this in a large pot as well

Total Time: 1 hour, 5 minutes, plus time to make the noodles

Prep Time: 5 minutes   **Cook Time:** 1 hour

2 to 3 pounds cubed stew beef, round steak, or London broil
Grandma's Homemade Noodles (see preceding recipe)
10 or more beef bouillon cubes OR 10 teaspoons beef bouillon powder

1. Cook the beef in a pressure cooker for about 40 minutes.
2. Add the noodles and enough water to cook them, and at least 10 beef bouillon cubes. Let the noodles swell by letting them simmer over low heat, then add more water so there is still an inch over the noodles before adding pressure. Cook under pressure for at least 15 minutes. Serve hot.

Chinese Noodles   Serves 4

Total Time: 25 minutes
Prep Time: 15 minutes   **Cook Time:** 10 minutes

Enough spaghetti, linguini, or other pasta for 4 servings
6 tablespoons sesame oil
6 tablespoons peanut butter
¼ cup water
3 tablespoons soy sauce
6 tablespoons tahini (optional; it can be hard to find)
2 tablespoons dry sherry
4 teaspoons rice wine vinegar
¼ cup honey
4 cloves garlic, minced
½ cup hot water
2 teaspoons hot pepper sauce, or to taste

1. Boil the noodles, then rinse in cool water and drain. Toss with 2 tablespoons of the sesame oil.
2. In a small saucepan over medium-low heat, combine the remaining 4 tablespoons sesame oil, the peanut butter, ¼ cup water, soy sauce, tahini (if used), sherry, vinegar, honey, garlic, ½ cup hot water, and the hot pepper sauce. Heat until warm, stirring until smooth. Taste and add more hot sauce if not spicy enough.
3. Toss the cooked noodles with the sauce just before serving.

STILL MORE BEANS, RICE, AND PASTA

Here are more recipes with beans, rice, and/or pasta that appear in other chapters.

Appetizers and Snacks
Black Bean and Corn Salsa, *page 127*
Assorted bean dips, *pages 129–131*
Black Bean Hummus, *page 132*

Salads
Assorted Bean Salads, *pages 156–158*

Soups and Stews
Assorted Bean Soups, *pages 168–169*

Meat Main Dishes
Potluck Burger 'n' Rice, *page 271*
Chicken and Sesame Noodles, *page 274*
Pork Chop Casserole, *page 290*

Canned Meats and Seafood
Chicken or Shrimp Paella, *page 312*
Couscous Chicken, *page 312*
Italian Chicken Pasta, *page 313*
Goulash, *page 316*
Rice or Pasta Salad with Ham, *page 321*

Meatless Main Dishes
Spaghetti Pie, *page 347*
Italian Pasta Skillet, *page 349*
Vegetarian Stuffed Peppers, *page 351*
Zucchini Black Bean Quesadilla, *page 353*

Beans, Rice, and Pasta

VEGETABLES

There's nothing better than fresh vegetables, whether just off a local truck, from the local market, directly from the garden, or even from the supermarket. Luckily, as cruisers we get our fair share of fresh vegetables.

But keep in mind that finding fresh veggies as cruisers outside the US is not like walking into a giant produce section of a modern US supermarket. Generally there are not many selections. If there are potatoes, there may be only one kind of red potato and one regular. If you can find fresh asparagus or lettuce at all, you likely won't have many choices. That doesn't make it bad; it just makes it more of an adventure.

COOKING VEGGIES IN SEAWATER

If you use seawater for cooking, remember that salt water boils at a slightly higher temperature than fresh water. Using seawater results in everything cooking faster—once the water is boiling. It may take slightly longer to boil. If you're using seawater to cook veggies, plan on slightly less time than the cooking times in this book. And *do not* forget that seawater already has salt, so reduce or eliminate any salt from the recipe.

FRESH VEGETABLE TIPS

Because there's no way to know where the vegetables you buy have been before you purchase them, it's best to always clean the veggies–even if you're going to peel them later. Wash them in a bleach and water solution (1 capful bleach to 1 gallon water) or a vinegar and water solution (3 parts water to 1 part vinegar) to remove any bacterial or chemical contaminants. Be sure to rinse thoroughly in plain water.

For complete information on buying, washing, and storing vegetables, see the chapter "Food Storage."

- **Asparagus.** Wash, rinse, and let dry. To prepare, snap off the tough end where it snaps easily. If you use a knife, it's much more difficult to find the correct spot.
- **Beets.** Wash thoroughly and rinse with fresh water. Be careful where you cut beets–they will stain countertops, cutting boards, and clothing. If the beets still have the tops attached, cut at least one inch above the beet to prevent the beet juice from escaping while boiling. Place the beets in boiling water, reduce the heat, and simmer for 15 to 20 minutes or more; they're done when a fork pierces them easily. Drain the beets, let cool, and rub the skins off with your hands under cold running water.
- **Cabbage.** Peel away any outer leaves that are wilting or bruised. Be sure to remove the core when cutting the cabbage in half.
- **Cucumber.** Wash and rinse. (Peeling is optional.) To decrease the "burp" factor, either cut the cucumbers into quarters and cut out the seeds, or buy so-called "English" or "burpless" cucumbers where they are available.

VEGETABLE COOKING CHART

Times in the chart are in minutes. For steaming and boiling, timing begins when the water boils after the vegetable is added to the water. If the amount of a vegetable is not specified, it is approximately 2 cups.

VEGETABLE	STEAM	BOIL	MICROWAVE	OTHER
Artichoke, whole	40–60	25–40	4–5 each	
Asparagus	8–10	5–10	4–6	
Beans, green	5–15	10–20	6–12	Stir-fry 3–4
Beets	n/a	20–30	n/a	
Broccoli, florets	5–6	4–5	4–5	Stir-fry 3–4
Broccoli, spears	8–15	5–10	6–7	
Cabbage, 2 wedges	6–9	5–10	10–12	
Carrots, sliced	4–5	5–10	4–7	Stir-fry 3–4
Cauliflower, florets	6–10	5–8	3–4	Stir-fry 3–4
Corn, on cob	6–10	8	3–4	
Corn, kernels	4–6	4–7	3–4	Stir-fry 3–4
Eggplant, diced	5–6	5–10	5–6	Bake 15
Greens, collard, mustard	30–60	18–20	4–6	Stir-fry 4–6
Mushrooms, whole	4–5	3–4 (in wine)	3–4	Stir-fry 4–5
Peas	2	2	2	Stir-fry 2–3
Peppers, bell	2–4	4–5	2–4	Stir-fry 2–3
Potatoes, diced	10–12	15–20	8–10	
Potatoes, whole	n/a	n/a	15	Bake 60 @ 350°F
Spinach	5–6	2–5	3–4	Stir-fry 3
Squash, sliced	5–10	5–10	3–6	
Squash, 2 halves	15–40	5–10	6–10	Bake 40 @ 350°F
Sweet potato	n/a	n/a	5	Bake 50 @ 350°F
Tomatoes	2–3	n/a	3–4	Bake 8–15 @ 350°F
Turnips, cubed	12–15	5–8	6–8	Stir-fry 2–3
Zucchini	5–10	5–10	3–6	Broil 5

- **Eggplant.** Wash and rinse carefully. Cut off each end and then cut into slices or quarters depending on your recipe. As a general rule, you do not need to remove the skin.
- **Green Beans.** Green beans purchased outside the US are often various types of string beans. Wash them and then snap off each end. If the bean has a string, be sure to remove it or the bean may be too tough to eat. The string (along one side) will be apparent when you snap off the ends; then you can just peel the string off the bean.
- **Herbs.** Wash all herbs thoroughly and dry on a paper towel. Most of the time you will pick the leaves off the stems. Fresh herbs seem to last longer if you don't cut them up for the recipe until you're ready to cook, and tearing them usually has better results than cutting them.
- **Lettuce.** Lettuce does not keep well aboard most boats, even at a dock unless it's very sheltered. Even the slightest motion of the boat results in bruised lettuce. Romaine lettuce seems to be a bit more hardy. Lettuce should be washed in a bleach solution (1 capful of plain bleach per gallon of water) and thoroughly dried.
- **Onions.** If an onion is cold, it usually will make you cry less when you're dicing or peeling it.
- **Peas.** Shell a pea by pressing your thumbs and forefingers against the pod to open it. Strip out the peas into a bowl. Wash the peas before cooking. Snow peas, used primarily in Asian cooking,

Vegetables

do not need to be shelled, but you should cut off any stems.

- **Potatoes.** Potatoes should be stored in the dark or they'll develop that funny green color. The green and any eyes are slightly toxic and may give you a stomachache, so be sure to peel any that are greenish and remove and discard the eyes.

- **Spinach.** Wash by swishing in cool water, then blot dry on paper towels. Remove the stem before preparing the spinach.

- **Squash—Spaghetti.** Buy a firm squash that's about 9 inches long and 5 inches in diameter—usually about 4 to 5 pounds. Make sure it does not have any soft spots. Green coloration in spaghetti squash means it's not ripe. It stores well for 4 weeks when whole and kept at room temperature, but after you cut it, be sure to refrigerate it (covered with plastic wrap or put in a plastic bag).

- **Squash—Summer and Zucchini.** In recipes these are generally interchangeable. Summer squash are yellow with larger seeds; zucchini are green and the seeds are much smaller. Wash, rinse, and chop. The skin is delicate and edible, and the seeds are not bothersome.

- **Squash—Winter, such as Butternut.** Wash and rinse. The easiest way is to simply cut the squash in half, scoop out the seeds, and bake the squash, cut side down, until tender. Scoop out the flesh with a sturdy spoon. The same cooking technique is used for acorn squash, but serve one half per person and let him or her scoop out the meat.

- **Tomatoes.** In some locales, you may not find canned tomatoes. No problem; you can use fresh. However, if they are going to be cooked, it's a good idea to peel them. The easiest way to "peel" a tomato is to cut an X in the bottom through the skin. Slip the tomato into boiling water for 10 seconds or less. Let it cool until you can handle it, and then the skin will slip right off. (Although blanching traditionally calls for plunging the hot tomato into ice water, I've found that it works just as well without doing that). If you need to remove the seeds so that a dish won't be as watery, cut the tomato in half and scoop out the seeds with a spoon.

BASIC VEGETABLE COOKING TECHNIQUES

From sear and steam to the oven to the grill, there are a variety of vegetable cooking techniques to entice even the pickiest eaters!

Steamed Vegetable Medley   Serves 6

You can use any vegetables you have for this medley. Any that take less cooking time than average should be added along with the mushrooms.

Total Time: 25 minutes
Prep Time: 10 minutes   **Cook Time:** 5 minutes

1 cup cauliflower florets
1 cup broccoli florets
1 cup diagonally cut carrot slices
1 cup halved green beans
1 medium red onion, sliced and separated into rings
1 cup sliced fresh mushrooms
1½ tablespoons butter or margarine
1 tablespoon lemon juice
¼ teaspoon dried basil, crushed
¼ teaspoon dried marjoram, crushed

1. Place the cauliflower, broccoli, carrot, green beans, and onion in a steamer insert in a saucepan. Or just put ½ inch of water in the bottom of the pan with the veggies; it's not quite as good, but it works. Cover and steam over boiling water for 10 minutes.
2. Add the mushrooms and steam for an additional 5 minutes, or until the vegetables are crisp-tender.
3. Meanwhile, melt the butter. Stir in the lemon juice, basil, and marjoram.
4. Drizzle the butter mixture over the vegetables and toss to combine. Serve hot.

Basic Sear and Steam Veggies   Serves 2

Searing and steaming is the one of the healthiest ways to enjoy your veggies.

Total Time: 12 minutes
Prep Time: 5 minutes   **Cook Time:** 7 minutes

Vegetables

2 tablespoons peanut oil, canola oil, olive oil, or vegetable oil

your choice of fresh veggies, julienned or chopped to the desired size

$1/4$ cup water

soy sauce, butter, balsamic vinegar, lime juice, lemon juice, or other preferred seasonings, for drizzling

1. Heat the oil in a heavy skillet over high heat. Sear the veggies for 3 minutes or less. Add the water and reduce the heat to medium-low. Cover the skillet and steam for 4 minutes, more or less, depending on how crunchy you prefer your veggies.
2. To add flavor, drizzle with your choice of seasonings. Serve hot.

Oven-Roasted Veggies
Serves any number

Very simple and delicious! Veggies are also great cooked on the grill (page 340).

Total Time: 45 minutes
Prep Time: 15 minutes
Roast Time: 15 to 30 minutes

a combination of almost any vegetables cut into bite-size pieces. Veggies that work well include zucchini, summer squash, bell peppers, mushrooms, carrots (slices or baby carrots), broccoli, onions (cut into chunks, not diced), green onions, green beans, asparagus, sweet potatoes (peeled and cut into chunks), chile peppers (but be careful!)

$1\frac{1}{2}$ teaspoons per person olive oil, canola oil, or vegetable oil

salt and pepper, seasoned salt, or Mrs. Dash, to taste

1. Preheat oven to 450°F (or as close to that as your oven will go).
2. Combine the veggies, oil, salt, and pepper. Toss to coat all the veggies with the oil. Place the veggies in a pan so that they aren't more than 1 inch deep (if they are deeper, they will take longer to roast).
3. Roast uncovered for 15 to 30 minutes, stirring every 10 minutes, until the veggies are golden

brown. Be sure to keep a watch as different veggies will take more or less time to roast.

POTATOES

Potatoes are another cruising staple. Enjoying them in a variety of ways keeps them from getting boring.

Basic Baked Potatoes
Serves any number

If you have a choice of type of potatoes, russet potatoes are best for baking. A good-quality russet potato is firm and has a textured skin with a few shallow eyes.

Make sure that the skin has a nice even brown tone without any greenish cast. If you're going to bake more than one potato, make sure that they're about the same shape and size so they'll be done at the same time.

Total Time: about 1 hour, depending on oven temperature (see below)

Russet potatoes or any good baking potato

1. Adjust the rack in your oven to the middle position and preheat oven to the desired temperature (see below).
2. Since potato skins are edible, you need to make sure that they are clean. Scrub each potato and rinse in chlorinated water. Dry thoroughly. Cut out any bruised or discolored parts. With a knife, pierce each potato 3 or 4 times. This releases the steam as it bakes. Otherwise, the potato may explode in the oven. Piercing also makes the potato flakier.

NOTE: Wrapping the potato in aluminum foil will cause the potato to be steamed instead of baked. The skin will be soft instead of crisp, and the potato texture will be more like that of a boiled potato than the flaky texture of a baked potato. If you like a really crisp skin, do nothing more before baking. If you prefer a softer skin, rub the potatoes with a little olive oil, canola oil, butter, or margarine. Then roll the potatoes in salt if desired (not for those watching their sodium intake).

3. Place the potatoes on the oven rack positioned in the center of the oven. It's fine to arrange the

Vegetables

potatoes around other things that are baking. For this reason, a range of temperatures and times is given below. Note that higher temperatures will generally cause the skins to be crispier.

BAKING TIME FOR MEDIUM POTATOES
(about the size of your fist)

TEMPERATURE	TIME
400°F	45 minutes
350°F	60 minutes
325°F	90 minutes

4. Larger potatoes will take longer. Test for doneness by piercing with a fork; if it slides all the way in easily, the potatoes are done.
5. To serve, hold a potato in your hand (in a pot holder) and slit it lengthwise. Gently squeeze the potato open and place it on a plate or in a serving dish. Serve hot.

Old-Fashioned Mashed Potatoes
Serves 2

Total Time: 20 minutes
Prep Time: 10 minutes   Cook Time: 10 minutes

2 medium potatoes, peeled* and diced
1 small onion, diced
butter, to taste
milk, to taste
salt and pepper, to taste

*If desired, leave the peels on for better nutrition and less waste.

1. Boil the potatoes and onion in a medium saucepan for 10 minutes. Drain, then mush the potatoes with a potato masher. Otherwise, cut the potato into smaller pieces and mush them with a fork. The result will be lumpier than with a potato masher, but still good. You can also use an electric hand mixer.
2. Stir in the butter, milk, salt, and pepper. Serve hot.

Variations: For yummy garlic mashed potatoes, add a diced clove of garlic to the potatoes and onion. More garlic makes even yummier garlic potatoes. Or use red potatoes with the skins on and mush them with

extra garlic, onion, and even a chile pepper for added flavor. Another idea: instead of milk, use a dollop of sour cream or plain yogurt. Chives added to any type of mashed/smushed potato will add flavor.

Garlic Smushed Potatoes and Veggies
Serves 4 to 6

The beauty of this recipe is that you can use any vegetables you have on hand. Plus it's a healthy way to use leftovers.

Total Time: 40 minutes
Prep Time: 20 minutes   Cook Time: 20 minutes

2 large potatoes (with skins on), cut into pieces
1 large onion, diced
2 cloves garlic, crushed (more if you like it garlicky, as I do)
1 cup chopped cabbage
1 carrot, peeled and diced or thinly sliced

NOTE: Use any leftover veggies you have, or any or none of the following. Your choice.

1 zucchini, peeled and chopped
1 cup chopped cauliflower
1 green bell pepper, diced
2 cups chicken broth (may be made from bouillon) or stock (page 164)
butter or margarine, to taste
1/4 cup sour cream (page 99), cream cheese, or milk, or to taste and for desired consistency
salt, ground pepper, seasoned salt, or any seasonings you desire

1. Place all the veggies in a large pan. Cover with the broth, adding water if necessary to cover the veggies. Cover the pan and bring to a boil. Reduce the heat and simmer until the veggies are "smushable"—about 10 to 12 minutes depending on what veggies you're using.
2. Drain the water (keep it for vegetable stock or other cooking, or use it to rinse the dishes) and leave the veggies in the pan. Smush them thoroughly with a potato masher or the back of a spoon. Add enough butter and sour cream to achieve the desired consistency. Add salt, pepper, and other seasonings to taste. Serve hot.

Special Potato Packets   Serves 2

Potato packets can also be cooked on the grill (page 340).

Total Time: 45 minutes
Prep Time: 15 minutes   **Bake Time:** 30 minutes

cooking spray or canola oil
1 medium onion, diced
$\frac{1}{2}$ green bell pepper, diced
2 cloves garlic, chopped or minced
$\frac{1}{2}$ jalapeño pepper, seeded and finely diced
2 small potatoes, julienned
butter, to taste
salt and pepper, to taste

1. Preheat oven to 350°F.
2. Spritz a piece of aluminum foil with cooking spray or use a bit of canola oil. Place the onion, bell pepper, garlic, jalapeño pepper, and potato on the foil. Add the butter, salt, and pepper, and fold up the foil (use a double fold on top so the packet doesn't leak). Bake for 30 to 45 minutes. Serve hot.

NOTE: The smaller the potato pieces, the quicker they will cook. If you like larger chunks, allow for a longer cooking time.

Stove-Top Red Potatoes   Serves 4

Total Time: 35 minutes
Prep Time: 15 minutes   **Cook Time:** 20 minutes

1 tablespoon olive oil, canola oil, or vegetable oil
1 medium onion, diced
$\frac{1}{2}$ cup diced green bell pepper
$\frac{1}{2}$ cup diced red bell pepper
dash of crushed red pepper flakes
4 medium red potatoes (with skin on), cubed
$\frac{1}{4}$ cup chicken broth (may be made from bouillon) or stock (page 164)
1 teaspoon Worcestershire sauce

1. Heat the oil in a skillet. Add the onion, bell peppers, red pepper flakes, and potato. Sauté over medium heat for 5 minutes.
2. Combine the broth and Worcestershire sauce and pour over the vegetables. Cover and cook for 10 minutes, or until the potato is tender. Uncover and cook until the liquid is absorbed. Serve hot.

Aly's Red Potatoes   Serves 4

Aly is Jan's daughter, who first served these great potatoes.

Total Time: 35 minutes
Prep Time: 5 minutes   **Bake Time:** 30 minutes

olive oil or cooking spray
4 to 6 red potatoes (with skins on), sliced $\frac{1}{2}$ inch thick
2 cloves garlic, minced
$\frac{1}{3}$ cup olive oil, canola oil, or vegetable oil
salt and pepper, to taste
crushed red pepper flakes, to taste

1. Preheat oven to 350°F. Spritz a baking dish with olive oil or cooking spray.
2. Place the potato slices in the dish and toss with the garlic. Drizzle with the oil. Season with the salt, pepper, and any seasonings you prefer. (We like crushed red pepper flakes, but be careful, they are spicy!)
3. Cover the dish with aluminum foil and bake until the potatoes are done, or about 30 minutes (test with a fork). Thinner sliced potatoes cook quicker, thicker slices take longer.

Variation: You can make this dish in a skillet on the stove top. The potatoes won't be crunchy on the outside, but they'll still be delicious.

Easy Scalloped Potatoes   Serves 6

Total Time: 1 hour, 30 minutes
Prep Time: 15 minutes
Cook Time: 1 hour, 15 minutes

cooking spray, olive oil, or canola oil
6 medium potatoes, peeled and thinly sliced
1 large onion, diced
$\frac{1}{2}$ cup chopped fresh chives OR 2 tablespoons dried chives (optional)
$\frac{1}{2}$ teaspoon salt
ground pepper, to taste
$\frac{1}{4}$ cup butter or margarine
1 cup milk

1. Preheat oven to 325°F.
2. Spritz a medium baking dish with cooking spray. Arrange the potato in layers, topping each layer

Vegetables

with the onion, a sprinkling of chives, and salt and pepper, and dotting each layer with butter. Repeat the layers until all the ingredients are used.

3. Pour the milk over all; cover and bake for 45 minutes. Then uncover and bake 30 minutes longer, or until the potato is tender when pierced with a fork and the top is golden brown. Serve hot.

Variation: If you prefer cheesy scalloped potatoes, simply sprinkle any shredded meltable cheese (cheddar, Monterey Jack, Colby, mozzarella) over each layer and over the top before baking. Also, to use this as a main dish, you can add up to 4 ounces of ham per person (pre-cooked or canned).

ARTICHOKES

Artichokes are not only delicious, but they also help lower cholesterol!

Cheesy Baked Artichoke Hearts
Serves 2 to 4

Total Time: 1 hour, 15 minutes
Prep Time: 30 minutes   Cook Time: 4 to 5 minutes

1 can (14 ounces) artichoke hearts, drained
1 clove garlic, minced, OR ¼ teaspoon garlic powder
¼ cup butter or margarine
salt and pepper, to taste
2 tablespoons flour
¾ cup milk
1 egg, slightly beaten
½ cup grated Swiss cheese or any mild cheese that will melt, such as mozzarella
1 tablespoon dry bread crumbs, finely crushed
1 teaspoon paprika

1. Preheat oven to 350°F.
2. Cut the artichoke hearts into bite-size pieces. Sauté the artichoke and garlic in the butter until both are golden.
3. Spritz a baking dish with cooking spray. Remove the artichoke and garlic from the pan and place in the dish, leaving as much butter in the pan as possible.

4. Stir the salt, pepper, and flour into the butter in the pan, then slowly add the milk. Cook over low heat until thickened, stirring constantly. Remove from the heat.

5. Slowly add the egg and half the cheese to the pan. Stir until smooth. Pour the sauce over the artichoke in the dish, and sprinkle with the remaining cheese and the bread crumbs and paprika. Bake for 30 minutes, or until the cheese is melted and golden. Serve hot.

Mushroom Artichoke Herb Casserole
Serves 4

Total Time: 55 minutes, including 5 minutes cooling time
Prep Time: 10 minutes   Cook Time: 40 minutes

1 can (16 ounces) artichoke hearts in water, drained
8 to 12 ounces fresh mushrooms OR 1 can (7 ounces) sliced mushrooms, drained
½ cup olive oil, canola oil, or vegetable oil
salt and pepper, to taste
1 cup Italian or herb bread crumbs (page 51)
¼ cup grated or shredded Parmesan cheese

1. Preheat oven to 350°F.
2. Cut the artichoke hearts into quarters. Clean and slice the mushrooms if needed.
3. Coat the bottom of a casserole dish with 1 tablespoon of the olive oil (reserve the remaining oil for later). Place a layer of artichoke hearts in the dish and top with a layer of sliced mushrooms. Sprinkle with salt and pepper. Top with part of the bread crumbs. Drizzle with 1 tablespoon of the olive oil.
4. Repeat the layers until all the ingredients are used. Top the last layer of bread crumbs with the remaining olive oil and sprinkle with the Parmesan. Cover with aluminum foil and bake for 30 minutes.
5. Remove the foil and continue baking until the top turns golden, or about 10 minutes more. Let cool for 5 minutes before serving.

Vegetables

Baked Artichokes and Brown Rice   Serves 4

Total Time: 1 hour, plus time to cook the rice if needed
Prep Time: 10 minutes
Cook Time: 45 minutes to 1 hour

cooking spray
1 jar (6 ounces) marinated artichoke hearts, drained and chopped into bite-size pieces
1 cup cooked brown rice
1 cup shredded cheddar or similar cheese
4 eggs
$1/2$ cup milk
$1/3$ teaspoon dry mustard OR 1 teaspoon prepared mustard
$1/8$ teaspoon paprika
salt and pepper, to taste

1. Preheat oven to 350°F. Spritz a baking dish with cooking spray.
2. Combine the chopped artichoke hearts, cooked rice, and cheese and pour into the baking dish.
3. Stir the eggs briskly with a fork. Add the milk and mustard; stir together and pour over the rice mixture. Sprinkle with the paprika, salt, and pepper.
4. Bake for 45 minutes to 1 hour, or until golden brown on top. Serve hot.

TIP: Make the dish ahead and store it in the refrigerator to bake later or even the next day. If you don't have room for the baking dish to sit flat, store the contents in a leakproof freezer bag or a leakproof plastic food storage container and transfer to a baking dish when you're ready to bake it.

ASPARAGUS

Fresh asparagus is a real treat when you find it, but even canned is a special treat!

Parmesan Asparagus   Serves 2

Total Time: 20 minutes
Prep Time: 5 minutes   **Bake Time:** 15 minutes

1 can (16 ounces) asparagus, drained, OR a bunch of fresh asparagus, prepared (page 190)
$1/2$ cup butter or margarine, melted
1 tablespoon lemon juice
$1/2$ cup grated or shredded Parmesan cheese

1. Preheat oven to 400°F.
2. If the asparagus spears are large, steam (page 191) them until almost tender. Arrange the spears in a baking dish and drizzle with the butter and lemon juice. Sprinkle with the Parmesan cheese. Bake for 15 minutes. If you're using large spears of fresh asparagus, they may need to bake a bit longer. Test with a fork after 15 minutes to see if they're tender. If not, bake a few minutes longer. Serve hot.

NOTE: This dish can be made on the stove top in a skillet with good results.

BROCCOLI

There are also several good broccoli salads in the "Salads" chapter.

Broccoli Penne   Serves 6

Total Time: 40 minutes
Prep Time: 10 minutes   **Cook Time:** 30 minutes

8 ounces penne pasta or other medium-size pasta
$2^1/2$ pounds broccoli florets
2 cloves garlic, minced
$1/3$ cup olive oil, canola oil, or vegetable oil
1 tablespoon butter or margarine
1 teaspoon salt
$1/4$ teaspoon ground pepper
Parmesan cheese, grated or shredded, to taste

1. Cook the pasta according to package directions while preparing the other ingredients. Drain the pasta and set aside.
2. Sauté the broccoli and garlic in the oil and butter until tender. Sprinkle with salt and pepper. Toss with the reserved pasta and serve topped with the Parmesan.

Vegetables

Sesame Broccoli   Serves 6

Total Time: 20 minutes
Prep Time: 15 minutes   Cook Time: 5 minutes

4 cups broccoli florets
3 tablespoons finely diced red bell pepper
2 teaspoons sesame seeds
dash of sesame oil or canola oil (optional)
2 tablespoons soy sauce
1 tablespoon water
2 teaspoons sugar
1/2 teaspoon ground ginger
1/4 teaspoon dry mustard OR 1 teaspoon prepared
    mustard

1. Steam the broccoli and bell pepper for 5 minutes,
   or until crisp-tender; place in a medium bowl.
2. Toast the sesame seeds if desired in medium-hot
   oil; set aside.
3. In a small pan combine the soy sauce, water, sugar,
   ginger, and mustard; stir well. Heat until just boiling. Pour the sauce over the prepared vegetables.
   Sprinkle with the prepared sesame seeds and toss
   to combine. Serve hot.

CORN

You can find canned corn almost everywhere, but try
one can of any local brand before stocking up on it—
in some places it's much tougher than what Americans and Canadians are used to.

Canned Corn Side Dish   Serves 4

Total Time: 25 minutes
Prep Time: 10 minutes   Cook Time: 15 minutes

1/3 cup finely chopped celery
1/3 cup finely chopped green bell pepper
1/2 cup finely diced onion OR 1 teaspoon onion
    powder
2 teaspoons olive oil, canola oil, or vegetable oil
1 can (16 ounces) corn, drained
1 can (8 ounces) tomato sauce
1 can (8 ounces) sliced mushrooms, drained, OR
    8 ounces fresh mushrooms, sliced

1 tomato, finely diced, OR 1 can (16 ounces) diced
    tomatoes, not drained
2 tablespoons brown sugar or white sugar
1 teaspoon garlic powder OR 4 cloves garlic,
    minced
1/2 teaspoon salt
ground pepper, to taste
cayenne pepper, to taste (optional)

In a large pan sauté the celery, bell pepper, and onion
(if using fresh) in the olive oil. Add the rest of the
ingredients. Mix thoroughly, cover, and simmer until
heated through. Serve hot.

Potluck Corn Casserole   Serves 8 to 10

Total Time: 55 minutes
Prep Time: 10 minutes   Cook Time: 45 minutes

cooking spray
1 can (16 ounces) creamed corn
1 can (16 ounces) whole corn, drained
2 eggs
1/2 cup butter or margarine, cut into 1/2-inch cubes
1 cup sour cream (page 99)
1 onion, chopped
1 box Jiffy corn bread mix OR 2 cups crushed Ritz
    or Club or similar crackers
salt and pepper, to taste

1. Preheat oven to 350°F. Spritz a casserole dish with
   the cooking spray.
2. In a medium bowl combine the creamed corn,
   whole corn, eggs, butter, sour cream, onion, corn
   bread mix, salt, and pepper. Cover and bake for
   45 minutes. Serve hot.

GREEN BEANS

Fresh green beans are a treat; canned green beans are
a cruising staple. In addition to the recipes here, be
sure to check out the other green bean recipes listed
in other chapters, such as the chapter "Salads."

Vegetables

Green Bean Casserole   Serves 6

Total Time: 40 minutes
Prep Time: 5 minutes   **Cook Time:** 35 minutes

cooking spray
2 cans (16 ounces each) French-cut green beans, drained, OR 2 cans (16 ounces each) regular-cut green beans, drained, OR 2 pounds fresh green beans, steamed until tender
1 can (10 ounces) cream of mushroom soup, undiluted (page 55)
1 tablespoon ground pepper, or to taste
1 can (3 ounces) onion rings OR 1 onion sliced thinly and sautéed in butter

1. Preheat oven to 350°F. Spritz an 8-inch square dish or loaf pan with cooking spray.
2. In a large bowl combine the beans, soup, ground pepper, and half the onion rings. Transfer to the baking dish and bake for 30 minutes, or until the mixture bubbles. Sprinkle the rest of the onion rings on top and bake another 5 minutes. Let sit for 5 minutes before serving.

Stove-Top Variation: Cook in a stove-top pan instead of a baking dish. Cook half the onion rings in a dry skillet over medium-high to high heat until they become dark golden and crunchy. Shake the pan frequently to keep them from sticking or burning. Top the green bean mix with a sprinkling of the toasted onion rings, and serve from the pan.

Fresh Green Beans and Bacon   Serves 2 to 4

OK, so bacon is not healthy at all, but this dish is good old-fashioned comfort food.

NOTE: When buying green beans in a foreign country, you may need to strip off the string to get rid of the tough fiber. See page 191 for instructions. No fresh green beans? See the variation below for using canned.

Total Time: 55 minutes
Prep Time: 10 minutes   **Cook Time:** 45 minutes

4 or 5 slices bacon
1 pound fresh green beans, washed, strings removed, and snapped into 1-inch pieces
1 small onion, diced
1 bouillon cube (beef or chicken)
ground pepper, to taste

1. Fry the bacon in a large skillet. Remove and drain the bacon but save the fat in the pan. Crumble the bacon and set aside.
2. Sauté the green beans and diced onion in the bacon fat. In the same pan, add enough water to cover the beans. Add the bouillon cube. Simmer until the water is evaporated (but be careful not to let the pan burn) and the beans are tender and cooked to the desired crispness.
3. Add the crumbled bacon and stir to combine. Add the ground pepper. Taste to see if the seasonings are right. You can add more pepper or some salt, but be careful since the bouillon cube contains salt. Serve hot.

Variation: If using canned green beans, fry the bacon and onion together, remove from the pan, and set aside. Heat the drained canned green beans in the bacon fat (it won't take very long). Remove from the heat and add the reserved bacon and onion. Sprinkle with ground pepper and serve.

Fresh Green Beans with Garlic   Serves 2

Total Time: 20 minutes
Prep Time: 5 minutes   **Cook Time:** 15 minutes

1 pound fresh green beans OR 1 can (16 ounces) green beans, drained
1 small onion, thinly sliced
2 cloves garlic, minced
2 teaspoons butter, margarine, olive oil, canola oil, or vegetable oil
1 tablespoon fresh thyme or oregano OR ½ teaspoon dried thyme, oregano, or Italian seasoning
salt, to taste
cayenne pepper, to taste
sliced almonds (optional, but very tasty)

Vegetables

1. Trim the fresh beans and steam for 5 to10 minutes, or until crisp-tender. Drain.
2. In a large skillet sauté the onion and garlic in the butter. Stir in the drained beans, thyme, salt, and cayenne, and simmer until the beans are the consistency you prefer. Add the almonds, if desired, just before serving.

Spicy Green Beans   Serves 6

Total Time: 25 minutes
Prep Time: 10 minutes   **Cook Time:** 15 minutes

5 tablespoons canola oil, olive oil, or vegetable oil
2 teaspoons whole cumin seed OR 1 teaspoon ground cumin
1 dried hot red chile OR dash of red chili pepper flakes
1-inch piece of fresh ginger, peeled and chopped, OR ¼ teaspoon ground ginger
10 cloves garlic, crushed or minced
2 teaspoons ground coriander
1 can (16 ounces) diced tomatoes OR 1 cup diced fresh tomato
1½ pounds fresh green beans, trimmed and snapped into 1-inch pieces, OR 2 cans (16 ounces each) green beans, drained*
1½ cups water
1¼ teaspoons salt
3 tablespoons lemon juice
1 (more) teaspoon ground cumin
ground pepper, to taste

1. Heat the oil in a large saucepan. Add the 2 teaspoons whole cumin seed (or 1 teaspoon ground cumin), the red chile, ginger, and garlic. Sauté for about 1 minute, stirring constantly.
2. Add the coriander, tomatoes, beans, water, and salt. Bring to a boil, then reduce the heat to a simmer. Cover and cook for 10 to 15 minutes, or until the beans are tender.
3. Add the lemon juice, the extra cumin, and ground pepper. Stir to combine. Increase the heat to high and cook until the liquid has boiled off, but be careful that the bean mixture doesn't burn.

NOTE: This dish can be really spicy. Reduce or add spice to suit your taste buds.

To make this dish with canned green beans, omit the water. And you don't need to cook the beans until tender; they already are.

ZUCCHINI, CHRISTOPHENE, AND SQUASH

We found squash in many locales, as well as small Tetra Paks of "canned" squash that are easy to stow and work well in many recipes—just be sure to drain them well.

Zucchini Cheese Casserole   Serves 8

Total Time: 1 hour, 25 minutes
Prep Time: 15 minutes
Bake Time: 1 hour, 10 minutes

dash of olive oil, canola oil, or vegetable oil OR cooking spray, butter, or margarine
18 saltine crackers, crushed, OR 1 cup bread crumbs
6 medium zucchini or summer squash, thinly sliced
2 tomatoes, diced, OR 1 can (16 ounces) diced tomatoes, drained
2 cups shredded cheddar or similar cheese
½ teaspoon salt
¼ teaspoon garlic powder
dash of ground pepper, to taste
1 large onion, slivered
3 slices bacon, fried and crumbled

1. Preheat oven to 350°F. Coat a large casserole dish with olive oil.
2. Sprinkle a layer of crushed crackers in the dish. Top with a layer of zucchini and tomato, then a layer of cheese (use half the cheese). Sprinkle with the salt, garlic powder, and ground pepper. Add a layer of onion and then the rest of the cheese.
3. Cover and bake for 1 hour. Remove the cover and sprinkle with the crumbled bacon. Return to the oven and bake, uncovered, 5 minutes longer, or until the cheese is melted and bubbly. Let stand for 5 minutes before serving.

Healthy Zucchini

Serves 6

Total Time: 35 minutes
Prep Time: 15 minutes   Cook Time: 15 minutes

6 small zucchini or summer squash, thinly sliced
1 onion, cut into thin slivers
1 red bell pepper or any bell pepper, finely diced
2 tablespoons olive oil, canola oil, vegetable oil,
     butter, or margarine
4 cloves garlic, minced
1 can (8 ounces) sliced mushrooms, drained, OR 8
     ounces fresh mushrooms, sliced
1 cup chicken broth (may be made from bouillon)
     or stock (page 164)
fresh cilantro, to taste
cayenne pepper, to taste (be careful!)
salt, to taste
ground pepper, to taste
2 tomatoes, diced, OR 1 can (16 ounces) diced
     tomatoes, drained
Parmesan cheese, grated or shredded (optional)

1. In a large skillet over medium-high heat, sauté the
   zucchini, onion, and bell pepper in the olive oil.
2. Add the garlic, mushrooms, broth, cilantro, cayenne, salt, and ground pepper. Increase the heat
   to high and cook until the broth is boiling. Then
   cover and reduce the heat to low. Simmer until the
   zucchini is tender but still a bit crunchy. Turn off
   the heat and add the tomatoes. Stir, cover, and let
   sit for 5 minutes, or until the tomatoes are heated
   through. Sprinkle with the Parmesan, and serve.

Stir-Fried Zucchini

Serves 2

*Gram flour (not "graham flour") has a nutty flavor. If
you use a substitute, compensate by adding more of your
favorite spice.*

Total Time: 30 minutes
Prep Time: 10 minutes   Cook Time: 15 minutes

1 large zucchini, with skin on
1 tablespoon gram flour (besan or chick-pea flour,
     not the same as "graham" flour) or regular flour
salt
¼ teaspoon turmeric powder
¼ teaspoon red chili powder
½ teaspoon ground cumin

½ teaspoon dried thyme or caraway seed, depend-
     ing on your preference
3 tablespoons canola oil or vegetable oil

1. Dice the zucchini into 1-inch pieces. Place in a
   medium bowl. Add the gram flour and spices to
   taste and mix well to coat.
2. Warm the oil in a skillet over medium-high heat
   until hot. Add the zucchini mixture and stir.
   Reduce the heat and cook until the flour coating is
   golden and the zucchini is tender when tested with
   a fork. Serve hot.

Baked Zucchini or
Summer Squash

Serves 2 to 4

Total Time: 50 minutes
Prep Time: 10 minutes   Bake Time: 35 to 40 minutes

2 medium zucchini
2 tablespoons olive oil, canola oil, or vegetable oil,
     or butter or margarine, melted
1 teaspoon dried oregano
¼ cup grated or shredded Parmesan cheese

1. Preheat oven to 350°F.
2. Slice the zucchini into ⅛-inch-thick to ¼-inch-
   thick slices. Toss with the oil and oregano. Arrange
   in a single layer on a baking sheet or in a shallow
   baking dish. Sprinkle with the Parmesan. Bake,
   uncovered, for 35 to 40 minutes. Serve hot.

Curried Zucchini
with Yogurt

Serves 2

*This is one of those recipes you have to try. It doesn't look
good on paper, but it's one of Dave and Carolyn's favorites. It's tasty even without the yogurt.*

Total Time: 20 minutes
Prep Time: 10 minutes   Cook Time: 10 minutes

4 or 5 small OR 2 medium zucchini
2 thick slices onion
1 teaspoon olive oil, canola oil, vegetable oil, but-
     ter, or margarine
⅛ teaspoon curry powder (or more to taste;
     page 47)
1 teaspoon sugar
¼ cup plain yogurt (page 101; optional)

Vegetables

1. Cut the zucchini into ¼-inch-thick slices. Separate the onion slices into rounds. Sauté the zucchini and onion in the oil until just golden.
2. Sprinkle with the curry powder and sugar. Cover and cook over low heat until tender, or approximately 5 minutes more.
3. Transfer the mixture to a serving bowl. (Do not leave it in the hot pan while you add the yogurt; the yogurt will curdle!) Drizzle the yogurt (if used) over the top. Serve hot.

Christophene au Gratin

Serves 2 as main dish or 4 as a side dish

Christophene is a type of squash common to Central America. Also called whiskiel in Belize and Guatemala, and chayote or chayotte in Mexico and the southwestern US, it has a mild flavor and a texture much like that of yellow squash. Be sure to remove the large seed in the middle.

Prep Time: 15 minutes
Boil Time: 20 to 30 minutes   Bake Time: 20 minutes

2 large christophenes
2 tablespoons butter, margarine, olive oil, canola oil, or vegetable oil
1 onion, minced
1 clove garlic, minced
½ hot chile pepper, seeded and minced
1 stalk celery, diced

1 green onion, diced, OR ¼ cup diced onion
½ teaspoon dried thyme
1 cup grated cheddar cheese
¼ cup grated or shredded Parmesan cheese
2 tablespoons dry bread crumbs
salt and pepper, to taste

1. Preheat oven to 375°F.
2. Cut the christophenes in half and remove the seed. Boil in water for 20 to 30 minutes, or until soft. Remove from the water and let cool.
3. Scoop out the pulp and set aside the shells (they will be used for serving). Dice or mash the pulp. Set aside.
4. Heat the butter and add the onion, garlic, hot pepper, celery, green onion, and thyme. Sauté for 5 minutes. Add the christophene pulp and sauté for another 5 minutes. Remove from the heat.
5. Add half of both cheeses and all the bread crumbs. Season with the salt and pepper.
6. Fill the christophene shells with the mixture. Place on a baking sheet and sprinkle with the remainder of the cheese. Bake for 20 minutes, or until the top is golden.

Christophene

Serves 2

Total Time: 20 to 25 minutes
Prep Time: 10 minutes   Cook Time: 10 to 15 minutes

1 large christophene
several cloves garlic or to taste, minced
½ medium onion, finely diced
1 cup chicken broth (may be made from bouillon) or stock (page 164)
salt and pepper, to taste

1. Cut the christophene in half and remove the large seed. Peel and cut into 1-inch chunks. Place the chunks in a saucepan, and add the garlic, onion, and broth. Bring to a boil over medium-high heat.
2. Reduce the heat to medium and steam the christophene until it is soft—usually 10 to 15 minutes. Add the salt and pepper, and serve hot.

Vegetables

Spaghetti Squash   Serves 4

Spaghetti squash tastes great and has just one-sixth the calories of pasta. It will last a month or more without refrigeration and is easy to cook. Use it for spaghetti and lasagna, and even in pasta salad!

Total Time: 45 minutes
Prep Time: 15 minutes   **Cook Time:** 30 minutes

1 spaghetti squash

1. Preheat oven to 350°F, if baking.
2. Cut the squash once around the middle, then cut each half in two lengthwise. Scoop the seeds from each piece.
3. To cook on the stove top, place the pieces in a pan large enough to hold them and add water to cover about halfway. Cover the pan and bring to a boil over high heat, then reduce the heat to low and simmer for about 20 minutes, or until a fork easily goes through the squash.
4. To bake, place the pieces in a baking pan and cover. Bake for about 30 minutes, or until fork tender.
5. To cook in a microwave, place the pieces cut side down on a plate or in a microwave-safe dish (you may have to cook it in two batches) and microwave on high for 7 to 10 minutes, or until fork tender.

You can cook a spaghetti squash whole, but it's easier to cut it into quarters so it will fit into a pot better. Plus it gets some of the "prep" done before the squash is hot.

The exact time will depend on the microwave oven power and the number of pieces being cooked.
6. Whatever method you choose, when the squash is cooked, remove one piece at a time and place it on a plate or cutting board. Run a fork lengthwise through the center of the squash, causing the squash to form "strands." Remove the strands and place them in a serving bowl; discard the skins. Gently squeeze any excess water out of the squash strands before serving.

CAULIFLOWER

There are also several recipes in the "Salad" chapter that use cauliflower.

Mashed Cauliflower   Serves 4

Mashing cauliflower makes it very similar to mashed potatoes but has far fewer calories and carbs. Three things we've learned from making it: (1) don't use any cauliflower stems because they're just too tough to have a nice consistency when mashed; (2) don't try to make these with a potato ricer—it won't mash them enough; (3) you don't have to add the cornstarch or flour, but the mixture will be thinner than mashed potatoes without it.

Total Time: 30 minutes
Prep Time: 10 minutes
Cook Time: 10 minutes to steam, 10 minutes to heat

1 head cauliflower, florets only
1 onion, diced
1 tablespoon cornstarch OR 2 tablespoons flour
¹/₃ cup heavy cream OR 4 tablespoons ranch dressing (page 161) OR ¹/₃ cup sour cream (page 99), half-and-half (*media crema*), or evaporated milk (page 99)
1 teaspoon sugar
³/₄ teaspoon salt
¹/₄ teaspoon ground pepper
¹/₈ teaspoon garlic powder
3 strips bacon, fried and crumbled (optional)

1. Steam the cauliflower and onion together for about 10 minutes, or until soft. Drain all the water, and mash the veggies with a potato masher.

2. Combine the cornstarch with the cream and mix into the mashed veggies. Add the sugar, salt, pepper, and garlic. Add the crumbled bacon if desired. Stir to combine.

3. Heat the mixture for 10 minutes over medium heat to thicken, stirring often. Serve as you would mashed potatoes.

Colorful Cauliflower   Serves 4 to 6

Total Time: 30 minutes
Prep Time: 15 minutes   Cook Time: 15 minutes

1 medium cauliflower, florets only
1 tablespoon olive oil, canola oil, or vegetable oil
½ cup diced red bell pepper or any color bell pepper you have
½ cup diced yellow bell pepper
3 or 4 green onions, diced
salt, to taste
cayenne pepper, to taste
½ cup shredded cheddar or other similar cheese
2 to 3 tablespoons chopped black olives (optional)

1. Place the cauliflower florets in a large saucepan with the olive oil. Add enough water (about ½ inch) to the pan to steam the florets. Add the bell peppers and green onion and sprinkle with the salt and cayenne. Steam until the veggies are crisp-tender. Remove from the heat, and drain.

2. Add the cheese and olives (if desired). Cover and let stand for 5 minutes, or until the cheese melts. Serve hot.

MUSHROOMS, BEETS, AND SUN-DRIED TOMATOES

Following are several great recipes for "miscellaneous" veggies.

Curried Canned Mushrooms   Serves 4

Total Time: 10 minutes

1 cup sour cream (page 99) or plain yogurt (page 101)
⅓ cup mayonnaise or Miracle Whip
2 tablespoons pickle relish (optional, but tasty!)

1 tablespoon curry powder (page 47; start with less and add to taste)
salt and pepper, to taste
2 cans (8 ounces each) mushrooms, drained
paprika, to taste

In a large serving bowl, combine the sour cream, mayonnaise, relish (if desired), curry powder, salt, and pepper. Stir in the mushrooms. Sprinkle with the paprika; cover and chill until ready to serve.

Sweet and Sour Beets   Serves 4

Carolyn's mother always called these "Harvard beets." She said they originated at Harvard University, but I can't find anything to support this, although there are many theories as to the origin of the name.

Total Time: 20 minutes, not including marinating time
Prep Time: 10 minutes   Cook Time: 10 minutes

½ cup sugar
1 tablespoon cornstarch OR 2 tablespoons flour
1 teaspoon salt
¼ cup water OR ¼ cup liquid from the beets
¼ cup cider vinegar or white vinegar
3 cups canned beets, drained and liquid reserved (about 2 cans of beets)*
2 tablespoons butter or margarine

1. In a large saucepan combine the sugar, cornstarch, and salt. Add the water and vinegar and stir until the mixture is smooth and the sugar and salt are dissolved.

2. Cook for 5 minutes over medium heat. Add the beets and let stand to marinate while you prepare the rest of the meal.

3. Just before serving, heat the beets to boiling and add the butter. Let it melt, and stir to combine. Serve hot.

*If you want to use fresh beets, you'll need 10 to 15 beets about 2½ inches in diameter. Place the beets in a large pan, cover with water, and boil for 45 minutes, or until tender. Drain, reserving ¼ cup of the cooking water for use as above, and let beets cool until they can be handled. When the beets are cool, slip off the skins and use the beets as directed in the recipe.

Vegetables

Sun-Dried Tomatoes

Yes, we know that a tomato is a fruit and not a veggie, but we couldn't figure out where else this recipe would fit in the cookbook. You may not want to invest the oven time, but if you have a taste for sun-dried tomatoes, you could try this recipe. I can't imagine that you couldn't dry the tomatoes in the sun just as easily.

Roma tomatoes cut into quarters or cherry tomatoes cut in half (smaller pieces dry faster than larger pieces)
coarse salt
olive oil, as needed
fresh basil or other herbs of choice, as needed

1. Preheat oven to 175°F.
2. Place the tomato pieces on a baking sheet, and sprinkle lightly with the coarse salt. Leave in the oven for 8 hours.
3. Remove from the oven and let cool. Store the tomatoes in a leakproof container filled with enough olive oil to cover the tomatoes. If you want to add herbs to the olive oil, feel free—fresh basil is good. Be careful as the herb flavors will intensify with time.

MORE WAYS TO PREPARE VEGETABLES

Almost every chapter contains numerous recipes that use vegetables. If you're interested in vegetable side dishes, you might want to take a look at these.

Salads

Almost all our salads incorporate veggies in some fashion. Here are some of our favorites:

Asian Cabbage Salad, *page 147*
Basic Creamy Coleslaw, *page 148*
Greek Salad, *page 151*
Japanese Cucumber Salad à la *Bruadair*, *page 152*
Broccoli Cauliflower Salad, *page 152*
Cucumber Onion Salad, *page 152*
Marinated Zucchini Salad, *page 153*
Carrot Raisin Salad, *page 154*
All-American Potato Salad, *page 154*
Oil and Vinegar Potato Salad, *page 155*
Black Bean, Corn, and Tomato Salad, *page 156*
Vegetable Salad à la *Que Tal*, *page 157*

Grilling

Grilled Veggies, *page 340*
Grilled Sweet Potato Slices, *page 341*
Potato Packets, *page 341*
Grilled Herbed Vegetables, *page 341*
Grilled Corn on the Cob, *page 342*

Vegetables

SAUCES, GRAVIES, MARINADES, AND RUBS

Many cooks often use packaged or bottled sauces, gravies, marinades, rubs, and so on. These are generally hard to find in cruising locales, so you have to make your own.

The cookbooks we have cruised with were short on many of these "basic" types of recipes and generally had only one recipe in a category–if it was covered at all. We've tried to provide a broad selection. Several of these recipes call for cooking in a double boiler. If you don't have a true double boiler, use a saucepan and a heat diffuser (also called a flame tamer; see page 15 in the chapter "Equipping a Galley") over the lowest possible heat. A flame tamer takes very little space and is useful for many things.

Tip: Some of the recipes here call for mixing flour or cornstarch with water. The easiest way to mix them is to put the liquid in a container with a tight-fitting lid, then add the flour or cornstarch, and stir, whisk, or shake. This is more effective than putting the liquid in last. And with cornstarch, using a cool liquid will produce smoother results than using a warm liquid.

Some of these recipes call for ingredients that are difficult to find in certain cruising locales. Because these ingredients typically don't take up much room and can be used for many recipes, Jan would bring them with her each year for their "commuter cruising" season, and Carolyn learned to stock up when she did find them or bring some back from trips to the US. Although availability seems to change from year to year, here's our quick list of things that are often hard to find:

- Dill pickle relish, grated horseradish, wasabi, liquid smoke, and cornstarch are not widely available.
- Worcestershire sauce is available everywhere, but it's called *salsa inglesa* in Spanish. Soy sauce is available everywhere and is often called *salsa chino* in Spanish.

Consider these recipes to be a starting point. For many, you may want to adjust the seasonings to your own taste. Other times, you may not have all the ingredients but can come close. Remember, the goal is to produce food that tastes good, not necessarily exactly how it is written in the recipe. These recipes will get you started and provide plenty of ideas.

Unless otherwise noted, these recipes each take 10 minutes or less to prepare.

BASIC WHITE SAUCE AND CHEESE SAUCE

White sauce is generally not used on its own but serves as the base for many other sauces, such as cheese sauce as well as most cream soups. Add herbs, spices, cheese, and more to suit your purposes. This recipe is useful when you don't have access to jarred sauces or sauce packets.

White Sauce

White sauce comes in three thicknesses, but they're all made the same way.

	#1 (THIN)	#2 (MEDIUM)	#3 (THICK)
Milk	1 cup	1 cup	1 cup
Flour	1 tablespoon	2 tablespoons	3 tablespoons
Butter	1 tablespoon	2 tablespoons	3 tablespoons
Salt	¼ teaspoon	¼ teaspoon	¼ teaspoon
Use for	Creamed vegetables Sauces	Cream soup base Scalloped dishes	Croquettes

Substitutions

Milk: use soy milk, evaporated milk, powdered milk (mixed according to package instructions), or half cream and half water for the same total amount

Butter: use margarine, olive oil, canola oil, or vegetable oil for the same total amount

My technique is not the "usual" approach, which involves adding the flour and the milk while the pan is still over the (hot) burner. My method, which mixes everything together at a cooler temperature, is far less likely to form lumps.

Melt the butter in a small saucepan over low heat. Remove from the heat, and add the flour and salt; mix thoroughly with a whisk or spoon, making sure there are no lumps.

Still off the burner, slowly mix in the milk, adding just a little at a time to prevent lumps. I start with adding about 2 tablespoons for the first couple of additions. Subsequent additions are slightly larger.

Turn the heat to medium and stir/whisk constantly as the sauce heats to boiling. Allow the sauce to boil for 1 minute; keep stirring. Note that the cooking time is important to eliminate the flour taste and to allow the sauce to thicken. Watch the trails left by the whisk or spoon as signs that the sauce is thickening.

Remove from the heat and add any spices or other ingredients, or use as directed in another recipe.

Cheese Sauce   Makes 1 cup

This sauce is delicious served over steamed vegetables such as broccoli, cauliflower, or zucchini. It also makes a good sauce for macaroni and cheese. This sauce is traditionally made with cheddar cheese or another "meltable" cheese to make a very smooth sauce, but I've even used crumbled feta and Roquefort; the sauce was a little lumpy, but the flavor was good.

1 batch White Sauce #1 (see preceding table)
¼ cup shredded cheese

After removing the white sauce from the heat, add the cheese and stir well until it melts (assuming it's a cheese that will melt). Serve immediately. If there are leftovers, refrigerate and heat before serving.

NOTE: If you're looking for a thicker cheese sauce with a consistency like Cheez Whiz or melted Velveeta, use White Sauce #2 or even #3.

HOLLANDAISE AND BUTTER SAUCES

Hollandaise is great on almost any steamed veggie or plain grilled or broiled meat; butter sauce is very quick and easy!

No-Fail Hollandaise Sauce   Serves 6

Hollandaise has the reputation of being hard to make and prone to failure. It doesn't have to be, though. The most important thing is to give it your full attention.

Total Time: 20 minutes

1 cup salted butter,* melted
3 egg yolks
1 tablespoon water
1 tablespoon lemon juice**
¼ teaspoon salt (only if you used oil or unsalted butter)
dash of ground pepper or cayenne (optional)
Montreal steak seasoning (page 219; optional)

*Butter produces a better result than margarine, although you can use the latter. Many margarines have water added to them. After melting the margarine, pour it into a clear container and let it settle for a minute. If there is clear liquid (water) on the

bottom, use only the melted fat on top, and add more margarine as necessary to total the full amount without the water. You can use olive oil, canola oil, or vegetable oil instead of the butter. These substitutions will change the flavor slightly, and it won't be a "true" hollandaise sauce, but it will still taste wonderful.

**Lime juice or limón (Key lime) juice can be substituted, as can white vinegar, but the flavor of the finished dish will be a little different.

1. Barely melt the butter; you want it warm but not hot. You should be able to comfortably put a finger in it. If you can't, let it cool before proceeding. Set aside.
2. Put the egg yolks into a cold pan (a small saucepan or skillet with a heavy bottom works best). Add the water and lemon juice. Mix thoroughly with a whisk, fork, or spoon.
3. Place the pan on the stove over the lowest possible heat. Keep stirring/whisking the egg mixture. Resist the temptation to turn up the heat to hasten the thickening.
4. When the eggs have thickened to the point where your whisk/spoon/fork leaves trails that are visible for a second (instead of immediately filling in), begin adding the melted butter about a tablespoon at a time. Pour in a little, stirring as you do until it's totally incorporated, then add a little bit more, stir like crazy, etc. Some recipes say that you can add the butter in a constant thin stream. I find it's *much* less likely to separate if I add just a bit at a time.
5. Keep stirring quickly with the pan over low heat until the sauce is thick—just slightly thinner than mayonnaise (it will continue to thicken after you take it off the heat).
6. If you used oil or unsalted butter, add ¼ teaspoon salt. You can also add a dash of ground pepper or cayenne. Depending on what you're serving the hollandaise over, a dash of Montreal steak seasoning (page 219) can also be good.
7. Serve immediately. If needed, you can keep hollandaise for a few minutes by putting a lid on the pan, but don't leave it on a hot burner. It's also *possible* to keep it over hot water, but it's very easy to overcook it if you do so!

Whole-Egg Hollandaise   Serves 2

This recipe was added by our editor at International Marine, Molly Mulhern, who once was a cook aboard Maine charter schooners!

Total Time: 15 minutes

1 egg (whole)
1 tablespoon butter, melted
1 tablespoon lemon juice

1. Break the egg into a heavy-bottom skillet or saucepan and place it on the stove at the lowest possible heat. Using a whisk or fork, start beating immediately. Continue to beat as the egg slowly begins to thicken. Resist the urge to turn up the heat to hurry things along.
2. When the egg has thickened to the point where you can see your "stirring track" for a couple of seconds, add the butter very slowly, stirring like crazy after each addition. Turn the burner off at this point; there is plenty of heat still in the pan, and you'll lessen the chance of overcooking the eggs. Add the lemon juice a little at a time, continuing to stir until it's all incorporated and the sauce is thick.
3. Serve immediately for the best results. If you need to keep the sauce for a few minutes, put a lid on the pan. If you're using an electric stove and the burner is still warm, remove the pan from the stove.

Mock Hollandaise Sauce   Makes 1 cup

Lower in fat and cholesterol than "real" hollandaise, this hollandaise has a slightly different taste and texture but is a healthier substitute.

1 cup mayonnaise or low-fat mayonnaise (do not use nonfat mayonnaise or Miracle Whip)
2 egg whites
2 tablespoons lemon juice, lime juice, or *limón* (Key lime) juice
½ teaspoon dry mustard
dash of salt

Place all the ingredients in a small saucepan, and beat with a wire whisk or fork until smooth. Cook over low to medium-low heat, stirring constantly, until thick. Do not let the mixture boil. Serve immediately.

Butter Sauce

This sauce is extremely easy to make and has endless variations. Vary the amount of butter by what it's being served with. Vegetables will take about 1 tablespoon butter per person, fish about 2 tablespoons, and pasta possibly more.

2 tablespoons butter per person (margarine or olive oil can be substituted, although the flavor will be different)

Melt the butter over very low heat; don't let it boil. Add any of the following for flavor (adjust seasonings to your own tastes):

Lemon Butter Sauce: Add ½ teaspoon lemon juice and a little grated lemon zest per person.

Italian Butter Sauce: Add ½ teaspoon Italian seasoning (page 48) and ⅛ teaspoon garlic powder per person.

Spicy Butter Sauce: Add a few drops of your favorite hot sauce, to taste. If you like spicy food, this is great on popcorn.

ALFREDO SAUCES

It's not hard to make your own Alfredo sauce, and who doesn't love pasta Alfredo? The ingredients are much easier to stow than a glass jar of sauce.

Alfredo Sauce   Makes 2½ cups

½ cup butter or margarine
2 cloves garlic, minced, OR 2 teaspoons minced garlic OR ½ teaspoon garlic powder
2 cups cream, half-and-half (*media crema*), or evaporated milk (not as good)
¼ teaspoon ground pepper
½ cup shredded Parmesan cheese*
¾ cup shredded mozzarella or similar cheese

*True shredded Parmesan cheese, often available in the refrigerated food section of a supermarket (or you can shred your own), produces much better results than the grated Kraft Parmesan in the green can. But you can use the grated form if it's all you've got.

1. Melt the butter in a saucepan over low heat. Add the garlic, cream, and ground pepper. Heat the mixture, stirring often; try not to let it boil.
2. Add the Parmesan, stirring constantly, and cook for about 8 minutes, or until the sauce has thickened and is smooth. Add the mozzarella and keep stirring until it is completely melted and the sauce is smooth. Serve the sauce over hot pasta.

NOTE: To make this sauce a little healthier, use olive oil instead of butter, and/or use evaporated milk instead of cream.

Healthier Almost Alfredo Sauce   Makes 2½ cups

1½ cups ricotta cheese (the closer to fat-free, the better; page 100)
¾ cup chicken broth (may be made from bouillon) or stock (page 164)
½ cup shredded (better) or grated Parmesan cheese
2 tablespoons lemon juice, lime juice, or *limón* (Key lime) juice
1 tablespoon butter or margarine
1 tablespoon minced garlic OR 1 teaspoon garlic powder
½ teaspoon ground pepper
⅛ teaspoon salt
1 tablespoon torn fresh basil OR 1 teaspoon dried basil

1. In a small saucepan combine the ricotta, broth, Parmesan, lemon juice, butter, garlic, ground pepper, and salt. Cook over medium-low heat until smooth and creamy.
2. Reduce the heat to low and stir constantly until the sauce is just warm. Do not let it come to a boil. Remove from the heat and mix in the basil. Toss with hot pasta and serve immediately.

Good add-ins include mushrooms, ham, chicken, green onions, and pine nuts. All but the pine nuts should be sautéed before adding to the sauce and pasta.

Sauces, Gravies, Marinades, and Rubs

PESTO AND MUSHROOM SAUCES

These sauces work well on a wide variety of foods—veggies, meats, and pasta all come quickly to mind.

Pesto Sauce   Makes about 1¼ cups

This sauce is a mainstay in many galleys. It is good to have on hand to drizzle over veggies or bake on top of salmon. Try it tossed with hot pasta to bring out the flavors of basil, garlic, and cheese. Pesto sauce is easier to make if you have a small blender or food processor. However, you can make pesto just by chopping the ingredients very finely. It will take longer to make and won't be as smooth, but the flavor will be excellent. Depending on your cruising locale, you may need to bring the pine nuts from home.

⅓ **cup pine nuts**

½ **cup torn fresh basil OR 3 tablespoons dried basil OR 3 tablespoons Italian seasoning***

5 cloves garlic OR 5 teaspoons minced garlic OR ¾ teaspoon garlic powder

¼ **cup shredded Parmesan cheese (if shredding yourself, use the finest shredder you have)****

⅓ **to ½ cup olive oil, canola oil, or vegetable oil (olive oil gives the traditional flavor)**

salt and pepper, to taste

*Using Italian seasoning will change the flavor slightly, but it will still be good. In many places where we cruised, we could get Italian seasoning but not basil or oregano.

**True shredded Parmesan that you buy in the refrigerated section of the grocery store (or shred yourself) will produce better results than grated Kraft Parmesan in the green can.

1. Preheat oven to 350°F.
2. Place the pine nuts on a cookie sheet or a piece of aluminum foil. Toast in the oven just until golden, which takes only a few minutes (the instant you start to smell them, it's time to remove them).

3. If you are using fresh basil, remove the stems and any damaged leaves.
4. If you have a food processor or blender, process the toasted pine nuts, garlic, basil, and cheese for about 30 seconds. Add the oil and continue to process until the desired consistency is reached; leave it thick to use as a dip or spread, thinner for pasta or as a sauce. Add the salt and pepper to taste.
5. To make by hand, crush the garlic and put it in a small bowl. Chop the toasted pine nuts and fresh basil as finely as possible and add to the bowl. Add the Parmesan and oil and mix together. Season with the salt and pepper.

Creamy Garlic Mushroom Sauce   Makes 1½ cups

This is great over grilled chicken or steak, but it is also yummy tossed with linguine or over steamed veggies.

1 cup sliced mushrooms OR 1 can (8 ounces) mushrooms, drained

3 cloves garlic, minced or crushed, OR 1 teaspoon garlic powder

2 tablespoons butter, margarine, olive oil, canola oil, or vegetable oil

1 cup red wine

1 teaspoon whole peppercorns, ground, OR ¼ teaspoon ground pepper

¼ **teaspoon salt**

2 tablespoons sour cream (page 99), cream, or evaporated milk (will be thinner)

1. Brown the mushrooms and garlic in the butter over medium heat until the mushrooms are golden.
2. Reduce the heat to medium-low and add the wine, ground pepper, and salt. Bring it to a boil, then reduce the heat and simmer for 5 minutes.
3. Remove from the heat and add the sour cream; mix well.

Mushroom Garlic Topping   Makes 1 cup

Be creative—try this on a good steak, grilled chicken breast, or baked asparagus or other veggies.

6 tablespoons butter or margarine
10 cloves garlic, minced, OR 3 tablespoons minced
    garlic OR 1 tablespoon garlic powder
6 cups mushrooms, sliced, OR 2 cans (8 ounces
    each) mushrooms, drained
1 teaspoon dried basil
1/4 teaspoon salt
ground pepper, to taste
2 tablespoons olive oil, canola oil, or vegetable oil

1. Melt the butter in a small pan, then add the garlic and mushrooms and cook over medium heat until the mushrooms are just golden, stirring occasionally.
2. Remove from heat and add the basil, salt, ground pepper, and oil. Stir to combine.

SAUCES FOR SHELLFISH AND FISH

It's not hard to make your own tartar or cocktail sauce, plus we have a fantastic coconut and curry dipping sauce!

Tartar Sauce   Makes about 1 1/2 cups

1 1/4 cups mayonnaise or Miracle Whip (regular or
    low-fat)
1/4 cup dill relish OR 1 dill pickle, finely chopped
2 sprigs fresh parsley, finely chopped, OR
    1/4 teaspoon dried parsley flakes (optional)
1 tablespoon lemon juice, lime juice, or *limón*
    (Key lime) juice
1 teaspoon dried onion flakes OR 1/4 teaspoon
    onion powder OR 1 tablespoon finely minced
    onion
1/4 teaspoon Worcestershire sauce

Mix all the ingredients. Store leftovers in the refrigerator.

Variation: To make Cajun Tartar Sauce, substitute sweet pickle relish for the dill relish. Slowly add up to 1 tablespoon horseradish, 2 teaspoons hot sauce, and/or 2 teaspoons Cajun seasoning. Be sure to taste as you add to ensure you don't inadvertently make it too hot.

Cocktail Sauce for Shrimp   Makes 1/2 cup

Even when it's hard to find horseradish, you can usually find wasabi paste. The taste isn't exactly the same, but the sauce is still good. Use about half the amount of prepared wasabi paste that you'd use for horseradish.

1/2 cup ketchup or chili sauce
1 tablespoon horseradish, or to taste (We like
    more. Lots more!)
squirt of lemon juice (optional)

Mix all the ingredients together. Store leftovers in the refrigerator.

Coconut-Lime-Curry Dipping Sauce   Makes 3/4 cup

Great with crab cakes or conch fritters, particularly if you substitute a hint of curry for other spices in the crab or conch. We also like a dollop of this sauce on sautéed or grilled fish fillets.

5 tablespoons lime juice, lemon juice, or *limón*
    (Key lime) juice
2/3 cup cream of coconut, such as Coco Lopez
    (about half a can)*
1 1/2 teaspoons curry powder (page 47)
1/4 teaspoon cayenne pepper
1/4 teaspoon salt
1/2 cup very finely diced green onion

*This is not the same as coconut milk; the consistency is different.

Combine all the ingredients. The flavor is improved if the sauce has a chance to sit for an hour or so before serving. It may be made ahead of time and refrigerated.

Sauces, Gravies, Marinades, and Rubs

MUSTARD SAUCES

If you can't find mustard sauces pre-made, they are easy to mix up yourself, and it's likely you've got the ingredients for at least one!

Honey Mustard Sauce   Makes ½ cup

This dipping sauce particularly enhances chicken tenders, but it's also good on crunchy broccoli or other veggies.

2 tablespoons honey
3 tablespoons prepared mustard (any type, depending on your taste)
1 tablespoon wine vinegar or other vinegar or lemon juice or lime juice

Combine all the ingredients; mix well.

Variation: For a milder sauce, add ¼ to ½ cup mayonnaise or Miracle Whip.

Hot Mustard Sauce   Makes ½ cup

Good on chicken strips or pork or with Chinese food.

6 tablespoons yellow mustard (any type is good, such as Spicy Brown, Coarse Grain, etc.)
2 tablespoons corn syrup (dark or light), molasses, or honey
4 teaspoons dry mustard
1½ teaspoons white vinegar
1 tablespoon mayonnaise or Miracle Whip
½ teaspoon soy sauce
½ teaspoon sugar
cayenne pepper (start with a couple of dashes and then taste, adding more if desired) or very finely minced fresh chile pepper OR red pepper flakes, to taste

1. Mix all the ingredients in a small saucepan over medium heat until the sauce is almost boiling.
2. Allow to cool before using. It's best if refrigerated for 4 to 6 hours. Refrigerate leftovers.

Orange-Mustard Sauce   Makes 1 cup

Good on pork, shrimp (especially coconut shrimp), chicken, and egg rolls.

½ cup orange marmalade
¼ cup prepared mustard (Dijon is best, but you can use other types or a mixture)
¼ cup honey
3 or 4 drops Tabasco sauce, hot sauce, or cayenne pepper

Combine all the ingredients and mix well.

RED WINE, STEAK, *CRIOLLA*, AND ENCHILADA SAUCES

The following recipes are all fairly easy to make and taste delicious!

Red Wine Sauce   Makes 1 cup

2 tablespoons chopped onion or green onion
2 tablespoons butter or margarine
1 tablespoon flour
2 tablespoons ketchup
¼ cup red wine
¾ cup beef broth (may be made from bouillon) or stock (page 165)
2 tablespoons soy sauce
1 teaspoon Worcestershire sauce
⅛ teaspoon ground pepper

1. Cook the onion in the butter over medium-low heat until soft. Don't let the onion brown. Add the flour, stirring it in well so there are no lumps, and cook for 1 minute. Add the ketchup and mix in thoroughly. Very slowly add the wine and broth, stirring constantly so that lumps don't form. Then add the soy sauce, Worcestershire, and ground pepper and cook for 3 minutes without letting it boil, stirring constantly.
2. Remove from the heat when ready to serve. Refrigerate any unused portion. It will generally last for a week to 10 days in a sealed container.

Steak Sauce   Makes a little less than 2 cups

Similar to A.1 Steak Sauce, which can be hard to find in many cruising areas.

$^1/_2$ cup raisins
$^1/_2$ cup orange juice
$^1/_4$ cup soy sauce
$^1/_4$ cup white vinegar, balsamic vinegar, or other vinegar
2 tablespoons prepared mustard (Dijon is best)
$^1/_4$ cup ketchup

1. Chop the raisins as finely as you can. If you have a meat grinder or food processor, use it.
2. Mix the chopped raisins, orange juice, soy sauce, vinegar, mustard, and ketchup in a small saucepan. Bring to a boil over medium-high heat while stirring. Keep stirring and boil for 2 minutes. Remove from the heat and let cool. This will keep well for 3 months in a tightly sealed container in the refrigerator.

Criolla   Makes the equivalent of one 8-ounce packet

Also called criolla sofrito, criolla *is available in many places in the Caribbean, Central America, and South America. It is usually sold in 8-ounce packets; this recipe can be substituted for one packet. It's not identical, but it's our closest approximation.*

Total Time: 20 minutes

$^1/_3$ cup finely minced onion
3 cloves garlic, crushed, OR 1 teaspoon garlic powder
$^1/_3$ cup finely minced green bell pepper or mild chile pepper
1 tablespoon canola oil or vegetable oil
$^1/_4$ teaspoon salt
$^1/_4$ teaspoon ground pepper
$^1/_2$ cup tomato sauce

Cook the onion, garlic, and bell pepper in the oil until translucent. Do not brown. Add the salt, pepper, and tomato sauce and simmer, covered, for 10 minutes.

Red Enchilada or Taco Sauce   Makes 2$^1/_2$ cups

2 tablespoons canola oil or vegetable oil
1 small onion, finely chopped
1 teaspoon dried red pepper flakes, or to taste
$^1/_2$ teaspoon dried oregano
1 tablespoon chili powder, or to taste
$^1/_2$ teaspoon dried basil
1 tablespoon ground cumin
1 tablespoon minced garlic OR 3 cloves garlic, minced, OR 1 teaspoon garlic powder
$^1/_3$ cup salsa (page 127) OR $^1/_4$ cup chopped tomato plus 1 tablespoon chopped green bell pepper
1 cup tomato sauce, chopped canned tomatoes, or diced fresh tomatoes
1 cup beef broth (may be made from bouillon) or stock (page 165)
1 teaspoon ground pepper

1. Mix all the ingredients. If a spicier sauce is desired, add some finely minced hot chile pepper or a bit of cayenne pepper or red pepper flakes. But be careful not to add too much; the flavors get stronger as the sauce sits.
2. If using this as an enchilada sauce, there is no need to cook it, as it will bake with the enchiladas. If using as a taco sauce, bring it briefly to a boil to fully mix the flavors.

Store any unused portion in the refrigerator in a sealed container. It will usually last 2 to 3 weeks.

ASIAN SAUCES

We have both always been able to find soy sauce, and with it we can make lots of other sauces.

Stir-Fry Sauce
Makes 1½ cups

This is a great sauce to add flavor to stir-fried food, whether veggies or meat and veggies. It also makes a great dipping sauce for veggies or chicken.

2 tablespoons cornstarch OR 4 tablespoons flour
  (sauce made with flour will be cloudy)
¼ cup water or pineapple juice
½ cup soy sauce*
½ cup chicken broth (may be made from bouillon)
  or stock (page 164)
⅓ cup rice wine, rice vinegar, or white vinegar
¼ cup sugar or packed brown sugar
1 tablespoon sesame oil
¼ teaspoon ground pepper
1 tablespoon minced garlic OR 1 teaspoon garlic
  powder
1 tablespoon minced fresh ginger OR 1 teaspoon
  ground ginger
2 tablespoons canola oil or vegetable oil

I find this dish too salty with the full amount of soy. Start with half the amount of soy sauce and add to taste.

1. Mix the cornstarch and water in a small bowl or cup; set aside.
2. Mix together the soy sauce, broth, wine, sugar, sesame oil, and ground pepper. If you are using garlic powder and ground ginger, add them and the canola oil now. Set aside.
3. If you are using minced garlic and minced fresh ginger, heat the canola oil in a skillet or saucepan over high heat. Add the garlic and ginger and cook briefly until they become fragrant, stirring constantly. This will take only 10 to 15 seconds.
4. Reduce the heat to low. Add the soy sauce mixture to the garlic and ginger in the pan and cook just until it comes to a boil. Slowly stir in the cornstarch mixture, mixing quickly so that lumps don't form. Allow it to come back to a boil. Cook until it thickens, or about 2 minutes.

Teriyaki Sauce
Makes 1¼ cups

¼ cup water
2 tablespoons cornstarch OR 4 tablespoons flour
  (sauce made with flour won't be clear)
¼ cup soy sauce
1 cup water
½ teaspoon ground ginger
¼ teaspoon garlic powder
5 tablespoons brown sugar
1 tablespoon honey

1. Mix the ¼ cup water and the cornstarch in a cup to dissolve. (Put the liquid in the cup or bowl first, then the cornstarch; it will be much easier to mix without lumps forming.) Set aside.
2. In a small saucepan combine the soy sauce, the 1 cup water, the ginger, garlic powder, brown sugar, and honey. Warm over medium heat until the sugar dissolves and the honey is melted.
3. Stir in the cornstarch mixture and bring to a boil, stirring constantly. Boil for 2 to 3 minutes, or until thick. If the sauce becomes too thick, add a little more water.

Sweet and Sour Sauce
Makes about 1¼ cups

1 cup pineapple juice
⅓ cup water
3 tablespoons vinegar (different types will give a
  different flavor)
1 tablespoon soy sauce
½ cup packed brown sugar or white sugar
3 tablespoons cornstarch OR 6 tablespoons flour
  (sauce made with flour won't be clear)

Mix all the ingredients in a saucepan and cook over medium-low heat, stirring constantly so lumps don't form, until the mixture boils. Boil for 1 to 2 minutes, or until the mixture thickens slightly.

Wasabi-Soy Sauce

This is my (Carolyn's) favorite accompaniment for sautéed fish. It's also very quick and easy!

wasabi paste
soy sauce

You can make this as spicy or mild as you wish. Start with a bit of wasabi paste about the size of a pencil eraser in a cup. Add 1 to 2 tablespoons soy sauce and mix together. Adjust the amounts of wasabi and soy sauce to your taste, and make as much as you need. This does not store well, so make only enough for one meal.

NOTE: Dave and I like spicy foods, so I use about a 1-inch strip of wasabi paste with 2 tablespoons soy sauce, but I'd recommend starting with less wasabi.

Peanut Sauce   Makes about 1¹⁄₂ cups

A quick version of the authentic Thai peanut sauce.

¹⁄₂ cup peanut butter (creamy produces the best result, but crunchy will work)
1 cup chicken broth (may be made from bouillon) or stock (page 164)
2 tablespoons lime juice, *limón* (Key lime) juice, or lemon juice
1¹⁄₂ tablespoons brown sugar or white sugar
1 tablespoon soy sauce
1 tablespoon minced fresh ginger OR 1 teaspoon ground ginger
dash of red pepper flakes OR cayenne pepper, to taste

1. Measure the peanut butter into a saucepan and begin warming it over low heat. Add the broth a little at a time, mixing thoroughly with each addition. Work hard to keep the mixture smooth.
2. Add the lime juice, brown sugar, soy sauce, ginger, and red pepper flakes, and stir well. Increase the heat to medium and cook about 5 minutes. Serve warm. Leftovers can be stored a few days in the refrigerator.

Thai Sweet Chili Sauce   Makes approximately ¹⁄₂ cup

This is good on its own and is also an ingredient in several other recipes.

1 tablespoon very finely minced red chili pepper, to taste*
¹⁄₂ cup vinegar (use cider vinegar for a sharper flavor, white for a milder taste)
1 teaspoon salt
1 tablespoon sugar
1 teaspoon finely minced garlic OR ¹⁄₄ teaspoon garlic powder

*Use any variety you like, depending on your own tastes and mild/spicy preferences. You can also use dried red pepper flakes; start with about ¹⁄₄ teaspoon and add more to taste.

1. Mix all the ingredients together in a saucepan. Bring to a boil over medium-high heat, stirring frequently. Cook until syrupy, or about 10 minutes, continuing to stir frequently.
2. Remove from the heat and let cool. Serve at room temperature.

BARBECUE SAUCE BASICS

Barbecue has vastly different flavors and meanings depending on where you live. We've included several barbecue sauce recipes.

The trick to using BBQ sauce when grilling meat is to turn the meat more often than you normally would so you don't burn the sauce. You want to barely blacken it on the grill lines so the sugar is carmelized, not charred. Be sure to save some of the BBQ sauce for dipping at the table.

But barbecue sauce is not just for grilling. Here are some other quickie ideas:

- Toss with shredded leftover chicken or pork to make barbecue sandwiches.
- Add barbecue sauce to a black bean/corn kernel/onion/chopped fresh tomato mixture and roll it up in a tortilla. Add shredded chicken or beef to make it a dinner-size meal.

Sauces, Gravies, Marinades, and Rubs

Alabama White BBQ Sauce

Makes about 3½ cups

This white BBQ sauce is unique in that it uses mayonnaise as its base instead of the more typical tomato or vinegar bases. Apply it only at the very end of the cooking—it will separate if heated too much. It's traditional on chicken and turkey, but it's also great on pork.

2 cups mayonnaise (low-fat is fine, but don't use nonfat or any type of Miracle Whip)
1 cup cider vinegar (you can substitute other varieties of vinegar, but the taste won't be the same)
2 tablespoons lemon juice or lime juice
3 tablespoons ground pepper
1 teaspoon salt
½ teaspoon cayenne, or to taste

1. In a small bowl mix all the ingredients together. If you have time to refrigerate the sauce for up to 8 hours, the flavor will only improve. But you can use it immediately and it will still be good.
2. Brush a little over pork, turkey, or chicken in the last few minutes of grilling. But reserve most of the sauce for use at the table.

BeerBQ Sauce

Makes about 2 cups

A sweet-spicy sauce that goes well with chicken or pork.

Total time: 1 hour

1½ cups ketchup
1 can (12 ounces) beer (don't use one with a particularly strong flavor)
¾ cup cider vinegar, white vinegar, or other type of vinegar (but other vinegars won't taste as sharp)
2 tablespoons dried onion flakes OR 1 small onion, finely minced
3 tablespoons brown sugar or white sugar
2 tablespoons Worcestershire sauce
2 cloves garlic, minced, OR ¼ teaspoon garlic powder
2 teaspoons ground cumin
1½ teaspoons salt
1½ teaspoons prepared mustard
½ teaspoon chili powder

dash of cayenne
dash of cloves

Combine all the ingredients in a saucepan and mix well. Simmer, uncovered, stirring occasionally, for about 55 minutes, or until thick. Store covered in the refrigerator, it will last a week or more.

Florida-Style BBQ Sauce with Citrus Juice

Makes 2 cups

The citrus juice in this sauce gives a tropical flair to almost anything. I've used this sauce on chicken, pork, beef, and even fish and seafood—it's wonderful on a grilled fish fillet!

Total Time: 20 minutes

1 tablespoon cornstarch (you can use 2 tablespoons flour as a substitute, but the sauce won't be clear)
¼ cup orange juice
¼ cup pineapple juice
¼ cup mango juice
1 cup ketchup
¾ cup packed brown sugar or white sugar
1 tablespoon prepared mustard (any variety)
¾ teaspoon ground pepper
1½ teaspoons onion powder

1. In a large enough saucepan to hold all the ingredients, mix the cornstarch with a little of the orange juice to make a thin, smooth paste. Slowly add more orange juice until the paste is diluted.
2. Mix in the remaining orange juice, the pineapple juice, mango juice, ketchup, brown sugar, mustard, ground pepper, and onion powder. Bring to a slow boil, then reduce the heat and simmer until the sauce thickens, or about 15 minutes.
3. Use it to baste meat on the grill, and also as an accompaniment at the table. Works well put in a squeeze bottle, such as an old plastic ketchup bottle. Any unused portion should be stored in the refrigerator and will last about 2 weeks.

Sauces, Gravies, Marinades, and Rubs

Memphis Barbecue Sauce
Makes about 2 cups

This is Carolyn's favorite. It is a very traditional spicy red barbecue sauce, similar to "Sweet Baby Ray's" or "Open Pit Original."

Total Time: 25 minutes

1/2 cup minced onion
4 cloves garlic, crushed, OR 4 teaspoons minced garlic OR 1/2 teaspoon garlic powder
1 1/2 teaspoons canola oil or vegetable oil
1/2 teaspoon celery seed, ground, OR 2 tablespoons very finely minced celery
1/2 teaspoon salt
2 cups ketchup
1/3 cup yellow mustard or other variety
1/3 cup cider vinegar, white vinegar, or balsamic vinegar
1/2 teaspoon cayenne pepper
1/3 cup molasses or honey
1/3 cup packed brown sugar or white sugar
1 tablespoon chili powder
1 tablespoon ground pepper
2 tablespoons Worcestershire sauce

1. Sauté the onion and garlic in the oil. If using celery instead of celery seed, sauté it too.
2. Add the celery seed (if using), salt, ketchup, mustard, vinegar, cayenne, molasses, brown sugar, chili powder, ground pepper, and Worcestershire. Simmer, uncovered, stirring occasionally, until the sauce thickens, or about 15 to 20 minutes.
3. We liked this even better after it sat overnight in the refrigerator. Store leftovers in the refrigerator.

No-Cook Barbecue Sauce
Makes 1 1/2 cups

This works well when brushed on meat as it is cooking. Making this no-cook sauce doesn't heat up the galley with a long simmering time. However, if you want to use it as a dipping sauce, you really need to cook it a bit—just bring it to a boil—so that the molasses melts and mixes with the other ingredients.

Total Time: 5 minutes

1/2 cup ketchup
1/3 cup prepared mustard (brown mustard is particularly good)
1/3 cup molasses or honey
1/4 cup Worcestershire sauce
dash of cayenne pepper*
1 teaspoon horseradish OR 1/2 teaspoon wasabi*
dash of cloves*
dash of hot sauce*

*Optional if you like a spicier sauce.

Mix all the ingredients together. Brush the sauce over meat as it is grilling.

South Carolina Mustard BBQ Sauce
Makes about 1 cup

This is wonderful on pork and goes well over pork chops and roast pork as well as barbecue.

Total Time: 45 minutes

1 cup yellow mustard*
1/2 cup white sugar
1/4 cup packed brown sugar or white sugar
3/4 cup cider vinegar (can substitute white vinegar, but it won't have as sharp a taste)
1/4 cup water
2 tablespoons chili powder
1 teaspoon ground black pepper
1 teaspoon ground white pepper or black pepper
1/4 teaspoon cayenne pepper
1/2 teaspoon soy sauce
2 tablespoons butter
1 tablespoon liquid smoke (optional)

*The plain yellow type is traditional; you can use other varieties, but they will not produce the traditional taste.

1. In a small saucepan, mix together the mustard, white sugar, brown sugar, vinegar, water, chili powder, black and white ground pepper, and cayenne. Simmer for 30 minutes.
2. Stir in the soy sauce, butter, and liquid smoke and simmer for another 10 minutes.

Sauces, Gravies, Marinades, and Rubs

North Carolina Vinegar-Based BBQ Sauce   Makes about 4 cups

This thin sauce is typically served at the table (often in a squeeze bottle) with pork—particularly pulled pork sandwiches.

1 teaspoon brown sugar or white sugar
2 cups cider vinegar or other vinegar (the flavor will be slightly different with other vinegar)
1 teaspoon salt
2 teaspoons ground pepper
1 teaspoon cayenne pepper, or to taste
1 cup ketchup
2 cups water
Tabasco sauce or hot sauce, to taste

Combine all the ingredients in a medium saucepan and bring to a boil. Reduce the heat and simmer, covered, for 15 minutes. Store tightly sealed in the refrigerator.

Southwestern Barbecue Sauce   Makes 3 cups

Most often used with beef, this sauce can be as mild or spicy as you wish. For a mild but flavorful version, use green bell pepper and add some cumin.

1 small onion, finely diced
2 cloves garlic, finely minced, OR 2 teaspoons minced garlic OR $1/4$ teaspoon garlic powder
1 tablespoon paprika
1 tablespoon chili powder
$1/4$ teaspoon salt
$1/4$ teaspoon ground pepper
1 tablespoon canola oil or vegetable oil
1 can (16 ounces) diced tomatoes, not drained, OR 1 can (16 ounces) whole tomatoes, diced, OR 2 or 3 large tomatoes, diced
1 can (6 ounces) tomato paste
$2/3$ cup white vinegar or other vinegar (the taste will vary depending on the vinegar)
$1/3$ cup finely chopped green chile pepper or bell pepper (choose your variety based on how spicy you want the sauce; you can use a combination)
$1/3$ cup packed brown sugar

2 tablespoons prepared mustard (Dijon is best, but others will work fine)
$1/2$ cup molasses or honey

1. Cook the onion, garlic, paprika, chili powder, salt, and ground pepper in the oil over medium heat until the onion is translucent. Don't brown the onion.
2. Add the tomato, tomato paste, vinegar, chile pepper, brown sugar, mustard, and molasses, and mix well. Bring the mixture to a boil. Reduce the heat and simmer, uncovered and stirring occasionally, for 20 minutes, or until the sauce thickens. If a totally smooth sauce is desired and a blender is available, you can puree the sauce until smooth. But it's great without blending. Refrigerate any leftovers.

Texas-Style Beef Barbecue Sauce   Makes 7 cups

This makes enough for a Texas-size get-together! I usually make a half batch—or even a quarter batch—for smaller groups. Being from Texas, it's designed for beef and is great on burgers as a change from the usual ketchup and mustard.

3 cups ketchup
3 cups water
1 cup cider vinegar
$1/2$ cup Worcestershire sauce
$1/4$ cup chili powder
3 tablespoons corn syrup OR $1/4$ cup sugar
3 tablespoons molasses or honey
3 tablespoons brown sugar or white sugar
2 tablespoons soy sauce
2 tablespoons paprika
2 tablespoons yellow mustard
$1/4$ cup lemon juice (juice from about 2 lemons), lime juice, or *limón* (Key lime) juice
1 teaspoon Tabasco sauce
1 teaspoon ground pepper
1 teaspoon liquid smoke (optional)
meat drippings*

*If you're grilling meat and don't pre-bake it in the oven and thus don't have drippings, substitute $1/2$ cup beef bouillon plus 2 tablespoons canola or vegetable oil.

Combine all the ingredients in a saucepan and simmer, uncovered, for 20 to 30 minutes, or until the sauce thickens. Serve warm or cool. Store leftovers in the refrigerator.

RUBS

Rubs add a lot of flavor and can be used on their own or with a barbecue sauce.

Sweet and Spicy Chicken Rub
Makes 1/2 cup

1/4 cup paprika
1 tablespoon sugar
1 tablespoon brown sugar or additional white sugar
2 teaspoons salt
1 teaspoon ground pepper
1/4 to 1/2 teaspoon cayenne pepper, or to taste
1 teaspoon dry mustard
1 teaspoon garlic powder, or to taste
1 teaspoon onion powder

Combine all the ingredients and stir well. Store in an airtight shaker.

Rib Rub Makes enough for 4 to 6 pounds of ribs

1/2 cup packed brown sugar
1 tablespoon salt
1 tablespoon chili powder OR 1/2 teaspoon cayenne pepper, or to taste
1/2 teaspoon ground pepper
1 teaspoon Old Bay Seasoning (page 48)
1 teaspoon onion powder
1 teaspoon garlic powder

Mix all the ingredients together. Rub it liberally over both sides of the ribs. Refrigerate the ribs for at least 2 hours before cooking to let the spices work into the meat.

Almost Montreal Steak Seasoning
Makes 1/2 cup

1 tablespoon ground black pepper (coarse ground is best)
1 tablespoon ground white pepper or black pepper
1 tablespoon salt (coarse or kosher if you have it)
1 tablespoon garlic powder
1 1/2 teaspoons dry mustard
1 1/2 teaspoons dried oregano (ground is best)
1 teaspoon ground cumin
1 teaspoon ground coriander
1/2 teaspoon dried red pepper flakes

Mix all the ingredients. The seasoning works best in some type of shaker. Liberally season the meat before grilling. Store leftover seasoning in a cool, dry place.

MARINADES

A marinade can add a whole new flavor to a meal—most often for meats or seafood, but you can also marinate veggies before roasting or grilling them.

Soy Chicken Marinade
Makes about 1 1/2 cups

1/2 cup olive oil, canola oil, or vegetable oil
1/2 cup plus 2 tablespoons honey
1/2 cup plus 2 tablespoons soy sauce
2 teaspoons ground cumin
1 teaspoon cayenne pepper, or to taste
1/2 teaspoon ground pepper
2 cloves garlic, minced

Mix all the ingredients together.

NOTE: To use the marinade, reserve about one-quarter of the mix to use later to baste the chicken as it cooks. Pour the rest into a leakproof plastic container or freezer bag. Add chicken breasts or cut-up pieces of chicken to the marinade. Seal the container tightly and refrigerate for 2 hours or more. When ready to cook, remove the chicken and discard the marinade (it's not safe to reuse). As the chicken cooks, occasionally baste the chicken with the reserved marinade.

Sauces, Gravies, Marinades, and Rubs

Worcestershire Chicken Marinade

Makes 1 1/2 cups, enough to marinate 2 to 4 chicken breasts

1 cup canola oil or vegetable oil
1/2 cup vinegar, any type
2 tablespoons mayonnaise or Miracle Whip
3 tablespoons Worcestershire sauce
2 tablespoons lemon juice, lime juice, or *limón* (Key lime) juice
1 tablespoon salt, or to taste
1 tablespoon ground pepper
2 tablespoons dried thyme
1 tablespoon garlic salt (page 47)

Mix all the ingredients together.

NOTE: To use the marinade, pour it into a leakproof plastic container or a freezer bag inside the plastic container. Put 2 to 4 chicken breasts in the marinade for 1 to 2 hours. Discard the marinade (it is not safe to reuse) and prepare the chicken however you like—on the grill, sautéed, or baked.

Zesty Chicken Marinades

Makes about 1 cup, enough to marinate up to 6 chicken breasts

1/4 cup cider vinegar or other vinegar (the flavor will be slightly different with other vinegar)
3 tablespoons dry mustard
3 cloves garlic, minced
1 tablespoon lime juice*
1 tablespoon lemon juice*
1/2 cup packed brown sugar
1 1/2 teaspoons salt
6 tablespoons olive oil, canola oil, or vegetable oil
ground pepper, to taste

Feel free to use all lemon or lime juice or limón (Key lime) juice if that's what you have.

Combine the vinegar, mustard, garlic, lime juice, lemon juice, brown sugar, and salt. Mix well, then add the olive oil and ground pepper. Stir to combine.

NOTE: To use the marinade, pour it into a large leakproof plastic container or a gallon freezer bag inside the plastic container. Add up to 6 chicken breasts and let them marinate overnight in the refrigerator. Discard the marinade after using (it's not safe to reuse) and cook the chicken as desired.

Teriyaki Marinade

Makes 1 1/4 cups

1/4 cup honey
1/2 cup soy sauce
1/4 cup canola oil or vegetable oil
1/4 cup teriyaki sauce (page 214)
4 cloves garlic, minced, OR 4 teaspoons minced garlic OR 1/2 teaspoon garlic powder
1/8 teaspoon ground ginger OR 1 tablespoon finely minced fresh ginger

Mix all the ingredients together.

NOTE: To use the marinade, pour it into a gallon freezer bag or leakproof plastic container. Add the meat of your choice and marinate overnight in the refrigerator; for fish, marinate only 1 hour. Discard the marinade after use; it's not safe to reuse.

Beef Marinade

Makes enough to marinate 4 to 6 steaks, depending on size

2 tablespoons minced garlic OR 6 cloves garlic, minced, OR 3/4 teaspoon garlic powder
2 tablespoons Worcestershire sauce
2 tablespoons balsamic vinegar, wine vinegar, or other vinegar
2 teaspoons prepared mustard (Dijon is best, but others will work)
2 tablespoons soy sauce
1/3 cup olive oil, canola oil, or vegetable oil
1/2 teaspoon ground pepper

Mix all the ingredients together.

NOTE: To use the marinade, pour it into a large leakproof plastic container, or a freezer bag inside the plastic container. Put your meat of choice in the marinade, close the container, and refrigerate for 4 to 24 hours. Steaks will be best if allowed to warm to room temperature before grilling. Discard the marinade after using; it is not safe to reuse.

Fajita Marinade

Makes enough for 6 chicken breasts or 2 to 3 pounds beef

For our fajita recipe, see page 269.

¼ cup olive oil, canola oil, or vegetable oil
1 teaspoon lime zest or lemon zest (use just the zest—the colored part of the rind; don't go too far into the white)
2 teaspoons Worcestershire sauce
1½ teaspoons ground cumin
1 teaspoon salt
¼ cup chopped fresh cilantro OR ⅛ cup dried cilantro, or to taste
½ teaspoon dried oregano
½ teaspoon ground pepper
2 cloves garlic, minced, OR 2 teaspoons minced garlic OR ¼ teaspoon garlic powder
1 cup beef or chicken broth (may be made from bouillon) or stock (pages 164–165)

Mix all the ingredients together.

NOTE: To use the marinade, pour the mixture in a leakproof plastic container or gallon freezer bag. Add the meat and marinate overnight in the refrigerator. Discard the marinade; it's not safe to reuse.

Kabob Marinade

Makes 3 cups

1½ cups canola oil or vegetable oil
¾ cup soy sauce
¼ cup Worcestershire sauce
½ teaspoon salt
1 teaspoon dried parsley flakes
1 teaspoon ground pepper
½ cup red wine vinegar, cider vinegar, or other vinegar (the flavor will be different with other vinegar)
2 tablespoons minced garlic OR 6 cloves garlic, minced, OR ¾ teaspoon garlic powder
½ cup teriyaki sauce (page 214)
½ cup honey
2 green onions, chopped (including green tops)

Mix all the ingredients together.

NOTE: To use the marinade, pour it into a large freezer bag. Add the kabob-size pieces of beef, pork, or chicken and let marinate overnight. Discard the marinade; it's not safe to reuse.

GRAVIES

Nothing says homemade like gravy!

Chicken or Beef Gravy from Pan Drippings

Makes 1½ cups

pan drippings from beef roast or roast chicken
water and bouillon powder or broth, as needed
¼ cup cold water
2 tablespoons flour*
salt and ground pepper, to taste

If you like darker gravy, brown the flour in a dry skillet over medium heat. Keep shaking the skillet until the flour is a medium-brown color (don't let it burn!).

1. Remove the roast beef or chicken from the pan and place it on a serving dish. Cover it with foil to keep warm while preparing the gravy.
2. Strain the pan drippings through a sieve and discard the pieces caught by the sieve. If you don't have a sieve, simply remove as many pieces of meat and "pan crust" as practical. The gravy won't be totally smooth, but it will have a great taste.
3. Remove as much fat from the drippings as practical. Then measure the remaining drippings. You need a total of 2 cups drippings for this recipe. If you have too much, you can either discard some, use proportionately more flour, or boil the drippings down to just 2 cups. If you don't have enough, add broth or water and the appropriate flavor of bouillon powder to make 2 cups.
4. Put the measured drippings into a saucepan. Pour ¼ cup cold water into a small, tightly lidded plastic container. Put the flour on top of the water (don't do it the other way around as it will not mix smoothly). Put the lid on the container and shake

until it is a smooth mixture. (You can also use a small bowl and whisk or stir the flour into the water, but I find that shaking is a more reliable way of avoiding lumps.)

5. Pour the flour and water slurry into the drippings, stirring as you do. Continue to stir as you bring the gravy to a boil over medium-high heat. Boil for a few minutes, or until the gravy has thickened. If you do have a few lumps, you can either mash them out with a spoon or pour all the gravy back through the sieve.

6. Add salt and pepper, to taste. Serve hot.

Chicken or Beef Gravy from Broth

Makes 3 cups

This method of mixing the flour and butter (or oil) without heat—just melting the butter and then turning off the heat while slowly adding the liquid—isn't typical. If you add the liquid too fast or with too much heat immediately, it's much more likely to form lumps. My favorite utensil for making gravy is a silicon spoon/spatula or the back of a regular spoon. Some people prefer a whisk, but I find it's harder to produce lump-free gravy with one.

½ cup flour
½ cup butter or margarine, softened, or canola oil or vegetable oil
½ teaspoon ground pepper
4 cups chicken or beef broth (may be made from bouillon) or stock (pages 164–165)

1. Combine the flour, butter, and ground pepper in a saucepan; blend to form a paste. Place the pan over low heat and stir until the butter is melted.
2. Turn off the heat and add the broth very slowly. Begin by adding just 1 tablespoon at a time, stirring constantly to prevent lumps. Then gradually add the rest of the broth, stirring continuously.
3. Turn the heat to medium-low. Slowly bring the gravy to a boil, stirring constantly to prevent lumps. Boil for just a few minutes and serve hot.

Ham Gravy

This is one of those recipes that isn't really a recipe; it's just "how I do it."

After baking a ham, remove it from the pan, scraping the "drippings" from the bottom of the ham back into the pan as you do so. Put the ham on a serving plate and cover with foil.

With a spoon or spatula, scrape all the good stuff from where it's sticking to the bottom of the pan, but leave it all in the pan (assuming the pan can be put on the stove. If not, scrape all the drippings and bits of good stuff into a saucepan). Put the pan over medium-low heat.

The next part is a bit of a judgment call depending on the volume of drippings that you have. Use ¼ cup flour for every 2 tablespoons of drippings in the pan. Sprinkle the flour over the drippings. Quickly stir the flour into the drippings, making sure to get out any lumps. Some people use a whisk; I prefer a spoon.

Slowly add water, a little at a time, stirring constantly so that lumps don't form. Bring the mixture to a boil; you may have to add more water as it thickens. If so, be sure to add the water very slowly so that lumps don't form.

Sausage Gravy

This is a breakfast favorite in Indiana and Illinois. Carolyn never saw it growing up in Michigan, but it was a staple for Jan, who grew up just south of Indianapolis.

1 pound bulk pork sausage, turkey sausage, chorizo, or other sausage*
2 tablespoons finely chopped onion
2 cups milk
5 or 6 dashes of Worcestershire sauce
salt and pepper
6 tablespoons flour

*If all you can find is sausage in plastic tubes, simply cut the end of the tube and squeeze out the sausage. If the sausage is in casings, remove the meat by slitting the casing and "unwrapping" the sausage. Discard the casings.

1. In a large skillet over medium-high heat, fry the sausage and onion until the sausage is done. Break it up into "crumbles" as it cooks. Drain off the fat.
2. As the sausage is cooking, combine the milk, Worcestershire, salt, and pepper in a medium bowl. Set aside.
3. Add the flour slowly to the sausage mixture in the pan, stirring constantly to coat the sausage. Fry over medium-high heat until golden.
4. Reduce the heat to low and slowly stir in the reserved milk mixture. (I usually stir in a quarter cup, mix it well, then another half cup, stirring until mixed and so on until all the milk mixture is incorporated.) Stir constantly until the gravy reaches the thickness you desire. Serve over your favorite biscuits—yum!

A FEW MORE SAUCES AND GRAVIES

Not everything fits neatly into just one chapter!

Appetizers and Snacks
Salsa, *page 127*
Pico de Gallo, page 128
Tangy Dipping Sauce, *page 135*
Tzatziki, page 136

Holiday Cheer
Giblet Turkey Gravy, *page 362*

SEAFOOD

Prior to cruising, neither of us knew the first thing about cooking seafood. Raised in the Midwest in the 1960s, we just weren't exposed to it. We each turned to our fellow cruisers and local fishermen, asking questions and learning as we went. We both love seafood now and fix it several times a week.

If you've never cooked seafood—or cooked only a few types or only from a freezer bag—don't worry. We give you all the information we wish we'd known, providing not just recipes but lots of preparation and cooking tips.

SEAFOOD SAFETY CONCERNS

All fresh seafood spoils very rapidly, so be sure to have adequate refrigeration available or eat it immediately. Fish should not smell, so avoid buying seafood that has anything but a fresh, salty odor. Some seafood such as crabs, mussels, and lobster should be bought only live.

Ciguatera Poisoning

Ciguatera is an illness caused by consuming fish that have eaten certain toxins that are commonly found on coral and algae in shallow reef areas in the tropics and subtropical waters. There is no way to pinpoint specific species to avoid eating, but in general it's our experience that the locals know exactly what fish might have the ciguatera poison and which are safe to eat. Ask other cruisers or locals before consuming any large fish such as barracuda or even grouper and snapper in certain areas of the world.

Puffer Fish Poisoning

Do not eat any puffer fish, porcupine fish (my favorite reef fish with its droopy wide-eyed innocence), or ocean sunfish. They contain high levels of deadly poisons almost everywhere in the world.

Mercury Poisoning

Most fish contain trace amounts of mercury. But humans can safely consume fish unless eaten in large quantities daily over a period of time.

Mollusks

Because mollusks are often filter feeders, certain conditions in the sea can affect the safety of their consumption. Red tide is known to adversely affect mussels along the New England Coast and West Coast of the US during warmer summer months. Again, local advice is warranted.

FISH

Fresh fish—whether caught off the back rail or from the dinghy, speared, or purchased from a local fisherman—has to be one of the great joys of "cruising," even if your cruising is on a local lake for the afternoon!

Filleting a Fish

So we finally caught or speared a fish. Now what? The "now what" kept us from trying to fish for a long time. It wasn't as hard as we'd feared, though, and the intimidation factor definitely wasn't worth all the "fish eating" potential we wasted by not fishing.

We prefer to fillet our fish rather than eating it whole or with the skin on. To fillet a fish merely means to cut off the meatiest part longitudinally so that you end up with a boneless side of fish. Follow these instructions. It will feel awkward at first, but after a few fish it will get easier. Larger fish are easier to fillet, so if you learn on fish purchased from a local fisherman, buy bigger rather than smaller.

Step 1. Get your utensils ready—you'll need a cutting board and a very sharp fillet knife. A good fillet knife is critical, so don't scrimp when buying it. We bought ours at a fishing-oriented sporting goods store along with a whetstone to keep it razor sharp. We also have a bucket with a line to dip fresh seawater from alongside the boat to keep our work area clean. We use our side deck, because our cockpit is too small, but all you really need is a flat space to work and access to water for cleanup.

Step 2. Lay the fish on its side on the cutting board and make a diagonal cut just behind the fish's gills.

Step 3. Make a shallow cut along the top of the fish, just off the centerline, from the front all the way to the back. Work the knife down as close to the ribs as possible so you don't lose the meat off the fillet.

Step 4. Continue to work the knife down the rib cage until you reach the bottom of the fish and can cut through the bottom of the fillet.

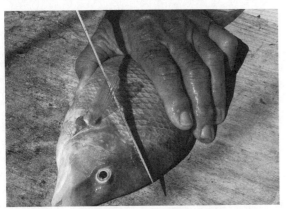
Using your sharp knife, cut diagonally behind the gills.

Slice almost halfway through the fish, just behind the gills.

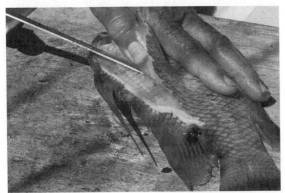
Slice along the rib cage until you can cut through the bottom of the fillet.

Remove the fillet from the carcass by cutting along the bottom.

Seafood

Step 5. Now you have one fillet, albeit with skin. If you don't want the skin, lay the fillet flat, skin side down, and carefully work the razor-sharp tip of the knife between the fillet and the skin, carefully slicing off skin as you go. Flip the fish over and cut a second fillet.

Step 6. Discard the remains with the guts intact. Depending on your cruising grounds, you may wish to discard a distance from your boat to keep away sharks. This is particularly important in the Bahamas. If you shower by jumping in the salt water first, you really don't want sharks waiting for things to be tossed overboard!

Step 7. Place the fillets in a bucket of seawater to clean them before putting them in a plastic food storage container. I rinse them with fresh water and a bit of lemon juice before I prepare them to grill or otherwise cook, or put in a freezer bag to freeze. Be careful not to use too much lemon juice or leave them soaking in it too long or you'll end up with ceviche (page 228)—great if you intend to have ceviche, a problem otherwise.

Step 8. Rinse the side deck, cutting board, and knife with seawater until clean. Wash the cutting board with a bleach solution and let it dry in the sun. The knife gets washed with dish soap and placed carefully back in its sleeve until hopefully tomorrow when we'll have another fish to enjoy.

Fish Recipes

I never thought having fish for dinner would get old, but when we were eating fish for almost every meal, we started searching for different ways to enjoy it. Hopefully this will give you some ideas!

Basic Fried Fish   Serves 2

Although we call this "fried fish," it is emphatically not deep-fried. Instead, the fillets are coated in egg and flour and then sautéed.

Total Time: 14 minutes
Prep Time: 10 minutes
Cook Time: 4 minutes (more for thicker fillets)

flour, cornmeal, or masa (corn flour, available everywhere in Central and South America)
salt and pepper, to taste
garlic powder, to taste
1 egg
splash of hot sauce (optional)
2 fillets of any type of fish
1 to 2 tablespoons olive oil,* canola oil, or vegetable oil (amount will vary with size of pan and how much is absorbed while cooking)

*Inexpensive olive oil may not get hot enough to quick-fry fish; good-quality extra-virgin olive oil is fine. If your olive oil smokes before it's hot enough to fry the fish, use canola oil instead.

1. Combine the flour, salt, pepper, and garlic powder; set aside.
2. Beat the egg with a bit of water and a splash of hot sauce, if desired.
3. Dip the fillets into the egg mixture, making sure that each side is coated. Then dredge the fillets in the reserved flour mixture.
4. Heat the oil in a skillet until a water drop sizzles. Add the fillets and sauté for approximately 2 minutes on one side, then 2 minutes on the other. You may need to add another tablespoon or two of oil when turning the fish. Depending on the size of your fish fillets and type of fish, cooking times will vary. Thicker fillets from denser fish such as swordfish or even grouper will take more time than snapper or hogfish fillets. Do not overcook. Fish should be opaque but still moist in the center. If you let it "cook until flakey," as specified in many cookbooks, it will be overcooked and dry.

NOTE: Some people prefer to fry fish fillets with the skin on. Try it both ways to determine your preference.

Variations:
- For extra-crisp fillets, coat them in the flour mixture first, then dip in the egg mixture, and finally dip in bread crumbs before placing in the hot oil.
- Add Cajun spice mix (page 46) to the flour mixture.

Sautéed Fish Fillets

One of the biggest mistakes in preparing fish is overcooking it. It should be just opaque. Fish continues cooking after you remove it from the pan, so be sure to remove it a couple of minutes before you think it's completely done. Err on the side of undercooking, as you can always put it back in the pan for another minute or so.

Total Time: Less than 12 minutes*
Prep Time: 2 minutes
Cook Time: Less than 5 minutes per side

*Cooking times for fish vary widely depending on the thickness of the fish fillets and the type of fish. Firmer, thicker fish such as tuna, swordfish, or mahimahi (dorado) may take as much as 5 minutes per side. Thinner, flakier fish such as hogfish, grouper, or snapper could take as little as 2 to 3 minutes per side.

fresh fish fillets
olive oil, canola oil, or vegetable oil
Winterlude's favorite seasonings: garlic powder and cracked black pepper
Que Tal's favorite seasonings: cracked pepper, no garlic powder, and served with wasabi-soy sauce (page 215)

1. Lightly coat both sides of the fillets with olive oil, and sprinkle with your preferred seasonings.
2. Heat a skillet to between medium and medium-high heat. Place the fillets in the skillet so they are not overlapping. Depending on the thickness and consistency of the fish, sauté for 2 to 5 minutes. Turn the fillets and sauté for 2 to 5 minutes longer. When done, the center should still be moist—similar to a medium-rare (beef) steak. Always err on the side of too little time—you can always put the fillets back in the pan, but you can't make tasteless dry fish appealing. Keep the fillets moving in the pan to make sure they don't stick. Serve immediately.

Aluminum Foil Beach Bake

This is every bit as good on the grill as it is on the beach with a bunch of friends in your favorite anchorage! When making the packets, it's best to use heavy-duty aluminum foil or double sheets of regular aluminum foil.

Total Time: 45 minutes
Prep Time: 15 minutes   **Cook Time:** 30 minutes

Serves however many packets you fix. We like to fix individual packets so they cook faster, but you can also put enough for two people in one packet. Ingredient amounts vary by the number of people to be served. Vary the vegetables by what you have available.

cooking spray
fish fillets (any type)
crushed or minced garlic or garlic powder, to taste
Beau Monde seasoning (page 46), Mrs. Dash (page 48), Old Bay Seasoning (page 48), or other seasoning mix you like
ground pepper, to taste
chopped onion, to taste
potatoes, peeled if desired, or yams, all coarsely chopped
chopped celery, to taste
chopped zucchini or summer squash, to taste
chopped tomato, to taste
olive oil, canola oil, vegetable oil, butter, or margarine
lemon juice, lime juice, or *limón* (Key lime) juice, to taste

1. For each packet, spread out a sheet of aluminum foil, making sure it's large enough to completely enclose everything you'll put in the packet and still have enough foil to fold over and seal. Spray the foil with cooking spray.
2. Rub each fish fillet thoroughly with a mixture of crushed garlic, Beau Monde seasoning, and ground pepper. Place the fish on the foil.
3. Chop the vegetables and spread over the fish. Drizzle a little olive oil and lemon juice over the veggies. Wrap the foil securely up, over, and around the prepared fish so the juices cannot escape. The best way to do this is to triple-fold the top and ends of the packets. If I'm worried about the juices escaping, I make a package, then overwrap with a second layer of aluminum foil. (If you use one layer of aluminum foil, keep the packets off the direct heat, and don't turn them so you don't lose juice.)

Seafood

4. Place the packet on the grill or just beside the coals, and turn occasionally. Total cooking time is about 30 minutes, but it depends on how hot the fire is and how large the packet is.

5. Open the packet occasionally to check the veggies for doneness. The total time will be influenced by whether a starchy veggie is included and, if so, how large the pieces are (the smaller the pieces, the quicker they will cook). When done, serve and eat right from the foil.

Basic Ceviche   Serves 4

Ceviche is a wonderful dish where the seafood is not cooked by heat but by the acid in lime or lemon juice. It's perfect on a hot day—a cold meal with no cooking heat!

There is no right or wrong way to make Ceviche. Experiment until you find a mixture that you love. For us, on Winterlude, the fresh cilantro makes the difference in the best ceviche and blah ceviche, so we don't make it unless we can get fresh cilantro. By contrast, Carolyn thinks cilantro tastes like soap, so she totally omits it!

Total Time: 1 hour, 15 minutes, including 1 hour marinating time (can be longer)
Prep Time: 15 minutes

1 pound fish fillets, tenderized conch, shelled and deveined shrimp, lobster meat, or a mixture (all raw, uncooked)
several limes, lemons, *limónes* (Key limes), or lime or lemon juice
2 large tomatoes
1 onion
chili pepper, to taste
2 cloves garlic, to taste
salt and pepper, to taste
cilantro (fresh is best), to taste

1. Cut the fish, conch, or lobster into small chunks. If you have large shrimp, cut them into smaller pieces.

2. Put the seafood in a bowl (not aluminum or other reactive material) with a tight lid or in a heavy, leakproof freezer bag. Cover the seafood with lime juice, seal the bowl or bag, and shake to coat all the pieces. You are not "cooking" the seafood/fish

in the conventional manner; rather the acid in the lime juice will "cook" the seafood.

3. Dice all the veggies very finely. Add them to the bowl or bag and shake gently. Season with the garlic, salt, ground pepper, and cilantro.

4. Chill for at least 1 to 2 hours, or preferably overnight. Serve cold with toasted bread or crackers.

Baked Parmesan Fish   Serves 4

Total Time: 30 minutes
Prep Time: 10 minutes   Bake Time: 15 minutes

cooking spray
1 egg
2 tablespoons milk
1/3 cup grated or shredded Parmesan cheese
2 tablespoons flour
1 teaspoon garlic powder
1/2 teaspoon paprika
1/4 teaspoon salt
1/8 teaspoon ground pepper
4 fish fillets, any type

1. Preheat oven to 350°F. Spritz a baking sheet with the cooking spray.

2. Beat the egg and milk in a shallow bowl and set aside. In a freezer bag, combine the cheese, flour, and spices.

3. Dip each fillet in the egg mixture, and shake off the excess. Place the fillet in the freezer bag with the cheese mixture and shake to cover, then remove the fillet and place on the oiled baking sheet. Bake, uncovered, for about 15 minutes, or until the fish appears opaque. Thicker fish fillets or steaks will take longer. Remember that the fish will continue cooking for a minute or two after you take it out of the oven.

Seafood

Grilled Fish Tacos
Serves 6

This version of fish tacos is from Southern California. The Mexican version is served with shredded cabbage, pico de gallo (page 128), and jalapeños.

Total Time: 30 minutes, plus 4 hours to marinate
Prep Time: 20 minutes
Grill Time: 8 minutes

1¾ pounds fish (any firm-fleshed fish, such as grouper or snapper)
⅓ cup lime juice*
3 tablespoons tequila*
cooking spray or oil
12 corn tortillas or flour tortillas, depending on your preference
salsa (page 127)
sour cream (page 99)

Cilantro Slaw
3 cups shredded green cabbage
3 cups shredded red cabbage
1 cup chopped fresh cilantro OR 8 tablespoons dried cilantro
½ cup lime juice or *limón* (Key lime) juice
1 tablespoon canola oil, vegetable oil, or olive oil
½ teaspoon cumin seed
1 teaspoon sugar
salt and pepper, to taste

*You can substitute ½ cup margarita mix (with or without alcohol) for the lime juice and tequila.

1. Rinse the fish, pat dry, and place in a freezer bag with the lime juice and tequila. Turn to coat. Refrigerate for up to 4 hours, turning occasionally to marinate.
2. Combine all the ingredients for the Cilantro Slaw. Stir. Cover and refrigerate for up to 4 hours.
3. Remove the fish from the marinade and discard the marinade. Spray the fish lightly with cooking spray or brush with oil. Grill over medium-hot coals, or sauté, turning once, until lightly browned and just opaque.
4. Heat the tortillas until soft. Place the grilled fish in the tortillas and add the Cilantro Slaw, salsa, and sour cream to taste. Serve at once.

David's Cioppino
Serves 2

Our friend David on Bruadair *was always coming up with fabulous new recipes from ingredients he just happened to have aboard. This was one of our favorites. Cioppino is an Italian-style fish stew that actually originated in San Francisco.*

Total Time: 35 minutes
Prep Time: 15 minutes   **Cook Time:** 20 minutes

1 small onion, diced
1 clove garlic, minced
1 tablespoon butter, margarine, olive oil, canola oil, or vegetable oil
1 can (10 ounces) tomato sauce with finely chopped onions/peppers/garlic
1 package *criolla* (page 213)
3 small fresh tomatoes, chopped
Italian seasoning, to taste (page 48)
dried marjoram, to taste
1 can (8 ounces) sliced mushrooms, not drained
1 chicken bouillon cube
fresh parsley, to taste
2 fish fillets
2 servings cooked pasta
Parmesan cheese, shredded or grated, for garnish

1. Sauté the onion and garlic in the butter. Add the tomato sauce, *criolla*, chopped fresh tomato, Italian spices, marjoram, and canned mushrooms with their juice. Crumble the bouillon cube into the pan and mix to combine. Bring to a boil, then turn down the heat to low. Simmer for 15 to 20 minutes, stirring occasionally. Then add the parsley; do not stir.
2. Arrange the fish fillets on top of the parsley. Cook for 2 to 4 minutes on each side, or until the fish turns opaque. The timing depends on the fish. Serve over pasta, and garnish with the Parmesan.

Seafood

Beer-Battered Fish   Serves 6

Total Time: 40 minutes
Prep Time: 10 minutes   **Cook Time:** 30 minutes

¾ cup beer (half a 12-ounce can)
¾ cup flour
½ teaspoon salt
¼ teaspoon dried oregano
¼ teaspoon dry mustard OR 1 teaspoon prepared
   mustard
¼ teaspoon cayenne pepper
¼ teaspoon ground pepper
6 fillets of any mild white fish
4 tablespoons canola oil or vegetable oil

1. To make a batter, mix the beer, flour, and spices in a shallow dish. Coat each fish fillet with the batter.
2. Heat 2 tablespoons of the oil in a skillet over medium-high heat until a drop of water sizzles. Fry the fish fillets to a golden brown on one side, usually 3 to 4 minutes. Remove the fillets temporarily.
3. Add the remaining 2 tablespoons oil to the skillet. Fry the other side of the fish fillets. Enjoy immediately to keep them from getting soggy.

Nut-Crusted Baked Fish   Serves 2

This is Carolyn's favorite way to prepare salmon, but this dish is good with many other types of fish as well.

Total Time: 30 minutes
Prep Time: 15 minutes   **Bake Time:** 15 minutes

cooking spray or oil
2 fish fillets
salt and pepper, to taste
1 tablespoon melted butter, margarine, canola oil,
   or vegetable oil
2 tablespoons prepared mustard (whole grain or
   spicy are best)
1 tablespoon honey
1 tablespoon dry bread crumbs (page 51)
2 tablespoons finely chopped walnuts, pecans, or
   almonds

1. Preheat oven to 400°F. Spritz a baking pan large enough to hold the fillets in a single layer with cooking spray. A shallow pan will give a crispier crust. If you don't have a baking pan, you can use a double layer of aluminum foil.
2. Place the fish fillets in the pan. If one side still has skin on it, place that side down. Sprinkle with salt and pepper.
3. In a cup or small bowl, mix the butter, mustard, and honey. Spread the mixture over the fish fillets, covering them as much as possible.
4. In another cup or small bowl, mix the bread crumbs and nuts. Evenly sprinkle the mixture over the fillets. Bake for 12 to 15 minutes, or until just done but not dry. Serve at once.

Greek Fish   Serves 4

Total Time: 40 minutes
Prep Time: 20 minutes   **Bake Time:** 20 minutes

cooking spray or olive oil
4 fish fillets, preferably grouper, snapper, or any
   firm-fleshed white fish
1 medium onion, thinly sliced
1 to 2 teaspoons dried dill OR 1 to 2 tablespoons
   chopped fresh dill
salt and pepper, to taste
2 tablespoons chopped fresh parsley OR
   1 teaspoon dried parsley flakes
¼ cup lemon juice, lime juice, or *limón* (Key lime)
   juice
1 tomato, chopped
½ cup crumbled feta cheese

1. Preheat oven to 350°F. Spritz a baking dish with cooking spray.
2. Place the fillets in the baking dish. It is much easier to serve if the fillets do not overlap.
3. Top the fillets with the onion slices, and sprinkle with the dill, salt, pepper, parsley, lemon juice, chopped tomato, and feta.
4. Bake, uncovered, for 20 minutes, or until the fish is just opaque. The actual baking time will depend on the thickness of the fish fillets.
5. Serve by sliding a spatula under each fillet and transferring it to a plate with all the toppings intact.

Seafood

Honey Ginger Fish
Serves 4

The fish is great with or without the wasabi.

Total Time: 35 minutes, including 15 minutes to marinate
Prep Time: 5 minutes
Bake or Grill Time: 15 minutes

5 tablespoons soy sauce
5 tablespoons orange juice*
¼ cup honey
1 teaspoon ground ginger
1 teaspoon garlic powder
¼ teaspoon wasabi paste, or to taste (optional)
1 green onion, sliced (including top)
4 fish fillets (or more as needed to serve 4 people)
cooking spray or olive oil

*Or pineapple juice—and you can include pineapple chunks or slices and bake or grill them alongside the fish.

1. In a large freezer bag or a non-reactive pan just large enough to hold the fillets, combine the soy sauce, orange juice, honey, ginger, garlic powder, wasabi, and green onion. Stir well. Add the fish fillets and turn to coat completely. Allow to marinate for 15 to 30 minutes, turning occasionally.
2. Preheat oven to 375°F. Spritz a baking pan with cooking spray.
3. If you'll be baking the fish, place the fillets in the baking pan and spoon a little of the marinade over each fillet. Bake for 12 to 15 minutes (depending on the size and thickness of the fillets), or until just done. If desired, spoon a little more marinade over the fish halfway through the baking.

NOTE: You may want to grill the fish instead of baking it. Instead of a pan, you can use aluminum foil, or wrap the fish in foil so it is easier to turn.

Kristiana Fish Bone Soup
Serves 2

Thanks to Doug and Rayene on Kristiana *for sharing my favorite fish bone soup recipe! Any leftover soup is even better the next day!*

Total Time: 1 hour, 20 minutes
Prep Time: 20 minutes   **Cook Time:** 60 minutes

2 good-size fillets of snapper, grouper, hogfish, or jack, cut into 1-inch cubes
center section of fish carcass (what remains after cutting fillets; no guts)
⅓ cup white vinegar
2 bay leaves
2 onions, diced
minced garlic (the more, the better), or to taste
1 teaspoon fresh or dried oregano
1 teaspoon fresh or dried thyme
1 green bell pepper, diced
olive oil
1 cup diced tomato, fresh or canned
1 can (16 ounces) coconut milk
2 servings cooked rice
fresh cilantro, for garnish
dash of Tabasco or hot sauce (optional)

1. Cube the fillets and set aside. Cut off and discard the head, tail, and all fins from the carcass.
2. Put the remaining carcass into a big pot; add enough water to cover the carcass. Add the vinegar, bay leaves, half the diced onion, half the minced garlic, and the oregano and thyme. Try not to dislodge any of the bones during the process so you have fewer in the soup.
3. Boil the carcass for 30 minutes. Let it cool, then remove the carcass. Pick any meat off the bones and set the meat aside until step 5.
4. Use a colander or strainer to strain the broth, or strain it through a clean rag or coffee filter. Discard everything in the strainer. Add water, if needed, to thin the broth to the desired consistency. Set aside.
5. In the soup pot, combine the rest of the onion and garlic and all the bell pepper. Sauté in olive oil for 5 minutes. Add the diced tomato, coconut milk, and the reserved fish broth and simmer for about 10 minutes. Add the reserved cubed fish fillets and any meat picked from the carcass. Cook for 5 more minutes, or until the fish is just opaque.
6. To serve, place the rice in bowls and ladle the soup over it. Top with the fresh cilantro. Add a dash of Tabasco or hot sauce if you like extra heat in your soup.

Seafood

Baked Salmon   Serves 2

Total Time: 35 minutes
Prep Time: 10 minutes   **Cook Time:** 12 to 15 minutes

cooking spray
2 salmon fillets or other fish fillets
2 tablespoons mayonnaise (Miracle Whip is not a
    good substitute)
1 teaspoon coarse-ground pepper or regular
    ground pepper
seasoned salt, to taste
1 teaspoon garlic powder
1 tablespoon grated Parmesan cheese
1/2 cup dry bread crumbs

1. Preheat oven to 350°F. Spritz a glass baking dish,
   nonstick cookie sheet, or piece of aluminum foil
   with cooking spray.
2. Place the fish, skin side down, in the baking dish.
   Cover the entire top of the fillets with mayonnaise.
   This keeps the fillets moist and prevents them from
   drying out in the oven. Make sure to get the mayonnaise all the way to the edges of the fillets.
3. Sprinkle the fillets liberally with the spices, cheese,
   and dry bread crumbs. Bake about 12 to15 minutes, uncovered. If you have a broiler, place the
   baked fillets under the broiler until the bread
   crumbs turn golden brown. If not, the fillets are
   good as is.

Cracked Pepper
Tuna Steaks   Serves 2

Total Time: 20 minutes
Prep Time: 10 minutes   **Cook Time:** 10 minutes

2 tablespoons coarsely cracked black pepper*
2 tablespoons sesame seeds
2 tuna steaks or any "meaty" fish fillets
4 teaspoons sesame oil or canola oil
4 cloves garlic, minced
4 tablespoons soy sauce
1/2 cup dry sherry or dry red wine
2 tablespoons chopped green onion
dash of red wine, if needed

You can use regular ground pepper, but it's not as good.

1. Combine the black pepper and sesame seeds on a
   plate. Press the tuna steaks into the mixture and
   turn until coated.
2. Heat the sesame oil in a large skillet over medium-
   high heat. Add the tuna steaks and sear about
   2 minutes on each side (less if you like it rare).
   Remember, as tuna cooks, it gets drier and tougher.
   The more pink, the more tender and juicy. Remove
   the steaks from the pan and cover with aluminum
   foil to retain heat.
3. Add a splash more oil to the pan, then add the
   garlic, soy sauce, sherry, and green onion. If too
   much liquid has boiled off, add a dash of red wine
   if necessary. Reduce the heat and simmer for about
   1 minute, or until the mixture is slightly reduced,
   scraping up any browned bits. Spoon the sauce
   over the reserved fish and serve at once.

Fish or Seafood Cakes

*This recipe is great for leftover cooked fish, shrimp, crab,
lobster, etc. It's a nice change! We (Jan) always threw the
small pieces of cooked fish that weren't consumed at dinner into a bag in the fridge. When we had enough, I made
fish cakes! The quantities are eyeballed—the only rule is
to use about the same amount of fish as mashed potatoes.
Also see our recipe for Meat, Seafood, or Fish Cakes using
canned meats (page 322).*

Total Time: 20 minutes
Prep Time: 10 minutes   **Cook Time:** 8 to 10 minutes

boneless fish fillets or cooked crab, shrimp, or
    lobster
mashed potatoes
1 onion, finely diced
1 red, green, or yellow bell pepper, finely diced
2 cloves garlic, minced
bread crumbs*
1 or 2 eggs, beaten
1 tablespoon mixed herbs, or to taste (whatever
    you like—I usually use garlic, basil, oregano,
    and thyme)
salt and pepper, to taste
peanut oil, canola oil, or vegetable oil

The quantity of bread crumbs will vary with the amount of fish/mashed potatoes. I use a sprinkling, work it in, and then add more until the consistency is substantial enough for the fish cakes to hold together.

1. Mix equal amounts of chopped fish/seafood and mashed potatoes. Add the onion, bell pepper, and garlic. Add enough bread crumbs and beaten egg for the mixture to hold together well enough to form patties. Add the mixed herbs, salt, and pepper.
2. Heat the oil in a skillet over medium-high heat. Form the mixture into patties and sauté in the hot oil. Drain on paper towels. Serve with cocktail sauce (page 211) or tartar sauce (page 211).

Fish Sausage

This is a very helpful "basic" recipe whenever you can't find sausage pre-made and have a hankering for it. A friend, Annie on Calliope, *says that she's made variations on this many times with meats other than fish—chicken, ground beef, pork—and uses it in any recipe calling for sausage. I (Carolyn) would keep a bag in the refrigerator with all the little leftover bits of fish that would fall off when Dave was filleting a fish. When it got full enough, I'd make fish sausage. This is also a great dish if you're catching a lot of fish and would like something "different." Here are a few ideas:*

- Instead of making it into patties, crumble it into a pan, brown it, and use in scrambled eggs.
- Change the spices to garlic, salt, ground pepper, oregano, and basil (or Italian seasoning) and use it in spaghetti sauce or lasagna.
- Add more chili powder or other "spicy" seasoning and call it Cajun sausage (also good in gumbo or jambalaya).
- Mix in diced potato, onion, and an egg and form it into patties (fish cakes!); cook in a little hot oil (hot is very important so the patties don't absorb the oil and become soggy). Very tasty!

Total Time: 15 minutes
Prep Time: 5 minutes   **Cook Time:** 10 minutes or so

3 cups coarsely ground raw grouper, triggerfish, or other "sticky" fish
1 teaspoon garlic powder
1 teaspoon dried thyme
1½ teaspoons chili powder
1 teaspoon ground sage
2 teaspoons poultry seasoning or ground sage
1½ teaspoons ground pepper
2 teaspoons salt
vegetable oil

1. Grind the fish in a meat grinder or finely chop it if it is not already ground. Combine the seasonings, then mix into the ground fish until evenly distributed. Shape the fish mixture into patties, or leave as is for use in other recipes. This may be stored several days in the refrigerator, or frozen.
2. To cook as sausage patties, thinly coat a skillet with vegetable oil. Cook the patties on one side until the edges turn white, then flip them over and cook until done.

SHRIMP

Fresh shrimp is a huge treat and often available right from the shrimp boats in the Caribbean or Mexico. If there's a shrimp boat in your anchorage, or at a shrimp dock, pull up in your dinghy and ask if they sell shrimp. If not, ask if they know if any of the other boats sell shrimp. You may need your own bag since shrimp boats are typically not in the business of selling consumer quantities of shrimp.

Also, in certain areas, there are shrimp farms; central Belize is a good example. Sometimes when they're in production, you can buy shrimp directly from the shrimp farm. A shrimp farm looks like a collection of very shallow ponds and a building where they process the shrimp, often in the middle of nowhere. We usually dinghy up and try to find someone to ask if we can buy some shrimp.

Shrimp 101

If you buy shrimp from a local fish market, make sure it is firm and doesn't smell. Shrimp should smell like the ocean, not like ammonia or anything else.

Seafood

Wherever you buy it, buy larger rather than smaller shrimp. They're easier to peel and eat and don't seem to be any "tougher" or less tasty than their smaller brothers and sisters.

If you get shrimp from a boat or farm, you're likely to get just an old grocery bag of them; they won't be cleaned or prepared at all. If this is a new experience for you (it sure was for us!), here's how to handle them:

Step 1. De-heading shrimp. To de-head the shrimp, grab the head firmly between your thumb and forefinger. Pinch it and give it a quick twist with your other hand—it should pop right off. Wash the shrimp in cold water. Discard the heads. If you're in an area with sharks (such as the Bahamas), you probably don't want to just dump the shrimp heads overboard!

Step 2. Preparing shrimp. Decide whether you're going to devein the shrimp. The dark vein running along the shrimp's back is its gastric vein. Usually they're small and don't make a taste difference. If you're like me and anal about the gastric vein, by all means devein it before cooking. The easiest way is to use the red plastic deveining tool available in stores with cooking gadget sections. The tool will come with easy instructions.

If you don't have a tool but want your shrimp deveined, peel them first, then run the tip of a sharp knife along the back of the shrimp, revealing the vein. You can dig it out with the knife tip or a toothpick. On *Que Tal*, Carolyn just used her thumbnail; she found it faster and easier with no risk of cutting the vein.

Step 3. Keeping shrimp. Shrimp should be kept cold, and cooked within the first couple of days, if not immediately.

Cooking Shrimp

Shrimp are delicious cooked in a variety of ways: boiling, steaming, grilling, sautéing, baking, or even deep-frying. Shrimp can be cooked with or without the shell, with the vein or deveined (see Step 2 above).

The most important thing about cooking shrimp is to cook them quickly to preserve the delicate flavor and texture. The easiest way to ruin shrimp is to overcook them.

Most shrimp, regardless of size, cook in about 3 minutes. The key is to make sure that the water, oil, or grill is HOT. When the shrimp are pink and curled like a "C," not an "O," they're done.

Shrimp can also be used in ceviche or other recipes calling for "cooking" via the acid in lime juice.

Boiling. This is probably the most common method of cooking shrimp.

1. In a large pot with a lid, heat about a quart of water with 3 tablespoons salt or other spices to boiling.
2. Add a pound of shrimp to the rapidly boiling water. Replace the lid.
3. Remove the pot from the heat. The shrimp will continue to cook in the hot water.
4. Timing is difficult because shrimp are easy to overcook. A rule of thumb is that the shrimp are done when they form a "C." If they're "O" shaped, they are overcooked. I usually start watching jumbo shrimp after 4 minutes, although they may take up to 7 minutes. Large shrimp take from 2½ to 5 minutes; medium shrimp are ready in 3 minutes or less.
5. If you are using the shrimp in a recipe, be sure to immediately place them in cold water to stop the cooking. Do not leave them in the hot water; they will continue to cook and turn rubbery.

Carolyn's Water-Conserving Method (not quite steamed, but not boiled either)

1. Put just half an inch of water in a saucepan. Add 2 tablespoons Old Bay Seasoning (page 48) and about 2 tablespoons white vinegar.
2. Bring to a full rolling boil over high heat.
3. Add up to 1 pound of medium shrimp (I prefer shelled so the spices really stick). Cover the pan and bring the water back to a full rolling boil.
4. The instant the water starts boiling, reduce the heat to low and begin timing 2 minutes very exactly.
5. After 2 minutes, turn off the heat, or remove the pot from the stove if you're using an electric stove. Leave the lid on the pot.
6. Time another 2 minutes.
7. Drain the water from the shrimp and serve at once. A lot of the spices should still be sticking to the shrimp.

NOTE: Large shrimp will take 2½ minutes in each stage; jumbo shrimp 3 to 3½ minutes in each. Frozen shrimp do not need to be thawed first; since you start timing when the water returns to a boil, the timing is the same.

Grilling. This is popular for cooking larger shrimp, or kabobs for smaller shrimp.

1. Heat the grill.
2. Spray the shrimp with cooking spray, or lightly brush with olive oil, then sprinkle with sea salt, garlic powder, and cracked black pepper.
3. Place the shrimp or kabobs on the hot grill.
4. Grill for 3 to 4 minutes, or until the shrimp are pink and "C" shaped. Turn once halfway into the cook time.
5. Remove from the grill and serve immediately.

Shrimp or Crab Boil Spice Balls   Makes 4 spice balls

Similar to Zatarain's Crawfish, Shrimp, and Crab Boil, a popular seasoning from New Orleans. Depending on where you are, some of the spices in this recipe may be hard to find. You can either stock up if you know you want to use this type of spice in your shrimp boils, or just bring a few packages of Zatarain's with you.

4 tablespoons mustard seed
3 tablespoons coriander seed
2 tablespoons whole allspice
2 tablespoons dill seed
1 teaspoon whole cloves
1 tablespoon crushed red pepper flakes
8 bay leaves
four 6-inch squares of clean cotton cloth
4 pieces of thin string

1. For each spice ball, put one portion of each spice in the center of each cloth square. Tie up the corners of each cloth square to make a ball. Crush the ball with your fingers to bring out the flavors.
2. Put a ball in a pot of boiling water before you add the shrimp or crab. See page 234 for boiling or steaming instructions.

Crab or Shrimp Boil Seasoning   4 tablespoons

This mixture is more like Old Bay Seasoning, which comes from the Chesapeake Bay area. As with the Shrimp or Crab Boil Spice Balls (see preceding recipe), you may need to bring some of the spices required for this seasoning with you. I was able to buy Old Bay Seasoning in major Caribbean markets such as Panama City, but Carolyn never found it on the Pacific side of Mexico or Central America.

1 tablespoon celery salt OR 1 tablespoon ground
    celery seed and 1 teaspoon salt
1 tablespoon ground pepper
6 bay leaves, finely crushed
½ teaspoon ground cardamom
½ teaspoon dry mustard
¼ teaspoon ground cloves
1 teaspoon paprika
¼ teaspoon ground mace

1. Mix all the ingredients together. A grinder or a mini food processor works well to ensure that all the ingredients are well mixed and powdery.
2. Put 1 tablespoon of the seasoning (or more if desired) in a quart of boiling water to boil shrimp or crab.

Spicy Sautéed Shrimp   Serves 2

Total Time: 15 minutes, including 5 minutes to marinate
Prep Time: 5 minutes   Cook Time: 4 to 6 minutes

1 tablespoon olive oil, canola oil, or vegetable oil
1 tablespoon lime juice
¼ teaspoon ground cumin
¼ teaspoon dried oregano
½ teaspoon salt
¼ teaspoon ground pepper
1 teaspoon minced garlic
red pepper flakes (optional)
½ pound shelled and deveined raw shrimp
    (page 234)

Seafood

1. Mix the oil, lime juice, and all the spices in a plastic bowl or freezer bag. Add the shrimp and toss to coat with the mixture. Let sit for 5 minutes to let the flavors absorb into the shrimp.
2. Warm a skillet over medium-high heat until a few drops of water dance on the surface. Add the shrimp mixture and cook, stirring every minute or so, until the shrimp are just pink and "C" shaped. Depending on the size of the shrimp and whether they are cold, this will take 4 to 6 minutes or less. Serve at once.

NOTE: The shrimp can also be grilled–either in an aluminum foil pouch or on skewers after marinating.

Low-Country Boil   Serves 6

Total Time: 50 minutes or so
Prep Time: 20 minutes   Cook Time: 30 minutes or so

2 pounds small red potatoes, quartered, with skin left on
4 medium onions, peeled and quartered or thick slivered
4 to 5 tablespoons Old Bay Seasoning (1 tablespoon for approximately each quart of water used; page 48)
hot sauce or cayenne pepper, to taste
2 lemons, quartered and squeezed into the pot, OR ¼ cup lime juice or *limón* (Key lime) juice OR ¼ cup white vinegar
4 tablespoons minced garlic
2 or 3 bay leaves
1 pound uncooked spicy smoked sausage links, cut diagonally into ¾-inch pieces
6 ears of corn, shucked and cut in half
2 pounds large fresh shrimp, peeled and deveined (page 234)
cocktail sauce (page 211; optional)

1. Add the potatoes and onions to a large pot and cover with water. Add the Old Bay Seasoning, hot sauce, lemon juice, minced garlic, and bay leaves. Put the lid on and bring the water to a boil. Boil for 5 minutes. Add the sausage and corn, and return to a boil. Cook 10 more minutes, or until the potatoes are almost tender.

2. Add the shrimp and cook for 3 to 7 minutes, or until they turn pink. The time depends on the size of the shrimp. Drain. Make sure to remove the bay leaves. Serve with cocktail sauce if desired.

Shrimp Scampi   Serves 2 to 4

Shrimp scampi is usually served over rice, but it's also good without.

Total Time: 17 to 19 minutes
Prep Time: 10 minutes
Cook Time: 7 minutes total, only 2 to 4 minutes for shrimp, depending on size

4 tablespoons minced fresh garlic OR 1¼ teaspoons garlic powder
⅓ cup butter, olive oil, canola oil, or vegetable oil
1 pound fresh shrimp, peeled and deveined (page 234)
6 green onions, chopped
¼ cup dry white wine
2 tablespoons lemon juice (fresh squeezed really enhances the flavor)
salt and pepper, to taste
fresh parsley, to taste
shredded Parmesan cheese, for garnish

1. In a large skillet over medium-high heat, sauté the garlic in the butter. Add the shrimp, green onion, wine, and lemon juice. Cook the shrimp for 1 to 2 minutes on each side; be careful not to overcook them.
2. Add the salt, pepper, and parsley. If desired, serve over rice and garnish with the Parmesan.

Beer Boiled Shrimp   Serves 6

These are delicious, but use a beer that will not overpower the flavor of the shrimp.

Total Time: 15 minutes

2 cans (12 ounces each) beer
2 tablespoons shrimp boil seasoning such as Old Bay (page 48) or Zatarain's (see Shrimp or Crab Boil Spice Balls, page 235)
2 pounds raw shrimp, either in shell or shelled and deveined (page 234)

1. Bring the beer and seasoning to a boil in a large pot (watch to keep it from boiling over). Add the shrimp, stir to mix, and cover.
2. Return the mixture to a full boil, then start timing 2 minutes. Turn off the heat and leave everything in the pan, covered, for another 2 minutes, or just until the shrimp are "C" shaped. Do not overcook. Drain immediately.
3. The shrimp may be served hot or chilled with shrimp cocktail sauce (page 211).

Simple Shrimp Creole   Serves 2 to 4

"Real" Louisiana creole cooks would shudder at this Simple Shrimp Creole recipe. Don't be fooled; it's nowhere as tasty as the real thing, but it's easy and quick, and it uses ingredients that are usually already aboard!

Total Time: 35 minutes, not including time to cook rice if needed
Prep Time: 15 minutes   Cook Time: 20 minutes or so

1 large onion, chopped
1 cup chopped celery
1 green bell pepper, seeded and chopped
2 cloves garlic, minced
¼ cup butter or margarine
1 can (16 ounces) diced tomatoes (if you have the spicy kind, so much the better!)
1 cup water
2 teaspoons dried parsley flakes
1 teaspoon salt
dash of cayenne pepper, to taste (optional)
dash of hot sauce, to taste
2 bay leaves
1 pound shrimp, peeled and deveined (page 234)

1. In a large skillet over medium-high heat, sauté the onion, celery, bell pepper, and garlic in the butter. Stir in the tomatoes, water, and spices. Simmer, uncovered, for 10 minutes.
2. Stir in the shrimp. Reduce the heat; cover and simmer for 3 to 7 minutes longer, or until the shrimp are pink and tender. The time will depend on the size of the shrimp.
3. Remove the pan from the heat and remove the bay leaves. Serve the shrimp over rice.

Shrimp and Pasta   Serves 4

Total Time: 40 minutes
Prep Time: 10 minutes   Cook Time: 30 minutes

8 ounces pasta, cooked and drained (I like multi-grain penne)
1 tablespoon minced garlic
¼ cup butter, olive oil, canola oil, or vegetable oil
1½ pounds shrimp, peeled and deveined (page 234)
2 cups half-and-half (*media crema*), evaporated milk, or cream
1 teaspoon minced fresh basil OR ½ teaspoon dried basil
¼ cup grated or shredded Parmesan cheese
¼ teaspoon ground pepper
¼ teaspoon red pepper flakes (optional)
fresh basil, for garnish (optional)
dash of Parmesan, for garnish (optional)

1. Boil the pasta while preparing the shrimp. Rinse the pasta with cool water to prevent overcooking.
2. In a large skillet over medium-high heat, sauté the garlic in the butter. Add the shrimp and continue to sauté for 3 to 5 minutes, depending on the size of the shrimp. Remove the shrimp from the skillet and keep warm.
3. Add the half-and-half to the pan. Bring to a boil, reduce the heat to low, and simmer, uncovered, for 15 minutes, stirring frequently. Remove the pan from the heat.
4. Add the reserved shrimp, the basil, Parmesan cheese, ground pepper, and red pepper flakes. Stir well. Add the cooked pasta and toss to mix.
5. Serve immediately, garnished with fresh basil and Parmesan, if desired.

CRAB

Finding, spearing, or buying a live crab from a local fisherman is always a big treat aboard. When we traded gasoline for the biggest crab I'd ever seen from a native Kuna fisherman in the San Blas Islands (Kuna Yala), Panama, there was no way that any pot on the boat was big enough! By snapping the legs off, we were able to engineer fitting the entire crab in the pot.

Seafood

Crab 101

If you're catching or spearing your own crab, be careful to avoid the pinching claws. It seems a no-brainer to make sure they're alive when you catch them.

Buy only live crabs from local fishermen because crab deteriorates quickly and you have no idea how long they've been dead in the bottom of a local's wooden *cayuco* (canoe).

We don't clean our crabs before cooking, but if you want to clean them prior to cooking, you can toss them in the boiling water for less than a minute. First turn the crab over and locate the triangular flap on the underside. Scrape or pull it off. Then flip the crab over and clean out the gills under the flaps over each leg. Rinse the crab and put it back into the boiling water.

Like shrimp, there are three basic ways to cook crab: boiling, steaming, or grilling. You can tell when a crab is done by the shell turning color—most varieties will turn bright red. If the crabs are smaller, they may float when they're done. Again, like shrimp, don't overcook or your crab will be rubbery.

Eating a Whole Crab

Eating crabs can be a real treat—an event, not just a meal, especially if you share it with friends. Just realize that it's going to be a major mess and plan accordingly. Ideally, you might take the cooked crabs to a picnic table nearby that you can line with old newspaper. But fear not, cockpits littered with leftovers after a crab dinner with friends do clean up the next morning. We tried to cover our table with paper towels, etc., to no avail. Realize that it's going to be messy and enjoy your crab!

Set out a large bowl of cocktail sauce (Jan's way—page 211) or melted butter (Carolyn's way). Everyone puts some on his or her plate—use large plates. You'll need a crab cracker, lobster cracker, or even a nutcracker or a knife. Have a trash can handy.

1. Put a crab on your plate.
2. Twist off the legs and claws and set them aside for later. If some crabmeat pops out, be sure to dip it in your cocktail sauce and savor it.

3. Turn the crab over on its back. Pull off the triangular apron on the bottom of the crab. Be careful — this is where the gunky stuff is. Underneath, you'll find the gills, guts, and "mustard." We remove them all and discard. It's reported that some people actually eat the mustard as a delicacy, but we're not brave enough to try it.
4. Use either your hands or a knife to break the chambers and then pull them apart to expose the crabmeat inside. If you can't quite reach it, use a knife, a fork, or even a cocktail swizzle stick.
5. After you've picked the body clean of all the meat you can reach, discard the shell and tackle the legs and claws. Crack the claws by using a hinged crab cracker or a nutcracker. If you don't have a cracker, a fork or knife can be used.
6. The best way to open a claw without a cracker is to put your knife, sharp side down, on the middle of the side of the claw. Use a mallet or hammer to gently tap the top side of the knife blade until it's about halfway through the shell. Then twist the blade to start opening the claw, and use your hands to snap the shell open. Enjoy the crabmeat, but avoid the cartilage. Be careful not to cut your hands or fingers on the sharp pieces of shell.
7. Use a pick or cocktail fork to pick through all the shell and cartilage and extract every last bit of the meat.

Enjoy your evening. Remember that this is an event, not just a meal. So take your time, savor everything, sip your beer or wine, and worry about cleaning up later.

Boiled Crab   Serves any number

Total Time: 8 to 12 minutes
Prep Time: 2 minutes
Cook Time: usually 6 to 10 minutes, depending on the size of the crab, and timing it after the water is boiling

salt, sea salt, or crab boil seasonings (page 235)
crabs

1. Fill your pot two-thirds full of water. If you're cruising in locales where the seawater is clear and clean, you can use seawater and omit the salt. Add the seasonings–use about $\frac{1}{2}$ cup per gallon of water for salt or sea salt; 1 tablespoon of Old Bay–type seasoning per quart of water.

2. Cover the pot and bring the water to a full boil. Add the crab either whole or in pieces, whatever fits. Don't bother to put the cover back on—you'll need to watch the crabs. The water will need to return to a boil after you put in the crabs. Many varieties of crab have shells that turn red when they're done. If your pot isn't crammed full, the crabs may float when they're done. So watch for the shells to turn red or float. Otherwise, boil them for between 6 and 10 minutes, depending on the size of the crab. Smaller Maryland blue crabs can be done in as little as 6 minutes. Larger crabs take longer.

3. Remove the crabs from the boiling water. Discard the water. Cool the crabs by running them under cool water in a colander, or just place them in a sink and douse them with cool water.

Steaming Crabs

Total Time: 12 minutes

crabs—as many as you have or will fit in your pot

Pour enough water into a steamer pan or other pan to cover the bottom of the pan. Bring the water to a boil. Toss in the crabs, cover the pan, and steam the crabs for 8 to 10 minutes, or until they turn red.

CLAMS AND MUSSELS

Although Jan wrote most of this chapter, she didn't have clams in the western Caribbean. She learned all about gathering and cooking clams from Carolyn during a summer visit to the Sea of Cortez aboard *Que Tal*.

Clams

In many cruising areas you can find your own clams or buy them freshly dug from local fishermen or kids. In some places, there are laws about collecting clams, so be sure to check with other cruisers or local authorities. Also, different locales have different species of clams, which require different methods of collecting. I'll talk about the method we used, but you'll probably need to ask cruisers in your area whether they can find them (Jan and David never did in the western Caribbean) and, if so, how. For example, in New England, it's traditional to rake for clams at low tide instead of diving for them.

Clams are filter feeders, so you don't want to eat any from highly polluted water. In particular, beware of collecting any from areas with inadequate septic or sewer systems, busy anchorages where boats are not using holding tanks, and anywhere there's a red tide. Ask locals if there's any doubt.

Further, although overcooked clams are tough and unpleasant to eat, raw or undercooked clams can be dangerous. They can be infected with the *Vibrio vulnificus* bacteria, which can cause serious illness and, in rare instances, death. The good news is that complete cooking destroys it.

When we were in the Sea of Cortez, we were told that we could collect clams for our own eating only. I'll give a brief description of how we found the most common type: *chocolates* (pronounced chock-oh-LA-tays; see photo). While these were the most common in the Sea of Cortez, we found everything from tiny clams called "wedgies"—about $\frac{3}{4}$ inch in diameter—to giant *amarillos* (Spanish for "yellows" because of their color) that were about 5 inches in diameter.

Chocolates *are usually about 3 inches across.*

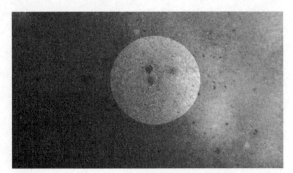

The two dark circles inside the light gray highlighted area are a clam. Without the highlighting, it can be very hard to see them when you're just starting out.

Chocolates are generally found in big white sand bays, generally in anywhere from 8 to 20 feet of water. You're going to have to snorkel and free dive to get them. Snorkel on the surface and look for two holes close to each other that are about the size of a pencil eraser. In the photo I've highlighted the clam holes. At first it can be very hard to distinguish them from dark-colored large bits of sand. Then dive and use your hand to dig in the sand (generally about 2 to 3 inches down) and grab the clam. Don't be surprised if the clam holes "disappear" as you dive down. The clams often pull in their feeding tubes in response to a disturbance in the water. Just dig where you remember them to be. When you find one, toss it in a mesh bag. The number of clams you need per person will depend on the size of the species.

Once you've collected your clams, it's best if you hang them overboard in the mesh bag for a day to release all the sand in them. Don't leave them for more than two days, though; they'll die if they don't get enough food. If you're going to be under way, put the mesh bag in a bucket of seawater and keep it in a shady place so that the water doesn't get too hot for the clams. As soon as you re-anchor, put the bag overboard again.

If you want to eat clams the same day you catch them, just rinse them well after steaming to get the sand out.

A couple of notes: Don't use any clams that have opened by themselves; they're bad. And if you want to freeze some for later use, it's best to steam them first and then freeze just the meat.

Steaming Clams. Most of the recipes start by steaming the clams to open them. If they are going to be cooked anyway, it's much easier than shucking them. To steam, put the clams in a pot with about a half inch of water (it's okay if the clams are piled up, but be sure the pot has about double the room that the clams take up). Cover and bring to a boil, and let boil until all the clams have popped open–typically about 5 minutes, but it depends on the size of the clams. Small varieties generally open faster than larger ones. Sometimes one or two clams will refuse to open, even with an extra minute or two of steaming. If so, just throw them out (accepted wisdom is that they are spoiled).

Once they are all opened, I usually dump them into a colander to drain the liquid and let them cool a bit before handling. You can also collect the liquid to use in other recipes.

If you don't have a colander, just use a spoon or tongs to fish the clams out and put them on a plate or cutting board. Let them cool until you can stand to touch the shells. I use a spoon or sometimes my fingers to remove the clam from the shell (some may just fall out on their own; others need to be helped).

Small clams can be eaten whole, while larger ones are better chopped up. I cut each one in quarters; you can chop them more finely, too.

Overcooking clams makes them tough, so I let the steaming cook them, then just barely heat them through when I add them to whatever dish I'm fixing.

One final note: I'm allergic to clams, but my husband loves them. Therefore, many of our clam recipes have you make the dish, then add the clams at the last minute and just warm them back up. Not only does this make it easy to remove a portion of the dish for anyone who doesn't want clams, it also prevents the clams from being overcooked.

Shucking Clams. Some recipes call for raw, shucked clams. The best tools for shucking clams are a table knife to open the shell and a sharper paring knife to cut the meat from the shell.

Hold a clam in the palm of your non-dominant hand with the hinged side against your palm. Hold the table knife in your other hand, and choke up on the blade for better leverage. Use the center of the

Seafood

Grilled clams are popular for beach parties.

knife against the center of the opening edge on the clam; you may even use a finger or two of the hand that's holding the clam to press the knife into the slit. Once the knife is in, give a little twist and the clam will pop open.

Once the shell is open, use the sharper knife if needed to cut the clam from the shell. Put the clam meat into a bowl of cool water while you're shucking the rest.

New England (White) Clam Chowder

Serves 2

Total Time: 25 minutes
Prep Time: 10 minutes   **Cook Time:** 15 minutes

1 small onion, diced
1 tablespoon minced garlic
1 can (8 ounces) mushrooms, drained (optional)
1 or 2 strips bacon, cut into 1-inch pieces (optional)
1 tablespoon butter or olive oil
ground pepper, to taste
1 large potato or 2 smaller potatoes
1 cup half-and-half (*media crema*), evaporated milk, cream, or milk
milk or water, as needed
clams, steamed and chopped if necessary (about ¼ to ½ cup per person; page 240)
dash of Tabasco or hot sauce (optional)

1. Sauté the onion, garlic, mushrooms, and bacon in the butter until golden. (If using bacon, there's no need to use butter.) Add the ground pepper.
2. At the same time, peel (or not, your preference) the potatoes and cut into 1-inch chunks so they cook faster. Boil them in salted water. When tender, drain off the water. Mash the potato with a fork; you're aiming for a lumpy consistency, not potato puree.
3. Add the onion mixture and half-and-half. Mix well. You may need to add some milk or water until it's the consistency of thick soup. Heat through. Right now you have potato soup.
4. Put half the clams into each of two bowls (this ensures that all the bowls have the same amount of clams) and pour the potato mixture over both. Some people like to add a dash of Tabasco.

NOTE: If someone is allergic to clams, pour his or her portion of the chowder into a bowl without adding the clams.

Manhattan (Red) Clam Chowder

Serves 6

Total Time: 60 minutes
Prep Time: 20 minutes   **Cook Time:** 40 minutes

1 cup chopped onion
½ cup chopped carrot
½ cup chopped green bell pepper
1 stalk celery, chopped
3 cloves garlic, minced, OR 1 teaspoon garlic powder
2 teaspoons olive oil, canola oil, or vegetable oil
3 cups diced potato, peeled or not, your preference
1 can (16 ounces) diced tomatoes, not drained, OR 2 large fresh tomatoes, diced
1 can (28 ounces) crushed tomatoes OR 4 fresh tomatoes, finely minced
1 cup steamed clam meat and its juice* (chop the clam meat if large) or canned clams and their juice

*Be sure to reserve the steaming water for further use.

1½ cups water from steaming, or the clam juice from canned clams
1 teaspoon sugar
½ teaspoon dried thyme
½ teaspoon dried basil
1 bay leaf
½ teaspoon salt, or to taste
ground pepper, to taste

Seafood

1. Sauté the onion, carrot, bell pepper, celery, and garlic in the olive oil in a large pot. Cook, stirring frequently, for 5 to 7 minutes.
2. Add the potato, diced tomatoes, crushed tomatoes, and reserved clam water/juice. Stir and bring to a boil.
3. Add the sugar, spices, salt, and ground pepper to taste. Reduce the heat and simmer for about 30 minutes, or until the potato is tender. Add the clams during the last 5 minutes of simmering.
4. Remove the bay leaf and serve.

Clam Appetizer   Serves 4

Total Time: 15 minutes
Prep Time: 5 minutes   Cook Time: 10 minutes

1 small onion, diced
1 tablespoon minced garlic
1 can (8 ounces) mushrooms, drained (optional)
1 or 2 strips bacon, cut into 1-inch pieces (optional)
1 tablespoon butter or olive oil
ground pepper, to taste
1 to 2 cups clams, steamed and chopped if necessary (page 240)
Tabasco sauce or hot sauce (optional)
shredded Parmesan cheese (optional)

1. Sauté the onion, garlic, mushrooms, and bacon in the butter until golden. (If using bacon, there's no need to use butter.) Add the ground pepper. Turn off the heat. Toss in the clams and cover the pan to just barely heat them through. Add the Tabasco and top with the Parmesan if desired.
2. Serve with crackers, corn chips, or bread (homemade onion bread is wonderful).

Variation: Save the clam shells, rinse out any sand, and refill with the onion and clam mixture. Top with a bit of any shredded cheese that will melt. Put under the broiler or on the grill just until the cheese is melted, then serve hot.

Linguine with Red Clam Sauce   Serves 4

Total Time: 25 minutes
Prep Time: 10 minutes   Cook Time: 15 minutes

3 cloves garlic, minced, OR 3 teaspoons minced garlic OR 1 teaspoon garlic powder
½ cup diced onion
¼ cup butter, margarine, olive oil, or canola oil
3 tablespoons olive oil, canola oil, butter, or margarine
½ cup chopped fresh parsley OR 1 tablespoon dried parsley flakes
¼ teaspoon dried oregano
1 teaspoon dried basil
1 can (16 ounces) diced tomatoes, not drained, OR 2 large tomatoes, diced
½ teaspoon salt
1½ cups chopped fresh steamed clams, plus ½ cup of the water they were steamed in, OR 1 can (16 ounces) minced clams, with liquid
1 tablespoon lemon juice
4 servings cooked linguine or other pasta

1. Sauté the garlic and onion in the butter and olive oil until soft. Add the parsley, oregano, basil, tomatoes, and salt, mixing well. Turn down the heat and simmer for 5 minutes.
2. Add the clams and steaming water and bring back to a boil. Add the lemon juice and cook for 1 minute. Add the cooked pasta to the pan and toss well. Serve hot.

Pasta and Clams   Serves 2

This is great with small clams, such as "wedgies" or butter clams, left whole.

Total Time: 20 minutes
Prep Time: 10 minutes   Cook Time: 10 minutes

4 ounces linguine or any other pasta
small onion or half a large onion, chopped
1 tablespoon minced garlic
1 can (8 ounces) mushrooms, drained
2 slices bacon, cut into 1-inch pieces
ground pepper, to taste
1 cup steamed clams, chopped if large
Parmesan cheese, for garnish

1. Cook the pasta while preparing the mushroom mixture. Drain the pasta and set aside.
2. Sauté the onion, garlic, mushrooms, bacon, and ground pepper. Toss with the linguine. Add the chopped steamed clams (or whole steamers) and toss. Sprinkle with Parmesan and serve.

Variation: Add a can of diced tomatoes to the onion mixture.

Greek Seafood Pasta   Serves 2

Frequently while cruising, "catch of the day" means that you don't have enough of one seafood to have a meal of it alone. I use this recipe—or variations of it depending on what I have available—to make a flavorful pasta dinner. Pair it with a salad and a glass of white wine for a special night!

Total Time: 40 minutes
Prep Time: 15 minutes   **Cook Time:** 25 minutes

2 green onions, finely chopped, OR ¼ cup chopped onion
2 cloves garlic, minced, OR 2 teaspoons minced garlic OR ¼ teaspoon garlic powder
2 tablespoons seeded and finely minced spicy chile pepper
2 tablespoons olive oil, canola oil, or vegetable oil
1 can (16 ounces) diced tomatoes, not drained, OR 2 large tomatoes, diced
1 bell pepper, cut into thin strips
3 tablespoons red wine vinegar or red wine
ground pepper, to taste
2 servings medium pasta (rotini or penne is good; fettuccine or spaghetti will work, too)
½ pound raw shelled shrimp
½ pound raw sea scallops
6 black olives, sliced (kalamata are good)
1 tablespoon capers, drained (optional)
4 ounces feta or other cheese, crumbled (the pasta won't be "Greek" without feta, but it will be good)
1½ teaspoons chopped fresh sage OR ½ teaspoon dried sage or poultry seasoning

1. Cook the green onion, garlic, and chile pepper in the oil over medium heat until soft. Add the toma-toes, bell pepper, vinegar, and ground pepper. Bring to a boil over high heat, then turn down and simmer, stirring occasionally, for 15 minutes.
2. At the same time, cook the pasta in the water as directed on the package. Drain and reserve 1 cup of the water. Keep the pasta covered and warm while finishing the sauce.
3. Add the shrimp to the sauce and cook for 2 minutes (time this so the shrimp are not overcooked). Add the scallops, olives, capers, feta, and sage to the sauce and cook for 2 minutes more. The shrimp should be just opaque.
4. Remove the sauce from the heat and add the pasta, tossing quickly. If needed, add some of the reserved pasta water to thin the sauce. Serve immediately.

Seafood Pasta Trio   Serves 6 to 8

If you have just one type of seafood, such as shrimp, merely increase the quantity and make the rest of the recipe as is. It won't be the same, but it will be delicious!

Total Time: 25 minutes
Prep Time: 10 minutes
Cook Time: 10 minutes for pasta and sauce simultaneously

1 tablespoon salt
16 ounces linguine or any pasta that's available
1 small onion, cut into small slivers
2 tablespoons minced garlic
1 teaspoon dried basil OR 4 teaspoons chopped fresh basil
1 teaspoon dried thyme
2 tablespoons olive oil, canola oil, vegetable oil, butter, or margarine
1 cup sliced mushrooms
1 cup diced fresh tomatoes OR 1 can (16 ounces) diced tomatoes, not drained
1 cup dry white wine
½ pound medium shrimp, raw but peeled and deveined (page 234)
½ pound raw sea scallops (page 245)
½ pound lobster meat, cooked and chunked (page 248)
lemon wedge (optional)
fresh basil, for garnish (optional)

1. Bring water to a boil in a large pot. Add the salt and cook the pasta. Drain and rinse.
2. At the same time, in a large pot sauté the onion, garlic, and spices in the olive oil. Add the mushrooms and tomatoes and stir well. Add the wine and simmer until the liquid is reduced by half. Add the shrimp and scallops; sauté over moderately high heat for 2 to 3 minutes, or until the shrimp are not quite done.
3. Add the pasta and the cooked lobster chunks to the other seafood. Turn off the stove, cover the pot, and let stand for 2 minutes more, or until the shrimp and scallops are done (the shrimp should be "C" shaped and the scallops opaque). Garnish with the lemon and fresh basil.

One-Pot Clambake   Serves 6

Great on board or anywhere you can't have a more traditional clambake. In fact, we loved doing it as a beach barbecue (put the pan on a grate over an open fire or on a grill) with all the boats in the anchorage, using whatever seafood and veggies anyone had. This is similar to the Low-Country Boil (page 236) but isn't quite as spicy. It's almost a regional difference, with this being more "northern" and the Low-Country Boil "southern." From a midwestern perspective, both are great!

Total Time: 35 minutes
Prep Time: 10 minutes   **Cook Time:** 25 minutes

1 large onion, diced
6 cloves garlic, minced
4 tablespoons olive oil, canola oil, or vegetable oil
½ teaspoon red pepper flakes
1 green bell pepper, diced
1 teaspoon salt
2 cups white wine
2 to 3 cups chicken broth (may be made from bouillon) or stock (page 164)
12 small red potatoes, scrubbed
1 sausage (smoked sausage, Polish kielbasa, etc.), cut into 1-inch pieces
2 or 3 ears of corn cut into 2-inch pieces
1 teaspoon Old Bay Seasoning (page 48) or other seafood seasoning

clams or any fresh seafood, such as fish fillets, mussels, small lobster tails, shrimp, or scallops, or a combination

1. In a large pot sauté the onions and garlic in the olive oil. Add the pepper flakes, bell pepper, and salt and sauté a few minutes longer. Add the wine and bring to a boil; boil until the liquid is reduced by half.
2. Add the broth, potato, and sausage. Cover and boil for 15 minutes, or until almost cooked through; then add the corn and seafood seasoning and boil for another 5 minutes.
3. Add the seafood, starting with items that take the longest to cook (scallops should go into the pot last). Cover the pot tightly with the lid after each seafood addition. The clambake is done when the clams have popped open. Serve immediately. This is good with crusty bread.

Mussels

Cousins to clams, mussels are of many different kinds, both seawater and freshwater. Mussels are commonly found in mid-tidal ranges in more temperate latitudes; they are not commonly found in the tropics.

But in case you happen to be cruising the US East Coast, New Zealand, or even the Far East (did you know that China produces more than 40 percent of the world's mussels?), here's some information on how to fix them.

- Always buy live mussels, as they spoil quickly and you never know how long they've been dead. To check to see if they're alive, tap the shell when they are in air—live mussels will tightly shut their shells when disturbed out of water.
- Mussels need to be cleaned thoroughly; scrub off any barnacles and remove the exterior "beard." Any mussels that are open and do not close when tapped should be discarded.
- As with much seafood, steaming is the easiest and one of the most delicious ways to fix mussels. To steam your mussels, try pouring an inch or so of white wine in the bottom of a large pan. You

can also use broth or plain water. Be careful of sodium—when the mussels open, they will release their own salty water, which will flavor the cooking water, wine, or broth. Place the mussels in the pan, cover, and heat the wine or water to boiling. After a few minutes, and when steam begins to escape from the lid, check to see whether the mussels are open. You can remove them as they open, ensuring that each mussel will be cooked perfectly. Any that do not open must be discarded.

- To bake or grill the mussels, they must be steamed first and then can be drizzled with olive oil and garlic and grilled or baked for another 5 to 7 minutes at 350°F or on a medium-hot grill.
- You can also use mussels in any of our clam recipes.

SCALLOPS

Jan never saw scallops in the western Caribbean; in the Sea of Cortez, Carolyn could always get them from local fishermen. It was illegal for non-Mexicans to harvest them, though. Laws may have changed.

In the Sea of Cortez, we bought at least a half-dozen different types of scallops, ranging from little ones less than ½-inch in diameter and about ¾-inch thick (slightly smaller than the ones usually sold in the US as "bay scallops") to monsters nearly 3 inches in diameter and up to 3 inches long—and in colors ranging from almost translucent to white, pink, and even tan.

Scallops 101

Scallops basically have two shells connected by a large muscle, which is the meat, and a bunch of "guts" that aren't attached to the shell. Fishermen sometimes sell scallops totally cleaned, sometimes whole (including the entire shell), and sometimes "partially cleaned" with one shell still on.

Rock scallops have one side of the shell firmly attached to a rock. To harvest them, the fisherman looks for one where the shell is slightly open. He sticks a long knife in and cuts the muscle from the shell on the side toward the rock. He then has a muscle attached to one shell and quickly can wipe off the

Catch of the day, as purchased from a local fisherman, often means a variety of different types of scallops (and a few clams). We dumped them on deck to see what we had and found at least four different types of scallops—all of which we had to clean!

Rock scallops, such as these, are cut off half the shell when they are collected. They just have to be sliced off the other half of the shell with a fillet knife and rinsed off.

guts. Sometimes the fisherman will cut off the other shell, or sometimes you'll buy it attached. If attached, just cut off the muscle with a fillet knife. Cut as close to the shell as possible so you don't miss any of the meat. Rinse off before using.

There are numerous types of scallops that are attached by the bottom end into the sand (often called "pin scallops") or are not attached at all (usually called "free swimmers"). These are all cleaned in a similar manner. See photos for the method.

Hold a scallop in your hand and wait for it to open slightly. Quickly stick a fillet knife in and run the tip along one side of the shell to cut off the muscle. Be careful not to cut your hand!

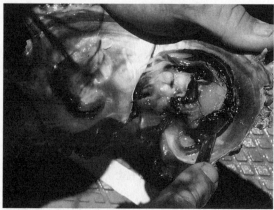

Now you can open the scallop and cut the second side off the shell.

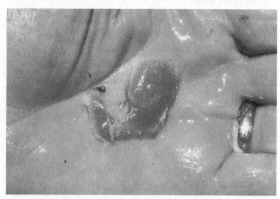

Discard the shell and guts and you've got a cleaned scallop. We were told by the local fishermen to throw the shells back in the water near the reef.

If the scallops are already cleaned, look for those that are firm. Fresh scallops should have no odor or be slightly sweet smelling, never fishy. If they're larger than 2 inches, consider cutting them in half before preparing.

Scallops should never be refrigerated longer than two days due to the fact that they are extremely perishable. You can, however, freeze them (after they've been cleaned) for a month or more. To freeze, simply put the cleaned scallops into vacuum-sealed or freezer bags and get out as much air as possible. While I don't add water, I don't try to dry them off, either. The moisture helps prevent freezer burn. Put just enough for one meal in one bag.

Cooking Scallops

About a year after we began cruising, a local fisherman offered us a dozen scallops. I found a recipe in my one "seafood" cookbook and proceeded to cook them according to the directions. I proudly served up my first effort at cooking fresh seafood. I bit into the first one and was appalled. Tough and rubbery, it resembled a pencil eraser.

Later that summer, our friends Robin and Martin aboard *The Cat's Meow* invited us to dinner. You guessed it—the main dish was scallops. But these were tender, sweet, and wonderful.

Robin told me the secret—don't overcook the scallops. It's actually more like barely cooking them. They should become just opaque, which takes only a minute or two. Robin's description has stuck with me: "You want to just introduce the scallops to warmth." Many recipes call for cooking scallops for 5 to 10 minutes (or more!) per side over high heat. Don't do it—they will be rubbery.

The best technique for cooking scallops that I've found is to prepare the sauce (or just a bit of melted butter or olive oil), then turn off the heat, add the scallops to the pan, stir just so that the scallops are covered with the sauce, then quickly put a cover on the skillet and let it sit for about 2 minutes until the scallops are just opaque. They must be served immediately and don't reheat well at all.

The Cat's Meow
Scallops   Serves any number

Total Time: 10 minutes

1 tablespoon butter per person (real butter is best, but you can use margarine or olive oil)
1 teaspoon minced garlic per person
three or four 2-inch scallops per person (adjust the number of scallops per person by the size of the scallops available)

1. Melt the butter over low heat, and add the garlic. Cook for 2 minutes.
2. Add the scallops, and stir to completely coat them with the butter. Cover the pan and turn off the heat (or remove the pan from an electric stove). Let sit for about 2 minutes, or until the scallops are just barely opaque. Serve at once. Some folks like to sprinkle them with ground pepper.

NOTE: If you have "baby" scallops (sold as "bay scallops" in the US, but they are not limited to bays in other parts of the world), use about ¼ cup per person. If you have fewer, make this dish as an appetizer.

Scallops in Creamy
Garlic Sauce   Serves 4

Total Time: 32 minutes
Prep Time: 15 minutes   Cook Time: 17 minutes

2 to 3 tablespoons butter or margarine
2 cloves garlic, minced
3 tablespoons chopped fresh parsley OR
      3 teaspoons dried parsley flakes
2 green onions, sliced thinly
¼ cup white wine (optional)
½ teaspoon salt
½ teaspoon ground pepper
½ cup cream, half-and-half (*media crema*), or evaporated milk (page 99)
1 pound scallops, cleaned (page 245)

1. Melt the butter in a pan over medium-low heat; add the garlic, parsley, green onion, wine, salt, and pepper. Cover and simmer for 10 minutes.
2. Remove the lid and stir in the cream. Continue heating, but do not boil, stirring constantly until the sauce begins to thicken. Turn off the stove and add the scallops; cover the pan and let sit for another 3 minutes. Do not overcook the scallops!
3. Serve immediately while the scallops are hot. Spoon any excess sauce from the pan and drizzle it over the scallops.

Scallops Carbonara   Serves 2

Total time: 30 minutes
Prep Time: 10 minutes   Cook Time: 20 minutes

4 strips bacon
½ red or green bell pepper, sliced, OR ¼ cup sun-dried tomatoes
½ cup sliced fresh mushrooms OR 1 can (8 ounces) mushrooms, drained
2 green onions, sliced (including tops), OR ¼ cup diced onion
1 clove garlic, minced
½ cup white wine, diluted chicken broth, or water
½ cup cream, half-and-half (*media crema*), or evaporated milk (page 99)
½ pound scallops, cleaned and patted dry
¼ cup grated Romano or Parmesan cheese
cooked pasta for 2 people (fettuccine is traditional, but you can use any type)
ground pepper, for sprinkling

1. Cook the bacon in a skillet until crisp. Drain on paper towels.
2. Drain most of the bacon fat from the pan, leaving just enough to sauté the vegetables. Place the bell pepper, mushrooms, green onion, and garlic in the pan and sauté over medium-high heat until golden brown.
3. Turn the heat to low, add the wine to the pan, and cook until the wine is reduced by approximately half. Add the cream and cook about 2 minutes, or until slightly thick.
4. Add the scallops and cheese, then crumble the drained bacon into the pan. Stir just to mix, then cover the pan and turn off the heat. Let sit for 2 to 3 minutes, or until the scallops turn just opaque. The time depends on the size of the scallops.
5. Add the cooked pasta to the pan, quickly toss, and serve immediately with a sprinkle of ground pepper.

Seafood

Breaded Scallops　Serves 2

Total Time: 15 minutes
Prep Time: 5 minutes　　　Cook Time: 2 minutes

$^1/_2$ pound scallops, cleaned and patted dry
$^1/_4$ cup seasoned bread crumbs (or mix about $^1/_8$ teaspoon Italian spices into plain bread crumbs)
1 tablespoon olive oil, canola oil, vegetable oil, butter, or margarine
shredded or grated cheese, for sprinkling (Parmesan or Romano is best, but any will work)

1. Roll the scallops in the bread crumbs.
2. Warm the olive oil in a skillet over medium-high heat. The oil is hot enough when a drop of water sizzles when flicked into the pan.
3. Add the scallops to the pan and sauté about 2 minutes, or until lightly browned. Quickly turn them and brown the second side. Immediately remove them from the heat and place them on a plate. Sprinkle with the cheese and serve immediately.

Balsamic-Glazed Scallops　Serves 2

Total Time: 30 minutes
Prep Time: 15 minutes　　　Cook Time: 15 minutes

1 tablespoon flour
$^1/_4$ teaspoon salt
$^1/_8$ teaspoon ground pepper
$^1/_2$ pound scallops, cleaned and patted dry
3 tablespoons balsamic vinegar
1$^1/_2$ tablespoons honey
$^1/_2$ teaspoon dried marjoram or oregano
1 tablespoon olive oil, canola oil, or vegetable oil

1. Combine the flour, salt, and ground pepper in a small plastic bag. Add the scallops and shake to coat completely. Set aside.
2. Mix the balsamic vinegar, honey, and marjoram in a small saucepan. Bring to a boil over medium-high heat and boil for 3 minutes. Set aside.
3. Heat the oil in a skillet until a drop of water sizzles. Add the scallops and briefly brown on each side and the scallops are just barely opaque. Turn off

the heat and pour the balsamic sauce over the scallops. Quickly stir, scraping the bottom of the pan to get the browned bits into the sauce. Serve immediately. Do not leave the scallops in the hot pan any longer than necessary. This is great over rice!

LOBSTER

No matter which kind of lobster you have—clawed lobster (northern or Maine lobster) or spiny lobster (the Caribbean variety)—to ensure a safe and tasty lobster meal, make sure the lobster is alive when you cook it (the exception is frozen lobster tails).

Lobster 101

There are many ways to cook lobster; the most common are boiling or steaming:

- **Boiling.** Place the live lobster in a pot of boiling water large enough to cover the entire lobster. You can include whatever seasonings you prefer —Old Bay, Zatarain's, sea salt, or plain salt. Use approximately a half cup of sea salt or 4 tablespoons of Old Bay to a gallon of water. Make sure the water is boiling when you put the lobster in the pot. Cooking time (see table) begins when the lobster goes in the pot. The shell should be bright red when you take it out. Tongs prevent burned fingers.
- **Steaming.** This is our preferred method. Sometimes submerging the lobster in water can turn the meat a bit mushy. Put an inch of water in a large pot and add salt. Bring to a boil and put the lobster in head down. It will take only 10 to 15 seconds for the lobster to die, and it will not be in pain. Leave enough space so you can see the bottom of the pan. Don't "layer" lobsters when steaming; use another pan or cook them in batches.

If you prefer lobster tails—a better size for many pans, or if you have too many to eat at once and want to freeze some—it's simple to turn your live lobster into a lobster tail.

1. Kill the lobster by swiftly inserting an ice pick between the eyes, with the lobster held firmly on a

cutting board or fish filleting board. Don't be surprised if the lobster emits a faint squealing sound.

2. Grab the body of the lobster in one hand and the tail as close to the body as possible with the other hand. Twist the tail off.

3. Throw away the rest of the body, unless it's a lobster with large claws—in which case, twist those off and keep them also.

4. You'll see a large "vein" coming out of the tail. Pull it out entirely. Occasionally you get lucky and it comes out as you twist off the tail; other times you may have to make a cut into the tail to find the vein and extract it.

5. Boil or steam the tail as above, or use it in one of the other recipes in this chapter. If you want to freeze the tail raw, double- or triple-wrap it in plastic freezer bags. The spikes on the shell tend to tear plastic bags, resulting in freezer burn.

The accompanying table shows cooking times for boiling or steaming live lobster, or a lobster tail. You can also use an instant-read meat thermometer; the internal temperature should be 180°F. The easiest way to know if the lobster is done is to look for the bright red shell. Do not overcook or you'll end up with dry, tasteless rubber. This table is useful only to give basic times. Remember, the lobster is done when the shell turns red.

LOBSTER WEIGHT	COOKING TIME
1 lb.	10–12 minutes
1–2 lbs.	12–20 minutes
2–3 lbs.	20–25 minutes
3–6 lbs.	25–28 minutes

See the following recipes for other ways to prepare lobster.

How to Eat a Lobster

Step-by-step instructions on how to eat a whole cooked lobster take the intimidation factor out of the experience. Be sure to put your lobster bib on first, or just stuff a full-size paper towel in the neck of your shirt. And be sure to set out a large empty bowl for shells.

A spiny lobster from the Sea of Cortez, freshly purchased from a local fisherman's boat and not yet cooked.

Savor your lobster in four easy pieces. We enjoy ours by saving the best for last and eating the parts in reverse order, so that's the way our steps are written. But you can choose to do the steps in any order.

Step 1. Twist off the claws. One is larger than the other, but both should twist off with a little bit of effort. Set aside for later. **NOTE:** Some lobster species don't have meaty claws, such as the spiny lobsters in the Sea of Cortez (pictured). With these, don't bother to twist off the claws, and skip Step 5.

Step 2. Roll the lobster onto its back and uncurl the tail. Grasp the lobster with both hands and twist off the tail. You may see green gunk inside; that's the lobster's liver and can be washed away in the sink or rinsed and dumped overboard for the fish to enjoy. Set aside the tail and attached flippers for later.

Step 3. Open the main part of the body by pulling the top part of the shell away from the rest. You can do this with your hands, or use a knife. Don't eat anything that's not white meat; although the liver (tomalley) and roe are edible, we choose not to eat them. There are some good bits of meat nestled in the body, but they're hidden beneath the thin, papery shells separating the meat. If you have the patience to pick them out, you'll end up with an extra half cup or so of lobster meat that those who skip this step will miss! Savor your first taste of lobster in fresh drawn butter (page 250) or cocktail sauce (page 211), whichever you prefer.

Seafood

Step 4. Twist off each leg. Because of their small size, they can be a challenge to eat. The easiest way we've found is to suck out the meat like you're sipping a straw. This meat is delicious, albeit hard to get at, so we'll leave that up to you. Now you're ready to savor what I think are the best parts—the claws and the tail.

Step 5. Use a lobster cracker or nutcracker to crack open the claws. If you don't have either aboard, use crab scissors, or try other suitable alternatives—a knife, a fork, pliers, a rock, or even tin snips or small wire cutters. If you're using something that's not normally used in the galley, wash the tool and dunk it in the leftover boiling water before using it on your food. (Beware that you may have to sharpen any tools not designed for use on a lobster before you can use them again!) Use a fork, knife, or specially designed lobster pick (a dental tool substitutes well if you have them aboard in your tool arsenal, but be sure to wash it thoroughly before and after using it on the lobster claw!).

Step 6. Twist off the little tail flippers on the lobster tail. Don't miss the tiny pieces of sweet, succulent lobster meat inside.

Step 7. With a sharp knife, slit the bottom of the lobster tail. Using your thumb, push out the tail meat. If it's a smaller tail, you may be able to push out the meat without slitting the bottom of the tail with a knife. Do not eat the dark vein running the length of the tail.

Buen provecho!

Steamed Lobster Tails   Serves 2

Total Time: 11 minutes
Prep Time: 5 minutes   Cook Time: 6 minutes

2 lobster tails, uncooked

1. Put ½ inch water in a pot and heat it to boiling.
2. Cut along the bottom of the lobster tails lengthwise, creating a slit in the shell for easier access later. (This is easiest to do with a good pair of kitchen shears rather than a knife.)

3. Drop the lobster tails in the boiling water and cover the pan tightly with a lid. Steam until the shells have turned bright orange and are curled up. Different sizes will require different times. In general, start with 2 minutes and recheck each minute. The meat should be firm and white. Do not overcook or the meat will be dry and tough.
3. Serve with cocktail sauce (page 211) or drawn butter with garlic (see below).

Drawn Butter

To make drawn butter, start with a stick of unsalted butter, and melt it over medium heat in a pan with as much garlic as you prefer. Slowly bring the butter to a boil. You don't want to burn the butter while the solids are separating. The milk solids will separate and sink to the bottom, and you can skim off the drawn or clarified butter and put in a separate cup for dipping.

Sautéed Lobster Tails   Serves 2

This is Carolyn's favorite way to prepare lobster, using butter instead of olive oil. The amount of butter needed will vary considerably depending on the size of the lobster tails.

Total Time: 15 minutes
Prep Time: 10 minutes   Cook Time: 5 to 6 minutes

1 tablespoon lemon juice
¼ cup butter, olive oil, or margarine
1 teaspoon salt (omit if using salted butter or margarine)
1 teaspoon paprika
ground pepper, to taste
1 teaspoon garlic powder
2 lobster tails, in the shell, uncooked

1. Combine the lemon juice, butter, and spices.
2. Split the lobster tails lengthwise, making two pieces. I found it was easiest to cut through the shells with kitchen shears, then through the meat with a sharp knife.
3. Cover the cut side of each half with the butter mixture, saving some for the pan.
4. Heat the remaining butter mixture in the pan until a drop of water sizzles. Place the lobster tails flesh or flat side down. Turn once and baste with the

butter in the pan, drizzling it into the open top side. Cook for 5 to 10 minutes, or until the tails are opaque and the shells curl or turn red. The time will depend on the size.

Szechwan Lobster   Serves 2

This recipe is courtesy of David on Bruadair. *If you like spicy food, this is oh-so-delicious!*

Total Time: 25 minutes
Prep Time: 15 minutes   **Cook Time:** 10 minutes

3 scallions, minced, OR 3 green onions, finely
    diced, OR ½ regular onion, finely diced
3 tablespoons sesame oil
2 to 3 cloves garlic, minced
2 teaspoons ground ginger
1 teaspoon red pepper flakes OR ¼ teaspoon
    cayenne pepper (start with less unless you like
    very spicy food)
2 tablespoons water
2 teaspoons cornstarch
2 tablespoons dry sherry
2 tablespoons sweet chili sauce (page 215)
2 tablespoons ketchup
½ pound lobster, steamed and cut into 1-inch
    chunks

1. Brown the scallion in the sesame oil. Add the spices and stir, then mix in the water, cornstarch, sherry, sweet chili sauce, and ketchup, and cook until the sauce thickens.
2. Add the lobster and stir until just heated through. Serve over rice.

CONCH

We normally buy our conch already cleaned from local fishermen so we don't have to mess with the cleaning. Since they're already cleaned, there's no way to tell how fresh they are. But trust your sense of smell. Fresh conch will smell salty, like ocean salt air, with no unpleasant odor. Conch should be a healthy coral pink color, not gray or brown.

Cleaning Conch

If you find a conch in the shell and want to try cleaning it yourselves, here's how.

- You will need a hammer, a regular screwdriver, a sharp fish fillet knife, a paring knife, maybe a table knife, and a cutting board.
- Kill the conch and remove it from the shell. To do this, find a spot on the shell between the third and fourth spiral from the top, where the shell spirals up to the end.
- Lay the conch on the side so the shell flare is facing up. Using a screwdriver and a hammer, tap a hole through the shell between the third and fourth spirals. The hole should be big enough for a paring knife to cut through the underlying muscle.
- Insert the paring knife into the hole. You should feel hard muscle. Cut through it. This will kill the conch and separate it from the shell. If you feel nothing hard and muscular, you're in the wrong spot. Try making your hole in a different spot.
- Grab onto the claw (also known as the operculum —the part you can see in the flare opening of the shell) and pull hard. The conch should pull right out of the shell.
- Use your sharp fish fillet knife and a cutting board and cut away the head–the black and yellow spotted part with the eyes. Holding the conch by the claw, cut off the mantle–the orange spotted "skin" and long, stringy, slimy "worm." Rinse in seawater to wash away the slime.
- Locate a dark vein on the bottom of the white muscle that is exposed after you've made the first two cuts. Cut out the vein.
- Slice through the dark tough skin that's still on the white muscle. You'll need to remove all the skin. Sometimes you can "skin" it by inserting a table knife under it, wriggling it, and then pulling it off. Otherwise, you may need to "peel" it with your sharp fillet knife. Rinse again.
- Cut off the claw, which should be the part you've been holding on to to accomplish the other steps. The claw can be eaten, but unless you're Bahamian, most choose to discard it in favor of the white meat.

Seafood

- Tenderize the meat by cutting through the muscle horizontally once or twice before pounding with a meat mallet (a piece of untreated lumber also works) until it's thin enough that you actually see holes through it, sort of Swiss cheesy. This pounding breaks down the muscle fibers and creates a tender steak.
- Refrigerate the cleaned conch immediately; it doesn't keep well.

Preparing Conch

The first time we prepared conch on *Winterlude*, it was an eye-opening experience! We were anchored in the Vivorillos Cayes, off the Honduran Mosquito Coast, literally in the middle of nowhere with three buddy boats. One of the boats, *Bruadair*, bought several pounds of cleaned conch from a local fisherman, and Conch 101 was initiated! None of us was a conch expert; in fact, I had never cooked conch before in my life.

Under the circumstances, we decided to have a party and entitled it "Conch 101." Each boat was allocated its share of the conch and had to devise a conch dish to share on the largest of the boats, *Blow Me Away*, for dinner. This was a challenge in the middle of nowhere with no conch recipes or other instructional materials in any of the cookbooks any of us had aboard.

One boat unearthed a conch fritter recipe that friends had given them years ago, and the other dug up a recipe for cracked conch. I decided that conch salad, which I had heard of but never fixed, couldn't be too different from ceviche. So began the adventure!

David, my partner and always a good sport, took our wood fish filleting board into the cockpit and began to pound the conch steak. We had no idea how long to pound the conch, only that it needed tenderizing. Luckily we had a tenderizing hammer aboard (a good investment since a lot of meat we buy in cruising locales isn't necessarily the highest quality). David pounded, turned the conch over, and pounded some more. He pounded until he literally broke the 1-inch-thick board into pieces. At that point we decided that maybe the conch had been tenderized sufficiently.

If you don't have the fortune to have your cutting board break, you'll know that the conch is tender enough when it looks lacy or like baby Swiss cheese with lots of small see-through holes.

David gave me the beaten-to-death conch, and I chopped it into tiny pieces. I marinated these conch morsels with lime juice, tomato, onion, celery, cucumber, green bell pepper, and Worcestershire and Tabasco sauces (Conch Salad, page 254).

Conch 101 was a big hit! We feasted that night under the full moon on cracked conch, conch salad, and conch fritters supplemented by ice and martinis aboard *Blow Me Away*. Good thing the weather cooperated for a few more nights in the Vivorillos Cayes!

Cracked Conch   Serves 4

Cracked conch is the island version of the gigantic fried pork tenderloin popular in the 1970s—not at all healthy, but yummy when the mood strikes.

Total Time: 25 minutes
Prep Time: 15 minutes   **Cook Time:** 10 minutes

1 teaspoon minced fresh cilantro
1 teaspoon minced garlic
salt and pepper (we like cracked black pepper), to
   taste
$1/2$ to 1 cup flour
1 or 2 eggs, beaten
2 tablespoons water
dash of Tabasco sauce or hot sauce
bread crumbs, as needed for dipping (page 51)
4 pieces conch, pounded and cut into strips
canola oil or vegetable oil

1. Mix the cilantro, garlic, salt, ground pepper, and flour in a pie pan or similar dish that the conch can be dipped into (or use a plastic bag). You can add or substitute spices as you prefer.
2. In another "dipping pan," beat the eggs with the water and add a dash of Tabasco. Put the bread crumbs in a third "dipping pan."
3. Dip the conch strips into the flour mixture, then the egg mixture, and finally the bread crumbs. Lay the strips on a plate or cutting board.

4. Heat ½ inch canola oil in a skillet over medium-high heat. Place the conch strips in the oil and fry until golden brown.

5. Drain on a paper towel and season with salt and pepper. Serve immediately with cocktail sauce (page 211) or Coconut-Lime-Curry Dipping Sauce (page 211).

Conch Fritters   Makes about 30 fritters

This recipe actually makes great "fritters" from almost any sort of seafood or meat. If you don't have all the spices, substitute accordingly. The fritters may not taste the same, but they will be good!

Total Time: 45 minutes
Prep Time: 30 minutes   **Cook Time:** 4 to 5 minutes

1 cup finely chopped cleaned and tenderized conch (page 252)
2 tablespoons *limón* (Key lime) juice, lime juice, or lemon juice
2 tablespoons tomato paste
2 eggs
½ bell pepper, any color, finely diced
½ cup diced onion
1 tablespoon minced garlic
1 tablespoon dried thyme
1½ tablespoons Italian seasoning OR ¾ tablespoon dried oregano and ¾ tablespoon dried basil
1 tablespoon celery seed OR 2 tablespoons celery salt and omit the salt below
1 tablespoon hot sauce, or to taste
1½ teaspoons salt (omit if using celery salt)
1½ teaspoons ground cumin
½ teaspoon ground pepper
1 cup flour
2 tablespoons baking powder (page 376)
milk, beer, or water, if needed to thin the batter slightly
canola oil or vegetable oil
lime, lemon, or *limón* (Key lime) wedges

1. Mix the conch, *limón* juice, and tomato paste together and set aside.

2. Beat the eggs slightly in a shallow bowl. Set aside.

3. In a large bowl combine the bell pepper, onion, garlic, thyme, Italian seasoning, celery seed, hot sauce, salt, cumin, and ground pepper. Add the conch mixture, the eggs, flour, and baking powder. After stirring, your batter should be thick enough to stick to the spoon. It will probably be too thick. If so, add a splash of beer, milk, or water a little at a time. If the mixture drips too easily off the spoon, it's too thin. Add flour, a small spoonful at a time.

4. Traditionally, fritters are deep-fried. Aboard *Winterlude*, I use my large frying pan since I don't have a deep fryer. Heat at least ½ inch oil (1 inch is better) in a large skillet over medium-high to high heat until a drop of water sizzles immediately. Whenever using hot oil, be extra careful in areas with boat wakes and movement. I use less oil to be safe—less oil, less to splash and burn me.

5. Because the oil temperature is so critical, test-fry the first fritter. Drop about a tablespoon of batter into the hot oil. Fry it for about 2 minutes, then turn and fry for another 2 minutes. You want it to be light brown on both sides. If the oil is too hot, the fritters will be too done on the outside and raw in the middle. If not hot enough, they'll be rubbery and greasy—yuck!

6. Remove the test fritter and place it on a plate lined with a paper towel. After a minute, cut into the fritter and see if the middle is doughy or done. If it looks right, go ahead and do the rest, a tablespoon at a time. If not, test another single until you get the timing and the oil temperature right. Discard the rejects.

7. As the fritters are done, drain them on the paper towel–lined plate. Serve immediately with lime or lemon wedges and hot sauce or Coconut-Lime-Curry Dipping Sauce (page 211).

Seafood

Conch Salad   Serves 4 to 6

As with ceviche, the conch is not "cooked" in the conventional sense. Rather the acid in the lime juice cooks the meat. It is delicious and very healthy.

Total Time: 4 hours, 20 minutes, including 4 hours
   to marinate (may be left longer)
Prep Time: 20 minutes

1 cup finely pounded and chopped conch meat
1 onion, finely diced
1 green bell pepper, finely diced
1 stalk celery, finely diced
¼ large cucumber, peeled, seeded, and finely diced
1 large tomato, finely chopped
2 tablespoons lime juice or *limón* (Key lime) juice
2 tablespoons wine vinegar, white vinegar, or
   balsamic vinegar
1½ teaspoons Worcestershire sauce
salt and pepper, to taste
hot sauce, to taste

Combine all the ingredients and place in a tightly sealed container or freezer bag.

Refrigerate for at least 4 hours, turning every half hour. Conch salad is best left overnight to marinate and can be left for 3 to 4 days. The longer it marinates, the better it tastes!

SEAFOOD IN OTHER CHAPTERS

Here are more recipes involving fish and seafood—many call for canned, but you can easily substitute fresh—that appear in other chapters:

MEAT MAIN DISHES

If you're cruising outside the US, you'll soon notice that meat—particularly beef—is often cut differently. It's not just translating the name of a cut into a foreign language; sometimes it's a whole different cut. As a result, our recipes rarely call for a specific cut of meat. We also provide information about the best cooking methods for various cuts as well as "cut charts" (pages 30–33) so that you can easily figure out what to substitute.

In this chapter you'll find sections for beef, poultry, pork, and even a few recipes for goat and lamb. In each section, you'll find food safety information, general cooking methods, and recipes. Many of our recipes work well with more than one kind of meat. While we've classified them by the kind of meat that is most often used, often you'll see an "or" or two for the meat in the ingredients list.

GENERAL FOOD SAFETY TIPS

In the sections dealing with various meats (beef, poultry, pork, goat, and lamb), we provide information on safe cooking temperatures and procedures specific to that kind of meat. When cruising, it's important to follow the USDA guidelines to avoid food poisoning, as medical help can be a distance away. If you're in a less developed area (particularly in small villages where meat may be sold from a freezer on someone's porch), you have little assurance of how the meat was handled on its way to you.

Four basic practices are applicable to all meats:

1. Cook meat thoroughly, in accordance with the USDA guidelines.
2. Clean your cutting board, knife, and other surfaces that raw meat touches with a mild bleach solution. Keeping a bleach water solution in a small spray bottle makes this convenient to do, so we actually do it.
3. Although we prefer using cloth rags for a lot of galley chores, we use paper towels to clean up raw meat juice. If you do use cloth rags, be sure to rinse them in a bleach solution after every contact with raw meat.
4. Don't re-use plastic bags that you use for raw meat.

Finally, if meat seems at all "iffy"—including, but not limited to, looking funny or smelling bad—don't buy it. And if you've already bought it, don't eat it (use it as fish bait instead). We both found that places with questionable meat almost always had excellent stocks of canned meat. And our "Canned Meats and Seafood" chapter has lots of ways to make great meals from it. You won't suffer from a lack of meat!

Bacteria can be found on raw or undercooked meat of any kind. They multiply rapidly at temperatures between 40° and 140°F (out of the refrigerator but before thorough cooking occurs). Freezing doesn't kill bacteria, but thorough cooking does. And be careful when thawing any kind of meat—either plan ahead and thaw it in the refrigerator, or cook it straight from its frozen state.

Thawing meat on the countertop is just asking for trouble; the USDA recommends against it. But if you do it anyway, be sure to cook the meat to the recommended temperature to be certain to kill all bacteria, and thoroughly sanitize anything that came in contact with the thawing or thawed meat.

BONING AND CUTTING MEAT

Boning your own meat isn't difficult. I find it much easier than filleting a fish! You'll probably find that you get better at it with practice, but the learning curve isn't steep. No, we're not going to give details of how to butcher a whole animal, as we've never run across a situation where we've needed to do that.

Cutting Up a Tenderloin

A tenderloin is a long sausage-shaped piece of meat. Cut a beef tenderloin to make filet mignon and a pork tenderloin to make boneless pork chops. Simply place it on a cutting board and slice straight across it, making slices of whatever thickness you prefer—typically 1 inch to 1½ inches. That's it! If you want to freeze them, it's best to put just one piece of meat per freezer bag to make it easier to thaw and use the exact number you want.

Simple Boning

In its simplest form, you simply cut one well-defined cross section of a bone out of a piece of meat, most likely beef but occasionally pork or ham. You can use

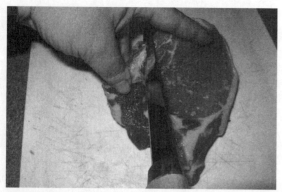

Boning a pork chop.

almost any sharp knife for this, but one with a blade about 6 inches long is best. My personal preference is to use my fish filleting knife, as in the photo.

Place the meat on a cutting board or plate. Pick up one edge in your non-dominant hand, at the place where you want the cut to begin—generally the place nearest the bone in question.

Cut down to the bone, then slice around the bone, angling the knife to leave as much meat as possible. When the meat and bone are separate, you're done!

Cutting Meat Off the Bone

This type of boning is where the meat surrounds one larger bone—think of boning a chicken drumstick or thigh (easy) or a pork shoulder (harder, but not difficult). Again, my preference is for a fillet knife, but a sharp chef's knife will do as well.

Place the piece of meat on a cutting board and look and feel to determine where the bone is. Generally, one side of the meat will be much closer to the bone, and that's the side to work from.

Slice down to the bone for the entire length of the bone. With chicken drumsticks and thighs, you can usually work your fingers around the bone and separate it from the meat. Other meats are more "attached" to the bone, and you'll have to slowly slice along the bone, using the tip of the knife and working your way around both sides of it until it comes free. Be careful of the fingers of your free hand; it's easy to cut a finger where you're holding the cut open to see what you're doing!

Boning a Chicken Breast

Whenever I've taught someone to bone a chicken breast, it seems that the first attempt is more about learning the physiology of the chicken, with the cuts not really going as intended. But with the second attempt, the process goes much more smoothly and produces a recognizable "boneless, skinless chicken breast." So don't give up. After you've done a couple, it actually gets easy!

Again, I like my fillet knife. And boning is easier to do than describe. Begin by working the tip of the blade under the bottom end of the rib bones, and slowly cut the meat away from the ribs. Now, the temptation is to hold the chicken breast in your hand, but that means that you are poking that knife tip right at your palm. Don't do it; work on a cutting board, and stay safe. Little by little, you can peel the meat back, and your cuts can become longer until the meat is totally separated from the bones.

To remove the skin, it's easiest to just use your fingers and work them between the meat and the skin, cutting with the knife only whenever fingers won't do it. If you have an Internet connection, see how to bone and skin the chicken breast on YouTube.com/TheBoatGalley.

Cutting Up a Whole Chicken

This is the big one. I'm going to assume that you have not bought a live chicken, or one that still has its innards or feathers. (If it has its head or feet, as happened to Jan on one memorable occasion, start by taking the heaviest knife you have and lopping off those body parts.) If someone is selling meat "whole," they know how to butcher it, and you can negotiate for them to do the serious work.

So I'm assuming that you're starting with what looks like a miniature version of a Thanksgiving turkey, and you want to cut it into the standard parts: wings, legs (thigh/drumstick), breast, and back.

Begin by checking if there is anything in the cavity of the chicken. Often there are packets with the liver or a gravy mix, or the neck might be stuffed in there. If you find anything, remove it.

Rinse out the cavity and the outside of the bird. Reach inside the cavity and pull out any loose bits you find. Most of them will be along the backbone (it's the very rough bone; the breastbone is smooth and located opposite the backbone). Usually, you'll have to pull away the "lights" (lungs)—they look like tiny pieces of liver. Even in the US, the lights are usually left in. It won't hurt you to leave them in or eat them, but you'll notice a different taste. I'll also usually find some loose bits of fat and maybe even some bone fragments.

I end up using three implements: a pair of kitchen shears, a heavy knife, and my fillet knife. If you don't have a pair of kitchen shears, don't try to substitute a pair of paper shears or sewing shears—they aren't heavy-duty enough and will break.

Start by setting the chicken on the cutting board, breast up. Reach inside the cavity and feel the upper surface. If it's smooth, the breast is up.

The first thing is to remove the legs. Take the fillet knife and cut the skin along the fold between the leg and the body on each side. Then hook each thumb over a "knee" with your fingers under the back of the chicken. Pull/rotate the legs outward while pushing up with your fingertips; you'll hear/feel a pop as the hip joints come apart (this is much easier to do than to describe). Then you can easily use the knife to cut through the joint and remove the legs. If you want to separate the thighs and drumsticks, simply cut through the knee joint; you can find it by bending the leg.

Cutting off the wings is next and is very straightforward. Pull one wing away from the body and use your other hand to feel where it's connected. I use the fillet knife to cut through the skin and meat to the joint, then the heavy knife—or sometimes the shears—to cut through the joint. Most people cut off the wing tips as there's almost no meat on them. They tend to burn, and they puncture plastic bags in the freezer!

Next, cut out the backbone (the really rough-feeling bone when you run your hand inside the cavity). Turn the chicken over so that the breast is down. Take the kitchen shears and cut closely along both sides of the backbone and remove it. There's not a lot of meat on it, but you can boil it and the neck (if included) for soup or broth.

What's left is the full breast section, which we'll turn into two breasts. Make a small cut from the neck down to the breastbone. Turn the breast section so the bones are facing up, and put your fingers underneath it with your thumbs over the top. "Pop" free the breast keel bone and cartilage (the long plastic-looking piece running up and down). Use your fingers to slide out the bone and cartilage; give it a good tug. Now cut right where that bone was to separate the two breasts. If desired, you can cut each breast in two crosswise with your kitchen shears or heavy knife. You're done!

Meat Main Dishes

Matching Cooking Methods to Beef Cuts Ensures Success

Beef Cut	Pan-Broil/Pan-Fry	Stir-Fry	Grill	Broil	Roast	Braise	Cook In Liquid
CHUCK							
Chuck 7-Bone Steak / Chuck Mock Tender Steak			*	*		●	●
Chuck Arm Steak						●	●
Chuck Eye Steak, *boneless*	●		●	●		●	●
Shoulder Top Blade Steak, *boneless*	●		●	●		●	●
Shoulder Top Blade Steak (Flat Iron)	●	●	●	●			
Shoulder Steak, *boneless*	*		*	*		●	
Shoulder Center Steak (Ranch)	●	●	●	●			
Shoulder Petite Tender Medallions	●						
Short Ribs						●	●
Chuck Pot Roast (Arm, Blade, Shoulder)						●	●
Shoulder Tender Petite Roast		●	●	●	●		
RIB							
Rib Steak / Ribeye Steak	●	●	●	●			
Rib Roast / Ribeye Roast			●		●		
LOIN							
Porterhouse/T-Bone Steak	●		●	●			
Top Loin (Strip) Steak / Tenderloin Steak	●	●	●	●			
Top Loin Roast, Tenderloin Roast			●		●		
SIRLOIN							
Sirloin Steak, Tri-Tip Steak / Top Sirloin Steak, *boneless*	●	●	●	●			
Tri-Tip Roast			●		●		
ROUND							
Top Round Steak	*	●	*	*			
Bottom Round Steak (Western Griller)	*		*	*			
Eye Round Steak	*	●	*			●	
Round Tip Steak, *thin cut*	●	●					
Sirloin Tip Center Steak	●	●	●	●			
Sirloin Tip Side Steak	*	●	*	*			
Eye Round, Bottom Round, Rump Roasts					●	●	
Top Round Roast / Round Tip Roast					●		
SHANK & BRISKET							
Brisket, Fresh or Corned						●	●
Shank Cross Cuts						●	●
PLATE & FLANK							
Skirt Steak	*	●	*	*			
Flank Steak		●	*	*			
OTHER CUTS							
Ground Beef	●		●	●	●		
Cubed Steak	●					●	
Beef for Stew							●
Beef for Kabobs			●	●			

* *Requires marinating for tenderization.*

BEEF

Outside the US, beef doesn't always come neatly packaged in plastic wrap. Thus, it's important to know what various cuts look like—many times they're not labeled in any language, let alone English—and also to rigorously follow food safety precautions.

Beef Cuts and Cooking Methods

Beef isn't cut the same from country to country. Use the chart on page 30, as well as the one left, to figure out close approximations for various cuts and determine what will work in a given recipe.

Safety Tips for Beef

In addition to the general tips on page 255, the USDA gives these tips for beef (modified to make them applicable to cruisers):

- Fresh beef should be stored at or below 40°F. Put fresh or frozen beef in a cooler with ice to transport to the boat if it will take longer than 10 minutes to get there or if the temperature will be over 100°F at any time.
- Most cuts of beef should be used within 3 to 5 days or else frozen. Liver, kidneys, tripe, and tongue should be used within 1 to 2 days. If kept continuously frozen, beef will last indefinitely.
- Ground beef is most susceptible to bacteria because more surface is exposed to the air and to the meat grinder. It's important to cook it thoroughly. The USDA recommends using an instant-read thermometer for hamburgers, meat loaf, and similar foods, and making sure the center of the meat patty reaches 160°F.
- Large "muscle" cuts such as steaks are less likely to be contaminated as they have been exposed to air and cutting boards only on their "outside" surfaces, and these cook the hottest. Consequently, steaks may be eaten medium rare with an internal temperature of 145°F. Unless you are 100 percent confident of how the meat has been handled, beef should not be eaten rare.

BEEF
Funded by The Beef Che

RECOMMENDED INTERNAL TEMPERATURES FOR SAFE MEAT CONSUMPTION

CUT AND DONENESS	USDA	MOST PEOPLE	APPEARANCE
Steaks, Roasts, and Chops—Rare	not rec.	120–125	Bright red center
Steaks, Roasts, and Chops—Med. Rare	145	130–135	Very pink center
Steaks, Roasts, and Chops—Medium	160	140–145	Light pink center
Steaks, Roasts, and Chops—Med. Well	—	150–155	Not pink
Steaks, Roasts, and Chops—Well Done	170	160+	Brown throughout
Ground Meat	160	160–165	Brown throughout

Beef Cooking Temperatures

With an instant-read thermometer, it's easy to cook steaks and burgers to the desired state of doneness. Whenever in doubt as to how safely meat has been handled, cook beef to an internal temperature of at least 160°F. See table above for recommended internal temperatures.

Tenderizing Beef

In many countries, beef doesn't have as high a fat content as in the US. That's great news for your health, not so great for tenderness, as fat is part of what makes beef tender. The other factor is the inherent toughness of the muscle fiber in a particular cut. There are a number of ways that you can make that fiber more tender.

The beef cooking chart, on page 258, is a good starting point for knowing what cuts need tenderizing when used in particular types of cooking. Combine this with the cut diagram (pages 30–31) to determine whether a particular cut tends to be tough and hence recommended only for moist cooking methods. Additionally, if the beef you buy has substantially less marbling (the very thin lines of fat running through the meat, not around the edges) than what you see in the cut chart, it will be less tender than what you are used to, and should be tenderized.

In all tenderizing, however, remember that you can't make a cut into something it's not. No amount of tenderizing will turn a chuck steak into a rib eye!

Long, Slow, Moist Cooking. The best way of tenderizing a tough cut of beef is simply to choose the correct cooking method: long, slow, and moist. That's why the tough cuts are used for pot roasts, stews, and Swiss steak. Cooking over low heat for 3 or 4 hours in a liquid will make almost any cut tender.

Pound the Meat. Pounding the meat with a tenderizing mallet is the second-best method and is often combined with long, slow cooking. A tenderizing mallet looks a bit like a hammer with a waffle face. If you don't have one, a regular hammer will also work.

Place the meat in a plastic bag and seal it, getting out as much air as possible (you don't have to use a bag, but it makes cleanup much easier, and there is less chance of contamination and food poisoning). Put the bagged meat on a sturdy, solid surface and begin pounding. Be firm, but—no—don't pound as hard as you can. You're not trying to flatten the cut. Thick pieces will take a little more pounding than thin ones, but generally just go over the meat once, flip it over, and do the same on the other side.

Grind the Meat. Ever wonder why hamburger is the cheapest beef? It's made from all the really tough pieces. Ground up, they're perfectly acceptable. If you have a meat grinder aboard, you can do the same thing. Otherwise, simply finely chop, dice, and mince the meat, throwing away the tough pieces of fibrous tissue that you come across.

Marinate the Meat. Any marinade with an acid in it—vinegar, citrus juice, and yogurt are common—will weaken the muscle tissue and tenderize it. Some marinades are specifically designed to tenderize as well as add flavor, such as our Tenderizing Marinade, below. Note, however, that marinades won't do as much good to a really tough cut as pounding and slow cooking will, but you can combine all three.

Pineapple, papaya, and kiwi contain chemicals that will also tenderize meat. Marinades containing any of

Meat Main Dishes

these can be quite effective, but you have to be careful not to marinate the meat too long or the outside can become mushy.

Tenderizing Marinade

This will make enough for up to 3 pounds of meat, but I've learned that you can't make much less even for less meat as the marinade must totally cover the meat.

¼ cup soy sauce

⅓ cup cider vinegar or other vinegar (cider vinegar is more acidic than other vinegars and will tenderize best)

¾ cup canola oil, vegetable oil, or olive oil

1 teaspoon garlic powder OR 2 tablespoons minced garlic

1 teaspoon ground pepper

½ teaspoon ground ginger, or more to taste

¼ cup honey

3 tablespoons Worcestershire sauce

Mix all the ingredients and immerse the meat in the marinade for 8 to 24 hours. I either put the meat and marinade in a plastic bag, then inside a bowl in the refrigerator, or—better yet—in a plastic storage container with a leakproof lid.

Use Powdered Meat Tenderizer. You can find powdered meat tenderizer near the other spices in most supermarkets and simply follow the instructions on the jar. (***NOTE:*** Meat tenderizer will also take the pain out of bee stings and many insect bites. Just sprinkle it on or make a paste with a little water.) However, many people don't like to use commercial meat tenderizer, us included, as it tends to make the outside of the meat mushy while the center remains tough.

Hamburger or Cheeseburger   Serves any number

Processed American cheese is traditional for cheeseburgers, and ketchup and mustard are the usual condiments. But you can use almost any type of cheese (if it doesn't make neat slices, just crumble it and mix it into the ground beef before making the patties) and virtually any toppings you can think of to create your own one-of-a-kind masterpiece. You don't need oil in the pan unless the

meat is very lean, as the salt we've specified to add to the pan will draw the fat and moisture out of the meat.

Total Time: 20 minutes (depends on number of burgers being made)

ground beef—1 pound will make 4 or 5 burgers

salt, for the pan

thin cheese slices for cheeseburgers, 1 slice per burger, if desired

1 bun per burger

1. Divide the ground beef into equal portions for the number of burgers desired. Use your clean hands to form each portion into a round patty about ¾ inch thick. Be careful to firm the edges so that loose bits of meat don't fall off.

2. Sprinkle a skillet with salt, and warm it over high heat until a drop of water sizzles. Quickly place the burgers into the skillet so that they don't overlap. Allow the burgers to brown on the bottom (generally about 3 minutes, but it depends on how hot your burner gets and the size of the patties), then flip them. Turn down the heat to medium-low and let the burgers cook through, typically about 10 minutes. If cheeseburgers are desired, place one slice of cheese on top of each burger shortly before it's done.

3. The meat should be brown throughout when done. Food poisoning is a definite possibility from undercooked beef, particularly ground beef. USDA guidelines call for ground meat to be at least 160°F in the center. (You can test your burgers with an instant-read thermometer, but you have to insert the tip only into the center of the burger and not all the way through it. In the latter case, the thermometer would read a higher temperature near the skillet.)

4. Remove the burgers from the skillet and serve on buns with ketchup, mustard, relish, and other condiments to taste.

Variations:

• Sprinkle the burgers with ground pepper, garlic powder, onion powder, Montreal steak seasoning, or Mrs. Dash as they are cooking.

• Sliced tomato, lettuce, mushrooms (raw or sautéed), grilled bacon strips, avocado slices, mayonnaise, and even barbecue sauce are good on a burger. Don't limit yourself to the traditional; use anything that sounds good!

Spaghetti Sauce   Serves 2 to 4

Making your own spaghetti sauce is easy!

Total Time: 1 hour
Prep Time: 15 minutes   **Cook Time:** 45 minutes

½ pound ground beef or ground turkey
½ medium onion, diced
1 tablespoon canola oil or vegetable oil
1 can (16 ounces) diced, stewed, whole, or Italian tomatoes, not drained, OR 2 or 3 tomatoes, diced
1 can (6 ounces) tomato paste OR 2 or 3 additional tomatoes, diced, plus a bouillon cube and omit the broth below
1 cup beef broth (may be made from bouillon) or stock (page 165)
1 teaspoon sugar
1 teaspoon garlic powder OR 1 tablespoon minced garlic
½ teaspoon ground pepper
1 teaspoon dried oregano
½ teaspoon dried basil
black olives, mushrooms (canned or fresh), green bell pepper, or green onion (optional)

Brown the ground beef and onion (and the optional mushrooms if using) in the oil. Add all the other ingredients and mix well. Simmer, covered, for about 45 minutes, stirring occasionally and adding more water if needed.

NOTE: If you're really pressed for time or you just don't want to heat up the boat, you can simmer the sauce for less time, but the flavors won't have mixed as well. By the same token, if it's a cold day and you have plenty of propane, the sauce can simmer for several hours.

Cruiser's Lasagna   Serves 4

By adding water to the sauce, the noodles do not have to be pre-cooked, thereby avoiding a lot of steam in the boat and also making the preparation faster. While there are

"no-cook" lasagna noodles that you can buy (often at a hefty premium), this technique of using uncooked lasagna noodles and adding an extra cup of water to the sauce can be used with any lasagna recipe.

Total Time: 1 hour, 10 minutes
Prep Time: 25 minutes   **Bake Time:** 45 minutes

½ to 1 pound ground beef or shredded chicken
1 tablespoon olive oil, canola oil, or vegetable oil
½ medium onion, diced
1 can (8 ounces) mushrooms, drained
½ green bell pepper, diced
4 cups spaghetti sauce (jarred or make your own, see preceding recipe—if you make your own, omit the above ingredients from this recipe, as they're already in your sauce)
1 cup water
lasagna noodles
4 cups raw spinach OR 1 can (16 ounces) spinach, drained
3 cups ricotta cheese (page 100) or cottage cheese
1 cup shredded or grated Parmesan cheese
1 cup shredded mozzarella cheese

1. Brown the ground beef in the oil with the onion, mushrooms, and bell pepper. Add the spaghetti sauce and water, and stir to combine. You don't need to heat the sauce through, although the baking time will be a little less if you do.
2. Pour ½ cup of the sauce into a 9"×13" pan and spread it out (it will be thin; that's okay). Place a layer of lasagna noodles on the sauce, with about a 1-inch gap between the noodles and also at the ends of the pan. The noodles will swell considerably as they bake.
3. Layer half the spinach, ricotta, Parmesan, sauce, and mozzarella. Add another layer of noodles, then repeat the layers with the other half of the ingredients. Cover the pan with aluminum foil.
4. Bake approximately 45 minutes at 350°F (oven does not need to be preheated). The lasagna is done when the sauce is bubbling at the edges and the cheese on top is melted. Let cool 10 minutes before cutting to serve.

Meat Main Dishes

Sloppy Joes
Serves 6 to 8

Total Time: 30 minutes, although the sauce can simmer far longer

1 pound ground beef
2 stalks celery, diced
$\frac{1}{2}$ to 1 medium onion, diced
1 tablespoon canola oil or vegetable oil
1 cup ketchup
1 tablespoon prepared mustard
2 tablespoons cider vinegar or white vinegar
2 tablespoons brown sugar or white sugar
1 teaspoon beef bouillon powder OR 1 beef bouillon cube OR $\frac{1}{4}$ teaspoon salt
ground pepper, to taste
$\frac{1}{4}$ teaspoon garlic powder
6 to 8 hamburger buns, tortillas, or other bread for sandwiches

1. Brown the ground beef, celery, and onion in the oil over medium-high heat.
2. Turn the heat to low, add the ketchup, mustard, vinegar, brown sugar, bouillon, ground pepper, and garlic powder. Stir well and cook, covered, for at least 10 minutes. Serve on buns with plenty of napkins!

Cabbage Lasagna
Serves 2

Tastes similar to lasagna but with the added vitamin C and fiber from the cabbage. A good alternative if you can't find lasagna noodles.

Total Time: 1 hour, 30 minutes, including 10 minutes to sit but not including time to make spaghetti sauce if needed
Prep Time: 20 minutes   Bake Time: 1 hour

1 small cabbage or $\frac{1}{2}$ large cabbage
$\frac{1}{2}$ pound ground beef, shredded chicken, or ground chicken or turkey
1 onion, diced
1 teaspoon garlic powder, or to taste, OR 3 cloves garlic, minced
$\frac{1}{2}$ teaspoon dried oregano OR 1 teaspoon Italian seasoning (page 48) and omit the basil
$\frac{1}{2}$ teaspoon dried basil

2 cups Spaghetti Sauce (see page 261 to make your own, in which case omit the garlic powder, oregano, and basil from this recipe, as they're in the sauce)
$\frac{1}{4}$ cup cooked rice
2 cups shredded mozzarella or similar cheese

1. Shred the cabbage. Steam until softened, then drain.
2. While the cabbage is cooking, brown the ground beef and onion, using a little bit of salt in the pan, then drain the fat. Mix in the garlic, oregano, and basil.
3. Grease the bottom of a loaf pan. Layer half the cabbage, half the meat, half the spaghetti sauce, half the rice, and half the cheese, then repeat the layers. Bake 1 hour at 350°F (no need to preheat oven). The lasagna should be bubbling at the sides of the pan when done. Let sit for 5 to 10 minutes before cutting.

Taco Casserole
Serves 6 to 8

This recipe comes from Jan's family. When I first read it, I thought there was a mistake—bake the lettuce? Sounds strange, but it tastes good! You can omit it if you prefer.

Total Time: 45 minutes
Prep Time: 10 minutes   Cook Time: 35 minutes

2 pounds ground beef
1 can (16 ounces) refried beans
1 envelope taco seasoning (page 49)
$\frac{1}{2}$ cup water
$\frac{1}{2}$ bottle hot taco sauce OR 1 cup tomato sauce plus hot sauce to taste (omit if you don't like spicy foods)
$\frac{1}{2}$ bag tortilla chips OR 6 tortillas (corn are best)
2 cups sour cream (page 99)
2 cups diced fresh tomato
shredded lettuce (optional)
2 to 3 cups shredded cheddar cheese, Mexican blend, or similar cheese

1. Brown the ground beef and drain any fat. Add the beans, taco seasoning, water, and taco sauce and mix well.

2. Place the chips (leave whole) in an ungreased casserole dish. Add the meat mixture, then cover with the sour cream, tomato, lettuce (if desired), and shredded cheese. Bake at 350°F for 20 minutes (no need to preheat oven).

Baked Ziti   Serves 4

Think of Baked Ziti as a variation of lasagna. Instead of layers, it's all mixed together. This is better than lasagna at potlucks where not everyone will be seated at tables because you don't have to use a knife to cut into your serving.

Total Time: 45 minutes, plus time to make spaghetti sauce if needed
Prep Time: 15 minutes   **Bake Time:** 30 minutes

4 servings ziti or other medium-size pasta (about 1 pound, uncooked)
1 jar (24 ounces) spaghetti sauce with meat OR 3 cups Spaghetti Sauce (page 261)
8 ounces ricotta cheese (page 100) or cottage cheese
$1/4$ cup grated or shredded Parmesan cheese
4 to 8 ounces shredded mozzarella or similar cheese

1. Cook the pasta according to package directions (typically about 7 minutes); drain. Place in an ungreased baking dish large enough to hold all the ingredients.
2. Pour three-quarters of the spaghetti sauce over the pasta. Add the ricotta, breaking it up as you add it, and the Parmesan and half the mozzarella. Toss together.
3. Pour the remaining spaghetti sauce over the top and sprinkle with the remaining mozzarella. Bake, uncovered, at 350°F (no need to preheat oven) until the mozzarella is lightly browned.

Ground Beef and Banana Curry   Serves 2

Total Time: 30 minutes (or can simmer up to 3 hours) plus time to cook rice if needed
Prep Time: 10 minutes   **Cook Time:** 20 minutes

$1/4$ to $1/2$ pound ground beef or other meat cut into bite-size chunks
$1/2$ medium onion, diced
1 tablespoon minced garlic OR 1 teaspoon garlic powder
1 can (16 ounces) diced tomatoes, not drained, OR 2 or 3 tomatoes, cut into chunks
1 banana, sliced
$3/4$ cup raisins or other dried fruit OR 1 cup chopped fruit such as mangoes, apricots, peaches, or apples
2 teaspoons curry powder (page 47), or to taste*
$1/2$ teaspoon salt
ground pepper, to taste
$1/2$ cup cashews or other nuts
2 servings cooked rice

Curry powder varies considerably in spiciness and heat. If you are not sure how hot yours may be, start with a half teaspoon and gradually increase to taste.

1. Brown the ground beef, onion, and garlic. Add the tomatoes, banana, raisins, curry, salt, and ground pepper. Stir to mix, then cover and simmer for 15 minutes. You can simmer it much longer to let the flavors blend, but, if so, don't add the banana and any other soft fruits you might be using until the last 30 minutes or so (they'll get very mushy otherwise).
2. Serve over rice, and garnish with the cashews.

Steak Under the Broiler   Serves any number

Grilling is really the best way to cook a steak. But if it's a nasty day out or you don't have a grill, this is the next best thing.

Special Equipment: Broiler
Total Time: 10 minutes

steak (any cut that is good for grilling [page 258]; best if at least $3/4$-inch thick)
garlic powder, ground pepper, Montreal steak seasoning (page 219), or other preferred seasoning

Meat Main Dishes

1. Steak cooks best when it starts out at room temperature. Sprinkle with the seasonings. Do not use salt on the meat until after it is cooked, as it will draw out moisture, leaving you with a drier steak.
2. You can either use a broiler pan or put the steak directly on the oven rack. If you put it directly on the oven rack, place another pan on the lower rack to catch the drippings. Adjust the rack so that the top of the steak will be about 4 to 6 inches from the broiler.
3. Preheat broiler for at least 5 minutes.
4. Place the steak under the broiler. Use the accompanying chart as a guide to how long in total to broil the steak. You will need to turn it over halfway through the cooking time; take it out from under the broiler to do so. If you try to do it right in the oven, you are likely to burn your hand on the hot walls of the oven. Also, it's best to use a spatula or tongs to turn the meat. Using a fork will pierce the meat surface and you'll lose those wonderful juices!
5. The exact length of time to cook your steak depends on how thick the steak is, how hot the broiler is, the distance from the broiler to the steak, and how rare/well done you like your steak.

APPROXIMATE TOTAL COOKING TIMES FOR STEAK (NOT PER SIDE)

	1-INCH THICK	1½-INCHES THICK
Rare	6–7 minutes	7–8 minutes
Medium	8–9 minutes	10–12 minutes
Medium-Well	10–11 minutes	13–14 minutes

The only way to know for certain when the steak is cooked to the preferred doneness is to make a small cut into the steak, although you'll lose some juices, or use an instant-read thermometer and the chart on page 259. It's better to check sooner rather than later; you can always put the steak back under the broiler, but it's impossible to "un-cook" it.

Tropical Beef Chunks   Serves 6

Total Time: 1½ hours
Prep Time: 30 minutes   Cook Time: 1 hour

1½ pounds chuck roast, chuck steak, round steak, or stew beef OR 4 or 5 chicken breasts
1½ teaspoons garlic powder
1 teaspoon paprika
2 tablespoons canola oil or vegetable oil
1 can (8 ounces or larger) pineapple chunks, drained and juice reserved, OR 1 cup fresh pineapple chunks (including juice from the pineapple)
1½ cups beef or chicken broth (may be made from bouillon) or stock (pages 164–165)
¼ cup wine vinegar or balsamic vinegar
½ cup sliced celery
½ cup halved onion slices (half circles)
½ cup green or other color bell pepper strips
2 large tomatoes, cut into wedges (optional, but don't substitute canned tomatoes)
1 tablespoon soy sauce
3 tablespoons brown sugar or white sugar
1 tablespoon cornstarch OR 2 tablespoons flour (sauce won't be clear if made with flour)
½ cup water

1. Cut the meat into 1-inch chunks. Sprinkle with the garlic powder and paprika. Brown the meat in the oil in a skillet over medium-high heat. Add the pineapple juice, broth, and half the vinegar. Cover and simmer about 1 hour, or until the meat is tender.
2. Have the vegetables ready. Mix together the remaining vinegar, the soy sauce, brown sugar, cornstarch, and water in a small cup before proceeding.
3. When the meat is tender, add the celery and onion; cover and cook 5 minutes. Add the bell pepper and cook another 5 minutes. Add the pineapple, tomatoes, and soy sauce mixture. Stir to mix. Turn the heat up to medium-high and bring to a boil, then turn the heat back down and simmer just until thickened, or about 3 minutes. This is good by itself, or served over rice.

Beef Stroganoff

Serves 8

Total Time: 2 hours
Prep Time: 1 hour   Cook Time: 1 hour

2 pounds round steak, chuck steak, or stew beef
1 pound fresh mushrooms OR 2 cans (8 ounces each) mushrooms (sliced or button), drained
1 large onion or 2 small onions, finely chopped
1/2 cup butter or margarine
1 can (10 ounces) condensed tomato soup, not diluted (page 55)
1 can (6 ounces) tomato paste
1 cup sour cream (page 99)
2 teaspoons beef bouillon powder OR 1 teaspoon salt
ground pepper, to taste
1 teaspoon Worcestershire sauce

1. Cut the meat into thin slices—aim for 1/8-inch thick. Clean the mushrooms if using fresh. The mushrooms may be sliced or left whole, depending on size.
2. Brown the meat, mushrooms, and onion in the butter in a large skillet. Reduce the heat to low and add the tomato soup, tomato paste, sour cream, bouillon, ground pepper, and Worcestershire. Mix well.
3. Cover the pan and simmer 1 hour, stirring occasionally. If desired, cook some rice or noodles at the same time.
4. This dish is traditionally served over rice or noodles, but it's also good on its own.

Goulash

Serves 2

Substitute rice for the pasta and you've got Spanish Rice!

Total Time: 35 minutes

2 cups medium-size pasta or macaroni
1 teaspoon beef bouillon powder OR 1 beef bouillon cube OR 1 teaspoon salt
salt, for skillet
1/4 to 1/2 pound ground beef
1/3 cup diced onion
1 can (8 ounces) mushrooms, drained and liquid reserved (optional)
1/2 to 1 tablespoon oil (if ground beef is especially lean)

1/4 green bell pepper, diced
1 can (16 ounces) diced tomatoes, not drained, OR 2 tomatoes, cut into chunks
ground pepper, to taste

1. Cook the pasta according to package directions, using beef bouillon powder in place of salt to add more flavor. Set aside.
2. As the pasta is cooking, sprinkle salt in a skillet and place on medium-high heat. Crumble the ground beef into the pan and add the onion and mushrooms (reserve the liquid for later). As the ground beef cooks, the salt will draw the fat from the meat, and the meat, onions, and mushrooms will cook in it. If the meat is particularly lean, add the oil so that the mixture sautés nicely. Cook until the meat is browned.
3. Add the bell pepper, tomatoes (including all liquid from the can), reserved mushroom liquid (if using), and ground pepper. When cooked, add the reserved pasta and mix well. Simmer 10 to 15 minutes, uncovered, to allow some liquid to boil off. Serve on plates or in bowls.

Swiss Steak

Serves 2

Total Time: 2 hours
Prep Time: 30 minutes   Cook Time: 1 1/2 hours

1/2 pound round steak or stew beef
2 tablespoons canola oil or vegetable oil
1 teaspoon beef bouillon powder OR 1 beef bouillon cube OR 1/4 teaspoon salt
1/4 medium onion, diced
1 stalk celery, cut into 1/8-inch slices
2 or 3 carrots, cut into 1/4-inch slices
1 can (16 ounces) diced tomatoes, not drained, OR 2 cups diced fresh tomato
ground pepper, to taste

Cut the round steak into 2 pieces. Brown the meat in the oil in a skillet over high heat. Sprinkle the bouillon powder over the meat, then spread the onion, celery, carrot, and tomato over the top. Sprinkle with the ground pepper. Cover and reduce the heat to low. Simmer for about 1 1/2 hours, or until the meat is thoroughly tender.

Meat Main Dishes

Pot Roast

Make this for a "nice" meal, then have sandwiches a couple of times, maybe on a passage?

Total Time: about 3 hours, depending on cut of meat. Cook stew beef only about an hour.
Prep Time: 40 minutes, part while cooking
Number of servings depends on size of roast. Allow ¼ **to** ⅓ **pound uncooked weight per person**

2 to 3 tablespoons canola oil or vegetable oil
4 to 6 pounds chuck roast OR 1-inch chunks of stew beef
1 slice onion about ¼ inch thick (used only for flavor), sliced in half to make half circles
salt and pepper, to taste
3 or 4 bay leaves
2 carrots or more per person
1 potato per person (if very large potatoes, use ½ per person)

1. In a skillet or Dutch oven, heat the oil over high heat. Add the meat and brown it so that it is dark brown on one side. Turn the meat over and brown the second side. The hot oil will spit some (wear an apron or at least a T-shirt), but resist the urge to turn the heat down until the meat is seared.
2. When the meat is browned on both sides, turn the heat to low and add the onion around the outside of the pan. Add water about ½ inch deep. Sprinkle salt and pepper over the meat and put the bay leaves in the water. Cover and simmer until the meat is almost tender when pierced with a fork, generally at least 2 hours, sometimes longer. Check occasionally to see if more water is needed.
3. Wash and peel the carrots and potatoes. Cut in half if they are particularly large. Place in the pan alongside the roast, or, if needed, lift the roast and put the veggies under it. Cover and simmer about 30 minutes longer, or until the carrot and potato are tender. The meat may be almost falling apart.
4. Rather than trying to slice the roast, I cut a section for each person and serve with the carrot and potato. Put a spoonful or two of the pan drippings over the potato—it's better than gravy!

American-Style Tacos   Serves 4 to 6

If you have a packet of taco seasoning, follow the directions there. If you don't have a packet, this recipe will closely duplicate the taste.

Total Time: 30 minutes
Prep Time: 20 minutes   **Cook Time:** 10 minutes

1 tablespoon chili powder
2 teaspoons onion powder OR 2 tablespoons dried onion flakes
1 teaspoon ground cumin
1 teaspoon garlic powder
1 teaspoon dried oregano
1 teaspoon sugar
½ teaspoon cornstarch
½ teaspoon salt
1 pound ground beef, ground turkey, or ground chicken
½ cup water
12 hard taco shells or 12 tortillas
onion bits, diced tomato, diced bell or chile pepper (mild or spicy), shredded lettuce, sour cream (page 99), diced avocado, *pico de gallo* (page 128), shredded cheese, and/or hot sauce (optional toppings)

1. In a small bowl combine the chili powder, onion powder, cumin, garlic powder, oregano, sugar, cornstarch, and salt. Set aside.
2. Brown the meat in a skillet over medium-high heat; drain the fat. Turn the heat to medium low and add the spice mixture and the water. Stir and bring to a low simmer, cooking until the sauce is thick, or about 10 minutes.
3. While the meat is simmering, heat the taco shells in a 350°F oven (no need to preheat oven); follow package instructions, or heat for about 5 minutes.
4. To serve, put a few spoonfuls of meat into each taco shell and let each person add toppings for him- or herself.

Mexican Squash and Ground Beef Skillet
Serves 2 or 3

A great one-pan meal! Prepare ahead for a passage meal and then just reheat.

Total Time: 45 minutes

1/2 **pound ground beef, ground turkey, or sausage**
salt, for skillet
3 **summer squash, zucchini, or similar squash, sliced**
3 **onion slices, about** 1/4 **inch thick**
1 **clove garlic, minced, OR 1 teaspoon minced garlic OR** 1/4 **teaspoon garlic powder**
1 **tablespoon canola oil or vegetable oil**
1 **can (16 ounces) diced tomatoes, not drained, OR 2 large tomatoes, diced**
1 **teaspoon chili powder**
1 **teaspoon ground cumin**
salt and ground pepper, to taste

1. Brown the ground beef in a skillet with a little salt (the salt will draw the moisture out of the meat and you won't need oil). Remove the meat from the pan and set aside.
2. Lightly brown the squash, onions, and garlic in the oil over medium-high heat. Add the cooked meat, tomato, chili powder, cumin, salt, and ground pepper and let simmer, uncovered, about 10 minutes. Some of the liquid will boil away, but it should not be dry. Serve in bowls.

Mexican-Style Tacos
Serves any number

Tacos that you get in Mexico are quite different from what's sold in US fast-food restaurants. Tacos in Mexico are delicious!

Total Time: 20 minutes

1/4 **pound meat per person—flank steak (***arrachera* **in Mexico), top sirloin, or other steak-quality beef**
salt and pepper, to taste
1 **tablespoon canola oil or vegetable oil**
soft taco shells (tortillas)—flour or corn

onion slices, diced tomato, diced bell or chile pepper (mild or spicy), shredded cabbage, sour cream (page 99), diced avocado, *pico de gallo* (page 128), shredded cheese, and/or hot sauce (optional toppings)

1. Slice the meat thinly into bite-size pieces and sprinkle with salt and pepper. Sauté in a skillet in oil until done.*
2. Although you can warm the tortillas in the oven or microwave, the taste is much better if you warm them individually on a grill or in a skillet. Preheat a dry pan over high heat (don't use any oil), and flip the tortilla after 10 to 15 seconds. Remove it from the pan after another 10 to 15 seconds. You should just start to see browned spots but no black spots. Repeat for the other tortillas.
3. Serve the meat with the tortillas and toppings and let everyone make his or her own .

* Or cook the meat on a grill, but wait to cut the meat until after it's cooked.

Meat Loaf
Serves 4

To use a standard 9"×5" loaf pan, double the recipe or cut the baking time about in half.

Total Time: 1 hour
Prep Time: 15 minutes   Bake Time: 45 minutes

1/2 **cup ketchup**
1 **teaspoon prepared mustard**
dash of Worcestershire sauce
ground pepper, to taste
1 **egg**
1/2 **cup dry bread crumbs (page 51)**
1 **pound ground beef**

1. In a large bowl combine the ketchup, mustard, Worcestershire, ground pepper, egg, and bread crumbs. Crumble the meat and add it to the bowl; mix thoroughly.
2. Place the mixture in a small loaf pan (about 6"×3"), pressing it in firmly. Bake for 45 minutes at 350°F (no need to preheat oven). If the top seems to be getting too browned, cover with aluminum foil toward the end of the baking time.

Meat Main Dishes

3. Remove from the oven and pour off the fat. Let the meat loaf sit about 5 minutes before slicing and serving.

Alternate method: Bake the meat loaf in muffin tins for about 30 minutes.

Beef Stew with Dumplings
Serves 4

You can use almost any combination of vegetables (fresh or canned) that you have. If you use canned, add them in the last few minutes of cooking (just before the dumplings) so they don't turn to mush. This dish is also good made with chicken cut into chunks, but cook only about 30 minutes after browning the chicken, and only until the veggies are tender.

Total Time: 1 hour, 45 minutes

2 tablespoons canola oil or vegetable oil
1 pound beef stew meat (usually chuck) or boned chicken, cut into 1-inch pieces
beef broth (may be made from bouillon) or stock (page 165); use chicken broth if you make the stew with chicken
ground pepper, to taste
3 bay leaves
dash of onion powder and/or celery powder (if not using onion or celery)
$1/4$ teaspoon dried ground thyme, or poultry seasoning if using chicken
3 to 4 cups or more of prepared vegetables: traditional veggies are diced onion, sliced carrot, sliced celery, potatoes cut in chunks (peeled or unpeeled, your choice). You can also use turnip, parsnip, peas, corn, peeled and chunked sweet potato, or broccoli or cauliflower florets
dumplings (page 280)

1. Heat the oil in a large skillet or Dutch oven over medium-high heat. Add the meat and brown it on both sides. Add the broth to cover the meat by at least 1 inch. Add the ground pepper, bay leaves, onion powder, and thyme. Cover and bring to a boil, then turn down the heat to low and simmer for about 30 minutes, or until slightly tender, while you prepare the vegetables.

2. Add the vegetables, and make sure there is still enough broth. If not, add more broth or water. Turn the heat up to medium while you prepare the dumpling mixture. The stew must be steadily boiling before adding the dumplings.

3. Drop the dumplings by the spoonful into the stew, quickly cover, and cook for 15 minutes. Don't lift the lid until the dumplings are done.

4. Remove the bay leaves. Serve the stew in bowls and give each person a dumpling.

Cabbage and Pasta (or Noodles)
Serves 4 to 6

This freezes well and tastes great on the second or third day, making it good to make ahead and reheat on a passage.

Total Time: 50 minutes, includes 10 minutes stand time
Prep Time: 20 minutes   Cook Time: 20 minutes

8 ounces wide noodles or other pasta
1 pound ground meat—any type —OR shredded meat from 3 or 4 chicken breasts
1 large onion, chopped
1 green bell pepper, chopped
minced garlic, to taste
1 tablespoon olive oil, canola oil, or vegetable oil
liberal amounts of ground pepper, salt or bouillon powder, ground cumin, ground cloves, and/or Worcestershire sauce
1 small head of cabbage OR $1/2$ large head, chopped
$1/2$ cup water

1. Cook the noodles according to package directions while preparing the meat and cabbage mixture. Drain the pasta and keep warm until ready to use.

2. Brown the meat, onion, bell pepper, and garlic (if desired) in the olive oil. Add the spices, cabbage, and water; stir to mix. Cover and bring to a boil, letting the mix steam until the cabbage is crisp-tender. Turn the burner down to low and add the cooked noodles; mix well until heated through. Remove from the heat, cover, and let stand for 10 minutes before serving.

Fajitas
Serves 4

Instead of the chili rub, you can use the Fajita Marinade (page 221). If you're in a hurry, slice the meat before marinating it, and marinate for just 30 minutes.

Total Time: 45 minutes

1 pound flank steak (*arrachera* in Mexico) or other tender cut of beef
1 tablespoon chili powder, or to taste, depending on how spicy the chili powder is
1 teaspoon beef bouillon powder OR $1/2$ teaspoon salt
$1/4$ teaspoon garlic powder
2 tablespoons canola oil or vegetable oil
2 bell peppers, cut into thin strips (use different colors if available)
1 cup thinly sliced red onion
8 tortillas, flour or corn
$1/2$ cup salsa (page 127) or *pico de gallo* (page 128)

1. Rub both sides of the steak with a mix of the chili powder, bouillon, and garlic powder.
2. Heat 1 tablespoon of the oil in a skillet over medium-high heat until a drop of water dances. Add the steak and cook about 5 minutes per side, or to the desired doneness. Remove the steak from the pan and place on a cutting board.
3. Heat the remaining 1 tablespoon oil in the skillet, and add the bell pepper and onion. Sauté, stirring often, until the vegetables are crisp-tender, or about 4 to 5 minutes.
4. While the veggies are cooking, slice the meat across the grain into very thin strips. Heat the tortillas according to package directions. When the veggies are done, remove them from the heat.
5. Divide the meat and veggies evenly among the tortillas. Add some salsa to each, and roll them up. Serve 2 to each person.

Ground Beef, Potatoes, and Carrots in a Skillet
Serves 2

Total Time: 30 minutes
Prep Time: 20 minutes   **Cook Time:** 10 minutes

$1/4$ to $1/2$ pound ground beef or ground turkey
$1/2$ medium onion, diced
1 tablespoon canola oil or vegetable oil
3 carrots, cleaned and cut into $3/4$-inch slices
1 large OR 2 small potatoes, peeled and cut into 1-inch chunks
$1/4$ cup water
1 teaspoon beef bouillon powder OR 1 beef bouillon cube OR $1/4$ teaspoon salt
ground pepper and garlic powder, to taste

1. Brown the ground beef and onion in the oil until about half browned. Add the carrot and potato and continue to brown the meat and vegetables.
2. Reduce the heat to low and add the water, bouillon powder, ground pepper, and garlic powder; stir to mix. Simmer, covered, for about 10 minutes, or until the carrot and potato are tender. Stir occasionally and add more water if the potato absorbs all of it. The mix shouldn't be soupy, but it shouldn't burn dry. If it's too wet, remove the cover and turn the heat to medium high and let a little water boil off.

Greek Beef and Eggplant
Serves 4

Many recipes call for salting eggplant and laying it on towels to pull out the moisture and "bitterness." I've never done this and never thought the eggplant was bitter.

Total Time: 40 minutes minimum
Prep Time: 15 minutes   **Cook Time:** 25 minutes

1 pound eggplant
1 pound ground beef, ground turkey, or sausage
1 small onion, diced
1 clove garlic, minced, OR 1 teaspoon minced garlic OR $1/8$ teaspoon garlic powder
1 tablespoon olive oil, canola oil, or vegetable oil
$1/2$ cup red wine, beef broth (may be made from bouillon), stock (page 165), or water
1 can (8 ounces) tomato sauce
$1/2$ teaspoon dried parsley
$3/4$ teaspoon dried oregano
$1/2$ teaspoon ground cinnamon
$1/4$ teaspoon ground pepper
1 cup shredded mozzarella or similar cheese (optional)

1. Peel the eggplant and cut it into ½-inch slices. Set aside.
2. Brown the ground beef, onion, and garlic in the olive oil over medium-high heat, breaking up the meat with a spoon. Drain off the excess fat.
3. Add the wine, tomato sauce, parsley, oregano, cinnamon, and ground pepper; stir to mix.
4. Place the eggplant slices on top of the meat in the skillet. You'll probably have to overlap them. Turn the heat down to low and cover the pan. Let simmer for about 20 minutes, or until the eggplant is tender.
5. Sprinkle with the cheese, put the lid back on the pan, and cook for 2 to 3 minutes more, or just until the cheese is melted. Serve at once.

New England Boiled Dinner

Also known as Corned Beef and Cabbage, New England Boiled Dinner is exceedingly simple to make. It's great on a cool day when you want to warm up the boat! Corned beef can be reheated numerous times and is also great for sandwiches.

Total Time: 3½ to 4½ hours
Serves 10 to 15—or makes lots of leftovers!

If the commercial corned beef didn't come with a little packet of spices, create your own spice mix (depending on your preferences and what's available): 1 tablespoon pickling spice, or a mix of peppercorns or ground pepper, mustard seed, celery seed or celery powder, onion powder (if you're not using quartered onions), bay leaf, dash of ground coriander, ground cloves, ground ginger, and/or ground allspice
4- to 6-pound corned beef (see next recipe)
variety of veggies, suitable for the number of people to be served: peeled potatoes, cabbage (cut in quarters), carrots and parsnips (whole or cut into 4-inch lengths), and/or turnips
onions (cut in quarters, more for flavor than to serve and eat)

1. Rub the spices into the corned beef. Place it in a Dutch oven or other large pan. Add water to cover the meat. Cover the pan, bring it to a boil, turn down the heat to low, and simmer for 3 to 4 hours,

or until the meat is tender when pierced with a fork.
2. Add the vegetables. If there is not enough room in the pan for the veggies, tuck them under the meat. Cover the pan, bring back to a boil, turn the heat down to low, and simmer for 20 to 30 minutes, or until the veggies are tender.
3. Cut the meat across the grain into slices ¼ inch to ⅜ inch thick. Serve with the veggies. Most people like butter or margarine on the potatoes and cabbage; I also like a dash of vinegar (preferably cider vinegar) on the cabbage.

How to Corn Beef

In many places, corned beef is impossible to buy except in little cans. But it's not hard to corn the beef yourself. Although beef brisket is the cut we're used to seeing corned, any cut that requires long, slow cooking is a candidate. You can even use stew meat and let it sit in the marinade for just 2 days. This method does not use saltpeter, which is also hard to find, so the meat won't have that bright pink color. The taste is the same, however.

Total Time: 1 week

½ cup kosher salt, sea salt, or other non-iodized salt
1 tablespoon peppercorns, cracked, OR 1½ teaspoons coarse ground pepper*
2 teaspoons ground allspice*
½ teaspoon ground thyme*
3 bay leaves, crushed*
3 cloves garlic, crushed or minced, OR 1 teaspoon garlic powder
4 to 6 pounds beef brisket or other beef roast

*You may substitute 2 tablespoons pickling spice for the pepper, allspice, thyme, and bay leaves.

1. Mix the seasonings together in a cup or small bowl.
2. Pierce the beef all over with a fork. Rub the seasonings into the beef. Place it in a freezer plastic bag and then put the bag inside a plastic storage container in case the bag should leak. Get as much air out of the bag as possible before sealing it. Place it in the refrigerator for 7 days, turning the bag over each day.

3. Before cooking, soak the beef in water for at least 2 hours to remove the salt; you may want to change the water a few times. Cooking times will vary with the recipe used for the corned beef. If you used stew meat (typically 1-inch cubes), cooking times will be considerably shorter than if an entire brisket is used.

Potluck Burger 'n' Rice   Serves 8

Total Time: 1 hour, 10 minutes to 1 hour, 55 minutes (depending on cooking method)
Prep Time: 10 minutes
Cook Time: 1 hour, 45 minutes in the oven or 1 hour in a skillet

1 to 1½ pounds ground beef
1 cup chopped celery
1 cup chopped onion
½ cup uncooked rice
1 can (10 ounces) cream of mushroom soup, undiluted (page 54)
2 cups water
1 can (8 ounces) sliced mushrooms, drained
2 tablespoons soy sauce

1. Brown the beef in a skillet with the celery and onion. Drain off the fat. Add the rice, mushroom soup, water, sliced mushrooms, and soy sauce to the skillet and stir to combine .
2. At this point, you can continue to cook this in the skillet, simmering over low heat for about 45 minutes, or until the rice is cooked through. Or you can place the mixture in a casserole with a lid and bake it at 350°F (no need to preheat) for about 1 hour and 45 minutes, or until it is bubbling and the rice is cooked through. While it is cooking (by either method), check periodically to see if it needs additional water. Different types of rice will take different amounts of water as well as different cooking times.

Liver and Onions   Serves 4

Total Time: 45 minutes
Prep Time: 20 minutes
Cook Time: 20 minutes (at a simmer)

4 slices bacon
1 onion, cut into slices
½ cup flour

1 teaspoon Mrs. Dash, seasoned salt, beef bouillon power, or garlic pepper
1 pound beef liver, sliced about ¼-inch thick
butter, margarine, canola oil, or vegetable oil
1 cup water

1. Cook the bacon in a skillet until crisp. Remove the bacon (but leave the bacon fat) and drain on paper towels on a plate. Set aside.
2. Over medium-low heat, cook the onion slices in the bacon fat until they are translucent and just beginning to be golden. Remove and set aside.
3. While the onion is cooking, mix the flour and Mrs. Dash in a pie pan or on a plate. Dredge the liver slices in the flour mixture.
4. When the onion is done, remove from the pan and set aside.
5. Turn the heat up to medium high. There should still be some bacon fat in the pan. If not, add a bit of butter to the pan. When it is hot, place the liver in the pan and quickly brown one side. Flip the liver and brown the second side.
6. Turn the heat down to low and add the water. Cover and simmer for about 20 minutes, or until the gravy forms and the liver is tender when pierced with a fork. Place the onion on top of the liver for last few minutes of cooking time, to warm through.
7. Serve with the bacon on the side. Or, if one person doesn't like liver, use the bacon to make them a bacon, lettuce, and tomato sandwich!

POULTRY

Chicken is a staple almost everywhere in the world and is usually easy to find in cruising locales. If you are limited on freezer space, buy boneless chicken or bone it before freezing it (page 256). If you're trying to eat healthier, note that many "old standby" recipes made with beef are equally good with chicken.

Less frequently found—and harder to use in most galleys—are turkey and Cornish game hens. Whole birds take up a lot of space in the refrigerator, although they can be good as a special treat for holidays. Ground turkey can be used in almost any recipe calling for ground beef, and is far healthier.

Meat Main Dishes

POULTRY COOKING TIMES

	OVEN—AT 350°F	STOVE TOP/SKILLET
Whole Chicken (4–7 pounds average)	20-25 minutes per pound, unstuffed (add 20–30 minutes if stuffed)	15-20 minutes per pound, unstuffed, covered (do not try to cook a stuffed bird on the stove top)
Cornish Game Hen (1½ pounds average)	50–60 minutes, unstuffed (add 10–15 minutes if stuffed)	35–40 minutes, unstuffed, covered (don't stuff)
Chicken Breast, bone-in	30–40 minutes	35–45 minutes
Chicken Breast, boneless, skinless	20–25 minutes	25–30 minutes
Whole Chicken Legs (thigh and drumstick)	50 minutes	50 minutes
Chicken Thigh	45 minutes	45 minutes
Chicken Drumstick	35 minutes	40 minutes
Chicken Wings	30–40 minutes if spaced in pan 40–50 if packed in sauce	35–45 minutes
Whole Turkey, fully thawed, unstuffed	About 15 minutes per pound, slightly less for large birds (over 15 pounds)	N/A
Whole Turkey, totally frozen	Add at least 50% more time than if fully thawed. Remember to remove the neck, liver, and giblet package when sufficiently thawed (the plastic package will melt during cooking).	N/A
Turkey Breast, fully thawed	20–25 minutes per pound	About 20 minutes per pound in Dutch oven with liquid

Poultry Cooking Times

In addition to the recipes that follow, the table above shows basic cooking times for poultry.

Food Safety Tips for Poultry

In addition to the general meat safety tips on page 255, the USDA gives these tips (edited to make recommendations applicable to cruisers):

- Chicken and other poultry should be stored at or below 40°F. Put fresh or frozen chicken in a cooler with ice to transport it to the boat if it will take longer than 10 minutes, or any time the temperature is over 100°F.

- Chicken and other poultry should be used within 1 to 2 days, or frozen. If kept continuously frozen, chicken will last indefinitely.
- The USDA recommends using an instant-read thermometer for all poultry and making sure the center of the meat reaches 165°F. Note that this is 5°F higher than for most other meat.
- The biggest food safety risk with poultry comes from cross-contamination. Always wipe down your cutting board with a bleach solution after cutting chicken on it.

Asian Skillet

Serves 4

Total Time: 25 minutes
Prep Time: 10 minutes   **Cook Time:** 15 minutes

4 chicken breasts or other cut of chicken
3 tablespoons cornstarch
$\frac{1}{2}$ cup chicken broth (may be made from bouillon) or stock (page 164)
1$\frac{1}{2}$ teaspoons cornstarch
1 tablespoon rice vinegar or white vinegar
2 tablespoons oyster sauce or soy sauce
1 tablespoon soy sauce
2 teaspoons brown sugar or white sugar
$\frac{1}{3}$ cup canola oil or vegetable oil
6 green onions, including tops, sliced
1 bell pepper, any color, seeded and diced
3 teaspoons chopped fresh ginger OR $\frac{1}{8}$ teaspoon ground ginger
2 tablespoons minced garlic OR $\frac{3}{4}$ teaspoon garlic powder
cooked rice (optional)

1. Bone and skin the chicken breasts and cut into 1-inch cubes. Place in a bowl or plastic bag. Add the 3 tablespoons cornstarch and toss or shake until the chicken is evenly coated. Set aside.
2. In a small bowl mix together the broth and the 1$\frac{1}{2}$ teaspoons cornstarch until smooth. Add the vinegar, oyster sauce, soy sauce, and sugar and mix well.
3. Heat the oil in a skillet or wok until very hot. Add the chicken cubes and sauté just until cooked through. Don't overcook or the chicken will be dry. Remove the chicken and place on a plate covered with paper towels to absorb the fat. Drain about half the fat from the skillet, leaving just 1 to 2 tablespoons.
4. Return the skillet to the stove over high heat. Add the onion, bell pepper, ginger, and garlic, and cook for about 2 minutes, or until the pepper is crisp-tender. Quickly add the chicken and broth mixture and cook, stirring constantly, for about 1 minute, or until the sauce thickens. Serve over rice if desired.

Breaded Dijon Chicken

Serves 6

Total Time: 1 hour
Prep Time: 25 minutes
Cook Time: 5 minutes to brown, 30 minutes to bake

6 chicken breasts, bone-in or boneless, skin removed
2 tablespoons Dijon mustard, spicy mustard, or yellow mustard
2 eggs
1$\frac{1}{2}$ cups dry bread crumbs (page 51)
1$\frac{1}{2}$ teaspoons garlic powder
1 teaspoon seasoned salt, sea salt, or regular salt
$\frac{1}{2}$ teaspoon ground pepper
$\frac{1}{2}$ teaspoon paprika
dash of cayenne pepper, to taste
canola oil or vegetable oil, for frying

1. Preheat oven to 400°F.
2. Rinse and pat the chicken breasts dry with paper towels. Set aside.
3. In a bowl large enough for dipping the chicken breasts, stir the mustard into the eggs until well mixed.
4. On a plate or in a plastic bag, combine the bread crumbs and all the spices.
5. Dip the chicken breasts into the egg/mustard mixture, and then coat with the seasoned bread crumbs; pat them into place. Set aside.
6. Cover the bottom of a large skillet with the oil, and place over medium-high heat. When the oil bubbles with a drip of water, place the breaded chicken breasts in the pan two at a time and cook both sides just until they turn golden brown. Don't completely cook them. Remove the chicken and blot any excess fat on a paper towel. Place on an ungreased cookie/baking sheet and bake for 30 minutes, or until cooked through. Remember that bone-in chicken breasts will take longer to cook than boneless.

Meat Main Dishes

Cheddar-Garlic Baked Chicken   Serves 4

Total Time: 1 hour
Prep Time: 20 minutes   Bake Time: 35 minutes

$\frac{1}{3}$ cup butter or margarine, melted
2 tablespoons minced garlic OR $\frac{3}{4}$ teaspoon garlic powder, or to taste
$\frac{1}{2}$ teaspoon seasoned salt or regular salt
$\frac{1}{2}$ cup to $\frac{3}{4}$ cup seasoned dry bread crumbs
$\frac{1}{2}$ cup shredded cheddar or other cheese
$\frac{1}{4}$ cup grated Parmesan or other cheese
$\frac{1}{4}$ teaspoon ground pepper
4 boneless, skinless chicken breasts

1. Preheat oven to 350°F. Grease a baking dish large enough for 4 chicken breasts.
2. In a bowl combine the melted butter with the garlic powder, and salt.
3. In another bowl or a plastic bag, combine the bread crumbs with the cheeses and ground pepper.
4. Dip the chicken into the butter mixture, then the crumb mixture. Place in the greased baking dish and bake, uncovered, for 30 to 35 minutes. Don't overbake or the chicken will be dry.

Chicken with Spicy Peach Sauce   Serves 4

You can also make this dish with canned chicken. Don't sauté it; just add it at the end and heat through.

Total Time: 25 minutes
Prep Time: 5 minutes   Cook Time: 20 minutes

4 boneless, skinless chicken breasts
$\frac{1}{4}$ cup butter or margarine
2 teaspoons cornstarch
$\frac{1}{3}$ cup balsamic vinegar, wine vinegar, or white vinegar
3 tablespoons sugar
$\frac{1}{4}$ teaspoon cayenne pepper, or to taste
$1\frac{1}{2}$ teaspoons chili powder, or to taste
$\frac{1}{2}$ teaspoon salt
2 teaspoons minced garlic
2 cups peeled diced peaches (fresh or frozen) OR 1 can (16 ounces) sliced peaches, drained

$\frac{1}{3}$ cup walnut halves, pecan halves, or whatever nuts you prefer, toasted

1. Sauté the chicken in the butter until golden brown. Remove from the pan and set aside.
2. Add the cornstarch to the pan and stir well so the cornstarch combines with the pan juices and lumps are eliminated.
3. Add the vinegar, sugar, cayenne, chili powder, salt, garlic, and peaches and cook over medium heat until thick and bubbly. Add the chicken and nuts and cook until the chicken is heated through. Serve over rice or pasta, if desired.

Chicken and Sesame Noodles   Serves 4

If you want to make this in a hurry, slice the chicken into thin strips before marinating, and marinate for only 30 minutes—it will also cook much faster this way.

Total Time: 3 hours, 40 minutes, including 3 hours to marinate
Prep Time: 15 minutes   Cook Time: 25 minutes

16 ounces pasta (angel hair is traditional, but spaghetti, penne, rotini, or other styles will work)
$\frac{1}{2}$ cup soy sauce
$\frac{1}{4}$ cup sesame oil, or to taste (I like more)
$\frac{1}{3}$ cup sugar
$\frac{1}{4}$ cup sesame seeds
3 green onions, thinly sliced

Marinade

$\frac{1}{4}$ cup soy sauce
$\frac{1}{4}$ cup teriyaki sauce (page 214)
2 cloves garlic, minced
1 teaspoon chopped fresh ginger OR $\frac{1}{2}$ teaspoon ground ginger
$\frac{1}{4}$ cup packed brown sugar
4 boneless, skinless chicken breasts
sesame oil, for cooking the chicken

1. Cook the pasta according to package directions; drain.
2. Stir together the $\frac{1}{2}$ cup soy sauce, the $\frac{1}{4}$ cup sesame oil, and the sugar until the sugar is dissolved. Pour over the pasta. Sprinkle with the sesame seeds

and green onion and toss to mix. Set aside so that the noodles are totally infused with the sauce.

3. Make the marinade for the chicken by mixing the soy and teriyaki sauces, garlic, ginger, and brown sugar until the sugar is dissolved.

4. Put the chicken in a large plastic bag and pour in the marinade. Marinate for at least 3 hours in the refrigerator.

5. Discard the marinade. Heat the sesame oil in a skillet over medium-high heat and sauté the chicken until done. Let cool. Slice the chicken into thin strips and serve over the sesame noodles.

Gumbo   Serves 4

This wonderful Cajun dish can be varied to suit whatever you have on hand. Gumbo can be made in two ways —okra gumbo, where the okra acts to somewhat thicken the sauce, and filé gumbo, where the filé powder helps to thicken the sauce and provides a subtle, unique flavor. (Filé powder is ground dried sassafras leaves and is used primarily for—you guessed it—filé gumbo.) Although filé powder used to be difficult to find outside Louisiana, you can now find it in the spice aisle in most US supermarkets. You can also easily buy it online. However, filé powder is virtually impossible to find outside the US. I've made this dish many times without it; while it doesn't taste quite the same, it's still a great dish!

Total Time: 1 hour, 30 minutes
Prep Time: 30 minutes   **Cook Time:** 50 minutes

4 servings cooked rice (cook while you're making the gumbo)
1 chicken breast, cut into 1-inch chunks, OR 1 can (6 ounces) chicken
4 to 6 ounces smoked sausage or bratwurst, cut into ¼-inch slices
¼ cup canola oil or vegetable oil, or more as needed
¼ cup flour
1 medium onion, diced
4 to 6 green onions, including tops, cut into ¼-inch slices
½ green bell pepper, diced
1 teaspoon minced garlic OR ¼ teaspoon garlic powder

2 cups chicken broth (may be made from bouillon) or stock (page 164)
⅛ teaspoon ground cloves*
⅛ teaspoon cayenne pepper*
¼ teaspoon ground thyme*
3 bay leaves*
1 tablespoon filé powder*
handful of raw shrimp OR 1 can (6 ounces) shrimp (optional)

*You can use a Cajun spice mix, Old Bay Seasoning, or even a blackening spice mix if you don't have the individual spices.

1. Cook the rice while you're making the gumbo.

2. In a medium to large pan (a heavy skillet or saucepan works best), brown the chicken and sausage in the oil. ***NOTE:*** If you use canned chicken, omit this step and add the chicken at the very end so it doesn't break up too much.

3. Remove the chicken and sausage from the pan, letting as much oil as possible drain back into the pan. Set the meats aside on a plate.

4. Make a roux by mixing the flour into the oil in the pan and stirring over medium heat until the mixture is slightly darker than peanut butter. If there was not much oil left in the pan after browning the chicken, add 1 to 2 tablespoons more. It is very important not to scorch or burn the roux. This is best avoided by turning the heat down as the roux darkens, and stirring it constantly.

5. Over medium-low heat, add the onion, green onion, bell pepper, and garlic and cook, stirring constantly, until the veggies begin to soften. Add the broth a little at a time, stirring constantly so the roux does not get lumpy. Bring to a boil, then reduce the heat to low and add the browned meats and the cloves, cayenne, thyme, and bay leaves. The consistency should be that of cream soup; add more water if necessary. Cover and simmer for 10 to 15 minutes.

6. Add the filé powder and mix well. If using canned chicken and/or shrimp, add it now. Cook to heat through, or until the shrimp is no longer raw. Remove the bay leaves and serve the gumbo in cups or bowls over rice.

Meat Main Dishes

Spanish Paella   Serves 6 to 8

Paella is a delicious delicacy that varies widely from region to region in Spain. Most varieties contain a mixture of seafood, chicken, and sausage, but you can use whatever you have. No clams or shrimp? Fine, use chicken and chorizo. No chorizo? Fine, make it with chicken, but be sure to taste and adjust the seasonings accordingly. Buen provecho!

Total Time: 1 hour, 15 minutes
Prep Time: 30 minutes   **Cook Time:** 45 minutes

¼ pound chorizo sausage, sliced
1 pound chicken, cooked and shredded
1 tablespoon olive oil, canola oil, or vegetable oil
1 large onion, chopped
1 green bell pepper, seeded and chopped
3 cloves garlic, minced
2 cups rice
3 cups chicken broth (may be made from bouillon) or stock (page 164)
¼ teaspoon saffron
¼ teaspoon dried oregano
salt and pepper, to taste
2 large tomatoes, chopped
¼ cup chopped fresh parsley OR 1 teaspoon dried parsley flakes
1 cup fresh, frozen, or canned peas
1 pound large shrimp
12 medium clams or mussels, in shells, well scrubbed (page 239)
lemon wedges

1. In a large skillet, sauté the chorizo over medium heat until browned. Stir in the shredded chicken.
2. Add the olive oil and cook the onion, bell pepper, and garlic until soft, but do not brown.
3. Add the rice, broth, saffron, oregano, salt, and pepper. Bring to a boil. Decrease the heat to low and cover the pan. Simmer for 20 minutes, or until the rice is tender (the cooking time will vary with the type of rice used).
4. As the mixture is simmering, preheat oven to 350°F.
5. Add the tomatoes, parsley, and peas to the rice mixture and cook 2 more minutes.

6. Put the mixture in the oven. You may be able to use your skillet if the handle won't melt; otherwise, transfer to a greased baking dish. Place the shrimp and clams on top and bake about 25 minutes, or until the clams open and the shrimp are curled and pink.
7. Throw away any clams that do not open. Garnish the paella with the lemon wedges and serve immediately.

Italian Chicken Breasts   Serves 4

Great dish for entertaining or to prepare ahead for a busy day or a passage.

Total Time: 1 hour
Prep Time: 25 minutes   **Bake Time:** 35 to 45 minutes

1 cup dry bread crumbs or finely crushed corn flakes
⅛ cup grated or shredded Parmesan cheese
1 teaspoon garlic powder
1 teaspoon Italian seasoning (page 48)
1 teaspoon seasoned salt, Mrs. Dash (page 48), or regular salt
½ teaspoon ground pepper
1 egg
2 tablespoons canola oil, olive oil, or vegetable oil
4 boneless, skinless chicken breasts (if you use bone-in, the cooking time will be longer)
1¼ cups spaghetti sauce or tomato sauce (if you use tomato sauce, double the seasonings listed above)
1 cup shredded mozzarella or other meltable cheese

1. In a dish suitable for breading, mix the bread crumbs, Parmesan, garlic powder, Italian seasoning, seasoned salt, and ground pepper. In another shallow dish, beat the egg.
2. Heat the oil in a skillet over medium-high heat until a few drops of water dropped into it sizzle. Coat both sides of each chicken breast with the egg so it is completely covered. Remove the breast and hold it over the dish to let any excess egg drain back. Then put the breast into the bread crumb mixture and again turn until it is totally coated. Place each breast into the hot skillet. Cook for about

5 minutes on each side, or until the coating is nicely browned. Note that the chicken will not be cooked through.

3. If you intend to finish baking the chicken later, place the breasts in a single layer in a plastic storage container (or place each one in a separate plastic bag) and refrigerate for up to 2 days.

4. When ready to bake, preheat oven to 350°F. While it's preheating, place the breasts in a single layer in a greased baking pan. Spread the sauce evenly over the chicken breasts, and top with the mozzarella. Bake 35 to 45 minutes, or until the chicken is done. The time will depend on the size of the chicken breasts and whether they just came out of the skillet or from the refrigerator.

5. If the cheese is not melted and golden when the chicken is done, put the pan under the broiler for a minute or two and cook just until the cheese is golden.

Oven-Baked
Barbecued Chicken   Serves 4

Total Time: 1 hour, plus time to make barbecue sauce if needed
Prep Time: 10 minutes   Bake Time: 50 minutes

4 boneless, skinless chicken breasts OR 3-pound whole chicken, cut into pieces (page 257)
seasoned salt or regular salt
garlic powder
ground pepper
2 cups bottled barbecue sauce or see barbecue sauce recipes (page 215)

1. Preheat oven to 350°F. Grease a baking pan.
2. Season the chicken on both sides with the salt, garlic powder, and ground pepper.
3. Place the chicken in the pan, cover with aluminum foil, and bake for 30 minutes (longer for bone-in). Remove from the oven and drain off any fat.
4. Drench the chicken in barbecue sauce. Bake, uncovered, for 20 more minutes, or until cooked through (longer for bone-in).

Simple Chicken Curry   Serves 2 to 4

Margaret Goodman, Jan's mom, loved making this Simple Chicken Curry for the family from the time she got the recipe from missionaries to India who visited their church. It's a great make-ahead recipe—prep it all and refrigerate up to 3 days, then bake when ready.

Total Time: 1 hour, 20 minutes
Prep Time: 20 minutes
Bake Time: 1 hour (cook rice at the same time)

1 cup chopped celery
1 cup chopped onion
1/2 cup chopped carrot
1/2 cup butter or margarine
2 teaspoons curry powder (page 47)*
2 teaspoons salt or chicken bouillon
ground pepper, to taste
1/2 cup flour
3 to 4 cups milk or soy milk
2 chicken breasts, cooked and cubed (you may substitute drained canned chicken)

If a less spicy curry is desired, substitute some turmeric and garam masala for all or part of the curry powder. If more flavor is desired, use more curry powder.

1. Cook the celery, onion, and carrot in the butter until soft. Mix in the spices. Slowly add the flour, stirring until the mixture becomes a paste. Add the milk slowly, stirring until the mixture thickens.
2. Remove from the heat and mix in the cooked chicken. Refrigerate to serve later, or transfer to a casserole with a lid and bake at 325°F (preheating oven is not necessary) for approximately 1 hour, or until bubbly.
3. If intending to serve over rice, cook the rice while the curry is baking. Serve the chicken curry over the rice.

Meat Main Dishes

Zesty Chicken Stir-Fry   Serves 4

Total Time: 40 minutes
Prep Time: 25 minutes   Cook Time: 15 minutes

1 pound boneless chicken, cut into 1-inch cubes
2 tablespoons olive oil, canola oil, or vegetable oil
1 clove garlic, minced, OR $\frac{1}{8}$ teaspoon garlic powder
$\frac{1}{2}$ teaspoon ground ginger OR 1 tablespoon fresh grated ginger
$3\frac{1}{2}$ cups chopped veggies, such as shredded cabbage, carrots, bell peppers, onions, jalapeño peppers (seeded and finely chopped), green onions, and/or celery

Sauce

$\frac{1}{4}$ cup orange juice
$\frac{1}{4}$ cup soy sauce
1 tablespoon rice wine vinegar or white vinegar
$\frac{1}{4}$ cup water
2 teaspoons sugar
1 tablespoon cornstarch

1. Mix the sauce ingredients in a cup or small bowl, making sure there are no lumps. Set aside.
2. Over medium-high heat, sauté the chicken in the oil with the garlic and ginger until the chicken is almost cooked through. Add the veggies and stir-fry about 3 minutes more, or until the veggies are crisp-tender.
3. Add the sauce, stirring constantly, and cook until thickened. If desired, serve the stir-fry over rice.

Sesame Chicken   Serves 6

Total Time: 25 minutes
Prep Time: 5 minutes   Cook Time: 20 minutes

6 boneless, skinless chicken breasts
1 tablespoon olive oil, canola oil, or vegetable oil
$\frac{1}{4}$ cup honey
$\frac{1}{4}$ cup soy sauce
$\frac{1}{2}$ cup water
1 tablespoons cornstarch
$\frac{1}{2}$ to 1 teaspoon ground ginger
$\frac{1}{2}$ to 1 teaspoon red pepper flakes, or to taste, OR $\frac{1}{4}$ teaspoon cayenne pepper
dash of sesame oil
3 tablespoons sesame seeds, toasted

1. Cut the chicken breasts into strips. Sauté in the olive oil until browned.
2. Mix together the honey, soy sauce, water, cornstarch, ginger, and red pepper flakes. Add to the chicken and cook until the mixture thickens slightly.
3. Add the sesame oil and sprinkle with the sesame seeds. Cover and simmer for 10 more minutes. Serve over rice if desired.

Whole Roast Chicken

Often a turkey won't fit into a boat oven, and it can be hard to find a turkey breast in many cruising locales. But a whole roast chicken works well, puts the same great smell in the air, and even looks like a miniature turkey on the table!

Total Time: about 3 hours, including time to clean chicken (cooking time depends on size)

1 whole chicken
2 to 4 tablespoons butter, margarine, canola oil, or vegetable oil
salt and pepper, to taste
celery salt or 6-inch piece of celery (optional)
onion powder or wedge of onion (optional)
1 teaspoon poultry seasoning OR $\frac{3}{4}$ teaspoon dried ground sage (or 3 teaspoons chopped fresh sage) plus $\frac{1}{4}$ teaspoon dried ground thyme (or 1 teaspoon chopped fresh thyme)

1. Preheat oven to 350°F .
2. Rinse the chicken cavity and remove the packet of giblets inside, if needed (see cutting up a whole chicken on page 257, but don't cut it up).
3. Rub the outside of the chicken all over with the butter. If possible, gently slip some of the butter under the skin on the breast. Put any remaining butter in the cavity.
4. Salt and pepper the inside of the cavity. Even if you are limiting your sodium intake, try to use at least a little salt. Without it, the chicken won't have any flavor.
5. Place the celery and onion in the cavity if they are being used.

6. If you have a roasting pan with a rack, use the rack. This will virtually eliminate problems with hot spots because the chicken won't be sitting in the pan, and all the skin will be crispy, not just the skin on the top. Otherwise, use any baking pan that the chicken will fit into. Place the chicken in the pan, breast side up (the rough backbone should be down and the smooth breastbone up). I prefer not to tuck the wings under the body or tie the drumsticks together. While tucking and tying makes a tidy little package, it also makes it harder to have the drumsticks and breast meat done at the same time.

7. Salt and pepper the outside of the chicken, then sprinkle the poultry seasoning over it (you can rub it in a little if you like). Don't put foil over chicken, and don't put water or any other liquid in the pan.

8. Put the bird in the oven and bake for approximately 20 minutes per pound. Unless the bird is really scrawny and lacking in fat, you don't need to baste it. If you decide you should baste it, brush it with butter every 30 minutes.

9. The best test for doneness is an instant-read meat thermometer, inserted into the thickest part of the thigh but not touching bone. It should read 165°F. If you don't have a meat thermometer, use all three of these tests: the skin should be a dark golden color; the juices should run clear without a rosy tint when the thigh is pierced with a fork; and the drumstick socket should feel loose when you try to wiggle it.

10. Remove the pan from the oven and put the chicken on a serving plate (a whole chicken will usually fit on a dinner plate). Put a piece of aluminum foil over the top to keep it warm, and let it sit about 20 minutes while you prepare the gravy and other side dishes. This "sit time" will make it much easier to carve as well as making the meat juicier.

11. The drippings in the pan will be carmelized and there won't be a lot of "juice." This makes extremely flavorful gravy even though there isn't much liquid. You'll have to add broth or water to make pan gravy (page 221).

12. Carve the chicken as you would a turkey.

Cornish Game Hens   Serves any number

Traditionally, Cornish game hens are served one to a person. However, serving one for every two people is becoming increasingly popular and can be quite romantic!

Total Time: 1 hour, 15 minutes
Bake Time: 1 hour

$1/2$ to 1 Cornish game hen per person
2 to 4 tablespoons butter, margarine, canola oil, or vegetable oil
salt and pepper, to taste
1 teaspoon poultry seasoning OR $3/4$ teaspoon ground dried sage (or 3 teaspoons chopped fresh sage) plus $1/4$ teaspoon ground dried thyme (or 1 teaspoon chopped fresh thyme)
celery salt or 3-inch piece of celery, and onion powder or wedge of onion (optional)

Prepare as for whole roast chicken (see preceding recipe) but bake for only 1 hour.

Sweet and Sour Chicken   Serves 4

Total Time: 1 hour

3 tablespoons soy sauce
1 tablespoon sherry, other white wine, or water
1 egg
$1/4$ teaspoon ground pepper
$1/4$ teaspoon garlic powder
$1/4$ cup cornstarch
1 pound boneless, skinless chicken breasts, cut into 1-inch pieces
$1/4$ cup canola oil or vegetable oil
1 can (20 ounces) pineapple chunks, drained and juice reserved
2 tablespoons cornstarch
$1/2$ cup sugar
$1/4$ cup ketchup
$1/4$ cup vinegar (any type)
1 tablespoon soy sauce
1 green bell pepper, cut into 1-inch pieces

1. If intending to serve over rice, cook the rice while preparing the chicken.
2. Mix together the 3 tablespoons soy sauce, the sherry, egg, ground pepper, garlic powder, and

Meat Main Dishes

the 1/4 cup cornstarch in a medium bowl. Add the chicken chunks and toss to coat.

3. Place the oil in a skillet over medium-high heat until a drop of water sizzles. Add the chicken mixture and cook until golden brown, periodically turning the chicken so it stays in individual pieces. Remove the chicken pieces and drain on a paper towel.

4. While the chicken is cooking, measure the reserved juice from the pineapple. Add enough water to make 1 cup. Place in a saucepan and add the 2 tablespoons cornstarch and the sugar, ketchup, vinegar, and the 1 tablespoon soy sauce. Stir well so there are no lumps. Bring to a boil and cook about 3 minutes, or until thick.

5. Add the drained chicken, pineapple chunks, and bell pepper and cook until heated through. Serve over rice if desired.

Chicken and Dumplings   Serves 4

Talk about comfort food! You can also start with bone-in pieces and boil the chicken until tender, then tear the pieces off the bones—discard the skin, bones, and any inedible bits—and put the chicken back in the broth.

Total Time: 1 hour (with boneless, skinless chicken breasts) or 3 hours (with bone-in pieces)

4 boneless, skinless chicken breasts, cut into 1-inch cubes
2 stalks celery, cut into 1/2-inch slices
4 carrots, sliced 1 inch thick
1 medium onion, diced
4 cups chicken broth (may be made from bouillon) or stock (page 164)
1/2 teaspoon ground pepper
Dumplings
1 cup flour
1 1/2 teaspoons baking powder (page 376)
1/4 teaspoon salt
2 tablespoons canola oil or vegetable oil, or butter, margarine, or shortening, melted
1/2 cup milk or water

1. Combine the chicken, celery, carrot, onion, broth, and ground pepper in a large pan. Bring to a boil, then reduce the heat and simmer, covered, about 30 minutes.

2. Mix the dumpling ingredients, stirring just enough to combine. Drop by spoonfuls (one per person) on top of the chicken stew. Cover the pan tightly and cook for 15 minutes over low heat—no peeking! Serve the chicken and dumplings immediately in bowls.

Cajun Chicken Pasta   Serves 2

Total Time: 30 minutes
Prep Time: 10 minutes   **Cook Time:** 20 minutes

2 boneless, skinless chicken breasts, cut into thin strips
2 teaspoons Cajun seasoning (page 46)
2 tablespoons butter, margarine, olive oil, canola oil, or vegetable oil
1 green onion, thinly sliced
1 cup cream, half-and-half (*media crema*), or evaporated milk (page 99)
2 tablespoons chopped sun-dried tomato OR 1 small tomato, diced
1/4 teaspoon dried basil
1/4 teaspoon salt
1/8 teaspoon garlic powder
1/8 teaspoon ground pepper
4 ounces linguine or other medium-size pasta, cooked al dente
1/4 cup grated or shredded Parmesan cheese

1. Place the chicken and Cajun seasoning in a bowl or plastic bag and toss to coat.

2. In a skillet over medium-high heat, sauté the coated chicken in the butter until golden brown, or approximately 3 to 4 minutes a side.

3. Reduce the heat to low, and add the green onion, cream, tomato, basil, salt, garlic powder, and ground pepper. Simmer until hot.

4. Pour over the hot linguine and toss with the Parmesan cheese.

Pan-Fried Chicken   Serves 4

Total Time: 30 to 45 minutes (depends on cuts of chicken used)

$1/2$ cup butter or margarine
4 pieces of chicken with bone in and skin on (can use boneless and skinless, but they're not as satisfactory)

1. Melt the butter in a skillet large enough to hold the chicken in a single layer. When melted, turn the heat up to high and wait for the butter to sizzle, but don't let it burn.
2. Carefully place the chicken in the skillet, skin side down (be careful not to burn your hand as the hot butter will spit when the chicken is added). Every minute or so, wiggle the chicken around in the pan so it doesn't stick.
3. When the chicken skin is medium-dark brown, flip the chicken over, cover the pan, reduce the heat, and simmer until the chicken is cooked through—typically another 15 to 20 minutes, but it can take a bit longer.
4. The best way to check for doneness is to use an instant-read thermometer, inserted into the meat away from bone. The chicken is done when the temperature reads at least 165°F.

Asian BBQ Chicken   Serves 4

This can also be made with canned chicken—but don't brown it. Just make the sauce, add the chicken, and heat just until warmed through.

Total Time: 45 minutes (cook rice at the same time)
Prep Time: 15 minutes   Cook Time: 30 minutes

4 boneless chicken breasts, cut into bite-size pieces, OR other chicken pieces, bone removed (page 256), cut into bite-size pieces
2 tablespoons olive oil, canola oil, or vegetable oil
1 clove garlic , crushed, OR 1 teaspoon minced garlic OR $1/8$ teaspoon garlic powder
$1/4$ teaspoon ground ginger
$3/4$ teaspoon crushed red pepper flakes, or to taste
$1/4$ cup apple juice
$1/3$ cup packed brown sugar or white sugar

2 tablespoons ketchup
1 tablespoon cider vinegar or other vinegar
$1/2$ cup water
$1/3$ cup soy sauce

1. Brown the chicken in the olive oil. Remove the chicken and set aside.
2. Add the garlic, ginger, red pepper flakes, apple juice, brown sugar, ketchup, vinegar, water, and soy sauce. Cook, stirring, over medium heat until the sugar is dissolved.
3. Put the chicken back in the pan and bring to a boil. Reduce the heat and simmer for 20 minutes. Serve over rice or pasta if desired.

Simple Caribbean Jerk Chicken   Serves 6

Total Time: 2 hours, 10 minutes, including 1 hour marinate time
Prep Time: 10 minutes
Bake Time: 45 minutes to 1 hour

1 envelope Italian salad dressing mix (page 161)
2 tablespoons brown sugar or white sugar
2 tablespoons canola oil, olive oil, or vegetable oil
2 tablespoons soy sauce
1 teaspoon ground cinnamon
1 teaspoon dried thyme
$1/2$ teaspoon cayenne pepper
$2^1/2$ pounds chicken pieces OR 6 boneless, skinless chicken breasts

1. Preheat oven to a 350°F.
2. Combine the salad dressing mix, sugar, oil, soy sauce, cinnamon, thyme, and cayenne. Mix well.
3. Put the chicken in a plastic freezer bag and add the spice mixture. Let marinate for 1 hour in the refrigerator. Remove the chicken and place in a baking pan or a skillet, then pour the marinade over the chicken.
4. Bake for 45 to 60 minutes, based on your oven, or simmer on the stove top for about 30 minutes, or until the chicken is cooked. Boneless, skinless chicken will cook faster than chicken with bones, so judge the time accordingly.

Meat Main Dishes

Basil Cream Chicken Pasta
Serves 4

Total Time: 25 minutes
Prep Time: 15 minutes   **Cook Time:** 10 minutes

1 pound boneless, skinless chicken breasts, cooked and shredded, OR 2 cans (6 ounces each) chicken, drained
1 onion, finely diced
¾ pound fresh mushrooms, sliced, OR 1 can (8 ounces) mushrooms, drained
2 tablespoons olive oil, canola oil, or vegetable oil
3 tablespoons butter, margarine, or oil
3 tablespoons flour
2 cups chicken broth (may be made from bouillon) or stock (page 164)
1 cup cream, half-and-half (*media crema*), or evaporated milk (page 99)
2 tablespoons minced fresh basil OR 2 teaspoons dried basil OR 2 teaspoons Italian seasoning (page 48)
¼ teaspoon ground pepper
4 servings fettuccine or any pasta you prefer, cooked and drained

1. Sauté the chicken, onion, and mushrooms in the oil for 4 minutes. Set aside. (If using canned chicken, sauté only the onion and mushrooms and add the chicken at the end so it doesn't turn to mush.)
2. In a large saucepan, melt the butter and slowly stir in the flour until smooth. Slowly add the broth and cream, stirring well after each addition so that lumps don't form. Stir in the basil and ground pepper. Bring to a boil; cook and stir for 2 minutes. Stir in the chicken mixture. Serve over the fettuccine or toss both together.

Chicken Teriyaki
Serves any number

Total Time: 2 hours, including 1½ hours to marinate
Prep Time: 5 minutes   **Cook Time:** 15 minutes

1 piece of chicken per person
2 tablespoons teriyaki sauce (page 214) per person

1. Place the chicken in a leakproof plastic bag or food storage container and add the teriyaki sauce. Marinate in the refrigerator for 1½ hours.
2. Preheat broiler or a grill. Remove the chicken from the marinade and place on the broiler pan. Discard the remaining marinade.
3. Broil for about 15 minutes, or until done, turning every 5 minutes. (The cooking time depends on the cuts used—boneless will take less time than bone-in.)

Chicken Potpie
Serves 6

This potpie is just as good as a casserole if you don't feel like making a piecrust.

Total Time: 1 hour, 20 minutes
Prep Time: 30 minutes   **Bake Time:** 40 to 50 minutes

1 cup diced potato
1 cup diced onion
1 cup diced celery
1 cup diced carrot
1 cup sliced mushrooms OR 1 can (8 ounces) mushrooms, drained (optional)
⅓ cup butter, margarine, olive oil, canola oil, or vegetable oil
½ cup flour
2 cups chicken broth (may be made from bouillon) or stock (page 164)
1 cup cream, half-and-half (*media crema*), or evaporated milk (page 99)
4 cups chopped cooked chicken OR 4 boneless, skinless chicken breasts, cooked and chopped, OR 6 servings canned chicken, drained
1 teaspoon salt or chicken bouillon powder
¼ teaspoon ground pepper
1 piecrust (page 425)

1. Preheat oven to 400°F.
2. Sauté the vegetables in the butter for 10 minutes, or until slightly browned. Sprinkle with the flour and cook for 1 minute, stirring constantly so there are no lumps.
3. Gradually stir in the broth and cream, again making sure there aren't lumps. Continue to cook the mixture over medium heat, stirring constantly, until thickened and bubbly.

4. Add the chicken and season to taste with salt and pepper. Stir well.

5. Pour into a shallow casserole and top with the piecrust. Cut slits to allow steam to escape. Bake for 40 to 50 minutes, or until the pastry is golden brown and the filling is bubbly and cooked through.

Chicken Enchiladas   Serves 4

For a slightly different version using canned beef or chicken, see page 311.

Total Time: 1 hour, 20 minutes
Prep Time: 50 minutes (less if using leftovers)
Bake Time: 30 minutes

4 boneless, skinless chicken breasts OR 1 pound
  beef chuck (allow longer to cook)
1/2 teaspoon dried oregano
1/2 teaspoon ground cumin
1/4 cup chopped onion
1 teaspoon garlic powder
1 tablespoon Worcestershire sauce
1 cup tomato sauce
1 teaspoon dried oregano
2 teaspoons chili powder, or to taste
1/2 teaspoon ground cumin (in addition to the
  above)
1/2 teaspoon ground pepper
1 can (16 ounces) enchilada sauce (page 213) OR
  salsa (page 127) OR an additional 1 cup tomato
  sauce and spices as above
12 tortillas, corn or flour
2 cups shredded cheddar or similar cheese

1. Place the meat in a skillet with 1/2 inch water. Add the oregano and the 1/2 teaspoon cumin; cover, bring to a boil, then turn the heat down and simmer until the meat is tender and can be pulled apart. This will take about 30 minutes for chicken breasts, longer for beef depending on the cut and thickness. You may need to add more water, particularly if using beef.

2. Shred the meat with a fork or your fingers, then place it in a small bowl and add the onion, garlic, Worcestershire sauce, tomato sauce, oregano, chili powder, another 1/2 teaspoon cumin, and the ground pepper.

3. Preheat oven to 350°F while continuing to prepare enchiladas.

4. Place a couple of tablespoons of enchilada sauce in a 9"×13" pan and tilt to cover the whole bottom thinly. Lay a tortilla on a plate and spoon a line of meat somewhat off center. Roll up the enchilada and place it in the pan, seam side down. Make the remaining enchiladas the same way and snug them against one another in the pan.

5. Spread with the remaining enchilada sauce, then top with the cheese. Bake for 30 minutes, or until the cheese is melted and the enchilada mixture coming out of the ends of each enchilada is bubbly.

6. Carefully remove the enchiladas from the pan with a spatula. This can be the trickiest part of making enchiladas—not to have them break while taking them out of the pan.

7. If desired, you can serve them with a dollop of sour cream (page 99) or guacamole (page 129) and a garnish of sliced olives or chopped green onion.

Chicken à la King   Serves 4

Total Time: 30 minutes

2 tablespoons butter, margarine, canola oil, or
  vegetable oil
1/2 cup flour
1/8 teaspoon ground pepper
2 cups milk
1 cup chicken broth (may be made from bouillon)
  or stock (page 164)
1 can (8 ounces) mushrooms, drained
2 cups cubed cooked chicken or turkey
1 can (16 ounces) peas, drained

1. Melt the butter in a saucepan over low heat. Add the flour and ground pepper, stirring well so there are no lumps. Slowly add the milk and broth, stirring constantly so that lumps don't form. Raise the heat to medium and continue to stir as the mixture comes to a boil and thickens.

2. When the mixture is thick, lower the heat to simmer and add the mushrooms, chicken, and peas. Stir to mix and cook for about 10 minutes, or until heated through.

3. This dish is usually served over toast, egg noodles, rice, or puff pastry, but it's also good on its own.

Meat Main Dishes

Salsa Chicken
Serves 4

Total Time: 45 minutes
Prep Time: 10 minutes   **Bake Time:** 35 minutes

4 servings of skinless chicken pieces (white or dark)
4 to 5 teaspoons taco seasoning mix (page 49)
1 cup salsa (page 127)
1 cup shredded cheese (cheddar is best; lots of others taste great)
2 tablespoons sour cream (optional; page 99)
1 green onion, sliced thinly (optional)

1. Preheat oven to 375°F.
2. Place the chicken and taco seasoning in a plastic bag and shake to coat. Remove the chicken and place in a single layer in a baking dish. Cover with the salsa and sprinkle with the cheese.
3. Bake for 25 to 35 minutes, or until the chicken is done. (The exact time will depend on what pieces were used.)
4. Arrange the pieces on plates or a serving platter, and top with a dollop of sour cream and a sprinkling of green onion.

Greek Chicken and Potatoes
Serves 2

Equally good baked or cooked on the stove top!

Total Time: 45 minutes
Prep Time: 10 minutes   **Cook Time:** 35 minutes

$1/4$ cup olive oil, canola oil, or vegetable oil
2 boneless, skinless chicken breasts, cut into 1-inch cubes, OR 1 can (6 ounces) chicken, drained
2 cups diced (1-inch cubes) peeled potatoes
3 cloves garlic, minced, OR 3 teaspoons minced garlic OR $1/4$–$1/2$ teaspoon garlic powder
1 chicken bouillon cube OR 1 teaspoon chicken bouillon powder
$1/3$ cup water
$1/4$ cup lemon juice, lime juice, or *limón* (Key lime) juice
1 teaspoon dried oregano
ground pepper, to taste

In the Oven
1. Preheat oven to 400°F.
2. Toss all the ingredients together in a large bowl or plastic bag, then transfer to a baking dish with a lid. Bake for 35 minutes.

On the Stove Top
1. Warm the olive oil in a skillet over medium-high heat. Add the chicken and potatoes and brown just slightly (if using canned chicken, don't add it here; add it just before serving and heat through).
2. Add the garlic, bouillon, water, and lemon juice and stir to combine. Sprinkle with the oregano and ground pepper; cover and turn down the heat. Simmer for about 30 minutes, stirring occasionally but being careful not to break up the potatoes. Add more water if needed—the dish should be moist but not soupy.

Ranch Chicken
Serves 4

Leftovers are great to slice and use in salads!

Total Time: 35 minutes
Prep Time: 5 minutes   **Bake Time:** 30 minutes

4 boneless, skinless chicken breasts
$1/2$ cup prepared ranch dressing (page 161)
$1/2$ cup dry bread crumbs or crushed crackers

1. Preheat oven to 400°F. (If your oven won't reach 400°F, bake longer at the highest temperature of your oven.)
2. Dip the chicken into the dressing and then into the bread crumbs. Place the pieces in a single layer in a greased baking dish.
3. Bake for about 30 minutes, or until no longer pink. (Check for doneness by making a small cut into the center of the meat.)

NOTE: You can easily use other cuts of chicken or bone-in pieces. Adjust the cooking time, as small cuts will cook faster and bone-in pieces will take longer. Don't overbake.

Chicken and Rice Casserole
Serves 4 to 6

Total Time: 1 hour, 30 minutes
Prep Time: 10 minutes
Cook Time: 1 hour, 20 minutes

1/2 to 1 cup uncooked rice
1 can (10 ounces) cream of mushroom or cream of chicken soup (page 54), not diluted
1 envelope Good Seasons Italian dressing mix (page 161)
2 cups water
1 to 1 1/2 pounds cut-up chicken (dark or light meat, bone-in or boneless)
ground pepper, to taste

1. Spread the rice in a greased baking dish. (If you are using a 9"×13" dish or pan, use 1 cup rice; if using a smaller pan, scale down the amount of rice proportionately.)
2. Mix the soup, dry Italian dressing mix, and the water. Set aside.
3. Arrange the chicken on top of the rice, and season with the ground pepper (don't use salt—there is a lot of salt in the soup and in the dressing mix). Pour the soup mixture over the chicken and rice.
4. Cover with aluminum foil and bake for 1 hour at 350°F (no need to preheat oven). Uncover and bake for 20 minutes longer, or until the liquid is absorbed and the rice is tender. This timing assumes bone-in chicken. Boneless breasts will take a total of about 45 minutes; uncover after about 25 minutes.

Chicken Livers
Serves 4

Total Time: 20 minutes

1 pound chicken livers
1 cup flour
1 teaspoon Mrs. Dash (page 48)
1/4 cup canola oil or vegetable oil
3 tablespoons butter, margarine, or oil
1 onion, sliced 1/4 inch thick
1/2 cup white wine (optional)

1. Rinse and drain the chicken livers.
2. Combine the flour and Mrs. Dash in a plastic bag. Add the livers, four or five at a time, and shake to coat. Remove and set aside until all are coated.
3. Heat the oil and butter in a skillet over medium-high heat until a drop of water sizzles. Add the onion and chicken livers. Sauté until browned (about 5 minutes)—don't overcook. If using wine, add it and simmer just a minute.

Variation: Flour the chicken livers as directed above, but instead of using the oil, cook 3 or 4 slices of bacon in a skillet until crisp. Remove the bacon and cook the livers and onion in the bacon fat. Just before serving, crumble the bacon over the livers and onion.

Turkey Meat Loaf
Serves 4

Cooking in a muffin tin shortens the cooking time, using less propane and putting less heat in the boat. But you can also bake it in a loaf pan—it will just take longer.

Total Time: 50 minutes
Prep Time: 15 minutes   **Bake Time:** 35 minutes

1 pound ground turkey, ground chicken, or ground beef
1/3 cup finely diced water chestnuts
3/4 cup dry bread crumbs
2/3 cup evaporated milk (page 99), milk, pineapple juice, or water
1/4 cup soy sauce
1/4 cup chopped green onion (including tops) or diced onion
1 egg, lightly beaten
2 teaspoons chicken bouillon powder OR 2 chicken bouillon cubes, crumbled
1 clove garlic, minced, OR 1 teaspoon minced garlic OR 1/8 teaspoon garlic powder

Oriental Sauce
1/3 cup ketchup
1/3 cup honey
2 tablespoons soy sauce
1/2 teaspoon minced garlic

Meat Main Dishes

1. Preheat oven to 350°F.
2. Combine all the meat loaf ingredients and mix thoroughly. Divide among 8 muffin cups and bake for 30 to 35 minutes, or bake in a loaf pan—an 8"×4" pan will take about an hour; a 9"×5" pan will take about 45 minutes.
3. While the meat loaf bakes, combine all the sauce ingredients in a small saucepan. Place over low heat, stirring frequently, until hot.
4. To serve, place 2 mini-meat loaves or meat loaf slices on each plate and drizzle a little sauce over the top.

Greek-Style Turkey Burgers
Serves 4 or 5

A nice change from typical hamburgers! See below to make them into "Almost Gyros."

Total Time: 25 minutes
Prep Time: 10 minutes   **Cook Time:** 15 minutes

1 pound ground turkey, ground chicken, or ground beef
1 cup crumbled feta cheese
$\frac{1}{2}$ cup chopped black olives
1 teaspoon dried oregano*
1 teaspoon dried parsley flakes*
1 teaspoon dried basil*
1 teaspoon onion powder OR 3 tablespoons very finely chopped onion
$\frac{1}{2}$ teaspoon garlic powder
ground pepper, to taste

*Or use 1 tablespoon Italian seasoning in place of the oregano, parsley, and basil.

Mix all the ingredients together, and form into 4 burgers. Grill, or cook in a skillet as you would for hamburgers (page 260).

Variation: For "Almost Gyros," add some chopped onion, chopped tomato, and *tzatziki* sauce (page 136). Serve in pitas, wrap in tortillas, or serve on hamburger buns.

Turkey Cordon Bleu Casserole
Serves 4 to 6

Using canned turkey (or chicken) and ham makes this quick to toss together. And if you don't have an oven—or don't want to heat it up—you can cook this on the stove top.

Total Time: 1 hour
Prep Time: 30 minutes   **Bake Time:** 30 minutes

4 cups cubed cooked turkey
3 cups cubed cooked ham
$1\frac{1}{4}$ cups shredded cheddar or other cheese that will melt
1 cup chopped onion
$\frac{1}{4}$ cup butter, margarine, canola oil, or vegetable oil
$\frac{1}{3}$ cup flour
2 cups cream, half-and-half (*media crema*), or evaporated milk (page 99)
$1\frac{1}{4}$ teaspoons dried dill (optional)
$\frac{1}{8}$ teaspoon dry mustard OR 1 teaspoon prepared mustard
$\frac{1}{8}$ teaspoon ground nutmeg
1 cup dry bread crumbs
2 tablespoons butter or margarine, melted
$\frac{1}{4}$ cup chopped walnuts (optional)

1. Preheat oven to 350°F.
2. Place the turkey, ham, and 1 cup of the cheese in a baking dish; set aside.
3. In a skillet or saucepan, cook the onion in the $\frac{1}{4}$ cup butter until soft. Add the flour and mix to form a paste. Turn the heat to low and slowly add the cream, stirring constantly so that lumps don't form. Slowly bring to a boil, still stirring, and let boil for 1 to 2 minutes, or until the mixture thickens.
4. Remove from the heat and add 1 teaspoon of the dill and the mustard and nutmeg. Pour over the turkey and ham in the baking dish and set aside.

5. Mix together the bread crumbs, butter, the remaining ¼ teaspoon dill, the remaining ¼ cup cheese, and the walnuts, if desired. Sprinkle over the meat mixture. Bake, uncovered, for 30 minutes, or until heated through—the mixture will be bubbling around the edges when done.

Variation: Cook the meat and sauce mixture in a skillet over medium-low heat for 20 minutes. Sprinkle with the cheese topping; cover and cook for 10 minutes, or until the cheese is melted.

Italian Turkey Burgers   Serves 4

Total Time: 30 minutes
Cook Time: 15 minutes

1 pound ground turkey or ground beef
2½ tablespoons Italian bread crumbs OR plain bread crumbs plus 1 teaspoon Italian seasoning (page 48)
1 tablespoon dried oregano OR ¼ cup finely chopped fresh oregano
2 teaspoons chopped sun-dried tomato OR 2 tablespoons finely chopped tomato, seeds removed
¼ cup red wine
1 teaspoon grated Parmesan cheese
1 clove garlic, minced, OR 1 teaspoon minced garlic OR ¼ teaspoon garlic powder, or to taste
salt and pepper, to taste
4 buns (optional)

1. Mix the turkey, bread crumbs, oregano, sun-dried tomato, wine, Parmesan, garlic, salt, and pepper. Form into 4 burgers. Cook on the grill or in a skillet as you would hamburgers (page 260).
2. Serve on buns, if desired. Good with sliced onion, sliced tomato, lettuce, and mayonnaise/Miracle Whip instead of the standard ketchup and mustard.

PORK

Pork chops, ribs, sausage, bacon—all are mouthwatering. Pork has a wonderful, almost sweet taste that's complemented by sweet and spicy flavorings and sauces, although it also can stand on its own.

In cooking pork, the important thing is not to overcook it if you're using a dry method such as grilling, but also to be sure to fully cook it. An instant-read meat thermometer makes this much easier.

Pork Food Safety Tips

In addition to the general meat safety tips on page 255, the USDA gives these tips for cooking pork (edited to make them applicable to cruisers):

- Raw pork should be stored at or below 40°F. Put fresh or frozen pork in a cooler with ice to transport it to the boat if it will take longer than 10 minutes, or any time the temperature is over 100°F.
- Raw pork should be used within 3 to 5 days or else frozen. If frozen, it's best eaten within 6 months.
- Ground pork—as in sausage—is most susceptible to bacteria because far more surface is exposed to the air and to the meat grinder. It is really important to cook ground pork thoroughly. The USDA recommends using an instant-read thermometer for sausage patties, meat loaf, and similar foods, and making sure the center of the meat patty reaches 160°F.
- In general, pork should be cooked to 160°F—it may still look pink at this point, but it's done. If you wait until it's gray throughout, it is likely to be overcooked and dry; this is why it's best to use a meat thermometer and not judge by appearance.

Meat Main Dishes

Today's Pork: Cooking Times and Temperatures

Method	Cut	Thickness/ Weight	Final Internal Temperature (Fahrenheit)	Total Cooking Time (Minutes)
Roasting Roast at 350°F. Roast in a shallow pan, uncovered	Loin Roast*, Bone-in or Boneless	2–5 lbs.	150°	20 per pound
	Crown Roast*	6–10 lbs.	150°	20 per pound
	Fresh Leg/Uncured Ham*	3½ lbs.	150°	20 per pound
	Shoulder Butt*	3–6 lbs.	160°	30 per pound
	Tenderloin* (roast at 425°–450°)	½–1½ lbs.	160°	20–30
	Ribs	--	Tender	1½–2 hours
	Ham, Fully Cooked	5–6 lbs.	140°	20 per pound
Broiling 4 inches from heat or **Grilling** over direct heat	Loin Chops, Bone-in or Boneless	¾ inch	160°	8–10
	Thick Chop	1½ inches	160°	12–16
	Kabobs	1 inch cubes	Tender	10–15
	Tenderloin*	½–1½ lbs.	160°	15–25
	Ribs (grill over indirect heat)	--	Tender	1½–2 hours
	Ground Pork Patties	½ inch	160°	8–10
Barbecue over indirect heat	Loin Roast*, Bone-in or Boneless	2–5 lbs.	160°	20 per pound
	Leg	3½ lbs.	160°	40 per pound
	Shoulder Butt	3–6 lbs.	160°	45 per pound
	Ribs	--	Tender	1½–2 hours
Sautéing Add a little fat to pan; sauté over medium-high heat	Cutlets	¼ inch	Tender	3–4
	Loin Chops, Bone-in or Boneless	¾ inch	160°	7–8
	Tenderloin Medallions	¼–½ inch	Tender	4–8
	Ground Pork Patties	½ inch	160°	8–10
Braising Cook, covered, with a liquid at a simmer	Chops or Cutlets	¼–1 inch	160°	8–15
	Cubes	1 inch	Tender	8–10
	Tenderloin Medallions	½–¾ inch	160°	8–10
	Shoulder Butt	3–6 lbs.	Tender	2–2½ hours
	Ribs	--	Tender	1½–2 hours
Stewing Cook, covered, with liquid at a slow simmer	Ribs	--	Tender	2–2½ hours
	Cubes	1 inch	Tender	45–60

Pork today is very lean and shouldn't be overcooked. The best test of doneness is to use an instant-read meat thermometer to check the internal temperature of your pork. We recommend cooking pork chops, roasts, and tenderloins to 160°F, which leaves the center pink and juicy.* Less tender cuts, like pork shoulder (butt) and ribs can be cooked long and slow, to render them tender.

  * For larger cuts of pork, such as roasts, cook to 150°F; remove from the oven or grill and allow to set for 10 minutes before slicing. The temperature of the roast will continue to rise to 160°F and the pork juices will redistribute throughout the roast before slicing.

Courtesy of the National Pork Board. www.otherwhitemeat.com

Skillet Pork Chop   Serves any number

Total Time: 10 to 20 minutes, depending on thickness of chops

1 pork chop per person, boneless or bone-in, best if $^3/_4$-inch to 1-inch thick
salt
ground pepper, to taste
$^1/_2$ cup water (approximate)

1. Sprinkle a skillet with salt, and place over high heat until hot. Place the chops in the pan and sear for 1 to 2 minutes, or until browned on the bottom. Flip and sear the other side for 1 minute more. As the chops sear, sprinkle with ground pepper.
2. Add water so there is about $^1/_4$ inch in the pan. Quickly cover and turn down the heat to low. Cook for 7 to 10 minutes, depending on the thickness of the chops and whether the bone is in (bone-in will take a little longer). Test for doneness with an instant-read meat thermometer (160°F minimum)—the pork chops will still be pink inside when done. Quickly serve and enjoy! For a treat, serve with the Southwest Spicy Salsa (page 332).

Pork Roast   Serves any number

Pork roast can be baked plain for the same amount of time, but this sauce adds flavor!

Total Time: depends on size of roast—10 minutes prep, 20 minutes per pound to bake, then 10 minutes standing before carving

pork loin roast, $^1/_4$ to $^1/_3$ pound uncooked weight per person
2 tablespoons honey or molasses
1 tablespoon soy sauce
1 tablespoon wine vinegar, balsamic vinegar, or white vinegar
1 teaspoon dry mustard OR 1 tablespoon prepared mustard
1 teaspoon salt
1 teaspoon garlic powder
$^1/_2$ teaspoon ground pepper

1. Place the pork on a roasting or baking pan.
2. Mix the honey, soy sauce, vinegar, mustard, salt, garlic powder, and ground pepper; spoon over the roast.
3. Bake, uncovered, about 20 minutes per pound at 350°F (no need to preheat oven). Every 30 minutes, spoon up some of the sauce from the pan and pour it back over the roast.
4. The roast is done when an instant-read thermometer reads 150°F (the temperature will continue to rise as the roast stands). Remove from the oven and let stand about 10 minutes before cutting into slices. Spoon a little of the sauce from the pan over each slice.

Sausage and Potatoes   Serves 2

You can make this with almost any type of sausage—Polish kielbasa, smoked sausage, chorizo, bulk sausage, breakfast links—whatever!

Total Time: 30 minutes

$^1/_2$ pound sausage
1 to 2 tablespoons canola oil, vegetable oil, butter, or margarine
$^1/_2$ medium onion, diced
2 medium potatoes, peeled and cut into $^3/_4$-inch cubes
salt and pepper, to taste

1. If not using bulk sausage, slice it about $^3/_8$-inch thick.
2. Heat the oil in a skillet over medium-high heat. (The exact amount of oil will depend on how much fat there is in the sausage and whether you're using a nonstick pan.)
3. When a drop of water sizzles in the pan, add the sausage, onion, and potato and cook, flipping occasionally, until the potato is a light golden brown.
4. Turn down the heat and add the salt and pepper —we like using a fair amount of pepper. Cover and cook for about another 10 minutes, or until the potato is fork tender. You may need to add a tablespoon or two of water—the mixture shouldn't be wet, but the inside of the lid should be covered with steam to cook the potato.

Meat Main Dishes

289

Carnitas
Serves 15 to 20

These are delicious, but they take time to cook, so make a large batch—perfect for a party!

Total Time: 4½ hours
Bake Time: 4 hours

4 to 5 pounds boneless pork
4 cups chicken broth (may be made from bouillon) or stock (page 164)
1 onion, quartered
1 tablespoon ground cumin
2 bay leaves
onion slices, diced tomato, diced bell or chile pepper (mild or spicy), shredded cabbage, sour cream (page 99), diced avocado, *pico de gallo* (page 128), shredded cheese, and/or hot sauce (optional toppings)

1. Trim any large pieces of fat from the meat, but leave some fat for flavor. Cut the meat into 1- to 2-inch cubes (smaller cubes will cook faster, but you don't want to make them so small that the meat isn't really in chunks).
2. Put the meat, broth, onion, cumin, and bay leaves in a large pot. The meat should be covered with liquid; if it's not, add more broth or water until it is. Cover and bring to a boil, then turn down the heat and simmer for about 3 hours, or until the meat pulls apart easily.
3. Drain the liquid from the pan, and remove the bay leaves and as much of the onion as practical. The next step is to "crisp" the outside of the cubes, and you can do this in the oven or on the stove top. In the oven, place the meat in a roasting pan, preferably in a single layer, and bake at 425°F for about 20 minutes. On the stove top, brown the meat in a large pan over high heat. Serve as you would Mexican-style tacos (page 267).

Pork Chop Casserole
Serves 4

This is also great made with chicken—bone-in or boneless, and skin on or off depending on your preference. The baking time is about the same in each instance.

Total Time: 1 hour, 10 minutes
Prep Time: 10 minutes   **Bake Time:** 1 hour

4 pork chops
1 cup uncooked rice
1 can (10 ounces) cream of mushroom or any cream-style soup, undiluted (page 54)
1 package dry onion soup mix (page 55)
2 cups water

1. Place the pork chops in a greased casserole dish. Layer the rice over the pork chops.
2. Dollop the mushroom soup over the chops and sprinkle generously with the onion soup mix. Pour water over all.
3. Cover tightly with aluminum foil. Bake at 350°F for 1 hour (no need to preheat oven). Serve hot.

Spicy Corn and Sausage Skillet
Serves 2

Total Time: 30 minutes
Prep Time: 20 minutes   **Simmer Time:** 10 minutes

1 cup chicken broth (may be made from bouillon) or stock (page 164)
¼ cup cream, half-and-half (*media crema*), or evaporated milk (page 99)
¼ teaspoon garlic powder
½ teaspoon salt
2 teaspoons ground pepper, or less to taste
¼ teaspoon Tabasco sauce, or less to taste
½ pound sausage (spicy is better!)
3 teaspoons canola oil or vegetable oil
1 cup diced onion
2 cups corn off the cob OR 1 can (16 ounces) corn, drained

1. In a small bowl, mix the broth, cream, garlic, salt, pepper, and Tabasco. Set aside.
2. In a large skillet, sauté the sausage until just lightly brown. Remove the sausage from the pan and place on paper towels to drain. Leave the pan drippings in the skillet.
3. Add the oil to the drippings in the pan. Warm until hot over medium-high heat. Add the onion and corn and sauté about 7 minutes, or until the onion and corn are just turning golden. Reduce the heat and add the sausage and the broth mixture. Stir to mix, then cover and simmer for 10 minutes. Best served in bowls.

Sesame Pork Stir-Fry
Serves 4 to 6

Total Time: 30 minutes, plus time to cook rice or pasta
Prep Time: 15 minutes   **Cook Time:** 15 minutes

1 tablespoon sesame oil, canola oil, or vegetable oil
1 pound pork (tenderloin, steaks, chops, or other cut), cut into thin strips
2 tablespoons sesame seeds, toasted
2 tablespoons honey
3 tablespoons soy sauce
1/2 teaspoon ground ginger
2 cups assorted vegetables—onion strips, chopped bell pepper, carrot slices, mushrooms, bamboo shoots, chopped asparagus, broccoli florets, or whatever is available (drain any canned veggies)

Warm the oil in a skillet over high heat. Add the pork and cook until browned, then reduce the heat to medium. Add the sesame seeds, honey, soy sauce, and ginger and mix well. Add the veggies and cook for 2 to 4 minutes, stirring, until they are crisp-tender. Serve over rice or pasta, if desired.

Baked Pork Chops
Serves 4

Total Time: 45 minutes (depends on thickness of chops)
Prep Time: 10 minutes   **Bake Time:** 35 minutes

cooking spray or oil
1/4 cup butter, margarine, olive oil, canola oil, or vegetable oil
1 cup Italian bread crumbs OR plain bread crumbs plus 1 tablespoon Italian seasoning (page 48)
1/4 cup shredded or grated Parmesan cheese
1 tablespoon dried oregano
1 1/2 teaspoons dried sage
1 teaspoon dried rosemary
1 teaspoon ground pepper
1/8 teaspoon salt
4 pork chops (the timing is for 1-inch-thick chops; adjust for thicker or thinner)

1. Preheat oven to 375°F. Spray a baking dish or cookie sheet large enough to hold the chops in a single layer with cooking spray, or wipe with oil.
2. Melt the butter and keep in a pan or dish for dipping the chops. Combine the bread crumbs, Parmesan, and spices in a pie pan, or place on a plate for breading.
3. Dip the pork chops in the melted butter and turn so that all sides are coated. Then dip them in the bread-crumb mixture. Place them in a single layer on the prepared pan.
4. Bake for 35 minutes, or until the chops are golden brown and cooked through.

Pork Tenderloin
Serves 2 to 4

As its name implies, tenderloin is an extremely tender piece of meat. As such, the more simple the cooking—as here—the better, as the meat is the star.

Total Time: 5 hours, 15 minutes, including 4 hours or more to marinate
Prep Time: 15 minutes   **Cook Time:** 50 minutes

1 garlic clove, minced
1 teaspoon salt
1/2 teaspoon ground pepper
1/4 teaspoon dried thyme
1 pound pork tenderloin
1 tablespoon olive oil, canola oil, or vegetable oil

1. Mix the garlic, salt, pepper, and thyme in a small bowl. Rub the mixture over the tenderloin and wrap in plastic. Refrigerate for 4 hours or overnight to marinate.
2. Preheat oven to 350°F.
3. In a skillet over medium-high heat, brown the tenderloin in the olive oil for approximately 4 minutes on each side.
4. Remove the tenderloin and place it in a greased baking pan. Add 1/2 inch water, then cover with aluminum foil and bake for approximately 45 to 50 minutes. Let the meat sit for 5 minutes before slicing. Cut into slices about 3/4 inch thick.

Meat Main Dishes

Baked Ham

When buying a ham, be sure to think about whether there is room in your refrigerator for it—or have a dinner party for all the boats in the anchorage to minimize the leftovers. If your ham is too big for your galley oven or pan, you can cut it in half or thirds so that it will fit.

Ham should be placed in a baking pan (typically a 9"×13") with about 1½ cups of liquid, then covered with aluminum foil and baked at 325°F for the time specified in the table below. The best way to know if it's done is to use an instant-read thermometer. Just below the cooking chart are several options if you're in a particularly hot area and don't want to bake the ham for hours!

Ham should sit for 10 to 15 minutes after being taken out of the oven, during which time the internal temperature will continue to rise. Thus, it's important to take the temperature just as the ham is coming out of the oven, particularly with uncooked or partially cooked hams that need to be fully cooked to be safe to eat.

As the ham is baking, check it periodically to make sure that additional liquid is not needed. Lots of different liquids can be used, but if you like ham gravy (as I do), you may want to stick with just plain water so as not to end up with a sweet gravy. Common liquids used to provide moisture in the baking pan include:

- Water
- Coca-Cola (see page 363 for recipe)
- Half pineapple or orange juice and half water

Some people stud the ham with whole cloves (if all you have is ground cloves, just sprinkle it over the top). Others lay pineapple slices or other fruit over the ham.

When the ham is done, remove it from the oven and let it sit while you make the gravy (see page 222). Cut into slices about ⅜-inch thick.

TYPE OF HAM	TIME PER POUND	INTERNAL TEMPERATURE
Fully Cooked Ham		
Whole—Boneless or Bone-In	15 to 18 minutes	135°F
Half—Boneless or Bone-In	18 to 24 minutes	135°F
Canned Ham	15 to 20 minutes	135°F
Picnic Ham	25 to 30 minutes	135°F
Uncooked or Partially Cooked Ham		
Whole—Boneless or Bone-In	18 to 20 minutes	155°F
Half—Boneless or Bone-In	22 to 25 minutes	155°F
Picnic Ham	30 to 35 minutes	155°–165°F
Fresh Ham	25 to 30 minutes	155°F

Avoiding the Heat

Baking a ham takes several hours, and that can really heat up the boat. While it won't actually be "baked" ham, you can considerably lessen the heat in one of several ways:

Pressure Cooker. If—and it's a big "if"—your pressure cooker is large enough, you can cook the ham in it. If you have a rack, use it, but it will work without it. Add about 2 cups of water and cook for about one-third the time shown in the chart above, but be sure to check the internal temperature, particularly for a ham that is not fully cooked.

Skillet

- Method 1: Cut the ham into slices, generally ½ inch to 1 inch thick. Put them in a skillet and add ½ inch water. Cover the pan and bring the water to a boil, then simmer for 10 to 20 minutes, depending on the thickness of the slice, or until done.
- Method 2: With a fully cooked ham, cut the slices and then sauté each one in a skillet over medium-high heat until slightly browned on each side.

Don't Cook. If your ham is fully cooked (sometimes labeled "ready to eat"), it actually does not need to be cooked again. You *can* eat it cold!

Ham Loaf   Serves 10 to 12

This loaf will feed 10 to 12—or provide plenty of leftovers. But if you make a half batch, it will bake in about an hour and still feed 4 plus, with some leftovers!

Total Time: 2½ hours
Prep Time: 15 minutes   **Bake Time:** 2 hours
Finish-Up Time: 15 minutes

1 pound each ground pork, ground beef, and
   ground ham
2 eggs
1 teaspoon dry mustard OR 1 tablespoon prepared mustard
ground pepper, to taste
1 can (10 ounces) condensed tomato soup
   (page 55)
1 cup dry bread crumbs
½ cup water

Sauce
1 cup medium white sauce (page 207)
juice drained from ham loaf after baking

1. Mix all the ham loaf ingredients, using half the can of soup. Reserve the remainder of the soup for the sauce.
2. Place the ham loaf in a loaf pan, cover with aluminum foil, and bake at 350°F for about 1¾ hours (no need to preheat oven).
3. About 5 minutes before the end of the bake time, make the white sauce and add the remaining tomato soup to it.
4. Remove the ham loaf from the oven. Here's the slightly tricky part: hold the ham loaf in the pan and tip the pan to drain the "juice" into the sauce mix. You have to be careful so that the ham loaf doesn't fall out of the pan in chunks. I usually use a spatula against the foil that covered the pan. If you have a flat grater that just fits the size of the pan, it also works well to hold it against the ham loaf while the juices run out. Return the ham loaf to the oven and cook for about 15 minutes more, or until done.
5. While the ham loaf is finishing baking, stir the juice into the sauce. If the sauce has cooled somewhat, warm it over low heat (it does not need to boil).

6. To serve, cut the ham loaf into slices. Top each slice with a dollop of sauce.

Ham and Veggie Pasta   Serves 2

Friends don't realize that I keep serving variations on the same recipe!

Total Time: 30 minutes

2 servings pasta (any medium-size or long pasta)
2 tablespoons olive oil, canola oil, or vegetable oil
4 to 6 ounces ham, cut into ¼-inch-wide strips
   about 2 inches long, OR 1 can (6 ounces) ham,
   broken into chunks
1 can (8 ounces) mushrooms, drained (use liquid
   as part of the pasta water)
4 green onions, cut into ¼-inch slices, OR ½ cup
   diced onion
½ green bell pepper, diced
10 black olives, cut in half
½ teaspoon Italian seasoning (page 48) OR
   ¼ teaspoon Old Bay Seasoning (page 48) OR
   ½ teaspoon Montreal steak seasoning (page
   219), OR ½ teaspoon garlic powder OR seasonings of your choice

1. Cook the pasta while preparing the ham and veggies; drain the pasta and set aside.
2. Heat the oil in a skillet over medium-high heat. Add the ham, mushrooms, and green onion and cook until lightly browned. Add the pasta, bell pepper, olives, and seasonings and toss to mix. Cook until just heated through (the bell pepper should be tender but still crisp).

Variations:
• Add a can of artichoke hearts, drained, when browning the ham.
• Add a can of diced tomato with the bell pepper.
• Add ¼ cup sun-dried tomatoes in olive oil with the bell pepper.
• Garnish with any sort of grated cheese.

Meat Main Dishes

Macaroni and Cheese with Ham   Serves 4

Total Time: 50 minutes
Prep Time: 30 minutes   Bake Time: 20 minutes

8 ounces macaroni or other medium-size pasta
4 tablespoons butter
4 tablespoons flour
$1/2$ teaspoon salt
ground pepper, to taste
2 cups evaporated milk (page 99), half-and-half (*media crema*), or milk
2 cups shredded cheddar or other cheese that will melt
8 ounces ham, diced (canned works well), OR 8 slices crisply cooked bacon
$1/2$ cup dry bread crumbs or cracker crumbs

1. Preheat oven to 400°F.
2. Cook the macaroni according to package directions; drain and set aside.
3. While the macaroni is cooking, melt the butter in a saucepan over low heat. Add the flour, salt, and ground pepper and mix into a paste. Still over low heat, very slowly add the evaporated milk, stirring constantly so there are no lumps. Continuing to constantly stir, raise the heat to medium and bring the mixture to a boil; boil for about 2 minutes, or until thick.
4. Reduce the heat to simmer and cook for 10 minutes, still stirring very frequently. Add the cheese little by little and simmer just until the cheese melts.
5. Add the pasta and ham and toss to coat with the cheese sauce.
6. Pour the mixture into a greased baking dish and sprinkle with the bread crumbs. Bake, uncovered, about 20 minutes, or until the top is golden.

Ham and Potato Casserole   Serves 4

Delicious either as a casserole or in a skillet on the stove top.

Total Time: 1 hour
Prep Time: 30 minutes   Bake Time: 30 minutes

1 cup cubed ($3/4$ inch) potato
$1/2$ cup chopped onion
2 tablespoons butter, margarine, canola oil, or vegetable oil
3 tablespoons flour
$1/8$ teaspoon salt
$1/8$ teaspoon ground pepper
$1^1/4$ cups milk
$1/2$ cup shredded Swiss or other cheese
2 cups cubed cooked ham OR 2 cans (6 ounces each) ham, broken up
1 cup soft bread crumbs (if you're baking this as a casserole)

1. Preheat oven to 400°F if baking as a casserole.
2. In a saucepan, cover the potato with water; cover the pan and bring to a boil. Reduce the heat to simmer and cook the potato until done, or about 5 to 7 minutes. Drain and set aside.
3. While the potato is cooking, cook the onion in the butter in a skillet over medium heat until the onion is glazed. Mix in the flour, salt, and pepper. Add the milk very slowly, stirring continuously so that lumps do not form. Cook until thick, then remove from the heat.
4. Add the Swiss cheese to the onion mixture and stir until the cheese melts and is totally incorporated. Add the ham and reserved potato and mix together gently so the potato doesn't break apart.
5. At this point, you can return the mixture in the skillet to the stove over low heat, and cook the ham and potato until just heated through. With this method, you don't use the bread crumbs. Or you can pour the mixture into a casserole and top with the bread crumbs; bake, uncovered, for 30 minutes, or until the bread crumbs are golden and the mixture is bubbling.

Ham Carbonara   Serves 4

If you're ever trying to come up with something appetizing to do with that can of Spam, no one will guess if you dice it up and substitute it for the ham in this dish!

Total Time: 30 minutes

4 servings pasta—angel hair is traditional, but any long or medium-size will work
1 medium onion, thinly sliced
1/3 cup olive oil, canola oil, or vegetable oil
1 cup cubed cooked ham (canned ham also works well)
1/2 cup chicken broth (may be made from bouillon) or stock (page 164)
1/4 cup butter, margarine, or oil
2 egg yolks, beaten
1/2 cup chopped fresh parsley (optional)
1/2 cup grated Parmesan or other hard cheese

1. Cook the pasta while preparing the rest of the dish; drain and set aside.
2. In a skillet over medium heat, cook the onion in the oil until it is just golden—more carmelized than browned. Add the ham, broth, and butter and heat through, stirring occasionally. Add the drained pasta to the ham mixture and toss to mix.
3. Add the egg yolks and quickly stir/toss, continuing to toss as the egg yolks set up. Don't let them set up totally.
4. Remove from the heat and sprinkle with the parsley and Parmesan cheese; toss to coat.

Variations: Add some minced garlic or garlic powder when cooking the onion. Many people like to add mushrooms and/or peas.

Asian Pork Tenderloin   Serves 6

Total Time: 9 hours, including minimum 8 hours to marinate
Prep Time: 30 minutes   **Bake Time:** 30 minutes

1/3 cup soy sauce
1/4 cup sesame oil
1/3 cup packed brown sugar
2 tablespoons Worcestershire sauce
2 tablespoons lemon juice, lime juice, or white vinegar
4 cloves garlic, crushed, OR 4 teaspoons minced garlic OR 1/2 teaspoon garlic powder
1 tablespoon dry mustard OR 3 tablespoons prepared mustard
1 1/2 teaspoons ground pepper
1 1/2 to 2 pounds pork tenderloin

1. Mix together the soy sauce, sesame oil, brown sugar, Worcestershire, lemon juice, garlic, mustard, and ground pepper.
2. Place the pork in a freezer plastic bag and add the soy sauce mixture marinade, turning the pork to coat with the marinade. Refrigerate for 8 hours.
3. Remove the pork from the marinade. Discard the marinade; it is not safe to reuse.
4. You can bake or grill the tenderloin. To bake, place the pork in a baking pan. Bake at 450°F for 25 minutes, or until a meat thermometer reads 160°F. To grill, place the tenderloin on the grill and cook for approximately 20 minutes, turning every 5 minutes, or until a meat thermometer reads 160°F.
5. Let the tenderloin stand for 5 minutes before slicing and serving.

Bacon and Tomato Pasta Florentine   Serves 2

Total Time: 30 minutes

2 servings pasta—rotini, penne, bow ties, linguine, spaghetti, or other pasta
6 slices bacon
1/2 cup diced onion OR 4 green onions, sliced 1/4 inch thick
1 can (8 ounces) mushrooms, drained (use liquid to cook the pasta)
1 can (16 ounces) diced tomatoes, not drained
1/4 teaspoon ground pepper
1 can (16 ounces) spinach, drained, OR 2 servings fresh or frozen spinach
pine nuts, for garnish (optional)

1. Cook the pasta according to package directions while preparing the bacon mixture. When the pasta is done, drain and set aside until needed.
2. Cut the bacon into 1-inch pieces and cook in a skillet until crisp. Remove the bacon from the pan (you can put it in the same pan as the cooked pasta). Leave about 3 tablespoons bacon fat in the pan, but discard any more than that.
3. Add the onion and mushrooms to the skillet and sauté over medium-high heat until golden. Add the tomato and ground pepper and cook until the liquid has reduced by half, stirring often.
4. Add the spinach, pasta, and bacon. Toss to mix. Cook just until heated through.
5. Sprinkle with the pine nuts and serve hot.

Pasta with Chorizo and Mushrooms
Serves 4

Total Time: 1 hour
Prep Time: 30 minutes

2 tablespoons olive oil, canola oil, or vegetable oil
6 green onions, including tops, sliced ¼-inch thick, OR ½ cup diced onion
2 cloves garlic, minced, OR 2 teaspoons minced garlic OR ¼ teaspoon garlic powder
½ pound mushrooms, sliced or not as you prefer, OR 2 cans (8 ounces each) mushrooms, drained
2 teaspoons paprika
½ teaspoon salt
dash of cayenne
3 medium tomatoes, diced, OR 1 can (16 ounces) diced tomatoes, not drained
1 green bell pepper (or any color pepper), diced
3 cups chicken broth (may be made from bouillon) or stock (page 164)
½ cup white wine
½ cup cream, half-and-half (*media crema*), or evaporated milk (page 99)
1 pound chorizo or other sausage, sliced ½ inch thick
1 pound uncooked angel hair pasta, spaghetti, linguine, or other pasta

1. Heat the oil in a skillet over medium-high heat. Add the green onion, garlic, mushrooms, paprika,

salt, and cayenne and cook until tender but not browned, stirring occasionally. Add the tomato, bell pepper, broth, wine, cream, and sausage. Stir to mix. Let the mixture come to a boil, then add the pasta. If using long pasta, break it in half as you add it. When the mixture boils again, turn heat down to simmer and cook, uncovered, until the pasta is done.
2. To finish in a skillet, cook for 10 to 15 minutes longer, letting some of the liquid boil away, until the sauce is thick.
3. To finish in the oven, pour the mixture into a baking pan and bake at 400°F (no preheating required) until the top is crisp, or about 15 to 20 minutes.

Chorizo Pasta
Serves 2

Total Time: 35 minutes
Prep Time: 10 minutes   Cook Time: 15 minutes

2 servings pasta
1 tablespoon olive oil, canola oil, or vegetable oil
¼ cup finely chopped red onion or any onion
½ teaspoon dried chili pepper flakes, or to taste
2 uncooked chorizo sausages, cut into bite-size pieces
2 ounces tomato paste (about ⅓ of a small can)
1 tomato, diced
¾ cup red wine
2 cloves garlic, minced, OR 2 teaspoons minced garlic OR ¼ teaspoon garlic powder
salt and pepper, to taste
fresh basil, for garnish (optional)

1. Cook the pasta according to package directions while preparing the sauce. Drain and set aside until the sauce is ready.
2. Heat the oil over medium-high heat. Add the onion, chili pepper flakes, and chorizo and cook until golden brown. Drain any excess fat.
3. Add the tomato paste, tomato, wine, and garlic and stir to mix. Bring to a boil, then reduce the heat and simmer for 15 minutes. Season to taste with salt and pepper.
4. Stir the pasta into the sausage mixture. If desired, garnish each serving with fresh basil.

Basil Bacon Cream Pasta · Serves 2

Total Time: 40 minutes
Prep Time: 15 minutes · Cook Time: 25 minutes

2 servings pasta (any type except very tiny)
4 slices bacon
1 clove garlic, very finely minced, OR $\frac{1}{8}$ teaspoon garlic powder
1 tablespoon cornstarch OR 2 tablespoons flour
1 tablespoon water
$1\frac{1}{2}$ cups cream, half-and-half (*media crema*), or evaporated milk (not as good; page 99)
2 teaspoons prepared mustard
$\frac{1}{4}$ cup shredded or grated Parmesan or other mild cheese
$\frac{1}{2}$ cup dry white wine
$\frac{1}{2}$ cup finely chopped fresh basil
4 green onions, chopped

1. While preparing the sauce, cook the pasta according to package directions.
2. Fry the bacon in a skillet until crisp, adding the garlic when there is sufficient bacon fat.
3. As the bacon is cooking, mix the cornstarch and water together in a small bowl. Add the cream, mustard, Parmesan, and wine. Set aside.
4. When the bacon is done, remove it and place it on a paper towel to drain. Pour off the excess fat from the pan, but leave a light coating. Add the cream mixture and warm it over medium heat, stirring constantly until the mixture boils. Turn the heat down to simmer and cook until the mixture is thick, carefully watching that it doesn't scorch.
5. Crumble the bacon into the sauce, then add the basil and green onion. Toss the pasta with the sauce. Serve hot.

Southwestern Frittata · Serves 2

Make a meatless version by omitting the bacon and using a little oil to cook the veggies.

Total Time: 15 minutes

3 strips bacon OR 4 ounces ham, diced (canned works well)
$\frac{1}{4}$ cup diced onion
$\frac{1}{4}$ green bell pepper, diced
minced hot chile pepper, to taste (omit if you don't want it too spicy)
1 clove garlic, minced, OR $\frac{1}{8}$ teaspoon garlic powder
6 eggs
$\frac{1}{2}$ cup milk
hot sauce, to taste
salt and pepper, to taste
1 tomato, diced
$\frac{1}{2}$ cup grated or shredded cheese (any kind)

1. Fry the bacon in a skillet until crisp. Remove and drain on a paper towel. Leave a thin film of bacon fat in the pan.
2. While the bacon is cooking, dice the onion, bell pepper, chile pepper, and garlic. Add to the bacon fat in the pan and cook over medium heat until the veggies are soft but not browned.
3. Beat the eggs with the milk, hot sauce, salt, and pepper. Add the egg mixture to the veggies in the pan. Crumble the bacon into the pan and mix slightly. Let the eggs cook until set on the bottom, then add the tomato and cheese. Drag a spatula through the eggs to mix. If needed, flip the eggs with the spatula so that the eggs will cook through.
4. Carefully lift the frittata out of the pan in two sections and place each on a plate to serve.

Hot Dogs and Variations

Hot dogs might be thought of as something primarily to throw on the grill or cook over a campfire. But if the weather is bad, you can cook them in a skillet, boil them, broil them, or microwave them for 30 seconds to 1 minute (be sure to poke them to let steam out).

Serving ideas:

- **Chili dogs:** Pour about $\frac{1}{4}$ cup chili (page 169) over each hot dog in its bun.
- **Bacon wraps:** Before cooking, wrap each hot dog in bacon, forming a spiral. Best cooked on the grill (watch for flare-ups from the fat), in a skillet, or broiled.
- **Sauerkraut:** Heat sauerkraut and serve over the hot dog in the bun.

Meat Main Dishes

- **Onion:** Cut onions in slices and cook slowly in a bit of butter or oil in a skillet until the onion is soft and glazed, not browned. Place under or over the hot dog.

Ribs in the Oven   Serves any number

The secret to falling-off-the-bone tenderness is long, slow cooking.

Total Time: 3½ to 4 hours

**½ to 1 full-slab baby back ribs per person
enough BBQ sauce to cover ribs (page 215)**

1. Preheat oven to 275°F.
2. Place the ribs in a baking pan and add about ½ inch water to the pan. Cover with aluminum foil and bake for 3 hours, or until the ribs are tender. Check occasionally to make sure there is still water in the pan or the ribs will be dry. Don't proceed with the next step until the ribs are tender, even if it means cooking them longer and delaying the meal!
3. Drain the water from the pan and arrange the ribs in a single layer if possible (you may need to use a cookie sheet). Cover with the BBQ sauce. Turn the oven up to 325°F and bake about 30 minutes more, adding more BBQ sauce if desired halfway through. Serve with plenty of napkins!

GOAT AND LAMB

In the US, goat is rarely eaten. When I was a child, my mom would serve lamb as an occasional "treat," but now lamb seems to be seen less and less in US supermarkets.

   In some other countries, however, goat and lamb are seen much more frequently than beef and sometimes more often than pork and chicken. I've eaten both while traveling. Neither one of us has much experience with either of these meats, yet we feel it's important to include a few recipes so that if these are the only meats you can get, you have an idea of what to do with it. Recipes come from family and friends.

Lamb/Mutton

Lamb is most tender when less than a year old; older than that and it's called "mutton" and really needs to be cooked by a long, slow moist-heat method, such as stewing or cooking as for a pot roast. Mutton can also be ground or finely diced and used as you would ground beef in virtually any recipe, although you may want to change the spices. In addition to the recipes here, lamb and mutton can be substituted for beef and chicken in many of the recipes in those sections. Traditional spices with lamb include rosemary, thyme, ground pepper, and occasionally oregano. Stews and long-cooking soups are particularly suited for mutton; lamb is good in kebobs.

   Lamb and mutton are covered by a whitish membrane called "fell." Most people prefer to remove this before cooking, as it has a strong flavor.

Goat

Many (most?) cruisers have not come across goat meat until they're in a developing country, but the reality is that in many of the areas that cruisers frequent, goats provide the main source of meat for the local population. Usually, you'll get goat meat from a backyard butcher. And no, there won't be any food safety inspectors. If you buy from the same person as all the locals, you're not likely to have problems—the locals don't want a food-borne illness any more than you do, and won't patronize someone who improperly butchers meat. But just to be on the safe side, be sure to thoroughly cook it!

   Goat, even when young, tends to be tough. Quite tough. It's often barbecued on a spit, and frankly most Americans don't like it as it tends to be dry as well as tough. If you cook goat for quite a long time with liquid, it will be moist and tender. Consider stewing to be the only good way to cook goat. Even stewed, young goat has a much more agreeable flavor than older goat; meat of male goats is extremely strong tasting, and most people not used to it from birth find it totally inedible.

Goat and Lamb Food Safety

In addition to the general meat safety tips on page 255, the USDA gives these tips for goat and lamb (edited to make recommendations applicable to cruisers):

- Fresh goat or lamb should be stored at or below 40°F. Put fresh or frozen lamb or goat in a cooler with ice to transport it to the boat if it will take longer than 10 minutes, or any time the temperature is over 100°F.
- Most cuts of goat and lamb should be used within 3 to 5 days or else frozen. Ground lamb (and presumably goat, were it ever found that way) should be used within 1 to 2 days. If kept continuously frozen, any meat will last indefinitely.
- Ground meat is most susceptible to bacteria, as far more surface is exposed both to the air and to the meat grinder. It is really important to cook it thoroughly! The USDA recommends using an instant-read thermometer for anything made with ground lamb and also "small cuts" such as kebobs, and making sure the center of the meat reaches 160°F.
- Large "muscle" cuts like chops are less likely to be contaminated as they have been exposed to air and cutting boards only on their "outside" surfaces, and these are what cook the hottest. Consequently, chops may be eaten medium rare with an internal temperature of 145°F . Unless you are 100 percent confident of how the meat has been handled, no meat should be eaten rare.

Greek Gyros

Makes 12 gyros

While lamb is the traditional meat for this dish, beef and chicken also work well. And while pitas can be hard to find, flour tortillas substitute well.

Total Time: 2½ to 4½ hours, including marinating time (*tzatziki* can be made in the same time, unless yogurt needs to be made)

Prep Time: 20 minutes for marinade, another 10 minutes to dice tomatoes

Cook Time: Depends on the method, but about 10 minutes

⅓ cup olive oil, canola oil, or vegetable oil
½ cup lemon juice, lime juice, or white vinegar
2 cloves garlic, minced, OR 2 teaspoons minced garlic OR ¼ teaspoon garlic powder
¼ teaspoon ground thyme
½ teaspoon ground oregano or Italian seasoning (page 48)
ground pepper, to taste
2 pounds boneless lamb, beef, or chicken, cut into 1-inch cubes
2 onions, cut into thinly sliced rings
12 pita breads or flour tortillas
3 tomatoes, diced
approximately 2 cups *tzatziki* sauce (page 136)

1. Mix together the olive oil, lemon juice, garlic, thyme, oregano, and ground pepper for a marinade. Separately marinate the meat and the onions, using about ⅔ of the marinade for the meat and the remainder for the onions. Marinate both for 2 to 4 hours in the refrigerator.

   Alternate Method for Onions: Don't marinate the onions, but cut the slices into quarters to be used raw.

2. Heat a skillet over medium-high heat. Drain and discard the marinade from the meat and onions. Sauté the lamb in the skillet, adding the onions about 5 minutes after the lamb. The exact cooking time will depend on how large the chunks of meat are, but the meat should be browned on the outside but still pinkish on the inside.

   Alternate Method for Cooking the Lamb: Place the lamb on kebob skewers and grill it. Use the onion raw, as above.

3. While the lamb is cooking, heat the pita bread until it is soft.

4. To serve, place a portion of the meat down the center of a pita and top with the tomato, raw onion, and *tzatziki*. Fold the sides over and secure with a toothpick.

   Alternate Method for Serving: Cut the pitas in half and open the pocket carefully to avoid tearing holes. Stuff with the meat, onion, tomato, and *tzatziki*.

Meat Main Dishes

Goat Stew
Serves 6

Total Time: 3+ hours, with on and off attention
needed

2 pounds boneless goat meat
1/2 cup white vinegar
1 teaspoon salt
1/4 cup olive oil, canola oil, or vegetable oil
5 cloves garlic, minced, OR 4 teaspoons minced
    garlic OR 1/2 teaspoon garlic powder
1 medium onion, diced
2 cups water
1/2 stick cinnamon OR 1/8 teaspoon ground
    cinnamon
3 bay leaves
1 tablespoon whole black peppercorns (optional)
ground pepper, to taste
4 teaspoons tomato paste
carrots, turnips, and celery (optional)
4 medium potatoes
1 bell pepper, cut into strips

1. Cut the meat into 1 1/2-inch cubes. Place in a bowl
   or plastic bag with the vinegar and salt. Let sit for
   about 45 minutes. (This is important to help tenderize the meat.) Drain the marinade from the
   meat, saving about half of it.
2. Heat the oil over medium-high heat and add the
   meat to brown it. When the meat is about halfway
   browned, add the garlic and onion and allow them
   to brown with the meat.
3. Add the reserved marinade, water, cinnamon
   stick, bay leaves, peppercorns, ground pepper, and
   tomato paste. Cover and bring to a boil, then lower
   the heat to simmer and cook until the meat can
   be pierced by a fork but is not yet fully tender, or
   about 1 hour and 20 minutes (but this can vary).
4. Prepare the carrots, turnips, celery, and potatoes, if
   desired, and cut them into large chunks. Add them
   to the pot; if needed, add more water. Cover, bring
   to a boil, and then turn down the heat to a simmer and cook for 30 minutes, or until the veggies
   and the meat are tender. If not, cook until they are
   before proceeding.

5. Add the bell pepper and cook for 5 to 7 minutes, so
   that it is still crisp.
6. Remove the cinnamon stick and bay leaves. Serve
   the stew in bowls.

Lamb Stew
Serves 4

Total Time: 2 1/2 hours
Prep Time: 30 minutes

1/4 cup flour
1/2 teaspoon ground pepper
1 pound boneless lamb stew meat, cut into 1-inch
    cubes
2 teaspoons olive oil, canola oil, or vegetable oil
1 medium onion, sliced thin
1/2 teaspoon ground thyme
1 teaspoon crushed rosemary
2 cups water
1 pound carrots, cut into 1-inch chunks, or whole
    baby carrots
2 cups diced potato
1 cup peas
1/2 teaspoon salt

1. Place the flour and ground pepper in a plastic bag,
   then add the lamb cubes and shake to coat.
2. Heat the oil in a skillet or Dutch oven over medium-
   high heat until a drop of water sizzles. Add the
   lamb and onion and cook until browned. Add
   the thyme, rosemary, and water. Bring to a boil,
   then turn down the heat to a simmer. Cook about
   1 1/2 hours, or until the meat is starting to get tender
   (it will cook another half hour, so you don't want
   it to be falling apart). Add the carrot, potato, peas,
   and salt. Cook for 30 minutes, or until the vegetables and meat are tender.

Broiled Lamb Chops
Serves any number

Special Equipment: A broiler is needed for this, or else
grill it for about the same time.

Total Time: 10 minutes

cooking spray or oil
1 lamb chop per person, about 1 inch thick (adjust
    broiling time if thicker or thinner)

1. Move the oven rack to about 4 inches from the broiler, and preheat broiler.
2. Spray the broiler pan with cooking spray, or brush with a little oil. Place the chops on the pan. Place it under the broiler for 5 minutes; then turn the chops over (remove the pan from the broiler to do so) and broil another 3 to 5 minutes. Be careful not to overcook—dry lamb is awful!

Marinated Lamb Chops   Serves 4

Total Time: 3 hours, 15 minutes, including 3 hours to marinate
Prep Time: 5 minutes

2 tablespoons soy sauce
1 tablespoon red wine vinegar or balsamic vinegar
2 tablespoons Worcestershire sauce
1 teaspoon dried oregano OR 1½ teaspoons Italian seasoning and omit the basil
½ teaspoon dried basil
½ teaspoon ground ginger
⅛ teaspoon garlic powder
⅛ teaspoon ground pepper
cooking spray
4 lamb chops, about 1 inch thick

1. Mix together the soy sauce, vinegar, Worcestershire, oregano, basil, ginger, garlic, and ground pepper in a plastic bag or leakproof lidded plastic bowl. Add the lamb chops and refrigerate for 3 hours, shaking occasionally.
2. Move the oven rack to about 4 inches from the broiler, and preheat broiler. Spritz with cooking spray. Place the chops on the greased broiler pan. Discard the marinade.
3. Place the pan under the broiler for 5 minutes; then turn the chops over (remove the pan from the broiler to do so) and broil another 3 to 5 minutes. Be careful not to overcook—dry lamb is awful!

NOTE: The chops may instead be grilled for about 4 minutes per side.

Lamb Meatballs with Curry-Tomato Sauce   Serves 2

Total Time: 45 minutes (cook rice at same time if desired)

½ pound ground lamb or any other ground meat
¼ cup dry bread crumbs
1 egg
½ teaspoon salt
½ teaspoon garam masala OR cumin
1 tablespoon olive oil, canola oil, or vegetable oil
¼ cup chopped onion
1 clove garlic, crushed or minced, OR ⅛ teaspoon garlic powder
½ cup very finely diced tomato or tomato puree
½ teaspoon curry powder, or to taste (page 47)
¼ teaspoon cayenne pepper, or to taste (some cayenne can be very spicy)
2 teaspoons sugar
1 tablespoon flour
1¼ cups chicken broth (may be made from bouillon) or stock (page 164)
½ cup half-and-half (*media crema*), evaporated milk (page 99), or milk

1. Make the meatballs by mixing the lamb, bread crumbs, egg, salt, and garam masala. Form the mixture into 1-inch balls.
2. Heat the oil in a skillet over medium-high heat until a drop of water sizzles. Add the meatballs and brown them, turning occasionally.
3. Remove the meatballs from the pan and set aside, but leave the drippings in the pan. Reduce the heat to medium; add the onion and cook until softened but not really browned.
4. When the onion is soft, add the garlic and cook for just 30 seconds or so. Add the tomato, curry powder, cayenne, and sugar. Mix and cook for a minute or two.
5. While the sauce cooks, mix the flour with an equal amount of broth in a cup to form a smooth paste. Add more broth, little by little, until you've added about ¼ cup (no need to be exact). Set aside.
6. Add the remaining broth to the skillet and stir it in. Bring to a boil, then turn the heat down to a simmer and let cook for 5 minutes.

Meat Main Dishes

7. Add the half-and-half and mix well. Then slowly add the flour mixture, stirring constantly so that lumps don't form. Bring it to a boil and cook a few minutes, or until the sauce thickens.

8. Lower the heat to a simmer and add the meatballs; cook just until heated through. Traditionally, this is served over rice.

ADDITIONAL MEAT MAIN DISHES

There are many "meat" dishes in other chapters that work well as a main dish:

Soups and Stews
Chili, *page 169*
Campfire Stew Casserole, *page 170*
Main Dish Minestrone, *page 172*
Taco Soup, *page 172*

Beans, Rice, and Pasta
Beef and Beans, *page 177*
Ham and Beans, *page 179*
Red Beans and Rice, *page 180*
White Chicken Chili, *page 180*
Southwestern Chicken, Beans, and Rice *page 181*
Jambalaya, *page 184*
Spanish Rice, *page 184*
Rice and Beans, *page 185*
Shipwreck Stew, *page 186*
Grandma's Homemade Beef 'n' Noodles, *page 188*

Canned Meats and Seafood
Almost all recipes in the chapter "Canned Meats and Seafood" can be made with fresh meat.

Grilling
Any of the meat recipes in the "Grilling" chapter; many can also be broiled, baked, or cooked on the stove top.

CANNED MEATS
AND SEAFOOD

Canned meats are great for cruising for several reasons. "Fresh" meat may look or smell suspect, or you may not have much (or any) refrigerator and freezer space. The good news is that it seems that the smaller and more remote the village, the greater the chance of finding a wide variety of canned meats. This is particularly true in fishing villages where few homes have electricity.

I buy most meats in 6-ounce cans that look like tuna cans—they're just right for one meal for two people. There's ham, chicken, turkey, tuna, crab, shrimp, corned beef, roast beef, corned beef hash, clams, salmon, oysters, and even chili—and we've had all of them at one time or another in the US, Mexico, and Central America. The recipes that follow are divided by the type of meat most often used, but many have several choices.

CANNED MEATS AND SEAFOOD BASICS

It's not hard to prepare great meals from canned meats. Through the years, I've learned a few tips to ensure good results:

- Add the meat as late in the cooking process as possible. It's already cooked, so all you have to do is warm it up.
- Once you've added the meat, stir as little as possible so it won't turn to mush. This is particularly true of chicken, turkey, and beef, and is one reason these meats shouldn't be added until the very

end of the cooking time, and can be just warmed through.
- Ham is the only meat that you need to "crumble" or break apart as you add it to the other ingredients. All other meats should be handled very gently.
- Don't overcook other ingredients to the point where they lose their texture and become a "blob" with the meat.
- Add one-half to one bouillon cube of an appropriate flavor to make up for the fact that you don't have drippings from browning the meat. The bouillon cube replaces salt in most recipes.
- Drain the liquid from the can and use it in the cooking process (ditto for any canned vegetables you use). It will add a lot more flavor than plain water.
- Some casseroles work well with canned meats; others don't. In general, ones using firmer meats such as ham and roast beef turn out the best.

You can create really good meals from canned meats, so there's no need to think of them as emergency rations. There are more than 70 great recipes designed just for canned meats in this chapter.

Once you're familiar with the techniques for using canned meats, you'll see that they can be used in lots of other dishes, including family favorites. And many of the recipes in this chapter can also be made with fresh meat; just adjust the cooking technique.

TUNA

Canned tuna is available everywhere. It's inexpensive, stores well, and lasts forever. Unfortunately most cruisers (like both of us) get stuck in a rut with recipes and think only of tuna salad or tuna noodle casserole as possibilities for the endless cans of tuna.

Over the years, however, we've discovered lots of tasty, easy recipes using tuna and commonly available ingredients that you probably already have aboard. We include more than 20 such recipes, and many of these dishes can be served in numerous ways. For example, any of the various "tuna salads" are good stuffed in tomatoes or served on a lettuce bed or on crackers as an appetizer. With all the variety, you shouldn't find yourself getting sick of tuna!

A word of warning. Outside the US and Canada, not everything that looks like tuna, in tuna-style cans, is really tuna! Read the label and ingredients carefully—in Spanish, tuna is *atún*. There are numerous other types of canned fish, such as mackerel (*jurel* in Spanish), which most Americans don't really like. Many times, if you ask the locals, they'll tell you that the fish in question IS tuna in the can when it is definitely not. Buyer beware!

Tasty Tuna Burgers   Serves 4

Try serving this with lettuce and a touch of horseradish or wasabi in mayonnaise.

Total Time: 15 minutes
Prep Time: 5 minutes   **Cook Time:** 10 minutes

12 ounces tuna, drained
2 eggs, beaten
$\frac{1}{2}$ carrot, grated
$\frac{1}{4}$ cup Italian seasoned bread crumbs (see page 51 for bread crumbs and add $\frac{1}{2}$ teaspoon Italian seasoning)
1 green onion, finely sliced
2 tablespoons chopped fresh parsley
dash of cayenne pepper
olive oil, canola oil, or vegetable oil
4 burger buns

1. Mix the tuna, eggs, carrot, bread crumbs, onion, parsley, and cayenne. Shape into 4 patties.

2. Heat the oil in a skillet over medium-high heat. Cook the patties for 5 minutes on each side, or until just lightly browned. Be careful when you turn them as they can easily fall apart. (For this reason, it's hard to grill them.) Serve each on a bun.

Middle Eastern Tuna Salad Pitas   Serves 4

If you're really pressed for time, you can eat these without the chill time.

Total Time: 1 hour, 15 minutes, including 1 hour chill time
Prep Time: 15 minutes

1 cup hummus (page 131)
12 ounces tuna, drained
$\frac{1}{4}$ cup mayonnaise (Miracle Whip can be used, but it is not nearly as satisfactory)
2 teaspoons sesame oil
$\frac{1}{4}$ cup finely chopped green onion
$1\frac{1}{2}$ teaspoons ground cumin
dash of cayenne pepper
salt, to taste
4 whole wheat or regular pita breads, cut in half for pockets
8 leaves lettuce
4 small tomatoes, thinly sliced

1. Combine the hummus, tuna, mayonnaise, sesame oil, green onion, cumin, cayenne, and salt. Taste; add more salt and cayenne if you want it spicier. Cover and refrigerate 1 hour to overnight.
2. Line each pita pocket with lettuce leaves and tomato slices. Scoop the tuna mixture into each pocket and serve.

Classic Tuna Salad   Serves 4

Jan and I have a slight disagreement on this recipe. I say that "classic" tuna salad has sweet pickle relish; she says it has dill pickle relish. Take your pick—or use whatever is available!

Total Time: 5 minutes
Prep Time: 5 minutes

12 ounces tuna, drained
$\frac{1}{2}$ stalk celery, diced
2 tablespoons pickle relish (sweet or dill) OR
    1 pickle, finely diced
1 teaspoon pickle juice
3 to 4 tablespoons mayonnaise or Miracle Whip
1 small onion, finely diced, OR 2 or 3 green
    onions, finely sliced
salt and pepper, to taste

Mix all the ingredients together. Serve as a sandwich with a slice of cheese and tomato or as a salad in a bowl with fresh sliced tomatoes surrounding the mound of tuna salad.

Tuna Melt
Serves 4

Total Time: 15 minutes
Prep Time: 10 minutes   **Cook Time:** 5 minutes

12 ounces tuna, drained
$\frac{1}{2}$ cup mayonnaise or Miracle Whip
2 tablespoons lemon juice, lime juice, or *limón*
    (Key lime) juice
1 stalk celery, finely diced
2 green onions, finely sliced, OR $\frac{1}{4}$ cup diced
    onion
1 tablespoon chopped fresh parsley
seasoned salt or Mrs. Dash (page 48), to taste
ground pepper, to taste
4 slices pumpernickel, rye, or any other bread
8 slices Swiss, mozzarella, or any white cheese that
    melts
4 slices tomato

1. Mix the tuna, mayonnaise, lemon juice, celery, green onion, and parsley. Add the seasoned salt and ground pepper.
2. Place the bread on a baking sheet and broil about 1 minute, or until lightly toasted. The exact time depends on your broiler. Remove from the heat.
3. Spread the tuna mixture on a bread slice. Place one slice of cheese and one slice of tomato on each slice of bread. Top the tomato with another slice of cheese. Broil for about 3 minutes, or until the cheese is melted. If you don't have a broiler in

your oven, you can bake the sandwiches at 350°F until the cheese melts, but remember to toast the bread first!

Tangy Tuna Salad Sandwich
Serves 2

Total Time: 15 minutes

6 ounces tuna, drained
1 tablespoon finely chopped red onion or any
    onion
1 tablespoon chopped fresh parsley
$\frac{1}{3}$ cup mayonnaise or Miracle Whip
1 teaspoon horseradish OR $\frac{1}{2}$ teaspoon wasabi
    paste (more if you like it spicier)
4 slices bread
4 leaves lettuce
4 thin slices tomato

Mix the tuna with the onion, parsley, mayonnaise, and horseradish. Spread on a slice of bread; add the lettuce leaves and tomato, and top with another slice of bread.

Tuna and Sweet Potato Patties
Serves 4

Total Time: 25 minutes
Prep Time: 15 minutes   **Cook Time:** 10 minutes

1 medium sweet potato, peeled and diced
12 ounces tuna, drained
2 eggs, beaten
2 tablespoons bread crumbs (page 51)
1 to 2 tablespoons chopped fresh parsley
salt and pepper, to taste
1 tablespoon olive oil, canola oil, or vegetable oil

1. Steam the sweet potato until tender. Drain. Place in a large bowl and mash with a potato masher. Add the tuna, egg, bread crumbs, and parsley and stir until well combined. Season with salt and pepper.
2. Shape the tuna mixture into 8 patties. Heat the oil in a skillet over medium-high heat. Sauté the patties for 3 to 4 minutes on each side, or until golden brown.

Canned Meats and Seafood

Grilled Tuna and Cheese Sandwich   Makes 2 sandwiches

Total Time: 10 minutes

2 slices any cheese—your preference
4 slices bread
3 ounces tuna, drained
butter or margarine, for grilling the sandwich

1. Put a slice of cheese on each of 2 slices of bread. Place half the tuna on top of each cheese slice. Top each with the other slice of bread. Butter the top side of the bread.
2. Heat a skillet over medium-high heat. When hot, place one or both sandwiches in the pan (depending on their size), butter side down. Grill about 2 minutes, or until golden. As the first side is grilling, butter the side that's now up.
3. Use a spatula to turn the sandwich over carefully so that the tuna doesn't spill out. Grill the second side until golden. Cut in half to serve. Grill the second sandwich if there was no room in the pan before.

Cold Macaroni Tuna Salad   Serves 4 to 6

Total Time: 1 hour, 30 minutes, including 1 hour chill time
Prep Time: 30 minutes

3 cups uncooked macaroni
1 cup peas
3 hard-boiled eggs, diced (page 108)
12 ounces tuna, drained
1 cup mayonnaise or Miracle Whip, or to taste
salt and pepper, to taste

1. Cook the macaroni; drain and rinse with cold water.
2. Mix the macaroni and peas. Gently stir in the eggs and tuna. Add the mayonnaise, salt, and pepper. Gently stir the macaroni into the tuna mixture. Cover and refrigerate for at least 1 hour.

Tuna Pasta Salad Without Mayonnaise   Serves 2

Total Time: 40 minutes

8 ounces penne or other pasta
zest and juice of 1 lemon
4 cloves garlic, minced
1/4 cup chopped fresh basil
6 ounces tuna in olive oil (not drained) OR
    6 ounces tuna in water, drained, plus 1/4 cup olive oil, canola oil, or vegetable oil
1 tomato, diced
2 green onions, finely sliced
2 tablespoons grated or shredded Parmesan or similar cheese
hot sauce, to taste
almonds or walnuts, toasted (optional)
salt and pepper

1. Cook the pasta while preparing the tuna mixture. Drain and rinse.
2. Combine the lemon zest and juice, garlic, basil, tuna, tomato, green onion, Parmesan, hot sauce, nuts, salt, and pepper. Taste, and adjust seasonings as needed.
3. Add the pasta and toss to coat.

Jalapeño Tuna Salad   Serves 4

Great stuffed in tomatoes, in a sandwich, or on crackers for an appetizer.

Total Time: 15 minutes

12 ounces tuna, drained
1/2 cup mayonnaise or Miracle Whip
1/4 cup finely chopped celery
1/4 cup finely chopped sweet onion or red onion
1/4 cup chopped fresh cilantro
1/4 cup jalapeño, seeded and chopped
salt and pepper, to taste

Flake the tuna with a fork into a large bowl. Add the remaining ingredients and stir well.

Curry Parmesan Tuna Serves 2

Total Time: 10 minutes
Prep Time: 10 minutes

6 ounces tuna, drained
6 tablespoons mayonnaise or Miracle Whip
1 tablespoon grated or shredded Parmesan cheese
3 tablespoons dill pickle relish or chopped dill
    pickle
dash of dried minced onion flakes
1/4 teaspoon curry powder (page 47)
1 tablespoon dried parsley flakes
1 teaspoon dried dill
dash of garlic powder

Mix together the tuna, mayonnaise, Parmesan, dill relish, and onion flakes. Stir well. Add the curry powder, parsley flakes, dried dill, and garlic powder and stir to combine.

Apple Tuna Salad Serves 2

Total Time: 25 minutes

1/3 cup mayonnaise or Miracle Whip
1/4 cup diced celery
1/4 cup finely chopped walnuts, pecans, or almonds
2 tablespoons minced onion or green onion
1 tablespoon sweet pickle relish or chopped sweet
    pickle
1 teaspoon sugar
1/4 teaspoon salt
1/4 teaspoon lemon pepper
6 ounces tuna, drained
1/4 cup chopped apple
1/4 cup chopped grapes (remove seeds if not
    seedless)
4 leaves lettuce

1. Combine the mayonnaise, celery, nuts, onion, relish, sugar, salt, and pepper; stir to combine. Add the tuna, apple, and grapes and mix well.
2. Put 2 lettuce leaves on each plate and top each portion with half the salad in a mound.

Black Bean Tuna Salad Serves 4

Substituting garbanzo beans for the black beans and/or vinaigrette for the mayonnaise is also good!

Total Time: 10 minutes
Prep Time: 10 minutes

12 ounces tuna, drained
1 can (16 ounces) black beans, drained and rinsed,
    OR Recipe-Ready Beans (page 176)
1 can (4 ounces) green chilies
3 tablespoons finely sliced green onion or diced
    onion
1 tablespoon chopped fresh cilantro OR
    1 teaspoon dried cilantro
1/2 cup mayonnaise or Miracle Whip
1/2 teaspoon chili powder
1/4 teaspoon ground cumin
1/4 teaspoon cayenne pepper
1/4 teaspoon salt
ground pepper, to taste

Flake the tuna with a fork. Mix in the beans, chilies, onion, and cilantro; stir to combine. Add the mayonnaise, chili powder, cumin, cayenne, salt, and pepper. Toss well.

Mediterranean Tuna Stuffed Tomato Serves 4

Total Time: 15 minutes

12 ounces tuna, drained
1/4 cup finely diced green bell pepper
1/4 cup finely diced red bell pepper
1/3 cup finely chopped pistachios, almonds, or
    other nuts
1 1/2 tablespoons capers, well drained, OR 1/4 cup
    chopped green olives
1/8 cup finely chopped onion
1 1/2 teaspoons dried parsley flakes
1/2 cup Greek Salad Dressing (page 151) or other
    vinaigrette dressing
1/3 cup grated or shredded Parmesan cheese
8 leaves lettuce
4 medium tomatoes

Canned Meats and Seafood

1. Mix the tuna, green and red bell pepper, pistachios, capers, onion, parsley flakes, salad dressing, and Parmesan in a medium bowl.
2. Line the individual plates with 2 lettuce leaves. Depending on the size of your tomatoes, hollow them out or cut into wedges and place on plates. Top each tomato with a mound of tuna salad.

Nicoise Salad   Serves 4

Total Time: 1 hour, 40 minutes
Prep Time: 40 minutes   Chill Time: 1 hour

1 cup green beans, cut into 2-inch lengths, cooked
    but still crisp
3 hard-boiled eggs, quartered (page 108)
1 small onion, sliced and separated into rings (red
    onion is best)
3 tomatoes, diced
1 clove garlic, minced
salt and pepper, to taste
1/3 cup black olives
12 ounces tuna, drained
lettuce leaves
anchovies, finely chopped (optional)
sardines, drained (optional)
cucumber, peeled, seeded, and diced
1 tablespoon chopped capers or green olives

Dressing
3 tablespoons olive oil, canola oil, or vegetable oil
1 tablespoon white wine vinegar, white vinegar,
    red wine vinegar, or balsamic vinegar
1 teaspoon finely chopped fresh parsley
1 teaspoon finely chopped chives
1/4 teaspoon dried tarragon
salt and pepper, to taste

1. Mix the olive oil, vinegar, herbs, salt, and pepper for the dressing. Set aside.
2. Toss the green beans, hard-boiled eggs, onion, tomato, garlic, salt, pepper, half the olives, and the tuna.
3. Arrange the lettuce leaves in the center of a serving dish. Place a mound of tuna salad on the lettuce, then top with the anchovies, sardines, cucumber, and capers. Pour the dressing over all.

Classic Tuna-Noodle Casserole   Serves 6

Total Time: 50 minutes
Prep Time: 20 minutes   Bake Time: 30 minutes

1 can (10 ounces) cream of mushroom soup, undiluted (page 54)
1 soup can full of water or milk
3 cups uncooked egg noodles
12 ounces tuna, drained
2 hard-boiled eggs, peeled and diced (page 108)
3 cups crumbled potato chips

1. Grease a casserole dish.
2. Bring the mushroom soup and water to a boil, stirring occasionally.
3. Layer half the noodles, tuna, eggs, mushroom soup, and potato chips. Repeat to form a second layer.
4. Bake, uncovered, at 350°F (no need to preheat oven) for 40 minutes, or until the noodles are tender.

Tuna Mushroom Casserole Without Canned Soup   Serves 6 to 8

Total Time: 1 hour
Prep Time: 30 minutes   Bake Time: 30 minutes

13 ounces egg noodles or other pasta
1 small onion, finely diced
1 stalk celery, finely diced
1 small red or green bell pepper, seeded and finely
    diced
1 tablespoon minced garlic
1/4 cup butter, margarine, canola oil, or vegetable
    oil
1/4 cup flour
2 1/2 cups half-and-half (*media crema*) OR 2 cups
    evaporated milk (page 99)
salt and pepper, to taste
1 cup sliced mushrooms (fresh, or canned and
    drained)
2 cups shredded cheddar or other cheese
12 ounces tuna, drained
3/4 cup bread crumbs or mashed cracker crumbs
1/4 cup grated or shredded Parmesan cheese

1. Preheat oven to 350°F.* Grease a 9"×13" pan.
2. Cook the noodles according to package directions while preparing the rest of the dish. Drain and set aside.
3. Sauté the onion, celery, bell pepper, and garlic in the butter for 3 minutes. Add the flour and stir slowly for 1 minute. Slowly add the half-and-half. Stir briskly until thickened and the sauce comes to a boil. Season with salt and pepper.
4. Add the mushrooms, cheddar, and tuna. Stir, breaking up the tuna as you do so. Add the cooked noodles.
5. Transfer to the greased baking dish. Sprinkle with the bread crumbs and Parmesan. Bake for 25 to 30 minutes, or until bubbly and golden brown.

Or you can serve this without baking—just heat it on the stove until the cheese melts.

Italian Tuna Casserole   Serves 4

Total Time: 55 minutes
Prep Time: 10 minutes   Cook Time: 45 minutes

4 cups medium pasta
1 large onion, diced
2 tablespoons olive oil, canola oil, or vegetable oil
2 cans (16 ounces each) diced tomatoes, not drained
4 tablespoons tomato paste
2 tablespoons Italian seasoning (page 48)
salt and pepper, to taste
1 can (8 ounces) mushrooms, drained (optional)
1/2 green bell pepper, diced (optional)
10 black olives, sliced (optional)
12 ounces tuna, drained
1 1/2 cups shredded cheddar or similar cheese
1 cup shredded mozzarella or similar cheese

1. Preheat oven to 350°F.
2. While preparing the rest of the dish, cook the pasta. Drain and set aside.
3. Sauté the onion in the olive oil until translucent. Add the diced tomato, tomato paste, Italian seasoning, salt, and pepper. Simmer, uncovered, for 15 minutes, or until the sauce has thickened slightly.

4. Stir in the drained pasta and any of the optional ingredients you are using. Add the tuna and mix very gently so that it doesn't turn to mush.
5. Transfer to an ovenproof dish and top with the cheddar and mozzarella. Bake for 25 minutes, or until the cheese on top is golden brown.

Tuna Mornay   Serves 4

Total Time: 1 hour
Prep Time: 30 minutes   Bake Time: 30 minutes

8 ounces dry macaroni, penne, or other pasta
1/2 onion, finely diced
4 tablespoons butter or margarine
4 tablespoons corn flour or white flour
salt and pepper, to taste
dash of cayenne pepper
2 cups milk or evaporated milk (page 99)
4 cups shredded cheddar or similar cheese
12 ounces tuna, drained and flaked
1/2 cup peas (fresh, frozen, or canned)
1/2 cup corn (fresh, frozen, or canned)
1/4 cup dry bread crumbs

1. Preheat oven to 350°F.
2. While preparing the sauce, boil the macaroni according to the package instructions, but add the chopped onion to the boiling water. Rinse, drain, and set aside.
3. Melt the butter over low heat. Remove from the heat. Add the flour, stirring constantly to form a paste. Season with the salt, ground pepper, and cayenne.
4. Add the milk gradually, stirring constantly. When all the milk has been added, place back over medium-low heat and stir constantly as the mixture thickens and boils. Boil for 1 minute, continuing to stir. Remove from the heat. Add half the cheese and stir until it melts. Stir in the tuna, peas, and corn. Add the pasta and toss gently until coated.
5. Transfer to a greased baking dish. Top with the remaining cheese and the bread crumbs. Bake for 30 minutes, or until the cheese is melted and the casserole is bubbling.

Stove-Top Tuna Penne   Serves 2

Total Time: 25 minutes
Prep Time: 15 minutes   Cook Time: 10 minutes

1 cup penne pasta, macaroni, or other medium-
    size pasta
1 small onion, diced
1/2 green bell pepper, diced
1 tablespoon butter, margarine, olive oil, canola
    oil, or vegetable oil
1 can (10 ounces) cream of mushroom soup
    (page 54)
6 ounces tuna, drained
1/2 cup white wine
2 tablespoons Worcestershire sauce
salt and pepper, to taste

1. Boil the pasta as directed on the package. Drain
   and set aside.
2. Sauté the onion and bell pepper in the butter.
   Turn the heat to low and add the soup, tuna, wine,
   Worcestershire, salt, and pepper; mix well. Cook
   about 10 minutes, or until heated through. Add the
   pasta and toss to coat.

Baked Brown Rice and
Tuna Casserole   Serves 6

A nice change from all the "tuna-and-pasta" dishes!

Total Time: 30 minutes, not including time to cook
    rice
Prep Time: 10 minutes   Bake Time: 20 minutes

2 cups diced celery
1 can (3 ounces) French fried onion rings OR
    1 small onion, diced
1 tablespoon butter or margarine
3 cups cooked brown or white rice, hot
12 ounces tuna, drained
3 hard-boiled eggs, diced (page 108)
3 tablespoons lemon juice
1 cup mayonnaise (do not substitute Miracle
    Whip)
salt and pepper, to taste

1. Preheat oven to 350°F.
2. Sauté the celery (and onion if you're using
   fresh onion) in the butter. Remove from the stove
   and add the cooked rice, tuna, hard-boiled egg,
   and lemon juice. Stir in the mayonnaise, salt, and
   pepper.
3. Transfer to a shallow greased baking dish. Top with
   the onion rings if you're using them. Bake, uncovered, for 20 minutes.

Tuna Bruschetta   Serves 2 to 4

Total Time: 25 minutes
Prep Time: 15 minutes
Cook Time: 8 to 10 minutes

1 cup shredded mozzarella or similar cheese
6 ounces tuna, drained
4 medium tomatoes, seeded and chopped
1/4 cup diced onion
2 tablespoons minced fresh parsley
1/2 teaspoon dried oregano
4 slices Italian bread or similar bread
2 tablespoons olive oil, canola oil, vegetable oil,
    butter, or margarine
2 cloves garlic, peeled and halved, OR 1/2 teaspoon
    garlic powder

1. Combine the cheese, tuna, tomato, onion, parsley,
   and oregano.
2. Brush both sides of the bread with the olive oil and
   rub the surface with the cut sides of the garlic (or
   sprinkle with the garlic powder).
3. Grill one side of each slice of bread in a skillet until
   golden brown. Flip the bread and top each toasted
   surface with the tuna mixture. Continue to grill
   until the cheese melts and the bread is toasted on
   the bottom.

Tuna Enchilada
Casserole   Serves 4 to 6

Total Time: 45 minutes
Prep Time: 20 minutes   Bake Time: 25 minutes

1¼ cups (10 ounces) red enchilada sauce (page 213)
⅓ cup water
8 corn tortillas
6 ounces tuna, drained and flaked
⅓ cup diced onion
2 cups shredded Monterey Jack or similar cheese
black olives, sliced

1. Mix the enchilada sauce with the water. Pour about ¼ cup of the mixture into a greased baking dish (round is good if you have it).
2. Pour the rest of the sauce into a dish big enough for dipping the tortillas. Dip 2 tortillas in the sauce and arrange in the casserole. Place one-third of the tuna and the onion and one-quarter of the cheese and sauce on the tortillas. Repeat twice so there are three layers total. Top with the rest of the sauce and cheese. Bake, uncovered, for 25 minutes. Sprinkle with the olives just before serving.

CHICKEN

Canned chicken must be handled very gently, so it doesn't break into mush.

Chicken Potpie   Serves 4

Total Time: 45 minutes
Prep Time: 15 minutes   Bake Time: 30 minutes

2 piecrusts (page 425), for top and bottom crust
2 cans (6 ounces each) chicken or other canned meat, drained and liquid reserved (see below)
1 can (16 ounces) mixed vegetables, drained and liquid reserved (see below), OR 1½ cups total fresh* and canned vegetables, such as carrots, potatoes, mushrooms, peas, and corn
2 tablespoons finely chopped onion
3 tablespoons canola oil, vegetable oil, butter, or margarine
4 tablespoons flour
¼ teaspoon ground pepper
2 cups liquid reserved from canned meat and veggies, supplemented with chicken broth or bouillon

*If using fresh veggies, cut into ⅜-inch pieces (if they are too large, they won't be done by the time the piecrust is golden).

1. Preheat oven to 425°F.
2. Place one piecrust in a 9-inch pie pan. Spread the chicken, mixed vegetables, and onion evenly over the crust. Set aside.
3. Mix the oil, flour, and ground pepper in a pan over medium heat. Add the reserved liquid and/or broth a little at a time, stirring constantly to prevent lumps and continuing to cook until it is thick and creamy. Pour over the chicken and vegetables in the pie pan.
4. Wet the edge of the piecrust, then place the top crust over the potpie and pinch the edges together. Cut three 1- to 2-inch air vents in the top crust. Bake for about 30 minutes, or until golden. If the crust begins to get overly dark, cover the entire potpie—or just the edges if you want—with a piece of aluminum foil toward the end of the cooking time.
5. Remove from the oven and cut into wedges. I find it works best to serve this in bowls to catch the gravy.

Chicken or Beef Enchiladas   Serves 2

Total Time: 30 minutes
Prep Time: 10 minutes   Bake Time: 20 minutes

1 cup canned black, pinto, or kidney beans, drained and rinsed, OR Recipe-Ready Beans (page 176)
½ cup diced onion or green onion, including tops
1 can (8 ounces) corn, drained (optional)
¼ cup sour cream (page 99) OR ½ cup refried beans
½ cup shredded cheese—Monterey Jack, Colby, or cheddar is best
1½ teaspoons chili powder
1 teaspoon ground cumin
½ teaspoon dried oregano
salt and pepper, to taste
1 can (6 ounces) chicken or roast beef, drained
4 small tortillas (flour or corn)
½ cup salsa (page 127), diced fresh tomato, canned diced tomatoes, or tomato sauce

1. Preheat oven to 350°F.
2. Mix the beans, onion, corn, sour cream, cheese, chili powder, cumin, oregano, salt, and pepper; stir to combine. Gently mix in the meat. Spoon the mixture onto the tortillas and roll them.
3. Place the enchiladas in a greased baking pan. Spoon any remaining mixture around and over the enchiladas. Spoon the salsa over the top. Bake for 15 to 20 minutes, or until the cheese is melted and mixture bubbles.

Chicken Salad Sandwiches   Serves 4

A little fancier than just chicken and mayo, this also stretches the chicken further and adds nutrients. Substitute ingredients with whatever you have available. Also look at the tuna salad recipes and substitute chicken for the tuna.

Total Time: 10 minutes

1 can (6 ounces) chicken, drained
1/2 apple, finely diced
1 carrot, finely chopped
10 grapes (seeded or seedless), sliced in half
1 cup mayonnaise, Miracle Whip, or ranch dressing (page 161)
1/2 cup chopped pecans
bread for 4 sandwiches
4 leaves lettuce

1. Mix the chicken, apple, carrot, grapes, mayonnaise, and pecans .
2. Make 4 sandwiches with the bread, 1 lettuce leaf per sandwich, and the chicken salad.

Chicken or Shrimp Paella   Serves 2

Total Time: 30 to 45 minutes (depends on type of rice used)

1 cup chopped onion or green onion
1 clove garlic, minced (or use garlic powder or garlic salt)
1 tablespoon canola oil, olive oil, or vegetable oil
2 tablespoons chopped fresh parsley OR 1 teaspoon dried parsley flakes (optional)
2 bay leaves

1 package saffron rice OR 3/4 cup brown or white rice (1 cup if using instant) and 1/4 teaspoon saffron
2 teaspoons lemon juice, lime juice, or *limón* (Key lime) juice
1/2 cup dry white wine or broth
2 cups chicken or shrimp broth (use liquid from canned meat—see below—and canned vegetables, then make up the remainder with bouillon and water)
1 to 1 1/2 cups chopped vegetables—carrots, green bell pepper, broccoli, zucchini, or mushrooms (fresh are best, but canned are acceptable)
1 can (6 ounces) chicken or shrimp, drained and liquid reserved

1. In a pan with a lid, brown the onion and the garlic in the oil. Add the parsley, bay leaves, and rice, stirring well to coat the rice. Add the lemon juice, wine, broth, and veggies; cover and simmer until all the liquid is absorbed and the vegetables are tender.
2. Turn off the heat. Add the meat to the pan and mix gently. Cover and let sit for 2 to 3 minutes to heat through.

Couscous Chicken   Serves 2

The ultimate in easy meals—great on a passage or in the middle of repairs!

Total Time: 5 minutes

1 cup water (use the liquid from the canned chicken and make up the rest with water)
dash of salt
2/3 cup couscous
1 can (16 ounces) diced tomatoes, not drained
1 can (6 ounces) chicken, drained and liquid reserved
1/2 teaspoon dried tarragon or dried oregano
salt and pepper, to taste

1. Bring the 1 cup water to a boil. Add a dash of salt and the couscous. Cover and turn off the heat—the couscous will cook itself in 5 minutes. Stir occasionally and check to see if more water is needed. Set aside.

2. At the same time, place the tomatoes in a small pan and heat to boiling. Add the chicken, tarragon, salt, and pepper, stirring gently so as not to break up the chunks of chicken. Turn off the heat and let stand for 2 to 3 minutes to heat the chicken through. Serve in bowls over the couscous.

Chicken and Dumplings   Serves 6

Total Time: 35 minutes

4 tablespoons canola oil, vegetable oil, butter, margarine, or shortening
3 tablespoons flour
$\frac{1}{2}$ teaspoon salt
1 cup milk, evaporated milk, or chicken broth
1 cup chicken broth (use the liquid from the canned chicken and vegetables and supplement with bouillon to total 1 cup)
1 can mixed vegetables, drained and liquid reserved (see above) OR fresh peas, carrots, or vegetables of your choice, cut into bite-size pieces (optional)
2 teaspoons chopped onion or green onion, including tops
2 cans (6 ounces each) chicken, drained and liquid reserved (see above)
dumplings (page 280)

1. Mix the oil, flour, and salt in saucepan or skillet with a lid and place over medium heat. Add the milk and broth a little at a time, stirring/whisking constantly to prevent lumps from forming. Continue to cook and stir until thick and creamy.
2. Stir in the vegetables and chopped onion. Very gently mix in the chicken and bring to a gentle boil.
3. Mix the dumpling ingredients, stirring just enough to combine. Drop by spoonfuls (one spoonful per person) on top of the chicken stew. Cover tightly and cook for 15 minutes over low heat. Don't lift the lid while the dumplings are cooking.
4. Ladle the stew and dumpling into a bowl and serve with the dumpling on top. Serve hot.

Chicken, Rice, and Beans Hash   Serves 4

Total Time: 45 minutes
Prep Time: 15 minutes   Cook Time: 30 minutes

1 onion, chopped
1 green bell pepper, chopped
3 or 4 cloves garlic, minced
1 packet *criolla* (page 213)
$\frac{1}{2}$ cup brown rice or other rice
1 cup chicken broth (may be made from bouillon), stock (page 164), or water
1 can (16 ounces) red kidney beans, drained and rinsed, OR Recipe-Ready Beans (page 176)
1 can (16 ounces) diced tomatoes, not drained, OR 2 large fresh tomatoes, diced
1 can (4 ounces) chopped green chile peppers
1 can (16 ounces) corn, drained
1 can (8 ounces) whole or sliced mushrooms, drained
1 tablespoon ground cumin
$\frac{1}{2}$ teaspoon cayenne pepper
1 tablespoon garlic powder
2 tablespoons Worcestershire sauce
2 cans (6 ounces each) chicken, drained
ground pepper, to taste
Parmesan cheese, grated

1. Sauté the onion, bell pepper, and garlic in the *criolla*.
2. Add the rice, broth, beans, tomatoes, chile peppers, corn, and mushrooms and mix well. Add the cumin, cayenne, garlic powder, and Worcestershire sauce. Cover and bring to a boil. Reduce the heat and simmer until the rice is done.
3. Add the chicken and just heat through. Sprinkle with the ground pepper and Parmesan and serve hot.

Italian Chicken Pasta

See Italian Tuna Casserole (page 309) and substitute chicken for the tuna.

Canned Meats and Seafood

Chicken and Apricots   Serves 2

A real family favorite! I make it about half the time with canned chicken and half with a boneless chicken breast, where I begin by cubing and browning the chicken, then preparing the dish as below.

Total Time: 20 minutes

1 cup water
dash of salt
²/₃ cup couscous
handful of dried apricots or white raisins
1 cup chicken broth (use reserved liquid from canned chicken; the remainder may be made from bouillon) or stock (page 164)
1 tablespoon oil
1 tablespoon flour
¹/₂ cup diced onion OR 1 tablespoon onion powder
¹/₂ teaspoon ground cinnamon
1 tablespoon honey
small handful of whole almonds
1 can (6 ounces) chicken, drained and liquid reserved
salt and pepper, to taste

1. Bring the water to a boil. Add a dash of salt and the couscous. Cover and turn off the heat—the couscous will cook itself in 5 minutes. Stir occasionally and check to see if more water is needed.
2. At the same time, boil the apricots in the chicken broth until softened and set aside.
3. Mix the oil and the flour in a medium saucepan or skillet. Add the onion and cook until browned. Add the apricot mixture slowly, stirring vigorously to avoid lumps from forming. Bring to a boil and add the cinnamon and honey. Cook until thickened to the consistency of gravy.
4. Add the almonds, chicken, salt, and pepper, stirring gently to keep the chicken intact. Cover and turn off the heat. Let stand 2 to 3 minutes, or until heated through. Serve over the couscous.

BBQ Chicken or Beef Sandwiches   Serves 2

Total Time: 10 minutes

¹/₂ cup barbecue sauce (page 215)
1 can (6 ounces) chicken, drained, or roast beef, drained and rinsed
2 buns, 4 slices bread, or 2 tortillas

1. Heat the barbecue sauce in a small saucepan or skillet over low heat. Add the chicken, shredding it as you do so. Stir and cook until heated through.
2. Warm the buns in the oven or toast in a skillet. Split the buns and fill with the chicken mixture. Serve hot.

BEEF

Canned roast beef can be used in all sorts of recipes, replacing ground beef as well as stew meat and roast beef.

Roast Beef Chili   Serves 2

Great with "Almost" Corn Bread (page 381), a tossed salad, and a cold bottle of beer!

Total Time: 20 minutes (better if cooked longer)

¹/₂ cup diced onion OR 1 tablespoon onion powder or dried onion flakes
¹/₄ green bell pepper, seeded and diced (optional)
1 tablespoon canola oil, vegetable oil, olive oil, butter, or margarine
1 can (10 ounces) roast beef, including the gravy
1 can (16 ounces) kidney beans, drained and rinsed, OR Recipe-Ready Beans (page 176)
1 can (16 ounces) diced tomatoes, drained, OR 2 fresh tomatoes, chopped
1 tablespoon chili powder, or more to taste
¹/₂ teaspoon ground cumin
¹/₄ teaspoon ground cinnamon (optional)

1. In a medium saucepan, sauté the onion and bell pepper in the oil over medium heat until golden. Add all the other ingredients and simmer, stirring occasionally.

2. This is best if simmered a half hour or more, or until the kidney beans start to split and the flavors are really melded. However, I've served it many times just as soon as it was heated though and it's still been pretty good.

Roast Beef Sandwich or Roll-Up

Serves 2

Total Time: 5 minutes

2 buns, 4 slices of bread, or 4 tortillas
1 can (10 ounces) roast beef, drained and rinsed
horseradish or wasabi (optional)
mayonnaise or Miracle Whip
lettuce leaves
onion slices, to taste

1. Warm the buns if desired.
2. If the roast beef is in large chunks, cut it into "slices" about ¼ inch thick. The roast beef may be heated if a hot sandwich is desired.
3. Mix a little horseradish, if desired, with the mayonnaise—exact amounts will depend on your preferences. Spread on the buns.
4. Arrange the lettuce leaves and onion on the buns, then top with the roast beef and the other half of the bun.

Pineapple Beef, Chicken, or Turkey

Serves 2

For the fresh meat version that I adapted this from, see Tropical Beef Chunks (page 264).

Total Time: 30 minutes

1 cup stock of appropriate flavor (use reserved liquid, then add water and bouillon to make the full amount needed)
½ teaspoon garlic salt, garlic powder, OR 2 teaspoons minced fresh garlic
1 teaspoon paprika (optional)
½ cup fresh or canned pineapple chunks (juice reserved)
¼ cup wine vinegar or wine
1 tablespoon soy sauce
3 tablespoons brown sugar or white sugar
1 tablespoon cornstarch

½ cup water
½ cup sliced celery
½ cup diced green bell pepper
½ cup diced onion
2 tomatoes, cut into chunks (optional)
1 can (6 to 10 ounces) roast beef, chicken, or turkey, drained and gravy/liquid reserved

1. Place the stock in a saucepan with the garlic salt, paprika, pineapple juice, and half the vinegar.
2. In a small bowl combine the rest of the vinegar, the soy sauce, sugar, cornstarch, and water; set aside.
3. Bring the mixture in the saucepan to a low boil and add the celery and bell pepper. Cook 5 minutes. Add the onion and cook 5 minutes more. Add the pineapple chunks and the reserved soy sauce mixture to the pan and bring to a boil; cook until the sauce thickens, stirring constantly to keep lumps from forming.
4. Turn off the heat and add the tomato and meat. Mix gently, taking care not to break apart the chunks of meat. Let sit, covered, for 2 to 3 minutes to warm through. This is great served over rice or couscous.

Vegetable Beef Soup

Serves 2

This is also good made with canned chicken.

Total Time: 10 minutes if using all canned veggies, 20 to 30 minutes with fresh veggies

1 can (16 ounces) mixed vegetables, drained and liquid reserved, OR 1½ cups total diced mixed fresh or canned vegetables, such as onions, carrots, celery, potatoes, green beans, green bell peppers, corn, okra, and/or peas
2 cups water, including any liquid reserved from the canned vegetables
2 teaspoons beef bouillon powder OR 2 beef broth cubes
1 can (10 ounces) roast beef, including gravy
spices, to taste, such as ground pepper, onion powder, and celery salt

1. If you're making the soup with all canned ingredients, place all the ingredients in a saucepan and heat through. If making with fresh veggies, cook the fresh veggies in water with bouillon powder and spices until the veggies are tender but not falling apart.

2. Add the roast beef and heat through. For a heartier meal, add dumplings (page 280). For more of a stew, use half the water.

Goulash or Spanish Rice   Serves 2

If you use pasta, it's goulash; with rice, it's Spanish rice. This is also good stuffed inside a green bell pepper and baked just until the pepper is tender.

Total Time: 30 minutes to 1 hour, depending on time to cook rice or pasta

1/4 cup diced onion or sliced green onion, tops included

1/4 green bell pepper, diced, OR 1 small can diced green chilies

1 can (8 ounces) sliced mushrooms (optional)

1 tablespoon canola oil or vegetable oil

1 can (16 ounces) diced tomatoes, not drained, OR 2 fresh tomatoes, diced

2 servings cooked rice or pasta

1/2 teaspoon Italian seasoning (page 48)

1 can (10 ounces) roast beef, including gravy

In a skillet, sauté the onion, bell pepper, and mushrooms in the oil just until light brown. Add the tomatoes, rice or pasta, spices, and roast beef. Cook until heated through.

CORNED BEEF

The small "sandwich" cans of corned beef can be used for lots of meals.

Corned Beef "Omelet"   Serves 2

Not really a true omelet but a layer of eggs with corned beef and melted cheese on top, served in wedges.

Total Time: 15 minutes

2 green onions, including tops, sliced, OR 2 tablespoons diced onion

2 tablespoons butter or margarine

4 eggs, beaten

1/4 cup milk

1 can (12 ounces) corned beef, cut into 3/4-inch cubes

1/2 cup shredded cheddar or similar cheese

ground pepper, to taste

1. In a skillet, sauté the onions in the butter until just golden.

2. At the same time, lightly beat the eggs and milk in a small bowl.

3. When the onions are golden, turn the heat to medium-low and add the beaten eggs. As the eggs set, lift the edges with a spatula, letting the uncooked egg flow underneath.

4. When the eggs are nearly set, sprinkle with the corned beef, cheese, and ground pepper. Cover the pan and turn off the heat. Let it stand for about 2 minutes, or until the corned beef is heated through and the cheese is melted.

5. Cut into wedges and serve.

Corned Beef Veggie
Criolla   Makes 4 small servings or 2 large

Total Time: 30 minutes

4 cloves garlic, minced

1 onion, diced

1 carrot, diced

2 potatoes, peeled and diced

1 green bell pepper, seeded and diced

1 jalapeño or other spicy chile pepper, seeded and finely minced

1/2 cup white wine or water

1/2 cup water

2 to 4 chicken bouillon cubes

dash of Worcestershire sauce, to taste

1 packet *criolla* (page 213)

1 can (12 ounces) corned beef

salt and pepper, to taste

1. Combine the garlic, onion, carrot, potato, bell pepper, and jalapeño in a saucepan. Add the wine, water, bouillon cubes, and Worcestershire sauce. Bring to a boil and cook for 15 minutes, or until the veggies are tender.

2. Add the *criolla* and corned beef, roughly breaking up the corned beef with the side of your spoon. Cook about 5 more minutes, or until thickened and the flavors are mixed. Add the salt and pepper to taste.
3. If you prefer more spice, add more Worcestershire sauce or even your favorite hot sauce.

Filipino-Style Corned Beef Hash

Serves 2

Total Time: 30 minutes

1 tablespoon canola oil, vegetable oil, butter, or margarine
1/2 cup diced onion
4 cloves garlic, minced, OR 1/2 teaspoon garlic powder
1 tomato, diced
1 large potato or 2 small potatoes, peeled and diced
1 can (12 ounces) corned beef
salt and pepper, to taste

1. Heat the oil in a large skillet over medium heat. Add the onion and garlic, and cook until tender.
2. Add the tomato and potato, and cook for 7 to 10 minutes, or until the potato is tender when pierced with a fork.
3. Add the corned beef, breaking it up with a spoon or fork as you do so. Season with salt and pepper. Cook for another 10 minutes, stirring frequently.

Corned Beef Sandwich Spread

Serves 2 or 3

Total Time: 10 minutes

1 can (12 ounces) corned beef
1 slice onion, finely diced
1/4 green bell pepper, finely diced
2 tablespoons canned corn, drained
2 tablespoons shredded or diced cheese
2 tablespoons ketchup, or to taste

1. Place the corned beef in a bowl and break it up with a fork or the side of a spoon. Add all the other ingredients and mix together.

2. Spread on bread for sandwiches, or on tortillas for roll-ups, or serve by itself.

Reuben Sandwich

Serves 1

Total Time: 10 minutes

2 slices corned beef from a can (easiest to cut if corned beef is refrigerated)*
1/3 cup sauerkraut, drained, or to taste
1 slice Swiss cheese (about the same size as the slices of bread)
2 tablespoons Thousand Island dressing (page 162) or Russian dressing
2 slices rye bread or other type of bread
1 tablespoon butter or margarine

Don't worry if the corned beef crumbles as you cut it, or if you can't refrigerate it. The sandwich will be a bit messier, but it will taste every bit as good!

1. Layer the corned beef, sauerkraut, cheese, and dressing on one slice of bread and top with the other slice. Lightly butter the top, using half the butter.
2. Warm a skillet over medium-high heat. Grill the sandwich as for a grilled cheese sandwich, using the other half of the butter before flipping over the sandwich. Place on a plate and cut in half to serve.

Corned Beef Scramble

Serves 1 or 2

Equally good for a hearty breakfast, lunch, or dinner.

Total Time: 20 minutes

cooking spray or 1 1/2 teaspoons olive oil, canola oil, vegetable oil, butter, or margarine
1/2 cup canned corned beef, crumbled
1/4 cup chopped onion
1/4 cup chopped mushrooms (drain if using canned mushrooms)
1/4 cup diced green bell pepper or other sweet or spicy pepper
1/4 cup chopped cooked potato
salt and pepper, to taste
2 eggs
3 tablespoons water or milk
3 drops hot sauce (optional), to taste

Canned Meats and Seafood

1. Spritz the skillet with cooking spray and place over medium heat. Add the corned beef, onion, mushrooms, bell pepper, potato, and a dash of salt and pepper and mix together. Cook until hot but not browned.
2. Beat the eggs, water, and hot sauce together. Pour into the skillet, letting the mixture run around the corned beef mixture. As the eggs begin to set up, use a spatula to lift them and let uncooked egg flow under to cook.
3. When cooked to your desired doneness, remove from the heat. Use a spatula to lift the scramble from the pan. Many people like to top it with a dollop of ketchup.

Cabbage and Corned Beef Soup

Serves 4

Total Time: 35 minutes
Prep Time: 15 minutes   Cook Time: 20 minutes

1 medium onion, diced
2 tablespoons canola oil, olive oil, or vegetable oil
$\frac{1}{2}$ head cabbage, cut into pieces about $\frac{1}{2}$ inch wide by 3 inches long
1 teaspoon dried oregano
1 teaspoon dried basil
2 cloves garlic, minced, OR $\frac{1}{2}$ teaspoon garlic powder
1 can (6 ounces) tomato paste
1 can (12 ounces) corned beef, cut into $\frac{1}{2}$-inch pieces
4 cups beef broth (may be made from bouillon) or stock (page 165)
salt and pepper, to taste

1. In a large pan over medium heat, sauté the onion in the oil for about 5 minutes. Add the cabbage and, stirring frequently, sauté another 10 minutes, or until the cabbage is tender but not mushy.
2. Turn the heat to low and stir in all the other ingredients. Cover and cook for 20 minutes. Ladle into bowls to serve.

CORNED BEEF HASH

You can make several quick dinners starting with a can of corned beef hash—or substitute canned roast beef hash.

Corned Beef Hash with Eggs

Serves 2

You'll need a skillet with a lid for this recipe, or use a piece of aluminum foil as a lid.

Total Time: 30 minutes

$\frac{1}{4}$ cup diced onion OR 1 teaspoon onion powder
1 tablespoon canola oil, vegetable oil, butter, or margarine
1 can (16 ounces) corned beef hash or roast beef hash
2 eggs
$\frac{1}{4}$ teaspoon ground pepper, or to taste (I like more)

1. Sauté the onion in the oil over medium heat until the onion is glazed. Turn the heat to medium-high and add the hash, breaking it up with the side of a spoon as you do so. The goal is a crispy crust on the hash, so resist the urge to keep stirring it. Let it cook for about 5 minutes, then gently lift the hash with a spatula and see if it's browned. If not, just put it back and let it cook a few minutes more.
2. When browned, turn one section at a time with a spatula. Then make two indentations in the top with the spoon and break an egg into each. Sprinkle the ground pepper over the top of the eggs and hash. Cover the pan and let the eggs cook for 2 to 3 minutes, or to the desired doneness.
3. Use a spatula to gently pick up the hash with the egg on top and place each section on a plate. Many people like a little hot sauce or ketchup over the top.

Hash Stuffed Pepper   Serves 2

Total Time: 1 hour, 15 minutes, including 10 minutes to stand before serving

Prep Time: 5 minutes   Bake time: 1 hour
Stand Time: 10 minutes

2 green bell peppers
1 can (16 ounces) corned beef hash or roast beef hash
ground pepper, to taste

1. Cut around the stem of the bell peppers and remove it and the seeds. Poke the knife into the bottom of each pepper a few times to allow cooking juices to drain.
2. Fill each bell pepper with the hash, adding ground pepper to taste as you go.
3. Place the peppers upright in a greased baking dish. Cover with foil. Bake at 350°F (no need to preheat oven) for 1 hour, or until the pepper is tender and the hash is heated all the way through. If desired, take off the foil during the last 15 minutes of baking so that the top will brown a little.
4. Remove from the oven and let stand for 10 minutes before serving.

Variation: Sprinkle a little shredded cheese over the top of the peppers 15 minutes before the end of the baking time. Leave the foil off for the remainder of the baking time.

Crustless Hash Quiche   Serves 4

Total Time: 45 minutes
Prep Time: 10 minute   Bake Time: 35 minutes

1 can (16 ounces) corned beef hash or roast beef hash
1 cup shredded cheese (Swiss is ideal but any will work)
1¼ cups milk
4 eggs
1 tablespoon flour
¼ teaspoon salt
¼ teaspoon ground pepper
1 teaspoon prepared mustard, or to taste, OR
    ⅛ teaspoon dry mustard

1. Preheat oven to 350°F.
2. Crumble the hash into a greased 9-inch square or round baking pan (a pie pan is likely to be too small) and sprinkle with the cheese.
3. In a small bowl, mix the remaining ingredients and spoon over the hash. Bake for 35 minutes, or until a knife inserted in the center comes out clean (depending on the pan, it can take up to 15 minutes longer).
4. Remove from the oven and let sit for 10 minutes before cutting into wedges. Serve warm.

HAM

Ham is probably the easiest canned meat to work with, as it doesn't tend to get mushy.

Stove-Top Scalloped Potatoes   Serves 6

Much faster than scalloped potatoes baked in the oven (page 195), but they lack that "crunchy" top.

Total Time: 1 hour, 15 minutes
Prep Time: 15 minutes   Cook Time: 1 hour

4 cups diced or sliced peeled potato
½ cup diced onion
2 teaspoons salt
1½ cups milk
2 cans (6 ounces each) ham, drained and broken into bite-size chunks
½ cup shredded cheddar or other meltable cheese
¼ cup dry bread crumbs or cracker crumbs (optional)

1. Combine the potato with the onion, salt, and milk in a pan. Cover and simmer over low heat for 30 to 40 minutes, or until the potato is tender.
2. Mix in the ham, and sprinkle the cheese and bread crumbs over top. Continue cooking, uncovered, for 15 to 20 minutes without stirring. Serve hot.

Canned Meats and Seafood

Jambalaya
Serves 2 to 4

Adding the optional beans and tomatoes makes this dish go further. If your spices are a little old, add more than what is called for. This dish should be spicy and flavorful but not uncomfortably hot. There are two other jambalaya recipes in this book: the "fresh meat" version that this recipe was adapted from (page 184) and a vegetarian jambalaya (page 183).

Total Time: 1 hour (30 minutes with instant rice)
Prep Time: 15 minutes
Cook Time: 45 minutes (15 minutes with instant rice)

$\frac{1}{2}$ onion, diced
$\frac{1}{2}$ green bell pepper, diced
1 tablespoon minced garlic OR $\frac{1}{2}$ teaspoon garlic powder
1 tablespoon butter, margarine, canola oil, or vegetable oil
3 to 5 green onions, chopped, including tops (optional)
1 can (8 ounces) mushrooms, drained and liquid reserved, OR 1 cup sliced fresh mushrooms
1 can (16 ounces) black, pinto, or kidney beans, drained and rinsed, OR Recipe-Ready Beans (page 176; optional)
1 can (16 ounces) diced tomatoes, not drained (optional)
$\frac{1}{2}$ cup brown rice or white rice OR 1 cup instant rice
$1\frac{1}{2}$ cups stock (use the reserved liquid from the meat [below], then add water and chicken or shrimp bouillon to make the full amount needed)
salt and pepper, to taste
$\frac{1}{8}$ teaspoon cayenne pepper
$\frac{1}{2}$ teaspoon chili powder
2 whole bay leaves
$\frac{1}{4}$ teaspoon dried thyme
$\frac{1}{8}$ teaspoon ground cloves
1 can (6 ounces) ham, chicken, shrimp, or oysters, drained and liquid reserved

1. Brown the onion, bell pepper, and garlic in the butter over medium heat.
2. Add the green onion, mushrooms, beans, tomato, rice, stock, salt, ground pepper, cayenne, chili powder, bay leaves, thyme, and cloves. Bring to a boil, then turn down the heat, cover, and simmer about 45 minutes (10 to 15 minutes for instant rice), or until the rice is cooked but still firm, stirring occasionally. If the rice is too liquid, remove the cover and turn up the heat to boil away some of the liquid. (All rice is different; you may have to add water.)
3. Add the meat; mix gently, cover, and let sit for 2 to 3 minutes to heat through. Serve in bowls.

Hobo Dinner
Serves 2

Total Time: 30 minutes

3 or 4 carrots, cut into 1-inch chunks
$\frac{1}{2}$ cup diced onion
$\frac{1}{2}$ green bell pepper, diced (optional)
1 large potato or sweet potato, peeled and cut into 1-inch chunks
1 tablespoon canola oil or vegetable oil
1 cup broth, including reserved liquid (use beef bouillon for ham, chicken bouillon for turkey and chicken)
1 can (6 ounces) ham, beef, chicken, or turkey, drained and liquid reserved
ground pepper and/or Mrs. Dash, to taste

1. Brown the carrot, onion, bell pepper, and potato in the oil. Turn the heat to low and add the broth and reserved liquid. Cover and cook until the carrot and potato are tender. If the liquid is not mostly evaporated, raise the heat, remove the lid, and cook until most of the liquid is gone.
2. Turn off the heat, gently stir in the meat and ground pepper, and let sit for 2 to 3 minutes with the lid on to heat the meat through.

NOTE: If you're doubling or tripling this recipe to feed more people, do not double or triple the broth. Use 1 cup plus the extra liquid from the additional cans of meat. Check the vegetables as they are cooking and add more water or broth only if needed.

Rice or Pasta Salad with Ham
Serves 2

Total Time: 30 minutes with instant rice or pasta; longer with regular or brown rice or if you wish to serve the salad chilled

2 servings rice or bite-size pasta (penne, rotini, bow ties, macaroni, etc.)
2 tablespoons minced onion
1 tomato, cut into 16 pieces, OR ¼ cup sun-dried tomatoes in olive oil
¼ green bell pepper, diced
5 black olives, cut in half
1 can (6 ounces) ham, drained and broken into bite-size bits
1 tablespoon olive oil, canola oil, or vegetable oil
2 tablespoons balsamic vinegar, red wine vinegar, cider vinegar, or other vinegar
1 teaspoon sugar

1. Cook the rice or pasta while chopping and prepping the other ingredients, drain.
2. Place the onion, tomato, bell pepper, olives, and ham in a bowl. Add the cooked rice or pasta and mix gently.
3. Sprinkle with the oil, vinegar, and sugar and mix gently. Serve warm (good on a cold day) or chilled.

Variations:
- Add a little shredded cheese to the top just before serving.
- Add 1 tablespoon pine nuts.
- Add cucumber—cut several slices ¼ inch thick, then cut each slice into quarters.
- Use chicken instead of the ham.

Pasta with Ham in Butter Sauce
Serves 2

This is never quite the same twice. There are lots of options depending on what is available.

Total Time: 30 minutes

pasta for 2 (fettuccine, rotini, spaghetti, penne—almost any type will work)
1 beef bouillon cube OR 1 teaspoon salt
2 tablespoons butter, margarine, olive oil, canola oil, or vegetable oil

2 cups total of any of the following:
- green onions, sliced, including tops, OR diced onion
- mushrooms, fresh or canned
- diced sweet bell or spicy chile peppers, any color
- sun-dried tomatoes, seeded and diced fresh tomatoes, or drained canned tomatoes
- artichoke hearts (in brine or marinated)
- small quantities of canned corn or peas

1 tablespoon minced garlic OR 1 teaspoon garlic powder
1 can (6 ounces) ham, drained and broken into chunks
shredded or grated cheese, for topping (optional)

1. Cook the pasta in sufficient water with a bouillon cube to the desired tenderness.
2. At the same time, melt the butter in a skillet and sauté the mixed vegetables. When just golden, add the garlic and ham and heat through.
3. Drain the pasta and add to the pan, tossing to mix. Serve in bowls, topped with a sprinkling of cheese.

Variations: This is also good with cooked bacon or 1 can (6 ounces) chicken (use chicken broth to cook the pasta).

Creamy Ham and Pasta
Serves 4

Total Time: 30 minutes

pasta for 4 people (bow tie, penne, rotini, fettuccine, spaghetti, or whatever you have)
4 tablespoons butter, margarine, olive oil, canola oil, or vegetable oil
½ cup minced onion OR 5 green onions, thinly sliced, including tops
2 cloves garlic, minced, OR ½ teaspoon garlic powder
2 cans (6 ounces each) ham, broken into bite-size bits
4 tablespoons flour
1½ cups half-and-half (*media crema*), evaporated milk, cream, or milk
½ teaspoon salt
¼ teaspoon ground pepper
½ cup shredded or grated Parmesan or similar cheese

1. Cook the pasta while preparing the sauce. Drain and set aside.
2. Melt the butter in a skillet. Turn the heat to medium and add the onion, garlic, and ham. Sauté until the onion is glazed and the ham is lightly browned.
3. Turn the heat to low and add the flour to the skillet. Stir with the back of a spoon to make a paste with the butter mixture. Add the half-and-half a little at a time, stirring constantly as the mixture thickens to avoid lumps from forming. The mixture should be a little thinner than you'd like the finished sauce to be; it will thicken with the cheese and also with sitting. If needed, add a bit more milk or water.
4. Add the salt, ground pepper, and cheese, continuing to stir frequently. When the cheese is melted, add the drained pasta to the sauce mixture and toss. Serve at once.

Variation: You can also add a can of mushrooms, drained. Sauté them with the onion.

CRAB

Canned crab adds variety and a touch of elegance to the menu.

Crab Dip or Crab Rangoon   Serves 6

A delicious treat for happy hour to celebrate a landfall, a successful repair, or the arrival of guests.

Total Time: 5 minutes for dip, 20 minutes for Crab Rangoon

8 ounces cream cheese, softened
½ teaspoon Old Bay Seasoning (page 48) or other crab/shrimp seasoning mix
few drops of Worcestershire sauce or hot sauce
1 can (6 ounces) crab, drained
crackers, wonton wrappers, or flour tortillas

1. To make the crab mixture, leave the cream cheese out of the refrigerator for a few hours to soften. Mix in the seasonings, then add the crab and mix well. Serve with the crackers.
2. To make Crab Rangoon (cruiser style), preheat oven to 350°F. Put a dollop of the crab mixture in the middle of each wonton wrapper; bring the cor-

ners together, and pinch together at the top. You can also use tortillas cut into quarters; you may have to use a toothpick to hold the corners together. Or you can spread the crab mixture on large flour tortillas, roll them up, and cut into ¼-inch slices to make pinwheels. Arrange on a cookie sheet (as close as you want—they won't spread out) and bake for 5 to 7 minutes, or until just golden brown. The insides should be warm but not hot enough to be runny.

Hot Crab Dip   Serves 4 as an appetizer

You can heat this in a saucepan over very, very low heat. Use a flame tamer (page 15) if you have one.

Total Time: 35 minutes, including 5 minutes to stand before serving
Prep Time: 5 minutes   **Bake Time:** 25 minutes

8 ounces cream cheese, softened
1 can (6 ounces) crabmeat, drained
1 green onion, including top, finely minced, OR 1 tablespoon finely minced onion
1 tablespoon lemon juice, lime juice, or *limón* (Key lime) juice
dash of hot pepper sauce OR ½ teaspoon shrimp/crab seasoning mix

1. Preheat oven to 350°F.
2. In a medium bowl, mash the cream cheese. Add all the other ingredients and mix thoroughly.
3. Place the mixture in a small greased baking dish (I use a 5-inch ovenproof bowl). Bake for about 25 minutes. Remove from the oven and let cool for 5 minutes. Serve with sturdy crackers or vegetable sticks, such as carrots.

Crab, Meat, Seafood, or Fish Cakes   Serves 2

This recipe is incredibly versatile, so you can probably find a combination of ingredients that will work even when the lockers are pretty bare. Adjust the spice quantities to your own preferences.

Total Time: 30 to 40 minutes

any of the following "binders," or a combination if you don't have enough of one:
- 1 medium potato, peeled, boiled, and mashed
- 2 slices bread, crumbled
- ½ cup flour
- ½ cup dry bread crumbs

any of the following "moisteners":
- 1 egg (the best way to help hold the cakes together)
- 2 tablespoons mayonnaise or Miracle Whip
- 2 tablespoons milk
- 2 tablespoons reserved liquid from canned meat

any or all of the following vegetables, but don't exceed the volume of meat (see below):
- ¼ cup chopped onion or green onion (including the tops)
- ¼ cup chopped green bell pepper
- chopped hot chile peppers, to taste
- ¼ cup canned corn, drained
- 1 can (4 ounces) whole or chopped mushrooms OR ½ cup chopped fresh mushrooms

any or all of the following spices:
- 1 teaspoon onion powder or onion salt (if no fresh onion or green onion was added)
- salt and pepper or Mrs. Dash (page 48), to taste

spices for fish or seafood (use any or a combination):
- 2 teaspoons Old Bay Seasoning (page 48)
- few drops hot sauce
- 2 teaspoons ketchup and ½ teaspoon horseradish
- 1 tablespoon salsa (page 127)

spices for ham:
- 2 teaspoons prepared mustard and ⅛ teaspoon ground cloves

spice for corned beef:
- 1 tablespoon ketchup

1 can (6 ounces) crab, ham, tuna, tiny shrimp, salmon, or corned beef, drained
flour, for dusting patties
2 tablespoons oil

1. Mix all the appropriate ingredients in a bowl, adding the meat last so it will stay in large pieces. The mixture should be firm enough to form into patties but still slightly moist. If not, add flour or liquid to achieve the right consistency.
2. Form into two or four patties about 1 inch thick and dust both sides of each patty with the flour (if you're out of flour, the patties will still taste fine but they won't brown as nicely).
3. Pour the 2 tablespoons oil into a skillet and heat until a few drops of water sizzle. If the skillet is not hot enough, the cakes will be greasy instead of having a nice crust.
4. Add the patties and cook for 5 to 7 minutes, or until browned and crusty on the bottom. Carefully turn them over and reduce the heat. Cook for 7 to 10 minutes, or until browned and crusty and cooked through.
5. Serve hot either plain or with hollandaise (page 207) or hot sauce (for fish and seafood), cocktail sauce (for shrimp, page 211), or mustard or pineapple sauce (for ham).

Variations:
- With ham, add 2 to 3 tablespoons crushed pineapple or pineapple bits.
- With corned beef, add 2 tablespoons sauerkraut, and use Russian or Thousand Island dressing for moistening.
- Add grated or small cubes of cheese to almost any meat.
- Use canned hash in place of meat and potatoes.

Mexican Crab Salad   Serves 4

Total Time: 15 minutes

1 can (6 ounces) crabmeat, drained
2 avocados, seeded, peeled, and diced
3 jalapeños, seeded and diced, or to taste
1 tablespoon minced garlic
¼ cup chopped fresh cilantro
juice of 4 *limónes* (Key limes) or 1 lime or 1 lemon
salt, to taste
cayenne pepper, to taste
4 tablespoons mayonnaise or Miracle Whip
4 large tomatoes, hollowed out*

If you don't have large tomatoes, serve the crab salad surrounded by tomato wedges.

1. Combine the crab, avocado, jalapeño, garlic, cilantro, lime juice, salt, cayenne, and mayonnaise; stir to mix.
2. Spoon the crab mixture into the tomatoes (depending on the size of the tomato, there will likely be some left over). Place each tomato on a plate and surround with any extra crab mixture. May be served immediately or refrigerated up to 2 hours.

Crab and Mushroom Quiche
Serves 6

Total Time: 1 hour, 15 minutes (plus time to make piecrust if needed)
Prep Time: 20 minutes   **Bake Time:** 45 minutes

9-inch piecrust in pie pan (page 425)
1 tablespoon olive oil, canola oil, vegetable oil, butter, or margarine
2 cloves garlic, minced
1 tablespoon finely minced green onion or onion
1 can (8 ounces) mushrooms (pieces, sliced, or button), drained
1 1/2 cups half-and-half (*media crema*), evaporated milk, cream, or milk
4 large eggs
dash of hot sauce
1 teaspoon Old Bay Seasoning (page 48) or other crab/shrimp seasoning
1 cup shredded cheese
1 can (6 ounces) crabmeat, drained

Make as for quiche (page 115).

Crab Salad
Serves 2

This can be served in many ways: as sandwiches, on a bed of lettuce, with crackers, or as a stuffed tomato. It's also good spread on a slice of bread and broiled until just golden.

Total Time: 10 minutes

1 can (6 ounces) crabmeat, drained
1/4 cup mayonnaise or Miracle Whip
1 tablespoon lemon juice, lime juice, or *limón* (Key lime) juice
1/4 teaspoon salt
1/2 cup finely diced celery

3 tablespoons thinly sliced green onion, including tops
1/2 teaspoon Old Bay Seasoning (page 48), optional
2 tablespoons shredded cheese, optional
5 grapes, cut in half (seed if not seedless), optional

Mix all the ingredients in a bowl. If desired, make ahead and refrigerate up to a day before serving.

SEAFOOD

Sometimes we just don't catch what we want. A few cans of seafood can help out!

Seafood and Tomato Casserole
Serves 4

Total Time: 1 hour, including stand time
Prep Time: 20 minutes
Bake Time: 30 minutes

2 cups canned shrimp, crab, tuna, and/or salmon, drained*
3 cups soft bread crumbs
2 tablespoons olive oil, canola oil, or vegetable oil, or melted butter or margarine
1/4 cup diced onion
1/2 teaspoon Old Bay Seasoning (page 48) or other seafood seasoning or ground pepper
1 teaspoon sugar
1/2 teaspoon salt
2 1/2 cups chopped tomato, most seeds removed, OR 1 can (16 ounces) diced tomatoes, drained
1/2 green bell pepper, seeded and diced
1 teaspoon lemon, *limón* (Key lime), or lime juice (optional) OR 1/2 teaspoon Worcestershire sauce (optional)
1 egg, beaten (optional)
1/4 cup white wine (optional)
1/2 to 1 cup shredded cheese, for topping

You can use just one or a mixture.

1. Preheat oven to 375°F.
2. In a large bowl combine the canned seafood, bread crumbs, oil, onion, Old Bay Seasoning, sugar, salt, tomato, bell pepper, and lemon juice. Add the egg and wine (if desired); mix thoroughly.

3. Spoon into a greased baking dish (a loaf pan works well). Sprinkle the cheese over the top. Bake, uncovered, for about 30 minutes, or until the cheese is melted and turning golden. The exact time will vary with the size of the pan and which of the optional ingredients are used. Remove from the oven and let stand for 10 minutes before serving.

Seafood Lasagna   Serves 8

If you don't have lasagna noodles, I've made this with bite-size pasta such as penne, rotini, or bow ties, and just mixed all the ingredients and put them in a casserole to bake.

Total Time: 1 hour, 30 minutes, including stand time
Prep Time: 30 minutes   **Bake Time:** 45 minutes

$1/2$ cup butter, margarine, canola oil, or vegetable oil
$1/2$ cup flour
2 cups milk or evaporated milk
2 cups shrimp broth,* chicken broth (may be made from bouillon), or stock (page 164)
3 green onions, including tops, thinly sliced, OR $1/2$ cup finely diced onion
1 teaspoon dried basil
2 cloves garlic, finely minced
1 cup shredded mozzarella or similar mild cheese
1 pound uncooked lasagna noodles
1 cup ricotta (page 100), cottage cheese, or other similar cheese
3 cans (6 ounces each) shrimp and/or crabmeat, drained
$1/2$ cup grated or shredded Parmesan cheese

Shrimp bouillon is available in many Latin American countries.

1. Preheat oven to 350°F.
2. Melt the butter over low heat, and stir in the flour. Stirring constantly, slowly add the milk and broth. Continuing to stir, turn the heat to medium and bring the mixture to a boil. Boil for 1 to 2 minutes, or until thick.
3. Turn the heat back down to the lowest possible setting and add the green onion, basil, garlic, and mozzarella. Continue to stir constantly until the cheese is melted.

4. Spread one-quarter of the cheese mixture in a 9"×13" pan. Place the uncooked lasagna noodles (generally it takes 3) over the top. Dab the ricotta over the lasagna, and top with another one-quarter of the sauce. Add another layer of lasagna noodles.
5. Sprinkle the seafood over the lasagna, and top with another one-quarter of the sauce. Add another layer of lasagna noodles. Top with the remaining sauce and sprinkle with the Parmesan. Bake, uncovered, for 45 minutes, or until bubbly and a fork can pierce the noodles. Remove from the oven and let stand for 15 minutes before cutting and serving.

Salmon Salad   Serves 4

A great cold dinner, particularly with some fresh bread!

Total Time: 15 minutes (better if you can make the dressing a few hours ahead and chill it)

Dressing
$1/2$ cup plain yogurt (page 101)
$1/4$ cup mayonnaise or Miracle Whip
1 tablespoon milk or water
1 teaspoon chopped fresh dill OR $1/2$ teaspoon dried dill
$1/8$ teaspoon onion powder

Salad
8 cups greens (spinach is great, but any greens will work)
1 cup cubed cheese (cheddar or Colby are preferred, but others are acceptable)
$1/2$ cup croutons (page 162)
1 tomato, seeded and diced
1 can (12 ounces) salmon, drained and broken into bite-size pieces
4 green onions, including tops, thinly sliced, OR $1/2$ cup diced onion

1. Combine the dressing ingredients in a plastic bowl with a tight lid. Mix well. If possible, refrigerate for a few hours to let the flavors mix (but it can be used immediately).
2. Mix the salad ingredients in a large bowl. Pour the dressing over the salad and toss. Serve immediately.

Canned Meats and Seafood

Salmon and Couscous Salad

Serves 4

Total Time: 20 minutes

1¼ cups* shrimp or chicken broth (may be made
    from bouillon) or stock (page 164)
1 cup couscous
2 green onions, including tops, thinly sliced
1 carrot, thinly sliced
¼ cup chopped walnuts or pecans
1 can (12 ounces) salmon, drained
¼ cup vinaigrette dressing (the dressing for the
    Greek Salad, page 151, or Carolyn's Vinegar
    and Oil, page 161, or Good Seasons Italian
    dressing, page 161, work well)

*Or use the amount of liquid specified for your brand of
couscous.

1. Place the broth and couscous in a medium pan.
   Cover, bring to boil, and turn the heat off. Let sit
   for 5 minutes while you prepare the green onion
   and carrots.
2. Add the green onion, carrot, nuts, and salmon to
   the couscous. Stir to combine, breaking the salmon
   into bite-size pieces.
3. Add the vinaigrette and toss. Serve plain or on a
   bed or greens or stuffed in a tomato. May be made
   ahead and refrigerated to serve cold.

Salmon Quesadillas

Serves 4

Total Time: 10 minutes

4 flour or corn tortillas
1 cup shredded cheese that will melt (cheddar and
    Colby are great)
1 can (12 ounces) salmon, tuna, or crab, drained
    and flaked
sour cream (page 99), *pico de gallo* (page 128),
    guacamole (page 129), and/or ranch dressing
    (page 161), optional toppings

1. Over medium heat, warm a dry skillet large enough
   to hold a tortilla laid flat. When hot, place 1 tortilla
   in the ungreased pan. Quickly sprinkle one-quarter
   of the cheese on half of the tortilla and top with
   one-quarter of the salmon. Fold the "bare" half of
   the tortilla over the top and lightly press it down
   with a spatula. Cook for about 1 minute, or until
   the bottom is lightly browned. Gently flip and cook
   another 1 to 2 minutes, or until lightly browned.
   Remove from the skillet and place on a plate.
   Repeat with the other tortillas and the remaining
   filling.
2. To serve, cut each quesadilla into three wedges.
   Serve with the optional toppings if desired.

New England Clam Chowder

Serves 6

Total Time: 50 minutes
Prep Time: 20 minutes

6 slices bacon, cut into 1-inch pieces
1 onion, diced
2 stalks celery, diced, OR ¼ teaspoon celery salt
2 cloves garlic, minced
2 bay leaves
⅛ teaspoon dried thyme
3 cups shrimp or chicken broth (may be made
    from bouillon) or stock (page 164)
4 medium potatoes, peeled and cut into 1-inch
    chunks
1 can (16 ounces) corn, drained
36 ounces canned clams,* drained, juice reserved
2 cups cream, evaporated milk (page 99), or milk
salt and pepper, to taste

*If you don't have enough clams, use fewer, or mix in
    some canned chicken or ham.

1. Fry the bacon in a large pot. Remove and set aside,
   but leave the bacon fat in the pot. Add the onion,
   celery, and garlic and sauté until tender.
2. Add the bay leaves, thyme, broth, potato, corn,
   and reserved clam juice. Continue to cook over
   medium heat until the potato is just tender—don't
   overcook or the potato will be mushy.

3. Turn the heat to low, and add the clams and cream. Add salt and pepper to taste. Heat just until warmed through—if you cook it too long, the clams will get tough (and the potato will get mushy)—stirring frequently so the cream doesn't scorch. Serve hot.

Linguine and Clam Sauce   Serves 2

You can make the same recipe with fresh clams, too. It's also good with canned ham, chicken, or shrimp in place of the clams.

Total Time: 30 minutes

1/2 pound linguine or other pasta such as spaghetti, fettuccine, penne, or rotini
2 tablespoons olive oil, butter, margarine, canola oil, or vegetable oil
1/4 teaspoon red pepper flakes
2 cloves garlic, minced, OR 1/2 teaspoon garlic powder
1 green onion, including top, finely sliced
1 teaspoon dried oregano
1 or 2 cans (12 ounces each) clams, not drained
1/2 cup white wine, milk, or water
1/4 cup cream, half-and-half (*media crema*), or evaporated milk (page 99)
1/3 cup Parmesan or Romano cheese or other hard cheese

1. Cook the linguine as directed on the package while preparing the sauce. Drain.
2. Heat the oil in a skillet over medium heat. Add the pepper flakes, garlic, and green onion. Sauté just until the onion is soft. Add the oregano, the juice from the clams, and the wine. Cook, stirring occasionally, until about half the liquid is gone.
3. Turn the heat to the lowest it will go—the clams will get tough if cooked very long or at high heat.

Mix in the clams and cream and cook about 2 to 3 minutes, or just until heated through.
4. You can serve by putting the pasta in bowls and covering it with the sauce, or by tossing the pasta and sauce in the pan and then serving it in bowls. Sprinkle with the Parmesan.

Variations:
- Add a can of drained mushrooms to the green onion when sautéing.
- Seed and dice a tomato and add it when adding the clams.

CANNED MEATS AND SEAFOOD IN OTHER CHAPTERS

The following recipes from other chapters use canned meat or seafood, or either can be easily substituted.

Appetizers and Snacks
Tuna and Bean Dip, *page 132*
Easy Smoked Tuna Dip, *page 132*
Cream Cheese and Tuna Dip, *page 133*
Spicy Tuna Dip, *page 133*
Crab Dip, *page 135*
Clam Dip, *page 136*
Seafood "Pizza," *page 140*
Curried Chicken Tidbits, *page 140*

Salads
Mediterranean Pasta Salad, *page 158*

Soups and Stews
Potato and Ham Soup, *page 170*

Seafood
Conch Fritters, *page 253*; substituting tuna makes an everyday fritter!

GRILLING

While relaxing in the cockpit and enjoying the sunset with a cool drink, there's nothing easier than lighting the grill on the back rail and savoring the tantalizing smells that soon waft through the cockpit and drift over the anchorage.

Grilling allows you to enjoy delicious food with a minimum of cleanup. Plus grilling keeps the heat out below decks. Perhaps this chapter will entice you into taking the plunge and lighting your grill.

You can grill just about anything you can cook on the galley stove or in the oven. Aboard *Winterlude*, our grill is totally separate from our propane stove. If our stove should fail or if we should run out of propane in the main tank, the grill is our backup. Operated from a separate canister of camping propane, the grill is not plumbed into the boat's propane supply.

We have had no trouble buying camping propane tanks anywhere in the northwest or southwest Caribbean. The easiest places to find them are hardware stores. Sometimes they are tanks used for propane blowtorches or other tools, but the fittings work with our grill.

Everyone can relate to grilling hamburgers, pork chops, chicken, and a nice thick, juicy steak, but what about grilling tuna, grouper, mackerel, and other fish as well as lobster, shrimp, and even the all-American favorite, pizza. It's delicious with made-from-scratch dough and toppings from what you already have aboard.

First, some general grilling tips:

- If you have a gas grill that's not piped to the main propane tank, always keep an extra camping bottle of propane fuel for the grill. There's nothing worse than a barely cooked steak and no propane! Aboard *Winterlude* we go through a camping propane canister every two weeks, so we stock several aboard. We store the extra camping propane tanks in our regular vented propane locker. If your propane locker won't hold them securely, make sure you wedge them in so they don't roll around under way.

- Keep a small squirt bottle of water nearby to douse flare-ups caused by fat dripping onto the grill.

- Let the grill come up to temperature before cooking. This is more important with charcoal than with gas. Meats in particular need to have the outside seared to keep the juices locked in.

- Resist the temptation to open the lid of the grill too often while cooking—all the heat will escape.

- Clean the grill grates periodically. A good grill brush will work wonders.

- Inspect your grill twice a year. In the harsh salt-water environment, the parts do fail. In particular we've replaced the starter, and we've rusted through two burners. Because we use our grill several nights a week, we carry several spare parts: a regulator, an ignitor, and a grill burner along with spare camping propane tanks.

We have included the section Step-by-Step Instructions for Grilling as a reference point for those unfamiliar with grilling. Please note that other successful grillers may have different methods, and that there is no one way to grill. The step-by-step instructions are from my husband, David's, 40 years of grilling success. Note that some recipes—such as pizza—call for other techniques, and we have detailed those in the recipes.

STEP-BY-STEP INSTRUCTIONS FOR GRILLING

Since there are two basic methods for grilling, we'll break out propane grilling steps from charcoal grilling steps.

Basic Step-by-Step Propane Grilling

1. Open the lid and take a look at the grill. David usually wire-brushes the grates. If it's been a while between cleanings, you may need to clean out the crumbs in the bottom.
2. Turn on the propane—it should always be in the off position when you're not using the grill—and flick the starter (if you have one) to get a flame. Aboard *Winterlude*, our automatic starter doesn't work, so David takes off one grate and uses a propane lighter (the type with a long tube; not a cigarette lighter), placing it at the front of the flame tube. It usually lights right away without a big explosion. Replace the grate.
3. If it doesn't light right away, turn off the propane for a couple of minutes to allow any accumulated propane to disburse. Then repeat step 2.
4. There's no need to preheat a propane grill. By the time we turn it on, grab the meat, and return to the grill, the flames are ready. If you want to make sure that the grate is hot enough to sear, you can wait a couple of minutes.
5. Adjust the flame for hot or medium temperature. There are no markings on our dial, so twisted all the way is high and anything less is less hot. Depending on what we're grilling, most times the dial is set closer to high in order to sear to begin the cooking.

6. Get whatever you're grilling and put it on the grill.
7. Close the cover.
8. Set a timer or a watch for 5 minutes. Usually after a minute and a half, David scoops up the meat just to make sure it's not sticking. At 5 minutes, flip it over. Usually you don't need to sear and move it again on the flip side, but sometimes he sears and moves it just to make sure it's not sticking to the grill.
9. Turn every 5 minutes. For complete instructions, see below.
10. The whole success to grilling is watching the time. From there it becomes experience to know which piece of meat and which timing produces the best results.

Basic Step-by-Step Charcoal Grilling

1. Open the vents on the bottom of the grill. Then open the vent on the top of the grill.
2. Remove the lid.
3. There's usually a grate under the charcoal and a grate that you're going to cook the food on. Take out the top (food) grate.
4. Pour in the charcoal. Whenever possible, we use Kingsford Charcoal and Kingsford Charcoal Lighter; anything else seems to inhibit starting and burning efficiently. Briquettes are usually stacked about two to four briquettes high and centered in the grill. Note that Weber and other grill manufacturers will tell you to put a ring of charcoal around the outside, leaving the center open. We don't use the ring because the center method produces a fire that's easier to light and quicker to be ready.
5. Douse the charcoal thoroughly with charcoal lighter. Most people don't use enough lighter fluid. David circles it around about eight to ten times.
6. Immediately light with a match. (Do not wait a few minutes for the charcoal lighter to "saturate.") Drop the match on the charcoal pile; it should light if you have adequate charcoal lighter saturating it.
7. Put the grate back on the grill, but leave the lid off.
8. In about 10 minutes the flame will have gone out and the briquettes will be getting white around

the edges. The top of the grate in the middle will be glowing pretty hot.

9. If after 10 minutes the briquettes aren't getting white around the edges, you may need to squirt the briquettes with more lighter. (If you didn't put enough charcoal lighter in originally, or if you're using inferior quality charcoal or charcoal lighter, it does happen.) Stand back and THROW the match into the hot coals. THIS IS DANGEROUS; BE CAREFUL!

10. By now, the fire has burnt off anything remaining on the grate from the night before, so take a wire brush and do a quick brush of the grate to give it a final cleaning.

11. In no more than 15 minutes, the charcoals should have a thin white coating of ash and be heating evenly.

12. Place the meat in the middle of the grill, put the lid on (the vent holes should still be open!), set the timer, and turn the meat every 5 minutes. (See in-depth instructions below.) After the first minute and a half, the heat will have seared in the juices, so move the meat slightly so it doesn't stick to the grill.

13. It's even more critical to monitor what's happening during cooking with a charcoal fire than a propane fire. Most tough meat is caused by not monitoring it closely enough.

14. After you're done cooking, close the bottom vents and then close the top vents. Put the lid back on. This way, the charcoal won't totally burn up, and you have some left for the next grilling. The burnt charcoal seems to act as a catalyst, allowing the grill to start faster the next time.

15. Clean out the bottom of the grill—where it catches all the ash and grease—about once a week.

Happy grilling!

GRILLING TIPS FOR STEAKS, CHICKEN, AND PORK

1. Start with room-temperature meat for the juiciest results.
2. Never leave meat unattended. Turn every 5 minutes—time it with your watch. The most common problem with grilling is not paying enough attention to the time. Chicken and pork chops tend to take about 15 minutes; turn them three times to be done. Hamburgers take about 15 minutes, a bit less for thinner burgers or for less done. Steak, depending on the thickness, takes 10 minutes or less. Pork loin or roasts take longer, but still turn them every 5 minutes.
3. After about a minute and a half, pick up the meat off the hot grill to prevent sticking.
4. Don't cut or puncture the meat even with a fork. Use tongs or a spatula. Inside juices are always on the lookout for an avenue of escape, rendering your dinner dry and tasteless.
5. After cooking, let the meat stand for 5 minutes off the grill. Don't cut into it right away or you'll lose the juices you worked so hard to save while grilling.

Experienced grillers simply eyeball steaks to know how long to grill for a particular doneness. If cooking multiple steaks, David redistributes "rare" to the outside, where the grill is cooler, after searing on the hot middle section to seal in the juices. The chart on the next page is simply a starting point if you're not experienced in eyeballing steaks.

BE CAREFUL—you can always put a steak back on the fire, but you cannot turn shoe leather into edible.

Note that times in the chart on the next page are for total time, not time per side. Don't forget David's 5-minute rule (or in the case of 1-inch thick, 8 minutes for rare—just split the time 4 minutes on one side and 4 minutes on the other side).

The best way to know when meat is done is to use an instant-read thermometer.

The USDA recommends cooking all whole cuts of meat, including steaks and pork, to 145°F as measured with a meat thermometer placed in the thickest part of the meat, then allowing the meat to rest for 3 minutes before carving or consuming. Ground

TOTAL NUMBER OF MINUTES FOR GRILLING STEAKS

STEAK THICKNESS ON A HOT FIRE	RARE	MEDIUM	WELL DONE
1" thick	8–10	10–12	15
1½" thick	10–14	16–20	22–26
2" thick	12–16	18–22	24–28

meats, including ground beef, veal, lamb, and pork, should be cooked to 160°F and do not require a rest time. The safe cooking temperature for all poultry products, including ground chicken and turkey, remains at 165°F.

Appearance of Cooked Pork

The new cooking recommendations clarify long-held perceptions about cooking pork. Historically, consumers have viewed the color pink in pork to be a sign of undercooked meat. If raw pork is cooked to 145°F and allowed to rest for 3 minutes, it may still be pink but is safe to eat and may be juicier!

GRILLED PORK

There are many great ways to prepare pork on the grill!

Ginger Beer Chops   Serves 4

Total Time: 6 hours, 15 minutes, including 6 hours to marinate
Prep Time: 5 minutes   Grill Time: 10 minutes

1 cup beer (two-thirds of a typical can or bottle— enjoy the rest ice-cold!)
¼ cup soy sauce
2 tablespoons brown sugar or white sugar
2 teaspoons grated fresh ginger OR ⅛ teaspoon ground ginger
4 boneless pork loin chops or other pork chops

1. Combine the beer, soy sauce, brown sugar, and ginger to make the marinade. Put the chops and the marinade in a leakproof freezer bag. Refrigerate 6 hours to overnight.

2. Remove the chops from the marinade and allow to return to room temperature before grilling. Discard the marinade.
3. Set the grill to medium, put the chops on the grill, and close the lid. Turn every 5 minutes. **Total Time:** 10 minutes for regular thickness chops; longer for thick cut. Check for doneness (see the USDA requirements on page 330).

Caribbean Pork Chops   Serves 4

Total Time: 6 hours, 20 minutes, including minimum 6 hours to marinate
Prep Time: 5 minutes   Grill Time: 10 to 15 minutes

1 cup chicken broth (may be made from bouillon) or stock (page 164)
½ cup orange juice
2 tablespoons dark rum
2 tablespoons lime juice, lemon juice, or *limón* (Key lime) juice
2 tablespoons brown sugar or white sugar
1 clove garlic, minced, OR ¼ teaspoon garlic powder
½ teaspoon salt
½ teaspoon ground ginger
¼ teaspoon ground nutmeg
¼ teaspoon ground cloves
4 boneless pork loin chops or other pork chops

1. Combine the broth, orange juice, rum, lime juice, brown sugar, garlic, salt, ground ginger, nutmeg, and cloves in a leakproof freezer bag; mix well. Add the chops, seal the bag, and refrigerate for 6 hours to overnight.
2. Remove the chops and discard the marinade. Let the chops come to room temperature before grilling.
3. Grill the chops on a covered grill for 5 minutes. Turn the chops, then grill for 5 more minutes. Test for doneness (page 330). If there is any question, turn and grill for another 5 minutes. Larger or thicker chops will take more than the initial 10 minutes, but do not overgrill.

Grilling

Pork Chops with Southwest Salsa
Serves 2

Both of us and our husbands had this on our first charter trip that we took together in the British Virgin Islands. It's delicious and brings back good memories every time we have it!

Total Time: 30 minutes, plus optional marinate time
Prep Time: 20 minutes   Grill Time: 10 minutes

Salsa
1 can (8 ounces) pineapple bits,* drained, OR
   1 cup diced fresh pineapple
1/2 cucumber, peeled, seeded, and diced
1 1/2 teaspoons lime juice, *limón* (Key lime) juice,
   or lemon juice
1 1/2 teaspoons brown sugar, honey, or white sugar
salt, to taste
1/2 jalapeño pepper or any other spicy chile pepper, seeded and minced, to taste, OR canned
   green chilies OR dash of cayenne pepper or hot
   sauce

Rub
1 1/2 teaspoons chili powder
1 1/2 teaspoons ground cumin
1 1/2 teaspoons ground pepper (course ground is
   nice)
1/4 teaspoon salt
2 pork chops, preferably thick cut, OR 1-inch-thick
   slices of pork tenderloin OR 4 chicken breasts

If you have chunks or slices of pineapple, chop them up a bit.

1. Make the salsa by mixing all the salsa ingredients. If you have time, make it ahead and refrigerate for a couple hours. Bring to room temperature before serving.
2. To make the rub, mix the rub ingredients and rub into both sides of the chops. Grill over a medium-hot grill for about 5 minutes per side (less for thinner chops, longer for chicken breasts). If you have any question about doneness, see page 330.
3. Serve with a generous dollop of salsa on top or on the side.

NOTE: This dish may instead be cooked on the stove or in the oven, if desired, or if a sudden thunderstorm makes grilling less appealing.

Spicy Grilled Pork Tenderloin
Serves 2

Total Time: 5 hours, including 4 hours to marinate
Prep Time: 10 minutes   Cook Time: 30 to 45 minutes

1 teaspoon salt
1 teaspoon ground pepper
1 teaspoon garlic powder
1 teaspoon dry mustard
1 teaspoon ground cloves
1 teaspoon cayenne pepper
1 teaspoon ground cinnamon
1 teaspoon ground cumin
1/2 pork tenderloin for every 2 people (1/4 to
   1/3 pound per person)
2 tablespoons olive oil, canola oil, or vegetable oil

1. Combine all the spices in a small bowl.
2. Lay the tenderloin on waxed paper or aluminum foil. Drizzle half of the olive oil over the tenderloin. Sprinkle with half the spice mixture. Turn the tenderloin, drizzle with the remaining olive oil, and sprinkle with the remaining spice mixture. Fold the waxed paper completely around the tenderloin and refrigerate for a minimum of 4 hours.
3. Remove the meat from the waxed paper and grill over medium heat with the lid closed. Cook for 15 minutes, then turn the meat and cook until done to your preference. We cook for a total of 20 to 30 minutes depending on the size of the tenderloin. Check for doneness (page 330). Let stand for 3 minutes before slicing and serving.

NOTE: if you're cruising in Belize, do not miss the pork tenderloins—two to a package and absolutely some of the best meat we found anywhere cruising. You may have to dig through the giant chest freezers to find them. Wallen's in Placencia has them in an easy-to-see display case.

Grilled Pork Tenderloin "Roast"

Serves 4

You can also bake the roast in an oven at 350°F for 30 to 40 minutes.

Total Time: 65 minutes, including 10 minutes to stand before serving
Prep Time: 15 minutes   **Cook Time:** 40 minutes

4 small red potatoes
¼ small head cabbage
1 small onion
½ cup sliced fresh mushrooms OR 1 can (8 ounces) mushrooms, drained
1 tablespoon olive oil, canola oil, or vegetable oil
1 pound pork tenderloin
½ cup Asian sesame dressing or Italian dressing (page 161)
¼ cup soy sauce
¼ cup Thai sweet chili sauce (page 215)

1. Julienne (cut into pieces about the size and shape of matchsticks) the potatoes, cabbage, onion, and mushrooms.
2. Grease a metal loaf pan with the olive oil. Put one-quarter of the onion slivers in the bottom. Place the pork tenderloin on top of the onion. Add the rest of the vegetables around and over the pork tenderloin.
3. Mix the salad dressing, soy sauce, and sweet chili sauce and pour over the pork tenderloin and vegetable mixture. Cover with aluminum foil.
4. Place the sealed pan on a medium grill. Close the lid, and grill for 40 minutes, watching carefully that the grill is not too hot. Test for doneness (page 330). Let stand for 10 minutes before carving the meat.

Billy's World's Best Ribs

Serves any number

In the unlikely event that you find ribs and have a strong enough craving to want to put up with the extra oven time, propane use, and heat in your galley, here's our favorite rib recipe! By the way, Billy is Jan's son—a Lieutenant in the US Navy. He introduced us to his ribs while in Annapolis celebrating his 2008 graduation from the US Naval Academy.

Total Time: 3 to 4 hours
Prep Time: 5 minutes
Cook Time: 2 to 3 hours bake time, 10 minutes on the grill

pork ribs (baby back ribs are best if available), allow at least 1 pound of ribs per person
orange juice
barbecue sauce (page 215; our favorite is Sweet Baby Ray's BBQ)

1. Preheat oven to 275°F.
2. Place the ribs in an ovenproof dish, preferably one large enough to hold them in a single layer. Cover with a combination of orange juice and your favorite barbecue sauce—stirred slightly to mix the flavors.
3. Cover the pan with aluminum foil and bake for 2 to 4 hours depending on the quantity of ribs. The low-temperature baking will make the ribs very tender as well as drive out part of the fat. Test for doneness by piercing with a fork—it should enter the meaty area very easily for "fall off the bone" ribs.
4. Remove the pan from the oven and transfer the ribs to a medium-hot grill. Baste with fresh barbecue sauce. Grill for 2 to 5 minutes per side, or just long enough on each side for the sauce to "crunch" up a bit.
5. Break out plenty of napkins, some extra dipping sauce, and enjoy!

Grilling

GRILLED CHICKEN

Chicken takes a slightly lower fire than beef to ensure that it's fully cooked.

Spicy Chicken Kabobs with Thai Peanut Sauce   Serves 4 to 6

Total Time: 6½ hours, including 6 hours to marinate
Prep Time: 20 minutes   Cook Time: 10 minutes

4 boneless, skinless chicken breasts or other chicken cuts

Marinade
2 tablespoons sesame oil, canola oil, or vegetable oil (the flavor will be different without sesame oil)
2 tablespoons canola oil or vegetable oil
¼ cup dry sherry or chicken broth (may be made from bouillon) or stock (page 164)
¼ cup soy sauce
2 tablespoons lemon juice or lime juice
2 teaspoons minced garlic OR ¼ teaspoon garlic powder
2 teaspoons minced fresh ginger OR ⅛ teaspoon ground ginger
½ teaspoon salt
½ teaspoon ground pepper
⅛ teaspoon Tabasco sauce or hot sauce

Spicy Peanut Sauce
½ cup minced onion (red onion is good)
2 tablespoons minced garlic OR ¾ teaspoon garlic powder
1 teaspoon minced fresh ginger OR ⅛ teaspoon ground ginger
4 teaspoons canola oil or vegetable oil
2 teaspoons sesame oil, canola oil, or vegetable oil
1 tablespoon red wine vinegar, white vinegar, or balsamic vinegar
1 tablespoon brown sugar or white sugar
⅓ cup peanut butter
½ teaspoon ground coriander
3 tablespoons ketchup
3 tablespoons soy sauce
1 tablespoon lemon or lime juice

½ teaspoon ground pepper
⅛ teaspoon Tabasco or other hot sauce
⅓ cup hot water—more if you want a thinner sauce

1. Cut the chicken into 1-inch chunks suitable for putting on kabob skewers. We use metal kabob skewers aboard, but you can also use wood skewers, but soak them in water for a half hour before using.
2. Combine all the marinade ingredients and add the chicken. A leakproof freezer bag works perfectly for marinating on a boat. Place in the refrigerator to marinate for 6 hours.
3. Just before grilling the chicken, make the peanut sauce. Sauté the onion, garlic, and ginger in the canola oil and sesame oil. Add the vinegar and sugar and stir until the sugar dissolves. Remove from the heat and add the remaining sauce ingredients. Set aside.
4. Remove the chicken from the marinade and discard the marinade. Thread the chicken on the skewers and grill for 5 minutes, then turn and grill for another 5 minutes. Serve with the Spicy Peanut Sauce over rice.

Jerk Chicken Kabobs   Serves 2

Total Time: 2 hours 30 minutes, including 2 hours to marinate
Prep Time: 15 minutes   Grill Time: 15 minutes

2 boneless, skinless chicken breasts or other cut of chicken
Jerk Chicken Marinade (purchased or recipe below)
1 small onion, cut into wedges
1 cup cherry tomatoes
1 green bell pepper, seeded and cut into 1-inch chunks
4 ounces fresh mushrooms
2 servings cooked rice

1. Cut the chicken into 1-inch chunks. Place the chunks into prepared Jerk Chicken Marinade–we prefer KC Masterpiece, or see below to make your own. Reserve part of the marinade for basting and dipping. Marinate for a minimum of 2 hours, turning frequently.

2. Alternate the marinated chicken chunks, onion wedges, cherry tomatoes, bell pepper chunks, and mushrooms onto kabob skewers. Brush with the jerk marinade. We use metal skewers, but if you use wood skewers, be sure to soak them in water for a half hour prior to making the kabobs.

3. Place the kabobs on the grill, turning every 5 minutes until done, for a total of 10 minutes. Baste with the fresh reserved marinade each time the skewers are turned. Serve over rice with the reserved marinade for dipping.

Homemade Jerk Marinade

½ cup orange juice
½ cup cider vinegar, white vinegar, or other vinegar
¼ cup soy sauce
¼ cup olive oil, canola oil, or vegetable oil
1 jalapeño pepper, seeded and minced
1 tablespoon brown sugar
1 teaspoon salt
1 teaspoon dried thyme
1 teaspoon ground cinnamon
½ teaspoon ground nutmeg
1 tablespoon ground allspice
1 tablespoon minced fresh ginger OR ½ teaspoon ground ginger
3 cloves garlic, minced, OR 1 teaspoon garlic powder, or more to taste
4 green onions, finely sliced, OR ½ small onion, finely diced

Mix all the ingredients in a bowl. Reserve half for dipping.

BBQ Honey Glazed Chicken   Serves 4

Total Time: 20 minutes
Prep Time: 10 minutes   **Grill Time:** 10 minutes

½ cup barbecue sauce (page 215)
1 tablespoon honey
¼ cup mayonnaise
2 cloves garlic, crushed, OR ½ teaspoon garlic powder
2 teaspoons grated fresh ginger OR ⅛ teaspoon ground ginger
4 boneless, skinless chicken breasts or other cut of chicken

Combine the barbecue sauce, honey, mayonnaise, garlic, and ginger. Generously brush on both sides of each chicken breast. Grill for approximately 5 minutes on each side (a total of 10 minutes), brushing more sauce on every few minutes.

NOTE: If the chicken breasts are larger, it might take an additional 5 minutes or a total of 15 minutes grill time. Other cuts, particularly ones with bones in, may take longer. Test for doneness (page 330).

Beer Can Chicken   Serves 4

Also known as "Drunken Chicken" or "Beer Butt Chicken," this produces the most flavorful and moist chicken and is perfect for a group! This may or may not work on your boat grill depending on the size of your chicken. It requires 10 to 12 inches of space between the grate and the lid. Even if it won't work on your boat's grill, you might be able to prepare it on a marina grill!

Total Time: 1 hour, 25 minutes
Prep Time: 10 minutes
Cook Time: 1 hour, 15 minutes

1 whole chicken
2 tablespoons olive oil, canola oil, or vegetable oil
2 tablespoons salt
1 teaspoon ground pepper
3 tablespoons of your favorite dry spice rub (page 219)
1 can beer (must be in a can)

1. Thoroughly wash the chicken and then wipe dry with paper towels. Rub the chicken lightly with oil, then rub inside and out with salt, ground pepper, and the dry rub. Set aside.

2. Wash the outside of the beer can. Open the can and enjoy a couple swigs so that the can is not totally full. Place the beer can on a solid surface. Grabbing a chicken leg in each hand, plunk the bird cavity over the beer can (put the can through the larger of the two openings); despite many cruisers calling this recipe "Beer Butt Chicken," you are actually putting the beer can into the neck opening.

3. Transfer the bird-on-a-can to the grill and place it upright in the center of the grate, balancing the bird on its two legs and the can like a tripod.

Grilling

4. Cook the chicken over medium-high, indirect heat (that is, no coals or lit burners directly under the bird), with the grill cover on, for approximately 1¼ hours, or until the internal temperature registers 165°F, or until the thigh juice runs clear when pierced with a sharp knife.
5. Remove from the grill, carefully extract the beer can (don't burn yourself), and let the chicken rest for 10 minutes before carving.

NOTE: Friends tried this on a large marina grill with a small turkey and a large Foster's beer can for Thanksgiving. It took forever to cook: 4+ hours!

Garlic Lime Grilled Chicken   Serves 2

Total Time: 5 hours, including 4 hours to marinate
Prep Time: 40 minutes   Cook Time: 15 minute

2 boneless, skinless chicken breasts or any cut of chicken (adjust grilling time)
⅓ cup soy sauce
¼ cup lime juice or *limón* (Key lime) juice
1 tablespoon Worcestershire sauce
2 cloves garlic, minced
dash of hot sauce
½ teaspoon ground pepper

1. Place the chicken in large leakproof freezer bag.
2. Mix together the soy sauce, lime juice, Worcestershire sauce, garlic, and hot sauce. Pour over the chicken in the bag, reserving a little to brush on the chicken at the end of the grilling time. Let the chicken marinate in the refrigerator for 4 hours, turning every 30 minutes. Remove the chicken from the bag, and discard the marinade.
3. Sprinkle the chicken with the ground pepper. Grill over medium-high heat for 5 to 6 minutes per side, brushing with the reserved marinade. Test for doneness (page 330).

GRILLED BEEF AND GROUND BEEF

Think grilling, and steaks and burgers automatically come to mind!

Grilled Meat Loaf Burgers   Serves 2

Total Time: 20 to 25 minutes
Prep Time: 10 minutes   Cook Time: 10 to 15 minutes

½ pound ground beef
1 egg
finely diced onion or onion powder, to taste
finely minced garlic or garlic powder, to taste
¼ cup cracker crumbs or dry bread crumbs
1 tablespoon Worcestershire sauce
1 tablespoon ketchup, or enough for desired consistency
salt and pepper, to taste

Mix all the ingredients together and form patties. Grill for 5 minutes on each side, or to desired doneness.

Beer Garlic Grilled Steak   Serves 2

This is not a tenderizing marinade, so choose a fairly good cut of beef! Flank steak is a good choice.

Total Time: 20 minutes plus overnight to marinate
Prep Time: 10 minutes
Grill Time: 10 minutes, depending on size

2 steaks (not necessarily the highest quality but at least decent)
2 cups beef broth (may be made from bouillon) or stock (page 165)
⅔ cup soy sauce
½ cup chopped green onion or onion
⅓ cup lime juice
¼ cup brown sugar or white sugar
2 cloves garlic, minced, OR ¼ teaspoon garlic powder
1 can (12 ounces) beer

1. Place the steaks in a leakproof freezer bag.
2. Combine the broth, soy sauce, green onion, lime juice, brown sugar, and garlic and pour over the steaks. Pour the beer over all and let marinate for 12 to 24 hours (more is better).

3. Remove the steaks and discard the marinade. Grill the steaks to the desired doneness (page 330). To serve, slice thinly across the grain.

Cumin and Lime Steak   Serves 2

Total Time: 6½ hours, including minimum 6 hours to marinate
Prep Time: 10 minutes   **Grill Time:** 10 minutes

¼ cup beef broth (may be made from bouillon) or stock (page 165)
¼ cup lime juice
1 tablespoon ground cumin
2 teaspoons ground coriander
2 large cloves garlic, minced, OR ¼ teaspoon garlic powder
⅛ cup olive oil, canola oil, or vegetable oil
2 rib-eye steaks or other steak

1. Mix the broth, lime juice, cumin, coriander, garlic, and olive oil for the marinade. Reserve a bit of the marinade for basting while grilling.
2. Pour the marinade over the steaks in a leakproof freezer bag; coat all sides of the steaks. Refrigerate for 6 to 24 hours, turning regularly. Remove the steaks and discard the marinade.
3. Grill the steaks (page 330), brushing with the reserved marinade while grilling.

Grilled Ground Beef Packets   Serves 2

You'll need two pieces of aluminum foil big enough to fold as a secure packet around the burger, potatoes, and onions. Heavy-duty aluminum foil works best if available. If not, use a double layer of foil.

Total Time: 45 minutes
Prep Time: 15 minutes   **Grill Time:** 30 minutes or so

cooking spray, olive oil, canola oil, or vegetable oil
2 ground beef patties
1 large onion, thinly sliced or julienned
2 small potatoes, skin on, thinly sliced or julienned
garlic powder
salt and pepper, to taste

1. Spritz the foil with the cooking spray. You will make one packet for each serving. Place a ground beef patty on the foil. Add half the onions and potatoes. Potatoes take longer to grill than the burger or onions, so the thinner the potato slices, the more likely that everything will be done at the same time.
2. Sprinkle with the garlic, salt, and pepper. Fold the foil up around the entire packet. Double-fold the top seam to hold in the juices and then double-fold each end.
3. Place on a medium-hot grill, close the lid, and grill for about 30 minutes. We generally do not turn the packets because the juices leak out when turned upside down. Because we do not turn them, it is imperative to have the grill *medium-hot*, not hot, or they will burn. The cooking time will vary considerably based on how big your burger is, how many veggies you have in the packet, and how thinly they're sliced. The potatoes and onion cook in the burger's own juice.

Grilled Oatmeal Burgers   Serves 2

Total Time: 20 minutes
Prep Time: 10 minutes   **Cook Time:** 10 minutes

½ pound ground beef
¼ cup ketchup plus 1 teaspoon Worcestershire sauce OR ¼ cup V-8 juice
¼ cup oats
1 egg
1 tablespoon finely chopped onion
salt and pepper, to taste

1. Mix all the ingredients together and form into patties. If the patties seem dry, add ketchup. If they're soupy, add more oats.
2. Place on a hot grill and grill for 5 minutes on each side, or less depending on how you prefer your burgers.

Grilling

GRILLING SEAFOOD AND FISH

Some of the best seafood and fish we've (Jan and David) ever eaten was cooked on our grill. Grilling fish is easy, if you select your fish carefully. It must be sturdy enough to withstand being grilled and flipped once. Tuna, swordfish, and other large fish steaks or fillets are easy. But you can also successfully grill grouper, hogfish, Spanish or cero mackerel, and many other types of fish. The secret is either having a big enough fillet or using aluminum foil. A common complaint about grilling seafood or fish is that the grill grates are too wide apart. In addition to using aluminum foil, you can buy a special grill insert if you plan to grill a lot of fish and seafood.

If you just want plain old grilled fish (which is about as tasty a treat as they come), wash the fresh fillets with fresh water. Add a bit of lemon juice to the fresh water to kill any smell. Then lightly brush the fillets with olive oil and any seasonings you prefer. Blackening spice or lemon pepper are both good, and garlic and ground pepper is our favorite.

You can also marinate your grilled seafood or fish, so try your favorite marinade.

You may or may not need to oil the actual grill grate. The only reason to brush the grate with oil is to keep the fillets from sticking. We've learned that if we brush our fillets with olive oil, they don't stick to the grill. Different grates act differently, so experiment with yours.

Bring the grill up to temperature, and turn the fish with a spatula every 2 to 3 minutes—depending on how big the fish fillets are—for a total of no more than 8 minutes.

Grilling seafood includes jerk shrimp kabobs or grilled lobster tail, both among our favorites. You'll soon have your own favorites.

The biggest mistake when grilling fish is overcooking, so watch the time on the grill.

Grilled Margarita Grouper   Serves 4

Total Time: 3½ hours, including 3 hours to marinate
Prep Time: 15 minutes   **Grill Time:** 8 minutes

⅓ **cup tequila***
½ **cup Triple Sec***
¾ **cup lime juice***
1 **teaspoon salt**
2 **or 3 cloves garlic, minced, OR** ½ **teaspoon garlic powder**
1 **tablespoon olive oil, canola oil, or vegetable oil**
1½ **pounds grouper fillets or any other white fish**
3 **medium tomatoes**
1 **medium onion**
1 **tablespoon minced jalapeño or other hot chile pepper**
2 **tablespoons chopped fresh cilantro OR 1 tablespoon dried cilantro**
1 **pinch sugar**
salt and pepper, to taste

Substitute prepared margarita mix for all of these. Use the mix with or without the liquor according to your preference.

1. Make the marinade by mixing the tequila, Triple Sec, lime juice, salt, garlic, and half the olive oil. Reserve a bit of marinade to brush on the fillets while grilling.
2. Put the fish fillets into a leakproof plastic bag and add the marinade to cover. Marinate for 3 hours in the refrigerator, turning each half hour.
3. To make the salsa accompaniment, finely dice the tomatoes, onions, chilies, and cilantro. Add the sugar, salt, and pepper to taste. Set aside.
4. Heat the grill to very hot. Remove the fish from the marinade and brush with the remaining olive oil. Sprinkle with pepper. Grill for 4 minutes or less per side, or until the fish just looks opaque. The cooking time will differ depending on the size of the fillets. Brush the rest of the reserved marinade on the fish. Enjoy with the salsa.

Basic Grilled Fish   Serves 2 to 4

Total Time: 1 hour, 20 minutes, including 1 hour to marinate
Prep Time: 10 minutes   **Grill Time:** 4 to 10 minutes

$\frac{1}{2}$ cup olive oil, canola oil, or vegetable oil
$\frac{1}{4}$ cup lemon juice or lime juice
2 teaspoons salt
$\frac{1}{2}$ teaspoon Worcestershire sauce
$\frac{1}{2}$ teaspoon Cajun seasoning (page 46)
2 to 4 servings of fish fillets, rinsed

1. Mix together the olive oil, lemon juice, salt, Worcestershire sauce, and Cajun seasoning.
2. Place the rinsed fish fillets and the marinade in a leakproof freezer bag, reserving a bit for basting. Place in the refrigerator for 1 hour.
3. Remove the fish and discard the marinade. Grill the fillets (page 338), basting after turning them.

Sesame-Crusted Tuna, Salmon, or Mahi Mahi   Serves 2

Total Time: 15 minutes
Prep Time: 5 minutes   **Grill Time:** 10 minutes

2 fillets of tuna, salmon, mahi mahi (dorado), grouper, or any firm white fish
salt and pepper, to taste
1 tablespoon sesame oil, olive oil, or canola oil (best with sesame oil)
sesame seeds, to coat fillets

1. Season the fillets with salt and pepper. Rub both sides with the sesame oil and coat the fillets with the sesame seeds.
2. Heat the grill to medium and grill the fillets for 3 minutes on each side, or until done (opaque). The doneness differs according to the type of fish. Tuna takes the least grilling; overgrilling will make it dry. Serve with Tangy Dipping Sauce (page 135).

Shrimp on the BBQ   Serves 2

Total Time: 1 hour, 20 minutes, including 1 hour to marinate
Prep Time: 15 minutes   **Cook Time:** 5 minutes

$\frac{1}{3}$ cup butter, melted
2 tablespoons olive oil, canola oil, or vegetable oil
1 teaspoon dried parsley flakes
1 teaspoon dried thyme
1 teaspoon dried cilantro OR 1 tablespoon minced fresh cilantro
3 tablespoons lemon juice or lime juice
3 large cloves garlic, minced
1 tablespoon finely chopped green onion or onion (green onion is best, but any you have will do)
salt and pepper, to taste
1 pound shrimp, unpeeled
lemon wedges

1. Combine the melted butter, olive oil, parsley, thyme, cilantro, lemon juice, garlic, green onion, salt, and pepper in a large bowl to make the marinade.
2. Add the shrimp. Let marinate at room temperature for 1 hour, stirring occasionally.
3. Turn the grill to medium. Thread the shrimp on kabob skewers. Grill for 2 minutes or less per side, or until the shrimp are curled like a "C," not an "O." Serve with lemon wedges and Cocktail Sauce for Shrimp (page 211).

Grilled Lobster Tails   Serves 2

Total Time: 15 to 20 minutes, depending on size
Prep Time: 10 minutes
Cook Time: 5 to 10 minutes, depending on size

1 or 2 cloves garlic, or to taste, OR $\frac{1}{4}$ teaspoon garlic powder
3 tablespoons butter or margarine, melted, or olive oil (butter is by far the best)
2 lobster tails, split lengthwise (page 248)

1. Mince the garlic and add to the melted butter.
2. Place the lobster tails on a hot grill, shell side down. Frequently baste with the garlic butter (which infuses down and pools in the shell). The lobster is done when the shells are red and the meat is white and tender—about 5 to 10 minutes, depending on size.

Grilled Shrimp Wrapped in Bacon

Serves 2

Total Time: 20 minutes
Prep Time: 15 minutes   **Grill Time:** 5 minutes

4 tablespoons olive oil, canola oil, or vegetable oil
2 tablespoons balsamic vinegar or wine vinegar
1 tablespoon Dijon mustard or other prepared mustard
20 medium to large shrimp, shelled and deveined (page 234)
5 bacon strips, cut into quarters

1. Mix the olive oil, vinegar, and mustard. Brush on each shrimp. Wrap each shrimp tightly in a quarter strip of bacon, using a toothpick to hold it together.
2. Grill over a hot fire for 3 to 5 minutes, or until crisp, turning once.

Easy Grilled Shrimp Scampi

Serves 4

Total Time: 20 minutes
Prep Time: 10 minutes   **Grill Time:** 5 to 10 minutes

cooking spray or melted butter
1½ pounds medium shrimp (about 48 medium shrimp, 12 per person), shelled and deveined (page 234)
salt and pepper, to taste
4 cloves garlic, minced, or more if you're a garlic lover
¼ teaspoon cayenne, or to taste
⅓ cup butter or margarine (butter tastes best)
lemon wedges

1. Spritz a large piece of heavy aluminum foil with cooking spray, or brush with butter.
2. Put the shrimp on the foil and season with salt and pepper. Sprinkle with the garlic and cayenne.

Cut the butter into bits and sprinkle on top of the shrimp.
3. Fold up the edges of the foil (but don't cover the top) so when the butter melts, it will simmer with the garlic and spices, flavoring the shrimp. Grill until the shrimp just curl into a "C" shape. Don't overgrill the shrimp or they will be tough and dried out. Serve with lemon wedges over rice.

GRILLING TIPS FOR VEGGIES

Grilled vegetables are wonderful because they complement pretty much any meat, chicken, or seafood, plus they keep the heat and mess out of the galley. Mixing and matching grilled vegetables creates an extremely appetizing array of oranges, reds, greens, yellows, and purples.

Grilling Vegetables Tips and Tricks

Sliced veggies such as potatoes or sweet potatoes usually take about 20 minutes to grill. Move them to the outside edges of the grill after starting the meat. Try starting the veggies about 10 minutes ahead of whatever meat you're grilling.

Another tip if you have a microwave available is to microwave potato chunks or slices for 3 minutes on high before you grill—they'll grill in about half the time.

Most vegetables can be cooked whole, but that's not the best way to grill them. Try cutting them up, making the pieces similar sizes so they cook evenly. Brush with olive oil or sesame oil.

Use nonstick cooking spray, or spritz with olive oil or canola oil before grilling to keep the veggies from sticking to the grill.

We usually season veggies with garlic powder and ground pepper after they're coated with cooking spray or oil. You can also use salt or other spices. Fresh herbs burn easily, so toss them in after the veggies are grilled.

You can make a vegetable packet using heavy-duty aluminum foil (or double regular foil). Spritz the foil with cooking spray or oil. Be sure the veggie pieces are similar sizes. Drizzling the veggies with olive oil and seasoning is a tasty favorite.

Grilling

Don't bother with baskets or kabob skewers (unless you're making kabobs). As long as the veggie pieces can't fall through the grill, they'll cook fine.

For vegetable kabobs, choose vegetables that have the same cooking time. Cherry tomatoes grill much quicker than carrot slices, for example, so a tomato and carrot kabob would not cook evenly unless you partially cook the carrots first.

Grilled Sweet Potato Slices   Serves 2

Total Time: 25 minutes
Prep Time: 5 minutes   **Grill Time:** 20 minutes

2 sweet potatoes
cooking spray, canola oil, or vegetable oil
garlic powder
ground pepper, to taste

1. Scrub the sweet potatoes (leave the skin on if desired) and cut slices ½ inch thick. Spritz both sides of the slices with cooking spray or brush with oil. Sprinkle with garlic powder and ground pepper. Or for a delicious sweet treat, sprinkle with cinnamon, then sprinkle with sugar just before serving.
2. Heat the grill and place the sweet potato slices around the edges of the grill (so the sugar doesn't burn). Grill for 15 to 20 minutes, turning every 5 minutes. Taste-test for doneness.

Potato Packets   Serves 2

Every bit as good made with sweet potatoes—actually, maybe even better!

Total Time: 35 minutes
Prep Time: 10 minutes   **Grill Time:** 25 minutes or so

cooking spray, butter, or oil
2 medium potatoes with skin on, cut into ½-inch cubes
1 onion (we prefer sweet onions, but use whatever you have), slivered
minced garlic, to taste
salt and pepper, to taste
butter, margarine, or olive oil

1. Spritz two large pieces of heavy-duty aluminum foil with cooking spray, or brush with butter or olive oil. If you don't have heavy-duty foil, use a double layer of regular.
2. Place 1 cubed potato and half the onion on each piece of foil. Sprinkle with garlic, salt, and pepper to taste. Top with a dollop of butter or a drizzle of olive oil.
3. Close the foil—double-fold the top seam, then double-fold each end seam. Place on the grill and cook with the lid closed for 20 to 25 minutes—the grill time will vary considerably based on the size of the veggie pieces. Check by opening the foil and testing with a fork. Be careful when opening the foil; the steam escaping will burn you.

Grilled Herbed Vegetables   Serves 4

Total Time: 30 minutes
Prep Time: 15 minutes   **Grill Time:** 10 to 15 minutes

2 tablespoons olive oil, canola oil, vegetable oil, or melted butter
1 clove garlic, minced, OR ¼ teaspoon garlic powder
2 tablespoons torn fresh basil OR 1 teaspoon dried basil
4 cups mixed vegetables, such as summer squash, christophene, zucchini, green beans, onion, any color bell peppers, sweet potatoes, and carrots
salt and pepper, to taste

1. Combine the oil, garlic, and basil. Add the veggies and toss.
2. Spoon the vegetable mixture onto an appropriately sized piece of heavy-duty aluminum foil (if you don't have heavy duty, use a double layer of regular foil). Bring the opposite edges together, and seal tightly with a double fold. Double-fold the ends to completely enclose the veggies.
3. Grill the packet over medium heat for about 15 to 20 minutes, or until the veggies are tender, turning once after 10 minutes. Be careful when opening the packet; the steam will have built up inside and will burn you if you're not careful. Season to taste with salt and pepper.

Grilling

Grilled Vegetables with Lemon Parsley Butter
Serves 4

Total Time: 18 minutes
Prep Time: 10 minutes   Grill Time: 8 minutes

8 cups assorted fresh vegetables, such as whole
    mushrooms and thickly sliced zucchini, toma-
    toes, carrots, bell peppers, onions, or whatever
    you have
olive oil spritzer bottle OR ½ cup olive oil, canola
    oil, or vegetable oil
garlic powder and ground pepper, to taste, or
    whatever seasonings you prefer

1. Preheat the grill to medium. Spray or toss all the
   veggies with olive oil and sprinkle with garlic powder and ground pepper. Grill, turning once, until
   everything is softened and a bit charred.
2. Serve with chilled Lemon Parsley Butter (see
   below).

NOTE: If your grill grate bars are too widely spaced to
hold the veggies, place them on a piece of aluminum
foil—lightly coated with oil to prevent sticking—and
set it directly on the grate.

Lemon Parsley Butter
2 tablespoons lemon juice
½ cup butter or margarine, softened
1 tablespoon chopped fresh parsley or dried pars-
    ley flakes

Stir the lemon juice into the softened butter. Add the
parsley and mix well. Chill for 1 hour.

Grilled Corn on the Cob
Serves 2

Total Time: 1 hour to 1 hour, 15 minutes, including
    30 minutes to soak
Prep Time: 45 minutes   Grill Time: 15 to 30 minutes

2 ears of corn, still in the husk
butter or margarine

1. Soak the corn, still in the husk, in water for 30
   minutes.
2. Pull back the outer husk and remove as much silk
   as possible.

3. Spread a bit of butter over the ear of corn to add
   flavor. Pull the husk back around the ear, making
   a cocoon, and tie the top of the wet husk together
   with wet string or something that won't burn to
   hold in the flavor.
4. Place the corn on a medium grill, close the lid, and
   grill for 15 to 30 minutes, depending on the heat.
   Keep the ears away from the hottest part. When
   the corn is done, the husks will almost be falling off
   and dried out.

Grilled French Fries
Serves 2

*To make it easier to grill, the potatoes are cut in slices
instead of the traditional "fry" shape.*

Total Time: 20 to 25 minutes
Prep Time: 5 minutes   Grill Time: 15 to 20 minutes

2 medium to large potatoes
olive oil, canola oil, vegetable oil, or cooking spray
garlic powder
ground pepper

1. Scrub the potatoes (leave the skin on if desired)
   and slice into ½-inch-thick rounds. Brush both
   sides of the slices with olive oil or spritz with cooking spray. Sprinkle with the garlic powder and the
   ground pepper.
2. Place the slices directly on the grill grate. Grill for
   15 to 20 minutes, turning every 5 minutes. Taste-
   test for doneness to make sure the slices are cooked
   through. Serve with ketchup and salt. Yum, instant
   French fries!

TIP: If you have a microwave and want to hasten the
cooking process, microwave the slices for a couple of
minutes before grilling.

Whole Grilled Onion
Serves 2 to 4

Total Time: 35 minutes
Prep Time: 5 minutes   Grill Time: 30 minutes

1 large sweet onion
1 beef bouillon cube
1 large clove garlic
grated or shredded Parmesan or other hard cheese

1. Peel the onion and cut off both ends. Hollow out the center of the onion about halfway.
2. Place the bouillon cube and the garlic in the center of the onion. Press in enough cheese to fill the hole to the top.
3. Place the onion on a large sheet of heavy-duty foil (or a double layer of regular foil) and gather toward the top.
4. Set the grill at medium-high and place the onion off to the side so it doesn't burn. Close the lid. Grill for 30 minutes, or until tender.

GRILLED PIZZA

When the weather is hot, pizza sounds good, but often you don't want to heat up the boat by baking it. It cooks just as well on the grill, and you'll make all the other boats in the anchorage jealous as the wind carries the aroma. Don't be surprised when friends "just happen" to drop by!

World's Best Pizza on the Grill

Total Time: 2 hours, 30 minutes, including homemade crust!
Prep Time: 2 hours, 15 minutes
Grill Time: 15 minutes or so

Crust
1 teaspoon yeast ($\frac{1}{2}$ packet; page 387)
$\frac{1}{2}$ cup warm water
1 pinch white sugar
1 teaspoon salt
$\frac{1}{2}$ tablespoon olive oil, canola oil, or vegetable oil
$1\frac{1}{2}$ cups flour or whole wheat flour
1 clove garlic, minced, OR $\frac{1}{4}$ teaspoon garlic powder
$1\frac{1}{2}$ teaspoons dried basil

Sauce
$\frac{1}{2}$ cup olive oil
1 teaspoon minced garlic
$\frac{1}{2}$ cup tomato sauce
1 teaspoon each dried oregano, dried basil, garlic powder, or whatever spices you desire

Toppings (vary according to your preference)
$\frac{1}{2}$ **cup chopped tomato**
small can sliced mushrooms, drained
pepperoni
onion, cut into slivers
bell pepper, cut into slivers
1 cup shredded mozzarella or similar cheese

1. If you're new to making bread, read Yeast Bread-making 101 (page 386) to learn the techniques for kneading, letting rise, and more.
2. To make the crust, dissolve the yeast in warm water with a pinch of sugar and let sit 5 minutes to proof (page 388). Mix in the salt, olive oil, flour, minced garlic, and basil. Knead for 8 minutes. The dough should be stiff but not too sticky. Form into ball and let rise until doubled— $\frac{1}{2}$ hour to 1 hour, depending on temperature. Punch down and knead again. Let rise again until double.
3. To make two "personal pizzas," divide the dough into two pieces and roll each one out to about an 8-inch round (or whatever shape fits on your grill; we can do two at once).
4. Mix the sauce ingredients together and set aside. Prepare the toppings.
5. Light the grill and heat to medium to medium-high. You'll need to experiment with the heat, since every grill is different. Brush the grill with olive oil, then brush the bottom of the crusts lightly with olive oil with garlic mixed in.
6. With your hands, lay the dough on the grill—it will rise almost immediately. Grill just long enough to get the bottom a bit browned. Then brush the top with the olive oil/garlic mixture. Using two spatulas, flip the crust over so the browned bottom is now on top.
7. Spread the sauce and toppings on the crust. Thinner layers of toppings seem to work best to get the entire pizza cooked before burning the bottom. Place the cheese as the last topping, then close the grill lid and bake until the cheese is bubbly. On our grill, the crust takes 5 minutes or less to bake and the pizza takes another 5 to 10 minutes to grill. Watch it closely so you don't burn it!

Grilling

MORE GREAT GRILLING RECIPES

The following recipes from other chapters are also good on the grill, or are good served with grilled food:

Appetizers
Tangy Dipping Sauce, *page 135*
Tzatziki, page 136

Sauces, Gravies, and Marinades
All but the first few recipes in this chapter are good with grilled food. In particular, see the barbecue sauces, starting on page 215.

Seafood
Aluminum Foil Beach Bake, *page 227*

Canned Meats and Seafood
Hobo Dinner, *page 320*

MEATLESS MAIN DISHES

When you're anchored in paradise, miles or days away from the nearest reprovisioning stop, and enjoying the snorkeling and lifestyle so much you just don't want to leave, you can stretch your provisions by including one or two meatless meals a week. And cutting back on the amount of meat eaten is a healthier lifestyle anyway.

Additionally, you're bound to make friends with vegetarian cruisers. If you invite them over for a meal, or even just for drinks, you want to be sure to have food they'll eat. If you're having a guest who says they're "vegetarian," be sure to find out what type of vegetarian and the specifics of what they do and don't eat.

Neither of us is vegetarian, although we both eat far less meat than we used to. And we both incorporate meatless main dishes into our meal planning—to stretch our provisions and for health reasons.

Most meatless main dishes include some form of legumes (beans), cheese, pasta, or a combination. They are typically low in fat and high in protein and fiber.

Here are 23 recipes for delicious meatless main dishes along with 17 additional meatless ideas in the cross-reference list.

CHEESY CASSEROLES

Before planning to serve any of these to your vegetarian friends, ask to be sure that they eat cheese—because some vegetarians avoid all foods that come from animals.

Macaroni and Cheese — Serves 4

Carolyn's grandmother's recipe, given to her mother in her wedding cookbook, is still a family favorite!

Total Time: 50 minutes
Prep Time: 30 minutes   **Bake Time:** 20 minutes

1 cup dry elbow macaroni
2 batches of White Sauce #1 (page 207)
1½ cups shredded cheese—cheddar, Monterey Jack, and Colby are traditional; Velveeta melts better. This dish is also good with feta, Roquefort, or even mozzarella, although the flavor is not at all traditional.

1. Preheat oven to 350°F.
2. Cook the macaroni according to package instructions. Drain and set aside.
3. While the macaroni is cooking, make the white sauce. Remove it from the heat and slowly add the cheese, stirring constantly until the cheese is melted (feta and Roquefort, if used, won't melt, so just mix them in). If the cheese does not completely melt now, don't worry—it will melt in the oven.

4. Add the drained pasta to the cheese sauce and transfer to a greased pan (a medium-size casserole is perfect, but you can use a 9-inch square cake pan or even a loaf pan if it's large enough). Bake, uncovered, for 20 minutes, or until bubbly and the top is slightly browned (the cooking time will probably be slightly longer in a loaf pan).

Bahamian Mac and Cheese　Serves 4

This has a heavy, cake-like consistency, not at all like the box mixes.

Total Time: 1 hour, including 10 minutes to stand before serving
Prep Time: 20 minutes　　　**Cook Time:** 30 minutes

2 cups uncooked elbow macaroni or other medium-size pasta
1 small onion, minced
1 green bell pepper, minced
1 clove garlic, minced, OR $\frac{1}{4}$ teaspoon garlic powder
$1\frac{1}{2}$ cups shredded cheddar or similar cheese
2 eggs, beaten
hot sauce, to taste
salt and pepper, to taste
1 teaspoon paprika
$1\frac{1}{2}$ cups evaporated milk (page 99)

1. Preheat oven to 350°F.
2. Cook the macaroni according to package instructions. When it is al dente, add the onion, bell pepper, and garlic, and cook for a minute or so, or until the veggies are softened.
3. Drain the macaroni, onion, pepper, and garlic; return them to the pot. Add half the cheese and stir until melted.
4. In a small bowl combine the beaten eggs, hot sauce, salt, pepper, and paprika. Stir the egg mixture and the milk into the mac and cheese. Spoon into a well-greased baking dish (about an 8-inch square pan or a loaf pan) and sprinkle the remaining cheese on top.
5. Bake, uncovered, for about 30 minutes, or until bubbling and browned around the edges. Remove from the oven and let sit for 10 minutes, then cut into squares and serve.

Cheesy Zucchini Enchiladas (Vegan Option)　Serves 4

For a vegan version, use oil instead of butter, soy milk instead of milk, and substitute 2 cups refried beans for the cheese. Excellent!

Total Time: 60 minutes
Prep Time: 25 minutes　　　**Cook Time:** 35 minutes

1 onion, diced
2 cloves garlic, minced, OR $\frac{1}{4}$ teaspoon garlic powder
1 tablespoon olive oil, canola oil, vegetable oil, butter, or margarine
3 cups diced zucchini (2 to 3 zucchini depending on size)
$\frac{1}{4}$ cup finely diced hot chile pepper, seeded, or to taste
1 teaspoon chili powder
$\frac{1}{4}$ teaspoon ground pepper
2 tablespoons butter, margarine, canola oil, or vegetable oil
2 tablespoons flour
$\frac{1}{4}$ teaspoon salt
1 cup milk
$1\frac{1}{2}$ cups shredded cheese (Monterey Jack, cheddar, or other similar cheese)
eight 8-inch flour tortillas
chopped tomato, for garnish

1. Preheat oven to 350°F.
2. Sauté the onion and garlic in the olive oil for 5 minutes. Stir in the zucchini, diced chile pepper, chili powder, and ground pepper. Cook for 3 to 5 minutes, or until the veggies are soft. Remove the zucchini mixture from the skillet and set aside.
3. Melt the butter in the skillet, then stir in the flour and salt. Very slowly add the milk while continuing to stir until thickened. Stir in the cheese.
4. Add half the cheese mixture to the zucchini mixture. Spoon zucchini-cheese mixture into each tortilla and roll up. Place the filled tortillas in a greased baking dish, open edge down. If there is any remaining zucchini-cheese mixture, place it in the dish around the enchiladas. Pour the remaining cheese sauce on top.
5. Cover and bake for 25 minutes. Sprinkle with the chopped tomato before serving.

Quesadilla Pie
Serves 4

Total Time: 45 minutes, including 5 minutes standing time
Prep Time: 10 minutes **Cook Time:** 30 minutes

1 can (4 ounces) chopped green chilies OR 2 to 4 tablespoons minced spicy chile pepper, or to taste
2 cups shredded cheddar or similar cheese
1 teaspoon chopped fresh cilantro OR ⅓ teaspoon dried cilantro
¾ cup flour
1 teaspoon baking powder (page 376)
dash of salt
1 tablespoon canola oil, vegetable oil, or melted butter or margarine
1½ cups milk
3 eggs
salsa (page 127), optional

1. Heat oven to 400°F. Grease a 9-inch pie pan.
2. Sprinkle the chilies, cheese, and cilantro on the bottom of the pan.
3. In a bowl, mix the remaining ingredients until well blended. Pour into the pan. Bake for 25 to 30 minutes, or until a toothpick inserted in the middle comes out clean. Let cool for 5 minutes. Top with salsa, if desired.

Cheesy Vegetable Casserole
Serves 2

Total Time: 1 hour, including 5 minutes sit time
Prep Time: 25 minutes **Bake Time:** 30 minutes

cooking spray or oil
2 tablespoons butter, margarine, canola oil, or vegetable oil
6 green onions, thinly sliced, including tops
2 tablespoons flour
dash of salt
dash of ground pepper
1½ cups milk
1 cup shredded Swiss cheese or other cheese
¾ cup bite-size pieces of broccoli
¾ cup small cauliflower florets
¾ cup sliced or diced carrot
¼ cup crushed crackers (buttery flavor if available)

1. Preheat oven to 350°F. Spritz a baking dish with cooking spray or brush with oil.
2. Melt the butter and sauté the green onion until translucent. Stir in the flour, salt, and pepper. Stir in the milk slowly. Simmer, stirring constantly, until thickened. Remove from the heat.
3. Add most of the cheese, reserving enough to sprinkle on top later. Stir until the cheese is melted. Stir in the vegetables.
4. Transfer the mixture to the prepared baking dish. Sprinkle with the reserved cheese and the cracker crumbs. Bake for 30 minutes, or until bubbly. Let cool for 5 minutes before serving.

PASTA-BASED DISHES

Pasta is a staple on most boats, as it lasts forever and can be stowed almost anywhere.

Spaghetti Pie
Serves 4

Total Time: 1 hour
Prep Time: 25 minutes **Cook Time:** 35 minutes

16 ounces spaghetti or similar pasta
½ cup butter or margarine, melted
1 egg
16 ounces shredded cheddar cheese
salt and pepper, to taste
1 medium onion, chopped
2 cloves garlic, minced
1 can (16 ounces) tomato sauce
1 tablespoon Italian seasoning (page 48), or to taste
1 cup grated Parmesan cheese

1. Preheat oven to 350°F.
2. Cook the spaghetti according to package directions while preparing the rest of the "crust." Drain.
3. Mix the melted butter, egg, cheddar cheese, salt, and pepper in a large bowl. Add the cooked spaghetti and mix well. Press into an ungreased baking pan approximately 9 inches square; set aside.
4. Sauté the onion and garlic. Add the tomato sauce and Italian seasoning. Pour over the spaghetti in the baking pan. Sprinkle generously with the Parmesan. Bake for 35 minutes. Let cool for 10 minutes before cutting and serving.

Meatless Main Dishes

Italian Pasta Fagioli (Beans and Pasta)　Serves 6

Total Time: 30 minutes
Prep Time: 15 minutes　　Cook Time: 20 minutes

1 cup ditalini* or other smallish pasta
1 medium onion, diced
1 medium hot chile pepper, seeded and minced, or
　to taste, OR 1 can (4 ounces) diced green chilies
1 carrot, diced
1 stalk celery, diced
1 tablespoon olive oil, canola oil, or vegetable oil
2 cloves garlic OR ¼ teaspoon garlic powder
1 can (16 ounces) diced tomatoes, not drained, OR
　2 fresh tomatoes, diced
1 can (16 ounces) cannelloni or Great Northern
　beans, drained and rinsed, OR Recipe-Ready
　Beans (page 176)
salt and pepper, to taste
1 cup water
¼ cup shredded or grated Parmesan cheese

*Ditalini are little tubes, about ¼ inch long and ¼ inch
　in diameter.

1. Prepare the pasta according to package directions.
　Drain and set aside.
2. While the pasta is cooking, sauté the onion, chile
　pepper, carrot, and celery in the olive oil until soft.
　Add the garlic, tomatoes, beans, salt, and pepper,
　then mix in the water and bring to a boil. Turn
　down the heat and let simmer about 15 minutes,
　or until most of the liquid has been absorbed. Add
　the pasta and the cheese and cook just until heated
　through.

Minestrone Pasta Salad　Serves 6

Total Time: 25 minutes, plus time to chill if desired

3 cups uncooked medium pasta shells or any other
　medium-size pasta
⅔ cup Italian dressing (page 161)
½ cup shredded Parmesan, cheddar, or other
　cheese
2 medium carrots, diced, OR 1 can (8 ounces)
　sliced carrots, drained

1 medium green bell pepper, chopped, OR 1 can
　(4 ounces) diced green chilies
1 can (16 ounces) red kidney beans, drained and
　rinsed, OR Recipe-Ready Beans (page 176)
1 can (16 ounces) garbanzo beans (chick-peas),
　drained and rinsed
1 can (16 ounces) diced tomatoes, drained

1. Cook the pasta. Drain and rinse with cold water.
2. Toss the pasta with all the other ingredients. You
　can eat the salad immediately, but we like it better
　chilled.

Southwest Meatless Lasagna　Serves 4

Total Time: 1 hour, including 10 minutes stand time
　(plus time to make Recipe-Ready Beans if needed)
Prep Time: 30 minutes　　Bake Time: 20 minutes

1½ cups chopped onion
3 cups chopped zucchini, peeled or unpeeled
3 teaspoons ground cumin
2 tablespoons olive oil, canola oil, or vegetable oil
1 can (16 ounces) diced tomatoes with green chil-
　ies OR 2 medium tomatoes, diced
1 can (16 ounces) black beans, rinsed, OR Recipe-
　Ready Beans (page 176)
1 can (16 ounces) corn, drained
1½ cups enchilada sauce (page 213)
½ cup chopped fresh cilantro OR 1 tablespoon
　dried cilantro
4 tortillas, of a size to fit your baking dish
1¼ cups shredded cheddar or similar cheese
salsa (page 127), optional
sour cream (page 99), optional

1. Preheat oven to 400°F. Grease a baking dish (round
　is better). Spritz a piece of aluminum foil to fit the
　baking dish with cooking spray.
2. In a large skillet sauté the onion, zucchini, and
　cumin with the oil for about 5 minutes. Stir in the
　tomatoes, beans, corn, and enchilada sauce and
　heat through. Remove from the heat and stir in the
　cilantro.

3. Put one tortilla in the baking dish. Top with one-third of the zucchini mixture, and sprinkle with one-quarter of the cheese. Do two more layers of tortilla, zucchini, and cheese. Top with the last tortilla and the remaining cheese.
4. Cover with the sprayed foil and bake for 20 minutes, or until bubbly around the edges. Let cool for 10 minutes. Cut into wedges and garnish with salsa and sour cream, if desired.

Italian Pasta Skillet   Serves 2

Total Time: 30 minutes

1 medium onion, diced
1 cup sliced mushrooms (fresh are best but canned will do)
1/4 cup butter, margarine, olive oil, canola oil, or vegetable oil
1 cup frozen sausage-style protein crumbles (optional)
1 can (10 ounces) condensed vegetable soup
1 cup uncooked bow-tie pasta or other medium-size pasta
2 cups fresh spinach leaves OR 1 can (16 ounces) spinach, drained
1/4 cup shredded mozzarella or any other meltable cheese
Parmesan cheese, for topping

1. Sauté the onion and mushrooms in the butter over medium heat. Add the protein crumbles, if desired. Stir in the soup. Cover and heat to boiling. Stir in the pasta, reduce the heat to medium-low, and simmer about 10 minutes, or until the pasta is done.
2. Add the spinach and cook until hot. Stir in the mozzarella. Serve hot, and sprinkle with the Parmesan.

VEGETABLE-BASED CASSEROLES

These are some of our favorite meatless meals, which are just fantastic if you've picked up veggies from a farmer's market.

Briam (Vegan Option)   Serves 4

Briam is a traditional Greek oven-roasted vegetable dish that can be adapted according to what is in season. Eggplant is often used in place of the zucchini—or you can use some of each. For a vegan version, do not garnish with feta.

Total Time: 1 hour, 30 minutes plus time to cool to lukewarm
Prep Time: 30 minutes   Cook Time: 1 hour

1/2 cup olive oil, canola oil, or vegetable oil
4 zucchini, unpeeled, cut in half lengthwise and sliced
10 small potatoes, skin on, thinly sliced
1 onion, chopped
2 cloves garlic, minced, OR 1/2 teaspoon garlic powder
5 green onions, sliced 1/2 inch thick
3 tomatoes, roughly chopped
1/2 cup chopped fresh parsley
1/2 bunch dill, chopped
1/3 cup lemon juice, lime juice, or white wine
1 teaspoon dried oregano
1 teaspoon dried rosemary
salt and pepper, to taste
feta cheese, for garnish (optional)

1. In a large bowl mix the oil, zucchini, potato, onion, garlic, green onion, tomato, parsley, dill, lemon juice, oregano, rosemary, salt, and pepper. Toss to coat everything with the oil and to distribute the spices.
2. Place in an appropriate pan and cook on the stove top over medium to medium-low heat, or in the oven at 350°F. Either way, cover the pan for the first 30 minutes, then remove the cover and let the liquid partially evaporate and the sauce to thicken (the liquid should form a thick sauce). Cook until all the vegetables are tender but not mushy—typically 20 to 30 minutes more. Do not add water, so keep checking frequently.
3. Serve lukewarm or at room temperature with a sprinkling of feta cheese, if desired.

Ratatouille (Vegan Option) Serves 4 to 8

Ratatouille is a French vegetable stew. Enjoy it hot, at room temperature, or chilled. It is also excellent as a side dish that will serve about 8.

Total Time: 1 hour, 30 minutes
Prep Time: 30 minutes   Cook Time: 1 hour or so

3 tablespoons olive oil, canola oil, or vegetable oil
1 large eggplant, unpeeled and diced
2 medium onions, chopped
1 large green bell pepper, seeded and diced
1 large red or yellow bell pepper, seeded and diced, OR diced green bell pepper
3 medium zucchini, cut in half lengthwise and sliced
2 cloves garlic, minced, OR ½ teaspoon garlic powder
½ teaspoon salt
½ teaspoon ground pepper
1 can (6 ounces) tomato paste OR foil packet of *criolla* (page 213)
2 tablespoons chopped black olives
3 tablespoons torn fresh basil OR 1 tablespoon dried basil

1. Drizzle the olive oil into a pan large enough to hold all the ingredients. Add the eggplant, onion, bell pepper, zucchini, garlic, salt, and ground pepper. Toss to thoroughly mix. Cover and cook over medium-low heat, stirring occasionally, for about an hour, or until the vegetables are tender but not falling apart, and not browned or mushy. The cooking time depends on the size of the vegetable pieces.
2. Stir in the tomato paste, olives, and basil. Cover for just a few minutes, or until heated through. Serve hot, or chilled if preferred.

Meatless Tamale Pie   Serves 2

Total Time: 1 hour, 15 minutes
Prep Time: 15 minutes   Bake Time: 1 hour

1 egg, beaten
⅔ cup milk
1 can (8 ounces) corn, drained
½ cup minced green bell pepper
1 onion, diced
½ cup diced tomato (fresh or canned)
1 can (4 ounces) sliced olives (optional)
1 teaspoon salt
¼ teaspoon ground pepper
¼ teaspoon paprika
¼ teaspoon chili powder
1 can (4 ounces) green chilies OR 2 tablespoons minced seeded fresh chilies, or to taste
½ cup yellow cornmeal or corn flour (masa harina)
¼ cup butter or margarine, melted, or canola oil or vegetable oil

1. Preheat oven to 350°F.
2. Combine all the ingredients and mix well. Pour into a greased casserole dish and bake for 1 hour, or until the mixture no longer jiggles when you move the pan.

Ratatouille Polenta Bake (Vegan Option)   Serves 6

Total Time: 1 hour, 15 minutes
Prep Time: 30 minutes   Bake Time: 45 minutes

1 cup water
½ cup polenta or cornmeal*
1 medium onion, chopped
1 medium bell pepper, chopped
1 clove garlic, minced
1 small unpeeled eggplant, diced (approximately 2 cups)
1 medium zucchini, diced (approximately 1 cup)
salt and pepper, to taste
1 can (14½ ounces) diced tomatoes
¼ cup grated or shredded Parmesan cheese
1 cup shredded mozzarella, Swiss, cheddar, or other shredded cheese

Or use ½ cup masa flour (Mexican corn flour) and just bring it and the water to a boil, then let it cool—it will thicken as it cools.

1. Bring the water to a boil. Add the polenta and boil vigorously for 1 minute. Turn the heat down and let simmer for 8 to 10 minutes—watch to make sure it doesn't boil dry, and add water if needed. You want

a pasty consistency, like grits; the polenta becomes the bottom layer of the dish, almost a crust. Turn off the heat and let it cool while making the veggie topping.

2. Preheat oven to 350°F. Spritz a skillet with cooking spray or brush with a dash of oil.

3. Cook the onion, bell pepper, and garlic over medium heat for about 2 to 3 minutes, or until translucent. Add the eggplant, zucchini, salt, and ground pepper. Turn the heat up to medium-high and sauté until the veggies are crisp-tender. Add the tomatoes and reduce the heat to low. Cook 2 to 3 minutes, or just until everything is heated through.

4. Spritz a baking dish (11½"×7½" is ideal, but you can substitute any size to fit the contents) with cooking spray, or brush with a dash of olive oil. Place the polenta on the bottom, pressing it in place like a crust. Add a generous sprinkling of Parmesan cheese, then add the veggies. Cover with aluminum foil and bake for 30 minutes. Remove from the oven and sprinkle with the shredded mozzarella. Return to the oven and bake, uncovered, for another 10 to 15 minutes, or until bubbly. Let cool for 5 to 10 minutes before serving.

Variation:

- For vegans, leave out both cheeses and add more tomatoes.
- For more flavor, add any veggies you have on hand. I like mushrooms in this dish. Just keep in mind the sauté times; the order you put the veggies into the skillet may change based on how long it takes a particular veggie to become "crisp-tender."

Easy Veggie Pie   Serves 6

Total Time: 1 hour, including 5 minutes stand time
Prep Time: 15 minutes   Bake Time: 40 minutes

2 cups chopped broccoli and cauliflower florets (or one or the other)
⅓ cup chopped onion or green onion
⅓ cup diced green bell pepper
1 cup shredded cheddar or similar cheese
½ cup baking mix (page 376)
1 cup milk
dash of salt

dash of ground pepper
2 eggs

1. Heat oven to 400°F. Grease a 9-inch pie pan.

2. Steam the broccoli and cauliflower just until crisp-tender (page 192). Drain and place in the prepared pan. Add the onion, bell pepper, and cheese.

3. In a separate bowl, combine the baking mix, milk, salt, ground pepper, and eggs; mix well. Pour over the vegetables in the pan. Bake for 40 minutes, or until golden brown and a toothpick inserted in the center comes out clean. Let cool 5 minutes before serving.

Vegetarian Stuffed Peppers (Vegan Option)   Serves 2

Total Time: 1 to 1½ hours, including 5 minutes stand time
Prep Time: 20 minutes   Cook Time: 45 to 60 minutes

1 clove garlic, minced, OR ¼ teaspoon garlic powder
1 onion, diced
2 carrots, diced
1 tablespoon olive oil, canola oil, or vegetable oil
3 or 4 Roma tomatoes or 1 large tomato or 2 medium tomatoes, diced, OR 1 can (16 ounces) diced tomatoes
1 can (8 ounces) mushrooms, drained and diced
1 cup tomato sauce
1 teaspoon Italian seasoning (page 48)
salt and pepper, to taste
2 cups cooked couscous (page 186) or cooked rice
4 large bell peppers

1. Preheat oven to 350°F.

2. Sauté the garlic, onion, and carrot in the olive oil until soft. Turn down the heat and add the tomatoes, mushrooms, tomato sauce, Italian seasoning, salt, and pepper; heat through. Add the couscous.

3. Cut the tops off the bell peppers (reserve the tops) and remove the seeds, but leave the pepper intact. Spoon the veggie/couscous mixture into the peppers and replace the tops. Set them in a baking dish, and bake for 45 to 60 minutes, or until the tops of the peppers are browned. Remove from the oven and let sit for 5 minutes before serving.

Vegetarian Green Curry (Vegan Option)   Serves 4

This is quite spicy. If you prefer a mild version, reduce the spices by half or more. Great served over basmati rice!

Total Time: 1 hour
Prep Time: 20 minutes   **Cook Time:** 40 minutes

1 pound potatoes, sliced thickly (peeled or not as you prefer)
1 pound green beans, cleaned and snapped in half, OR 1 can (16 ounces) green beans, drained
5 tablespoons butter or margarine, or canola oil for a vegan version
1 onion, chopped
5 cloves garlic, minced, OR 1 teaspoon garlic powder
2 teaspoons ground turmeric
1 tablespoon ground cumin
1 tablespoon ground coriander
½ teaspoon paprika
½ teaspoon cayenne, or to taste
¼ teaspoon ground cinnamon
1 zucchini, sliced
1 pound spinach, washed and chopped
1½ tablespoons grated fresh ginger OR 1 teaspoon ground ginger
4 tablespoons minced green chile peppers or other spicy chile peppers, or to taste
2 tablespoons lemon juice
¾ cup water
salt and pepper, to taste

1. Boil the potato and green beans (don't boil canned green beans) in salted water for 5 minutes. Drain and set aside.
2. Melt the butter over low heat, then increase the heat and sauté the onion and garlic for 5 minutes. Add the spices and sauté for a few more minutes. Add the potato, green beans, zucchini, spinach, ginger, chilies, lemon juice, water, salt, and pepper. Stir well, then bring to a boil. Turn down the heat and simmer, uncovered, stirring frequently, until most of the water is gone and the veggies are tender.

BEAN/LENTIL-BASED MAIN DISHES

Beans are a great way to add fiber to your diet!

Meatless Hoppin' John (Vegan Option)   Serves 10

Hoppin' John is a southern rice and bean dish, adapted from a traditional West African dish. Hoppin' John is traditional on New Year's Day. It's thought to bring a prosperous and lucky year.

Total Time: 40 minutes
Prep Time: 10 minutes   **Cook Time:** 30 minutes

1 cup corn OR 1 can (8 ounces) corn, drained
3 medium carrots, thinly sliced
½ cup chopped green bell pepper
½ cup chopped red bell pepper
½ cup chopped yellow or orange bell pepper
¼ cup chopped onion
4 cloves garlic, minced
1 tablespoon olive oil, canola oil, or vegetable oil
¾ cup cooked long-grain brown rice
1 can (16 ounces) black-eyed peas, rinsed and drained
1 can (16 ounces) diced tomatoes, drained
2 tablespoons chopped fresh parsley
3 teaspoons chopped fresh thyme OR 1 teaspoon dried thyme
salt and pepper, to taste
¼ teaspoon crushed red pepper flakes
hot sauce, to taste

Sauté the corn, carrot, bell pepper, onion, and garlic in the olive oil until crisp-tender. Add the cooked rice, black-eyed peas, and diced tomatoes and bring to a boil. Reduce the heat and simmer until heated through. Add the spices and hot sauce, and simmer 5 minutes longer. Let cool for 5 minutes before serving.

Tomato Veggie Bean Curry
(Vegan Option)   Serves 2

Total Time: 30 minutes
Prep Time: 10 minutes   Cook Time: 20 minutes

1 onion, diced
1 tablespoon olive oil, canola oil, or vegetable oil
1 can (10 ounces) tomato sauce OR 1 can
    (6 ounces) tomato paste plus ¾ cup water
1 tablespoon curry powder OR ½ teaspoon garlic
    powder, or to taste (page 47)
1 can (16 ounces) diced tomatoes OR 2 fresh toma-
    toes, diced
2 cups cooked garbanzo beans (chick-peas) or
    lentils, drained
4 cups diced veggies (carrots, peas, green beans,
    broccoli, bell peppers—whatever you have)
    OR 2 cans (16 ounces each) mixed vegetables,
    drained
1 cup cooked brown rice or other rice

Sauté the onion in the olive oil. Add the tomato
sauce, curry powder, diced tomato, garbanzo beans,
and diced veggies. Simmer, uncovered, until most
of the liquid has evaporated. Top with a spoonful of
cooked brown rice and serve.

Chick-Pea Masala
(Vegan Option)   Serves 2

Total Time: 20 minutes, plus time to prepare rice
Prep Time: 10 minutes   Cook Time: 10 minutes

1 medium onion, chopped
2 tablespoons olive oil, canola oil, or vegetable oil
1 clove garlic, minced, OR ¼ teaspoon garlic
    powder
1 tablespoon curry powder (page 47)
1 tablespoon tomato paste
1 can (16 ounces) garbanzo beans (chick-peas),
    drained, 3 tablespoons liquid reserved
1½ teaspoons lemon juice
½ teaspoon salt
ground pepper, to taste
red pepper flakes, to taste (optional)
2 servings cooked rice

1. Sauté the onion in the oil until translucent.
   Reduce the heat and add the garlic, curry powder,
   and tomato paste. Stir and simmer until heated
   through.
2. Add the garbanzo beans with their 3 tablespoons
   liquid, the lemon juice, salt, ground pepper, and
   pepper flakes. Simmer for 5 minutes, or until
   heated through and the garbanzo beans are soft.
   Serve over the rice.

Zucchini Black
Bean Quesadilla   Serves 2

Total Time: 40 minutes
Prep Time: 15 minutes   Cook Time: 25 minutes

1 pound zucchini, grated
1 can (16 ounces) black beans OR Recipe-Ready
    Beans (page 176)
6 ounces shredded Monterey Jack or similar
    cheese
1 green onion, sliced thinly
½ jalapeño pepper, seeded and minced
8 flour or corn tortillas (8 inch is best)
salsa (page 127) and/or sour cream (page 99),
    optional

1. Combine the zucchini, beans, cheese, green onion,
   and jalapeño pepper.
2. Place a dry skillet over medium-high heat until
   hot. Put one tortilla in the ungreased pan and
   spread one-quarter of the bean mix on it. Top with
   a second tortilla. Cook over medium-high heat for
   about 2 to 3 minutes, or until the cheese melts and
   the tortilla is golden brown. Then very carefully
   flip the quesadilla. (If the cheese is sufficiently
   melted, the filling will stay inside the quesadilla.)
   Cook another 2 to 3 minutes. Remove from the
   pan and keep warm. Repeat to make the remaining
   quesadillas.
3. Serve with the salsa and/or sour cream, if desired.

Meatless Main Dishes

Spicy Zucchini Casserole (Vegan Option)

Serves 4

For a vegan version, omit the cheese.

Total Time: 1 hour, plus time to cook rice and/or Recipe-Ready Beans if needed
Prep Time: 20 minutes   **Cook Time:** 35 minutes

2 tablespoons olive oil, canola oil, or vegetable oil
3 zucchini, unpeeled, cubed
1 cup diced onion
1 teaspoon garlic salt (page 47)
1 teaspoon paprika
1 teaspoon dried oregano
$\frac{1}{2}$ teaspoon cayenne pepper, or to taste
2 cups cooked rice
1 can (16 ounces) pinto beans OR Recipe-Ready Beans (page 176)
$2\frac{1}{2}$ cups salsa (page 127)
$1\frac{1}{2}$ cups shredded cheddar or similar cheese

1. Preheat oven to 350°F.
2. Warm the oil over medium-high heat. Add the zucchini and onion; sauté for 10 minutes. Stir in the garlic salt, paprika, oregano, and cayenne. Mix in the rice, beans, and salsa, and cook just until heated through. Mix in 1 cup of the cheese.
3. Transfer to a 9-inch square baking pan and top with the remaining cheese. Cover with aluminum foil. Bake for 20 minutes, or until the cheese is melted and bubbly.

Lentil Chili (Vegan Option)

Serves 6

Total Time: 1 hour, 30 minutes
Prep Time: 20 minutes
Cook Time: 1 hour, 10 minutes

1 large onion, diced
2 cloves garlic, minced, or to taste, OR $\frac{1}{4}$ teaspoon garlic powder
2 tablespoons olive oil, canola oil, or vegetable oil
1 cup dry lentils
1 pouch *criolla* (page 213)
4 cups water
1 tablespoon chili powder

1 tablespoon ground cumin
dash of paprika
salt and pepper, to taste
1 cup diced carrot
1 green bell pepper, diced
1 can (8 ounces) sliced mushrooms, drained, OR 8 ounces fresh mushrooms
1 can (16 ounces) diced tomatoes, not drained, OR 2 cups diced fresh tomatoes
1 can (4 ounces) chopped green chilies OR fresh chilies, seeded and minced, to taste
hot sauce, to taste

1. Sauté the onion and garlic in the olive oil in at least a 3-quart pan. Add the lentils, *criolla*, water, and spices. Cover and bring to a boil. Reduce the heat and simmer for 30 minutes.
2. Add all the veggies and continue simmering for another 30 minutes, or until the veggies are crisp-tender. Taste and add hot sauce or more spices as needed.

MEATLESS MAIN DISHES IN OTHER CHAPTERS

For more meatless recipes, check out these ideas in other chapters.

Breakfast and Brunch

Salads

Soups and Stews

Rice, Beans, and Pasta

POTLUCK

Everyone loves a good cruiser potluck, but finding a recipe with ingredients on hand that no one else is making can be challenging. With a little ingenuity, you can bring something different that will be much appreciated by everyone attending.

This chapter provides creative ideas as well as general potluck tips, plus important allergy awareness information.

TWELVE TIPS FOR A PERFECT POTLUCK

1. Be imaginative when scheduling a potluck. Most are at happy hour or evening hours, but in some areas cruisers enjoy Sunday brunch potlucks as well. But why limit a brunch to Sundays?
2. When doing your major provisioning, think ahead about potluck recipes and buy the ingredients. Make sure you consider one or two possibilities that do not require fresh ingredients–such as Pineapple Angel Food Cake (page 407) or BBQ Baked Beans (page 181).
3. When planning your contribution, consider the potluck setup and how the food is to be served. Does your dish need to be finger food by necessity, or can it be more of a meal? Keep in mind that it doesn't matter how delicious your gazpacho might be if the potluck is held where everyone is standing. It's very difficult to eat soup while standing!
4. Even if your potluck is "only" on a beach, is it possible to put something between two dinghies to

create a makeshift table if no other flat surface is available?
5. Be sure to bring your own "chairs"—5-gallon buckets upside down make fine seats if you don't have foldable chairs aboard.
6. Think about how you will transport your dish. Deviled eggs in a plastic egg tray designed to hold the eggs in place may allow you to get the eggs to the potluck without major damage, but a simple dinner plate of deviled eggs is bound to be a slippery mess in a dinghy!
7. Consider whether your dish needs to be kept warm or cold and whether you have the appropriate insulated containers aboard. Making a dish that is delicious regardless of serving temperature may be preferable since food can sit for a while until it's all consumed. If you don't have an insulated container, wrap your warm dish in a towel to hold in the heat.
8. If the weather is very hot, consider making something that won't spoil—for example, potato salad with vinegar and oil (page 155) instead of mayonnaise. Or bring non-perishables such as cookies, bread, or a batch of pickled cucumbers and onions.
9. Unless there's a spot for everyone to sit (preferably at a table), under no circumstances should you bring something that requires cutting with a knife!
10. Make sure to bring your plates, plastic ware (or silverware), napkins, cups, condiments, and any

serving utensils or potholders needed for your dish.

11. It's easier to bring disposable plates, cups, and plastic ware–unless there's no place to dispose of it (as in the San Blas islands in Panama). Carolyn prefers "real" plates and silverware and just brings a plastic grocery bag for carrying the dirty items back to the boat.

12. If you need to use plastic wrap to cover your dish, spritzing it first with cooking spray will help to keep the plastic wrap from sticking to the top of the dish. This is especially good for cupcakes, cakes with frosting, deviled eggs, and similar foods.

FOOD ALLERGIES

If you or someone on your boat suffers from food allergies, potlucks seem more like a minefield than a party. Eating the wrong thing can have serious consequences: breathing difficulties, swelling of the lips and throat, abdominal cramps and vomiting, and possibly death. When medical help is hours or days away, food allergies are very scary.

To make potlucks more inviting to those with food allergies, the best thing that you can do is to place a small card next to your dish listing *every* item that went into it. The second best thing is to at least place a small sign beside a dish that contains one of the eight most common allergens:

- **Milk/dairy products,** including cheese, yogurt, butter, margarine, and cream. Plain mayonnaise does not contain milk, contrary to what most people think.
- **Eggs.** In addition to the obvious, eggs are a major ingredient of mayonnaise (and Miracle Whip). They're also in almost all baked goods, including bread, cakes, cookies, and often crackers.
- **Peanuts.** Those who are allergic to peanuts often cannot be anywhere near peanuts or any dishes containing peanut butter or peanut oil. This is considered to be the most severe food allergy.
- **Tree nuts,** such as almonds, cashews, or walnuts.
- **Fish or shellfish,** including such things as clam juice. (Watch out for Bloody Marys made with Clamato juice!)

- **Soy,** including soy sauce. Many crackers and processed meats contain soy, as do most margarines.
- **Wheat/gluten**—notably, anything with flour.

Don't be annoyed if someone asks detailed questions about ingredients in a dish. And if someone has a food allergy, don't press them to eat anything if they say they'd prefer not to risk it.

PERFECT POTLUCK QUICK IDEAS

We've included a comprehensive "Potluck Cross-Reference List" (next section) for gazillions of ideas on recipes that you could make and bring to a potluck. But if you're just looking for some quick ideas, here are some:

- Any homemade bread or muffins. Braided Bread (page 396) is particularly good.
- Any homemade cookies (page 414)
- Vinegar and Oil Potato Salad (page 155)
- Fresh Veggies with Dip (starting on page 124). Choose any dip.
- Black Bean, Corn, and Tomato Salad (page 156)
- Basic Oil and Vinegar Coleslaw (page 148)
- Killer Bread (page 139)
- Chipotle Cream Cheese Dip and Crackers (page 133)
- Hummus Without Tahini (page 131) or Black Bean Hummus (page 132)
- Garlic Smushed Potatoes and Veggies (page 194)

POTLUCK CROSS-REFERENCE LIST

Here's a comprehensive list of ideas for recipes in this book that are perfect for taking to a potluck. Remember to select your potluck recipe with consideration for the weather (too hot or too cold) and the setting for the potluck as well as your method of transportation to the potluck.

Breakfast and Brunch
Breakfast Casserole, *page 115*
Quiche in General, *page 115*
Apple Breakfast Bread, *page 118*
Gingerbread Muffins, *page 118*
Streusel Coffee Cake, *page 119*

HOLIDAY CHEER

Holidays are always special and always involve great food, whether you're gathered around the dining room table with dozens of family members or anchored in paradise with no other boats in sight. One of the things we often missed aboard was a selection of festive holiday recipes, not to mention basic recipes for what to do with that turkey breast we found in one of the little *tienda* freezers. Every holiday is an adventure to see what we can find in the local *tiendas* and what we can make out of it to create a special meal. The 34 recipes in this chapter, plus more than 40 other recipes listed in the "More Holiday Cheer" cross-reference list, provide a good start to your holiday planning.

Holiday Cheer differs a bit from the basic premise of *The Boat Galley Cookbook* in that the ingredients in these holiday recipes may not be readily available in popular cruising grounds. If you really want to ensure that you have green beer on St. Pat's Day, you may need to bring green food coloring with you, so plan holiday celebrations in advance and take the critical ingredients with you.

Besides holidays calling for special cuisine, cruisers are often looking for reasons or themes for gatherings. Here's a calendar with some of our favorite excuses for get-togethers. If someone in the anchorage has satellite radio, sporting events are always a great excuse for a party, too.

Whenever	Howl at the Moon Party (aka Full Moon Party)
	Friday the 13th Party
	Birthday
	Luau
January	Super Bowl—date varies
	Chinese New Year—sometime between January 20 and February 20
February	Groundhog Day—February 2
	Valentine's Day—February 14
	Mardi Gras—date varies, Tuesday before Ash Wednesday
March	St. Patrick's Day—March 17
	Spring Equinox—March 20 or 21
	Passover—date varies, March to April
April	April Fool's Day—April 1
	Easter/*Semana Santa*—date varies, March to April
	Earth Day—April 22
May	May Day—May 1
	Kentucky Derby—1st Saturday in May
	Cinco de Mayo—May 5
	Mother Ocean Day—May 8
	National Nutty Fudge Day—May 12
	Indianapolis 500—Sunday of Memorial Day weekend
	Memorial Day—last Monday in May
June	Father's Day—3rd Sunday in June
	Summer Solstice—June 20 or 21
July	Canada Day—July 1
	Independence Day (US)—July 4
	Chocolate Day—July 7

continued

August	International Beer Day—August 5
September	Labor Day—1st Monday in September
	Rosh Hashanah—date varies
	Yom Kippur—date varies—September to October
	Talk Like a Pirate Day—September 19
	Fall Equinox—September 22 or 23
October	Thanksgiving (Canada)—2nd Monday of October
	Halloween—October 31
	Oktoberfest—usually early October, pick a date and have a party!
November	Day of the Dead/All Souls' Day—November 2
	Veterans Day—November 11
	Thanksgiving Day (US)—4th Thursday of November
December	Hanukkah—date varies
	Winter Solstice—December 21 or 22
	Christmas—December 25
	Kwanzaa—December 26 to January 1
	Boxing Day—December 26
	New Year's Eve—December 31

Happy Holidays!

TIPS FOR "RE-SIZING" RECIPES

Especially during the holidays, you may need to serve more or fewer people than in the original recipe. No problem. Here are a few tips to help you get the exact number of servings you need.

Doubling or halving a recipe is easy, right? Just divide by two or multiply by two. But this can lead to some interesting fractional amounts of ingredients. In these cases, I usually try to re-size the recipe to use entire cans.

Probably the hardest thing to double or halve is eggs. If the original recipe calls for 3 eggs and you want to halve it, you'll need to use one egg and then beat the other egg and measure half. Here's an alternative if there are other liquid ingredients in the recipe:

A typical egg will measure ¼ cup or slightly less. Add together the total volume of the eggs and another liquid in the original recipe. For example, if it called for 1 egg and ¾ cup milk, the total would be 1 cup. So for a half recipe, I need ½ cup of egg and milk together. Break an egg into a measuring cup, then add enough milk (or whatever liquid is in the recipe) to total ½ cup.

Seasonings can be tricky when revising recipes. If you're doubling the recipe, consider using 1½ times the amount of seasoning and then tasting before adding the rest. If you're halving the recipe, start with a little less than half. You can always add more.

When changing recipe quantities, you'll also need to think about pan size. In general, consider the pan size in the original recipe and size up (or down) so that the amount in the pan is consistent. For more information on changing pan size, please see page 8.

TURKEY: TIPS, TECHNIQUES, AND RECIPES

Thanksgiving and, to a lesser extent, Christmas are traditional times for having turkey.

Cooking a Turkey

Before buying a turkey, whether fresh from a butcher or frozen, consider whether it will fit in your refrigerator (or plan in advance for an alternative, such as at the marina restaurant). Also consider whether the turkey will fit in your oven. If it won't, consider a whole roast chicken as a great alternative (page 278).

Fresh Turkey. It would be rare where we were cruising to see a fresh turkey, but just in case, the USDA recommends buying fresh turkey only if it will be cooked within two days.

Thawing a Frozen Turkey. It's important to safely thaw a frozen turkey. If you don't have enough freezer room, choose a turkey breast or another type of meat for your holiday celebrations. You can thaw a turkey either in cold water or in your refrigerator—if you have a large enough refrigerator. If you buy a frozen turkey and don't have enough freezer space to keep it safely frozen until the holiday, allow it to thaw via the cold water method below and then cook it immediately.

- **Refrigerator thaw instructions:** You may not have a refrigerator space large enough to defrost a turkey, but cruisers are nothing if not resourceful. We've seen cruisers talk the local dive shop that has a drinks refrigerator into thawing their turkey, as well as asking friends ashore to do this for them.

  Keep the turkey in its original wrapper, and place it in a tray in case the juices leak during thawing. Plan to thaw it for about 24 hours for every five pounds of turkey. Yes, a ten-pound turkey will take about two days to thaw.

  Do not thaw your turkey at room temperature since the chance of bacteria growth increases. Cooking may not destroy all the bacteria, so be on the safe side!

- **Cold water thaw instructions:** Submerge the turkey in its wrapper in a tub of cold water. Allow 30 minutes per pound to thaw in cold water. Do not use warm or hot water.

Roasting a Turkey

1. Preheat oven to 325°F.
2. Check the wrapper to see how much the turkey weighs. Then determine the approximate cooking time from the table below.
3. Remove the giblet bag and the neck from the turkey cavity. Wash the turkey inside and out and pat dry with paper towels. (Brining a turkey involves submerging it overnight in salt water to preserve moisture, but it's almost impossible on a boat, so we have deliberately not included it here.)
4. Place the turkey breast side up in a roasting pan. Insert a meat thermometer in a thigh (unless you have an instant-read type, which should not be left in the oven). Add ½ cup water to the roasting pan (optional). Add any other ingredients you want—we prefer placing the turkey on 2 or 3 stalks of celery and including wedges of onion in the baking pan. You can also loosen the skin and rub any spices you prefer—Cajun or otherwise—between the skin and the flesh.
5. Cover the turkey with a loose "tent" of aluminum foil to keep it from drying out. Remove the foil after 1½ hours of baking and brush the skin with olive oil or canola oil to enhance browning.

6. Bake until the meat thermometer reads 165°F. If you don't have a meat thermometer and your turkey didn't come with a pop-out indicator, you can test for doneness by moving one of the drumsticks. If it moves easily and separates from the body, the turkey is done.
7. Take the turkey out of the oven and let sit for 20 to 30 minutes before carving to retain the juices.

Here are the USDA Recommended Cooking Guidelines for turkey. (Always use a meat thermometer.)

Unstuffed	8–12 pounds	2¾ to 3 hours
	12–14 pounds	3 to 3¾ hours
	14–18 pounds	3¾ to 4¼ hours
	18–20 pounds	4¼ to 4½ hours
	20–24 pounds	4½ to 5 hours
Stuffed	8–12 pounds	3 to 3½ hours
	12–14 pounds	3½ to 4 hours
	14–18 pounds	4 to 4¼ hours
	18–20 pounds	4¼ to 4¾ hours
	20–24 pounds	4¾ to 5¼ hours

Tips on Roasting a Turkey Breast

Turkey breasts have more of a tendency to dry out than a full turkey. So here are some tips to help ensure that a turkey breast is moist and tasty.

- Bake in a large enough roasting pan to allow air to completely circulate around the turkey breast. The pan should be shallow, no deeper than about 2 inches. We like to place celery stalks under the meat to allow air circulation until the juices fill up the space.
- Wash the turkey before baking and pat dry with a paper towel.
- An oven cooking bag keeps the moisture in, but you'll need to plan ahead and stock turkey cooking bags as they are not readily available. Follow the directions and cooking time given in the bag instructions—there are differences between brands.
- Before roasting, insert a meat thermometer (unless you have an instant-read type, which should not be left in the oven). The turkey breast

Holiday Cheer

is done when the meat thermometer reads 170°F (note the slightly higher temperature than for a whole turkey).

- After taking the breast out of the oven, let it sit 20 minutes to ensure that the juices have a chance to distribute throughout the entire breast.
- If you don't have a meat thermometer, pierce the meat with a fork. If the juices run clear, the turkey breast is done. Be sure to pierce close to the middle of the meatiest part of the bird.

APPROXIMATE ROASTING TIMES FOR A TURKEY BREAST AT 325°F*

2–3 pounds	1½ to 2 hours
4–6 pounds	1½ to 2¼ hours
7–8 pounds	2¼ to 3¼ hours

*Boneless turkey breasts require about 20 minutes per pound at 325°F.

Roast Turkey Breast

Time and servings depend on size of breast (see above).

1 turkey breast
½ cup butter or margarine, melted
¼ cup dry white wine or apple juice
1½ teaspoons dried thyme OR 2 tablespoons chopped fresh thyme
1 teaspoon salt
1 teaspoon paprika
2 cloves garlic, minced

1. Place the turkey breast, skin side up, in a roasting pan. Insert a meat thermometer. Roast, uncovered, for 1 hour at 325°F (no need to preheat oven).
2. At the end of the first hour, mix the butter, wine, thyme, salt, paprika, and garlic. Remove the turkey from the oven and brush with half the mixture. Return it to the oven and roast until done (see roasting times above), basting every 20 minutes with the rest of the mixture.
3. Remove the turkey from the oven and let stand for 15 minutes before carving. Meanwhile, make the gravy as for Chicken or Beef Gravy from Pan Drippings (page 221) or Giblet Turkey Gravy (page 362).

Blackened Turkey Breast   Serves 10

Blackened turkey breast can be a delicious treat, but you will need room in your refrigerator to marinate it overnight, which may be a problem. If you have a cooler and access to ice, you could marinate it in the cooler overnight.

Total Time: 3 hours, not including 24 hours marinate time
Prep Time: 20 minutes
Cook Time: 2 to 3 hours approximately; check with a meat thermometer

8-pound boneless turkey breast
3 tablespoons butter, melted, or canola oil or vegetable oil
¾ cup Cajun spice (page 46)
1 small onion (we prefer Vidalia if available), thinly sliced

1. Loosen the skin of the turkey breast and brush with the butter or oil, under the skin first and then over it. Cover with the Cajun spice and sliced onion. Wrap in foil or plastic wrap and refrigerate for 24 hours.
2. Uncover the breast and discard the onion slices. Bake at 350°F (no need to preheat), uncovered, until the internal temperature reaches 170°F— approximately 18 minutes per pound.

Giblet Turkey Gravy

Total Time: 20 minutes
Prep Time: 5 minutes   **Cook Time:** 15 minutes

4 to 5 cups of pan drippings from roasting the turkey (use giblet water and broth to make the total amount needed)
turkey scraps or cooked giblets* (leave these out if you prefer gravy with no "stuff")
3 chicken bouillon cubes, or more to taste
½ cup cold water
3 tablespoons flour

*To cook the turkey giblets, first rinse them in water. Then place the giblets you wish to use in a sauté pan with some onion slivers and celery chunks for flavor. Cover with water and bring to a boil, then reduce the heat and simmer until the meat is firm, usually 1 to 2 hours. Chop the meat into small pieces to use in *the gravy. The stock is flavorful, so if you don't have enough pan drippings from the turkey, use the stock to make up the difference.*

1. Heat the pan drippings, turkey scraps/giblets, and bouillon cubes to boiling. Meanwhile, pour the cold water into a small bowl and mix in the flour.
2. Turn down the heat under the pan and add the flour mixture, stirring constantly until it is thickened. Let boil 3 minutes, stirring constantly, to thoroughly cook the flour so the gravy won't taste "pasty." This makes a fairly thin gravy. If you prefer thicker gravy, increase the amount of flour you mix into the water.

HOLIDAY HAM RECIPES

Ham is also traditional for holidays.

Holiday Ham Balls   Makes about 18 balls

Total Time: 55 minutes
Prep Time: 30 minutes   **Cook Time:** 25 minutes

3 cups baking mix (page 376)
1½ cups finely chopped cooked or canned ham
4 cups grated cheddar or similar cheese
½ cup grated Parmesan cheese
2 teaspoons dried parsley flakes
2 teaspoons spicy brown mustard
1 tablespoon milk or pineapple juice

1. Heat oven to 350°F. Lightly grease a large baking pan.
2. Combine all the ingredients; the mixture will be very stiff. If needed, add a tiny bit more milk until the mixture forms a dough that can be made into balls.
3. Shape the mixture into 1-inch balls. Place about 2 inches apart on a baking sheet. Bake for 20 to 25 minutes, or until browned. Immediately remove from the pan and serve warm.

Holiday Ham Coca-Cola   Serves 8

Total Time: 2 hours
Prep Time: 30 minutes   **Bake Time:** 1½ hours

5-pound boneless ham or any other ham (adjust cooking time, page 292)

whole cloves
½ cup packed dark brown sugar
½ cup honey
1 can (12 ounces) Coca-Cola (not Diet Coke)
1 can (8 ounces) pineapple rings, drained and juice reserved

1. Preheat oven to 350°F.
2. Using a sharp knife, crosscut the surface of the ham, forming a crosshatch pattern about ¼ inch deep and 1 inch apart. Insert 1 clove into each "X." Place the ham, fat side up, in a roasting pan.
3. Mix the brown sugar, honey, and Coca-Cola together. Pour three-quarters of the mixture over the ham. Bake for 1½ hours, basting every 20 minutes with extra sugar/honey/Coke mixture. If you use all the mixture, baste by spooning the liquid up from the bottom of the pan.
4. During the last 20 minutes of baking time, baste with the reserved pineapple juice as well as the original liquid. If desired, decorate the ham with pineapple rings (use two or three toothpicks to hold each ring in place) or just serve with pineapple rings surrounding the ham.
5. Cook a fully cooked ham to an internal temperature of 135°F, uncooked hams to 155°F. (See page 288 for full details on safe temperatures.)

Holiday Ham Glaze   1½ cups

Use on fresh ham or canned ham.

Total Time: 25 minutes
Prep Time: 15 minutes   **Cook Time:** 10 minutes

½ cup packed brown sugar
½ cup butter or margarine
½ cup dark rum or light rum
¼ cup molasses
3 tablespoons spicy prepared mustard or other prepared mustard
1 tablespoon cider vinegar or other vinegar
½ teaspoon ground cinnamon
½ teaspoon ground pepper

Mix all the ingredients together and bring to a boil, stirring constantly. Reduce the heat and simmer for 5 to 10 minutes. Drizzle over the ham while the glaze and the ham are warm.

Holiday Cheer

CHICKEN RECIPES

We find chicken is often easier to prepare on a boat than turkey or ham.

Virginia's Flaming Festive Chicken

Serves 4

Virginia is a friend who has shared a number of great recipes with us over the years and kindly consented to our using them here.

Total Time: 45 minutes (prepare the rice at the same time)
Prep Time: 10 minutes   **Cook Time:** 35 minutes

¼ cup flour
1 teaspoon salt
4 boneless, skinless chicken breasts or any chicken breasts you have, skin removed
¼ cup plus 2 tablespoons butter or margarine
½ cup dry white wine
½ cup chicken broth (may be made from bouillon) or stock (page 164)
1 jigger (1 to 2 ounces) brandy
8 ounces shredded mozzarella or any white cheese

1. Mix the flour and salt. Use it to lightly dust the chicken breasts. Shake off any excess flour.
2. Melt ¼ cup of the butter in a large skillet. Add the chicken breasts and sauté for 6 minutes on each side. Turn only once. Pour in the wine and broth. Cook slowly, uncovered, until the liquid is reduced, leaving only enough in the pan to keep the chicken from sticking. Add the brandy and ignite with a match.
3. When the flames go out, add the remaining 2 tablespoons butter and let it melt. Sprinkle the chicken with the shredded mozzarella. Place under the broiler until browned. If you don't have a broiler, you can omit this step; just leave the pan on the stove over low heat until the mozzarella melts. It won't look as good, but it will taste the same. Serve over rice.

Chicken Surprise

Serves 8

Not quite as good as a Thanksgiving turkey with all the trimmings, but it fits easily into a cruiser oven, and the aroma is very similar to a traditional Thanksgiving morning with baking chicken, dressing, and gravy. We enjoyed this for Thanksgiving while checking out of Livingston, Guatemala, sitting on a dock waiting for high tide at 3 P.M. to cross the infamous Rio Dulce bar.

Total Time: 2 hours
Prep Time: 30 minutes   **Cook Time:** 1½ hours

¾ loaf of bread
2 to 3 pounds of bone-in chicken (dark or light) OR 1½ to 2 pounds boneless chicken OR similar amount of cooked chicken meat*
1 can (8 ounces) sliced mushrooms, drained
1 can (8 ounces) water chestnuts, drained
1 can (10 ounces) condensed mushroom soup, undiluted (page 54)
1 tablespoon flour
1 cup diced celery
2 tablespoons chopped onion, or to taste
2 eggs
dash of sage, to taste

If using previously cooked chicken, you will also need 6 cups chicken broth (may be made from bouillon) or stock (page 164)

1. Tear the bread into bite-size pieces and allow to sit out overnight to dry.
2. Boil the chicken until it is falling off the bone—about 30 minutes. Cool. Reserve 6 cups of the broth; skim off the fat and discard it.
3. Preheat oven to 350°F.
4. Pick the chicken off the bone. Grease a large baking dish and place the chicken in it.
5. Mix 2 cups of the reserved broth, the mushrooms, water chestnuts, soup, and flour in a saucepan and bring to a boil, then reduce the heat and simmer for 10 minutes. Pour over the chicken in the baking dish.
6. To make the dressing, sauté the celery and onion. Combine the pieces of dried bread, 4 cups of the reserved broth, the eggs, celery, onion, and sage. Pour the mixture over the chicken in the baking dish and bake for 1 hour.

Leftovers Holiday Hash   Serves 4

Total Time: 1 hour, 15 minutes
Prep Time: 20 minutes   Cook Time: 55 minutes

¼ cup canola oil, olive oil, or vegetable oil
¼ cup flour
⅔ cup diced onion
⅓ cup diced celery
¼ cup diced red bell pepper
¼ cup diced green bell pepper
1 tablespoon minced garlic
3 cups diced turkey, chicken, roast beef, ham, or any leftover meat
3 cups chicken broth (may be made from bouillon) or stock (page 164), kept hot
1½ teaspoons chopped fresh basil
1½ teaspoons chopped fresh thyme
⅔ cup diced potato
½ cup diced carrot
½ cup sliced green onion
¼ cup chopped fresh parsley
salt and pepper, to taste

1. In a large pan over medium-high heat, warm the oil. Slowly add the flour and stir constantly until it becomes a golden brown roux. Add the onion, celery, bell pepper, and garlic. Cook for 3 to 5 minutes, or until the vegetables are crisp-tender.
2. Add the meat and blend into the roux. Add the hot broth, one cup at a time until a stew-like consistency is achieved. Add the basil and thyme. Bring to a boil, then reduce the heat and simmer for 30 minutes. Add the potato, carrot, green onion, and parsley. Return to a simmer and season to taste with the salt and pepper.
3. Cook an additional 10 to 15 minutes, or until the potato and carrot are tender. Add more broth as needed to retain the correct consistency. Serve over rice, if desired.

HOLIDAY APPETIZERS

Here are a few very special treats!

Pineapple Cheese Ball   Serves 6 to 8

Total Time: 20 minutes using alternate method and no chill time
Prep Time: 20 minutes

1 package ranch dressing mix (page 161)
16 ounces cream cheese, softened
1 can (8 ounces) crushed pineapple, drained
2 green onions, thinly sliced
1 cup shredded cheese (Monterey Jack or Colby are good)

1. Mix the package of ranch dressing mix with the softened cream cheese until well mixed. Then add all the other ingredients and mix well. Chill for about 20 minutes, or until the mixture is firm enough to shape.
2. Form the mixture into a ball. If desired, cover the ball with chopped nuts or parsley and chill at least 2 hours before serving.

Alternate Method: If you don't want to wait or don't have a refrigerator, mix all the ingredients together and place in a small bowl to serve.

Coconut Shrimp Appetizers   Serves 6 to 8

Combining hot oil and a moving boat is not a safe idea. Burns can be very serious. We recommend that you use this recipe only if you're in a calm anchorage or marina with no potential of large boat wakes. An even better idea is to use a marina kitchen if one is available.

Total Time: 20 minutes
Prep Time: 15 minutes   Cook Time: 5 minutes

½ cup flour
salt, to taste
24 raw jumbo shrimp, peeled and deveined (page 234)
2 eggs, beaten
1½ cups shredded coconut
canola oil or vegetable oil, for frying
1 cup cocktail sauce (page 211)
¼ cup crushed pineapple, or more to taste

1. Combine the flour and salt. Roll the shrimp in the seasoned flour, then dip in the beaten egg and roll in the coconut to cover thoroughly.
2. Heat the oil to about 350°F. Fry the shrimp in the hot oil until browned and cooked through—about 3 minutes. Deep-frying is best, although it's not practical in a galley. I just put some canola oil in a skillet and fry one side of the shrimp at a time. Be careful not to overcook; start with about 1½ minutes on each side.
3. Drain the shrimp on paper towels. Mix the cocktail sauce with the crushed pineapple to taste. Serve the shrimp with the cocktail sauce on the side.

Holiday Cheese Ball   Serves 6 to 8

Total Time: 15 minutes using alternate method with no chill time
Prep Time: 15 minutes

16 ounces cream cheese, softened
1½ cups shredded sharp cheddar or similar cheese
½ cup chopped green onion or chopped dill pickle
2 tablespoons mayonnaise
1 teaspoon Worcestershire sauce
½ cup finely chopped walnuts, pecans, almonds, or other nuts

Combine the cream cheese, cheddar, green onion, mayonnaise, and Worcestershire with a potato masher, food processor, or your hands (Carolyn's technique). Shape into two small balls and roll in the nuts. You could make one large ball, but then each serving would have fewer nuts on the surface. Wrap in plastic wrap or place in a plastic bag and chill for several hours or overnight to let the flavors blend.

Alternate Method with no refrigeration: Make the cheese mixture as above. Place it in a small bowl or spread it on a dinner plate and cover with the nuts. Serve at once.

VEGETABLE ACCOMPANIMENTS

Here are a few traditional recipes from our families.

Sweet Potato Casserole   Serves 6

Total Time: 40 minutes
Prep Time: 10 minutes   **Bake Time:** 30 minutes

3 cups cooked mashed sweet potatoes
½ cup milk
1 cup sugar
2 eggs, beaten
1 teaspoon vanilla extract

Topping
1 cup packed brown sugar
1 cup chopped pecans or walnuts
½ cup flour
4 tablespoons butter or margarine, softened

1. Preheat oven to 400°F.
2. Mix the sweet potatoes, milk, sugar, eggs, and vanilla. Pour into a greased 2-quart casserole.
3. Mix together the topping ingredients and sprinkle over the casserole. Cover and bake for 30 minutes.

Classic Corn Bread Dressing   Serves 8

Total Time: 1 hour, 5 minutes
Prep Time: 20 minutes   **Cook Time:** 45 minutes

1 small onion, diced
2 stalks celery, diced
½ loaf bread, torn into pieces and left out overnight to dry
3 cups crumbled corn bread (page 381)
turkey or chicken broth (may be made from bouillon) or stock (page 164)
dried sage, to taste
salt and pepper, to taste
2 cans (6 ounces each) water chestnuts, drained and chopped
1 egg, beaten

1. Sauté the onion and celery in water until soft.
2. Mix together the torn bread, crumbled corn bread, and cooked onion and celery in a bowl large enough to hold all the ingredients and still be able to mix them.

3. Heat the turkey broth to boiling. Pour over the bread mixture; use enough broth to make the bread moist but not soupy. Stir in the sage, salt, and pepper. Mix in the water chestnuts. Stir in the beaten egg.
4. Transfer to a greased 9"×13" pan or large casserole. Bake, uncovered, at 350°F (no need to preheat oven) for 45 minutes, or until the top is golden brown.

Cranberry Green Bean Casserole
Serves 6 to 8

Total Time: 1 hour
Prep Time: 15 minutes   Cook Time: 45 minutes

2 cans (16 ounces each) green beans, drained (we prefer French cut, but any will do)
1 can (10 ounces) cream of mushroom soup, undiluted (page 54)
3/4 cup milk
1 teaspoon soy sauce
1/4 teaspoon ground pepper
1 teaspoon onion powder
1/2 cup sliced fresh mushrooms OR 1 can (8 ounces) sliced mushrooms, drained
6 ounces dried sweetened cranberries
1/2 cup slivered almonds (optional)
1 can (3 ounces) French fried onions OR 1 cup fresh onion slivers, sautéed

1. Preheat oven to 350°F.
2. Mix the green beans, soup, milk, soy sauce, ground pepper, onion powder, mushrooms, cranberries, almonds (if desired), and half the onions in a large casserole or baking dish. Cover and bake for 30 minutes. Uncover and stir to mix well.
3. Sprinkle with the remaining onions and bake, uncovered, for another 10 to 15 minutes, or until the onions are deep golden.

NOTE: You can make this on the stove top—just simmer all the ingredients except the onions in a saucepan until the mixture is warm and the flavors have had a chance to meld. At the same time, toast the onions in a dry pan until deep golden, then sprinkle them over the top as you serve. If you're using fresh sautéed onion slivers, just mix them in with the other ingredients as you heat the dish.

SALADS FOR TRADITIONAL HOLIDAYS
Here are some more family favorites!

Waldorf Salad
Serves 8

Total Time: 4 hours, 20 minutes
Prep Time: 20 minutes

2 apples, cored and diced
1 can (8 ounces) pineapple chunks, drained
1 medium pear, cored and coarsely chopped
1/2 cup thinly sliced celery
1/2 cup halved seedless red grapes
1/2 cup walnut pieces
2 kiwifruit, peeled, halved lengthwise, and sliced (optional)
1 cup mayonnaise or plain yogurt (page 101)
1 tablespoon lemon juice
1 tablespoon honey or sugar
1 tablespoon milk, to thin dressing if necessary (optional)
lettuce leaves (optional)

1. Toss together the apple, pineapple, pear, celery, grapes, walnuts, and kiwifruit slices in a large bowl.
2. In a small bowl combine the mayonnaise, lemon juice, and honey; fold gently into the fruit mixture. Add the milk if necessary to thin the dressing. Cover and chill for 4 hours. Serve on lettuce leaves if desired.

Fruited Pudding Salad
Serves 6 to 8

Total Time: 4 hours, 15 minutes
Prep Time: 15 minutes

1 can (20 ounces) pineapple chunks
1 can (12 ounces) mandarin oranges
1 box (4 servings) instant vanilla pudding
2 bananas, sliced
1 can (16 to 20 ounces) fruit pie filling (cherry or your preference)

1. Drain the fruits, reserving the pineapple and orange juice. Mix the pudding into the reserved juice; it will be thick.
2. Fold in the drained fruit, bananas, and pie filling. Chill 4 hours before serving.

Holiday Cheer

Baked Pineapple   Serves 4

Total Time: 40 minutes
Prep Time: 10 minutes   **Cook Time:** 30 minutes

$\frac{1}{2}$ cup butter or margarine
1 can (20 ounces) crushed pineapple, not drained
2 cups sugar
1 cup cracker crumbs (I like graham cracker
  crumbs, but any type will do)

1. Preheat oven to 350°F.
2. Melt the butter. Stir in the pineapple, sugar, and all
   but a small amount of cracker crumbs for garnish.
   Mix well, and pour into a greased 8-inch square
   pan. Sprinkle with the remaining crumbs and bake
   approximately 30 minutes.

Holiday Spicy Cranberries   Serves 4

Total Time: 30 minutes, including 10 minutes to cool
  before serving
Prep Time: 10 minutes   **Cook Time:** 10 minutes

1 can (16 ounces) whole-berry cranberry sauce
$\frac{1}{4}$ cup water
$\frac{1}{2}$ cup peeled, seeded, and diced orange or canned
  mandarin oranges, drained and diced
$\frac{1}{4}$ teaspoon salt
$\frac{1}{8}$ teaspoon ground cloves
$\frac{1}{4}$ teaspoon ground ginger
$\frac{1}{4}$ teaspoon ground cinnamon

Mix all the ingredients in a saucepan. Bring to a boil,
stirring until the sugar is dissolved. Reduce the heat
and simmer for another 5 minutes. Remove from the
heat and let cool 10 minutes. Serve warm or chilled.

BREADS

Homemade bread of any variety was a holiday staple
in my (Carolyn's) family, but I developed this recipe
for cruisers who craved hot cross buns.

Hot Cross Buns   Serves 12

*These are traditionally served during Lent. Some cruising
friends complained that they could not buy hot cross buns
in remote locations and wanted to learn how to make
their own. This is my adaptation, with notes on substitutions for several of the ingredients. Currants and candied
fruit can be hard to come by. Substitute any type of dried,
canned, or fresh fruit—cranberries, dates, prunes, and
apricots are particularly good. Or you can make them
with all raisins. Also, if you don't have all the spices, use a
mix of those that you do have.*

Total Time: 3 to 4 hours, depending on how long the
  dough takes to rise

$\frac{3}{4}$ cup milk, warm but not hot
2 teaspoons yeast (1 packet; page 387)
$\frac{1}{2}$ teaspoon white sugar
$\frac{1}{4}$ cup brown sugar or white sugar
1 teaspoon ground cinnamon
$\frac{1}{4}$ teaspoon ground cloves
$\frac{1}{4}$ teaspoon ground allspice
$\frac{1}{4}$ teaspoon ground nutmeg
$\frac{1}{2}$ teaspoon salt
2 eggs
$\frac{1}{4}$ cup butter or margarine, softened, or vegetable
  oil
4 cups white flour (approximately)
$\frac{1}{2}$ cup candied fruit and/or candied zest OR any
  other dried, canned, or fresh fruit
$\frac{1}{4}$ cup currants or raisins

Optional Egg Glaze
1 egg
1 tablespoon water

Hot Cross Bun Frosting
$\frac{1}{2}$ cup confectioners' sugar
1 tablespoon milk or water

1. Mix the milk, yeast, and white sugar. Let proof for 10 minutes (page 388). Add the brown sugar, spices, eggs, and butter. Mix well. Add half the flour and mix for 5 minutes, or until smooth. Add the candied fruits and currants. Slowly add the remaining flour, kneading when the dough becomes too stiff to mix by hand. Knead for 10 minutes to fully develop the gluten to produce a very soft bread.
2. Place the dough in an oiled bowl and turn it so that it's completely coated with oil. Cover with a plastic bag and let rise until doubled in size.
3. Divide the dough into 12 equal pieces, and roll each into a ball. Lightly grease a 9"×13" pan and place the dough balls in the pan in four rows of three, equally spaced. Cover the pan with a plastic bag and let rise until the balls are doubled in size.
4. Preheat oven to 400°F.
5. Lightly beat the egg and water to make the egg glaze. Very gently brush it over the tops of the buns, taking care not to deflate them. Bake for about 15 minutes, or until golden brown. Remove from the pan and place on a wire rack or plate(s) to cool.
6. Mix the confectioners' sugar and milk to form the frosting. Make a cross with the frosting on the top of each bun, extending from the center of each side to the center of the opposite side. The easiest way to make the crosses is to drip glaze from the tip of a spoon. You can also put the glaze into a small plastic bag and cut off a tiny corner to form a nozzle.
7. Serve the buns warm or cool.

TRADITIONAL HOLIDAY DESSERTS

Of course, you can make these any time!

Almost Pecan Pie   Serves 6 to 8

This pie is for those times when you just can't find pecans but would love a taste of something similar for the holidays!

Total Time: 1 hour to 1 hour, 15 minutes, plus time to make piecrust if needed
Prep Time: 15 minutes (plus piecrust)
Bake Time: 45 minutes to 1 hour

3 eggs
1 cup corn syrup
½ cup sugar
2 tablespoons butter or margarine, melted
1 teaspoon vanilla extract
¼ teaspoon salt
¾ cup oats (quick-cooking oats are best, but if regular is all you have, bake them in an ungreased pan at 325°F for 55 minutes to 1 hour before adding them to the filling)
one 9-inch piecrust, unbaked (page 426)

1. Preheat oven to 350°F.
2. Beat the eggs with a fork or an eggbeater. Stir in the corn syrup, sugar, butter, vanilla, and salt until the sugar and salt are dissolved. Stir in the oats. Pour the mixture into the piecrust. Bake for approximately 45 minutes, or until a toothpick inserted in the middle comes out clean. (See note above for regular oats.) My boat oven takes longer to bake this pie, so I check it at 45 minutes and continue checking it every 5 minutes until the toothpick comes out clean.

Pecan Pie   Serves 6

Total Time: 1 hour to 1 hour, 15 minutes
Prep Time: 15 minutes
Bake Time: 45 minutes to 1 hour

3 eggs
1 cup corn syrup (dark is best, but light will work)
⅔ cup sugar
⅓ cup butter or margarine, melted
1 teaspoon vanilla extract
1¼ cups pecan halves
one 9-inch piecrust, unbaked (page 426)

1. Preheat oven to 350°F.
2. Beat the eggs with a fork, whisk, or eggbeater until frothy. Stir in the corn syrup, sugar, butter, vanilla, and pecans. Pour the filling into the piecrust. Bake for 45 minutes, or until a toothpick or knife inserted in the middle comes out clean. Start watching it at 45 minutes and check it every few minutes.
3. If you have trouble with the crust burning, you can cover the edge of the crust with aluminum foil for the first half of the baking time and take it off for the last half.

Holiday Cheer

Miniature Pecan Pies   Serves 8

My (Jan) mom's favorite pecan pie. Great for a potluck celebration, where everyone wants to sample several desserts.

Total Time: 45 minutes
Prep Time: 20 minutes   **Cook Time:** 25 minutes

Crust
3 ounces cream cheese, softened
1/2 cup butter or margarine, softened
1 cup flour

Filling
3/4 cup packed brown sugar
1 tablespoon butter or margarine
1/4 teaspoon salt
1/2 teaspoon vanilla extract
1 egg
1/2 cup chopped pecans

1. To make the crust, blend the cream cheese, butter, and flour. Chill for 1 hour. Shape into 24 balls, each 1 inch in diameter. Put one in each cup of a miniature nonstick (or greased) muffin pan. With your fingers, press down on the bottom and sides of the ball to make a pastry shell.
2. Preheat oven to 350°F as you begin making the filling.
3. To make the filling, mix all the filling ingredients. Spoon into the shells so each is approximately three-quarters full. Bake for 25 minutes. Do not overbake.

Margaret's Christmas Cookie Dough   Yield depends on cookie size

Another family favorite from Jan's mother.

Total Time: 40 minutes
Prep Time: 30 minutes   **Bake Time:** 8 minutes or so

1 1/2 cups confectioners' sugar
1 cup butter or margarine, softened
1 egg
1 1/2 teaspoons vanilla extract
2 1/2 cups flour
1 teaspoon baking soda
1 teaspoon cream of tartar (page 47)
colored sugar (optional)

1. Preheat oven to 350°F.
2. Cream the confectioners' sugar and butter. Add the egg and vanilla and mix thoroughly.
3. Combine the flour, baking soda, and cream of tartar. Add the flour mixture to the butter and sugar mixture.
4. Roll out the dough for cookie cutter cookies or drop as balls. Decorate with colored sugar if available.
5. If you want to make your own colored sugar, you will need to have food coloring aboard. To color the sugar, just mix food coloring into white sugar drop by drop until the color you want is achieved. It's easiest if you put the sugar and color into a tightly lidded plastic container or zipped plastic bag and then shake. You can let the sugar dry or use it right away.
6. Bake the cookies until lightly browned. Since the size will vary widely depending on whether you make cookie cutter cookies or drop cookies, it's important to watch the first batch closely to determine the baking time for your oven.

Thanksgiving Glazed Apple Cookies   Makes 2 to 3 dozen

This is our (Jan) family's favorite dessert for Thanksgiving. My brother and I have contests over who can eat more of these glazed apple cookies.

Total Time: 1 hour
Prep Time: 20 minutes   **Bake Time:** 8 to 9 minutes

1/2 cup shortening, butter, or margarine
1 1/3 cups packed brown sugar
1 egg
1/2 teaspoon salt
1 teaspoon ground cinnamon
1/3 teaspoon ground nutmeg
1/2 teaspoon ground cloves
2 1/2 cups flour
1 cup chopped, peeled, and cored apple
1 cup raisins, or more to taste
1 teaspoon baking soda
1/4 cup milk

1. Preheat oven to 375°F.
2. Cream the shortening. Add the brown sugar gradually, then add the egg. Beat well.
3. Sift the salt, cinnamon, nutmeg, and cloves (if you don't have a sifter, put them through a strainer). Stir into the brown sugar mixture, then stir in half the flour. Add the apple and raisins and mix well, then add the baking soda, the remaining flour, and the milk. Stir to combine.
4. Drop by teaspoonfuls on a greased cookie sheet. Bake for 8 to 9 minutes.

Glaze

1 cup confectioners' sugar
1 tablespoon butter or margarine, melted
1 teaspoon vanilla extract
2 tablespoons milk

1. Combine all the ingredients and beat well.
2. Frost the cookies. I usually make 1½ times the frosting to have enough. If you prefer, spread the frosting very thinly so this recipe may make enough.

EASTER EGGS

Dyed Eggs

International kids in anchorages are a blast! They each have their own traditions for Easter eggs, and adults can have as much fun as the kids.

Total Time: 5 minutes   **Prep Time:** 5 minutes

½ cup boiling water
1 teaspoon white vinegar
10 drops food coloring
hard-boiled eggs

1. For each color wanted, combine the water, vinegar, and food coloring. Mix the standard colors to make other colors—half yellow and half red make orange, blue and green make turquoise, etc.
2. Dip the hard-boiled eggs into the solutions. Tongs are easiest, but a slotted spoon works okay. After dipping the eggs, let them dry in an egg carton or on waxed paper.

ST. PATRICK'S DAY RECIPES

For some reason, cruisers from all over love to celebrate St. Patrick's Day!

St. Patrick's Day Green Beer

Total Time: Depends on how long it takes you to drink your green beer!
Prep Time: 1 minute

Light-colored beer, chilled
clear drinking glass
5 to 6 drops green food coloring

Pour half the chilled beer into a drinking glass. Add the food coloring. Pour the rest of the beer into the glass. Drink, enjoy, repeat!

Rueben Casserole   Serves 6

Total Time: 1 hour
Prep Time: 15 minutes   **Cook Time:** 45 minutes

1½ to 2 cups diced corned beef (about 8 ounces; you may use canned)
16 ounces sauerkraut, fresh or canned, drained, rinsed, and pressed dry (about 1 cup pressed)
2 tablespoons finely diced onion
1 cup shredded Swiss cheese
1 cup shredded cheddar cheese
½ cup Thousand Island dressing (page 162)
¼ cup mayonnaise
⅛ teaspoon ground pepper
3 slices rye bread or other bread
2 tablespoons butter or margarine, melted

1. Preheat oven to 350°F. Spritz an 8-inch square baking dish with nonstick cooking spray or brush with olive oil.
2. Combine the corned beef, sauerkraut, onion, cheeses, dressing, mayonnaise, and ground pepper. Stir until well blended. Transfer to the prepared baking dish.
3. Tear the bread into pieces and roll in your hands until you have mostly bread crumbs. Mix with the melted butter and sprinkle over the baking dish.
4. Bake for 45 minutes, or until bubbly and the top is browned. Let sit for 5 minutes before serving.

Holiday Cheer

MISCELLANEOUS OTHER HOLIDAY RECIPES

A few more good recipes . . . and excuses for a party!

Oktoberfest Bratwurst
Serves 10

If you're lucky enough to find bratwurst, enjoy this recipe for Oktoberfest. If not, the recipe works well with any other type of sausage.

Total Time: 35 minutes
Prep Time: 5 minutes   **Cook Time:** 30 minutes

10 fresh bratwurst sausages
2 onions, thinly sliced
1 cup butter
6 cans (12 ounces each) beer (or enough beer to
    cover the sausages in the pan)
1½ teaspoons ground pepper
10 bratwurst rolls or hoagie rolls

1. Prick the sausages with a fork to prevent them from exploding when heated. Put the sausages, onion, butter, beer, and ground pepper in a large pan and simmer for 15 to 20 minutes over medium heat.
2. Transfer the sausages to a medium-hot grill and grill for 10 minutes, turning every 5 minutes. Serve on the rolls along with the onions scooped out of the beer broth.

Chicken and Pork Adobo
Serves 4 to 6

Adobo is the Philippines national dish and a luau favorite in Hawaii. Unlike many "American" recipes, the meat in this adobo is cooked thoroughly and then browned.

Total Time: 4 hours, 10 minutes, including 3 hours
    to marinate
Prep Time: 3 hours, 15 minutes
Cook Time: 55 minutes

2 pounds boneless chicken, cut into bite-size
    pieces
1 pound boneless pork, cut into bite-size pieces
½ cup white vinegar
½ cup soy sauce
¼ teaspoon ground pepper
1 teaspoon brown sugar
5 cloves garlic, crushed
3 bay leaves
salt, to taste
olive oil, canola oil, or vegetable oil, to brown the
    meat
cooked rice (optional)

1. In a pan or plastic container, combine the chicken, pork, vinegar, soy sauce, ground pepper, brown sugar, garlic, bay leaves, and salt. Cover and marinate in the refrigerator for 3 hours.
2. Remove from the refrigerator and place the meat and marinade in a skillet. Bring to a boil, then simmer over low heat for 30 minutes. Uncover and simmer for an additional 15 minutes, or until most of the marinade has evaporated and the chicken and pork are cooked.
3. Add a trace of olive oil to the skillet. Turn up the heat and brown the meat. Serve with the rice if desired.

NOTE: This recipe can be made with only chicken or only pork as well as this combination.

Dirt Cake (Groundhog Day)
Serves 8 to 10

These ingredients may be hard to find unless you're in a good-size city. And you also need to have refrigerator space to chill the cake. But if you can manage it, this is a great centerpiece for Groundhog Day!

Total Time: 30 minutes, plus chill time
Prep Time: 30 minutes

4 tablespoons butter or margarine
8 ounces cream cheese, softened
1 cup confectioners' sugar
2 packages (4 servings per package) vanilla or
    French vanilla instant pudding
3½ cups milk
12 ounces whipped topping
1 package (20 ounces) Oreos or other chocolate
    sandwich cookies

1. Soften the butter and cream cheese. Cream them together with the confectioners' sugar.

2. Mix the pudding with the milk, then stir in the whipped topping. Add the butter/cream cheese/sugar mixture and stir to combine.

3. Mash the entire package of Oreos with a rolling pin, wine bottle, hammer (lightly), or your hands. Layer the crumbled cookies in the bottom of a nonstick (or greased) cake pan or a lidded plastic container or bowl. (This dessert is not baked, so the container does not have to be heatproof.) Add a layer of the pudding mixture, then more crumbled cookies, then more pudding mixture. Crumbled cookies should be the top layer.

4. Chill for 3 hours before serving. Try to find a small plastic toy that resembles a groundhog to stick in the "dirt" so it looks like he's emerging from hibernation.

Variations

- Put the cake ingredients in anything resembling a flowerpot and add a few artificial flowers for the first day of spring.
- Spread the cake ingredients on a cookie sheet and add "gravestones" made from note cards or paper for Halloween.

Mint Julep   Makes enough for 32 drinks

This is the official drink of the Kentucky Derby. Serve it in silver mint julep cups or any other cup or glass.

Total Time: 10 minutes, plus overnight to marinate

2 cups sugar
2 cups water
6–8 sprigs fresh mint (difficult to find, but you never know)
crushed ice
Kentucky whiskey

1. Make a simple syrup by boiling the sugar and water together for 5 minutes. Cool and place in a covered container with 6 to 8 sprigs of fresh mint, then refrigerate overnight.

2. Make one julep by filling a julep cup with crushed ice, adding 1 tablespoon of the mint syrup and 2 ounces of Kentucky whiskey. Stir rapidly. Garnish with a sprig of fresh mint.

Kentucky Hot Brown (Kentucky Derby)   Serves 4

Total Time: 30 minutes
Prep Time: 15 minutes
Cook Time: 15 minutes (5 minutes to fry the bacon)

½ cup plus 2 tablespoons butter or margarine
6 tablespoons flour
3 cups milk
½ cup shredded or grated Parmesan cheese
1 egg, beaten
salt and pepper, to taste
2 cups sliced fresh mushrooms, or canned and drained mushrooms
4 slices bread, toasted
1 tomato, thinly sliced
1 pound cooked turkey, thinly sliced
8 slices bacon, fried

1. Melt the ½ cup butter in a skillet. Stir in the flour. Slowly stir in the milk and 6 tablespoons of the Parmesan cheese. Stir in the egg and heat to thicken, but do not allow it to boil.

2. Remove from the heat and season with salt and pepper to taste. Set aside.

3. Heat the remaining 2 tablespoons butter and sauté the mushrooms. Set aside.

4. Preheat the broiler, or preheat oven to 400°F.

5. To make a hot brown, place a slice of toast on an ungreased cookie sheet. Cover the toast with one-quarter of the sautéed mushrooms and sliced tomato. Place one-quarter of the turkey onto each hot brown and top with one-quarter of the sauce. Sprinkle with one-quarter of the remaining Parmesan cheese. Repeat for the other three hot browns.

6. Place the cookie sheet under the broiler and broil until the sauce is speckled brown and bubbly. (If cooking in the oven, bake about 15 minutes.) Remove from the broiler and crisscross each hot brown with 2 strips of fried bacon.

MORE HOLIDAY CHEER

Lots of recipes in other chapters are also good for holidays and parties.

Beverages
Easy Eggnog (Christmas), *page 97*

Appetizers and Snacks
Various mexican dips (Cinco de Mayo), *starting on page 124*
Reuben Dip (St. Patrick's Day), *page 137*
Creamy Corned Beef Dip (St. Patrick's Day), *page 137*
Buffalo Chicken Dip (Super Bowl party), *page 138*
Deviled Eggs (every holiday!), *page 139*

Salads
Asian Cabbage Salad (Chinese New Year), *page 147*
Thanksgiving Cabbage Salad (Thanksgiving), *page 150*
Firecracker Salad (Fourth of July), *page 153*
All-American Potato Salad (Fourth of July), *page 154*
German Potato Salad (Octoberfest), *page 155*
Black Bean Corn Tomato Salad (Cinco de Mayo), *page 156*
Picnic Pasta Salad (Fourth of July), *page 159*
Hawaiian Ham Salad (luau), *page 160*

Soups and Stews
Spicy Black Bean Soup (Cinco de Mayo), *page 168*
Egg Drop Soup (Chinese New Year), *page 171*

Beans, Rice, and Pasta
White Chicken Chili (Super Bowl), *page 180*
Jambalaya (Mardi Gras), *page 184*
Fried Rice (luau), *page 185*
Chinese Noodles (Chinese New Year), *page 189*

Vegetables
Old-Fashioned Mashed Potatoes (Thanksgiving), *page 194*

Seafood
Fish Tacos (Cinco de Mayo), *page 229*
Shrimp Scampi (Valentine's Day), *page 236*
Shrimp Creole (Mardi Gras), *page 237*

Meat Main Dishes
Asian Skillet (Chinese New Year), *page 273*
Whole Roast Chicken (Thanksgiving or Christmas instead of roast turkey), *page 278*

Canned Meats and Seafood
Corned Beef Omelet (St. Patrick's Day), *page 316*
Cabbage and Corned Beef Soup (St. Patrick's Day), *page 318*
Jambalaya (Mardi Gras), *page 320*

Grilling
Caribbean Pork Chops (luau), *page 331*
Beer Can Chicken (International Beer Day), *page 335*

Quick Breads, Muffins, and Biscuits
"Almost" Irish Soda Bread (St. Patrick's Day), *page 380*
Beer Bread and Variations (International Beer Day), *page 382*

Yeast Breads
Braided Bread (Thanksgiving, Easter, Christmas), *page 396*
Totally Decadent Cinnamon Rolls (Christmas), *page 402*

Sweet Tooth
Gingerbread Cake (Christmas), *page 412*
No-Bake Booze Balls (Christmas), *page 423*
Pumpkin Pie (Thanksgiving), *page 427*
Sweet Potato Pie (Thanksgiving), *page 429*

QUICK BREADS, MUFFINS, AND BISCUITS

Everything in this chapter is made with baking powder or soda, not yeast. You'll find recipes for muffins, biscuits, and a variety of loaf breads including "Almost" Corn Bread (page 381) and "Almost" Irish Soda Bread (page 380) for those times when you have a craving but just can't find all the authentic ingredients.

Consider this chapter even if you don't have an oven. Quick breads can easily be baked on the stove top in an Omnia oven (page 75) or Dutch oven (page 76).

TROUBLESHOOTING UNSATISFACTORY RESULTS

Following are the two most common problems with quick breads:

- Making anchors. If your bread or muffins don't rise or are heavy, chances are your baking powder has gone bad. See page 376 to test it and page 51 for substitutes.
- Burnt bottoms. Burning the bottom of your baked items before the top is fully done is a common problem with the smaller size of boat ovens. See the chapter "Equipping a Galley," the section Stoves and Ovens: Using and Troubleshooting (page 14).

ADAPTING RECIPES TO MAKE HEALTHIER VERSIONS

We've provided "healthier" versions of a few of our favorite recipes—fewer calories, lower fat, less sugar, more fiber. Depending on your particular needs, you may also want to lower the sodium and/or the cholesterol.

My experience has been that there are no hard-and-fast rules in trying to make a particular dish healthier and still have it taste good. It generally takes a certain amount of experimentation. One important key is not to try to totally take an offending substance out of a dish, but simply to reduce it to an acceptable level.

Start by substituting unsweetened applesauce for some of the fat, and Splenda for some of the sugar. I usually start by substituting less than half the total amount–generally, only about a quarter. In subsequent batches, I increase the amounts if I find the results satisfactory. I've found that the results generally are not satisfactory if I try to swap the entire amount. Also, in many baked goods, I have to add an extra egg.

If you're watching sodium, try "Lite Salt" (in the same aisle as the salt; we found it even in small towns in Mexico). You can often cut the amount of salt in half as well. Using half the original amount of salt *and* using Lite Salt results in one-quarter the original amount of sodium.

Egg yolks can be a significant source of cholesterol. In baking, you can almost always replace whole eggs with two egg whites, or you can use Egg Beaters.

Increase fiber by using a bran cereal or whole wheat flour instead of white flour.

To give an example of a "healthier" recipe, compare our Zucchini Bread (page 383) and Healthier Zucchini Bread (page 384). The regular version has raisins and walnuts, and the healthier version has just raisins. The numbers below are for one slice, which is $\frac{1}{10}$ of the loaf. Cholesterol is higher in the "healthier" version due to the extra egg; it can be decreased by using egg whites or Egg Beaters.

	HEALTHIER	REGULAR
Calories	115	315
Total Fat	4.2 g	15.5 g
Saturated Fat	0.5 g	1.3 g
Cholesterol	43 mg	21 mg
Sodium	124 mg	124 mg
Total Carbohydrates	19.6 g	41.3 g
Dietary Fiber	3.4 g	1.3 g
Sugars	9.7 g	24.3 g

You can experiment with any of the recipes in this chapter or even family favorites—just make changes incrementally. Whatever your health concerns, it's possible to modify recipes so that you don't have to go without. And we often prefer the taste of the healthier versions!

TIPS FOR BAKING POWDER AND BAKING SODA

Baking powder reacts with water to give volume to baked goods (double-acting baking powder, which is what is usually sold commercially, reacts a second time with heat). Just the humidity in the air is enough moisture to make it react. Store your baking powder in double plastic bags or another airtight container, and take it out just long enough to measure the amount needed; then put the container back in the bags and seal them. If baking powder is hard in the container, or has formed lumps, be suspicious that it is no longer "active" and should be tested before using it.

To test if baking powder is still good, place one teaspoon in a container with a half cup of water. If it bubbles, as shown in the photo above, it is still good.

In some places, baking soda is called bicarbonate of soda. If you can't find it in grocery stores, try pharmacies—that's where we found it in El Salvador!

See the chapter "Food Substitutions" for substitutions for baking powder (page 51) and baking soda (page 51).

BISCUITS

Here are recipes to make your own baking mix (similar to Bisquick, in case you have favorite recipes calling for it), as well as five recipes for biscuits.

Baking Mix   Makes 2 cups of mix

Use this as a substitute for Bisquick or Jiffy Baking Mix.

Total Time: 10 minutes

1 $\frac{5}{8}$ cups flour
$\frac{1}{4}$ cup powdered milk
2 $\frac{1}{2}$ teaspoons baking powder (see previous section)
$\frac{3}{4}$ teaspoon salt
$\frac{1}{2}$ cup shortening

Combine the flour, milk, baking powder, and salt in a bowl. Cut in the shortening with two knives, a fork, or a pastry blender until the mixture resembles coarse sand.

Store in a tightly closed container in a cool place (double plastic freezer bags work well).

Baking Powder Biscuits

1 cup Baking Mix (above)
$1/3$ cup water

1. Preheat oven to 425°F.
2. Combine the baking mix with the water and mix well. Drop by spoonfuls onto a greased pan and bake for 10 to 15 minutes. The baking time will depend on the size of the biscuits.

No-Roll Classic Biscuits

Makes 6 biscuits

Much more boat friendly than trying to roll out biscuits and cut them. If you don't have cold butter or margarine, use our Quick Biscuits recipe (page 378) instead.

Total Time: 30 minutes
Prep Time: 10 minutes   **Bake Time:** 20 minutes

1 cup flour
$1/2$ teaspoons baking powder (page 376)
dash of salt
2 tablespoons cold butter, cut into small pieces
6 tablespoons milk

1. Preheat oven to 400°F.
2. Mix together the flour, baking powder, and salt in a bowl. Cut the butter into the flour mixture using two knives, a fork, or a pastry blender until the mixture looks like coarse crumbs. Very gently stir in the milk until a soft dough forms—don't over-mix.
3. Place the dough on a greased cookie sheet or other flat pan or a double layer of aluminum foil. With floured hands press the dough into a 6"×9" rectangle. Handle the dough as little as possible. Cut the dough into 6 biscuits without actually cutting them apart. Bake for about 15 to 20 minutes, or until golden.

Variation: For cheese biscuits like those served at Red Lobster, add $1/2$ cup shredded cheese along with the butter. Vary the type of cheese according to what will go well with the rest of the meal. For example, use mozzarella or Parmesan with an Italian meal.

Classic Biscuits

Makes 6 biscuits

If you don't have cold butter or margarine, use our Quick Biscuits recipe (page 378).

Total Time: 22 minutes
Prep Time: 10 minutes   **Bake Time:** 12 minutes

1 cup flour
2 teaspoons baking powder (page 376)
$1/2$ teaspoons sugar
$1/2$ teaspoon salt
$2/2$ tablespoons cold butter or margarine
6 tablespoons cold milk

1. Preheat oven to 425°F.
2. Mix the flour, baking powder, sugar, and salt in a bowl. Cut in the butter with a pastry blender, fork, or two knives until crumbly. Add the milk and stir until the mixture forms a ball. Add a bit more milk if necessary to make a soft dough.
3. Roll or pat the dough to 1 inch thick. Cut it into circles with a biscuit cutter, an empty can (washed, of course), or the floured rim of a glass. You can also make square biscuits (with no waste) by cutting the dough with a floured knife.
4. Arrange the dough shapes on a greased cookie sheet or a piece of aluminum foil. Bake for 10 to 12 minutes, or until browned.

Buttermilk Biscuits

Makes 6 biscuits

Total Time: 22 minutes
Prep Time: 10 minutes   **Bake Time:** 12 minutes

Special Equipment: This recipe requires an oven that can get up to 450°F.

1 cup flour
$1/8$ teaspoon baking soda
$1/2$ teaspoons baking powder (page 376)
$1/2$ teaspoon salt
3 tablespoons very cold butter
6 tablespoons buttermilk (page 99)

1. Preheat oven to 450°F.
2. Mix together the flour, baking soda, baking powder, and salt in a bowl. Cut the butter into the flour mixture using two knives, a fork, or a pastry blender until the mixture looks like coarse crumbs.

Quick Breads, Muffins, and Biscuits

Very gently stir in the buttermilk until a soft dough forms—don't overmix. Add a little more buttermilk if the dough seems dry.

3. Turn the dough onto a floured board. Gently pat the dough until it's about ½ inch thick. Use a round cutter to cut the biscuits, or cut the dough into squares with a floured knife.

4. Place the biscuits on a greased cookie sheet, pie pan, or sheet of aluminum foil. If you like biscuits with soft sides, position them so they touch one another. If you like "crusty" sides, place them about 1 inch apart—these will not rise as high as the biscuits that are close together.

5. Bake for 10 to 12 minutes, or until light golden brown on top. Be careful not to overbake.

Quick Biscuits   Makes 4 to 6 biscuits

Quick and easy drop biscuits!

Total Time: 20 minutes
Mix Time: 5 minutes   **Bake Time:** 15 minutes

1 cup flour
2 teaspoons baking powder (page 376)
½ teaspoon salt
³⁄₈ cup milk
2 tablespoons canola oil or vegetable oil

1. Preheat oven to 400°F.
2. Mix the flour, baking powder, and salt in a bowl. Add the milk and oil and mix well. Depending on your flour, you may need to add a few teaspoons more milk. The batter should be thick enough to clump around the spoon and pull away from the bowl, but there shouldn't be any problem incorporating all the flour.
3. Drop spoonfuls of batter onto a greased pan, cookie sheet, or aluminum foil. Bake for 15 minutes.

Variation: For cheese biscuits, add ½ cup grated or shredded cheese along with the oil.

Shortcake Biscuits

Add 2 tablespoons sugar to the recipe for Quick Biscuits, above.

MUFFINS

It almost seems that muffins were created with boat galleys in mind. They're designed to be quickly mixed by hand, and they bake quickly. Add in the fact that most are forgiving about many ingredients. No dates? Use raisins! No wonder that muffins are a staple aboard many boats.

In addition to these four basic recipes and variations, virtually any quick bread recipe in this chapter can be baked in muffin tins. With any recipe, be sure to do the following:

- Grease the tins or use a cooking spray.
- Fill each cup no more than two-thirds full. Although you can fill them fuller and get big, high tops when cooking ashore, it's not a good idea to try this on a boat. Any little movement of the boat and you'll have batter spilling out of the pan and burning in the oven.
- Fill the empty cups in the muffin tins about half full of water. If they are dry, they will get very hot, and the adjacent muffins are likely to burn. But be very careful when taking muffins out of the oven not to spill that hot water on yourself.
- If using a quick bread recipe, bake the muffins at the same temperature, but start checking for doneness at about half the original time.

Banana Bran Muffins   Makes 12 muffins

Total Time: 35 min
Prep Time: 10 minutes   **Bake Time:** 20 to 25 minutes

1 cup All-Bran cereal or Raisin Bran cereal
1 cup mashed banana
²⁄₃ cup milk or water
⅓ cup packed brown sugar or white sugar
¼ cup canola oil or vegetable oil
1 egg
1 teaspoon vanilla extract
1½ cups flour (white, whole wheat, or a mixture)
1 tablespoon baking powder (page 376)
½ teaspoon salt
½ teaspoon ground cinnamon (optional)
¾ cup raisins or chopped dates (optional)
½ cup walnuts or pecans (optional)

1. Preheat oven to 375°F.
2. Mix the cereal, banana, and milk in a large bowl, then let sit for 5 minutes to allow the cereal to soften. Mix in the brown sugar, oil, egg, and vanilla.
3. Mix together the flour, baking powder, salt, cinnamon, raisins, and walnuts in a small bowl. Add the flour mixture to the banana mixture and stir just until mixed.
4. Spoon the batter into greased muffin cups, filling them two-thirds full and filling any empty cups half full of water. Bake for about 25 minutes, or until a toothpick inserted in the center comes out clean.
5. Let the muffins cool in the pan for a couple minutes, then transfer them to a wire rack or plate.

Basic Muffins and Variations   Makes 10 to 12 muffins

Total Time: 35 minutes
Prep Time: 10 minutes   **Bake Time:** 25 minutes

1 egg
½ cup milk
¼ cup canola oil or vegetable oil
1 teaspoon vanilla extract
1½ cups flour
½ teaspoon salt
2 teaspoons baking powder (page 376)
½ cup sugar

Optional add-ins and variations:
• 1 cup well-drained fresh or canned fruit
• 1 cup raisins or other dried fruit
• 2 bananas, peeled and mashed
• 1 cup flaked coconut
• Substitute ¼ cup orange juice for half the milk.
• Use whole wheat flour instead of white flour.
• Add 1 teaspoon garlic powder and/or onion powder and decrease the sugar slightly.
• Add ½ teaspoon dried basil and/or dried oregano and decrease the sugar slightly.
• Add ½ cup grated cheese.

1. Preheat oven to 375°F.
2. In a small bowl beat the egg. Add the milk, oil, and vanilla.

3. In a larger bowl, mix the flour, salt, baking powder, and sugar. Add the milk mixture and stir just until mixed. Add any of the optional add-ins desired.
4. Spoon the batter into greased muffin cups, filling them two-thirds full and filling any empty cups half full of water. Bake for about 25 minutes, or until a toothpick inserted in the center comes out clean. Let the muffins cool in the pan for a couple minutes, then transfer them to a wire rack or plate.

Corn Muffins   Makes 12 muffins

If you don't have cornmeal—which is next to impossible to find outside the US—see "Almost" Corn Bread (page 381).

Total Time: 40 minutes
Prep Time: 15 minutes   **Bake Time:** 25 minutes

½ cup butter or margarine, softened
⅔ cup sugar
¼ cup honey
2 eggs
½ cup milk
1½ cups flour
¾ cup cornmeal
½ teaspoon baking powder (page 376)
½ teaspoon salt
¾ cup whole-kernel corn (canned, fresh, or frozen)

1. Preheat oven to 375°F.
2. Mix the butter, sugar, honey, eggs, and milk in a large bowl. Add the flour, cornmeal, baking powder, and salt and mix just until incorporated. Add the corn and stir to combine.
3. Spoon the batter into greased muffin cups, filling them two-thirds full and filling any empty cups half full of water. Bake for about 20 minutes, or until a toothpick inserted in the center comes out clean.
4. Let the muffins cool in the pan for a couple minutes, then transfer them to a wire rack or plate.

Quick Breads, Muffins, and Biscuits

Orange-Raisin Bran Muffins

Makes 10 to 12 muffins

Total Time: 30 minutes
Prep Time: 15 minutes   Bake Time: 12 to 14 minutes

1¼ cups white flour or whole wheat flour
½ cup Raisin Bran cereal OR cornflakes, Wheaties, or similar cereal plus 2 tablespoons raisins
½ cup sugar
1½ tablespoons baking powder (page 376)
½ teaspoon salt
1 egg
½ cup milk or water
¼ cup canola oil or vegetable oil
½ cup orange juice or other sweet juice, such as pineapple, mango, papaya, or cranberry
extra raisins, dates, and/or chopped nuts (optional)

1. Preheat oven to 375°F.
2. Mix all the ingredients in a bowl until just combined.
3. Spoon the batter into greased muffin cups, filling them two-thirds full and filling any empty cups half full of water. Bake for about 15 minutes, or until a toothpick inserted in the center comes out clean. Let the muffins cool in the pan for a couple minutes, then transfer them to a wire rack or plate.

QUICK BREADS

Although we give a pan size for each recipe, don't fret if you don't have the correct size or even the "correct" shape. Round pans work just as well as loaf pans and vice versa. Just check our tips for changing pan size (page 8). Any of our quick breads can also be baked as muffins (page 378).

Irish Soda Bread

Serves 8

Total Time: 1 hour, 10 minutes
Prep Time: 20 minutes   Bake Time: 50 minutes

1¾ cups flour
¼ cup sugar
¼ teaspoon baking soda
1 teaspoon baking powder (page 376)

½ teaspoon salt
1 egg
1 cup sour cream (page 99)
1 tablespoon caraway seeds (optional)
⅓ cup raisins (optional)

1. Preheat oven to 350°F.
2. Mix the flour, sugar, baking soda, baking powder, and salt in a bowl.
3. In a small bowl beat the eggs and stir in the sour cream. Add to the flour mixture and stir just to combine. The batter will be very thick.
4. Add the caraway seeds and raisins, if desired, and stir well with a spoon or knead them in with your hands.
5. Transfer the batter to a greased 9"×5" loaf pan or a 9-inch pie pan. Dust the top with enough flour so that you can pat the batter evenly in the pan without it sticking to your hands. Bake for 50 minutes, or until a knife or toothpick inserted in the center comes out clean. Great served warm, but let it cool slightly before slicing.

"Almost" Irish Soda Bread

Serves 6 to 8

This recipe uses baking powder instead of the traditional baking soda and buttermilk or sour cream. It also works well if the recipe is cut in half and baked in a small dish for two to four people. Try it with our Cheddar Butter (page 386).

Total Time: 40 to 50 minutes
Prep Time: 10 minutes   Bake Time: 30 to 40 minutes

1½ cups whole wheat flour or other flour
1 tablespoon baking powder (page 376)
¼ teaspoon salt
¼ cup sugar
2 eggs
½ cup milk
⅓ cup canola oil or vegetable oil, or butter or margarine, melted

1. Preheat oven to 350°F.
2. Mix the dry ingredients in a medium bowl. In a small bowl, beat the eggs slightly, then add the milk and oil and mix well. Add to the dry ingredients and stir just until mixed.

3. Spread in a greased 9-inch pie pan or 9"×5" loaf pan and bake for 30 to 40 minutes, or until golden brown on top or a toothpick inserted in the center comes out clean.
4. Cut into wedges and serve hot. Leftovers get hard in 24 hours, even in an airtight container.

Variation: Add 1 tablespoon caraway seeds and/or ¼ cup raisins or other diced moist dried fruit such as dates or apricots.

Garlic, Herb, and Mustard Soda Bread
Makes 1 loaf

Total Time: 55 minutes
Prep Time: 5 minutes   Bake Time: 50 minutes

2 cups white flour
1 cup whole wheat flour
1 tablespoon baking powder (page 376)
1 teaspoon garlic powder
1 tablespoon mixed herbs or Italian seasoning (page 48)
½ teaspoon salt
1 teaspoon prepared mustard (spicy or whole grain varieties are best)
2½ cups water
1 tablespoon canola oil or vegetable oil

1. Preheat oven to 400°F.
2. Mix together the flours, baking powder, garlic powder, herbs, and salt.
3. In a small bowl, mix together the mustard, water, and oil. Add to the flour mixture and stir until just mixed.
4. Pour into a greased 9"×5" loaf pan. Bake for 45 to 50 minutes, or until a knife inserted into the center comes out clean. Let cool in the pan for 10 to 15 minutes before serving.

Traditional Corn Bread
Serves 6 to 8

Traditional corn bread requires true cornmeal and an oven that can get up to 450°F. For a good, boat-friendly alternative, see "Almost" Corn Bread (see next recipe).

Total Time: 35 minutes
Prep Time: 10 minutes   Bake Time: 25 minutes

2 tablespoons shortening or bacon drippings
1½ cups cornmeal
3 tablespoons flour
1 teaspoon salt
1 teaspoon baking soda
2 cups buttermilk OR 2 tablespoons vinegar and enough milk to total 2 cups
1 egg

1. Preheat oven to 450°F.
2. Place the shortening in a 9-inch skillet with an ovenproof handle or an 8-inch square baking pan. Place in the oven for about 3 minutes, or until the shortening is melted. The skillet will be very hot when the shortening is melted—be careful!
3. While the shortening is heating, in large bowl combine the cornmeal, flour, salt, and baking soda. Add the buttermilk and egg and mix well.
4. Carefully pour the batter into the prepared skillet. For a crunchy bottom crust, it's important that the pan be as hot as possible when you pour in the batter, so don't remove the pan from the oven until you're ready for it. Bake for 22 to 25 minutes, or until the surface cracks and the edges are light golden brown and are pulled away from the side of the pan. Serve hot.

"Almost" Corn Bread
Serves 2 to 4

This recipe uses the corn flour (masa) that is sold everywhere in Mexico to make tortillas. The resulting bread isn't as coarse as true corn bread, but it makes a tasty alternative.

Total Time: 35 minutes
Mix Time: 10 minutes   Bake Time: 25 minutes

½ cup corn flour*
1½ teaspoons baking powder (page 376)
½ teaspoon salt
2 tablespoons sugar
1 egg
2 tablespoons canola oil or vegetable oil, or butter or margarine, melted
⅜ cup milk or water

Make sure to get the corn flour with no added ingredients, not a "corn tortilla mix."

Quick Breads, Muffins, and Biscuits

1. Preheat oven to 350°F.
2. Mix the corn flour, baking powder, salt, and sugar in small bowl. In a cup or small bowl, beat the egg slightly and add the oil and milk. Add to the corn flour mixture, stirring just until completely mixed. The batter will be thick.
3. Transfer to a greased small baking dish (I use a 5-inch soup bowl that's ovenproof; you can also mound up the batter in the center of a greased pie pan). Bake for 25 minutes, or until a toothpick inserted in the center comes out clean.
4. Cut into 4 wedges and serve hot.

Beer Bread and Variations
Makes 1 loaf, about 10 slices

Total Time: 50 minutes
Prep Time: 5 minutes   Bake Time: 45 minutes

3 cups flour
1 tablespoon sugar
1 teaspoon salt
1 tablespoon baking powder (page 376)
2 tablespoons chopped fresh dill OR 2 teaspoons dried dill
1 cup grated cheddar or other cheese
12 ounces (1½ cups) beer (use part water if needed)
1 egg and 2 teaspoons water, beaten (optional glaze)

1. Preheat oven to 375°F.
2. Combine the flour, sugar, salt, baking powder, dill, and cheddar in a large mixing bowl. Slowly stir in the beer and mix just until combined. The batter will be thick.
3. Transfer to a greased 9"×5" loaf pan. Brush with the egg glaze, if desired, and bake about 45 minutes, or until golden brown and a toothpick inserted in the center comes out clean.
4. Cool in the pan on a wire rack for 10 minutes, then remove from the pan and cool for 10 more minutes. Serve warm or at room temperature.

Variations:
- **Garlic and Herb:** Eliminate the dill. Add 1 teaspoon each dried rosemary, dried oregano, dried thyme, and garlic powder to the basic mix.
- **Rosemary and Feta:** Eliminate the dill and cheddar. Add 2 teaspoons dried rosemary and ¾ cup crumbled feta cheese (about 4 ounces) to the basic mix.
- **Italian:** Eliminate the dill and cheddar. Add 1 teaspoon each dried basil, dried oregano, and garlic powder and ½ cup grated Parmesan or Romano cheese to the basic mix.

Healthier Banana Bread
Makes 1 loaf, about 10 slices

Total Time: 1 hour
Prep Time: 15 minutes   Bake Time: 45 minutes

1⅔ cups whole wheat flour
1 teaspoon baking powder (page 376)
1 teaspoon baking soda
1 teaspoon salt
1 teaspoon ground nutmeg
1 teaspoon ground cinnamon
1 egg
⅓ cup unsweetened applesauce (if yours is sweetened, use ¼ cup less sugar)
1 tablespoon canola oil or vegetable oil
1 teaspoon white vinegar
½ cup white sugar OR use Splenda for up to half the total amount of sugar
½ cup packed brown sugar or white sugar
1 tablespoon honey
2 cups mashed ripe banana (2 to 4 bananas, depending on size)
½ cup raisins or other dried fruit such as diced dates, cranberries, or diced apricots (optional)
½ cup chopped walnuts or pecans (optional)

1. Preheat oven to 350°F.
2. In a large bowl mix together the flour, baking powder, baking soda, and spices.
3. In a small bowl beat the egg, applesauce, oil, vinegar, white sugar, brown sugar, honey, banana, raisins, and walnuts. Add to the flour mixture and stir to combine.
4. Pour into a greased 9"×5" loaf pan and bake for about 30 minutes, or until a toothpick inserted into the center comes out clean.
5. Cool in the pan at least somewhat before slicing, but it's great served warm.

Banana Bread Makes 1 loaf, about 10 slices

Total Time: 1 hour, 20 minutes
Prep Time: 15 minutes   Bake Time: 55 minutes
Stand Time: 10 minutes

1 cup sugar
2 ripe bananas, peeled and sliced
1/2 cup butter or margarine, softened
2 eggs
1 3/4 cups flour
1 teaspoon baking powder (page 376)
1/2 teaspoon baking soda
1/2 teaspoon salt
1/2 cup chopped walnuts

1. Preheat oven to 350°F.
2. Mix the sugar, bananas, butter, and eggs in a large bowl. Add the flour, baking powder, baking soda, and salt, and beat well. Add the nuts and stir to combine.
3. Place the batter in a greased 9"×5" loaf pan and bake for 55 to 60 minutes, or until a toothpick inserted near the center comes out clean.
4. Cool in the pan for 10 minutes before slicing.

Pumpkin Bread Makes 1 loaf

This is great for holidays instead of pumpkin pie!

Total Time: 90 minutes
Prep Time: 20 minutes   Bake Time: 70 minutes

1 cup canned pumpkin*
1 1/2 cups sugar
1/2 cup water
1/2 cup canola oil or vegetable oil
2 eggs
1 2/3 cups flour
1 teaspoon baking soda
2 teaspoons baking powder (page 376)
1/2 teaspoon salt
2 teaspoons ground cinnamon
1/4 teaspoon ground nutmeg
1 cup raisins and/or dates (optional)
1/2 cup chopped nuts (optional)

This is about half of a typical can of pumpkin; I use half a can and save the other half for another batch rather than worry about whether it's exactly 1 cup.

1. Preheat oven to 350°F.
2. In a large bowl combine the pumpkin, sugar, water, oil, and eggs. Mix well. Add the flour, baking soda, baking powder, salt, cinnamon, nutmeg, and raisins and nuts if desired; stir until combined.
3. Pour the batter into a greased 9"×5" loaf pan. Bake for 60 to 70 minutes, or until a toothpick inserted in the center comes out clean. Cool slightly in the pan before cutting.

Zucchini and/or Carrot Bread Makes 1 loaf, about 10 slices

Total Time: 2 hours, 10 minutes
Prep Time: 40 minutes   Bake Time: 90 minutes

1/2 cup canola oil or vegetable oil
1 egg
2 tablespoons milk or water
1 cup sugar
1 cup grated raw zucchini (about 1 small zucchini), summer squash, or carrot (or a mix)
1 teaspoon vanilla extract
1 1/2 cups flour
2 teaspoons baking powder (page 376)
1/2 teaspoon salt
1 tablespoon ground cinnamon
1/2 cup chopped nuts (optional)
1/2 cup raisins or diced soft dried fruit, such as chopped dates or chopped apricots (optional)

1. Preheat oven to 325°F.
2. Mix the oil, egg, milk, sugar, zucchini, and vanilla in a large bowl.
3. Mix in the flour, baking powder, salt, cinnamon, and nuts and raisins, if desired, just until incorporated. Do not overmix.
4. Pour into a greased 9"×5" loaf pan and bake for 90 minutes, or until a toothpick inserted in the center comes out clean. Cool in the pan.

Quick Breads, Muffins, and Biscuits

Healthier Zucchini and/or Carrot Bread

Makes 1 small loaf

Total Time: 55 minutes
Prep Time: 20 minutes (including "sit" time)
Bake Time: 35 minutes

2 tablespoons canola oil or vegetable oil
1/2 cup unsweetened applesauce
2 tablespoons water or milk
2 tablespoons sugar
1/2 cup Splenda
1 cup grated zucchini and/or carrot
1 cup All-Bran (the kind that looks like little sticks, not flakes) or Bran Buds
2 eggs
1/2 cup whole wheat flour
1 tablespoon baking powder (page 376)
1 teaspoon salt
1 tablespoon ground cinnamon
1/2 cup raisins and/or walnuts (optional)

1. Preheat oven to 325°F.
2. Mix the oil, applesauce, water, sugar, Splenda, zucchini, and All-Bran. Let sit for 10 minutes to let the All-Bran soften.
3. Mix in the eggs. Add the flour, baking powder, salt, cinnamon, and raisins or nuts, if desired. Stir until just combined.
4. Pour into a greased 8"×4" loaf pan and bake for 30 to 35 minutes, or until a toothpick inserted in the center comes out clean. For a large loaf pan (9"×5", which seems to be the size sold most often in the US), make 1½ times the recipe and bake for about 45 minutes.

Cheese Bread

Serves 8

This is a wonderful easy bread that's a perfect accompaniment to a salad or quiche.

Total Time: 1 hour
Prep Time: 15 minutes   Bake Time: 45 minutes

1/3 cup butter or margarine
1 cup milk
1 cup flour
1/4 teaspoon salt
4 eggs
1 tablespoon cream, sour cream (page 99), evaporated milk (page 99), or milk
1 teaspoon dry mustard OR 2 teaspoons prepared mustard
1/2 cup plus 3 tablespoons grated Swiss cheese or other cheese

1. Preheat oven to 375°F.
2. Heat the butter and milk in a heavy saucepan over medium heat. Mix in the flour and salt, stirring constantly until the mixture comes away from the sides of the pan.
3. Remove from the heat and add the eggs, one at time, beating them in to the dough.
4. In a small bowl combine the cream, mustard, and the ½ cup cheese and stir in to dough.
5. Transfer the dough to a greased 10-inch pie pan and sprinkle with the remaining 3 tablespoons cheese. Bake for 30 minutes, then reduce the heat to 350°F and bake for 10 to 15 minutes longer, or until a toothpick inserted in the center comes out clean. Depending on your cheese, a bit of it might stick to the toothpick, but no dough should stick. Bake a bit longer if necessary.
6. Cut into 8 wedges and serve.

ADDITIONAL QUICK BREADS, MUFFINS, AND BISCUITS

Here are a few quick breads that are found in other chapters.

Breakfast and Brunch
Apple Breakfast Bread, *page 118*
Gingerbread Muffins, *page 118*
Streusel Coffee Cake, *page 119*

Meat Main
Dumplings (in Chicken and Dumplings, *page 280*)

YEAST BREADS

Homemade bread is a wonderful treat and fairly easy to make. It is always well received at pot-lucks, can often be bartered for fish, shrimp, or even lobster, and is a great thank-you gift to anyone who has helped you.

We've included a large section of tips and step-by-step instructions to ensure your success. Don't let breadmaking scare you!

Even if you don't read through all the tips below, just know to avoid the two most common causes of ending up with something better suited to anchoring the dinghy:

- Dead yeast. If your bread doesn't rise the way it should, try buying new yeast. (Also read about how to avoid "killing" yeast, page 386.)
- Too much flour. If your loaf is heavy and dry, use a little less flour the next time.
- No oven? You can have fresh-baked bread even without an oven. Read about several ways to bake on the stove top or on the grill in the "Special Galley Cooking Techniques" chapter.

BREAD DIPS AND SPREADS

Spreads and dips make a good alternative to straight butter or margarine. Dips work well as an appetizer as well as with a meal. Also see our Jams and Spreads in the "Breakfast and Brunch" chapter (page 121).

Garlic–Olive Oil Bread Dip

Total Time: 35 minutes, including 30 minutes "sit" time
Prep Time: 5 minutes

$\frac{1}{2}$ cup olive oil or vegetable oil
1 teaspoon salt
$\frac{1}{4}$ teaspoon ground pepper
1 teaspoon minced garlic OR $\frac{1}{2}$ teaspoon garlic powder
1 teaspoon Italian seasoning (page 48)

Mix all the ingredients and let sit for at least 30 minutes—longer is better. Refrigerate leftovers if saving for more than a day.

Oil and Vinegar Bread Dip

Total Time: 35 minutes, including 30 minutes "sit" time
Prep Time: 5 minutes

1 cup olive oil
$\frac{2}{3}$ cup balsamic vinegar OR white or wine vinegar plus 1 tablespoon sugar
1 tablespoon minced garlic OR 1 teaspoon garlic powder
$1\frac{1}{2}$ tablespoons dried basil
1 tablespoon dried oregano
1 teaspoon dried thyme
1 teaspoon salt
$\frac{1}{4}$ teaspoon ground pepper

1. Mix all the ingredients and let sit for at least 30 minutes—longer is better.
2. Leftover dip can be saved, although if you want to keep it more than a day, it should be refrigerated.

Other Olive Oil Dip Ideas. Mix any of the following with olive oil, and let sit at least a half hour before serving:

- grated Parmesan cheese
- fresh or dried rosemary
- finely chopped fresh tomato or sun-dried tomato
- chopped olives (black or green)

Cheddar Butter   Makes 1½ cups

Total Time: 5 minutes

½ cup butter or margarine, softened
1 cup shredded cheddar, Parmesan, mozzarella, or similar cheese
¼ teaspoon garlic salt or garlic powder OR 1 clove garlic, minced
½ teaspoon Worcestershire sauce

Mix all the ingredients. Store in the refrigerator, but let warm to room temperature before spreading.

Honey Butter

⅓ cup honey
½ cup butter, softened (margarine can be used, but it's not as good)

Add the honey to the softened butter. Mix well. Serve at room temperature.

Jam Butter

¼ cup jam or jelly (apricot or peach are good, but almost any kind will work)
½ cup butter, softened

Add the jam to the softened butter; mix well. Serve at room temperature.

Other Butter Spreads. Finely chop or grind any of the following and mix into butter (best), margarine, or cream cheese:

- dill
- cheese (grated hard cheese or blendable soft cheese)
- sesame seeds or sesame oil
- garlic and/or onion (fresh, dried, or powder all work well)
- red pepper flakes or finely chopped sweet or spicy chile peppers

YEAST BREADMAKING 101

Carolyn has made bread since she was a little kid. Jan began making it only after she started cruising. Her first attempts were like lead dinghy anchors (Jan's words, not mine!). As a result of Jan's problems and questions, we've put together the following information for novice breadmakers, starting with basic principles and concluding with a step-by-step guide. According to Jan, if she could do it, anyone can!

Before We Begin . . .

Below we've provided a few notes on the time involved and various ingredients for making bread. Don't be intimidated—we tell you ways to work with whatever you've got.

- **Time.** We like to give a time estimate for recipes, but this is hard to do with bread since the air temperature and the yeast potency play such large roles in how long it takes for the bread to rise. In general, plan on at least two hours to make yeast bread, or longer if you're a beginner or in a cold climate.
- **Water.** Water used in baking bread should be warm, to encourage the yeast to multiply and allow the dough to rise. However, hot water will kill the yeast. The ideal temperature is between 100° and 115°F. If you're in the tropics, don't worry about the water temperature, as the dough will rise well in the warm air. If you're in a cool to cold location, using warm water will significantly speed the rising time. A basic rule of thumb is if you can't hold a finger in the water for a five count, it's too hot.

  Many cruisers use bleach in their water tanks to purify the water. Heavily chlorinated water can inhibit yeast action and keep bread from rising. If you can smell the chlorine in the water, there's

Different Types of Yeast

Buying and using yeast can be confusing—there's compressed yeast, cake yeast, active dry yeast, bread machine yeast, rapid-rise yeast, instant yeast, and now pizza yeast. Do you really need to buy different types for different recipes?

The primary difference in yeasts is whether they have to be first mixed with water and proofed (see page 388), or whether they can be added directly to the dry ingredients. Some types of yeast are designed to rise more rapidly and/or have various dough conditioners mixed in, which make them somewhat more suited for one type of dough than another.

Although some types of yeast have been developed to be mixed into the dry ingredients, the important thing is that (at least as far as I know) there are *no* types that are hurt by first proofing them. I always proof the yeast in water to make sure that it's good. I never want to waste ingredients by mixing an entire recipe and then discovering that it won't rise. But proofing yeast is especially important on a boat, where yeast storage may not be ideal and where it can be a while before I get more flour—particularly specialty flours.

So the simple answer is that if you use a recipe that calls for proofing the yeast, or first dissolving it in water, it doesn't matter what type of yeast you use. And if the recipe calls for mixing yeast with the dry ingredients, but you don't have the right type of yeast for that, you can substitute the type that you do have by first dissolving it in water and then adding the yeast and water mixture to the dry ingredients.

Cake Yeast

"Cake" means that it comes in a cake, not that it's used for making cakes. It's sold refrigerated and lasts only about two weeks, even when kept in the refrigerator. Cake yeast is usually used in commercial bakeries. It's occasionally found in small cakes in grocery stores. One small cake is equivalent to a packet, or $2\frac{1}{4}$ teaspoons of bulk yeast.

Cake yeast *must* be dissolved in water before adding it to the dry ingredients. Be sure to proof it due to its short life!

Active Dry Yeast

Active dry yeast has been generically referred to as "yeast" for years. In the US, it's usually sold in strips of three little packets (one packet equals $2\frac{1}{4}$ teaspoons of bulk yeast). Outside the US, it's usually sold in bulk in foil-covered bricks. Whether you buy it in packets or in bulk bricks, the yeast is the same.

Active dry yeast must be dissolved in water before using; it's best to not just mix it with warm water but to actually proof it so you know it's good.

Rapid Rise/Bread Machine/Instant Yeast

These are all names for the same thing, which is most often sold in jars in the US, although you may find it in packets or even in foil-covered bricks.

It's a different yeast strain than active yeast, and rapid-rise yeast and bread machine yeast often have a tiny bit of dough conditioner added. There are two notable differences in this yeast: first, you don't have to dissolve it first in water (you can put it in with the dry ingredients and then mix in the water and other liquids), and if you mix it with the dry ingredients, you have to let the dough rise only once instead of twice before shaping it.

According to the manufacturers, if you dissolve the instant yeast in water first, you'll have to let the dough rise twice before shaping it. While that does produce the best results, I'll go on record as saying that when I'm in a hurry, I'll let the dough rise only once no matter what type of yeast I've used! And the results are still pretty good.

You can use bread machine yeast when making bread by hand with no problem. I often do this, as bread machine yeast is much cheaper per loaf where I live than the individual packets of regular yeast.

enough to interfere with your yeast. Don't add bleach to your tanks right before making bread unless you have a tap with a charcoal filter (to remove the chlorine) or another source of water.

You can use all sorts of other liquids in place of water, such as milk or fruit juice. The cooking water from vegetables, rice, or pasta also works well and adds some nutrients as well as good flavor.

Yeast Breads

- **Milk.** If you use milk that has not been pasteurized, it needs to be scalded and then cooled before using it in bread in order to alter a protein that will otherwise keep the yeast from rising properly. If you use pasteurized milk, powdered milk, canned milk, or boxed milk, it has been heated in the processing and you don't need to scald it.
- **Yeast.** Although Americans are used to buying yeast in packages, it is sold in bulk in most other places. Two teaspoons of bulk yeast is roughly equivalent to one package. All yeast needs to be stored in a dark, cool place—the refrigerator is ideal—as heat will kill it. Also, yeast will not rise without a source of sugar—white or brown sugar, honey, molasses, or corn syrup. Salt is needed so that the loaf does not collapse during baking.

How to Proof the Yeast

Few home cooks bother to proof their yeast to make sure that it is still active, but it is essential on a cruising boat. In many small stores, it's hard to determine whether you are buying fresh yeast, or how it has been stored. And if you are in the tropics, the heat can quickly kill yeast. While keeping the yeast in the refrigerator will help you, it's no guarantee that your bread will rise properly.

To proof yeast, mix together the required liquid, sugar, and yeast. Let sit for 10 minutes in a warm place, and then check the mixture. It should be foamy, or bubbly, as in the photo. If not, or there are only a few bubbles, the yeast is dead. Your bread won't rise,

After 10 minutes, the yeast mixture will be very foamy if the yeast is good.

and you might as well throw out the mixture and not waste any more ingredients. If the yeast proofs well, continue with the recipe.

A quick note: some cookbooks also use the term "proof" to mean the final rising of a yeast bread before it goes in the oven. Don't mix up the two!

Basic Proportions in Breadmaking

While there are lots of variations in bread recipes, the basic proportions remain roughly the same. This information is helpful if you have to improvise:

- A recipe that begins with 1 cup of water or other liquid will make a nice-size loaf in an 8"×4" pan or a not-very-thick loaf in a 9"×5" pan. Using 1½ cups of water will make a full loaf in a 9"×5" pan.
- For every cup of water, use 2 to 3 teaspoons bulk yeast (or one package).
- Use at least as much sugar, honey, molasses, or corn syrup as yeast. Splenda and other sugar substitutes won't work; you must use at least twice as much agave syrup as the amount of yeast, and it still doesn't do as well as the other sugar sources.
- Use about 1 teaspoon of salt per cup of water. Even if you are cutting back on salt intake, you need to use some salt in bread as the loaves are prone to collapse without it. Bread also tastes very flat without salt.
- The amount of flour will vary considerably with the type. In general, it takes about 3 cups of wheat flour for 1 cup of water, but only about 1½ cups of corn flour (not cornmeal, but the corn flour found in much of Latin America).
- A single loaf made from 1 cup of water will bake for approximately 30 minutes in a 350°F oven. The time may depend on the pan used, the loaf shape, and the type of flour. A larger loaf will take longer.

Step-by-Step Instructions

After proofing the yeast, the next step is to mix in the flour and then, typically, knead the dough, let it rise, sometimes "punch it down" and let it rise again, then shape it, put it in a pan for the final rise, then bake it . . . and then eat!

Most first-time breadmakers think that there are all sorts of secrets and tricks to making bread. There aren't. The only two things to remember are to make sure your yeast is good by proofing it, and not to add too much flour. Everything else is flexible.

While I've mixed bread dough in a dented aluminum saucepan with a soup spoon (and it turned out just fine), my preference is for a sturdy but relatively short metal mixing spoon and a plastic bowl. A metal spoon is much easier to clean than the wooden spoons favored by many, and a plastic bowl makes it easy to tell when you've got about the right amount of flour mixed in—the dough will come away from the sides in a nice ball (that does not happen with a metal or glass bowl). But the important thing to know is use whatever you have—it'll be fine!

Equally important, don't worry if the bread rises faster than anticipated or if you're away from the boat and don't punch it down or shape it right when you "should." If the dough rises an extra time, or gets so high that it falls back in on itself, it is truly not a problem. Bread dough is incredibly forgiving, and the finished product will be just fine.

One quick tip if you're a newbie: make white bread the first few times, then move on to other types. While it's not as healthy as whole wheat or some other types, white bread is the most forgiving and hence perfect for learning. After you've made a couple of loaves, you'll know what the dough looks and feels like at the various stages, making it easier to work with other flours.

And now, since many of the terms used in bread-making may be a little unfamiliar, here is my attempt to demystify the process:

Mixing the Dough to Develop Gluten. Gluten is the stuff that gives bread dough its elasticity. Bread that you can cut or tear without a lot of crumbs from the bread itself (not the crust, which always produces crumbs) is high in gluten; bread that tends to crumble is low in gluten. Gluten is developed by working the flour/water mixture in the initial mixing and in subsequent kneading.

The type of flour used and how it was processed determine how much gluten can be developed. So-called "bread flour" is high in gluten; "cake flour" is low. It is quite difficult to develop gluten from flours other than wheat. Thus, if you use specialty flours,

you must also use at least half wheat flour for your bread to have a satisfactory texture (unless you're trying to make gluten-free bread, which is outside the scope of this cookbook).

My experience has been that flours bought outside the US aren't particularly consistent in their gluten content, even from one bag to another of the same brand. Thus I take a little more care to develop the gluten in the dough. *Mixing the dough for at least five minutes when it is about the consistency of cake batter, before adding the final bit of flour, gives good results.* This is really the only "trick" I know for creating great results. You'll notice that as you keep mixing, the texture of the dough will change—it will become very smooth, almost satiny. Gluten is further developed in the kneading.

For some recipes—pizza being the best known—having a stretchy dough is critical. If you make these items regularly, you may want to purchase a gluten additive. It is generally stocked with the specialty flours. There are also many online sources.

Although high-gluten breads have a wonderful soft texture, they also get stale faster than lower-gluten breads. Lower-gluten breads tend to be heavier, crumble more easily, and have more of an "artisan bread" texture. Both are great, so the development of the gluten is really a worry only if you're making something–such as pizza or Danish–that requires it.

How Much Flour? If you're using a plastic bowl, mix in the flour until the dough just forms a ball in the center of the bowl, with very little dough left on the sides or bottom. In a metal or glass bowl, use your judgment—some dough will always adhere to the sides of the bowl. You do *not* want to add flour until you can't mix any more in; if you do, you'll have added too much, and the bread will be heavy and won't rise properly.

My experience is that many bread recipes I find in other cookbooks call for too much flour. If I use the total amount they specify, the dough does not rise nicely and the bread is heavy. Instead of blindly adding the amount of flour specified in a recipe, use your own judgment. The dough should be as thick as most cookie doughs, such as for chocolate chip cookies or peanut butter cookies.

Yeast Breads

I feel like I'm on a soapbox here, harping about not adding too much flour, but bread truly isn't hard to make, yet most people who aren't happy with their results have simply used too much flour. You're much better off to use too little than too much, so don't fret—just keep the dough about the consistency of cookie dough and the bread will be fine.

Kneading. Many people, and even some cookbooks, have the impression that the purpose of kneading is to mix in additional flour. It isn't. The purpose of kneading is to further develop the gluten in the dough. In kneading, you want to be very careful *not* to knead much more flour into your dough.

Most cookbooks have you sprinkle flour on a counter, put the dough on the flour, sprinkle more flour over the top, and then knead. This just isn't suited for a galley, as it can be extremely messy if the boat rolls at the wrong minute or a gust of wind comes through a porthole. (One tip if you do knead the dough on a counter: turn off any fans in the vicinity before sprinkling flour.) Further, many galleys don't have a large countertop at a convenient height.

Instead, try kneading the bread right in the bowl. And if your bowl is plastic, it will help you resist the temptation to add too much flour, as the dough won't stick to the bowl. (If you have a plastic cutting board, another alternative is to knead the dough on it so the dough doesn't stick.)

To knead dough in a bowl, start by washing your hands. Then lift the dough and sprinkle some flour under it. Lower the dough and sprinkle just a little more flour over the top. Take your hand and fold one side of the dough to the center of the bowl and push down with your knuckles or the heel of your hand. Turn the bowl a quarter turn, then fold and press the dough in the same way. Keep working your way around the bowl until the dough is no longer sticky—you may have to add a little more flour. You don't want the dough sticky, but you don't want to add so much flour that the dough feels dry and crumbly. You are generally better off erring on the side of too little flour. Typically, the dough should be kneaded for five to seven minutes. It will be a nice smooth ball when you are done.

If you don't want to deal with kneading, you can make no-knead bread (page 399), which uses far less yeast and develops gluten by very long, slow rising (16 to 24 hours). This bread requires no kneading at all—you handle it only enough to shape it into loaves.

Rising Dough. Once the dough is kneaded, take it out of the bowl and set it aside for a minute. Rinse out the bowl—it doesn't have to be perfectly clean—and add a couple tablespoons of oil. Put the dough back in the bowl, wiggle it around to fully coat the bottom of the dough with oil, then flip it over. If you don't completely cover the dough with oil, the outside will dry out, and you'll have hard bits in your finished loaf.

Cover the bowl with anything that will keep off bugs and such. My favorite is to put the bowl inside a plastic grocery bag and tuck the ends of the bag under the bowl. Place it in a warm spot—this will help the dough to rise faster.

Some recipes call for letting the dough rise once in the bowl, then shaping it and putting it in the pan, whereas other recipes call for "punching it down" or kneading it a second time. As a girl, when my mom would tell me to punch it down, I'd do exactly that: make a fist, bring it back to my shoulder, and put everything I had into a punch. Well, I never ruined a loaf of bread, but you don't need to be quite so violent. Just use your hand and gently tap the dough down, then re-cover the bowl and let the dough rise again.

If the recipe calls for a second kneading, I usually do it right in the bowl without adding any extra flour if I can help it. I remove the dough for a minute while I re-oil the bowl, and put the dough back in and turn it all around to cover the dough with the oil, and then cover the bowl again.

Pans. While most of us are used to loaves of bread baked in "loaf" pans, most breads can be baked on cookie sheets, in casserole dishes, and in all sorts of other baking dishes–or even on a double layer of aluminum foil. It will still taste great!

The pans should be greased. You can form your dough into almost any shape you want. To make a regular loaf, it's easiest to flatten the dough into a square or rectangle with one side slightly shorter than the length of the loaf pan. Roll up the dough into a long roll and put it in the pan with the seam on the bottom.

You can also make one large ball and bake the bread in a casserole dish or ovenproof skillet, or on a cookie sheet or a piece of aluminum foil. Make little balls for rolls, or flatten them out to make hamburger buns. And braided bread is always a hit—any dough can be split in three, rolled into strands, and braided. Check our recipe for braided bread (page 396).

Sometimes a recipe will call for greasing the pan, then dusting it with cornmeal. The cornmeal is not critical—nice, yes, but not critical. You can omit it entirely or use oats instead. The bread will be fine.

Baking. Most breads are baked in a preheated oven. However, if you are really pressed for time and want to dramatically shorten the time for rising after forming, you can put your loaves into a cold oven, then turn it on and let the dough rise as the oven comes up to temperature. The loaf won't rise quite as nicely as if baked traditionally, but you have to add only 5 to 10 minutes to the baking time versus 30 minutes or more for rising at room temperature.

Testing for Doneness. The most foolproof way to test a loaf for doneness is to use an instant-read thermometer and insert it in the center of the loaf (be careful not to push it down too far—you want the tip right in the center of the loaf). Unless a particular recipe specifies otherwise, the bread is done when the internal temperature reaches 190°F.

If you don't have an instant-read thermometer, the first half of the test is simply the look at the top of the bread—is it a deep golden color verging on brown? Of course, if you're making a dark bread, this can be almost impossible to tell. Second, lightly rap on the loaf with your knuckles. When the bread is done, it will sound hollow. Admittedly, the first time or two you do this, you'll be wondering whether or not it really sounds hollow--but with a bit of experience, this is a very reliable test.

Cooling. To keep the crust crisp after baking, remove the bread from the pan and cool it on a rack. Leaving it in the pan will trap steam and make the crust soft. Aboard *Que Tal*, we didn't have room to take cooling racks, so I improvised: putting a few table knives between the loaf of bread and the counter or cutting board works well.

Crusty Bread. If you want a soft bread with a crunchy crust, the trick is to have a moist dough and bake it in a hotter-than-normal oven. The recipes for Onion Bread (page 395) and No-Knead Bread (page 399) are perfect for this, but almost any bread's crust will be improved by making sure not to use too much flour. Be sure to take the loaf out of the pan to cool, and don't store it in a plastic bag or in the refrigerator—otherwise, the crust will be soft.

You can also brush a loaf with a beaten egg (or just the egg white) before baking it, but the "crustiness" produced is different.

Storing Bread. Homemade bread does not keep well, due to the lack of preservatives. It's best eaten within a few hours of coming out of the oven. Storing homemade bread is somewhat problematic. If you put it in a plastic bag, it will mold very quickly (especially in a hot climate), but if you don't, it will get dry and stale equally as fast. The best thing I've found is to store it on end, with the cut side down, on a plate. If you do put it in a plastic bag, make sure that the bread is completely cool first. If you have room in your refrigerator, you can put it in a plastic bag in the refrigerator (but note that it will make the crust soft).

Yeast Breads

WHITE, WHEAT, AND RYE BREAD RECIPES

Let's move on to the good stuff—recipes for fantastic homemade bread!

Basic White Bread   Makes 1 loaf

If this is your first time making bread, or you have not had good results in the past, please read Yeast Breadmaking 101 (page 386) for more detailed step-by-step directions.

1 cup warm water
2 teaspoons yeast (1 package; page 387)
2 teaspoons sugar
1 teaspoon salt
1 tablespoon canola oil or vegetable oil
3 cups white flour, or more as needed

1. Mix the water, yeast, and sugar. Let sit for 10 minutes in a warm spot to proof (page 388). Add the salt, oil, and 2 cups of the flour. Mix for at least 4 minutes to develop the gluten—the dough will become smooth and satiny. Add the remaining flour as needed to make a stiff dough. Knead until the dough becomes smooth and elastic; do not add too much flour.
2. Put the dough in an oiled bowl and turn the dough so it is completely coated with the oil. Cover the bowl and let the dough rise until it is doubled, then punch it down. Let rise until doubled again, then form into a loaf and place in a greased 8"×4" loaf pan. Cover and let rise again. Meanwhile, preheat oven to 350°F.
3. Bake for 40 minutes.

Whole Wheat Bread   Makes 1 loaf

Please read the section Yeast Breadmaking 101 (page 386) for more detailed step-by-step directions.

1 cup warm water
2 teaspoons yeast (1 package; page 387)
2 teaspoons sugar
1 teaspoon salt
1 tablespoon canola oil or vegetable oil

1 to 1½ cups whole wheat flour
1½ cups white flour

1. Mix the water, yeast, and sugar. Let sit for 10 minutes in a warm spot to proof (page 388). Add the salt, oil, and 1 cup of each type of flour. Mix for 10 minutes or more—it is harder to develop gluten from whole wheat flour, and extra effort here will pay off in the finished product. Knead the dough until it becomes smooth and elastic, being careful not to add so much flour that the dough becomes dry.
2. Put the dough in an oiled bowl and turn the dough so that it is completely coated with the oil. Cover the bowl and let the dough rise until it is doubled, then punch it down. Let rise until doubled again, then form into a loaf and place in a greased 8"×4" loaf pan. Cover and let rise. Meanwhile, preheat oven to 350°F.
3. Bake for 40 minutes.

Whole Wheat-Corn Flour Bread   Makes 1 large loaf

Please read the section Yeast Breadmaking 101 (page 386) for more detailed step-by-step directions.

1½ cups warm water
3 teaspoons yeast (1½ packets; page 387)
1 tablespoon sugar
2 teaspoons salt
2 tablespoons canola oil or vegetable oil
1 cup whole wheat flour
1½ cups white flour
½ cup corn flour

1. Mix the water, yeast, and sugar. Let sit for 10 minutes in a warm spot to proof (page 388).
2. Add the salt, oil, whole wheat flour, and 1 cup of the white flour. Mix 10 minutes or more—it is harder to develop gluten from whole wheat flour (and the corn flour won't contribute any). A little extra effort here will pay off in the finished product.
3. When the dough is smooth and elastic (it will still be very wet), mix in the corn flour. Then add the remaining flour as needed and knead into the

dough, being careful not to add so much flour that the dough becomes dry. Because of the wide variety of flours—you're using three types here—it's difficult to say exactly how much flour you'll have to add. Always err on the side of less flour! Knead until the dough becomes smooth and elastic.

4. Put the dough in an oiled bowl and turn the dough so that it is completely coated with the oil. Cover the bowl and let the dough rise until it is doubled, then punch it down. Let rise until doubled again, then form it into a loaf and place it in a greased pan. Cover and let rise. Meanwhile, preheat oven to 350°F.

5. Bake for 40 minutes.

White or Whole Wheat Rolls
Makes about 12 rolls

Virtually any yeast bread dough can be shaped into rolls. Bake for about half the time that a loaf would take.

1. Use the recipe for White Bread (page 392) or Whole Wheat Bread (page 392), but increase the sugar to $^1/_4$ cup and double the amount of butter or oil.

2. To shape the rolls, do one of the following:

   • Make $1^1/_2$-inch balls and place on a greased cookie sheet, well spaced out. Let rise as usual, then bake for 15 to 20 minutes in a 400°F oven.

   • Make 1-inch balls and place about 1 inch apart in a greased baking pan. As the rolls rise, they will touch. Bake about 30 minutes at 375°F. Pull apart to serve.

   • Make $^3/_4$-inch balls and place two or three balls in each cup of a greased muffin tin. Let rise as usual, then bake about 15 minutes in a 375°F oven.

Swedish Rye Bread
Makes 1 loaf

Please read the section Yeast Breadmaking 101 (page 386) for more detailed step-by-step directions.

$1^1/_4$ cups warm water
2 teaspoons yeast (1 package; page 387)
$1^1/_2$ teaspoons salt
2 tablespoons molasses
$^1/_4$ cup packed brown sugar

2 tablespoons butter, margarine, or oil
1 tablespoon grated orange zest (or use orange juice instead of the water)
$^1/_2$ teaspoon anise seed or caraway seed (if available)
2 cups rye flour
$2^1/_4$ cups white flour

1. Mix the water, yeast, salt, molasses, brown sugar, and butter in a bowl. Let sit for 10 minutes to proof the yeast (page 388). Add the zest, anise seed, and half of both flours. Mix for 10 minutes to develop the gluten. Add the remaining flour a little at a time until the dough is stiff. Knead the dough in the bowl until it becomes smooth and elastic, being careful not to add so much flour that the dough becomes dry.

2. Remove the dough from the bowl, rinse and oil the bowl, then return the dough to the bowl, turning it to cover with the oil. Place the bowl in a plastic bag and let the dough rise in a warm spot until it is doubled in size. Punch down and let rise again.

3. Shape the dough into a round loaf and place it on a greased cookie sheet or in a round pan (or shape it as a loaf and bake it in a loaf pan). Meanwhile, preheat oven to 375°F.

4. When doubled in size, bake for 35 minutes.

Dark Rye Bread
Makes 1 large loaf

Please read the section Yeast Breadmaking 101 (page 386) for more detailed step-by-step directions.

$1^1/_2$ cups warm water
4 teaspoons yeast (2 packets; page 387)
$^1/_2$ cup molasses or honey
2 teaspoons salt
2 tablespoons butter or margarine, melted, or oil
2 tablespoons caraway seed
$^1/_4$ cup unsweetened baking cocoa
2 cups rye flour
2 cups white and/or whole wheat flour

1. Mix the water, yeast, and molasses. Let sit for 10 minutes to proof (page 388). Add the salt, butter, caraway seed, cocoa, and half of both flours. Mix for 5 to 10 minutes to develop the gluten.

Yeast Breads

Add the remaining flour a little at a time until the dough is stiff, then knead in the remaining flour, taking care not to add so much flour that the dough bcomes dry.

2. Remove the dough from the bowl, rinse and oil the bowl, then return the dough to the bowl, turning the dough to cover with the oil. Place the bowl in a plastic bag and let the dough rise in a warm spot until doubled in size. Punch it down and let rise again.

3. Shape the dough into a round loaf and place it on a greased cookie sheet or in a round pan (or shape it as a loaf and bake it in a loaf pan). Meanwhile, preheat oven to 375°F.

4. When the dough is doubled in size, bake for 40 minutes.

"Almost" Rye Bread

Rye flour is virtually impossible to find in many cruising locales, and it is heavy and bulky to bring from trips home. But relatively large containers of caraway or anise seed easily fit inside a suitcase. With the seeds, most people don't notice that there's no rye flour in my "Almost" Rye Bread!

To make "Almost" Rye, use the recipe for Swedish Rye Bread (page 393), Pumpernickel Bread (see following recipe), or Dark Rye Bread (page 393) and substitute whole wheat flour for the rye flour. If you don't have molasses, use honey or sugar.

SPECIALTY BREADS

While we call these "Specialty Breads," they're actually variations on the basic breads above.

Pumpernickel Bread   Makes 1 loaf

Please read the section Yeast Breadmaking 101 (page 386) for more detailed step-by-step directions.

1 cup warm water
3 teaspoons yeast (1½ packets; page 387)
¼ cup molasses, honey, brown sugar, or white sugar

2 teaspoons salt
2 tablespoons butter or margarine, melted, or canola oil or vegetable oil
2 tablespoons caraway seed or anise seed
1½ cups rye flour
1½ cups white and/or whole wheat flour

1. Mix the water, yeast, and molasses in a bowl. Let sit for 10 minutes to proof the yeast (page 388). Add the salt, butter, caraway seed, and half of both flours. Mix for 5 to 10 minutes to develop the gluten. Add the remaining flour a little at a time until the dough is stiff. Knead the dough in the bowl until it becomes smooth and elastic, being careful not to add so much flour that the dough becomes dry.

2. Remove the dough from the bowl, rinse and oil the bowl, then return the dough to the bowl, turning the dough to coat it with oil. Place the bowl in a plastic bag and set it in a warm spot to let the dough rise. When it is doubled in size, punch it down and let it rise again.

3. Shape the dough into a round loaf and place it on a greased cookie sheet or a round pan (or it can be made as a loaf and baked in a loaf pan). Meanwhile, preheat oven 375°F.

4. When the dough is doubled in size, bake for 40 minutes.

Raisin Bread   Makes 1 loaf

Please read the section Yeast Breadmaking 101 (page 386) for more detailed step-by-step directions.

¾ cup water or milk
¼ cup butter, margarine, canola oil, or vegetable oil
1 cup raisins
¼ cup sugar
1 teaspoon salt
2 teaspoons yeast (1 package; page 387)
2 eggs (if unavailable, use an extra ½ cup water or milk)
3½ to 4 cups white flour
2 tablespoons canola oil or vegetable oil

Yeast Breads

NOTE: This recipe makes 1 large loaf (9"×5" pan). If your pan is smaller, decrease the water or milk by ¼ cup and the flour by approximately 1 cup to make a smaller loaf.

1. Heat the water and butter to almost boiling. Put the raisins in a large mixing bowl and add the hot liquid to plump the raisins (this is particularly helpful if the raisins are somewhat dried out). Allow to cool until just warm to the touch.
2. Add the sugar, salt, and yeast; mix well. Put the eggs in a cup or small bowl and beat just enough to break the yolks, then add them to the raisin mixture.
3. Add 2 cups of the flour and mix for 8 minutes to help develop the gluten. Continue mixing in more flour until the dough is stiff. Knead the dough in the bowl, using additional flour as necessary but not so much that the dough becomes dry.
4. Remove the dough from the bowl. Rinse the bowl, add oil, and put the dough back into the bowl, turning the dough to completely coat it with oil. Cover the bowl with a plastic bag and place it in a warm spot to rise.
5. When the dough is doubled in size, punch it down and allow it to rise again. When it is doubled in size again, shape it into a loaf and place it in a greased 9"×5" loaf pan. Allow to rise again.
6. When the dough has almost doubled in size, preheat the oven to 375°F.
7. Bake for 40 to 45 minutes, or until it is golden brown and sounds hollow when tapped.

Onion Bread   Makes 1 loaf

This bread requires no kneading but the ingredients must be mixed longer.

1 cup warm water
2 tablespoons sugar
2 teaspoons yeast (1 packet; page 387)
1 teaspoon salt
¼ cup dried minced onion OR 1 packet French onion soup mix OR 1¼ cups diced fresh onion

2 tablespoons canola oil, vegetable oil, butter, or margarine*
2½ cups flour

*Using olive oil instead of vegetable oil will overpower the flavor of the onions and is not recommended.

1. Mix the water, sugar, and yeast. Let proof for 10 minutes (page 388). Mix in the salt, onion, and oil. Add half the flour and mix for 10 minutes to develop the gluten. Add the rest of the flour and mix for 3 minutes. The dough should be slightly wet.
2. Cover the bowl with a plastic bag and let rise for 30 minutes. Punch down the dough, and let it rise again for about 30 minutes.
3. Form the dough into a desired loaf shape (it can be baked in a loaf pan, a small bowl, or a casserole), using little to no additional flour. Grease a pan and place the loaf in pan. Cover with a plastic bag and let rise for 30 minutes.
4. Shortly before the end of the rising time, preheat oven to 350°F.
5. Bake for 40 minutes, or until golden brown.
6. Cool in the pan for 5 to 10 minutes, then remove from the pan. Best when served warm, but also makes great sandwiches and toast.

Dill Bread or Onion-Dill Bread

Use the Onion Bread recipe (above), but use half the onion (or omit it entirely) and add 1 tablespoon dried dill (leaves or ground). This makes wonderful hamburger buns—form the dough into 2-inch balls, flatten them to about ½ inch thick, and bake on a cookie sheet, in a 9"×13" pan, or on sheets of aluminum foil for about 15 to 20 minutes, or until golden brown. (The baking time varies considerably depending on your pan and how thick the buns are.) The dough is also good as a loaf, baked as for Onion Bread, above.

Yeast Breads

Braided Bread

I can't tell you how many loaves of this bread I've made—probably hundreds! It was my mom's favorite to go with just about any "special" meal, and it's my favorite, too. Please read the section Yeast Breadmaking 101 (page 386) for more detailed step-by-step directions.

1¼ cups warm water
2 teaspoons salt
4 teaspoons yeast (2 packages; page 387)
¼ cup sugar
2 tablespoons canola oil or vegetable oil
4 cups flour (white flour produces the best results)
1 egg
sesame seeds or poppy seeds

1. Mix the water, salt, yeast, sugar, and oil in a large bowl. Add 1 cup of the flour; mix well and let stand for 10 minutes to proof (page 388).

2. Add one more cup of the flour and mix with a spoon for 6 minutes (you really have to mix it that long to develop the gluten necessary to be able to braid the dough). The dough should be very elastic and come away from the sides of the bowl.

3. Add one more cup of flour and again mix until the dough is smooth and elastic. Don't worry about kneading it now. Just cover the bowl with a plastic bag and let the dough rise for 30 to 45 minutes, or until approximately doubled.

4. Although I normally knead the dough right in the bowl, it's hard to do with this one. Instead, I take a 9"×13" pan or a cookie sheet with sides and sprinkle it with about ¼ cup flour. (The sides contain the flour mess and make cleanup a lot easier.) Then turn the dough onto the flour and sprinkle with another ¼ cup or so. Knead the dough gently, working in a little more flour. The dough should still be very soft and stretchy. If in doubt, err on the side of the dough being too moist.

5. Rinse out the bowl and oil the inside of it. Place the dough in the bowl, turning the dough so that it is completely coated with oil. Cover the bowl with a plastic bag and again let the dough rise until doubled. Don't bother cleaning the flour pan just yet—you'll use it again later.

6. Wash your hands and oil them. Lift the dough out of the bowl and knead it right in your hands, just folding one section under at a time. The dough should still be very soft and stretchy. Do not add any more flour unless the dough is so moist that it is not really "dough." As you knead, the dough may tear a bit. That's okay. Continue to knead for a total of 10 minutes. Think of this as a poor man's (or woman's) fitness center! You may need to add more oil to the bowl, in which case remove the dough, add the oil, then return the dough to the bowl, turn it to coat the dough with oil, and place the plastic bag back over the bowl. Let the dough rise until doubled.

7. Turn the dough onto the floured pan and cut the dough into three equal pieces. Roll each piece into a strip about 18 inches long. If the strip breaks, pinch it back together. I have better luck rolling the dough on the counter than trying to squeeze it into a strip going hand over hand in midair.

8. Grease a cookie sheet or a long piece of aluminum foil. Lay the three strips of dough on the cookie sheet and pinch them together at one end. Starting there, braid the strands together. When you reach the other end, pinch the ends together and tuck them under just an inch or so. Then go back to the top and tuck under the pinched end there, too.

9. Beat the egg in a small bowl or cup until it is slightly frothy. Use your fingers to lightly spread the egg all over the braided loaf. Don't press down hard, and don't worry if some of the egg puddles in the nooks and crannies and on the cookie sheet. I've tried using brushes, spoons, and other utensils, and they just don't work as well as fingers. Apply the egg liberally, as the dough will expand considerably as it rises.

10. Wash your hands, then sprinkle the loaf liberally with the seeds. Allow to rise until doubled in size.

11. If you begin preheating your oven to 350°F at about the time that you begin the final rising, it will be ready about when the loaf is risen (the exceptions being in very warm and cold climates).

12. When the loaf is doubled, bake for about 35 minutes. If you made a very long, skinny loaf, it may take a little less time, and a short, fat loaf will take a little more. The loaf is done when the egg wash is a light brown color (darker than golden) and the loaf sounds hollow when tapped.
13. Loosen the loaf from the pan by sliding a spatula or knife under it all around. Remove the bread from the hot pan as soon as possible. Serve warm or cool. Don't try to cut it, but just tear off sections.

NOTE: If you want to make a double recipe, you can either make two loaves or make four ropes and do a four-strand braid (under two, back over one).

Soft Italian Breadsticks
Makes 24 breadsticks

Please read the section Yeast Breadmaking 101 (page 386) for more detailed step-by-step directions.

Total Time: 35 minutes

1 cup warm water
2¼ teaspoons yeast (1 packet; page 387)
2 tablespoons sugar
3 tablespoons butter or margarine, softened
1½ teaspoons salt
1 teaspoon Italian seasoning (page 48)
1 teaspoon garlic powder
3 cups flour
2 tablespoons butter or margarine
¼ cup grated Parmesan cheese (optional)

1. Mix the water, yeast, and sugar. Let sit for 10 minutes in a warm spot to proof (page 388). Add the 3 tablespoons softened butter, the salt, Italian seasoning, garlic powder, and half the flour. Mix well. Add the remaining flour as needed to make a stiff dough. Knead until the dough becomes smooth and elastic, being careful not to add so much flour that the dough becomes dry.
2. Put the dough in an oiled bowl and turn the dough so that it is completely coated with the oil. Let rise until doubled, then punch down the dough. Let it rise again until doubled.
3. To form breadsticks, cut the dough into 24 equal portions. Roll each into an 8-inch-long rope. Place

2 inches apart on a greased cookie sheet. Cover and let rise in a warm place for about 20 minutes, or until doubled. Meanwhile, preheat oven to 350°F.
4. Bake for 15 minutes, or until golden.
5. Just before the end of the baking time, melt the 2 tablespoons butter. When the breadsticks are done, remove them from the oven and immediately brush with the melted butter and sprinkle with the Parmesan. Serve warm.

Refrigerator Crescent Rolls
Makes 24 to 30 rolls

This recipe was given to Jan as a wedding present from Virginia Vogel, our Y-Flyer sailing friend and neighbor, who was happy to have us include it here. I've rewritten some of the method to make it more boat friendly. You can store the dough up to a week, using a little at a time whenever you want rolls. Don't skimp on the sugar or use artificial sweetener—sugar is needed to keep the yeast alive during the storage period.

Total Time: 45 minutes
Prep Time: 30 minutes   **Bake Time:** 10 to 15 minutes

4 teaspoons yeast (2 packets; page 387)
1 cup warm water
½ teaspoon plus ½ cup sugar
1 egg
¾ cup hot water
1 tablespoon salt
3 tablespoons butter or margarine
5 cups flour
Extra melted butter or margarine, to brush tops of rolls (optional)

1. Place the yeast, warm water, and the ½ teaspoon sugar in a mixing cup and stir to combine. Let it proof (page 388) as you prepare the other ingredients. Beat the egg in another cup.
2. Mix together the hot water, the ½ cup sugar, the salt, and butter in a large bowl, and stir to dissolve the sugar. Before adding the yeast mixture, make sure that this sugar mixture has cooled sufficiently so that the yeast won't be killed. An easy test is whether you can comfortably hold a finger in the mix for 5 seconds.

3. Add the yeast mixture and egg to the large bowl. Also add half the flour. Stir vigorously for at least 8 minutes. Slowly add the rest of the flour. The dough should be sticky. Knead the dough just until it is smooth—don't knead it too long.

4. Pour 1 tablespoon oil into a large plastic bowl with a tight-fitting lid and add the dough, turning it so that the entire surface is coated. Place the lid on the bowl. The dough will keep well in the refrigerator for a week or more.

5. When ready to use, divide the dough into thirds. Roll one-third of the dough into about a 10-inch circle. Brush with the melted butter, then cut the circle into wedges. For larger rolls, make eight wedges, and for smaller rolls make ten wedges. If you don't want to bake that many rolls right now, just put the extra wedges back in the bowl with the rest of the dough, and put it all back in the refrigerator until the next time you want rolls.

6. Roll up each wedge starting at the wide end. Dip the top of the roll in the melted butter. Place the rolls on a greased cookie sheet (or a piece of aluminum foil) with the point of the roll on the bottom. Let rise about 15 minutes before baking. While the rolls are rising, preheat oven to 350°F.

7. Bake for 10 to 15 minutes, or until the rolls are brown on top. Remove immediately from the pan. Best served warm!

Doug's Easy Focaccia Bread   Makes 1 loaf

From our friends on Kristiana.

¾ cup warm water
2½ teaspoons yeast (1 package; page 387)
1 teaspoon sugar
1¼ cups white flour
1¼ cups rye flour
½ teaspoon salt
2 tablespoons caraway seed
1 tablespoon olive oil

1. Combine the warm water, yeast, and sugar in a small bowl or measuring cup. Let sit about 5 minutes to proof (page 388).

2. In a large bowl, combine the flours, salt, and caraway seed. Add the yeast mixture and oil, then mix as best you can—you won't be able to mix in all the flour. Knead for 10 minutes to mix in the remaining flour and to develop the gluten.

3. Put a half-dollar-size puddle of oil in a clean bowl, then add the dough and wiggle it around to coat all surfaces. Cover the bowl (a plastic grocery bag works well) and let the dough rise in a warm place until doubled in size.

4. Form the dough into a round, flat shape about ½ inch thick. Place on a greased cookie sheet and let rise until doubled. Meanwhile, preheat oven to 350°F.

5. Bake for 18 to 20 minutes.

Variations: Use whole wheat or white flour instead of rye flour, and any of the following additions instead of the caraway seed: 1 teaspoon Italian seasoning, ½ cup sliced or chopped olives, 1 teaspoon dried dill, ¼ cup shredded cheese, and /or ½ cup raisins or other chopped dried fruit.

Italian Herb Focaccia   Serves 8 to 12

Total Time: usually just over 1 hour

1 cup warm water
1 teaspoon sugar
2½ teaspoons yeast (1 packet; page 387)
2½ cups white flour
1 teaspoon garlic powder
1 teaspoon dried oregano
½ teaspoon dried thyme
½ teaspoon dried basil
1 teaspoon salt
¼ teaspoon ground pepper
1 tablespoon olive oil
olive oil, to brush top of bread
grated Parmesan cheese (optional)
shredded mozzarella or other cheese that melts well (optional)

1. Mix the warm water, sugar, and yeast. Let stand 10 minutes to proof (page 388). While it is proofing, mix the flour and spices in a large bowl. Add

the yeast mixture and olive oil. Mix well. Knead for about 3 minutes.

2. Oil a bowl, place the dough in the bowl and turn the dough until it is coated with oil. Cover the bowl and let the dough rise for about a half hour.

3. Oil a cookie sheet and your hands. Turn the dough onto the cookie sheet and press it into a circle about ½ inch thick. Lightly coat the top of the dough with the olive oil, then sprinkle with the cheeses. Preheat oven to 425°F and let the dough rise while the oven preheats.

4. Bake for 15 minutes. To serve, cut into wedges. This bread does not keep well.

Variation: Add ¼ cup sliced black olives to the dough.

No-Knead Bread

No-Knead Bread is an "artisan" bread with a thick, crunchy crust and a coarse texture. The secrets to success are a very long, slow rising; a wet dough; high-temperature baking (oven must be able to reach 450°F); and a preheated pan. The pan must have a lid. Since you're preheating the pan, it's impossible to use aluminum foil as a "lid" without burning yourself.

Total Time: about 1½ hours plus 14+ hours to rise

3 cups flour
¼ teaspoon yeast (page 387)
1¼ teaspoons salt
1½ cups water
cornmeal, oats, or wheat bran (optional)

1. In a large bowl combine the flour, yeast, and salt. Add the water and stir until blended; the dough will be shaggy and sticky. Don't be alarmed that it doesn't look like "typical" bread dough. Cover the bowl with plastic wrap and let the dough rest at least 12 hours, preferably about 18 hours, at room temperature (or about 70°F). The dough is ready when its surface is dotted with bubbles.

2. Sprinkle a work surface with flour (using a cookie sheet or 9"×13" pan as your work surface will make cleanup easier) and turn the dough onto it, scraping the bowl to get all the dough. Sprinkle a little flour over the top of the dough. Gently and quickly shape the dough into a ball. Coat it with flour and

cornmeal, then put it back into the bowl and let it rise until doubled—typically about 2 hours. Half an hour before the end of the rising period, preheat oven to 450°F and put an empty pan that will be large enough to hold the dough (I use an oven-proof skillet; remember that it must have a tight-fitting lid) into the oven so that it preheats (no need to have the lid on it).

3. When the oven is up to temperature, carefully remove the pan. Unless it's a very well-seasoned Dutch oven, pour a little oil into it so that the bread won't stick. Turn the dough into it. It won't look like a pretty loaf, but that's okay. Shake the pan a bit if the dough is really lopsided, but then quickly put the lid on the pan and put it back in the oven.

4. Bake for 30 minutes, then take off the lid and bake for 20 to 30 minutes more, or until the top is very crusty and a dark golden brown. If you have an instant-read thermometer, insert it into the center of the loaf. When the bread is done, it will read at least 210°F.

5. Remove the bread from the pan to cool. Although it's tempting to cut into it immediately, wait at least 15 minutes and it will be much easier.

Pizza   1 deep-dish or 2 thin-crust pizzas

No pizza parlor? Make your own pizza as a special treat to celebrate good times! Before making the pizza dough, read the information about developing gluten (page 389), as it is very important to a good pizza crust, particularly if you want a thin-crust pizza.

Total Time: 2½ to 3 hours, depending on rising time, oven temp, pizza style, etc.

Crust
2 teaspoons yeast (1 packet; page 387)
¾ cup warm water
½ teaspoon sugar
1 teaspoon salt
1½ tablespoons olive oil, canola oil, or vegetable oil
2 cups flour—half white and half whole wheat is good, but you can use all of either one
Pizza Sauce (see below), and any toppings desired

1. Mix the yeast, water, and sugar in a large bowl and proof for 10 minutes (page 388). Stir in the salt, oil, and half the flour. Mix for at least 5 minutes, or until the dough is very smooth and stretchy. Gradually add the remaining flour, continuing to mix until the dough is stretchy after each addition. Be very careful not to add so much flour that the dough becomes dry.

2. Oil the bowl and your hands. Knead the dough for 5 minutes in the oiled bowl (make sure that the dough is coated with oil on all sides) and don't add any additional flour. Cover the bowl with a plastic bag. Let the dough rise until doubled in size, which will take 30 to 60 minutes depending on the temperature.

3. Oil your hands again and knead the dough again for 3 minutes in the oiled bowl, turning the dough so that it is coated with oil. Again let it rise until doubled, about 30 minutes. Meanwhile, preheat oven to 450°F if possible. If not, preheat it to as hot as your oven will get.*

4. Divide the dough into two or more parts, depending on pan sizes and the type of crust desired. This recipe will make one deep-dish pizza in a 9"×13" pan, one "pan pizza"–style crust on a larger cookie sheet, or two thin-crust pizzas in 9"×13" pans. Use any size pan you have—for example, a pie pan makes a good pizza for one or two people. You can even make pizza on a piece of aluminum foil (put a cutting board under the foil to transfer the pizza and the foil to and from the oven rack).

5. Lightly oil the pan(s) and pat out the dough to form the crust. Pre-bake the crust for 5 to 10 minutes so that it won't get soggy when you add the toppings. The exact time for pre-baking depends on your oven temperature and the thickness of your crust—hotter temps and thinner crusts need less time. The crust should not brown at all.

6. Remove the crust from the oven and quickly add the Pizza Sauce and other desired toppings. Return the pizza to the oven and bake for 10 to 25 minutes. The time depends on the oven temperature, crust thickness, and toppings. When done, the crust should be nicely browned and the cheese melted and golden—you know what a pizza should look like!

Pizza is best baked at 425° to 450°F. You can still make a good pizza if your oven will bake at 350°F, but the crust will be a little drier.

NOTE: While mozzarella is traditional, you can use almost any variety of cheese that will melt. In Mexico, those marketed as "quesadilla" cheese are always a good choice, and generally considerably cheaper. Additionally, you can make pizza with no cheese— I make them without cheese because of Dave's allergy to all milk products. The best way to do this is to put half the sauce on the pizza, then the toppings, then the rest of the sauce.

Alternate Pizza Crust

Use the recipe for Italian Herb Focaccia Bread (page 398) and shape the dough into a pizza crust. You can also use the above recipe for pizza crust, but add the herbs specified in the Italian Herb Focaccia for a more flavorful crust.

Pizza Sauce

This is generally enough for the crust above, depending on your preference.

1 can (12 to 16 ounces) tomato sauce
1 tablespoon olive oil
1/2 teaspoon salt
1/2 teaspoon dried basil
1/2 teaspoon dried oregano
3 to 4 cloves garlic, crushed, OR 1/2 teaspoon garlic powder
1/2 teaspoon onion powder OR 1 teaspoon dried onion flakes
1 teaspoon brown sugar or white sugar
2 tablespoons red wine, balsamic vinegar, or other vinegar

Mix all the ingredients together and blend well. If you have extra sauce, store it tightly covered in the refrigerator.

Hamburger Buns

Use the recipe for Basic White Bread (page 392), Whole Wheat Bread (page 392), Onion Bread (page 395), or Dill Bread (page 395). If you like soft buns, use milk in place of the water in the recipe.

1. Preheat oven to 375°F.
2. To shape the buns, make 1½-inch balls and place them on a lightly greased cookie sheet. Press down to flatten. Let rise for 10 to 15 minutes and press down again. The circles should be between 3 inches and 4 inches in diameter. Let rise another 10 minutes, then bake for 15 to 20 minutes.

BREAKFAST ROLLS AND COFFEE CAKES

Here are some great treats for special days . . . but then, every day on a boat is special, isn't it?

Cinnamon-Raisin Coffee Cake   Serves 10 to 12

Please read the section Yeast Breadmaking 101 (page 386) for more detailed step-by-step directions.

1 cup warm water
2 teaspoons yeast (1 package; page 287)
¼ cup sugar
1 egg
1 teaspoon salt
2 tablespoons butter or margarine, melted, or canola oil or vegetable oil (do not use olive oil)
3 cups white flour, or more as needed
2 tablespoons butter or margarine (optional)
1 tablespoon ground cinnamon
¼ cup sugar
1 cup raisins or other chopped dried fruit
½ cup walnuts or pecans (optional)

Glaze (optional)
½ cup confectioners' sugar
1 tablespoon milk or water

1. Mix the water, yeast, and sugar. Let sit for 10 minutes in a warm spot to proof (page 388). Add the egg, salt, the 2 tablespoons melted butter, and 2 cups of the flour. Mix well. Add the remaining flour as needed to make a stiff dough. Knead until the dough becomes smooth and elastic, being careful not to add so much flour that the dough becomes dry.
2. Put the dough in an oiled bowl and turn the dough so that it is completely coated with the oil. Let rise until doubled, then punch down the dough. Let it rise until doubled again.
3. Turn the dough onto a cookie sheet or countertop. Roll it into a rectangle about 15"× 24" (use a wine bottle as a rolling pin, or just pat it into the appropriate shape). Dot the surface with bits of butter, if desired, then sprinkle with the cinnamon, sugar, raisins, and walnuts (if desired), making sure to evenly cover the entire surface.
4. Roll the dough into a long log. Place it in a greased 9-inch round pan, forming a circle as you do and pinching the ends together. (If you don't have a round pan, you can use a cookie sheet, but the coffee cake won't hold its shape as well.)
5. Use kitchen shears or a very sharp knife to cut through the log almost to the bottom at 1¼-inch intervals. Gently twist each slice 90 degrees so that it lies facing up and overlapping its neighbor on one side. Let rise until doubled in size. Meanwhile, preheat oven to 350°F.
6. Bake for about 45 minutes. Remove from the pan and let cool on a wire rack or plate. While still warm, mix the confectioners' sugar and milk to make the glaze, if desired. Drizzle over the coffee cake from the tip of a spoon. This is best when served warm, but it can be baked the night before.

Yeast Breads

Totally Decadent Cinnamon Rolls
Makes 8 large rolls

Very similar to those found at Cinnabon's and various coffee shops, these are loaded with calories (about 800 calories each, including the frosting) and fat (more than 30 grams), so they're not for every day. But they can't be beat for a special occasion! Please read the section Yeast Breadmaking 101 (page 386) for more detailed step-by-step directions.

Total Time: 3 hours

Dough
1/2 cup water
3 3/4 teaspoons yeast (1 1/2 packets; page 387)
1/4 cup sugar
2 1/2 tablespoons butter or margarine, softened
1/2 cup milk
2 eggs
1/2 teaspoon salt
3 1/2 cups flour, sifted
1/4 cup raisins (optional)
1 tablespoon canola oil or vegetable oil

Filling
1 cup butter or margarine, melted
1 1/2 cups packed brown sugar
3 tablespoons ground cinnamon
3/8 cup chopped walnuts

1. To make the dough, mix the water, yeast, and sugar in large mixing bowl; let proof 10 minutes (page 388). Add the butter, milk, eggs, and salt and mix well. Add half the flour and mix well. Add the raisins, if desired, and all but 1/2 cup of the remaining flour. Mix well. The dough will be quite sticky and begin to leave the sides of the bowl.
2. Sprinkle 1/4 cup of remaining flour into the bowl and knead the dough right in the bowl for about 10 minutes, or until the dough is smooth. Add more flour if needed. (The dough should still be soft and almost sticky.)
3. Turn the dough out of the bowl and rinse the bowl. Add the oil and swish it around to coat the bowl completely. Shape the dough into a ball and put it in the bowl, turning it so that it is completely coated with oil. Cover the bowl and let the dough rise until doubled, about 45 minutes.
4. Near the end of the rising time, make the Filling by mixing together the butter, brown sugar, and cinnamon. Set aside.
5. Roll the dough into a 12"× 20" rectangle. (The dough will be thin.) Spread the entire rectangle of dough with the filling mixture, and then sprinkle with the walnuts. Roll the rectangle tightly starting with the short side. Turn it over so that the seam is on the bottom. Cut the roll into 8 equal pieces approximately 1 1/2 inches each.
6. Grease a 9"× 13" pan. Place the rolls side by side in the pan. Cover with a plastic bag and let the dough rise for 30 to 40 minutes, or until doubled in size. Meanwhile, preheat oven to 350°F.
7. Bake for about 35 minutes, or until the rolls are browned and the filling is bubbling. Allow to cool for 10 minutes, then invert the rolls onto a cookie sheet. Allow the butter and sugar mix to drip from the pan onto the rolls—use a spatula to scrape the pan to get it all.
8. If desired, when the rolls are cool, spread them with the Cinnamon Rolls Frosting (below).

Cinnamon Rolls Frosting
It is almost impossible to make this frosting without an electric mixer.

1/2 cup butter, softened
4 ounces cream cheese, softened
1 1/2 cups confectioners' sugar
1 teaspoon vanilla extract

Beat the butter and cream cheese together. Add the confectioners' sugar and vanilla and whip until light and fluffy.

PRETZELS

In some places, buying pretzels is hit-and-miss. But my (Carolyn) Dave loves them! Solution: make them yourself.

Hard Pretzels   Yield depends on pretzel size

While it is possible to make these pretzels into small twists (see directions for Soft Pretzels, but work with very thin ropes about 8 inches long), it's much easier to simply make sticks.

Total Time: About 1½ hours

1¼ cups warm water
2 teaspoons yeast (1 packet; page 387)
1 teaspoon salt
1 tablespoon sugar
¼ cup butter or margarine, melted, or oil
4 cups white flour
1 egg
coarse salt, kosher salt, or regular salt

1. Preheat oven to 350°F.
2. Mix the water, yeast, salt, sugar, and butter. Let proof 10 minutes (page 388). Mix in the flour and knead until the dough is smooth. Don't let it rise.
3. Pinch off a 1-inch ball of dough. Roll it between your hands until it is a long rope about half the diameter you wish the finished pretzels to be. Lay the rope down on a cookie sheet and cut it into sticks about 3 inches long. Move the sticks slightly apart.
4. Lightly beat the egg and brush it over the top of the pretzels, then sprinkle with the coarse salt. Bake immediately (don't let them rise) for 45 minutes to an hour (depending on the size of the pretzels), or until dark brown. These pretzels keep well if you let them cool completely, and then put them in a plastic bag and squeeze out as much air as possible before sealing the bag.

Soft Pretzels   Makes 10 to 12

Total Time: About 1 hour

1½ cups warm water
2 teaspoons yeast (1 packet; page 387)
1 teaspoon salt
1 tablespoon sugar
4 cups white flour
1 egg
coarse salt, kosher salt, or regular salt

1. Preheat oven to 425°F.
2. Mix the water, yeast, salt, and sugar. Let proof 10 minutes (page 388). Mix in the flour and knead until the dough is smooth. Don't let it rise.
3. Pull off pieces slightly larger than a golf ball and roll each one between your hands until it forms a rope about 18 inches long.
4. To form a traditional pretzel shape, hold the center of each rope in one hand and twist the free ends together (one complete turn) about halfway down. Lay the pretzel down on a cookie sheet and flip the twist over the loop to form the traditional pretzel shape, as shown below. You can also form them into circles or sticks. Repeat to make all the pretzels.

5. Lightly beat the egg and brush it over the top of pretzels, then sprinkle with the coarse salt. Bake immediately (don't let them rise) for 12 to 15 minutes, or until brown. Serve warm with mustard.

NOTE: These do not store well. Enjoy immediately!

Yeast Breads

MORE YEAST BREADS

A few yeast bread recipes made their way into other chapters:

Special Galley Cooking Techniques
Baked bread on the grill, *page 78*

Breakfast and Brunch
Homemade Bagels, *page 119*
English Muffins, *page 120*
English Muffin Bread, *page 121*

Rice, Beans, and Pasta
Black Bean Pizza Dough, *page 178*

Grilling
Grilled Pizza, *page 343*

Holiday Cheer
Hot Cross Buns, *page 368*

SWEET TOOTH

Everyone loves sweets! And they're not just for your own enjoyment. Sweet treats are always welcome as an introductory hello to a new boat in an anchorage or as a fond farewell to cruising friends when you part ways. And sweets at a potluck often are devoured before the meal even begins!

Many of our recipes use oil instead of shortening or butter. Oil is easier to mix in by hand, it's easier to store since it doesn't require refrigeration, and it's generally healthier. We've included made-from-scratch cakes, piecrusts, and pies as well as more than 25 cookie recipes. And if it's too hot to contemplate heating up the boat by lighting the oven (or if you're running low on propane), there are even seven no-bake cookie recipes to satisfy your sweet tooth! Don't feel like cookies? There are many extras, such as from-scratch cheesecake made without cream cheese just in case you can't find it. Plus the ultimate treat for kids—Peanut Butter Play-Doh!

CAKES, FROSTINGS, AND OTHER TOPPINGS

There are several challenges in making a cake aboard a cruising boat, but our recipes are designed to overcome them: they're easy to mix with just a spoon, they're forgiving of ovens that aren't true to temperature, they're flexible about pan sizes, and we provide lots of frosting alternatives that don't require an electric mixer. If needed, read more about solving oven problems (page 15) and changing pan sizes (page 8).

With these recipes and tips, you'll have great results even if you've never made a cake from scratch before!

Chocolate Cake   Serves 6 to 8

Total Time: 45 minutes
Prep Time: 10 minutes   **Bake Time:** 35 minutes

$1^{1}/_{2}$ cups flour
$1/_{4}$ cup unsweetened baking cocoa
$3/_{4}$ cup sugar
1 teaspoon salt
$2^{1}/_{2}$ teaspoons baking powder (page 376)
1 egg
$1/_{2}$ cup milk or water
$1/_{4}$ cup canola oil or vegetable oil, or butter or margarine, melted
1 teaspoon vanilla extract, fruit juice, or liqueur of your choice

1. Preheat oven to 350°F.
3. Mix the flour, cocoa, sugar, salt, and baking powder in a large bowl. Mix the egg, milk, oil, and vanilla in a cup or small bowl. Add the egg mixture to the flour mixture and stir until well combined.
4. Pour the batter into a greased 9"×5" loaf pan.* Bake for 30 to 35 minutes, or until a toothpick inserted in the center comes out clean. Let cool at least 15 minutes before cutting.

For an 8-inch or 9-inch round or square pan, double the recipe and bake for about the same time.

Yellow Cake
Serves 6 to 8

This cake won't be as "yellow" as one from a box mix, which has yellow coloring added. If you have yellow food coloring, you can add up to 1 teaspoon.

Total Time: 45 minutes
Prep Time: 10 minutes   **Bake Time:** 35 minutes

1½ cups flour
¾ cup sugar
1 teaspoon salt
2½ teaspoons baking powder (page 376)
1 egg
½ cup milk or water
¼ cup canola oil or vegetable oil, or butter or
   margarine, melted
1 teaspoon vanilla extract, fruit juice, or liqueur of
   your choice

1. Preheat oven to 350°F.
2. Mix the flour, sugar, salt, and baking powder in a large bowl. In a small bowl, mix the egg, milk, oil, and vanilla. Add the egg mixture to the flour mixture and stir until well combined.
3. Pour the batter into a greased 9"×5" loaf pan.* Bake for 30 to 35 minutes, or until a toothpick inserted in the center comes out clean. Let cool at least 15 minutes before cutting.

*For an 8-inch or 9-inch round or square pan, double the recipe and bake for about the same time.

White Cake
Serves 6 to 8

Total Time: 45 minutes
Prep Time: 10 minutes   **Bake Time:** 35 minutes

1½ cups flour
¾ cup sugar
1 teaspoon salt
2½ teaspoons baking powder (page 376)
2 egg whites (you can use 1 whole egg, but the cake
   won't be pure white)
½ cup milk or water
¼ cup shortening, melted (this will produce the
   "whitest" cake), or canola oil or vegetable oil,
   or butter or margarine, melted
1 teaspoon Triple Sec or other clear liqueur with
   agreeable flavor or vanilla extract

1. Preheat oven to 350°F.
2. Mix the flour, sugar, salt, and baking powder in a large bowl. Mix the egg whites, milk, shortening, and Triple Sec in a cup or small bowl. Add the egg mixture to the flour mixture and stir until well combined.
3. Pour the batter into a greased 9"×5" loaf pan.* Bake for 30 to 35 minutes, or until a toothpick inserted in the center comes out clean. Let cool at least 15 minutes before cutting.

*For an 8-inch or 9-inch round or square pan, double the recipe and bake for about the same time.

Spice Cake
Serves 6 to 8

Good without a frosting or with just a dusting of confectioners' sugar, but if you want a decadent treat, add the topping from Betty Macy's Oatmeal Cake (page 411).

Total Time: 45 minutes
Prep Time: 10 minutes   **Bake Time:** 35 minutes

1½ cups flour
¾ cup sugar
1 teaspoon salt
2½ teaspoons baking powder (page 376)
½ teaspoon ground cinnamon*
¼ teaspoon ground nutmeg*
⅛ teaspoon ground cloves*
¼ teaspoon ground allspice*
1 egg
½ cup milk or water
¼ cup canola oil or vegetable oil, or butter or
   margarine, melted
1 teaspoon vanilla extract, fruit juice, or liqueur of
   your choice

*If necessary, substitute 1 teaspoon ground cinnamon or ground allspice for all the spices.

1. Preheat oven to 350°F.
2. Mix the flour, sugar, salt, baking powder, and spices in a large bowl. Mix the egg, milk, oil, and vanilla in a cup or small bowl. Add the egg mixture to the flour mixture and stir until well combined.
3. Pour the batter into a greased 9"×5" loaf pan. Bake for 30 to 35 minutes, or until a toothpick inserted in the center comes out clean. Let cool at least

15 minutes before cutting. (For an 8-inch or 9-inch round or square pan, double the recipe and bake for about the same time.)

Mayonnaise Cake   Serves 9

Total Time: 45 minutes
Prep Time: 20 minutes   **Bake Time:** 25 to 30 minutes

½ cup unsweetened baking cocoa
2 cups flour
1½ teaspoons baking soda
¼ teaspoon salt
1 cup sugar
¾ cup mayonnaise (do not use Miracle Whip)
1 cup water
1 teaspoon vanilla extract

1. Preheat oven to 350°F.
2. Mix the cocoa, flour, baking soda, and salt in a small bowl or measuring cup. In a medium bowl, cream together the sugar and mayonnaise. In another cup or small bowl, mix the water with the vanilla.
3. Add the flour mixture to the mayonnaise mixture, alternating with the water mixture. Beat well after each addition.
4. Grease and flour a 9-inch square pan and pour in the batter. Bake for 25 to 30 minutes, or until a toothpick inserted in the center of the cake comes out clean.

Hot 'n' Gooey Chocolate Cake   Makes 10 to 12 servings

Can be served warm with Hot Fudge Sauce (page 410) and whipped cream.

Total Time: 1½ hours, including 15 minutes to cool
Prep Time: 15 minutes   **Bake Time:** 1 hour

½ cup plus 1 tablespoon canola oil or vegetable oil
4 eggs
1 cup sugar
1 cup flour
½ cup unsweetened baking cocoa
2 teaspoons baking powder (page 376)
⅛ teaspoon baking soda
½ cup milk
1 teaspoon vanilla extract

1. Preheat oven to 350°F. Grease and flour a 9-inch tube pan or Bundt pan or 9"×13" cake pan (shake out excess flour).
2. Beat the oil, eggs, and sugar in a large bowl until the mixture is light and lemon colored. In a medium bowl mix the flour, cocoa, baking powder, and baking soda. Add the flour mixture to the egg mixture, alternating with the milk and vanilla. Beat until well blended.
3. Pour the batter into the prepared pan. Bake about 1 hour, or until a toothpick inserted in the center of the cake comes out clean. Let cool for 10 to 20 minutes in the pan. Invert the cake onto a platter if using a tube or Bundt pan. If using a 9"×13" pan, leave the cake in the pan.

Pineapple Angel Food Cake   Serves 12

For those who can get box mixes, this simple cake doesn't require an electric mixer and tastes great without frosting!

Total Time: 40 minutes
Prep Time: 10 minutes   **Bake Time:** 30 minutes

1 box angel food cake mix
1 can (20 ounces) crushed pineapple, with juice

1. Preheat oven to 350°F.
2. Combine the cake mix and pineapple with juice— nothing else!
3. Pour the batter into an ungreased 9"×13" pan, and bake for 30 minutes.

Carrot Cake and Cream Cheese Frosting   Serves 12 to 15

The cream cheese frosting is difficult (but not impossible) to make without an electric beater. The cake is still great without it!

Total Time: 1 hour, 15 minutes (plus time to let cool and frost, if desired)
Prep Time: 20 minutes   **Bake Time:** 45 minutes
(See notes on next page to make a smaller cake)

Sweet Tooth

Cake

2 cups flour
2 teaspoons baking soda
1 teaspoon baking powder (page 376)
1 teaspoon salt
2 teaspoons ground cinnamon
1¾ cups sugar
1 cup canola oil or vegetable oil
3 eggs
1 teaspoon vanilla extract
2 cups shredded carrot*
1 cup coconut (flaked or shredded)
1 cup chopped walnuts
1 can (8 ounces) crushed pineapple, drained

Frosting

¼ cup butter or margarine, softened
8 ounces cream cheese, softened
2 cups confectioners' sugar

*You can shred the carrot using a grater or a vegetable peeler.

1. Preheat oven to 350°F. Grease and flour a 9"×13" pan.
2. Mix the flour, baking soda, baking powder, salt, and cinnamon together in a large bowl. Make a well in the center of the dry ingredients and add the sugar, oil, eggs, and vanilla. Mix with a spoon until smooth. Stir in the carrot, coconut, walnuts, and pineapple.
3. Pour the batter into the prepared pan and bake for about 45 minutes, or until a toothpick inserted in the center of the cake comes out clean. Don't panic if the center of the cake sinks a little as it bakes—that's normal.
4. This cake is good as is, or dust the top with confectioners' sugar if desired. If you want to frost it, let it cool first.

NOTE: To make an 8-inch square cake (9 smaller servings), make half a batch, using 2 eggs and only ⅞ cup oil. Roughly divide the can of pineapple in half. The baking time is approximately the same. To make a 9"×5" loaf cake (6 servings), make one-third of a batch. Begin checking for doneness at 35 minutes.

Sweet Tooth

5. To make the frosting, cream the butter and cream cheese until smooth. This is hard without an electric mixer, but it can be done if you're feeling strong and the cream cheese is very soft. Add the confectioners' sugar and beat until creamy. If you're mixing it by hand, you'll be more than ready for a piece of the cake by the time you're done!

White Buttercream Frosting

2 cups

This frosting is much easier to make with an electric beater. Without one, use very soft shortening and butter and the back of a spoon to work in the confectioners' sugar, then use the spoon with a more normal beating motion to fluff up the frosting before putting it on a cake. (Let the cake cool before frosting it.)

Total Time: 10 minutes

⅓ cup shortening (you can use all butter, but the frosting won't be as "white")
⅓ cup butter or margarine (if unsalted, add ⅛ teaspoon extra salt)
¼ cup cream, half-and-half (*media crema*), evaporated milk, or milk
⅛ teaspoon salt
1½ teaspoons vanilla extract, almond flavoring, or flavored liqueur such as Triple Sec
3½ cups confectioners' sugar, sifted (may need slightly more or less)
2 to 4 drops food coloring (to make colored frosting, if desired)

1. Beat the shortening and butter together in a large bowl until they are totally blended. Add the cream, salt, and vanilla and beat again to combine.
2. Add 2 cups of the confectioners' sugar and mix well. Continue adding confectioners' sugar ½ cup (or less) at a time until you reach the consistency you want (if the batter becomes too stiff, add a few drops of cream, milk, or water). Add the food coloring if desired (don't add too much or the frosting will curdle) and beat until the color is uniform.

Chocolate Buttercream Frosting
2 cups

See note above to make this frosting without an electric mixer.

Total Time: 10 minutes

$^1/_2$ cup butter or margarine, softened
$^1/_3$ cup cream, half-and-half (*media crema*), evaporated milk, or milk
$1^1/_2$ teaspoons vanilla extract, almond flavoring, Triple Sec, or orange juice
$^1/_2$ cup unsweetened baking cocoa (you can use up to $^3/_4$ cup for a darker chocolate frosting)
$2^1/_2$ cups confectioners' sugar (you may need slightly more or less)

1. Cream the butter in a medium bowl. Add the cream and vanilla and blend well.
2. In a small bowl combine the cocoa and confectioners' sugar until totally blended. Add to the butter mixture, starting with about half the confectioners' sugar mixture and adding more a little at a time. If needed, add a few more drops of cream or a little more confectioners' sugar to reach the desired consistency.

Drizzle Frostings

Drizzle frostings are a great alternative to traditional frostings on a boat. Basically, they're like the frosting you see drizzled on the top of coffee cakes and pastries. Mix the ingredients and then let the frosting run off a spoon in a pretty pattern all over the top of the cake (or cookies). For all the drizzle frosting recipes, add confectioners' sugar or a few drops of water to make the frosting thicker or thinner as needed.

Peanut Butter Chocolate Drizzle

This is actually a "double drizzle"!

Chocolate Drizzle
2 ounces chocolate chips OR milk chocolate bar

Melt the chocolate chips and drizzle the chocolate over the cake. (Or you can substitute the Chocolate Drizzle made from cocoa, below.)

Peanut Butter Drizzle
$^3/_4$ cup confectioners' sugar
$^1/_4$ cup creamy peanut butter
milk, as needed

Mix the confectioners' sugar and peanut butter, then add milk a little at a time until the mixture is thin enough to drizzle. Drizzle it over the Chocolate Drizzle (above) or Cocoa Chocolate Drizzle (below) in an overlapping pattern.

Cocoa Chocolate Drizzle

3 tablespoons unsweetened baking cocoa
1 cup confectioners' sugar
4 teaspoons butter or margarine, melted
2 tablespoons milk or water, or as needed

Mix the cocoa and confectioners' sugar in a bowl. Add the butter and half the milk and beat until smooth. Add more milk a little at a time, beating well after each addition, until the desired consistency is reached.

Tangerine Drizzle

juice from 4 or 5 tangerines OR $^1/_4$ cup orange juice
$^3/_4$ cup confectioners' sugar

Mix the juice and confectioners' sugar. If desired, decorate with some tangerine or mandarin orange sections and/or add a drop *each* of yellow and red food coloring to make the drizzle a pale orange.

Clove Drizzle

Good on a chocolate or spice cake.

$^3/_4$ cup confectioners' sugar
$^1/_4$ teaspoon ground cloves
sprinkling of ground cinnamon
3 to 4 tablespoons water, or as needed

Mix the confectioners' sugar, cloves, and cinnamon. Add 2 tablespoons of the water, then add more a little at a time until the consistency is right.

Sweet Tooth

Other Easy Drizzles

- Nutella—thin with a little milk
- honey
- Chocolate Syrup (page 410), good with a few nuts sprinkled over the top
- Butterscotch Sauce (page 410)
- Hot Fudge Sauce (page 410)
- caramel *dulce de leche* (caramel-flavored sweetened condensed milk found in Latin America and in the Latin food sections of large supermarkets in the US)

Butterscotch Sauce

Total Time: 10 minutes

2 cups packed brown sugar
1/2 cup cream or evaporated milk
4 tablespoons butter or margarine
1/4 cup corn syrup (dark or light)

1. Mix the brown sugar, milk, butter, and corn syrup in a medium saucepan. Warm over medium heat until the sugar is dissolved, stirring frequently.
2. Turn the heat to high and bring to a full rolling boil. Turn off the heat and allow to cool slightly, stirring occasionally. Serve warm. Keep any unused portion in the refrigerator and warm slightly before using.

Chocolate Syrup

Total Time: 10 minutes, plus time to cool

1/2 cup unsweetened baking cocoa
1 cup water
2 cups sugar
1/8 teaspoon salt
1/2 teaspoon vanilla extract

1. Mix the cocoa, water, sugar, and salt in a large saucepan. Warm over medium-low heat until the sugar is dissolved, stirring frequently.
2. Turn the heat to high and bring the mixture to a full rolling boil. Reduce the heat to medium-low and continue boiling for 3 minutes. (Time this— boiling the syrup too long or not long enough will have unsatisfactory results.)

3. Remove from the heat and stir in the vanilla. Allow to cool, then store in a tight-lidded container. Keep any unused portion in the refrigerator.

Hot Fudge Sauce

Total Time: 15 minutes

1/2 cup unsweetened baking cocoa
1 cup sugar
1 cup corn syrup (dark or light)
1/2 cup evaporated milk, half-and-half (*media crema*), or cream
2 tablespoons butter or margarine
1/4 teaspoon salt
1 teaspoon vanilla extract

1. Combine the cocoa, sugar, corn syrup, milk, butter, and salt in a large saucepan. Warm over medium-low heat until the sugar is dissolved, stirring frequently.
2. Turn the heat to high and bring the mixture to a full rolling boil. Reduce the heat to medium-low and continue boiling for 3 minutes. (Time this— boiling the fudge sauce too long or not long enough will have unsatisfactory results.)
3. Remove from the heat and stir in the vanilla. Allow to cool, then store in a tight-lidded container. Keep any unused portion in the refrigerator.

3-Minute Microwave Chocolate Mug Cake   Serves 2

Great for those who have a microwave! You'll need one microwave-safe coffee mug for this cake.

Total Time: 5 minutes
Prep Time: 2 minutes
Bake Time: 3 minutes at 1,000 watts

4 tablespoons flour
4 tablespoons sugar
2 tablespoons unsweetened baking cocoa
1 egg
3 tablespoons milk or water
3 tablespoons canola oil or vegetable oil
3 tablespoons chocolate chips (mini chips are best), optional
1/8 teaspoon vanilla extract

1. Place the flour, sugar, and cocoa in a microwave-safe mug and combine well. Add the egg and mix thoroughly. Pour in the milk and oil and blend well. Add the chocolate chips, if desired, and the vanilla and mix again.
2. Put the mug in the microwave and cook for 3 minutes at 1,000 watts (the time may vary with the microwave and whether you're running it from shore power, a generator, or an inverter). The cake will rise over the top of the mug, but don't be alarmed! Allow it to cool a little, and tip the cake out onto a plate (you may have to run a knife around the edge to get it out). Cut it into two pieces and serve warm.

Betty Macy's Oatmeal Cake

Serves 8 to 10

Another of our Y-Flyer sailing friends, Betty lives on the same lake we do. Her oatmeal cake is always a crowd-pleaser at our fleet parties!

Total Time: 60 minutes
Prep Time: 20 minutes
Bake Time: 30 minutes, plus 5 minutes under a broiler

Cake
1¼ cups boiling water
1 cup oats (old-fashioned, quick cooking, or instant are equally good)
½ cup shortening, butter, or margarine, softened
1 cup packed brown sugar
1 cup white sugar
1 teaspoon vanilla extract
2 eggs
1½ cups flour
¼ teaspoon salt
1 teaspoon baking soda
½ teaspoon ground cinnamon

Topping
¼ cup butter or margarine, softened
½ cup packed brown sugar
¼ cup cream, half-and-half (*media crema*), evaporated milk, or milk
½ teaspoon vanilla extract
1⅓ cups flaked or shredded coconut
½ cup chopped pecans or walnuts

1. Preheat oven to 350°F.
2. Pour the boiling water over the oats and let stand while making the cake.*

*IMPORTANT: The first time I made this cake, I tried to cook the oats with the water in a pan as though I were making oatmeal for breakfast. But there's a lot less water in this recipe, and the oats scorched—badly—before I realized it. Learn from my mistake: put the oats in a small bowl, then pour the boiling water over them and let sit. It will form a thick glob—that's fine.

3. Use the back of a spoon to cream together the shortening, brown sugar, white sugar, and vanilla in a medium bowl. If the shortening is soft, it's easy to mix it in by hand. Add the eggs and beat so that the mixture is well combined.
4. Add the oat mixture and use your spoon to break up the "blob" a bit. Then start mixing and the blob will break into small pieces—it's okay if the mixture is still a little lumpy.
5. Mix together the flour, salt, baking soda, and cinnamon in a measuring cup or a small bowl, then add it to the oat mixture. Stir until it's all mixed in, and then beat 20 to 30 strokes so that it's a little fluffy.
6. Pour the batter into a greased 9"×13" pan and bake for 30 to 40 minutes, or until a toothpick or knife inserted into the center comes out clean.
7. While the cake is baking, mix the Topping ingredients in a small bowl.
8. When the cake is done, quickly spread the Topping on it, then put it under a broiler (if you have one) for about 5 minutes, or until the Topping bubbles. If you don't have a broiler, let the cake cool somewhat (it doesn't have to be totally cool) while you put the Topping mixture into a small saucepan over medium heat until it just starts to boil, stirring occasionally. Spread it over the partially cooled cake. Serve warm or at room temperature.

Sweet Tooth

Chocolate Upside-Down Cake

Serves 8 or 9

This was Carolyn's great-grandmother's recipe from homesteading in the Dakotas and has been a favorite in our family for generations.

Total Time: 55 minutes
Prep Time: 20 minutes   **Bake Time:** 35 minutes

Cake

1 cup flour
2 teaspoons baking powder (page 376)
1/4 teaspoon salt
1 1/2 tablespoons unsweetened baking cocoa
3/4 cup sugar
1/2 cup milk
2 tablespoons butter or margarine, melted, or
    canola oil or vegetable oil
1/2 teaspoon vanilla extract
1/2 cup chopped nuts

Topping

1/2 cup packed brown sugar (if not available, use
    white sugar and a smidge of honey or molasses)
1/2 cup white sugar
5 tablespoons unsweetened baking cocoa
1 cup boiling water

1. Preheat oven to 350°F.
2. Place all the cake ingredients in a large bowl and stir to mix. Scrape the batter into an ungreased 8-inch square pan (a 9"×5" loaf pan also works well). Let sit while you prepare the Topping, which can be made in the same bowl (you don't need to wash the bowl after pouring out the batter).
3. For the Topping, mix all the Topping ingredients together and spoon over the batter in the baking pan. The batter may start to float to the surface—that's what makes it "upside down" (sometimes it happens immediately, sometimes in the oven as it bakes). Bake for 35 minutes, or until the top is uniformly dry, although the Topping mixture may bubble around the sides. Don't overbake! Allow to cool.
4. To serve, cut the cake into pieces and slip a spatula under one slice. Carefully lift it out of the pan and flip it upside down onto a plate—the gooey

Topping will now be on top. Generally not all the Topping will have come out of the pan. If this happens, scrape out the extra and smooth it over the top of the slice. Repeat for all the slices.

Gingerbread Cake

Serves 9

Total Time: 1 hour, 5 minutes
Prep Time: 20 minutes   **Bake Time:** 45 minutes

cooking spray or oil
1/2 cup shortening, butter, or margarine, softened
1/3 cup white sugar or packed brown sugar
2/3 cup molasses
2 eggs
1 3/4 cups flour
1/2 teaspoon salt
1 tablespoon baking powder (page 376)
1 1/2 teaspoons ground ginger
1 teaspoon ground cinnamon
1/2 teaspoon ground nutmeg
1/4 teaspoon ground cloves
2/3 cup milk

1. Preheat oven to 350°F. Spritz an 8-inch square pan with cooking spray or wipe with oil.
2. In a medium bowl, cream together the shortening, sugar, molasses, and eggs. If you don't have an electric beater, use very soft shortening (but not melted) and mix in the sugar, then the molasses, until well combined. Then add the eggs and beat until light.
3. In a measuring cup or a small bowl, mix together the flour, salt, baking powder, and spices. Pour the milk into another measuring cup.
4. Add half the flour mixture and half the milk to the shortening mixture and beat until well combined. Then add the remaining flour mixture and the rest of the milk and beat again until well mixed and light.
5. Spread the batter into the greased pan. Bake for 35 to 45 minutes, or until a toothpick inserted into the center comes out clean. Let cool for at least 5 to 10 minutes.
6. The cake may be served warm or at room temperature. Cut it into 9 pieces. Great with whipped cream (hard to find in many locations) or a dollop

of sweetened vanilla yogurt (page 101) or frozen yogurt (page 103).

Gingerbread-Beer Cake   Serves 9

A half batch nicely fills a loaf pan—use just one egg instead of three eggs, and add an extra 2 tablespoons of beer. This cake tends to stick, so take care when preparing the pan. Instead of cooking spray and oil, you can line the pan with aluminum foil (or waxed paper) and leave the excess folded over the sides to lift out the cake after it is baked. Don't forget to grease the foil.

Total Time: 1 hour, 5 minutes
Prep Time: 15 minutes   **Bake Time:** 50 minutes

1 cup beer (dark is great), coffee, water, or milk
1 cup molasses
$\frac{1}{2}$ teaspoon baking soda
2 cups flour
$1\frac{1}{2}$ teaspoons baking powder (page 376)
2 tablespoons ground ginger
1 teaspoon ground cinnamon
$\frac{1}{4}$ teaspoon ground cloves
$\frac{1}{4}$ teaspoon ground nutmeg
$\frac{3}{4}$ cup canola oil or vegetable oil (olive oil has too strong a taste)
1 cup packed brown sugar or white sugar
1 cup white sugar
3 eggs

1. Preheat oven to 350°F. Prepare a 9-inch square pan with cooking spray, or grease it well and dust with flour.
2. Boil the beer and molasses in a large saucepan. (Use a larger pan than seems necessary; the mixture will foam up when you add the baking soda.) Turn off the heat and mix in the baking soda.
3. Pour the beer mixture into a medium bowl and let cool while you prepare the flour mixture.
4. Mix the flour, baking powder, and spices in a small bowl or measuring cup; set aside.
5. Add the oil to the beer mixture and mix well. Add both sugars and combine well. At this point, the mixture should be close to room temperature. If it is warmer, wait for it to cool a bit more before adding the eggs (you don't want them to cook in the bowl).
6. Add the eggs to the beer mixture and beat until the mixture is light. Beat in half the flour mixture until well combined, then beat in the other half.
7. Pour the batter into the prepared pan and bake for 45 to 50 minutes. To test for doneness, insert a toothpick in the center. When the cake is done, some crumbs will stick to the toothpick when you remove it. If the toothpick is covered with batter, the cake needs to bake a little longer. Do not over-bake—the cake will be overdone and dry if the toothpick is completely clean.
8. Let the cake cool at least partially in the pan (until you can touch the pan comfortably), then lift out the cake with the foil or waxed paper if used. Otherwise, just leave the cake in the pan. Cut into pieces when you are ready to serve. This is great warm!

Holding Ground
Mud Cake   Serves 6

Here's a great cake that uses no eggs or milk. It comes all the way from Gringo Bay, Rio Dulce, Guatemala, and Jennifer Lindeen! You may add ground cinnamon for a "Mexican" taste, glaze it with Cocoa Chocolate Drizzle Frosting (see page 409), or add instant coffee for a mocha flavor.

Total Time: 40 minutes
Prep Time: 10 minutes   **Bake Time:** 30 minutes

$1\frac{1}{2}$ cups flour
3 to 5 heaping tablespoons unsweetened baking cocoa
1 teaspoon baking soda
1 cup sugar
$\frac{1}{2}$ teaspoon salt
$\frac{1}{3}$ cup canola oil or vegetable oil
1 tablespoon white vinegar
1 teaspoon vanilla extract
1 cup cold water, orange juice, or milk

1. Preheat oven to 350°F. Grease a round cake pan, an 8-inch square pan, or even a loaf pan.

Sweet Tooth

2. In a large bowl combine the flour, cocoa, baking soda, sugar, and salt. In a small bowl combine the oil, vinegar, vanilla, and water. Add the oil mixture to the flour mixture and stir to combine thoroughly.

3. Pour the batter into the prepared pan and bake about 30 minutes, or until a toothpick inserted in the center comes out clean.

Pineapple Upside-Down Cake

Serves 6 to 8

Total Time: 45 minutes
Prep Time: 15 minutes   Bake Time: 30 minutes

2 tablespoons butter or margarine, softened
3 tablespoons brown sugar or white sugar
1 can (8 ounces) pineapple (see instructions on draining in step 3 below) or other canned fruit OR ¾ cup chopped (bite size) fresh fruit OR ¾ cup chopped dried fruit*
¼ cup broken nuts (optional)
1 cup flour
1½ teaspoons baking powder (page 376)
½ teaspoon salt
¾ cup white sugar
1 egg
¼ cup canola oil or vegetable oil, or butter or margarine, melted (do not use olive oil as it has too strong a flavor)
½ cup milk
½ teaspoon vanilla extract

This is good made with peaches, mandarin oranges, raisins, dates, apricots, apples, cranberries, or strawberries, but almost any type of fruit can be used.

1. Preheat oven to 350°F.
2. In a small bowl mix the butter and brown sugar. Spread the mixture in the bottom of an ungreased 9"×5" loaf pan.

3. Drain the pineapple (if desired, reserve the juice and use it in place of part of the milk in the cake). If using pineapple rings, lay them in the bottom of the pan so they are not overlapping. Otherwise, spread the fruit over the butter/brown sugar mixture. Sprinkle with the nuts and set aside.

4. Combine the flour, baking powder, salt, and white sugar in a small mixing bowl. In a cup or small bowl, beat the egg slightly and add the oil, milk, and vanilla. Add the egg mixture to the flour mixture and stir to combine well.

5. Pour the cake batter over the pineapple in the pan. Bake for 30 minutes, or until a toothpick inserted in the center comes out clean.

6. Let the cake cool in the pan before serving. The cake can be served warm, but it's hard to remove from the pan until it cools at least somewhat. Flip the pieces as you place them on a plate so that the pineapple side is up.

COOKIES: TRADITIONAL, NO-BAKE, AND BAR

Everybody loves cookies, but most people find them hard to make on a boat. We've come up with 27 great-tasting, boat-friendly cookie recipes:

- Almost all are easy to make without an electric mixer.
- Some are baked "traditionally" in batches—good on a cool day!
- Bar cookies baked in a pan all at once are good on a warm day!
- No-bake cookies are good if you don't have an oven or if it's a really hot day.

If your oven has hot spots, be sure to read about troubleshooting oven problems (page 15), and strongly consider getting a baking stone—it will make all your baked goods turn out much better.

Dishpan Cookies   Makes about 3 dozen

Total Time: About 1 hour, depending on how many cookies you can bake at once
Prep Time: 20 minutes
Bake Time: 7 to 8 minutes per batch

1 cup white sugar
1 cup packed brown sugar, or white sugar plus a touch of molasses or honey
1 cup canola oil or vegetable oil (olive oil has too strong a taste)
2 eggs
1 teaspoon vanilla extract (optional)
2 cups flour
1 teaspoon baking soda
1 teaspoon salt
1/2 cup oats (instant or regular work equally well)
1 1/3 cups cornflakes, Wheaties, Raisin Bran, or similar cereal
2/3 cup flaked or shredded coconut*
2/3 cup (4 ounces) chocolate chips*
1/3 cup raisins*
1/3 cup chopped walnuts or pecans*

For all these ingredients, substitute a total of 1 1/2 to 2 cups chopped nuts, chopped moist dried fruits, and/or chocolate bits, chunks, or candies (M&M's are great)—any combination works well!

1. Preheat oven to 400°F.
2. In a large bowl mix the sugars and oil. Add the eggs and vanilla; mix well. Add the flour, baking soda, and salt, and stir to combine. Add the cereals and mix thoroughly. Add the coconut, chocolate chips, raisins, and nuts (or any substitutes); mix well.
3. Shape the mixture into 1 1/2-inch balls and arrange on an ungreased cookie sheet or aluminum foil; bake for 7 to 8 minutes. The cookies should be golden, but soft and moist, not hard. Transfer to a wire rack to cool. Store in an airtight container.

Peanut Butter Cookies   Makes about 3 dozen

Total Time: 45 minutes
Prep Time: 10 minutes
Bake Time: 9 minutes per batch (three batches)

1 cup packed brown sugar or white sugar
1/2 cup canola oil or vegetable oil (olive oil has too strong a flavor)
1 cup peanut butter
1/4 teaspoon salt
1/2 teaspoon vanilla extract (optional)
2 tablespoons milk or water
1 egg
1 3/4 cups flour
2 teaspoons baking powder (page 376)

NOTE: If you first measure the brown sugar, then the oil, then the peanut butter, you won't have anything sticking in the measuring cup.

1. Preheat oven to 375°F.
2. In a medium bowl mix the brown sugar, oil, peanut butter, salt, vanilla, milk, and egg. Add the flour and baking powder and mix well.
3. Shape the dough into 1-inch to 1 1/4-inch balls and place on a greased cookie sheet, or grease a double sheet of aluminum foil. Use a fork to flatten the cookies, as shown in the photo. Bake for 9 minutes, then transfer to a wire rack to cool.

Sweet Tooth

Ginger Snaps
Makes about 2 dozen

Total Time: 1 hour
Prep Time: 15 minutes
Bake Time: 10 minutes per batch, plus time to cool the cookie sheet between batches

²/₃ cup canola oil or vegetable oil (olive oil has too much flavor)
¹/₂ cup white sugar
¹/₂ cup packed brown sugar or white sugar
¹/₄ cup molasses
1 egg
1 teaspoons vanilla extract
2 cups flour (you can use up to half whole wheat flour)
2 teaspoons baking soda
¹/₄ teaspoon salt
1 teaspoon ground cinnamon
1 teaspoon ground ginger
¹/₂ teaspoon ground cloves
extra sugar to sprinkle over top

1. Preheat oven to 375°F.
2. Mix the oil, sugars, molasses, egg, and vanilla.
3. In a small bowl mix the flour, baking soda, salt, and spices so that the baking soda and spices are evenly distributed. Add the flour mixture to the molasses mixture.
4. Shape the mixture into 1-inch balls (the mixture will be soft) and place 3 inches apart on a greased cookie sheet (as they bake, the cookies will become 3-inch flat circles). Sprinkle some sugar over each cookie. Bake for 9 minutes.
5. Let cool on the cookie sheet for a minute or two before moving to a wire rack or plate.

Chocolate Drops
Makes about 3 dozen

Total Time: 1 hour
Prep Time: 15 minutes
Bake Time: About 12 minutes per batch, plus time to cool the cookie sheet between batches

2 cups sugar
³/₄ cup canola oil or vegetable oil
³/₄ cup unsweetened baking cocoa

4 eggs
2 teaspoons vanilla extract
2¹/₃ cups flour
2 teaspoons baking powder (page 376)
¹/₂ teaspoon salt
1 cup confectioners' sugar

1. Preheat oven to 350°F.
2. In a large bowl stir together the sugar, oil, and cocoa. Add the eggs and vanilla and beat well. Add the flour, baking powder, and salt, and mix well. The dough will be soft.
3. Drop the dough by teaspoonfuls onto a greased cookie sheet and sprinkle with the confectioners' sugar. Bake about 12 minutes, or until the tops are slightly cracked. Remove the cookies from the pan to cool, and let the pan cool completely before dropping another batch onto it. If the pan is still warm, the mounds of dough will melt into a large "puddle."

Honey-Nut Oatmeal Cookies
Makes about 2 dozen

Total Time: 45 minutes
Prep Time: 15 minutes
Bake Time: 8 minutes per batch, plus time to cool the cookie sheet between batches

²/₃ cup honey
1 egg
¹/₄ cup canola oil or vegetable oil
1 cup flour (white, whole wheat, or a mixture are all good)
1 cup oats (regular or instant)
¹/₂ teaspoon baking powder (page 376)
¹/₄ teaspoon salt
²/₃ cup chopped walnuts or pecans
¹/₃ cup dried cranberries (optional) or other chopped dried fruit

1. Preheat oven to 350°F.
2. Mix the honey, egg, and oil in a medium bowl. Add all the remaining ingredients and mix well.
3. Drop the dough by teaspoonfuls onto a greased cookie sheet. Bake about 8 minutes. Remove the pan from the oven and let sit for about 2 minutes

to allow the cookies to firm up a bit before removing them to cool. Let the pan cool before putting another batch onto it.

Chocolate Chip Cookies
Makes 2 to 3 dozen

If you don't have an electric mixer, make sure that the shortening is very soft (but not melted). This recipe can be used to make traditional cookies or bars.

Total Time: 1 hour
Prep Time: 15 minutes
Bake Time: 9 minutes per batch for individual cookies, or 20 minutes for bar cookies

1 cup shortening, butter, or margarine, softened
3/4 cup white sugar
3/4 cup packed brown sugar
1 teaspoon vanilla extract
2 eggs
2 1/4 cups flour
1 teaspoon baking soda
1 teaspoon salt
2 cups (12 ounces) chocolate chips*
1 cup chopped nuts (optional)

*If you can't get chocolate chips, chop up dark chocolate or milk chocolate bars, or use M&M's or Reese's Pieces. The cookies won't be traditional Toll-House cookies, but they will still be good!

1. Preheat oven to 375°F.
2. Cream the shortening and sugars in a large bowl. Add the vanilla and eggs and beat well. In a measuring cup mix the flour, baking soda, and salt. Gradually add the flour mixture to the sugar mixture, stirring well after each addition. Add the chocolate chips and nuts (if desired) and mix well.
3. Drop by spoonfuls onto a greased cookie sheet. Bake about 9 minutes, or until the edges are golden but the centers are still fairly pale (assuming you like really soft, melt-in-your-mouth cookies). Remove the pan from the oven and let the cookies sit for about 2 minutes to firm up before moving them to wire racks. Let the pan cool before dropping the next batch of dough onto it.

Variation: Instead of making cookies, make bars! Spread the dough in a 9"×13" pan and bake for 20 to 25 minutes. Cut into bars when cool. Every bit as good, with a lot less oven time!

Margaret's Chocolate Chip Cookies
Makes 2 to 3 dozen

Margaret is Jan's mother. To mix the dough by hand, use very soft butter (but not melted).

Total Time: 1 hour
Prep Time: 15 minutes
Bake Time: 15 to 20 minutes per batch

2 1/2 cups flour
1 teaspoon baking soda
1 cup butter or margarine, softened
1/4 cup white sugar
3/4 cup packed brown sugar
1 teaspoon vanilla extract
1 box (4 servings) vanilla instant pudding mix
2 eggs
2 cups (12 ounces) chocolate chips
1 cup chopped nuts (optional)

1. Preheat oven to 300°F.
2. Mix the flour and baking soda. Set aside.
3. Combine the butter, the sugars, vanilla, and pudding mix in large bowl; beat until smooth and creamy. Beat in the eggs. Gradually add the flour mixture, then stir in the chocolate chips and nuts (if desired). The batter will be stiff.
4. Drop by rounded teaspoonfuls about 2 inches apart onto an ungreased cookie sheet. Bake for 15 to 20 minutes, depending on your oven. Be sure to watch the first batch—these cookies should be soft. If baked too long, they will be hard and tough.

Soft Sugar Cookies

Makes about 2 dozen

Total Time: 45 minutes
Prep Time: 15 minutes
Bake Time: 6 minutes per batch, plus time to cool the cookie sheet between batches

2 eggs
²/₃ cup canola oil or vegetable oil
2 teaspoons vanilla extract
³/₄ cup white sugar
2 cups flour
2 teaspoons baking powder (page 376)
¹/₂ teaspoon salt
sugar, for sprinkling

1. Preheat oven to 400°F.
2. In a medium bowl beat the eggs, oil, vanilla, and sugar. Mix in the flour, baking powder, and salt, taking care that all are completely incorporated.
3. Drop by teaspoonfuls on an ungreased cookie sheet. Sprinkle sugar over the top of the cookies. Bake for 6 minutes, or just until barely golden. Remove the pan from the oven and let the cookies sit about 2 minutes to firm up before moving them to wire racks. Let the pan cool before dropping the next batch of dough onto it.

Soft Snickerdoodle Cookies

Makes about 2 dozen

Total Time: 1 hour
Prep Time: 20 minutes
Bake Time: 10 minutes per batch, plus time to let the cookie sheet cool between batches

1 cup butter or margarine, softened
1¹/₂ cups sugar
2 eggs
2³/₄ cups flour
2 teaspoons cream of tartar
1 teaspoon baking soda
¹/₄ teaspoon salt
3 tablespoons sugar
3 teaspoons ground cinnamon

1. Preheat oven to 350°F.
2. Cream the butter and the 1¹/₂ cups sugar in a large bowl. Add the eggs and beat well to blend. Combine the flour, cream of tartar, baking soda, and salt in a small bowl. Add the flour mixture to the butter mixture, stirring until well combined.
3. If possible, chill the dough in the refrigerator for about 10 minutes. This will make the dough much easier to work with, but it is not strictly necessary.
4. While the dough is chilling, mix the 3 tablespoons sugar and the cinnamon in a small flat dish.
5. Shape the dough into 1-inch balls and roll them in the cinnamon sugar, then place them on an ungreased cookie sheet. Place the remaining dough in the refrigerator while the first batch bakes.
6. Bake the cookies for about 10 minutes and then transfer them to a wire rack immediately. Allow the pan to cool to room temperature before making another batch.

Soft Raisin Cookies

Makes about 4 dozen

If you'll be mixing the dough by hand, make sure that the shortening is very soft (but not melted).

Total Time: 1¹/₄ hours
Prep Time: 20 minutes
Bake Time: 12 minutes per batch

2 cups raisins
1 cup water
1 cup shortening, butter, or margarine, softened
1³/₄ cups sugar
2 eggs
1 teaspoon vanilla extract
3¹/₂ cups flour
1 teaspoon baking powder (page 376)
1 teaspoon baking soda
1 teaspoon salt
¹/₂ teaspoon ground cinnamon
¹/₂ teaspoon ground nutmeg
¹/₂ cup chopped walnuts (optional)

1. Preheat oven to 350°F.
2. Bring the raisins and water to a boil in a small saucepan. Turn down the heat and let simmer for 3 minutes to plump up the raisins. Turn off the

heat and let the raisins sit until needed—don't drain the water!

3. Cream the shortening and sugar in a large bowl. Add the eggs and vanilla and beat thoroughly. Add the dry ingredients and mix well. The dough will be very stiff. Add the nuts (if desired) and the plumped raisins, including the water that the raisins were boiled in. Mix well to combine.

4. Drop the dough by teaspoonfuls onto greased cookie sheets. Bake for 12 minutes, or until just golden brown. The centers should still be soft. Remove the pan from the oven and let the cookies sit for about 1 minute to firm up, then remove them to a plate to cool. Allow the pan to cool to room temperature before making another batch.

Zucchini Cookies
Makes about 2 dozen

Almost anywhere we cruised, we could get zucchini. In Latin American countries, you can often get zucchini in 250 ml (1 cup) Tetra Paks in the canned vegetable section of the grocery store. Buy some and keep them on hand for these treats! Where christophene (chayote) is a popular local squash, you can substitute it for the zucchini.

Total Time: 45 minutes
Prep Time: 15 minutes
Bake Time: 8 to 10 minutes per batch

1/4 cup butter or margarine, softened
1/2 cup packed brown sugar
1/2 cup white sugar
1 egg
1 1/2 cups grated zucchini
2 cups flour (whole wheat or white)
1 teaspoon baking soda
1/2 teaspoon salt
1 tablespoon ground cinnamon
1 pinch ground cloves
1 pinch ground nutmeg

1. Preheat oven to 375°F.
2. In a large bowl cream together the butter and sugars. Add the egg and beat well. Stir in the zucchini.
3. Mix together the flour, baking soda, salt, cinnamon, cloves, and nutmeg in a cup or small

bowl, then stir the flour mixture into the zucchini mixture.

4. Drop the dough by teaspoonfuls onto a greased cookie sheet. Bake for 8 to 10 minutes, or until just golden. Remove the pan from the oven and let the cookies sit for about 1 minute to firm up, then remove them to a plate to cool. Allow the pan to cool to room temperature before making another batch.

Sweet Potato Cookies
Makes about 3 dozen

Total Time: About 1 hour
Prep Time: 20 minutes
Bake Time: 15 minutes per batch

1 cup mashed sweet potato*
1/4 cup milk
1 egg
4 tablespoons butter or margarine, melted, or canola oil or vegetable oil
1 1/4 cups flour
2 teaspoons baking powder (page 376)
1/2 cup sugar
1/2 teaspoon salt
1 teaspoon ground cinnamon
1/2 cup raisins

Peel and boil the sweet potato, or bake it and then peel it. Mash it with a fork.

1. Preheat oven to 375°F.
2. Mix the mashed sweet potato, milk, egg, and butter. Stir in the remaining ingredients, making sure that all the flour is incorporated.
3. Drop the dough by teaspoonfuls onto a greased cookie sheet. Bake 15 minutes, or until golden. Remove from the cookie sheet to cool. Allow the pan to cool to room temperature before making another batch.

Sweet Tooth

Cookie-Cutter Sugar Cookies with Hard Icing
Makes about 3 dozen

These are much more labor intensive to make than any of the drop cookies, but they are good for a special occasion or on a rainy day with kids. If you don't have a cookie cutter, you can either cut the dough into squares or make a pattern from paper and cut around it. Easy shapes to cut include pumpkins for Halloween, hearts for Valentine's Day, Christmas trees for Christmas, and flags for the Fourth of July.

Total Time: About 2 hours

Cookies
1 cup butter or margarine, softened
1 cup sugar
2 eggs
1 teaspoon vanilla extract
3 $\frac{1}{4}$ cups flour
$\frac{1}{2}$ teaspoon baking soda
$\frac{1}{2}$ teaspoon baking powder (page 376)
$\frac{1}{2}$ teaspoon salt

Frosting
2 cups sifted confectioners' sugar, or as needed
1 tablespoon milk, or as needed
1 tablespoon light corn syrup
$\frac{1}{2}$ teaspoon vanilla extract
food coloring

1. Preheat oven to 400°F.
2. In a large bowl cream the butter, sugar, eggs, and vanilla until light and fluffy.
3. In a measuring cup or small bowl, mix together the flour, baking soda, baking powder, and salt. Add to the butter mixture one-third at a time.
4. Grease a cookie sheet. Lightly flour wherever you'll be rolling out the dough (I like to use a jelly roll pan to contain the mess). Roll the dough about $\frac{1}{4}$ inch thick. If you don't have a rolling pin, use a wine bottle (or other round bottle) or a piece of clean PVC pipe.
5. Cut the dough into desired shapes using cookie cutters or a pattern and knife. Use a spatula to transfer the cookies to the greased cookie sheet—space them about 2 inches apart. Bake from 4 to 6 minutes, or until the cookies are set but not darkening.
6. Remove the pan from the oven and let the cookies sit for 1 to 2 minutes until they're fully set (removing them immediately will cause them to break). Transfer to a wire rack or plates and allow the cookies to cool totally before frosting them. Allow the pan to cool to room temperature before making another batch.
7. While the cookies are cooling, prepare the Frosting. In a small bowl mix together the confectioners' sugar and milk. Add the corn syrup and vanilla and beat until the frosting is glossy. If needed, add a few drops more milk to thin the frosting to a nice spreading consistency. If the frosting is too thin, add 1 to 2 tablespoons more confectioners' sugar.
8. Divide the frosting into as many small bowls as you want colors, and use the food coloring to tint each one.
9. Frost the cookies using a knife or clean paintbrush. Further decorate with sprinkles, Red Hots candies, flaked coconut,* crushed hard candies, crushed graham crackers, or chocolate bits. Allow the frosting to completely harden before moving the cookies.

*To color coconut, put it in a tightly lidded container or freezer plastic bag with a few drops of the desired food coloring. Shake the container until all the coconut is colored.

Coconut Macaroons

The easiest and fastest cookies ever. Great for making with young kids since they're so simple to prepare!

Total Time: 30 minutes
Prep Time: 5 minutes
Bake Time: 10 minutes per batch
Makes 2 to 3 dozen cookies (depending on size, and on how many the kids eat while mixing . . .)

1 can (14 ounces) sweetened condensed milk (Eagle Brand in the US, Lechera Dulce in Latin America)
4 cups coconut (shredded or flaked)

1. Preheat oven to 350°F.
2. Mix the condensed milk and coconut thoroughly. I usually end up using my hands. Drop by spoonfuls onto a greased cookie sheet. These cookies don't spread during baking, so you can space them pretty close together—about 1 inch apart.
3. Bake for about 10 minutes, or until golden brown. Remove the pan from the oven and let the cookies cool just 1 minute to firm up, then transfer to a wire rack or plate to cool completely. (If you take them off the cookie sheet too soon, they'll fall apart; leave them too long and they'll stick.)

Variation: Add a few drops of food coloring for holidays, such as orange (a drop of red and yellow) for Halloween or red for Valentine's Day.

Molasses Cookies with Grape Jelly   Makes 4 to 5 dozen

Total Time: 1½ hours
Prep Time: 30 minutes
Bake Time: 12 minutes per batch

1 cup shortening, butter, or margarine, softened
2 cups packed brown sugar or white sugar
½ cup molasses
2 eggs
⅔ cup cold coffee
4½ cups flour
1 teaspoon baking powder (page 376)
1 teaspoon baking soda
1 teaspoon salt
¼ teaspoon ground ginger
1 teaspoon ground cinnamon
extra sugar, for sprinkling
grape jelly, as needed

1. In a large bowl cream the shortening and brown sugar. Add the molasses, eggs, and coffee and beat until light.
2. In a small bowl mix together the flour, baking powder, baking soda, salt, and spices. Add to the butter mixture one-third at a time and mix well.
3. Preheat oven to 350°F and grease a cookie sheet.
4. Lightly flour wherever you'll be rolling out the dough (I like to use a jelly roll pan to contain the mess). Roll the dough about ⅜ inch thick. If you don't have a rolling pin, use a wine bottle (or other round bottle) or a piece of clean PVC pipe.
5. You can use a cookie cutter and cut the dough into 3-inch rounds, or simply cut the dough into 3-inch squares—that way, you don't have scraps that have to be re-rolled, which tends to make them dry as they absorb more flour.
6. Use a spatula to transfer the cookies onto the prepared cookie sheet and space them at least 1 inch apart. Sprinkle the top of each with sugar and put ½ teaspoon grape jelly in the center of each one. Bake about 12 minutes, then remove the pan from the oven and let the cookies sit for 1 to 2 minutes, or until fully set (removing them immediately will cause them to break). Transfer to a wire rack or plates to cool. (Don't eat the cookies immediately—the grape jelly gets really hot and can burn your mouth.)

Chocolate-Oatmeal No-Bake Cookies   Makes about 1 dozen

Total Time: 10 minutes

1 cup sugar
¼ cup butter or margarine
¼ cup unsweetened baking cocoa
¼ cup milk
2 tablespoons peanut butter (creamy or crunchy), optional
1½ cups oats (instant or quick cooking are best, but you can use old-fashioned)

1. Combine the sugar, butter, cocoa, milk, and peanut butter (if using) in a medium pan. Bring to a boil, stirring constantly, and boil for 3 minutes. Remove from the heat and stir in the oats.
2. For "cookies," drop by teaspoonfuls onto waxed paper or aluminum foil coated with cooking spray. Let cool. For "bars," line a pan (I use a 7-inch frying pan) with aluminum foil and spray with cooking spray. Turn the mixture into the pan and press it down. Let cool, then cut into individual pieces.

Variation: If you don't have oats, you can use cornflakes, Rice Krispies, or any similar cereal.

Sweet Tooth

No-Bake Peanut Butter Rice Krispies Treats   Makes about 18 squares

Total Time: 15 minutes

6 cups Rice Krispies or Cocoa Krispies cereal
1 cup packed brown sugar
1 cup corn syrup
1 cup peanut butter (creamy or crunchy)

1. Put the cereal in a large bowl; set aside.
2. In a small saucepan combine the brown sugar, corn syrup, and peanut butter and stir constantly over low heat until everything is melted. Turn up the heat to medium and bring just to a boil. Immediately remove the pan from the heat and pour the mixture over the cereal in the bowl. Stir to combine.
3. Press the mixture into a greased 9"×13" pan or onto a cookie sheet or even just an oiled piece of aluminum foil or waxed paper. Let cool, then cut into squares.

No-Bake Rice Krispies Treats   Makes about 18 squares

Total Time: 20 minutes

3 tablespoons butter or margarine
1 package (10 ounces) regular marshmallows OR 4 cups miniature marshmallows
6 cups Rice Krispies

1. Place the butter and marshmallows in a large saucepan over low heat, stirring pretty much constantly, until the marshmallows are totally melted.
2. Remove the pan from the heat and add the Rice Krispies. Quickly, while the mixture is still warm, stir until the cereal is totally coated.
3. Press the mixture into a greased 9"×13" pan or on a cookie sheet or even just an oiled piece of aluminum foil or waxed paper. Let cool, then cut into squares.

Variation: Kids like to "sculpt" the mixture into various creations. Make sure to grease their hands, or more "dough" will stick to them than will make it into "treats." You can also tint the marshmallow mixture with food coloring for various holidays—such

as orange (a drop each of red and yellow) for Halloween, then make pumpkin-shaped balls, and use a little green candy for the stem, red and green balls for Christmas, etc.

No-Bake Cookies   Makes 20 large or 40 small

Total Time: 20 minutes

1 cup packed brown sugar or white sugar
1/2 cup margarine or butter
1/2 cup corn syrup
2/3 cup peanut butter (creamy or crunchy)
1 teaspoon vanilla extract
2 cups cornflakes, Raisin Bran, or similar cereal
2 cups Cheerios, Chex, or similar cereal
1 cup flaked coconut
1/2 cup chopped nuts

1. Combine the brown sugar, margarine, and corn syrup in a large saucepan and bring to a boil. Let boil for 1 minute.
2. Remove the pan from the heat and add the peanut butter and vanilla, stirring well. Add the remaining ingredients and thoroughly mix.
3. While the mixture is still warm, drop by spoonfuls onto waxed paper—make any size cookie you like!

No-Bake Cornflake Cookies   Makes about 2 dozen

Total Time: 15 minutes

5 1/2 cups cornflakes
1 cup sugar
1 cup corn syrup
1 cup peanut butter (creamy or crunchy)

1. Put the cereal in a large bowl; set aside.
2. In a small saucepan combine the sugar, corn syrup, and peanut butter and stir constantly over low heat until everything is melted. Turn up the heat to medium and bring just to a boil. Immediately remove the pan from the heat and pour the mixture over the cereal in the bowl. Stir to combine.
3. Drop by spoonfuls onto a piece of waxed paper, greased aluminum foil, or a greased cookie sheet. Let cool before eating.

Sweet Tooth

No-Bake Orange Cookies

Makes about 3 dozen

Total Time: 45 minutes

1 box (15 ounces) vanilla wafers
1/2 cup butter or margarine, softened
2 cups confectioners' sugar
1 can (12 ounces) frozen orange juice concentrate OR 1 1/4 cups orange juice or other fruit juice
1 cup chopped nuts
shredded coconut or confectioners' sugar, to coat the cookies

1. Crush the vanilla wafers as for No-Bake Booze Balls, below.
2. In a medium bowl combine the crushed wafers, butter, confectioners' sugar, orange juice, and nuts and mix well until totally combined.
3. Form the mixture into 1-inch balls, then roll them in the shredded coconut. Place the balls on a plate or a piece of waxed paper to dry for an hour. Store in a tightly lidded container.

Quick Variation: Sprinkle shredded coconut (or confectioners' sugar) in the bottom of an ungreased 8-inch square pan. Press the cookie mixture into the pan, then sprinkle more coconut over the top. Cut into 1-inch squares and spread them out to dry.

No-Bake Booze Balls

Makes 2 dozen

These were always a Christmas tradition, and then I realized that they're good anytime! They're great when it's hot out, as you don't have to cook or bake anything! To crush the vanilla wafers, place them in a heavy-duty plastic bag (a batch at a time if you have small bags) and roll them with a rolling pin or wine bottle (or crush them any other way you can—the finer they are, the better). If you have a food processor or blender, those work really well to crush the wafers.

Total Time: 45 minutes, plus 1 hour drying time before storing

3 cups crushed vanilla wafers
1 cup confectioners' sugar
1 cup finely chopped nuts (walnuts or pecans are most often used)

2 1/3 tablespoons unsweetened baking cocoa
3 tablespoons corn syrup
1/2 cup rum, bourbon, Triple Sec, Grand Marnier, or other liquor, or orange juice or other fruit juice (okay, then they're not "Booze" Balls)
additional confectioners' sugar, for coating the cookies

1. Place the crushed wafers in a bowl and add the confectioners' sugar, nuts, and cocoa. Mix well.
2. In a small cup, mix the corn syrup and rum (the rum helps to thin the corn syrup so it will be easier to mix with the wafer mixture). Add the rum mixture to the wafer mixture and combine thoroughly—the dough will be very stiff.
3. Form the mixture into 1-inch balls, then roll them in additional confectioners' sugar. Place the balls on a plate or a piece of waxed paper to dry for an hour. Store in a tightly lidded container.

Quick Variation: Sprinkle confectioners' sugar in the bottom of an ungreased 8-inch square pan. Press the cookie mixture into the pan, then sprinkle with more confectioners' sugar. Cut into 1-inch squares and spread them out to dry.

Brownies

Makes 10

Total Time: 35 minutes
Prep Time: 15 minutes   Bake Time: 15 to 20 minutes

1 1/2 squares (1 1/2 ounces) unsweetened chocolate
1/4 cup butter or margarine (oil does not work well)
2/3 cup sugar
1 egg
1/2 teaspoon vanilla extract*
1/3 cup flour
1/4 teaspoon salt
chopped nuts (optional)

For variety, substitute Kahlua, Amaretto, rum, or other flavored liqueur (orange, mint, and cherry flavors are all good).

1. Preheat oven to 350°F. Prepare a 9"×5" loaf pan: If you have aluminum foil, lay a 12-inch-long sheet across the pan so that the extra extends over the sides (this makes it much easier to remove the

Sweet Tooth

brownies from the pan, but it is not essential). Grease the foil with cooking spray or wipe with oil. Otherwise, grease and flour the pan.

2. Melt the chocolate over low heat or in microwave set at medium-low power (the time will vary, but start with just 15 seconds and adjust from there).

3. Transfer the melted chocolate to a medium bowl. Add the butter and stir until the butter is melted and well mixed in. Add the sugar, egg, and vanilla and stir to combine. Add the flour, salt, and nuts and mix well.

4. Spread the batter in the prepared pan and bake for 15 to 20 minutes. To test for doneness, insert a toothpick in the center. When the brownies are done, some crumbs will adhere to the toothpick when you remove it. If the toothpick is covered with batter, the brownies need to bake a little longer, but the brownies will be overdone and dry if the toothpick is completely clean.

5. Let the brownies cool at least partially in the pan (until you can touch the pan comfortably), then lift them out using the foil or waxed paper if used. Otherwise, just leave them in the pan. Cut them into squares when you are ready to serve. These are great warm!

NOTE: A doubled batch nicely fills an 8-inch square pan (bake for 25 to 30 minutes), and a triple batch will fill a 9"×13" pan (bake for 30 to 35 minutes).

Potluck Brownies   Makes 16

Total Time: 35 minutes
Prep Time: 10 minutes   Bake Time: 25 minutes

½ cup butter, melted
½ cup unsweetened baking cocoa
1 cup sugar
2 eggs
2 teaspoons vanilla extract
½ cup flour
¼ teaspoon salt
optional add-ins: chocolate chips, miniature marshmallows, Reese's Pieces, nuts, chopped M&M's, chopped maraschino cherries—use your imagination!

1. Preheat oven to 350°F. Grease an 8-inch square pan.

2. Combine the melted butter, cocoa, and sugar and stir until totally mixed. Add the eggs one at a time and stir well. Add the vanilla, flour, and salt and stir just until you no longer see flour. The batter can be somewhat lumpy—do not overmix. Fold in the optional ingredients, if desired.

3. Spread the batter evenly in the prepared pan and bake for approximately 25 minutes—do not over-bake or you will have dry brownies.The toothpick test should yield moist crumbs instead of being clean. Let the brownies cool before cutting into squares.

NOTE: For a double recipe, use a 9"×13" pan and add a few minutes to the baking time.

Cocoa Brownies   Makes 10

Total Time: 40 minutes
Prep Time: 10 minutes   Bake Time: 30 minutes

1 cup sugar
⅓ cup canola oil or vegetable oil
2 eggs
1 teaspoon vanilla extract
⅔ cup flour
⅜ cup unsweetened baking cocoa
½ teaspoon baking powder (page 376)
¼ teaspoon salt
¼ cup chopped walnuts or pecans (optional)

1. Preheat oven to 350°F. Prepare a 9"×5" loaf pan as for Brownies (page 423).

2. Mix the sugar and oil in a medium bowl. Add the eggs and vanilla and mix well.

3. Combine the flour, cocoa, baking powder, and salt in a small bowl or measuring cup. Add to the sugar mixture and stir to combine. Add the nuts and mix well.

4. Spread the batter in the prepared pan and bake for 25 to 30 minutes. The toothpick test should yield moist crumbs instead of being clean.

5. Let the brownies cool at least partially in the pan (until you can touch the pan comfortably), then lift them out using the foil or waxed paper if used.

Sweet Tooth

Otherwise, just leave them in the pan. Cut them into squares when you are ready to serve. These are great warm!

Pumpkin Pie Squares Makes 18 squares

These are great for a Thanksgiving or Christmas get-together!

Total Time: 1 hour, 45 minutes (includes three baking times, but you're prepping the next step while it bakes)

Crust
1 cup flour
$\frac{1}{2}$ cup oats—instant or quick cooking
$\frac{1}{2}$ cup packed brown sugar
$\frac{1}{2}$ cup butter or margarine, softened

Filling
2 cans (15 ounces each) pumpkin
2 cans (12 ounces each) evaporated milk (page 99)
4 eggs
$1\frac{1}{2}$ cups sugar
2 teaspoons ground cinnamon
1 teaspoon ground ginger
$\frac{1}{2}$ teaspoon ground cloves
1 teaspoon salt

Topping
$\frac{1}{2}$ cup packed brown sugar
$\frac{1}{2}$ cup chopped pecans or walnuts
2 tablespoons butter or margarine, softened

1. Preheat oven to 350°F.
2. Mix the crust ingredients in a small bowl. Press into an ungreased 9"×13" pan and bake for 20 minutes. Do not turn off the oven when done.
3. While the crust is baking, prepare the filling by mixing the filling ingredients in a medium bowl. Beat well.
4. When the crust is done, remove the pan from the oven and pour the filling over the crust. Return the pan to the oven and bake for 45 minutes. The filling will *not* be done at this point.
5. While the filling is baking, mix the topping ingredients in a small bowl. At the end of the 45-minute

baking period, sprinkle the topping over the filling. Return the pan to the oven and bake another 15 to 20 minutes, or until a knife inserted in the filling comes out clean (some of the topping may stick to it, but none of the filling should). Let cool before cutting into squares.

NOTE: This is a custard-type filling and should be kept in the refrigerator if it will be kept longer than a day.

PIES

While pies seem labor-intensive, many can be made fairly quickly. And everyone loves them at potlucks. I once saw a cruiser trade a slice of homemade apple pie for two lobsters! For a quick alternative, sometimes I don't bother with the piecrust. Many pie fillings, particularly in non-fruit pies like pumpkin pie and pecan pie, can be baked directly in a pan or even in individual cups (or in a muffin tin). While maybe not a true "pie," it tastes great!

Piecrust Notes and Tips

We've included several different piecrust recipes:

- **Classic Piecrust.** The basic shortening and flour type is the hardest to work with and still get really flaky results. The shortening, water, and even the dough as you work with it all must be kept cold.
- **No-Fail Piecrust.** The addition of an egg makes it easier to work with.
- **Cookie or cracker crusts.** These are easy to make if you can find suitable crackers or cookies, and if the crust complements your filling. They can't be used for a two-crust pie, though.

Rolling Out a Crust and Making the Pie

To roll out a piecrust, the easiest way is to use two sheets of waxed paper. Lay one sheet down, sprinkle a few tablespoons of flour over it, shape the dough (or half the dough if you're making a two-crust pie) into

Sweet Tooth

a ball, and place it in the middle of the waxed paper sheet. Sprinkle a little more flour over the top, then lay down the second sheet of waxed paper.

Since I doubt you have a rolling pin aboard, find something cylindrical that's about 10 inches long (a wine bottle, water bottle, piece of PVC, whatever—it won't be touching the piecrust). Use your "rolling pin" and begin at the center, rolling to each edge in turn—don't try to reach the final thickness all at once, but rather aim to reduce the thickness by one-third each time. Check that the crust is large enough by holding your pie pan over the crust—because of the pan's sloping sides, the crust should be about 1 inch larger all around than the pie pan.

When the crust is rolled to the correct size, gently peel off the top sheet of waxed paper. Put the pie pan upside down on the crust, then turn the whole thing right side up. Remove the second sheet of waxed paper and gently fit the piecrust into the pan. If it's a one-crust pie, flute the edges (that is, press down gently with the tines of a fork, making a pretty pattern that also anchors the crust to the pan so it doesn't shrink as it bakes) and bake as directed (either empty or filled).

For a two-crust pie, place the filling into the bottom piecrust, then roll out the top crust just as you did the first one. When it's the right size, again remove the waxed paper from the top. Slide a hand under the bottom waxed paper and flip the crust into position on top of the pie. Peel off the second sheet of wax paper.

If you don't use waxed paper, once the crust is rolled to the correct size, the easiest way to transfer it to the pan is to fold it in half—or even in quarters—and then place it on the pan and unfold it. You can do this for both the top and bottom crust.

Use your finger to run a dab of water along the edge of the piecrusts between the two layers—it will mix with the flour in the crust to form a "glue" that will hold the two crusts together. Cut the crusts off evenly about ½ inch larger than the pie pan, then use the tines of a fork and gently press down all around the edge to seal the pie. (Some people press with their fingers instead of a fork.) Cut a few 2- to 3-inch slits in the top piecrust to let steam and bubbling juices escape as the pie bakes.

If you desire a "sugared top" on your pie, brush the top crust with milk, then lightly sprinkle sugar (and cinnamon if desired) over the milk.

Classic Piecrust
Makes two 9-inch piecrusts

Total Time: 20 minutes (unbaked)

2½ cups flour
1½ tablespoons sugar
1¼ teaspoons salt
⅔ cup shortening (the colder the better)
½ cup butter or margarine, chilled
6 tablespoons ice water or cold water
2 teaspoons cider vinegar or white vinegar

1. Blend the flour, sugar, and salt in a medium bowl. Add the shortening and butter, cutting both into small pieces as you do. Use a pastry blender to mix the pieces into the flour. If you don't have a pastry blender, use a table knife in each hand and keep cutting through the shortening until the mixture resembles coarse meal. Do not use the back of a spoon to just mash it all together—the piecrust will be tough.
2. Pour the water and vinegar over the flour mixture and quickly mix with a fork until it all clumps together. If it is too dry, add additional water 1 teaspoon at a time.
3. Divide the dough into two, make each half into a ball, and roll out as described in Rolling Out a Crust and Making a Pie (page 425).

No-Fail Piecrust
Makes two 9-inch piecrusts

Total Time: 20 minutes (unbaked)

3 cups flour
½ teaspoon salt
1 cup shortening
1 egg
5 tablespoons cold water, or as needed
1 teaspoon cider vinegar or white vinegar

1. Blend the flour and salt in a medium bowl. Add the shortening and use a pastry blender to mix it into the flour. If you don't have a pastry blender, use a

table knife in each hand and keep cutting through the shortening until the mixture resembles coarse meal.

2. In a small bowl combine the egg, water, and vinegar, beating well so that the egg is well broken up. Pour the egg mixture over the flour mixture and quickly mix with a fork until it all clumps together. If it is too dry, add additional water 1 teaspoon at a time.

3. Divide the dough into two, make each half into a ball, and roll out as described in Rolling Out a Crust and Making the Pie (page 425).

Vanilla Wafer Piecrust

Makes one 9-inch piecrust

Crush the vanilla wafers as described in No-Bake Booze Balls (page 423).

Total Time: 15 minutes

1¼ cups vanilla wafer crumbs
3 tablespoons sugar or Splenda
3 tablespoons butter or margarine, melted

Mix all the ingredients right in your pie pan and press the mixture to cover the bottom and sides evenly. It's helpful to chill the crust for a few minutes before filling it, but it's not strictly necessary.

Variation: Use chocolate wafers instead of vanilla wafers.

Graham Cracker Piecrust

Makes one 9-inch piecrust

Make the graham cracker crumbs as described in No-Bake Booze Balls (page 423).

Total Time: 15 minutes

1¼ cups graham cracker crumbs
3 tablespoons sugar or Splenda
3 tablespoons butter or margarine, melted

Mix all the ingredients right in your pie pan and press the mixture to cover the bottom and sides evenly. It's helpful to chill the crust for a few minutes before filling it, but it's not strictly necessary.

Pumpkin Pie

Serves 8

Total Time: 1 hour, 15 minutes (plus time to make piecrust)
Prep Time: 15 minutes   **Bake Time:** 1 hour

¾ cup sugar
½ teaspoon salt
1 teaspoon ground cinnamon*
½ teaspoon ground ginger*
¼ teaspoon ground cloves*
2 eggs, beaten slightly
2 cups pumpkin puree (just pumpkin, not the prepared "pumpkin pie filling")
1½ cups evaporated milk, cream, half-and-half (*media crema*), or milk
1 unbaked piecrust (page 426)

Or substitute 2 teaspoons pumpkin pie spice for all these. I like a spicier pie than many and use about double these amounts.

1. Preheat oven to 425°F.
2. Mix the sugar, salt, spices, eggs, pumpkin, and evaporated milk in a medium bowl. Stir to combine well.
3. Pour the filling into the piecrust and bake for 15 minutes. Do not remove the pie from the oven, but reduce the oven temperature to 350°F and bake for 40 to 50 minutes longer, or until a knife inserted near the center of the pie comes out clean.
4. Allow the pie to cool at least one hour before cutting and serving. Best when served warm. Ideally, leftovers should be refrigerated to reduce the chances of food poisoning.

Sweet Tooth

Cherry Pie   Makes one 9-inch pie

Total Time: 1 hour, 15 minutes (plus time to make the piecrust and/or pit the cherries)
Prep Time: 15 minutes (plus time to make the piecrust and/or pit the cherries)
Bake Time: 1 hour

two uncooked 9-inch piecrusts (page 426)
4 cups cherries (either sweet or sour), pitted
1 cup sugar (1¼ cups for sour cherries)
1 teaspoon lemon juice if using sweet cherries
¼ cup flour
½ teaspoon ground cinnamon

1. Preheat oven to 425°F. Place one piecrust in a 9-inch pie pan.
2. Mix the cherries, sugar, lemon juice (if using), flour, and cinnamon by putting them all in a large freezer plastic bag and flipping it all around so that the cherries are evenly coated (you can mix in a bowl, but the bag works really well). Put the cherry mixture in the pastry-lined pie pan.
3. Put on the top crust, seal the edge, and cut vents as described in Rolling Out a Crust and Making the Pie (page 425). Bake for 25 minutes, then reduce the heat to 350°F (without removing the pie from the oven) and bake for 25 to 30 minutes more, or until cherry juice is bubbling from the vent holes in the top crust and the crust is a deep golden brown.

Pecan Pie   Makes one 9-inch pie

Total Time: 55 minutes (plus time to make the piecrust, if needed)
Prep Time: 10 minutes
Bake Time: 45 minutes

one 9-inch piecrust, unbaked (page 426) (the pie is also good without a crust)
3 eggs
1 cup corn syrup
⅔ cup sugar
⅓ cup butter or margarine, melted (do not substitute oil)
1 teaspoon vanilla extract
1¼ cups pecan halves or pieces

1. Preheat oven to 350°F. Place the piecrust in a pie pan and trim if needed.
2. Beat the eggs with a whisk or fork to break up the yolks. Stir in the corn syrup, sugar, butter, and vanilla. Add the pecans and mix well. Pour the mixture into the crust.
3. Bake for about 45 minutes, or until a knife inserted in the center of the pie comes out clean.

Coconut Cream Pie   Makes one 9-inch pie

Meringue is harder to make without an electric mixer, but people have done it for years.

Total Time: 30 minutes (plus time to make piecrust)

Special Equipment: To make the optional meringue, you'll need a broiler and either a whisk, a hand eggbeater, or (best) an electric beater.

Filling
⅔ cup sugar
⅓ cup flour
2 cups milk
2 egg yolks (reserve whites for meringue, below)
1 cup shredded coconut
1 teaspoon vanilla extract
1 teaspoon butter

Meringue (optional)
2 egg whites (best if at room temperature)
4 tablespoons sugar
⅛ teaspoon cream of tartar (optional, but it helps form high peaks)

1. Place the piecrust in a 9-inch pie pan.
2. Mix the sugar, flour, milk, and egg yolks thoroughly in a saucepan so that there are no lumps. Warm over medium heat (resist the temptation to turn the heat up—it's very easy to scorch this mixture) until it comes to a boil, then boil for 1 minute. Remove the pan from the heat and add the coconut, vanilla, and butter. Mix well, then pour into the piecrust.
3. To make the meringue (optional), beat the egg whites, sugar, and cream of tartar in a bowl until stiff peaks form. A "stiff peak" is one that stands straight up without slumping when you remove the beater. For the best results, don't stop beat-

Sweet Tooth

ing once you begin—this can be a real problem if you're using a hand eggbeater or a wire whisk, as your arm will get tired!

4. Drop the meringue by small spoonfuls over the top of the pie—you want little peaks all over. Place the pie under a preheated broiler and watch carefully. Remove when the tops of the peaks turn golden brown. Allow to cool somewhat before cutting.

5. Instead of meringue, you can eat the pie plain or topped with a dollop of ice cream, vanilla yogurt (page 101), or frozen yogurt (page 103).

6. Keep the pie in the refrigerator. I suggest putting it in its own plastic tub so that nothing falls on it and it can't move too much with any motion of the boat.

Sweet Potato Pie   Makes one 9-inch pie

This makes an excellent substitute for pumpkin pie when you can't get pumpkin!

Total Time: 1 hour, 10 minutes (plus time to make the piecrust and cook the sweet potatoes)
Prep Time: 15 minutes   Bake Time: 55 minutes

one 9-inch unbaked piecrust (page 426)
$1/3$ cup butter or margarine, softened
$1/2$ cup sugar
2 eggs, lightly beaten
$3/4$ cup evaporated milk, half-and-half (*media crema*), cream, or milk
2 cups peeled, cooked, and "smushed" sweet potatoes
1 teaspoon vanilla extract
$1/2$ teaspoon ground cinnamon
$1/2$ teaspoon ground nutmeg
$1/4$ teaspoon salt

1. Preheat oven to 425°F.
2. Place the piecrust in a pie pan and trim any excess from the edges.
3. Mix the butter and sugar in a bowl. Add the eggs and mix well. Add the milk, sweet potato, vanilla, and spices and stir to combine. Pour the mixture into the piecrust.

4. Bake for 15 minutes. Without removing the pie from the oven, lower the heat to 350°F and bake another 35 to 40 minutes, or until a knife inserted in the center of the pie comes out clean. Refrigerate any leftover pie.

OTHER DESSERTS

Yum! Here are some of our favorites that don't fall into any of the other categories.

Cheesecake   Makes one 9-inch pie

This is one cheesecake that can be made without a mixer—but you'll definitely have a workout! If mixing this by hand, the cream cheese must be really soft or it will be very hard to blend in.

Total Time: 1 hour (plus time to make the crust)
Prep Time: 20 minutes   Bake Time: 40 minutes

16 ounces cream cheese, softened
$1/2$ cup sugar
$1/2$ teaspoon vanilla extract
2 eggs
1 graham cracker piecrust (page 427), vanilla wafer piecrust (page 427), or chocolate wafer piecrust (page 427) in a 9-inch pan

1. Preheat oven to 350°F.
2. Cream the cream cheese, sugar, and vanilla. Add the eggs and beat until there are no lumps and the mixture is all the same consistency.
3. Pour the filling into the piecrust and bake for 40 minutes. Note that you can't test for doneness with a toothpick or knife as they'll cause the cheesecake to crack. Instead, wiggle the pan a little on the oven rack—only the center of the cheesecake should jiggle, and only just a little bit. Let cool before cutting and serving.

Sweet Tooth

"Almost Cheesecake" Makes 1 cheesecake

This is much easier to mix by hand than true cheesecake, and I actually prefer its flavor!

Total Time: 45 minutes
Prep Time: 20 minutes

1/3 cup butter or margarine
1 1/2 cups graham cracker crumbs or crushed vanilla wafers or similar cookies
2 tablespoons sugar
1 can (14 ounces) sweetened condensed milk (almost 2 cups), page 99
1 cup sour cream (page 99)
1/4 cup lemon juice or lime juice
1 can (16 to 20 ounces) cherry pie filling or other similar pie filling*

*Or the cheesecake can be made without the pie filling on top and simply topped with fresh fruit just before serving.

1. Preheat oven to 350°F.
2. As the oven preheats, put the butter in an 8-inch square pan and put it in the oven for a minute or two to melt the butter.
3. When the butter is melted, remove the pan from the oven and add the crumbs and sugar. Mix well with a fork, then press the crumb mixture into the bottom of the pan. Bake the crust for 7 minutes.* Remove the pan from the oven and set aside if the filling isn't quite ready, but don't turn off the oven.
4. While the crust is baking, mix the sweetened condensed milk, sour cream, and lemon juice together. When the crust is finished baking, spread the filling over the crust. If using pie filling (it can be very hard to find in some cruising grounds), spoon it over the top.
5. Bake on the lowest oven rack for about 25 minutes, or just until the filling is set and doesn't jiggle when gently shaken. This cheesecake can be served warm (let it cool at least somewhat), at room temperature, or chilled. To store it more than a few hours, it should be refrigerated.

* If the oven isn't quite up to temperature yet, go ahead and bake the crust for 7 minutes as the oven is pre-heating—you're just getting the crust to set a bit so the filling won't soak into it.

NOTE: For a 9" × 13" pan, make a double batch. It will probably need to bake 30 to 35 minutes at 350°F (the crust will still bake for just 7 minutes).

Fruit Crumble   Serves 2

Total Time: 25 minutes
Prep Time: 10 minutes   **Bake Time:** 20 minutes

3/4 to 1 cup fruit,* not drained, and cut into bite-size chunks
1 tablespoon flour OR 1 1/2 teaspoons cornstarch if fruit is particularly juicy
2 tablespoons butter or margarine, softened
2 tablespoons flour
2 tablespoons brown sugar
3 tablespoons oats (any type)
2 tablespoons broken walnuts or pecans (optional)
dash of ground cinnamon (optional)
3 drops vanilla extract (optional)

*You can use fresh, canned, or frozen fruit—blueberries, strawberries, and peaches are traditional, but you can also use apples, mandarin or regular oranges, pineapple, mango, and pretty much anything else.

1. Preheat oven to 375°F.
2. Put the fruit in a small baking dish. If the fruit is particularly juicy, mix in the flour or cornstarch to thicken it. Bake for 10 minutes while preparing the topping.
3. To make the topping, in a small bowl or cup combine the rest of the ingredients until they form a crumbly mixture. Sprinkle it over the fruit and bake another 10 minutes.
4. You can serve the crumble warm or chilled. It's even more decadent with a dollop of yogurt (page 101), frozen yogurt (page 103), or ice cream on top!

Chocolate Pudding
Serves 4

Total Time: 10 minutes, plus time to cool

½ cup powdered milk
⅓ cup sugar
2½ tablespoons cornstarch
2½ tablespoons unsweetened baking cocoa
dash of salt
1 cup milk or cream
1 teaspoon butter or margarine
¼ teaspoon vanilla extract

1. Combine the powdered milk, sugar, cornstarch, cocoa, and salt in a saucepan. Add the milk and bring to a boil over medium-low heat, stirring constantly and watching closely so it doesn't scorch.
2. Mix in the butter and vanilla, then pour the mixture into four small bowls. Let cool before serving. You can serve the pudding warm, at room temperature, or chilled. It should be refrigerated if it will not be eaten within a couple hours after it's made.

Chocolate Truffles
4 dozen

To make these you really need a refrigerator or a cold climate. If you can't refrigerate the truffles, they're just too soft to handle if the temperature is over 50 degrees in the galley.

Total Time: 3+ hours, including a minimum 2 hours refrigeration time

3 cups (18 ounces) semisweet chocolate chips
1 tablespoon vanilla extract
1 can (14 ounces) sweetened condensed milk
flaked coconut, chocolate sprinkles, colored sprinkles, unsweetened baking cocoa, or finely chopped nuts, to coat truffles (optional)

1. Melt the chocolate chips over very low heat or at low power in a microwave. Add the vanilla and sweetened condensed milk and stir until everything is totally blended. Chill about 2 hours, or until the chocolate mixture is firm enough to handle.
2. Shape the mixture into 1-inch balls—a melon baller is ideal for this, or you can use a teaspoon. The more you use your hands, the more the chocolate will melt and become a sticky mess.

3. If desired, roll the balls in coconut, sprinkles, cocoa, or nuts. If the weather is over 70°F, keep the truffles in the refrigerator until just ready to serve. To store until serving, put a layer of waxed paper or aluminum foil between the layers so they don't stick together.

Yogurt Fruit Chill
Serves 4

Total Time: 1 hour, 15 minutes
Prep Time: 15 minutes
Chill Time: 1 hour

1 cup plain or vanilla yogurt (page 101)
1 tablespoon lemon juice
1½ teaspoons poppy seed (optional)
1 teaspoon grated orange zest
½ medium cantaloupe, peeled and seeded*
lettuce leaves
1 cup fresh blueberries*

If you want larger servings, cut up an entire cantaloupe and use 2 cups of blueberries.

1. Combine the yogurt, lemon juice, poppy seed, and orange zest. Stir well, then cover and chill thoroughly.
2. Cut the half cantaloupe lengthwise into 16 slices. Arrange 4 slices on each of 4 lettuce-lined serving plates; top each with ¼ cup blueberries. Spoon the chilled yogurt mixture over the fruit.

"Almost" Tootsie Rolls
Makes 4 dozen

Great recipe to make with kids—they love both the making and the eating! Double or triple the recipe to compensate for the number that will be consumed while making them.

Total Time: 15 minutes

2 tablespoons butter or margarine, softened
½ cup unsweetened baking cocoa, or as needed
3 cups confectioners' sugar
1 teaspoon vanilla extract or orange juice
¾ cup powdered milk, or as needed
½ cup corn syrup

1. Mix all the ingredients together. Knead the mixture as you would for bread—I do it right in the bowl.

2. Roll the mixture into rope shapes and cut into desired lengths—I usually make them about 1½ inches long. If the dough is too soft, add more powdered milk or cocoa powder.

3. If the candies are not being eaten immediately, cut waxed paper into rectangles about 2 inches by 3 inches and place each candy lengthwise on one square. Roll it up and twist the ends, as with a Tootsie Roll. Store in a cool place.

Pudding (or Pie Filling) Fruit Salad
Serves 10

Total Time: 10 minutes, plus 2 hours chill time
Prep Time: 10 minutes

1 can (16 ounces) peach slices, not drained, OR 2 cups sliced peaches (peeled or not, your preference)
1 can (20 ounces) pineapple chunks, not drained, OR 2 cups fresh pineapple chunks
1 box (4 servings) vanilla instant pudding mix
1 pound strawberries, stemmed and quartered
1 pint blueberries
1 bunch seedless grapes, sliced in half
1 banana, sliced

1. Drain the juice from the canned peaches and pineapple into a small mixing bowl. Add the dry vanilla pudding mix and stir until smooth.

2. In a large bowl combine the sliced peaches, pineapple chunks, and the juice/pudding mix. Stir in the strawberries, blueberries, and grapes and toss lightly. Chill.

3. Slice in the banana just before serving, and toss to coat.

Variation: For the Pie Filling Fruit Salad, omit the pudding mix and add a can of cherry pie filling.

Marshmallow Fluff
Makes 8 cups

Best made with an electric mixer. It's possible to make it with a rotary beater (also called a hand-crank egg-beater), but your arms will be tired and the results won't be as good.

Total Time: 10 minutes

3 egg whites
2 cups light corn syrup (you can use dark, but the fluff won't be pure white)
½ teaspoon salt
2 cups confectioners' sugar
1 tablespoon vanilla extract

1. In a large bowl beat the egg whites, corn syrup, and salt on high speed for 10 minutes, or until thick. Gently add the confectioners' sugar and beat on low speed until mixed, then add the vanilla and again mix at low speed until well combined.

2. Use this in any recipe calling for marshmallow cream:

JAR SIZE	CUPS OF FLUFF
7½ ounces	2½ cups
16 ounces	5 cups

3. Keep in the refrigerator for up to a week, or you can freeze the leftovers for several months.

Freezer Treat
Serves 2

Total Time: 5 minutes, plus time to freeze (depending on freezer, can be 2 to 6 hours)

⅓ cup powdered milk
2 teaspoons unsweetened baking cocoa
2 teaspoons sugar or Splenda
½ cup unsweetened crushed canned pineapple, drained, or fresh pineapple or other sweet fruit cut into bits

1. Combine the milk powder, cocoa, and sugar. Stir in the pineapple until well combined.

2. Pour the mixture into a small plastic container with a tight lid and freeze until firm. Some boat freezers can't get cold enough to totally freeze this—it's still good even if it's slushy.

FUDGE

We've included four different recipes, so you'll be able to make whatever type of fudge you remember from your childhood. Depending on where you cruise, you may not find the brands of cocoa and chocolate that you're used to, but part of the fun of cruising is discovering new foods and trying them out. Some may be higher quality, some lower. But when you're in a gorgeous anchorage, it all tastes good.

Unless you're eating the fudge right away, store it in an airtight container. The types of fudge that require refrigeration to set up should be kept refrigerated; others don't **have to** be, but they will benefit if you're in a hot climate.

Old-Fashioned Chocolate Fudge   Makes one 8" or 9" pan of fudge

You must have a candy thermometer to make this fudge successfully.

Total Time: 20 minutes, plus about 2 hours chill time

3 cups sugar
$1/2$ cup unsweetened baking cocoa
1 can (12 ounces) evaporated milk (page 99) OR
    $1^{1}/_{2}$ cups of milk
$1/4$ cup butter or margarine
1 teaspoon vanilla extract
$1/2$ cup chopped nuts (optional)

1. Grease a pie pan or an 8-inch or 9-inch square pan.
2. Mix the sugar, cocoa, and evaporated milk in a saucepan over medium heat, and bring to a boil, stirring occasionally. Continue to heat until the mixture reaches 240°F on a candy thermometer (don't try to judge it by eye—you really need a thermometer). Do not stir after the mixture boils—stirring will cause the mixture to "sugar"—that is, to form large sugar crystals so that the fudge won't have that super creamy texture.
3. When the mixture reaches 240°F, remove from the stove. Stir in the butter, vanilla, and nuts. Pour the mixture into the prepared pan, and chill the fudge until it's hardened. Depending on how cold your refrigerator is and what size pan you used, it will take anywhere from 1 to 4 hours.

NOTE: If you have kids aboard, the step where you add the vanilla is a good science demonstration. The fudge mixture stops boiling when you take it off the stove, but when you add the vanilla (assuming you use real vanilla with alcohol in it), the vanilla will vigorously boil when added to the hot mixture, showing that the boiling point for alcohol is much lower than for the fudge mixture.

Marshmallow Fluff Fudge   Makes one 9"x13" pan of fudge

You must have a candy thermometer to make this fudge successfully.

Total Time: 30 minutes, plus cooling time (depending on temperature in boat galley)

3 cups sugar
$3/4$ cup butter or margarine
$2/3$ cup evaporated milk
2 cups (12 ounces) chocolate chips, butterscotch chips, white chocolate chips, or peanut butter chips, or 2 cups peanut butter (crunchy or creamy)
1 jar (7 ounces) marshmallow fluff (about $2^{1}/_{2}$ cups; page 432)
1 cup chopped nuts
1 teaspoon vanilla extract

1. Butter a 9"×13" pan and set aside.
2. Mix the sugar, butter, and evaporated milk in a saucepan. Bring to a boil over medium-high heat, stirring constantly. Use a candy thermometer and watch for the mixture to reach 230°F.
3. When the mixture reaches 230°F, remove the pan from the heat. Stir in the chocolate chips a few at a time and keep stirring until they are all melted. Add the marshmallow fluff, nuts, and vanilla and gently stir in.
4. Spread the mixture into the prepared pan. Allow it to cool to room temperature and then cut it into 1-inch squares.

Sweet Tooth

Uncooked Fudge   Makes 30 pieces

Total Time: 45 minutes, plus at least 2 hours chill time (can be made without the refrigerator time, but it will be very soft)

3 cups confectioners' sugar
3 ounces cream cheese, softened
½ cup butter or margarine, softened
½ cup unsweetened baking cocoa
1 teaspoon vanilla extract
1 cup chopped nuts, such as walnuts, pecans, macadamia nuts, or even peanuts

1. In a bowl thoroughly mix the confectioners' sugar, cream cheese, butter, and cocoa. If mixing by hand, use the back of a sturdy spoon against the side of the bowl to cream the items.
2. Mix in the vanilla and nuts and stir to combine thoroughly.
3. Roll the mixture into ropes and cut into pieces 1 inch long. It's best if the pieces can be chilled for several hours to firm up, but the fudge will still taste good without chilling—the pieces will just be soft.

Peanut Butter Fudge   Makes one 9"×13" pan of fudge

This recipe does not work well without a refrigerator or an icebox where you can chill the mixture (unless it's below 35°F outside and you can put it on deck in a place where birds won't get to it).

Total Time: 25 minutes, plus about 2 hours chill time

4 cups sugar
1 cup milk or evaporated milk (page 99)
2 cups peanut butter (crunchy or creamy)
1 tablespoon butter or margarine
1 tablespoon vanilla extract

1. Butter a 9"×13" pan and set aside.
2. Mix the sugar and milk in a saucepan. Have the other ingredients measured out and ready.
3. Heat the sugar mixture over medium-high heat, stirring constantly, until it comes to a boil. Stop stirring, and time it—using a watch—for 4 min-

utes. Remove from the heat. Stir in the peanut butter, butter, and vanilla and thoroughly mix.
4. Spread the fudge mixture in the prepared pan and refrigerate until firm, or about 2 hours.

PEANUT BUTTER "PLAY-DOH"

Remember, whatever the kids make with this "Play-Doh" is edible! This makes one fun afternoon!

Prep Time: 5 minutes
Play Time: hours and hours

2 cups peanut butter
2 cups powdered milk
1 cup honey or corn syrup

1. Combine all the ingredients—the mixture will be very stiff.
2. Give your child a piece of waxed paper, a cookie sheet or a piece of aluminum foil (it will help considerably in the cleanup), and the Play-Doh and let the fun begin!

MORE SWEETS, PLEASE!

Try these tempting sweets found in other chapters, too.

Breakfast and Brunch
Yogurt Granola Parfait, *page 106*
Gingerbread Muffins, *page 118*
Streusel Coffee Cake, *page 119*

Appetizers and Snacks
Sour Cream Dip for Fruit, *page 137*

Holiday Cheer
Fruited Pudding Salad, *page 367*
Baked Pineapple, *page 368*
Almost Pecan Pie, *page 369*
Pecan Pie, *page 369*
Miniature Pecan Pies, *page 370*
Margaret's Christmas Cookie Dough, *page 370*
Thanksgiving Glazed Apple Cookies, *page 370*

Sweet Tooth

Sweet Tooth

TOPIC INDEX

See Recipe Index on page 440

RECIPE INDEX